Pre-Registration Segment

LAND, STRUCTURES AND REAL ESTATE TRADING

Land, Structures and Real Estate Trading
© 2012 Real Estate Council of Ontario

DISCLAIMERS

This Course Has Been Approved By The Registrar Under The *Real Estate And Business Brokers Act, 2002.*

 Real Estate Council of Ontario
3250 Bloor Street West
Suite 600, East Tower
Toronto, ON M8X 2X9

International Standard Book Number: 978-0-9780344-3-6
Content Development: Ontario Real Estate Association and Acronamic Learning Systems Inc.
Design and Graphics: Automation Plus Ltd.

Printing and Binding: MediaLinx Printing Group

 MIX
Paper from
responsible sources
FSC
www.fsc.org   FSC® C008820

Reprint: January, 2012

ROLE OF THE REGISTRAR UNDER REBBA 2002 IN EDUCATION

The Registrar under the *Real Estate and Business Brokers Act, 2002* (REBBA 2002) is responsible for setting the educational requirements for individuals who wish to obtain and maintain registration as a real estate salesperson or broker. In order to trade in real estate in Ontario, real estate salespersons, brokers and brokerages must be registered with the Real Estate Council of Ontario (RECO) under REBBA 2002. Before beginning a career as a real estate salesperson, individuals are required to complete the required pre-registration courses.

The Registrar, through an Educational Services Agreement, had designated the Ontario Real Estate Association as the organization authorized to provide the pre-registration, articling and broker educational program. All registration-related courses of study, including associated course content, must be approved by the Registrar prior to being offered to students.

DESIGNATE

The Ontario Real Estate Association, through its OREA Real Estate College, takes great pleasure in delivering this program on behalf of the Registrar pursuant to an Educational Services Agreement between the Real Estate Council of Ontario and the Ontario Real Estate Association.

The course curriculum supports the Real Estate Council of Ontario's mandate to protect the public interest through the development of skilled and educated real estate professionals by providing students with timely, comprehensive, accurate and up-to-date education that will allow them to succeed in the real estate marketplace. The OREA Real Estate College fulfills many of its responsibilities to the Registrar, the public of Ontario and the real estate profession by providing learning opportunities so that individuals, either contemplating registration or currently holding registration, can receive appropriate and timely training.

The real estate profession makes a valuable contribution to the economy of Canada and the welfare of its people. Congratulations on taking the first step towards real estate registration in Ontario. The Real Estate Council of Ontario and the Ontario Real Estate Association hope that the successful completion of this *Land, Structures and Real Estate Trading* course will inspire and motivate you to pursue advanced educational offerings throughout your new career.

ACKNOWLEDGEMENTS

A course of this scope is only possible with the assistance of many dedicated professionals committed to the advancement of real estate skills and knowledge. A special note of thanks is owed to the Ontario Real Estate Association for its ongoing forty-year commitment to excellence in real estate education.

A further debt of gratitude is owed to various government departments and agencies who assisted with information and published materials. Appropriate references are included within text materials.

The terms REALTOR® and MLS® are identified as design marks in this publication. No attempt has been made to designate all words or terms in which proprietary rights might exist. The inclusion, definition, or description of a word or term is provided for general information purposes only and is not intended to affect any legal status associated with the word or term as a trademark, service mark or proprietary item.

Course Materials

Check that all required course materials are included. Contents vary based on course delivery selection.

	CORRESPONDENCE	ONLINE	CLASSROOM
Land, Structures and Real Estate Trading Textbook	●		●

If any materials are missing, call Course Administration Services at (416) 391-6732 or (866) 411-6732.

The Hewlett Packard 10BII

Real Estate as a Professional Career, Land, Structures and Real Estate Trading, The Real Estate Transaction – General, The Residential Real Estate Transaction and *The Commercial Real Estate Transaction*, as well as various advanced programs, require detailed financial calculations. Calculations are illustrated using **HP 10BII** keystrokes. The use of the **HP 10BII** is not an endorsement of the product, but a practical decision for consistent content presentation. Students may select other calculators, but no assistance or support is provided. Students using such calculators are well advised to compare computational capabilities with required course calculations.

Examination

An examination follows completion of *Land, Structures and Real Estate Trading*. See College Program Standards in the *Student Handbook* for full details regarding examination locations, rules, policies and procedures.

Other Resources

Instructor Support Line (866) 444-5557
Clarification regarding *course content only*.

Missing Course Materials (416) 391-6732 (866) 411-6732
Course Administration Services

College Education Centre (866) 411-6732 (Toronto)

My OREA Community—Education Forums

OREA encourages the use of the Education Forums as a learning tool. This can be found on our website at **www.orea.com**. Log in to "My Portfolio" using your student ID and password. Once logged in, click on the *My OREA Community* link. If you do not already have a "My Portfolio" password, please contact the College Education Centre. This positive exchange of content information with an expert who will answer posted questions can be practical and extensive. Participation in the forum is specific to each course and fellow students are encouraged to join the discussions. Privacy is protected.

REAL ESTATE TRADING
CONTENTS AT A GLANCE

SECTION II   123
Planning and Land Use

CHAPTER 4
Municipal Planning   124

CHAPTER 5
Land Use Restrictions   154

SECTION III   197
Structural Types and Components

CHAPTER 6
Structures and Components   198

CHAPTER 8
Mechanical Systems and Insulation 270

SECTION VI   505
Introduction to Real Estate Trading

CHAPTER 15
Trading and Agency Relationships   506

CHAPTER 16
Representation   546

APPENDIX

INTRODUCTION

ABOUT THIS TEXT

Land, Structures and Real Estate Trading expands knowledge of what products the real estate professional will be trading in the marketplace. The course consists of six sections, each highlighting different perspectives on these products. The program begins with an indepth analysis of property ownership including how land is described and registered in Ontario, followed by planning and key land use restrictions.

The next section concentrates on typical structures found in the Ontario marketplace, along with an illustrated description of key components, mechanical systems and finishes/features. The focus then shifts to detailed analysis of property valuation by means of the direct comparison, cost and income approaches, key considerations about the structure of mortgages and mortgage financing techniques and, lastly, an introduction into how property is traded pursuant to the *Real Estate and Business Brokers Act, 2002*.

Various text features and study aids are included to make this a rewarding learning experience, while building a solid foundation for advanced materials in *The Real Estate Transaction – General*.

Learning Features

Chapter content summaries and **learning outcomes** detail the learning journey in each chapter.

Key terms are boldfaced with the most significant glossary terms highlighted in page margins. All glossary terms and associated definitions are found in the *Appendix: Glossary*.

Illustrations simplify and summarize complex topics. A picture is worth a thousand words. Detailed subject matter often requires visual enhancements to ensure complete understanding.

Curiosities offer novel ideas or explanatory details, while satisfying the inquisitive nature in us all. The element of discovery can expand awareness and consolidate subject matter.

Market Memos are interspersed to bring reality to the subject matter. If a topic involves value, the memo may address new technologies that are revolutionizing the valuation process. If the topic details economic trends, the memo may highlight a specific indicator together with statistical data.

Perspectives bring fresh outlooks and consolidate complex topics, usually using a story line. Everyday occurrences of real estate practitioners often complement the subject matter.

Cautions identify special concerns including situations where prudence is required and practices that can lead to dire consequences if pursued.

Each **Focus** concentrates on additional details for a particular topic. These informative descriptions bridge the gap between academic discussions and today's realities.

Study Aids

Notables highlight key topics in each chapter to assist students with review and study efforts, along with a summary of key glossary terms.

Strategic Thinking questions are included to assist in preparing for a new sales career.

A **Chapter Mini-Review** is provided with each chapter for personal review and assessment. The mini-review is a warm up for active learning exercises.

Active Learning Exercises are included at the end of each chapter. Various testing formats are used including multiple choice, fill-in-the-blanks, matching, short answer and form completion exercises.

The **Appendix** contains the *Glossary* as well as *all* solutions (including solutions for chapter mini-reviews and active learning exercises).

Additional Resources

 The online *Guide to REBBA 2002* is a key resource for information about the *Real Estate and Business Brokers Act 2002* and associated *Regulations*. This resource is strongly recommended, but is not required for examination purposes. The online *Guide to REBBA 2002* can be accessed at **www.reco.on.ca/onlineguide**.

 Web Links are provided for general interest regarding selected chapter topics. Knowledge of website content is not required for examination purposes.

problem-solving with fictional characters and scenarios. Students must evaluate circumstances, make suggestions, correct errors and learn important lessons in preparation for the marketplace. Questions are posed that require introspection, strategic thinking, application of techniques and explanation of procedures.

HOW TO MAXIMIZE LEARNING

Make the Text Priority One	• Carefully review each chapter including every topic, illustration and example.
Follow the Learning Path	• Topics are logically sequenced by section and topics within chapters. • While creativity is encouraged, most students are advised to follow the pre-set order.
Access Additional Resources	• The online *Guide to REBBA 2002* and *Web Links* can be very helpful in clarifying and expanding chapter topics. *These resources are not required for examination purposes.*
Study Key Terms	• Clearly understand all boldfaced terms included in the primary text. These are also summarized at the end of each chapter and detailed in *Appendix: Glossary.*
Complete all Questions/ Exercises	• Practice makes perfect. Complete all chapter mini-reviews and exercises. Solutions are provided in the *Appendix.* • Suggestion: Use a blank sheet of paper as an answer sheet where feasible, leaving the chapter mini-reviews and exercises blank for follow-up review.
Continuously Review	• When in doubt, review. Repeat readings, mini-reviews and active learning exercises as often as required. • Don't move forward without fully understanding all content. • Learning has a lot in common with building blocks. Start with a good foundation and a sound structure will emerge. • Remember, knowledge is cumulative. Don't skip any chapters.
Prepare for the Exam	• The examination tests subject matter covered in the primary text. No surprises…if you diligently study the materials. • Exam questions vary, but not the underlying purpose. Emphasis is on understanding concepts, techniques and procedures. • Don't expect a mere recital of facts.

PROPERTY OWNERSHIP

The listing and selling of real estate are intrinsically tied to ownership. Listing agreements and agreements of purchase and sale must clearly set out what extent of ownership is being marketed and sold.

Current legislation, procedures and terminologies affecting ownership arise from centuries of English law and tradition. To compound matters, real estate developments and usages have become complex. Little wonder that recent decades have witnessed the explosion of legislation, regulations and rules that directly or indirectly affect how property titles are described, registered and transferred.

Section I contains three chapters. Chapter 1 focuses on the evolution of ownership including basic rights, scope of ownership and alternatives available. Particular emphasis is placed on the degree, quantity, nature and extent of interest that accrues when someone buys a property.

Chapter 2 expands the discussion to include methods of land description and descriptive devices such as surveys, reference plans, registered plans and condominium declarations and descriptions.

Chapter 3 focuses on land registration including procedures and documents used for title registration.

The Evolution of Ownership

Introduction

An unmistakable chill greets the first morning light. Four hardy figures emerge from the shadows of the cool autumn dawn; a soft mist drenches the low hanging bows of weathered, towering pines. Clear Humber River waters amble by. No, these are not early risers jogging before breakfast; these are men of purpose—Gunter's Chain in hand.

The well-worn chain, a full 66 feet in length with 100 links, is repeatedly drawn tight and marked—one hundred times for each concession. The leader, a rough seasoned surveyor from the old country, carefully checks and confirms each chain. The sound of axes, voices and occasional curses break the serenity. Then, gradually the group move on pursuing imaginary lines in the forest.

This is 1792 and the survey crew is setting out another township. Crude wooden markers, slashed underbrush and footprints are all that remain. Once again, the task is repeated; another 100 lengths of chain and another concession marked.

After 100 lengths, a special 66-foot chain measurement places the road allowance for others soon to follow. In the midst of dense woods, these pioneers are setting out ownership boundaries. Sidewalks, street lamps and homes will follow in their footprints, long lost in history.

Once concessions are mapped in one direction, then lots appear along these future roads. Twenty lengths of chain and a new lot for some future owner is born. Every five lots a road allowance is created (66 feet or 1 chain). Neighbours will some day travel back and forth with horse and buggy; much later, a quick trip to the mall. But for the moment, the forest grows still again. All evidence of the surveyors, save and except the markers, will be lost in time.

While surveys produced physical property boundaries, centuries of English law were necessary to codify the rights and limitations associated with ownership. Logically, England is the starting point for any discussion of Canadian ownership.

This chapter begins with traditions that began many centuries ago in English law and continue with us today.

Learning Outcomes

At the conclusion of this chapter, students will be able to:

- Describe basic legal concepts and principles that have developed from English law into the present day system of ownership.
- Identify and explain key ownership terms involving estates in land, concurrent ownership, joint tenancy and tenancy in common.
- Identify and explain key provisions relating to the distinct status afforded matrimonial homes under the *Family Law Act*.
- Discuss various ownership options commonly found in the present Ontario real estate marketplace including condominiums, co-operatives, co-ownership arrangements and partnerships.
- Describe and distinguish between real estate, real property and personal property.
- Describe various ownership rights and fractional (lesser) interests encountered in the marketplace with particular emphasis on air, surface and mineral rights, riparian rights, easements and rights-of-way.
- Identify and discuss government as well as private limitations imposed on landowners with particular emphasis on expropriation and restrictive covenants.

doctrine of tenure, and the subsequent doctrine of estate (see *Growth of Estates*). For the majority of provinces, the present-day system of land holding has its roots in English medieval law. At one time, every part of Canada was a colony under English law. The method of establishing English law depended entirely on how those lands became colonized. Ontario became a colony because of direct British settlement and consequently English statute and common law were established immediately.

The Feudal System of Tenure

To fully appreciate today's ownership structure, a brief overview of British feudalism is necessary. After the fall of the Saxon empire in 1066 to King William of Normandy, a military regime was imposed on the entire English countryside. Under this regime, a land-holding system was instituted known as feudalism. Through this system, King William appointed approximately 1,500 tenants-in-chief who became the King's principal tenants of all England, thus becoming in turn the lords of the land (or landlords) of the entire domain. The tenants-in-chief, who were the principal lords of the realm, did not own the land, but were merely tenants of their king. Payment by services of different kinds was demanded by the sovereign for allowing the lords to occupy these large tracts of land. The lords, in return, were allowed to sublet.

A system of parcelling land was established that allowed the respective tenants to pay with goods and services. This system was one of tenure, or the holding of land subject to some superior right rather than ownership. The type of tenure held was related to the duties owed to the landlord, the payment exacted became traditional with each type of tenure so that if one knew the nature of services due, one could identify the type of tenancy held.

Doctrine of Estates

The earliest use of the word *estate* is found in the medieval Year Book, where lawyers of the time were found to use this term in their reports to describe the interest that a tenant held in his land. Estate, connected with the Latin word status, was used to convey the legal position. The recognition of estates in land law arose through legal action that brought disputes over ownership before the royal courts. Before the Norman conquest of 1066, the jurisdiction of the royal courts was rather narrow, since the administration of local justice was left to the lords of the realm who made it a very profitable business.

After 1066, King William saw fit to intervene frequently between the tenants-in-chief and their subtenants, thereby establishing a more or less uniform system of rights, which is said to have led to the establishment of the principle of common law. Modern law was developed as a result of the many disputes brought before the royal courts. These actions, where interests in the property were recognized, became known as real estates, thus leading to the phrase real estate in modern usage to define interest in, or rights to, land.

As mentioned, two terms are focal: tenure and estate. **Tenure**, a medieval English term, involved the holding of land without ownership—a right to possess (not own) subject to payment; i.e., to an overseeing lord of the land and ultimately the king.

However, of particular interest to practitioners is the term estate. An **estate** can be generally described as the status or extent of rights associated with tenure. Those rights (e.g., the right to pass on tenure from parent to child) formed the building blocks of modern real estate law. Countless court disputes and decisions concerning property gradually evolved under common law to become known as real estates; hence our current terminology.

> **Common Law**   That part of the law that is formulated, developed and administered by the common law courts, mostly unwritten and founded originally on common customs. Common law is based on principles more so than specific rules and has developed over the centuries using legal precedents as opposed to statutory provisions set out by parliamentary decree.

Differing estates in land have arisen to suit particular purposes. Fee simple provides the most rights with the least limitations. For example, a young couple buying a home in a new subdivision will typically acquire fee simple ownership. However, many other more limited types of ownership exist; e.g., life estate and future estate, not to mention a tenant renting a property by way of a leasehold estate.

A Thousand Years in the Making   HISTORICAL FOCUS

What began as feudal relationships dating back to the Magna Carta in England was gradually transformed into legal status. As time passed, rules and procedures were handed down from generation to generation. Customs turned into law, property rights evolved from common law courts and modern real estate law came into being.

Property Ownership Unfolds	Estates (Interests) Are Classified	Limitations Of Ownership Evolve	Extent Of Ownership Codified
• English feudal system of tenure develops • Doctrine of estates formalized • English tradition embodied in Canadian Law	• Definition of property more precisely defined *fee simple estate* (or *freehold estate*), established as highest form of ownership; i.e., contains the greatest rights • Complementary estates arise; e.g. estate to uses, leasehold and life estate • Co-ownership interests unfold; e.g., joint tenancy and tenants in common	• Interests less than estates appear • Rights of one owner over another exercised; e.g., easement • Restrictive covenants are formalized • Government restrictions expand (e.g., taxation, expro-priation, right to regulate) • Profit a prendre develops; the right to enter and take something	• Fixtures and chattels differentiated • Crown restrictions delineated • Riparian rights established • Fractional rights determined

THE EVOLUTION OF REAL ESTATE OWNERSHIP

organized alphabetically. Two are included for descriptive purposes only, as they have fallen into disuse or are no longer valid.

Title

The means of evidence by which the owner of land has lawful ownership thereof.

Fee Simple

The highest estate or absolute right in real property.

Estate to Uses	The estate to uses concept was at one time a method of holding ownership. Normally, such ownership was obtained by deed, will or possession. Estate to uses flowed from trust ownership in which **title** was in the name of a registered owner who may have held title as a trustee for the real or beneficial owner. This concept gave rise to estate to uses where ownership was held for a future buyer and was often used to avoid a dower right. Dower right has been largely replaced by provincial legislation concerning spousal rights in regard to land ownership. Consequently, estate to uses has fallen into disuse.
Fee Simple	The highest estate or absolute right in real property. The holder of such a **fee simple** estate has the most rights and fewest limitations and can use, sell, lease, enter or give away the property, or refrain from any of these rights. This bundle of rights, known as ownership, is subject to restrictions imposed by laws of governing authorities. Fee simple is alternatively referred to as fee simple title, estate in fee simple or simply freehold ownership. The term *simple*, sometimes misunderstood based on modern usage, refers to the general concept of being unconstrained.
Fee Simple with Conditions	Fee simple can be created so that it terminates under certain conditions. A determinable fee simple is one that automatically terminates on the occurrence of some event, which may never happen. While prevalent historically, such arrangements are infrequently found and may be considered contrary to law and public policy. **EXAMPLE** A tract of land might be dedicated for educational purposes and would revert back if such use was ever terminated. Another example of fee simple with conditions would be a grant from the grantor to Smith and his heirs so long as the property is used as a farm. The fee simple interest will cease and the land will revert to the grantor or the heirs if the land ceases to be used as a farm.
Fee Tail	This historical fee restricted the inheritability of land to a limited class of heirs, such as the eldest male. Such provisions, often found in old deeds/ wills, are no longer valid.

reversion when the grantor of the life estate reserves the balance for himself. If, however, the grantor gives the balance to a third party, the remaining portion is called a *remainder*.

The life estate and the estate in remainder co-exist. The life tenant and the person entitled to the remainder both have an interest in the property from the beginning of the life estate. The difference is that the person with the remainder cannot use the property so long as the life estate exists, while the life tenant is restricted in what he/she can do with the property. In a general sense, the life tenant is responsible for current obligations and has the benefit of current assets while the ultimate owner has the capital benefits and obligations. If, however, the life tenant and the person with the remainder are in agreement, the property may be dealt with in any manner they choose; e.g., sell the property, tear down buildings or dig up the land, because their combined interests form the entire fee simple.

> the end of a life estate.

Leasehold Estate	A **leasehold estate** is an interest in land for a definite period of time— a week, a month, a year, 99 years or any other specific period of time. The estate cannot, however, be longer than the estate from which it was granted. In a leasehold estate, the person to whom the interest is granted is called the lessee or tenant, and the grantor of the interest is called the lessor or landlord. These individuals are governed partly by old established rules of common law and partly by provincial tenancy legislation.
Life Estate	A grantor in a deed or will may grant an interest in the lands to someone for a lifetime period. That **life estate** interest will cease on the death of the named individual: for example to Jones for his life. The grantor may specify rights and obligations that affect the life tenancy; e.g., use of the land, limitations on alterations/improvements and payment of usual expenses such as taxes and maintenance. This type of estate often arises under the terms of a will.

Leasehold Estate

An interest in land for a specified period of time.

Life Estate

An ownership right to an individual for a lifetime period.

Life Estate: An Old Idea Turned New

CURIOSITY

Historically, life estates played a significant role in rural Canada. Often, a son or daughter was granted the farm by will from a deceased parent, provided that the remaining parental spouse was permitted to reside in the home (or a portion thereof) for his or her life. The interest would cease upon the demise of the person holding the life estate.

In recent years, retirement developments have kindled renewed interest in life estates. These projects, often referred to as life equity developments, provide independent residential units designed for seniors who acquire a life interest in the specific unit. The price paid is often referred to as an occupancy purchase price submitted at point of taking possession.

Occupants reside in the home for their lifetimes, subject to a monthly fee for ongoing expenses; e.g., operation and management of the project, property maintenance and property taxes. Upon death, the life estate is terminated. The unit is then marketed for a subsequent life estate. Termination provisions vary, but typically the estate of the original life estate receives a percentage of the price received from the subsequent life estate, the balance attributable to marketing, administrative and related costs.

For centuries, only freehold interests evolved, with little regard for leasehold. However, common law now embraces a wide range of leasehold rules, rights and procedures impacting both residential and commercial properties.

The fundamental difference involves time. In fee simple, ownership is for an indeterminate period of time. With leasehold, time is finite and is capable of being made certain. Detailed discussion of leasehold estates and lease agreements are addressed in a subsequent unit.

CONCURRENT OWNERSHIP

Concurrent ownership arises when two or more persons have a right of ownership at the same time. Concurrent interests normally fall into two primary categories:

- Joint tenancy; and
- Tenants in common.

Concurrent ownership can be disposed of by agreement of the owners. If concurrent owners cannot agree as to the disposition of the property, an application can be made to the court that then leads to the forced sale of the property and distribution of proceeds.

Concurrent Ownership

Two or more persons having ownership at the same time.

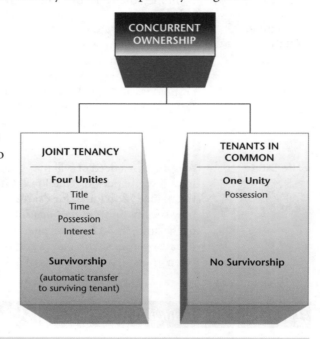

> **EXAMPLE**   *Concurrent Ownership*
>
> The buyers, James Jones and Judy Jones, purchase a home as joint tenants and draft the offer in both names. Accordingly, the deed is prepared showing both parties as owners in joint tenancy. As such, Mr. and Mrs. Jones have concurrent ownership of the property.

Joint Tenancy

Joint tenancy involves ownership of land by two or more persons whereby, on the death of one, the surviving tenant or tenants acquire the whole interest in the property.

Joint Tenancy

Ownership of land by two or more persons whereby, on the death of one, the survivor or survivors take the whole estate.

CREATION

In joint tenancy, all the owners have the same size of interest, the same possession and the same title to the land. Described alternatively, joint tenants between themselves have

I leave my fee simple in 123 Main Street to my five nephews equally.

However, stating that the five nephews are to hold the interest in the property equally is not enough to create a joint tenancy. A presumption exists that a grant of land to two or more people will be a tenancy in common unless clear intent is evident that it be a joint tenancy. Where co-owners exist on a deed, the assumption is that they are tenants in common unless the title specifies otherwise.

FOUR UNITIES

Even though a clear intention exists to create a joint tenancy, one will not be formed unless the four unities are satisfied. If these conditions are not satisfied, then a tenancy in common has been created.

TITLE All joint tenants must derive their title from the same instrument; e.g., deed or will.	**EXAMPLE** *Unity of Title* Buyer James Jones acquires an interest in a home and subsequently transfers one-half interest in the property to his spouse, Judy. If the ownership is not obtained at the same time by the same document, Jones and his spouse will own the property as tenants in common. However, James Jones can transfer the title of the property to *James Jones and Judy Jones as joint tenants and not as tenants in common.*
TIME The interest of each joint tenant must begin at the same time.	**EXAMPLE** *Unity of Time* Buyer James Jones acquires one-half interest in the home on Monday and his wife Judy receives the remaining portion on Tuesday. In this case, James Jones and his wife will be tenants in common and not joint tenants, as their interests were not received at the same time.
POSSESSION Each joint tenant is entitled to undivided possession of the whole of the property and none holds any part separately to the exclusion of the others. Perhaps a clearer way to explain unity of possession is to say that it gives all joint tenants an interest in all of the property, but an exclusive interest in none of the property.	**EXAMPLE** *Unity of Possession* If Jones and Smith own two acres of land as joint tenants, they both own two acres—not one person one acre and the other person the other acre. In addition, neither has an exclusive right to any particular part of the land as they both together own the whole. Accordingly, one joint tenant cannot maintain an action in trespass against the other.
INTEREST The interest of each joint tenant must be identical in nature, extent and duration.	**EXAMPLE** *Unity of Interest* If three brothers hold the fee simple in a property as joint tenants, each has a one-third interest in the fee simple.

and there is a clear intention that a joint tenancy should exist, then a joint tenancy will be created.

> **EXAMPLE 1**   *Ownership of Specific Area*
>
> Buyer James Jones and Judy Jones purchase a duplex at the same time and by the same document. However, James insists that the lower unit be specifically owned by Judy and that he will hold title to the upper unit. In this case, joint tenancy cannot apply as both parties must have an undivided interest in the property. Neither can specifically point to one portion of the lands and improvements and claim ownership to those specific areas.

> **EXAMPLE 2**   *Different Ownership Interests*
>
> Buyers James Jones and William Jones are purchasing an investment property and want to create two-thirds and one-third interests, as they are not contributing equally to the purchase. They also inform the lawyer that they would like to acquire title as joint tenants. The lawyer explains that joint tenancy is not possible as the same quantity of ownership would not be demonstrated.

SURVIVORSHIP

> **Right of Survivorship**
>
> The distinguishing feature of joint tenancies which provides that, where land is held in undivided portions by co-owners, upon the death of any joint owner, his interest in the land will pass to the surviving co-owner, rather than to his estate.

The **right of survivorship** is an important aspect of joint tenancy in that the interest of the deceased tenant (owner) is automatically transferred to the surviving tenant (owner). This means that, if one joint tenant dies, his/her interest does not pass to his/her estate (such as a personal representative or to heirs) but passes directly to the surviving joint tenant or tenants.

Joint tenancy is often encountered when a husband and wife obtain title to the family home as joint tenants. In such cases, on the death of either spouse, the survivor is automatically entitled to immediately receive full title to the property. The joint tenancy is thus an advantage to the surviving spouse because the house does not form part of the deceased's estate where it could become entangled in problems of settling the estate.

A joint tenant cannot bequeath his or her interest by means of a will because the transfer to the other joint tenant is automatic at death. Effectively, the deceased joint tenant's interest ceases to exist.

> **EXAMPLE**   *Joint Tenancy—Survivorship*
>
> If James and Judy Jones are joint tenants in fee simple, and Judy dies, James immediately becomes the owner of the whole interest. This is true even if Judy tries to dispose of it by will. The right of survivorship takes precedence.

SPOUSAL INTEREST

> **Matrimonial Home**
>
> Special status given to selected properties pursuant to the *Family Law Act*.

The general rule concerning right of survivorship in a joint tenancy is subject to an important exception. Under provincial legislation, if a married person dies owning an interest in a **matrimonial home** jointly with someone other than his/her surviving spouse, the joint tenancy is deemed to be severed immediately before the time of death.

Consequently, the interest becomes a tenancy in common and thereby provides a basis for the appropriate spousal interest in the assets of the deceased spouse's estate. Additional information regarding spousal rights and ownership of a matrimonial home is provided later in this chapter.

tenants in common as a result of that agreement.

A joint tenant may destroy the right of survivorship before his/her death without the consent of the other joint tenant(s). This process, called severance, turns the joint tenancy into a tenancy in common with the other tenant or tenants. Even after an act of severance, if there are two or more other tenants remaining, they still remain joint tenants with each other, but are tenants in common with the person who holds the severed interest. The most common method of severance is by a joint tenant granting his/her interest to a third party. The grant has the effect of turning the interest transferred into a tenancy in common with the remaining interests.

Other modes of severance exist, such as when all the joint tenants mutually agree to end the joint tenancy and instead hold their interests as tenants in common. For example, with a marriage separation, the joint tenancy termination can be mutually agreed upon as part of the separation agreement. A joint tenancy may also terminate by partition; i.e., splitting the land by means of an application to a court. If proper grounds exist, the court will order that the property be divided according to the joint tenancy. When it would be impractical to divide the property into different sections, as the case would be for a residential home, the court can order that the property be sold and the proceeds divided up.

The termination or severance of a joint tenancy has a significant impact on property ownership and must be done properly. A lawyer should always be consulted.

EXAMPLE   *Joint Tenancy—Termination*

Jones, Smith and Taylor are joint tenants. If Jones sells his share to Wilson, then Wilson becomes a tenant in common (one-third) with Smith and Taylor (two-thirds). Smith and Taylor remain as joint tenants. If Smith dies, Taylor will become the owner of the two-third interest and will hold it as a tenant in common with Wilson (two-third ownership by Taylor and one-third ownership by Wilson).

TENANTS IN COMMON

Tenants in common involves concurrent ownership of land by two or more persons. However, unlike joint tenancy, the interest of a deceased person does not pass to the survivor, but is treated as an asset of the deceased's estate. Tenancy in common requires only the unity of possession as opposed to joint tenancy, which must have the four unities. Each tenant in common is entitled to the same rights over the property and the use of the whole property.

Since the only unity that is required is that of possession, tenants in common may hold different interests and acquire those interests in different ways. It is quite possible to have two tenants in common each owning ¼ of the property and the third tenant in common owning the balance, namely ½ of the property.

No right of survivorship exists under a tenancy in common as the tenants/owners hold separate interests. Therefore, upon the death of one of the owners in a tenancy in common arrangement, the interest in the land passes to that individual's estate and does not automatically transfer to the remaining tenants.

Each tenant in common may sell or lease his/her undivided interest to another or dispose of it by will. A tenancy in common arrangement can therefore be terminated by the sale of one tenant's interest to the other tenant(s), the sale of the entire property to another party or the dissolution of the tenancy in common relationship by a court order.

> **Tenants In Common**
>
> Ownership of land by two or more persons; unlike joint tenancy in that interest of deceased does not pass to the survivor, but is treated as an asset of the deceased's estate.

properties pursuant to provincial legislation. The *Family Law Act* recognizes the concept of an equal partnership-marriage relationship and provides a code for the orderly and equitable settlement of the spouses' affairs when a marriage breaks down, or when a spouse dies, by an equalizing of the net family properties.

Practitioners require a general knowledge of legislative provisions concerning matrimonial homes and related matters, as issues regarding spousal rights often arise in the listing and selling of residential property. Five topics are addressed, but salespersons and brokers are encouraged to refer to the Act and seek legal counsel for further information.

Family Law Act

Part I of the *Family Law Act* deals with equal division of property on the marriage breakdown or death with stated exclusions; e.g., property inherited or received as a gift. Part II details the rights of the non-owner spouse to equal possession of the matrimonial home and sets out rights of possession of that home, the designation of a matrimonial home and limitations on ability to encumber or dispose of the matrimonial home.

Practitioners must be aware of various statutory provisions relating to spouses, particularly in the signing of documents such as the listing and the agreement of purchase and sale (including waivers).

Part II of the Family Law Act, provides a definition of a matrimonial home.

> *Every property in which a person has an interest and that is or, if the spouses have separated, was at the time of separation ordinarily occupied by the person and his or her spouse as their family residence is their matrimonial home.*

Based on this definition, there can be more than one matrimonial home, (e.g., a home in the city and a home in the country) however, properties previously occupied and then vacated by the spouses would not normally fall under the definition of a matrimonial home. Spouses can choose to limit the number of matrimonial homes by jointly designating one or more properties as their matrimonial home(s).

Designation

A designation of a home as a matrimonial home essentially means that the property is deemed to be the family residence at the time of designation. Any property can be designated by both spouses as a matrimonial home by joint registration. All other matrimonial home property is then released from the protection of Part II of the *Family Law Act* and issues concerning possession and the consent of the non-owner spouse are eliminated. The designation does not remove such property from the calculations of net family property and the resulting equalization payment in the case of divorce. If only one spouse completes a designation, all of the remaining matrimonial homes retain their status despite that registration.

The *Family Law Act* effectively alters common law. In joint tenancy, the interest of a joint tenant passes immediately upon the death of that individual to the other tenant(s). However, where a spouse dies owning an interest in a matrimonial home as a joint tenant with other person(s), the joint tenancy is deemed to be severed immediately before the time of death. Consequently, a tenancy in common is created that requires the inclusion of the deceased person's interest in his/her estate.

- I am not a spouse.
- We are spouses of one another.
- The person consenting below is my spouse.
- The property is not ordinarily occupied by me and my spouse, who is not separated from me, as our family residence.
- I am separated from my spouse and the property was not ordinarily occupied by us at the time of our separation as our family residence.

A mortgage also includes a choice of various statements regarding spousal rights under the *Family Law Act* when the mortgagor is an individual.

> **EXAMPLE**   *Designation*
>
> Sam and Trisha have agreed to separate and have put their residence up for sale with ABC Realty Inc. Meanwhile, they have equalized net values as required by the *Family Law Act* with the exception of one property. Trisha owned a duplex before marrying Sam and an agreement was signed concerning this matter at the time of the marriage. The value of the property was estimated at $389,000 and, in the event of divorce, Sam would only receive his proportionate share of any increase from that value. Sam and Trisha lived in this property before acquiring their new house.
>
> For purposes of the divorce action, their current home is the matrimonial home. The duplex, while having the matrimonial home status for a specified period, reverted to its prior status once the new home was purchased. However, for purposes of an equalization payment, the duplex has increased in value by approximately $60,000. Accordingly, a payment of $30,000 from Trisha to Sam would be factored into the final equalization process.

Family Property

The Act sets out procedures for the equal division of property on marriage breakdown or death. Property acquired during the marriage is equally divided between the spouses, subject to the provisions of any valid domestic contract signed by the spouses and subject to any court order. Each calculates the value of his/her own property, after deducting the net value of the property that he/she brought into the marriage, excluding the matrimonial home.

The spouse with the greater net value pays the other an amount to equalize their holdings. The right to equalization also occurs on the death of a spouse. The surviving spouse does not have to accept the benefits under the will or intestacy and has six months to elect to take the equalizing payment instead. Certain exclusions apply to the net family property concept:

- Property excluded in a valid domestic contract.
- Amounts received during marriage from court awards.
- Amounts received during marriage from insurance proceeds.
- Property inherited or received as a gift.
- Increases in the prior listed items may be included unless the donor specifically made provision that the increase would not form part of the recipient's net family property.

possessory rights to the matrimonial home. This right relates only to possession and does not affect ownership. The right to possession by the non-owner spouse continues until the spouses have agreed to the contrary or until the court orders otherwise.

Non-Owner Right to Possession

Both spouses have an equal right to possession of a matrimonial home. The Act confirms the rights of the non-owner spouse to equal possession of a matrimonial home. This right is a personal one and is not an interest in land. The Act further provides that the spouse has the right to be notified of any proceedings by a third party that could affect that possessory right. The registered owner cannot dispose of, or encumber, the matrimonial home without the consent of the other spouse.

> **EXAMPLE** *Non-Owner Right to Possession*
>
> Sam and Trisha have recently separated and are obtaining a divorce. The matrimonial home is owned by Sam and is currently valued at $250,000, less an outstanding mortgage of $180,000. The couple have agreed to list the property at $259,900, with Trisha retaining possession until the point of sale. If the property does not sell within three months, the listing price will be reduced in line with recommendations from the listing salesperson. At the point of sale, the equity remaining following discharge of the mortgage and all related costs, will be added to their net family property. The fact that Trisha was neither a tenant in common nor a joint tenant with her husband in the matrimonial home is irrelevant. The *Family Law Act* protects the rights of non-owner spouses in this situation.

Other Provisions

- Part III of the Act addresses support obligations that go beyond the scope of this text. The definition of a spouse for this purpose is expanded to include those who have cohabited for more than three years or who cohabit and are the natural or adoptive parents of a child or children. Same-sex partners are also included under provisions of Part III.
- Part IV relates to agreements between those who are married, are to be married, are cohabiting or are separating. Basically, a contract can deal with ownership in, or division of, property. However, a domestic contract cannot limit a spouse's possessory rights in the matrimonial home, except in a valid separation agreement.
- Part V addresses claims by dependents for remedies covering losses suffered through the injury or death of the spouse upon whom they are dependent.
- Part VI should be highlighted as it deals with changes to some doctrines of common law that are no longer appropriate. A spouse, married or common-law, can bring a court application for support to determine ownership rights and to restrain the other spouse from depleting the property. The court can determine the ownership and order property sold or transferred to a spouse. Consequently, the prudent practitioner will have all parties sign legal documents such as a listing agreement, agreement of purchase and sale, a waiver and other forms dealing with real property, to ensure that all possible parties are consenting to the transaction.

and $140,000 respectively, excluding the matrimonial home. Following deduction of the initial contributions of $25,000 each, the net value for equalizing purposes is $75,000 (Sam) and $115,000 (Trisha). Accordingly, Trisha will pay Sam $20,000 to equalize their values. Trisha did inherit property from her parent's estate amounting to $50,000 but this is not included, as per Part I of the Act. Sam and Trisha also entered into a domestic contract at the time they were married which excluded that eventuality.

While awaiting the final divorce, Sam leaves the matrimonial home and attempts to secure a loan against the property for $20,000 to assist with unexpected costs. His lawyer advises that it is not possible owing to provisions of Part II of the *Family Law Act*. Alternatively, he wants to sell the property, but Trisha refuses. The lawyer advises Sam that he cannot disrupt Trisha's possession of the property even though her name may not be on title to the property. Ultimately, the spouses arrive at a mutual agreement that permits the property to be offered for sale. The listing salesperson has both Sam and Trisha sign the listing agreement before marketing the property.

OWNERSHIP ALTERNATIVES

Many ownership alternatives now exist to meet the demands of an increasingly complex marketplace. For example, both residential and commercial buyers and sellers have embraced condominiums representing a combination of differing *estates (interests)*. The condominium buyer not only acquires a fee simple interest in a unit, but also has a co-ownership interest as a tenant in common relating to the common elements. Other less well known ownership options include co-operatives and co-ownership. Further, real estate acquisitions can also be viewed in terms of ownership arrangements; such as partnerships or limited partnerships acquiring property or corporations.

Condominium

A **condominium**, either freehold or leasehold, enables a person or other entity to share in the ownership and operation of a residential or commercial complex, while having negotiable title to an individual unit. The remainder of the property is held jointly as tenants in common, thereby allowing ownership of differing interests (typically, but not always, based on the proportionate size of the unit in relation to the overall sum of all units). A unit owner can sell his or her respective unit, but the unit ownership and tenants in common ownership of the common elements must be sold as a package and cannot be severed by separate deed.

Condominium is not a new concept. The term *condominium* originated in Roman law referring to joint dominion or co-ownership. This form of ownership was introduced in Ontario approximately 40 years ago. The original *Condominium Act* in Ontario dates from 1967. This statute received only minor changes until significant modification and additions occurred upon proclamation of the *Condominium Act, 1998*—a substantial document containing 189 sections. The updated Act represented a compilation of proven procedures and concepts from previous legislation, combined with new and innovative approaches to the expanding world of condominium ownership, such as common elements, phased, vacant land and leasehold condominiums.

> *Condominium*
>
> The fee simple ownership of a specified amount of space (the unit) in a multiple dwelling or other multi-occupancy building with tenancy in common ownership of portions used jointly with other owners (the common elements).

including surveys of the land and improvements). A condominium is created in law which both the declaration and the description are registered. The owner of the land invokes the *Condominium Act* through this registration process. Registered encumbrancers, such as mortgagees and lien holders, must consent in the declaration to the invocation of the Act.

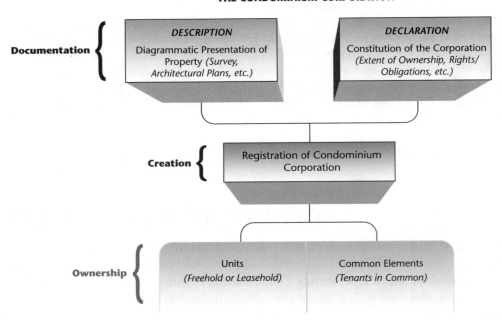

THE CONDOMINIUM CORPORATION

A corporation without share capital is automatically formed upon incorporation in which members are the unit owners. The land registrar for the applicable land registry office gives the corporation a name and sequential number; e.g., Waterloo South Condominium Corporation 986. The corporate objects focus on management of the property and corporation assets. These functions are paid for by unit owners through common expenses, in proportions specified in the declaration.

The corporation has a duty to effect unit owner compliance under the Act, the declaration and the by-laws and has the power to own, acquire, encumber and dispose of real and personal property according to the by-laws. The corporation does not provide limited liability. The unit owners are personally liable for all the debts and obligations of the condominium corporation.

Condominium ownership specifics, including drafting agreements of purchase and sale, are fully detailed in *The Residential Real Estate Transaction.*

WEB LINKS

Condominium   The *Condominium Act* is administered by the Ministry of Government and Consumer Services. For additional information, go to *www.mgs.gov.on.ca* and search under *Consumer Protection.* The Act (as with all other Ontario legislation) is accessed at *www.e-laws.gov.on.ca.*

ted to acquire a share in the corporation (in the case of an equity co-op). A housing co-operative is an incorporated business, pursuant to the *Co-operative Corporations Act* in Ontario. Currently, Canada has more than 2,100 housing co-operatives with approximately 25% of those located in Ontario. Generally, the co-op provides a high level of security of tenure, not typically found in rental properties. Co-operative housing has proven attractive to individuals seeking to avoid the uncertainties of the rental market, while deriving the benefit of combined financial resources in the acquisition of affordable housing. Co-operatives originally gained popularity with university campuses, as they provided affordable accommodation for students.

Co-ops, as member-controlled organizations, are managed by a board of directors consisting of elected persons from the membership. Members pay a monthly housing charge to cover mortgage and operating costs. Housing charges rise with increases in operating costs, unlike rents that respond to market conditions, operating costs and provincial legislative controls in some instances; e.g., *Residential Tenancies Act*.

In Ontario, a housing co-operative is formed to own real property. Members may or may not hold shares in the co-operative depending on whether the property is an equity or non-profit co-operative. In both instances, members do not own specific units, however, they are protected by means of rights as set out in occupancy agreements (or similarly worded documents).

corporation and members have a lease for a specific unit. A co-operative can be either with share capital (equity co-operative) or without share capital (non-profit co-operative).

EQUITY CO-OPERATIVE (WITH SHARE CAPITAL)

An equity co-op involves a corporation that owns the land and buildings with members as shareholders in the corporation. Ownership is by way of a share certificate in combination with an occupancy agreement relating to a specific unit. The occupancy agreement may also provide for exclusive use of parking or locker spaces, as would be the case in a condominium. Co-operatives and condominiums must be clearly differentiated. In the former, an individual holds shares in a corporation; in the latter, ownership is by way of title to a specific unit.

NON-PROFIT CO-OPERATIVE (WITHOUT SHARE CAPITAL)

Equity co-ops must be differentiated from non-profit co-operatives. A non-profit housing co-operative in Ontario (i.e., without share capital) has the primary objective of providing housing for its members without the purpose of gain for those members. At point of a dissolution, the co-operative will distribute any remaining property, after payment of debts and liabilities, in one or more non-profit housing co-operatives or charitable organizations.

NOTE: The Financial Services Commission of Ontario (FSCO) regulates registration of organizations who conduct business as co-operatives under the *Co-operative Corporations Act*. The FSCO is an arm's length agency of the Ministry of Finance that became operational in July 1998 under the *Financial Services Commission of Ontario Act, 1997*.

Additional details concerning co-operatives including financing and drafting agreements of purchase and sale are located in *The Residential) Real Estate Transaction*.

 WEB LINKS
Financial Services Commission of Ontario   For additional information concerning how to register a co-operative, go to the Financial Services Commission of Ontario web site at **www.fsco.gov.on.ca**.

owning a recreational property or ten investors owning a plot of land. Many variations are possible. For example, in a multi-unit co-ownership building, individuals may receive a deed in addition to an occupancy agreement. The deed represents the proportionate interest held in the building in relation to other tenant in common owners, but does not relate to a specific unit within that structure.

The issuance of a deed, however, does not alleviate certain troublesome situations including the joint liability with other owners in regard to a blanket mortgage, the difficulty of securing secondary financing and other issues that go beyond the scope of this text. Legal advice is strongly encouraged. Co-ownership arrangements should be clearly differentiated from partnerships. A partnership, be it general or limited, *is the relation that subsists between persons carrying on a business in common with a view to profit (Partnerships Act, Sec. 2)*. According to that Act, where two or more persons own property jointly (e.g., joint tenancy, tenancy in common, joint property, common property or part ownership) *does not of itself create a partnership as to anything so held or owned, whether the tenants or owners do or do not share any profits made by the use thereof (Partnerships Act, Sec. 3)*. In other words, the existence of a partnership is very much dependent on the agreement between the parties that establishes such an arrangement. The joint ownership of land does not necessarily mean that a partnership exists.

Partnership

A **partnership** represents another ownership alternative that is essentially a contractual relationship. As mentioned, the mere co-ownership of property does not in itself create a partnership. The partnership is personal and all assets (including property) acquired within the partnership cannot be disposed of without the express consent of the partners. In fact, failing such an agreement, partnership assets remain as such, unless the partnership is dissolved/terminated pursuant to the *Partnerships Act*. In the case of co-ownership, an individual's holdings are not subject to such constraints (unless agreed otherwise) and can be sold as a distinct interest.

A partnership is created by the prospective partners entering into a partnership agreement that can be oral or written. Partnerships must be registered under the *Business Names Act*. Certain advantages as well as disadvantages are identified with partnerships. Increased capital resources and improved borrowing power can result when two or more persons form a partnership. Partnerships also tend to have low start-up costs and are easy to form. The primary disadvantages are individual liability for all debts of the partnership incurred during the term of the partnership and the binding authority of one partner over all other partners. When terminating, unless the partners can agree as to who is the remaining partner, the partnership commonly ceases to exist with dissolution handled pursuant to the *Partnerships Act*.

LIMITED PARTNERSHIP

A limited partnership is an investment arrangement that limits a partner's liability to the amount invested while also limiting the profit he/she can make. To better understand limited partnerships, a brief recap of partnerships is required. Generally, under common law, a partner is jointly and severally responsible for the debts of the partnership. In addition, a partner can bind his/her other partner on decisions made for the partnership.

Limited partnerships must be registered and have at least one general partner, whose liability is not restricted. The limited partners enter into an agreement whereby their liability is restricted to individual capital investment. Limited partners must be passive investors and turn over the management and general operation of the project to the general partner.

> **EXAMPLE**   *Limited Partnership*
>
> Developer Reed wishes to undertake a residential development involving a 30-acre tract of land. To fund the project, Reed will invest the sum of $1,000,000. He prepares detailed plans and financial projections concerning the project and its overall feasibility and creates a corporation for the sole purpose of acting as general partner for the project.
>
> Based on presentations to investors, Reed is able to secure eight commitments ($250,000 per investor) to raise the necessary equity of $3,000,000 required by the lender considering the project. Developer Reed's new company becomes the general partner, with the individual investors taking on limited partner status in the development of the land. The limited partners each have a 8.33% interest in the venture.

LIMITED VS. GENERAL PARTNER

The liability of a limited partner in a limited partnership is confined to his/her investment. Further, the limited partner does not have a voice in the management of the partnership and is viewed as a passive investor. The general partner manages the operation and is liable for all debts. The general partner, in the case of real estate, is usually a developer who allows other individuals (limited partners) to participate in a project to raise necessary funding.

The general partner typically prepares projections indicating the viability of the project and consequential benefits to be obtained by the limited partners. He or she may also incorporate a shell corporation, the assets of which are limited to those sums contributed by the limited partners. Under such an arrangement, if the project was unsuccessful, the limited partners would have no recourse or power to force the general partner to fulfill obligations. Therefore, limited partners may look beyond the terms of the partnership agreement to ensure that the general partner supplies sufficient additional guarantees to secure the limited partners' positions.

> **EXAMPLE**   *Limited Partner*
>
> Investor McKay has been approached to invest $20,000 in a land development project in which he, as a limited partner, will receive a return based on his proportionate interest in the entire project. The developer, as a general partner, is prepared to invest $100,000 in the project together with five other limited partners (each contributing $20,000). The developer will oversee and manage the development through a corporation specifically formed for this project.
>
> McKay will participate in all profits in proportion to his contribution. The partnership has $200,000 ($100,000 + 5 limited partners @ $20,000) therefore McKay's proportionate interest is:
>
> $$\$20,000 \div \$200,000 = 0.10 \text{ or } \mathbf{10\%}$$

To fund the project, the developer will invest $1,500,000. He also prepares detailed plans and financial projections concerning the project and its overall feasibility, and incorporates a corporation for the sole purpose of completing this project.

Based on presentations to investors, he is able to secure sufficient commitments ($300,000 per investor) to raise the necessary equity of $3,000,000 required by the lender who is contemplating financing the project. Reed becomes the general partner, with the individual investors taking on limited partner status in the land development.

NOTE: Additional ownership options relating to commercial properties (e.g., joint ventures, syndicates and trusts) are discussed in *The Commercial Real Estate Transaction*.

SCOPE OF OWNERSHIP

Real Estate vs. Real Property

Real Property

Tangible and intangible attributes of land and improvements.

Real estate typically refers solely to tangible aspects of property, while **real property** includes both tangible (land and improvements) and intangible (rights). Property is further viewed as either real or personal. Real property is immovable, while **personal property** is movable; e.g., chattels. Rights associated with real property are key to value. For example, appraisers must precisely identify what rights are being analyzed when establishing value. Any significant limitation concerning rights can dramatically impact that value.

Differentiation between real and personal property is also important. Generally, all property, except land and the improvements thereon, are considered to be personal property. For real estate practitioners, personal property normally includes various chattels on the property that are referred to as consumer goods; e.g., refrigerators, stoves, drapes, house maintenance equipment, clothing, books and furniture. A **chattel** is viewed as movable and, therefore, is considered to be personal property. As such, furniture in a home is not included in the purchase price, unless specifically stated as an inclusion. However, the legal nature of a chattel changes when it becomes fixed to the real property. Whether chattels become fixtures depends largely on circumstances.

Fixtures are typically included as they are attached to the property. If such is not the intention, those items must be excluded when drafting an offer. The issue of chattels included and fixtures excluded is a key consideration for real estate practitioners. A more detailed discussion of issues relating to fixtures versus chattels is addressed in *The Real Estate Transaction – General*.

Ownership Dimensions

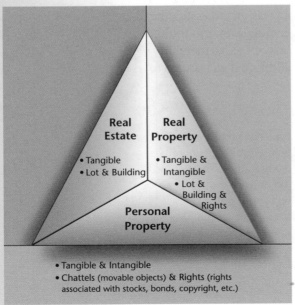

Real Estate
• Tangible
• Lot & Building

Real Property
• Tangible & Intangible
• Lot & Building & Rights

Personal Property

• Tangible & Intangible
• Chattels (movable objects) & Rights (rights associated with stocks, bonds, copyright, etc.)

plans to vacation in the area. Consequently, various personal items are being offered as part of the purchase price. These are described as 'included' on a schedule attached to the seller representation (listing) agreement. Salesperson Lee has also completed a list of excluded items to avoid any possible confusion during negotiations with a prospective buyer.

EXAMPLE   *Fixtures*

Seller Smith wants to retain the dining room chandelier that is now permanently affixed to the ceiling, along with the decorator rods in the living room. Salesperson Lee informs Smith that both fixtures should be clearly excluded in the seller representation (listing) agreement, as well as in any agreement of purchase and sale to ensure that no confusion exists from the buyer's perspective.

EXAMPLE   *Chattels*

Thomson is selling his recreational property and advises Salesperson Lee that various items are not included in the sale. While understanding that chattels are moveable and fixtures are fixed to the property and improvements thereon, Lee must ensure that there is no confusion in relation to these items with either Thomson or a potential buyer. He prepares and attaches a schedule to the listing itemizing all excluded chattels. This list includes a 14 foot aluminum fishing boat, two outboard motors (5 HP and 10 HP), fishing tackle boxes, assorted rods/reels, two space heaters in the guest cabin, various lawn ornaments and outside furniture.

the improvements thereon.

Fixtures

Permanent improvements to property that may not be removed at the expiration of the term of lease or tenure.

Chattels

Personal property which is tangible and moveable.

Rights and Fractional (Lesser) Interests

The legal journey that began in feudal England is strewn with countless disputes and resolutions. These formed the foundation for today's rights and limitations regarding estates in land. Property rights are most commonly referred to as the **bundle of rights**. Each right in this imaginary bundle represents a separate and distinct privilege of ownership; i.e., the right to sell.

Bundle of Rights

Rights of ownership associated with the possession, use, enjoyment and disposition of real estate.

Dissecting the Bundle of Rights	RIGHTS FOCUS

Dissecting Ownership Rights

Legally speaking, the bundle of rights is normally discussed in terms of rights to use, sell, occupy, dispose of by way of gift or the right not to do any of the above. But consider how many valuable rights can flow from a single property:

- The right to lease the property to one or more tenants.
- The right to sell or lease air rights or surface rights.
- The right to sell or otherwise deal with mineral rights.
- The right to dispose of the property in numerous ways: develop a residential subdivision, residential or commercial condominium, or perhaps a timeshare.
- The riparian right to access adjacent watercourses.
- The right to grant an easement or right-of-way to another over the owned land.
- The right to allow others to access and take crops on the land (profit a prendre).

The list goes on and on! Even those to whom a right is granted may have further fractional interests; e.g., a tenant with the right to sublet to a subtenant.

world of modern real estate.

AIR RIGHTS

Air rights represent a fractional interest within a fee simple estate relating to the rights to use space above the physical surface of the land. Land can actually be divided into three horizontal spaces: sub-surface, surface and air rights. Air rights, as with other fractional interests, can become a separate unit of real property and consist of fee rights that can be sold or leased. The rights associated with the interest relate to the use, control and regulation of that space.

Air rights are normally acquired to permit the construction of bridge approaches, piers, elevated streets and sidewalks, and in some cases, entire building structures. From appraisal and brokerage perspectives, air rights are marketable and can be valued in the marketplace. Air rights can have substantial value depending on the highest and best use attributable to that space; e.g., construction of a skyscraper or multi-level building above an existing use such as a railroad. However, if such use is restricted to a ground level parking lot or pedestrian promenade, the air rights may be of limited value.

SURFACE RIGHTS

Surface Rights

Rights associated with ground level as opposed to mineral or air rights.

Surface rights (also referred to as ground level rights) involve the right to use and otherwise alter the surface of real property, as opposed to other fractional (partial) interests such as mineral rights and air rights. For example, certain parcels of land in Ontario may include surface rights, but not mineral rights on or below the land. The extent of ownership that accompanies a particular parcel of land is a legal issue that should be addressed through a title search conducted at the applicable land registry office. See *Chapter 2: Legal Land Description.*

MINERAL RIGHTS

Mineral Rights

Rights regarding minerals on or below the land.

Mineral rights involve the right to enter or use lands for the purpose of removing minerals located therein. Typically, such rights involve a range of activities including exploring, drilling, extracting or otherwise removing such materials. Minerals can be broadly described as including gas, oil, gold, silver and precious metals but not generally deemed to include sand, gravel or stone.

Practitioners involved in recreational properties may encounter titles in which mineral rights are sold or reserved by the Crown. Legal advice is required.

Mining Leases/Crown Land Leases

The Ministry of Natural Resources (MNR), in addition to patenting Crown lands, grants mining leases and crown land leases. In both instances, leases are recorded by a numeric recording system unique to the Ministry. If a legal description is available (as it is for most areas of the province except certain northern regions), the MNR can cross reference the information and locate property by the registry or land titles description.

Crown Patents

Original deed issued from the Crown (government) representing the root of title for a particular property.

Mining leases issued after 1940 can be found, as is the case with **Crown patents**, in the Official Documents Section of the Ministry. All pre-1940 mining documents were registered in the appropriate land registration office as was the case with land leases on Crown land.

RIPARIAN RIGHTS

Owners of land bordering the shore of a navigable lake may have certain rights. **Riparian rights** are associated with access to the water, as opposed to ownership of the bed of the lake or river, and can include rights associated with the:

- access to and from the water from their own lands;
- natural flow and quality of water, subject to the same rights of riparian neighbours;
- increased ownership through natural accretion processes;
- navigation in the navigable waters along with those of the general public;
- right to control trespass originating from the water;
- right to drain one's property;
- right to take water without interrupting the same rights of riparian neighbours; and
- right to protect the bank or shoreline from erosion (with approval) but not to interfere with the rights of adjacent riparian ownership.

Real estate practitioners will typically encounter riparian rights in the listing, marketing and selling of recreational properties. Such rights are deemed to be natural rights by reason of ownership, as they arise from the natural state of the property in conjunction with the abutting watercourse.

EASEMENT—OVERVIEW

An **easement** is a right enjoyed by one tenement over another tenement, for example, one land owner with a right over another land owner, usually granted for a special purpose rather than for the general use and occupation of the land. An easement is an interest that runs with the land.

Once granted, an easement attaches to the land and binds subsequent owners. An easement must have both a **dominant tenement** (land that benefits from the easement) and a **servient tenement** (land that serves or is subject to the easement). Separate ownership of the dominant and servient tenements must exist and the right must confer a benefit on the dominant tenement. The two tenements need not be adjoining.

Registration

Agreements relating to easements are usually registered against titles to both properties. However, such is not always the case, for example, when statutory easements are involved (see subsequent details). The title to an adjacent property may have to be searched before determining if a particular property benefits from a registered easement over another's land. These agreements may be registered as instruments on their own and appear on the title under that particular name, or they may be registered by way of a caveat (a warning or notice on title).

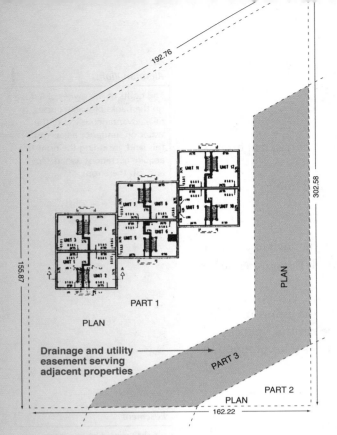

or semi-detached home), an encroachment agreement (e.g., when one owner has inadvertently built a fence over the adjoining owner's land), a right-of-way for pedestrians or vehicles, or a utility agreement granting a utility company the right to place and maintain utility lines, pipes or equipment.

Party wall agreements and rights-of-way warrant further discussion. Registered owners of adjoining parcels of land (e.g., semi-detached houses in which each side has a separate title) may enter into a party wall agreement. The agreement will declare the dividing wall between the dwelling units a party wall and set out the rights, privileges and covenants that exist in respect of the party wall. These will usually be the same for both parties. Therefore, a party wall agreement is similar to a mutual easement. Legal descriptions and characteristics of party walls varies by provincial jurisdiction.

A mutual (shared) side drive is also commonly found in certain market areas. This strip of land shared by adjoining neighbours is used as a joint driveway by both parties, created by an easement on each property. Mutual drives are a potential source of confusion, or worse, litigation. Real estate salespeople require a clear understanding of the exact location of the mutual drive and any obstructions related thereto. Practitioners are also well advised to make careful inquiry if there have been any difficulties or disputes with the drive. What may initially appear as minor confusion can later grow into major legal obstacles and litigation.

Right-of-Way

The **right-of-way** is also a frequently encountered form of easement; e.g., the right to pass over the land of another or make use of a designated strip of land. While a right-of-way is seemingly distinct from an easement, in reality, it is only a matter of terminology as both possess the same legal characteristics.

A right-of-way is an easement that includes the right to enter upon the lands of the servient tenement for the purpose of maintaining the easement and making repairs. Typically, such maintenance and repairs involve public utilities such as telephone, railway, telegraph, gas and oil rights. Often such rights-of-way are referred to as statutory easements if the right is created by the authority of a statute; e.g., a public utilities act, pipeline act or power corporation act. A typical utility easement is illustrated.

tive with ABC Realty Inc., noticed a storm sewer easement cutting diagonally across the rear yard.

The easement, according to the owner's recollection, contains an underground storm sewer that services higher portions of the subdivision in which his home is located and drains into the sewer network in the lower part of town. In this instance, the municipality is the dominant tenement (benefits from the easement) and Smith's property is the servient tenement (subject to the easement).

THE DOMINANT TENEMENT

A dominant tenement is the estate or interest in land that derives benefit from an easement over a servient tenement, as in a right-of-way. An easement must confer a benefit on the dominant tenement. As long as the easement properly serves the dominant tenement, the dominant and servient tenements need not be adjoining. The owner of the dominant tenement has no right to enlarge the use for which the easement was granted.

An illustration is provided showing a right-of-way over Lot 2 (the servient tenement) as an interest attached to Lot 1 regarding access to a lake.

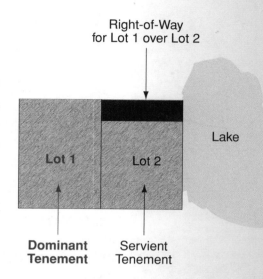

SERVIENT TENEMENT

The servient tenement involves land over which an easement exists in favour of a dominant tenement.

EXAMPLE   *Right-of-Way*

Seller Smith owns a cottage on Big Lake. The listing salesperson noted that access to the property was by way of a private easement over an adjacent property owned by Williams. The right-of-way forms part of the title. In this instance, Williams property is the servient tenement and Smith's property is the dominant tenement. The precise wording for the servient tenement easement follows:

Subject to an easement in, over and along the most westerly 40 feet of even width through Lot Number 9 and running southerly from the road allowance between Concession IX and X in the said Township of Anytownship to the waters of Big Lake.

Express Grant	The easement can be created ... ...g privilege, (a right-of-way or easement), in favour of another owner.
Prescription	An individual can obtain a right-of-way or easement by adverse possession, also known as by prescription or squatters' rights, in certain circumstances if the usage of the right-of-way was open and continuous for a specified period of time.
Implication	Best described by using an example. Assume that a sale of land adjoining the seller's land causes a parcel of land to be landlocked, the law implies that a purchaser would have an easement over the seller's remaining land by way of necessity. Another example would involve mutual support. A shared docking area by two cottagers would naturally preclude the ability of one party to destroy his/her portion of the docking facility to the detriment of the other's structure.
Statute	Easements created by statute involve groups such as public utilities and telephone companies who gain the right to string wires, install equipment and maintain services by virtue of various provincial statutes. A statutory easement is created by the authority of the statute and does not require a dominant tenement.

TERMINATING AN EASEMENT

Merge

An easement is extinguished if the ownership of both dominant and servient tenements merge.

> **EXAMPLE**   *Termination—Merge*
>
> Seller Smith, a cottage owner, has an easement over his neighbour's vacant piece of land for purposes of accessing a road, without which Smith could only get to his property by boat. Uncomfortable with this situation, Smith approaches the neighbour offering to buy the property to make one large cottage lot. Upon closing the sale, Smith's original easement is extinguished as the properties merge into one parcel of land.

Release

The person entitled to the benefit of an easement may release it to the servient tenement by removing the easement from the title.

> **EXAMPLE**   *Termination—Release*
>
> Seller Smith has a precisely described easement across a neighbour's property for purposes of accessing a rear lane. With the passage of time, the lane has become unuseable and Smith no longer requires access. Further, neighbour Jones wishes to build a garage on the rear of his property that would obstruct the easement. The neighbours agree to extinguish the easement by signing and registering appropriate documents.

Ceasing of Purpose

If the purpose of the easement disappears, so does the easement.

> **EXAMPLE**   *Termination—Ceasing of Purpose*
>
> Seller Smith owns a right-of-way to a cottage. The right-of-way subsequently becomes a public thoroughfare and the easement ceases to exist given this change. The easement would also disappear if it is abandoned by an actual intention to abandon (not merely by non-use).

Right vs. License   CURIOSITY

What is the difference between a right and a license? Consider an example involving an easement. An easement is a right (an interest in land). A license is a contractual arrangement with specific limitations and typically a specific expiry date.

Easement

Smith, as the owner of one property, may have the right (dominant tenement) to cross another's land (servient tenement) in order to access the lakefront in a recreational development. This right is documented and passes with title to the property.

License

Smith, as the owner, might grant a specific license to a developer to enter his lands for a specified period to remove topsoil from a defined area on the land. Once the time period has expired, no further right exists. In this instance, Smith has granted a license to the developer.

PROFIT A PRENDRE

Profit a prendre involves the right to enter upon a property based on a written agreement and take something from it, such as crops, minerals or timber. This right can, in some instances, pass with title upon the sale of the property.

> **EXAMPLE**   *Harvesting Crops*
>
> Owner Smith entered into a lease arrangement with Jones for 200 acres of farmland that is currently being used for the production of corn. Originally, Smith had planned to harvest the crop, but instead decided not to pursue farming and return to his city employment. Jones, already possessing the necessary harvesting equipment, leases the property as of July 20xx for five years. The lease specifically provides that Jones, for an agreed annual rental sum, shall remove the existing crop during the current year and thereafter harvest crops for the remaining four-year period.

ADVERSE POSSESSION

Rights can also arise through adverse possession of land provided that certain conditions are in place. Adverse possession occurs when an individual, not the owner, takes possession of the property, hostile to, and without the consent of the owner and remains in exclusive possession using the land like an owner and ignoring the claims of other persons including the owner. It is possible, by adverse possession, for an occupier of land to extinguish the title of the owner. The possessor then becomes, in effect, the owner of the land.

Background

Title by adverse possession began in medieval times, given the number of large estates and the fact that absentee landowners and squatters often entered and stayed on those lands for long periods. With the introduction of more accurate surveys, the number of squatters has become smaller. Under common law, a person can acquire possessory title to lands under certain circumstances by taking possession of the lands for a period of time as set out in the applicable provincial law of limitations.

The possession must be open, exclusive and continuous for a period, without the consent of the owner, but with the owner's knowledge. Adverse possession ceases to be effective if interrupted by the owner before the limitation period has elapsed, or if the adverse possessor abandons the land before the limitation period has expired, as the law considers that possession has returned to the owner.

Current Status

Practitioners must exercise caution in all matters regarding adverse possession. As background, possessory title in Ontario is only granted under the *Registry Act* (see subsequent chapter for additional description). No title by adverse possession can occur under land titles. In provinces still under the registry system (e.g., Maritime Provinces and parts of Ontario and Manitoba) statutes set out limitation periods beyond which an owner loses the right to regain possession of his/her land. In Ontario, for those areas under the registry system, the period is ten years as set out in the *Limitations Act*. The statutory period can vary by province. The onus of proof rests with the individual claiming adverse possession. Expert legal advice is strongly recommended regarding such matters.

The principle behind the law of limitations is that a person who has a right of action against another must pursue it within a time period or lose the right. He/she must not keep the other party in indefinite jeopardy of being sued. No title by adverse possession can occur in British Columbia, Alberta and Saskatchewan (and those parts of Manitoba and Ontario which are under the land titles systems) as these jurisdictions have provided by statute that the title of the registered owner cannot be extinguished by adverse possession.

EXAMPLE   *The Laneway*

Buyer Jones acquires a one-acre rural lot in Ontario based on measurements and a survey provided by Seller Smith. Without precisely measuring the property, both parties assume that the lot includes a small laneway on the westerly edge of the lot. The abutting neighbour, next to the laneway, is also under the same impression and consequently no formal consent is required as everyone assumes that Smith owns the property in question. In fact, the laneway is not owned by Smith, but by the neighbour. A few days following closing the sale under the *Registry Act*, Jones erects a fence between the lane and the neighbour. Under common law, the lands in question might be acquired by Jones through adverse possession if such possession was open, exclusive and continuous for a time period as set out in provincial legislation, without the consent of the owner but with the owner's knowledge.

ENCROACHMENT

An encroachment is a form of possessory right that arises from the unauthorized intrusion onto the lands and property of another. The right to an encroachment by one landowner over an adjoining owner's property is sometimes granted by express written agreement; e.g., when a window sill, eave, deck, porch or chimney extends over a side yard area. This is particularly common in older urban areas where side yards can be particularly narrow. When the overhang is no longer present, the encroachment ceases to exist. No right to substitute an encroachment exists if one is lost, except by further agreement.

EXAMPLE *The Garage*

Salesperson Lee, when listing Smith's cottage property, is reviewing various documents and notes an apparent encroachment involving one of the accessory buildings. Smith acknowledges that the garage encroaches a few feet on a public right-of-way. However, he adds that the municipal by-law enforcement officer has acknowledged the fact and felt that the municipality would not require its relocation. In any event, a local contractor would do the job for approximately $3,000 if it was necessary.

Lee insists that a reference to the encroachment be included in the remarks section of the listing. The seller agrees to the following wording:

> *Beautifully maintained and upgraded cottage only 45 minutes drive from Southville. Note: Single-car garage encroaches onto adjacent right-of-way. Estimated cost to move: $3,000. Seller will arrange at no cost to buyer. Call listing salesperson for further information.*

Ownership: From Tenure to Fractional Interests

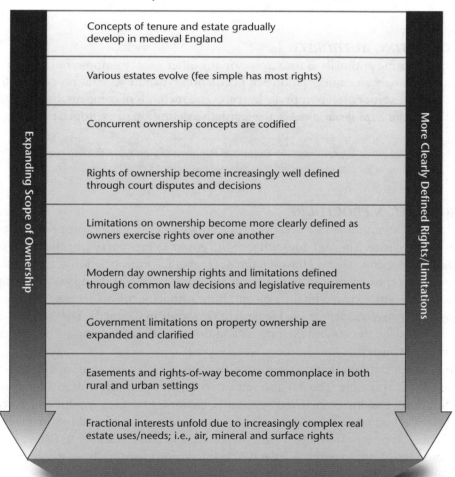

Concepts of tenure and estate gradually develop in medieval England

Various estates evolve (fee simple has most rights)

Concurrent ownership concepts are codified

Rights of ownership become increasingly well defined through court disputes and decisions

Limitations on ownership become more clearly defined as owners exercise rights over one another

Modern day ownership rights and limitations defined through common law decisions and legislative requirements

Government limitations on property ownership are expanded and clarified

Easements and rights-of-way become commonplace in both rural and urban settings

Fractional interests unfold due to increasingly complex real estate uses/needs; i.e., air, mineral and surface rights

Expanding Scope of Ownership

More Clearly Defined Rights/Limitations

OWNERSHIP LIMITATIONS

Expropriation

Taking of private property by the state for public use, with fair compensation to the owner, through the exercise of the right of eminent domain.

Escheat

The reversion of property to the state in the event the owner thereof dies leaving no will.

While rights are many, so also are limitations—government limitations top the list. Today's real estate owner is impacted by a myriad of legislative provisions. Primary government limitations can be grouped under four categories:

- Right to regulate (various federal and provincial statutes impacting land ownership, such as land planning, which are discussed later in this course (sometimes referred to as *police power*)).
- Right to levy taxes (see *Real Estate as a Professional Career*).
- Right to take private property (**expropriation**).
- Right to have ownership returned if no heir can be found (**escheat**).

Expropriation

Expropriation involves the taking of private property by the state for public use, with fair compensation to the owner, through the exercise of the right of eminent domain. Eminent domain is the right of a government or municipal quasi-public body to acquire private property for public use. Eminent domain is acquired through a legal action called condemnation or expropriation in which the appropriate body determines the use is a public use and decides the price or compensation to be paid to the owner.

EXPROPRIATING AUTHORITY

The expropriating authority is the Crown or any other agency empowered by provincial legislation, namely an expropriation act. Legislation typically sets out procedures for application to expropriate, appropriate hearings and methods of compensation. In Ontario, according to the *Expropriations Act*, the legislative definition of expropriation is:

> . . . the taking of land without the consent of the owner by an expropriating authority in the exercise of its statutory powers . . . (Expropriations Act, R.S.O. 1990, as amended, Sec. 1.)

EXPROPRIATION PROCEDURE

The Ontario *Expropriations Act* sets out procedures concerning the expropriation of lands within the province. This Act does not give the power to expropriate, as that power is found in the relevant statute. However, the Act makes the expropriation activity public by requiring the expropriating authority to obtain confirmation of the approving authority. Following the notice served by the expropriating authority, the owner may request a hearing (unless overridden by the Lieutenant Governor in Council). The Act then details the use of inquiry officers and the powers and duties of the approving authority (the appropriate Ministry).

If the expropriation is approved, the registration of a plan concerning the lands in question is then possible. The Act also sets out compensation methods involving special considerations; e.g., losses incurred by tenants, business loss, prepayment of a mortgage, injurious affection when the owner's rights are prejudiced or reduced in some way and special costs. Appeal procedures are also detailed, as well as the ability to issue a warrant concerning resistance to entry. A federal Act concerning expropriations exists that can affect land in Ontario, but such matters go beyond the scope of this text.

Real estate practitioners are rarely involved in expropriation matters. However, an example is provided as background information. This fictitious scenario involves a situation in which a government agency requires additional land from an adjacent owner.

EXAMPLE   *The Smith Expropriation*

A government agency, adjacent to Smith's property, wishes to expropriate a small section of Smith's rear yard along with the land of adjoining neighbours to provide expanded area and buffer zones for a new, badly needed, building addition. See the *Perspective*: *The Expropriation Process* for the detailed discussion of the procedure including rights concerning compensation and the awarding of damages.

Escheat

Escheat is the reversion of property to the state or some agency of the state in the event that the owner dies intestate (leaving no will) and having no legally qualified heir to whom the property may pass by lawful descent. Escheat remains as one of few examples in existence today of the old tenurial relationship. The owner, as tenant to the Crown who retains paramount claim to all land within the realm, is not able to fulfill the services required during tenure. Therefore, the land escheats to the lord and original grantor.

Intestacy and Real Estate Negotiations   CURIOSITY

Intestate is a legal term referring to a deceased person who has died without a will. Real estate practitioners are occasionally involved with estate properties and the assets of a deceased person. While the disposition of such assets can be complex, intestacy (where a will has not been made or cannot be found) often poses even greater challenges. Two provincial statutes provide direction for solicitors involved in such estate proceedings. The *Succession Law Reform Act* sets out provisions concerning entitlement to property of a deceased individual who has not made a will. However, the Act is limited only to who has that right to the property. The *Estates Administration Act* addresses the role of a personal representative and the ability to dispose of real property on behalf of a deceased person with no will or who has a will that does not set out a specific authority to dispose of the deceased's property. Issues concerning both testacy (having left a valid will) and intestacy situations go well beyond the role of real estate practitioners. Legal advice should be sought to ensure that an individual authorizing a property for sale (e.g., signing a listing) has the authority to do so and that the ultimate sale will involve a marketable title.

Private Limitations

Limitations on rights commonly extend beyond government intervention. Various **restrictive covenants** may be placed on property. For example, a developer may restrict the type of homes to be built, a condominium declaration may dictate whether satellite dishes can be placed on unit exterior walls, deed restrictions can require that buildings be painted in accordance with approved colours and subdivisions may forbid the parking of motor homes or commercial vehicles in driveways. In recent years, deed restricted subdivisions have become commonplace as developers and owners alike seek the assurances of uniformity and defined standards beyond municipally-enforced zoning by-laws.

> **Restrictive Covenants**
>
> A limitation placed upon the use of property, contained in the deed.

RESTRICTIVE COVENANTS

A restrictive covenant is a limitation placed on the use of property contained in the title for that property. More specifically, a restrictive covenant is a contract between two land owners, by which the person obtaining the promise (the covenantee) acquires the right to restrain the covenantor from putting the land to certain specific uses. Such contracts between landowners run with the land and can involve a wide array of limiting conditions regarding a property. Restrictive covenants have certain characteristics:

The Expropriation Process PERSPECTIVE

Application

- The expropriating authority serves a notice of application on each registered owner, including Smith.
- The notice is made by registered mail or personal delivery, or three consecutive publications of notice in the local newspaper.
- Each property owner must be served, including all joint tenants.

Hearing

- If Smith wants a hearing, he must notify the expropriating authority within 30 days.
- The inquiry officer sets a time and place for a hearing and notifies the parties.
- The expropriating authority makes documents, plans and other relevant items available prior to the hearing.
- The hearing is held and the inquiry officer determines if the expropriation is fair, reasonable and sound in achieving objectives of the expropriating authority.
- The hearing report and opinion are filed with the approving authority.
- The inquiry officer must consider whether the taking of this specific land is reasonably defensible and not whether the expropriating authority's policy decision to expropriate is fair.
- The approving authority considers the report but is not bound by it, approves or does not approve the report, and subsequently delivers a decision including reasons within 90 days of the inquiry officer's report to Smith and other neighbouring residents affected.

Expropriation Plan

- Within three months of approval, a survey plan is registered against the lands by the expropriating authority.
- The expropriating authority becomes the owner by statutory vesting.

Compensation

- The expropriating authority attempts to come to an agreement with the owner(s) concerning compensation.
- If no agreement, the authority serves a notice of expropriation within 30 days of the registration of the expropriation plan.
- Compensation is assessed as of the date of plan registration unless Smith serves notice, within 30 days of receiving the notice of expropriation, and wants the value determined as of the notice of hearing or upon the service of the notice of expropriation. Given market volatility, Smith's choice can directly impact value.

Value of Expropriated Land

In expropriation, the common law market value approach applies; e.g., willing buyer and willing seller not under undue pressure.

Damages

Damages can be awarded under one or more of the following categories.

Disturbance

- Potential for claim owing to disturbance; e.g., business losses, cost of relocation, loss of profit or rent, loss of trees, loss of parking spaces, depreciation, loss through a forced sale of trade fixtures or other losses than can be proven.
- Usual to add five percent to the market value for damages;
- Value of other items; e.g., loss of personal amenities, relocation costs, legal/survey costs, business losses and goodwill may be considered.

Injurious Affection

- Claims such as loss of access to other land, road or dock retained by owner, loss of landscaping and parking areas, delay of construction, denial of access to business premises, damage to crops, dirt and noise from construction, and relocation of a creek bed or erosion caused by alterations by expropriating authority, less an added value contributed by those alterations.

Relocation Difficulties

- Claims for special problems facing the owner in relocation; e.g., additional costs of construction resulting from more stringent building codes or expenses incurred in complying with current zoning laws, and compensation to find a residence of equivalent accommodation to that expropriated.
- Special circumstances concerning financing; i.e., difference in interest rate as a result of relocation.

Payment to Others

- Tenant may be entitled to part of the disturbance cost.

Payment

- Payment made if no disagreement.
- If no settlement on compensation, authority serves notice within three months of registration of the survey plan.
- Notice includes amount offered for compensation and copy of the appraisal report.

Negotiations and Arbitration

- If unable to agree, either may serve notice of negotiations on the other.
- Board of negotiation meets with the parties to resolve.
- If not resolved or negotiations waived, parties can proceed to arbitration by service of a notice of arbitration.
- Appeal can be made to the Court of Appeal and from there to the Supreme Court of Canada.

Possession

- If no agreement on possession, the authority serves the owner with a notice of planned possession of at least three months in the future.
- A judge may adjust the date based on special circumstances; e.g., removing crops.

If the authority decides that the expropriated land is not necessary for its purposes and has not paid the owner, the authority can advise the owner of that fact. The owner then has the option of taking the property back or requiring the authority to pay for it. If expropriation is completed and monies paid and the authority wishes to sell, the owner may have a first right of refusal on the terms of the best offer received by the authority.

- A dominant tenement (benefited land) and a servient tenement (burdened land) must exist.

- The covenant must be negative in nature and represent a burden on the covenantor's land. No positive or affirmative covenant can be imposed on the land, unless by statute.

- The covenant must directly benefit or enhance the value of the covenantee's land.

- Both the covenantee's and covenantor's land must be clearly defined, the agreement between the owners should state that a covenant is being imposed, and titles to both benefited and burdened lands must be registered (unless provided otherwise by statute).

- The covenant must be reasonable in nature and not arbitrary or contrary to the public interest.

Historically, restrictive covenants were widely used in residential areas to regulate the uses to which land could be put. Typical restrictive covenants prohibited the use of land for other than residential purposes, limited building on the land to one-family dwellings and required minimum frontage per house.

A prudent buyer who intends to use the lands for a specific purpose would be wise to do some preliminary title investigations and zoning enquiries before completing his/her offer to purchase. This research is particularly important because, if the restriction is being complied with at the time of purchase, it cannot be used as an objection to title unless appropriate provisos are added to the agreement to protect the buyer. Exact wordings in preprinted agreements/contracts concerning restrictive covenants will vary.

Restrictive covenants are usually created by express promises contained in the grant of the property to the buyer who has previously agreed to accept title subject to these covenants. Restrictive covenants are often found in subdivisions, where all the owners are obliged to conform to various stipulations. These served as the forerunners of municipal by-laws. Real estate practitioners should be aware of all restrictions that affect any subdivision in which they are marketing homes so that they can provide accurate information to buyers.

EXAMPLE   *The Subdivision Home*

Buyer Jones is considering a resale property owned by Seller Smith. Various restrictive covenants were imposed on buyers within this subdivision when the new homes were first marketed. These restrictive covenants run with the land and must be assumed by Jones. The following is a brief list for example purposes:

- Six foot maximum height for fences and only permitted in side and rear yard subject to front yard setback requirements.

- Prohibited use of television antennas.

- All fuel to be supplied by pipeline as opposed to individual fuel tanks.

- No unauthorized removal of trees or other significant vegetation, or alterations to drainage.

- Prohibition of clotheslines.

- Property restricted to single-family residence.

- Prohibition against the storage of motor homes, except in enclosed areas.

- No alteration to front elevations of houses or exterior colours on houses, without approval.

- In the case of alterations to vegetation, house elevations and exterior colours on house, such plans must be first approved by the developer or his nominee; such approval not to be unreasonably withheld.

The Cellular Transmission Tower   LEGAL FOCUS

Two salespersons jointly listed a commercial property. The seller informed them that a lease existed with a telecommunications company for a cellular transmission tower and equipment shed. He also informed them that a service access agreement existed and provided the salespeople with a sketch indicating the tower location on the property. However, a copy of the ten-year lease with a further ten-year option was not given to them.

The buyers, owners of adjacent property, wanted the site for retail development including a big box operation. The salespeople furnished the buyers with an out-of-date survey, which failed to show the tower, shed and easement. The buyers assumed that the tower was part of the seller's operation and made no further enquiries. An offer was prepared and accepted at $825,000. When title was searched, the lease was discovered. The salespeople told the buyers that the lease could be cancelled, but such was not the case. Apparently, the tenant had refused and the seller was unable to terminate the agreement. However, the buyers wanted the property and sued for specific performance with an abatement in price.

The Court held that the listing salespeople fell below the standard expected of professional practitioners and that losses suffered by the seller were caused by them. An abatement of $75,000 was granted and the seller was ordered to complete the sale.

Reference   Suntract v. Chassis, Unreported Case—Digested from Full Text Judgment.

The Value of Rights   PERSPECTIVE

Today's real estate market is driven by the bundle of rights. Real estate is valuable and fractional interests increasingly play a pivotal role in how land is developed and used. Here's a few examples:

Special buyer and seller needs can be served by dividing up land in creative ways, whether it's a condominium in Toronto or a vacation timeshare in Collingwood. Have you noticed cellular receivers on top of commercial buildings? The landlords are collecting extra revenue by not only renting to tenants, but also to telecommunications companies. Ever thought about the small retailer kiosks in shopping mall concourses? Just a few of many creative ways to productively use real estate rights.

Sure, everyone knows about mineral rights, but have you ever looked deeper into the concept of fractional interests? What about second floor walkways over public roads that connect shops in downtown Toronto? Air rights are involved and those rights have value. What about below-ground concourses? Don't forget about bridges with property below. Vertical division of real estate is everywhere.

An even more complex picture unfolds with easements and rights-of-way. Property in Ontario has all sorts of easements and rights-of-way ranging from narrow private cottage access roads to a shared recreation facility between two condominium towers. Don't forget about the miles of communication and hydro cable flowing through downtown office buildings. As with all real estate, value is involved.

Don't forget about the seniors market. Retirement properties range from homes on leasehold land to retirement villages in which aging tenants have leasehold interests combined with meal packages and special care facilities. Meanwhile, the younger set are busily dividing up cottage properties into co-ownership arrangements where several families divide up occupancy so that everyone has a chance to enjoy lakeside tranquility at a reduced cost.

SECTION I   PROPERTY OWNERSHIP

KNOWLEDGE INTEGRATION

Notables

- In Canada, two doctrines of law relating to land ownership have arisen: the original doctrine of tenure and the subsequent doctrine of estate.

- Various types of estates have evolved in modern real estate.

- Concurrent ownership focuses on joint tenancy and tenants in common. Be fully conversant in similarities and differences.

- The *Family Law Act* provides for a distinct status involving matrimonial homes that can impact the listing and selling process, particularly relating to signing of certain documents.

- Many ownership alternatives exist including condominium, co-operatives, co-ownerships and partnerships.

- Real estate, as with real property, includes the tangible, physical elements. However, real property also includes intangible rights.

- Personal property is movable and can include tangible and intangible elements.

- Several rights associated with real property are most commonly described as a bundle of rights; e.g., the right to use, sell, give or otherwise dispose of property.

- Fractional interests in real estate have proven increasingly important in our modern, complex society.

- Pay particular attention to rights-of-way, easements and restrictive covenants.

- Ownership limitations arise from both government and private sources.

- Government limitations include the right to regulate, to take private property, to levy taxes and to have ownership returned if no heir can be found.

- Many limitations imposed by private sources are accomplished by way of restrictive covenants.

Glossary

Air Rights	Fee Simple	Real Property
Bundle of Rights	Fixture	Restrictive Covenant
Chattel	Fractional Interest	Rights
Concurrent Ownership	Future Estate	Right of Survivorship
Condominium	Joint Tenancy	Right-of-Way
Co-operative	Leasehold Estate	Riparian Right
Crown Patent	Life Estate	Servient Tenement
Dominant Tenement	Matrimonial Home	Surface Rights
Easement	Mineral Rights	Tenants in Common
Escheat	Partnership	Tenure
Estate	Personal Property	Title
Expropriation	Profit a Prendre	

Web Links

Web links are included for general interest regarding selected chapter topics.

Condominium	The *Condominium Act* is administered by the Ministry of Government and Consumer Services. For additional information, go to **www.mgs.gov.on.ca** and search under *Consumer Protection*. The Act (as with all other Ontario legislation) is accessed at **www.e-laws.gov.on.ca**.
Financial Services Commission of Ontario	For additional information concerning how to register a co-operative, go to the Financial Services Commission of Ontario website at **www.fsco.gov.on.ca**.
Ministry of Northern Development and Mines	Go to the Ministry of Northern Development and Mines website (**www.mndm.gov.on.ca**) for additional information regarding mining activities within Ontario.

Strategic Thinking For Your Career

Questions are included to assist in developing your new career. No answers are provided.

1. Can I briefly explain differences between joint tenancy and tenancy in common?

2. Why is it important to differentiate between real property and personal property? How does this affect the way properties are listed and agreements drafted?

3. What is the best way to discuss the issue of fixtures and chattels with sellers and ensure that appropriate listing details are accurate? What items in a home might be incorrectly assumed to be fixtures, but the seller thinks of them as chattels?

4. What questions should I ask sellers that will reveal restrictions, easements or other limitations affecting ownership of properties?

5. What types of fractional interests are actively bought, sold or leased in my local market area?

6. If a buyer or seller asked me to describe an easement, could I provide a simple explanation of a dominant and a servient tenement?

Chapter Mini-Review

Solutions are located in the Appendix.

1. The major distinction between real property and personal property is the feature of mobility.

   ◯ True   ◯ False

2. Fee simple ownership is the highest estate in real property and includes the most rights and fewest limitations.

   ◯ True   ◯ False

3. An estate to uses involves granting an interest in real estate to someone for a lifetime period.

   ◯ True   ◯ False

4. A matrimonial home represents a distinct status afforded to a property pursuant to the *Family Law Act* in recognition of the equal partnership-marriage relationship.

   ◯ True   ◯ False

5. In the case of an easement, the land receiving the benefit is known as the dominant tenement.

   ◯ True   ◯ False

6. Property inherited or received as a gift is included when applying the net family concept for the equal division of property on marriage breakdown.

   ◯ True   ◯ False

7. Expropriation is the taking of land without consent of the owner and may be done without compensation to the owner.

   ◯ True   ◯ False

8. According to the doctrine of escheat, an individual's property will automatically revert to the Crown if he dies intestate.

   ◯ True   ◯ False

9. If two individuals own a parcel of vacant land as joint tenants and one dies with or without a will, the interest in the property will revert to the remaining joint tenant.

   ◯ True   ◯ False

10. The power to regulate includes the government's right to regulate privately owned property.

    ◯ True   ◯ False

11. A condominium is created through the registration of a declaration and description.

    ◯ True   ◯ False

12. Housing co-operatives in Ontario can be either equity co-operatives or private corporation co-operatives.

    ◯ True   ◯ False

13. The act of severance can change a joint tenancy into a tenancy in common.

    ◯ True   ◯ False

14. Air rights could be alternatively described as a fractional interest of fee simple ownership.

    ◯ True   ◯ False

15. Personal property of a seller may be included as chattels in a transaction.

    ◯ True   ◯ False

16. A limited partnership need not have a general partner, but must have one or more limited partners.

    ◯ True   ◯ False

Active Learning Exercises

Solutions are located in the Appendix.

■ Exercise 1   Real Estate Ownership (What was the Question?)

Complete the correct question for each of the following answers.

1.1   A grant of an interest in land for the lifetime of that individual.

What is a (an) [_____] ?

1.2   A form of ownership in which two or more persons have the same interest, the interest begins at the same time, possession is undivided and title is granted from the same instrument.

What is [_____] ?

1.3   Rights associated with owners of land on the banks of watercourses to take advantageous use of water on, under or adjacent to their land.

What are [_____] ?

1.4   A TV satellite dish that is not permanently affixed to the property and is not deemed to be a fixture.

What is a (an) [_____] ?

1.5   An interest in land, referred to as a type of tenement, that includes the owner's right to cross another person's land.

What is a (an) [_____] ?

1.6   Restrictions in a subdivision that control the type of construction and style of homes within that development.

What are [_____] ?

1.7   A government right to regulate property ownership.

What is [_____] ?

1.8   The Crown or any person authorized by statute to expropriate land.

What is a (an) [   ] ?

1.9   A legal authority to create an easement that is typically used when granting such rights to a public utility or telephone company.

What is a (an) [   ] ?

■ Exercise 2   Multiple Choice

2.1   Real property is the freehold ownership of land and improvements, consisting of tangible and intangible elements. Which of the following would NOT be considered real property?

    a.   An exotic flowering tree planted on the land, but protected by a movable greenhouse.

    b.   An owned underground sprinkler system.

    c.   A boat firmly secured by ropes inside a boathouse that is an improvement (outbuilding) on the land.

    d.   The fruit ripening on a pear tree.

2.2   Which of the following statements is NOT true with respect to a fee simple estate?

    a.   An estate in fee simple can be held by several persons.

    b.   An estate in fee simple is the most extensive estate or quantity of ownership of land.

    c.   An estate in fee simple cannot be held by more than one person.

    d.   In a fee simple estate, the rights of ownership are the most extensive and the limitations the smallest of any estate in land.

2.3   The distinguishing feature of joint tenancy is the right of survivorship. Which of the following best reflects that statement?

    a.   Upon the death of one of the joint tenants, his or her interest in a property automatically passes to the spouse named in the deceased's will.

    b.   The interest in a property held in joint tenancy is not an interest in the land; it is merely a right to use the land for a certain time period.

    c.   Upon the death of one of the joint tenants, his or her interest in the property will automatically pass to the other joint tenants and not to the heirs of the deceased.

    d.   The joint owners hold different interests in the property and have the right to pass their respective interests to surviving spouses upon death.

2.4 Which of the following is a characteristic of joint tenancy?

a. Owners must obtain title at different times.

b. Owners are all entitled to simultaneous possession of the property.

c. Owners must obtain title from different people.

d. Owners must each have different quantities of interest.

2.5 Which of the following does NOT apply to the *Family Law Act*?

a. Sets out the orderly and equitable settlement of spouses' affairs in a marriage breakdown.

b. Provides for the orderly division of property in a marriage breakdown.

c. States that spouses cannot contract out of the equalizing system to establish and distribute value.

d. Establishes certain non-owner spousal rights regarding possession of the matrimonial home.

2.6 Which of the following is NOT a characteristic of a restrictive covenant?

a. The parcels of land affected by the benefit and burden must be owned by the same person.

b. The covenant must be negative in nature.

c. The covenant, in order to run with the land, cannot be contrary to public interest.

d. There must be dominant and servient tenements.

2.7 Which of the following is a characteristic of an easement?

a. An easement does not run with the land.

b. An easement remains if both dominant and servient tenements are purchased by the same person.

c. The dominant tenement need not directly adjoin the servient tenement but must be reasonably close.

d. An easement must confer a burden on the dominant tenement and be reasonably necessary for its use and enjoyment.

2.8 Which of the following is NOT generally viewed as an interest in land that is less than an estate?

a. Right-of-way.

b. Life tenancy.

c. Profit a prendre.

d. Easement.

2.9 Which of the following statements is correct?

a. A partnership is a contractual relationship that may involve the ownership of property.

b. An equity co-operative involves a non-profit corporation, without share capital, that owns the land and buildings.

c. In a condominium, unit owners are not liable for the debts and obligations of the condominium corporation.

d. A limited partnership need not be registered.

■ Exercise 3 Selling the Matrimonial Home

Bill and Susan Weston appear headed for a legal separation and are considering listing their home. Bill is adamant that the property go on the market immediately. Susan opposes this approach, given disruption for the children midway through the school year. A few additional background facts are also relevant. The Westons purchased the home two years ago for $335,000, after three years in rental accommodation. The current outstanding mortgage balance is $258,000.

The conversation was casual until the discussion shifted to getting the property on the market. Susan reiterated her concerns. Bill retorted quickly:

> *Listen, this has got to be done. Just give me the listing and I'll sign. She doesn't have to! If we can get $355,000 we're out of here. Susan will get her 50% and that's that.*

While the Westons clearly need legal advice, point out any concerns you have with Bill's comments based on requirements concerning matrimonial homes.

■ Exercise 4   The Easement

Smith and Jones are neighbours. Smith wants access across Jones' property during the summer months to reach his cottage lot. While another access route is possible, extensive work would be required to install a usable road.

4.1   Based on information provided in this chapter, briefly outline the elements or characteristics necessary to create an easement.

4.2   What would happen to the easement if Smith bought Jones' property and merged the two properties at some future point in time?

4.3 Smith and Jones will probably create an easement by express grant. Briefly outline three other approaches by which an easement might be created.

4.4 If Smith and Jones merely agree verbally to the easement, do you foresee any problems in that arrangement? Be specific with reference to chapter materials.

■ Exercise 5   An Ownership Decision

John and Mary Williams have finally found their dream home. As the salesperson, you are just getting ready to prepare the agreement of purchase and sale. In the midst of inserting their names as buyers, John asks *"what is the difference between joint tenancy and tenants in common?"*

Answer his question with due regard to both similarities and differences between these two forms of concurrent ownership. Include a brief description of how joint tenancy can be terminated.

■ Exercise 6   Restrictive Covenants

The following case provides insight into restrictive covenants that run with the land. List five typical restrictive covenants that might be found on title to properties in Ontario.

The Moxhay Plan

The leading case on restrictive covenants is Tulk v. Moxhay (1948, 2P.H., 774). This case dealt with land known as Leicester Square in London, England. The land was sold to a man named Elms who covenanted to keep the centre of the square in good repair, uncovered with any buildings. Elms diligently looked after the square, but in due course ownership passed to the hands of an enterprising gentleman, Mr. Moxhay.

Moxhay freely admitted having knowledge of the covenant but proposed to erect commercial buildings in the centre of the square. Tulk, who owned nearby land, brought action to restain Moxhay's plans. Tulk was successful, as the court held that the covenants constituted a restrictive covenant. Accordingly, the burden of that covenant ran with the land. Moxhay, even though he had not signed the covenant, was bound to it.

Restrictive covenants sometimes cover entire areas and prescribe that only buildings of a certain price range can be built on the land.

CHAPTER 2

Legal Land Description

Introduction

Legal land description is a complex issue that goes well beyond the normal scope of real estate practitioners' activities. Surveyors, planners, lawyers and a host of other professionals constantly face intricate issues involving the proper and complete legal description of land.

However, an understanding of basic description methods is necessary in the overall listing, marketing and sale of real estate. For study purposes, emphasis is placed on selected aspects of land description most frequently encountered by practitioners.

Topics addressed include lots, concessions and townships, metes and bounds descriptions, surveys, reference plans and selected approaches to registering developments; i.e., registered plans of subdivisions and condominiums. In particular, emphasis is placed on the Surveyor's Real Property Report and associated standards and content requirements imposed on surveyors. Road systems are also broadly described in advance of specifics in subsequent chapters and *The Residential Real Estate Transaction* regarding such matters as entrance permits, access roads and shore road allowances.

This chapter flows from historic fundamentals underlying Ontario descriptions to the unfolding world of geographic information systems (GIS). Digital technology is bridging the gap between traditional word-based land description methods and the power of graphic presentations.

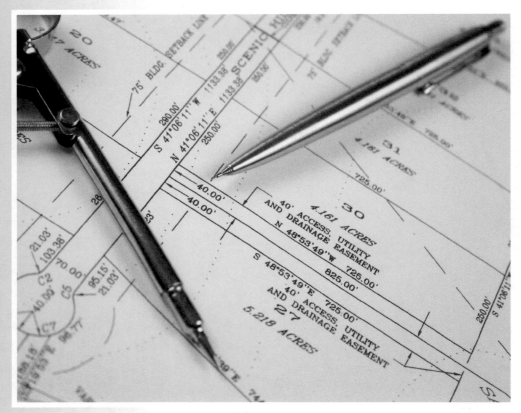

Learning Outcomes

At the conclusion of this chapter, students will be able to:

- Outline the basis of modern land descriptions based on counties, townships, concessions and lots.
- Differentiate various township structures that form the basis of land descriptions in Ontario.
- Apply basic principles and procedures involved with metes and bounds descriptions when describing property.
- Detail fundamental requirements concerning Ontario surveys as set out in the *Surveys Act* and the *Surveyors Act*.
- Identify different types of surveys with particular emphasis on components making up the Surveyor's Real Property Report (Part 1—Plan of Survey; Part 2—The Written Report).
- Describe the major components in reference plans, plans of survey, registered plans of subdivision and condominiums.
- Describe three broad categories of road systems within the province and highlight key legislation impacting properties adjacent to highways.
- Describe the fundamental structure of a geographic information system as it relates to the mapping of real estate and associated layers of information.

LAND DESCRIPTION METHODS

Descriptive Fundamentals

A legal land description is a written identification and formal depiction of land in order that the property can be precisely located. From a practitioner's perspective, the legal land description ensures that the property being purchased is, in fact, the same one being offered for sale. Further, this description is required for related activities; e.g., arranging a mortgage.

- Primary documents containing the legal land description include the deed and survey. Practitioners should always rely on primary source documents.
- Secondary documents (such as assessment notices and municipal tax bills) also include this information. Practitioners should not rely on secondary source documents.

Land is described for legal purposes in a precise manner, according to a formula, so that one piece of land cannot be mistaken for another. As such, the difference between land description and legal description is somewhat blurred and, in fact, both terms are generally viewed as synonymous for purposes of real estate discussions. In a legal document, a description such as the lot with the white stucco house or 43 Enroy Court would not be sufficient. Land description, therefore, must include the most complete legal identification of the property. This wording is then used for registration in the appropriate land registration office.

The Basis of Modern Land Descriptions

The basis for modern methods of land description lies in the original **survey** of the province completed in 1792. At that time, Governor Simcoe divided Ontario into counties. He hired teams of surveyors to trek through the bush to mark out the actual boundaries. The **county** boundary often followed a river or lake, but in most cases was a straight line through the bush. The counties were then divided into smaller parcels referred to as **townships**. Many townships were square, although topography sometimes necessitated a rectangle or an irregular line on one or more township sides due to natural boundaries.

> **Township**
>
> Division of a county into several distinct areas for administrative purposes.

Each township was in turn divided into strips of land known as **concessions**, numbered in Roman numerals beginning with I. Each concession was separated from the next one by a road allowance. The road allowance was not always converted into an actual road, but remained as public property. Each concession was further divided into **lots**, running at right angle to the concessions and numbered in Arabic numerals from 1. The lots were sometimes divided by a road allowance (usually every 5th lot) or simply by a lot line . A parcel of land could then be described as the entirety of the lot and concession.

> **Concession**
>
> Strips of land making up a township, each separated by a road allowance.

> *Lot 5 in Concession III in the Township of Anytownship, in the County of Anycounty.*

Differing Township Structures

Practitioners should be aware of special considerations regarding the development of townships. Differing structures dictate how townships are laid out, as well as the size and shape of township lots. The single front and double front township configurations were introduced in 1783 and 1818 respectively, with sectional townships following in 1835. Single front townships normally contained 200 acre lots, while double front townships were usually patented in 100 acre half-lots.

SINGLE FRONT TOWNSHIP

The **single front township**, ... of the township systems, was laid out in southern Ontario between 1783 ... was found generally on the banks of navigable lakes and rivers. ... system varied from time to time. Lots were 20 chains (1,320') by ... d contained 200 acres. A standard road allowance was 1 chain ...

... ries and the fronts of the concessions were run with posts ... t corners of the lots. No provisions existed for check ties ... the original survey. Consequently, the road allowances between ... were usually found to jog at the fronts of the concessions.

... OWNSHIP

... **front township** refers to a township where the original survey laid out ... lots to be 30 chains (1,980') by 66.67 chains (4,400') and were usually ... f-lots containing 100 acres. The township boundaries and the centre-line ... llowances between the concessions were run with posts planted on each ... road to mark the front corners of the lots. As with single front townships, no provisions existed for check ties across the concessions in the original survey and road allowances often jogged at the fronts of the concessions.

SECTIONAL SYSTEM TOWNSHIP

The **sectional township** system of land division involved 1,000-acre sections and was introduced in 1835. In this arrangement, lots were designed to be 20 chains by 50 chains and to contain 100 acres. This system was the first township system in which an attempt was made to check the survey by means of cross ties between concessions. Not only were the centre-lines of the road allowances between concessions surveyed but also the centre-lines of the road allowances between every fifth lot, thus forming surveyed sections of 10 lots with each section containing a total area of 1,000 acres.

Land Measurement

The measurement of land was based on the old chains and links system. A chain is 66 feet, 100 links make a chain and 80 chains equal one mile. Each concession was 100 chains across, or 1 ¼ miles. As time passed, many farmers divided the land among their sons. Such divisions could be easily described as long as the parcel was ½ or ¼ of an overall lot; e.g., land could be described as:

> *The South East ¼ of Lot 5, Concession III, Township of Anytownship, in the County of Anycounty.*

This system of describing land as part of a concession lot is still the basis for land descriptions in Ontario today. The system can be used to describe a lot containing as few as 50 acres. However, this description would only be approximate, and to comply with present-day conveyancing standards, property normally must be re-surveyed and measured more accurately. To describe smaller parcels, further refinements are necessary.

FRACTIONAL DESCRIPTIONS

As the provincial population grew, the demand for sm... with land registration systems gradually encountering m... lots. Initially, legal descriptions were based on dimensions w... directions and descriptions were prepared without benefit of s...

An excerpt from a typical description dating from the early 18... increased

> ALL AND SINGULAR that certain parcel or tract of land and premises situate,...
> being in the Township of Anytownship in the County of Anycounty and being c...f
> of part of Lot 4, Concession IV in the said Township and being more particularly
> described as follows:
>
> COMMENCING at a point in the northern limit of the road allowance
> between concessions III and IV distance 198 feet measured westerly there
> along from the South East corner of said Lot 4....

The lack of exact directional bearings could cause conflict between the printed word and what existed on the ground. Metes and bounds descriptions and associated surveys helped eliminate a great deal of confusion through improved wording precision:

> Commencing at a point in the northern limit of the said road allowance distant 198
> feet measured on a bearing of South 60 degrees 10 minutes thirty seconds West there
> along from the South East corner of said Lot 4...[partial description only]

The reader now possessed sufficient details to confirm boundaries exactly by means of a re-survey of the property. Unfortunately, written metes and bounds descriptions were often complex and surveys lacking sufficient reference to abutting properties could prove confusing. As a result, various requirements were added to recording acts and regulations associated with registry and land titles systems.

VISUAL PLANS

Detailed surveys with improved standards are now required in support of fractional descriptions and new developments require formal surveys of the entire subdivision including all lots. A severance of land in rural areas now must be fully described by means of a reference plan (see subsequent discussion) identifying the severed property as a PART. The legal description, while still referring to lot and concession, is now supported by a visual reference plan filed in the land registration office. A typical description might read as follows:

> Part of Lot 25, Concession IV, more particularly described as PART 2 on Reference Plan
> 99R-1832, Township of Anytownship.

In the case of subdivision lots, the entire plan is allocated a number based on when it was registered and individual lots are simply described numerically. For example, Mr. Smith purchases Lot 27 in the Anycity Heights subdivision. The legal description would be:

> Lot 27, Plan 99M-165, City of Anycity.

SECTION I   PROPERTY OWNERSHIP

The lot number designates his property and the plan number informs the searcher of the following: the land registration office is identified by the number (in this case 99), the plan can be found under land titles (frequently indicated by the letter **M**) as opposed to registry and the plan number being #165 (the 165th plan registered in that land registration office) is filed accordingly within the land titles records for that land registration office. This example is provided for illustration purposes only. Variations exist across the province.

Ensuring Accuracy in Today's Marketplace   FOCUS

Land description in Ontario has progressed well beyond Simcoe's original plan of townships, concessions and lots, but the fundamentals remain, particularly for practitioners in rural areas. However, for their urban counterparts, problems began to surface with more complex divisions of land typically found in built-up areas.

- Initially, descriptions were simple and straightforward. A 200-acre farm could be quickly identified by lot and concession.

- Irregular parcels were ultimately carved out of concession lots by means of metes and bounds descriptions.

- Increasingly, written descriptions were supported by surveys. The survey has now all but replaced metes and bounds descriptions given the advantage of graphic display over words.

- Surveys became a necessity to clearly denote not only the boundaries, but also physical improvements situated on the land, together with limitations to rights of ownership.

- Given increasingly complex land use plans, registered plans were required to better describe specific lots within a registered plan of subdivision, or in the case of a condominium, to identify the unit location within the condominium plan.

METES AND BOUNDS

Metes and bounds is a system of written land description whereby all boundary lines are set forth by use of terminal points and angles; metes referring to a limit or limiting mark (i.e., distance) and bounds referring to boundary lines (i.e., directions). All descriptive text and illustrations are based on metes and bounds descriptions as recorded in land registry.

Metes and bounds descriptions arose from a necessity to sever land originally described by means of township surveys that were generally patented as whole lots or fractional parts of lots. As demand increased for smaller lots, severances were required. Until recently, new severances that did not form part of a plan of subdivision were generally described by means of a metes and bounds description. Often land descriptions were provided by the seller or buyer without benefit of a survey.

An example is provided representing an early form of metes and bounds description. While the wording does provide general direction and dimensions enclosing the property, the description lacked specific directions (i.e., degrees, minutes and seconds as set out in compass directions).

> *ALL AND SINGULAR* that certain parcel or tract of land and premises situate, lying and being in the Township of Anytownship in the County of Anycounty and being composed of part of Lot 4, Concession III in the said Township and being more particularly described as follows:
>
> *COMMENCING* at a point in the northern limit of the road allowance between concessions II and III distant 198 feet measured westerly there along from the south east corner of said Lot 4;
>
> *THENCE* westerly continuing along the northern limit of said road allowance a distance of 330 feet;
>
> *THENCE* northerly parallel to the eastern limit of Lot 4 a distance of 264 feet;
>
> *THENCE* easterly parallel to the northern limit of the said road allowance a distance of 330 feet;
>
> *THENCE* southerly parallel to the eastern limit of Lot 4 a distance of 264 feet more or less to the place of commencement.

Many variations of metes and bounds descriptions are found given the lack of rigid rules in historical land description and registration. Two of many examples are provided for illustration purposes.

EXAMPLE	*Historical Variations*
Land has been described as that part of a lot lying to one side of a described line (preamble omitted).	Land has also been described by reference to the perpendicular width of a rectangular part of a rectangular lot (preamble omitted).
That part of Lot 3 lying South of a straight line drawn from a point in the Western limit of the lot, distant 950 feet measured northerly there along from the South West corner of the said lot, to a point in the Eastern limit of the said lot, distant 1,200 feet measured northerly therealong from the South East corner of the said lot.	*That part of Lot 5 which lies North of a line parallel to and perpendicularly distant 69 feet, measured southerly, from the Northern limit of said lot.*

Directions and Quadrantal Bearings

In circumstances previously outlined, a real possibility existed that the location of the property as described in the deed might not agree with the actual position of the property on the ground. In older crown patents and many earlier deeds, the dimensions were given in chains, links, rods, perches or poles and the areas were occasionally provided in square chains.

In the example provided, the directions are given in quadrantal bearings. Quadrantal bearings are a method of expressing the direction of a line in terms of the acute angle it makes with the north-south line chosen as the reference line for that particular survey. For example, the lines having bearings of North 20 degrees 49 minutes 30 seconds West and South 20 degrees 49 minutes 30 seconds East both form angles of 20 degrees 49 minutes 30 seconds with the north-south line used for this description.

In older surveys, the north-south direction may have been determined either by astronomic observations, by using magnetic north as shown on a compass or merely by arbitrarily assuming a direction to be North. Today's surveys must comply with rigid legislative and professional surveyor requirements.

For example, the *Registry Act* and the Standards for Surveys of the Association of Ontario Land Surveyors require the bearings to be determined by astronomic observation or derived from a line of known astronomic bearing.

> *ALL AND SINGULAR that certain parcel or tract of land and premises situate, lying and being in the Township of Anytownship in the County of Anycounty and being composed of that part of Lot 7, Concession IV, described as follows:*
>
> > *PREMISING that the northern limit of the road allowance between Concessions III and IV as shown on Plan 899 registered in the Land Registry Office for the Registry Division of Anycounty has a bearing of North 69 degrees 10 minutes 30 seconds East and relating all bearings herein thereto;*
> >
> > *COMMENCING at a point in the northern limit of the said road allowance distant South 69 degrees 10 minutes 30 seconds West, 369.72 feet measured therealong from the South East corner of the said Lot 7;*
> >
> > *THENCE North 20 degrees 49 minutes 30 seconds West, a distance of 300.00 feet to a point;*
> >
> > *THENCE South 69 degrees 10 minutes 30 seconds West, a distance of 200.00 feet to a point;*
> >
> > *THENCE South 20 degrees 49 minutes 30 seconds East, a distance of 300.00 feet more or less to a point in the Northern limit of said road allowance;*
> >
> > *THENCE North 69 degrees 10 minutes 30 seconds East, a distance of 200.00 feet more or less to the point of commencement.*

Analyzing a Metes and Bounds Description

A typical metes and bounds description is illustrated, along with a supporting sketch. Such descriptions are straightforward, if read with reference to a few key concepts:

Direction	The reference to degrees, minutes and seconds represents very accurate compass directions. The division of degrees into 60 parts called minutes, and minutes into a further 60 parts called seconds, enables the draftsman to be very accurate in describing the angle. One can imagine that the less accurate the initial compass direction is at its starting point, the greater the error along its line of extension.
Distance	With respect to distances, notice that even where the description is so accurate that the measurements are given in hundredths of a foot, the expression **more or less** is still used. Some measurements are said to be more or less to allow for minor error. The reason is that the description must completely enclose the parcel of land. There can be no gaps.
Enclosing the Property	The line running from West to East along the South of the parcel must get to a point in the Westerly limit of the road allowance. Similarly, when the description proceeds Northerly along the road, the measurement is not as important as the fact that the line must reach the place of commencement.

More or Less

Term often found in a property description intended to cover slight, unimportant or unsubstantial inaccuracies of which both parties are willing to assume the risk.

Location	The description establishes the location of the property in general terms. The third paragraph establishes a point of commencement, and the description proceeds to indicate the perimeter of the parcel by setting out directions and distances.
Compass Bearings	The bearings are compass directions. The first direction is always true north or south. A survey will always indicate the compass direction in relation to north. This is followed by instructions to swing away a certain number of degrees (minutes and seconds) in an easterly or westerly direction.

ALL AND SINGULAR that certain parcel of land and premises situate lying and being in the Township of Anytownship, in the County of Anycounty and being composed of part of Lot 8, Concession IX in said Township, more particularly described as follows:

PREMISING that the Westerly limit of the road allowance between Concessions IX and X has a bearing of North 45 degrees 11 minutes, 30 seconds West and relating all bearings herein thereto;

COMMENCING at a point in the westerly limit of said road allowance distant 462.48 feet measured on a bearing of South 45 degrees 11 minutes 30 seconds East along the Westerly limit of said road allowance from the Northeast angle of said lot 8;

THENCE South 38 degrees 15 minutes 22 seconds West a distance of 120.36 feet to a point;

THENCE South 44 degrees 03 minutes 40 seconds East a distance of 113.26 feet to a point;

THENCE North 43 degrees 09 minutes 52 seconds East a distance of 120.18 feet, more or less, to a point in the said Westerly limit of the road allowance;

THENCE North 45 degrees 11 minutes 30 seconds West along said Westerly limit of road allowance a distance of 114 feet, more or less, to the point of commencement.

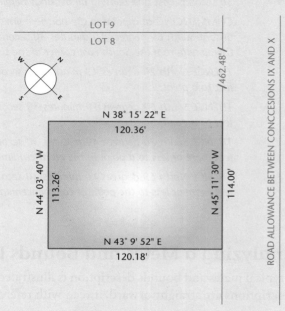

Directions and Bearings

To clarify the directions indicated, follow these steps to create the diagram as illustrated below.

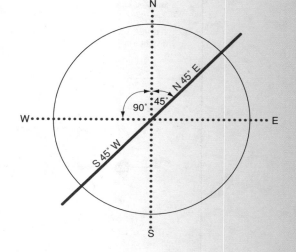

1. Draw a circle.

2. Draw a line from top to bottom and mark the top north and the bottom south.

3. Draw a horizontal line intersecting the first line at the centre of the circle.

4. Mark the right end of the line where it cuts the circle east and the other end west.

5. Draw a line from the centre of the circumference halfway between north and east; i.e., dividing this quarter of the circle in two. A circle contains 360 degrees, each degree contains 60 minutes, each minute contains 60 seconds; between north and east is a quarter of a circle or 90 degrees. By dividing this quarter in two, a line is created that is described as north 45 degrees east.

6. Extend this line to a point on the circle halfway between south and west. This is known as the back or reverse bearing, or south 45 degrees west.

One line has two descriptions, one of which indicates one direction and the other the exact opposite. Therefore, in reading a description, one can tell which direction on the straight line is being followed.

A Written Walk Around the Property   METES AND BOUNDS FOCUS

All metes and bounds descriptions start at a point of reference on the property and progress around the property, ultimately returning to the original point of reference (point of commencement); i.e., a written walk around the property that includes metes (the distance) and bounds (boundary lines; i.e., directions).

The diagram (see facing page) illustrates a vacant piece of land having four boundaries. For this example, the descriptive starting point is the upper right hand corner of the property. In four successive steps, the walk of the property is completed. To better understand directions being taken, a small compass circle has been placed over the four sequential changes in direction. Note how the description changes as we move in various directions, ultimately returning to the point of commencement.

The compass circle shows four quadrants—Southwest, Southeast, Northeast and Northwest—each having 90 degrees. All bearings (directions) are taken from the north-south bearing line that represents 0 degrees. The direction of travel is identified by the quadrant; the exact number of degrees is determined in relation to the north south line.

Students are sometimes confused when the metes and bounds description references a "southerly" direction when walking and yet the survey shows a northerly bearing. The explanation is simple. Every line has two descriptions, one in relation to North and one to South. In a survey, all references relate to the angle (bearing) in relation to the northerly direction of the north/south line. Therefore, all bearings relate to degrees from north (either east or west). However, when the property is described by metes and bounds, the walk around the property makes us face in various directions (some northerly and some southerly based on the shape of the property) before returning to the point of commencement.

Metes and Bounds Description

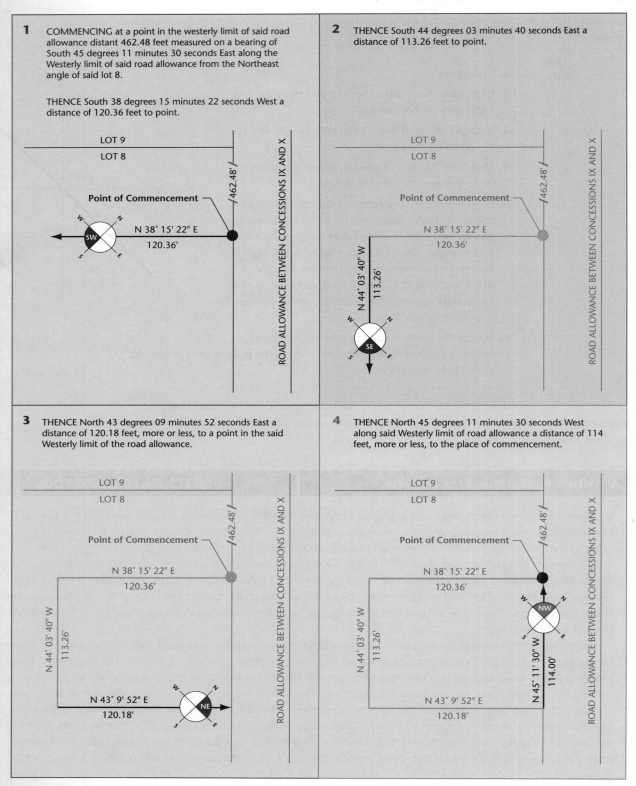

1 COMMENCING at a point in the westerly limit of said road allowance distant 462.48 feet measured on a bearing of South 45 degrees 11 minutes 30 seconds East along the Westerly limit of said road allowance from the Northeast angle of said lot 8.

THENCE South 38 degrees 15 minutes 22 seconds West a distance of 120.36 feet to point.

2 THENCE South 44 degrees 03 minutes 40 seconds East a distance of 113.26 feet to point.

3 THENCE North 43 degrees 09 minutes 52 seconds East a distance of 120.18 feet, more or less, to a point in the said Westerly limit of the road allowance.

4 THENCE North 45 degrees 11 minutes 30 seconds West along said Westerly limit of road allowance a distance of 114 feet, more or less, to the place of commencement.

SURVEYS

A survey, prepared by an Ontario Land Surveyor, depicts accurate mathematical measurements of land and improvements. Several types of surveys exist. Technically, land surveying is referred to as cadastral surveying. Cadastral, as an adjective, generally refers to the division of land; e.g., townships, concessions and lots. Therefore, a cadastral survey is a visual presentation showing boundaries, dimensions and other relevant information for a specific piece of property.

Many surveys exist ranging from construction surveys (i.e., structural layout of buildings, bridges, roads, etc.) to topographical surveys (i.e., land contours and elevations). Practitioners will most typically encounter four types of surveys when involved in the listing and selling of residential and commercial real estate.

- Surveyor's Real Property Report
- Reference Plan (R-Plan)
- Plan of Survey
- Plan of Subdivision

Surveyors are also involved in the preparation of the *description*, one of two documents required for condominium registration. The other required document is the *declaration*.

Ontario Surveys

Surveyors in Ontario are subject to both the *Surveys Act* and the *Surveyors Act* in the establishment and/or re-establishment of lines, boundaries and other components of surveys. The term survey is not statutorily defined other than descriptively referenced in the *Surveys Act*. The Association of Ontario Land Surveyors has determined that a survey contains four components:

- Research
- Measurement
- Monumentation
- Plan and/or Report

The determination of boundary lines made by the surveyor is not necessarily based on a description in the deed or an earlier survey plan. He/she must consider the best evidence available and re-establish the boundary on the ground in the location where it was first established.

To establish the true boundaries of the property, the surveyor's mandate is to follow the rules of evidence based on precedent setting court cases. The courts have established the weight or priority of evidence as follows:

- Natural boundaries; e.g., rivers.
- Original monuments; e.g., stone, iron bars and other items set during the first running of lines.
- Physical evidence of ground takes precedence over written evidence in transfer/deed.

SURVEYS ACT

The *Surveys Act* sets out requirements for the establishment and/or re-establishment of survey items such as lines, boundaries and corners. The *Surveys Act* consists of 11 parts that describe methods and procedures regarding front and rear townships, single and double front townships, sectional townships and plans of subdivision. A valid survey is defined by the Act:

> *No survey of land for the purpose of defining, locating or describing any line, boundary or corner of a parcel of land is valid unless made by a surveyor or under the personal supervision of a surveyor. (Part I, Sec. 2, Surveys Act, R.S.O. 1990).*

SURVEYORS ACT

The Association of Ontario Land Surveyors, as the governing body for land surveyors in the province, operates under the provision of the *Surveyors Act*. Regulation 42/96, passed under this Act, should be of general interest to real estate practitioners in that it sets out standards of practice concerning field surveys and plans, while allowing some professional discretion by individual surveyors.

PART I: Interpretation

Definitions relating to surveying.

PART II: Field Survey Standards

Establishes accepted terminology for members of the Association of Ontario Land Surveyors licensed to engage in the practice of cadastral surveying.

Part II sets out field survey standards; i.e., practice parameters and minimum guidelines. For example, surveyors must prepare field notes for every survey containing a clear and detailed account of everything found, observed and done in the field in the course of and relevant to the survey.

PART III: Plans

Applies to plans executed by a registered member surveyor while engaged in the practice of cadastral surveying. For example, the plan must be drawn on translucent linen or on translucent plastic material, rectangular in size, signed by the surveyor, drawn to a scale sufficient for clarity, prepared to a drafting standard that will permit legible and accurate copies and not drawn in colour.

Part III also includes extensive practice requirements concerning items shown on a survey; e.g., rights-of-way, radius, arc length, cord length and chord bearing of each curved line, straight line distances and bearings, north point and scale to which the plan is drawn.

PART IV: Surveyor's Real Property Report

Describes the components included in a surveyor's real property report. For purposes of this Regulation, a surveyor's real property report is a survey that locates a building or structure in relation to the boundaries of a unit of land. This report must consist of a plan of survey and a written report. If these two items are separate, a note must be inserted indicating that the written report is to be read in conjunction with the plan. The plan shall also include a note specifying the name of the client. In addition to the requirements of Part III, the surveyor's real property report shall show:

- All buildings and structures, the foundations of all buildings and structures under construction and their distances from the boundaries of the land.
- The number of storeys of all buildings and their external construction materials.
- The municipal address of the property, if any.

WEB LINKS

Land Surveyors   For more information concerning the Association of Ontario Land Surveyors, go to the Association's web site at **www.aols.org**.

Surveyor's Real Property Report

This report, traditionally referred to as a building location survey, consists of two parts:

- Part 1—Plan of Survey; and
- Part 2—The Written Report.

The **Surveyor's Real Property Report** is completed in accordance with the Standards for Surveys of the Ontario Land Surveyors Association and represents a full survey of the property, with the exception that complete monumentation is not required. Only the front angles of the property must be monumented. This survey does, however, show everything that might affect title to the property as well as enjoyment of the property by the owner.

To be complete and accurate, the Surveyor's Real Property Report must have the following:

- The municipal address and information regarding the land titles or registry office designations.
- The dimensions and bearings of all property boundaries, as determined by a field survey, according to the standards for surveys of the Ontario Association of Land Surveyors.
- The designation of adjacent properties, roads, lands, etc.
- The location and description of all pertinent improvements on the property, along with the setbacks to the property boundaries. The projection of overhangs and eaves are also noted, as well as fences, driveways, walkways, swimming pools, trees, etc.
- The location of any easements or rights-of-way that may affect the property.
- The location and dimensions of any visible encroachments onto or off the property (hydro lines, telephone, etc.).
- The location of survey monuments found and placed.
- A note indicating for whom the plan is prepared.
- Certification by an Ontario Land Surveyor.
- Written report.

A typical residential survey (Part 1) identifying lot boundaries and the structure is illustrated.

> **Surveyor's Real Property Report**
>
> A plan of survey consisting of two parts: Plan of Survey and The Written Report.

Survey

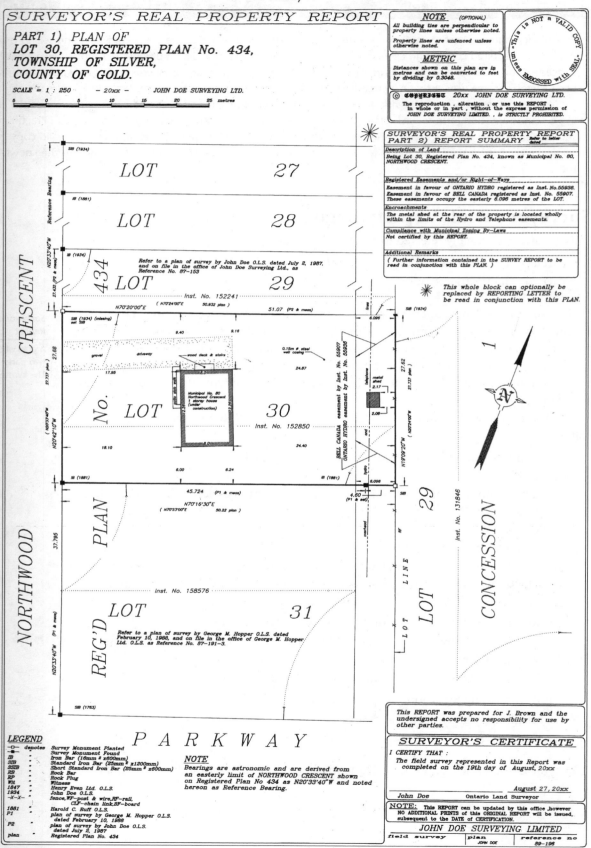

SECTION I

PROPERTY OWNERSHIP

Reference Plan

A **reference plan** is a survey that provides a graphic illustration of property pursuant to requirements as set out in the *Registry Act* or *Land Titles Act*. Often referred to as an R-Plan, the reference plan is not a plan of subdivision, but rather a plan of survey that meets requirements as set out in the *Surveys Act*. The reference plan was introduced as a graphic illustration of the land and associated metes and bounds description to permit a more effective, less complex method of describing property.

A reference plan normally describes more than one area with each area identified as a part; e.g., PART 1, PART 2, etc. Buildings may or may not be shown on reference plans. A typical legal description shown on a reference plan is provided by way of example. The reference plan provided is identified as 99R-1033. The first number identifies the applicable registry office (in this case, a fictitious 99 is used) followed by the sequentially assigned number for that specific reference plan (in this case, being the 1033rd plan deposited in the applicable land registry office).

> **Reference Plan**
>
> A survey that normally describes more than one interest in land (each interest identified as a Part), which is deposited in a Land Registry Office.

> *Legal Description Based on Reference Plan*
>
> *Part of Lot 2, Concession I, Township of Anytownship, designated as PART 2 on a Reference Plan deposited in the Land Registry Office for the Registry Division of Anycounty as 99R-1033.*

With few exceptions, all changes to land now require a reference plan to be deposited in the land registration office. Reference plans are normally required for:

- Severance of an existing lot or parcel. The reference plan is for descriptive purposes only, as a formal consent for a land severance is required.
- Any instrument that is submitted for registration within the land registry office and the description is sufficiently vague or complex in the opinion of the land registrar.
- First application (first registration) under the *Land Titles Act*.

A reference plan is not a plan of subdivision within the meaning of the *Planning Act*. A sample reference plan is illustrated on the following page. Reference plans are particularly useful when dealing with convoluted or multi-sided parcels, as complex metes and bounds descriptions can be avoided and replaced with a visual portrayal of the property.

Plan of Survey

A **plan of survey** largely resembles the overall format and content of a reference plan with two major differences. First, the plan cannot be deposited as a separate document with the title in a land registration office, as it lacks certain certificates and other items required by the *Registry Act* or *Land Titles Act*. Second, a survey normally describes a specific property while a reference plan usually describes several. A plan of survey is typically provided only to the client or others upon that client's instruction, with the original plan being retained by the surveyor. As mentioned previously, a plan of survey is Part 1 of the Surveyor's Real Property Report.

Reference Plan

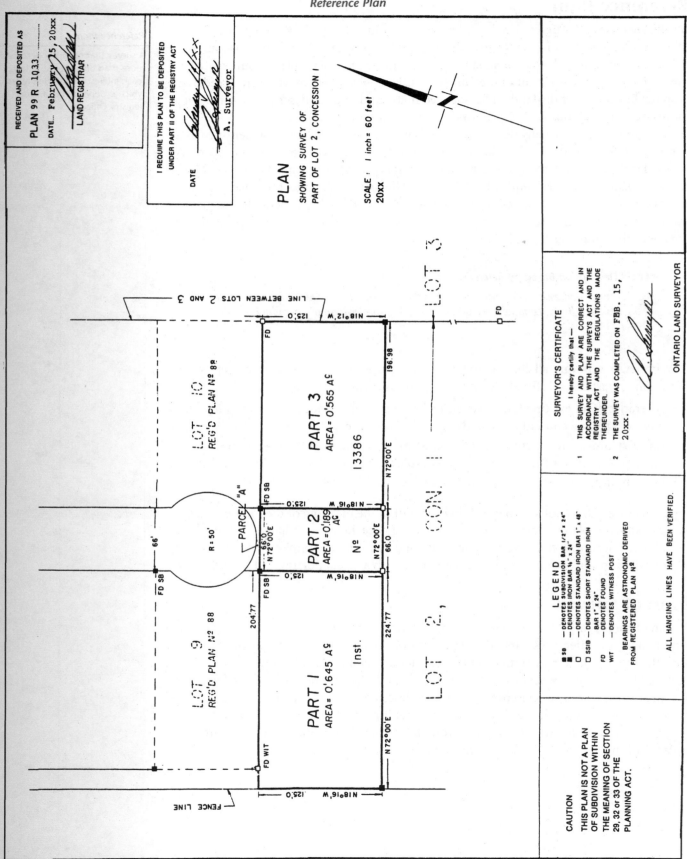

Plan of Subdivision

A registered **plan of subdivision** is prepared by an Ontario Land Surveyor showing lots, blocks or parcels of land intended to be dealt with separately, as such separation has been fully approved by appropriate municipal authorities and registered in the land registry office.

> **Plan of Subdivision**
>
> A detailed survey indicating lots, blocks of land, road allowances, etc.

Plans of subdivision are assigned numbers at time of registration. Subdivision plans divide the land into various numbered or named subdivision units such as lots, blocks, streets and road allowances. A registered plan of subdivision creates a new geographic identity for the land. For example, a property might have been previously described as Part of Lot 2, Concession III, Township of Anytownship, County of Anycounty. Upon registration as a subdivision, the legal identity would change; e.g., Registered Plan 99M-165, County of Anycounty.

Plans of subdivision arose from the need for smaller units of land, in addition to severances from township lots by means of written descriptions. At point of registration, each plan is assigned a number. See the illustration on the following page for an example in which Plan 485 is registered from an under-developed block of land (Block 195) contained within an older registered plan (Plan 450). Additional details concerning the registration process for subdivisions is provided under planning and land use discussions later in this course.

Compiled Plans   CAUTION

A compiled plan is a visual depiction of adjoining lands that originated as a method to clarify written metes and bounds descriptions in Ontario land registration offices. Compiled plans were designed for general information and guidance only. For the most part, they do not constitute plans of survey, but certain exceptions exist. Compiled plans were officially discontinued in 1985, but are worthy of note as such plans may still appear when reviewing land registry records. The vast majority of these were developed directly from documented descriptions in the land registration office with no inspection of the lands.

Two types of compiled plans were used:

- The Land Registrar's Compiled Plan (LRCP) is NOT a plan of survey, but simply a visual indexing system to typically identify several adjacent properties. The exact extent of ownership for such properties was established by metes and bounds descriptions.

- The Municipally Ordered Compiled Plan (MOCP) is similar to the LRCP but was requested by municipalities to assist in land development.

Fortunately, the current conversion of paper-based registry records to electronic land titles records will eliminate all compiled plans in the near future.

Plan of Subdivision

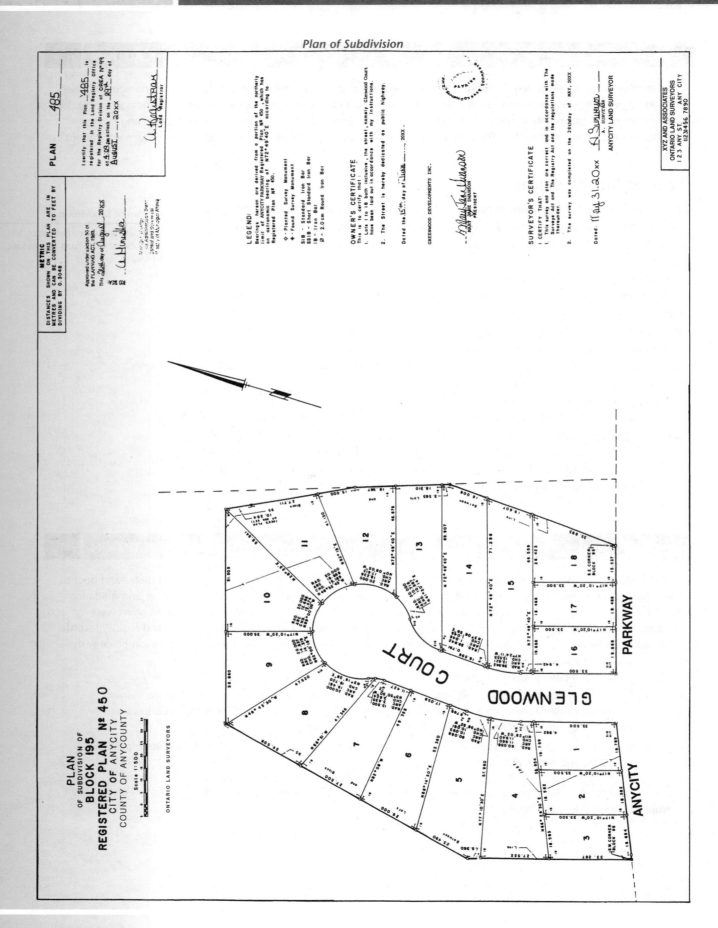

Condominium

A **declaration** and a **description** must be registered in order for a **condominium** corporation to legally come into existence. The *Condominium Act* sets out procedures for registering both documents in the land registry office. The description includes all the plans for the condominium.

DESCRIPTION

The description is a diagrammatic presentation of the property and any structures within the condominium corporation. This includes such items as the plan of survey, architectural plans and structural plans, along with other legislative requirements. The *Condominium Act* specifically sets out the following requirements:

- A plan of survey showing the perimeters of the land and buildings.
- Architectural building plans (including an architect's certificate that all buildings are in accordance with the regulations under the Act).
- Structural plans (if there are any) along with an engineer's certificate that all buildings are in accordance with the regulations under the Act.
- Boundaries of all units in relation to the buildings and other monumentation.
- Diagrams depicting the shape/dimensions of each unit and location in relation to other units and the structure as a whole.
- A certificate signed by an Ontario land surveyor stating that the unit diagrams are substantially correct.
- A description of all interests appurtenant to the land that are included with the property.
- Any other material that may be required under the Act.

DECLARATION

The description should be clearly differentiated from the declaration, which is best described as the constitution of the condominium corporation. The Act outlines both required and optional items. If any item in the declaration is inconsistent with the Act, the provisions of the Act prevail.

Declaration content varies according to condominium type; e.g., standard, phased, vacant land, common element and leasehold. Selected items required in the declaration are listed below.

- Statement that the *Condominium Act* governs the land and appurtenant interests.
- Consent of mortgagees.
- Proportionate interest of each unit in the common elements.
- Proportionate interest of each unit in allocating contribution to common expenses.
- Address for service, municipal address and mailing address (if different from service and/or municipal addresses).
- Parts of common elements used by one or more designated units and not by all owners.
- Common expenses of the condominium corporation.
- Conditions or restrictions concerning occupation or use of units and/or common elements.
- Responsibilities of the condominium corporation consistent with its objects and duties.
- Allocation of obligations to maintain units and common elements, including repairs after damage, in accordance with the Act.

Declaration

A condominium document required for registration that sets out the responsibilities of the owners and condominium corporation.

Description

A diagrammatic presentation of the condominium property and structures on that property.

NOTE: Standard, phased, vacant land, common element and leasehold condominium types are fully described in *The Residential Real Estate Transaction*.

WEB LINKS

Condominium   The *Condominium Act* can be accessed at ***www.e-laws.gov.on.ca.***

ROAD SYSTEMS

Ontario's road systems form an important dimension within the overall scheme of land description. As briefly described earlier, road allowances were established between concessions. Legally, roads are described in much the same way as other land by being designated as such on plans of subdivision, identified on reference plans and described in surveys.

The original road allowances provided the rudimentary structure for what is now an extensive road system of provincial, county, township and municipal roads throughout the province. Over 16,000 kilometers of paved roads currently exist in Ontario. In fact, survey work involving new roads and construction/upgrading of existing roads is a special area of expertise. Many road allowances established under township systems remain unopened. Individuals contemplating the use of such road allowances should seek guidance from the local municipality, as various requirements and standards must be met. Legal advice is also strongly encouraged.

Road Categories

PROVINCIAL HIGHWAYS

Ontario's provincial highways can be broadly grouped under three categories beginning with the 400-series King's Highways (e.g., controlled access highways such as the 400 and the 401). The King's Highways are typically either two or four-lane undivided paved roads with numbers ranging from 2 to 169.

NOTE: This numbering system also includes alternate routes identified as either A or B (e.g., Highway 7A).

Secondary Highways are generally inferior to King's Highways and are used primarily to service small communities in more distant Northern and Central Ontario locations. Lastly, tertiary roads were introduced in the 1960's to provide access to remote areas in the province with the intention of ultimately upgrading these routes to Secondary Highways.

COUNTY ROADS

County roads are usually numbered in Ontario and are typically marked with trapezoid-shaped signs, often including both the county road number and the county or region responsible for updating and maintenance. Most county roads are built to provincial highway standards. In the late 1990's, many provincial highways were downloaded from provincial to county/regional responsibility. Some roads were further downloaded to the municipal responsibility as part of an overall restructuring of responsibilities within the province.

Road Map—Selected Area of Ontario

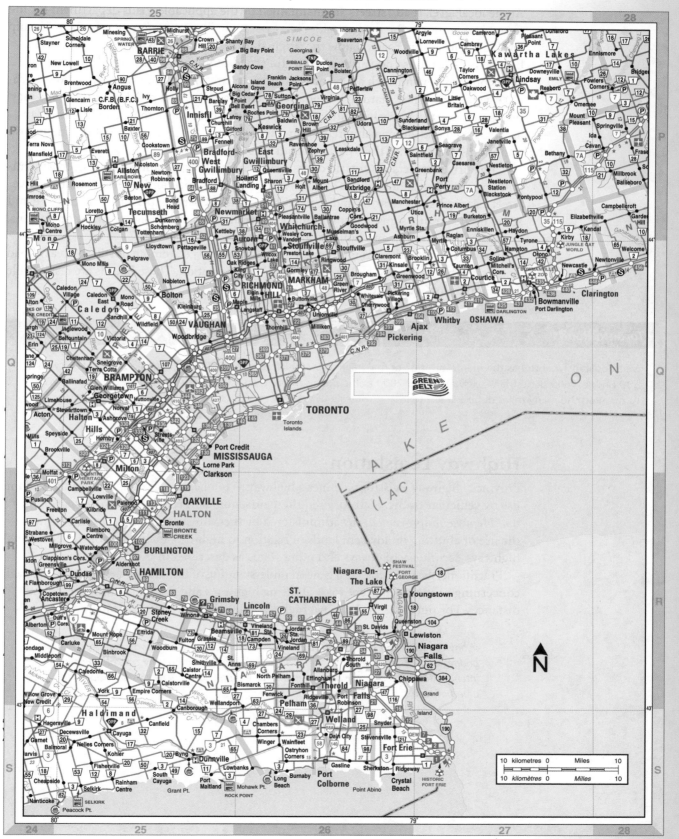

Source: Ontario Ministry of Transportation

TOWNSHIP AND MUNICIPAL ROADS

At the local level, roads/streets are maintained by the applicable roads department for the municipal authority, be it a township, incorporated village, town or city. At the township level, most township roads follow the original township layout with road allowances between concessions and various connecting roads. Other township roads may involve roads opened beyond such allowances in order to circumvent natural obstructions such as large hills, or follow natural boundaries such as a river bank or lake. Lastly, roads may be assumed by the township within plans of development once these subdivision plans are registered and all township requirements are met. Similarly, municipalities in Ontario maintain streets within their particular jurisdictions.

Large urban centers in Ontario operate substantial transportation services departments with expanding responsibilities and activities including road and sidewalk maintenance, street cleaning, snow clearing and road salting, on-street parking permits, construction and street events, traffic signs, pavement marking, traffic signals, red light camera operations, construction planning and policies, and pedestrian/cycling issues.

In areas in which there is no municipal organization (i.e., remote northern areas) Road Boards can be established by the Ministry of Transportation. These Boards are responsible for maintaining such roads.

Toronto Roads	CURIOSITY

Metropolitan Toronto has the mammoth task of maintaining 5,300 kilometers of roads, 7,100 kilometers of sidewalks, 530 bridges, 600 pedestrian crosswalks, over 2000 traffic signals, more than 4,000 bus shelters and 1 million signs, not to mention the many miles of bike lanes, trails and routes.

Source: Transportation Services, City of Toronto.

Highway Legislation

Provincial highway legislation defines a highway as public passage designed or intended for use by vehicular traffic. Statutory requirements, pursuant to the *Public Transportation and Highway Improvement Act* administered by the Ministry of Transportation, impact the use of abutting or adjacent lands in relation to highways including controlled-access highways, secondary highways and other roads as described in the Act.

Practitioners should possess a general understanding of limitations that may be imposed concerning property adjacent to or abutting highways and that fall within prescribed distances. For purposes of the Act, a highway is expansively defined as including:

> *...any common and public highway, street, avenue, parkway, driveway, square, place, bridge, viaduct, trestle or any other structure incidental thereto, any part of which is intended for or used by the general public for the passage of vehicles and includes the area between the lateral property lines thereof.*

PERMITS

A permit issued by the Minister is required for various activities near a highway designated as the King's Highway; e.g., placing, erecting or altering buildings, fences, gasoline pumps or other structures; the placing of trees, shrubs or hedges; the displaying of signs, notices or advertising devices; the use of land for various purposes that cause individuals to congregate in large number such as a theatre or fairground; the displaying, selling or offering for sale of goods or merchandise; and the construction or use of any private road, entranceway, gate or other structure as a means of access to the highway.

Part II of the Act relates to highways that are designated as controlled-access highways and includes more stringent requirements; i.e., greater minimum distances for activities already outlined above. A King's Highway can be designated as a secondary highway (Part III) in which case the regulations that apply to a King's Highway will also apply with necessary modifications as set out in the Act. County roads (Part VII) fall under the jurisdiction and control of the county and are subject to applicable rights and powers granted to municipalities under the *Planning Act*. Further, the county may prohibit or regulate matters concerning the placing, erecting or altering of any gas pump, the displaying of signs and notices, and the construction or alteration of any private road, entranceway, gate or other structure or facility that permits access to a road as defined in the Act.

Practitioners should also be aware that developers involved with land development proposals may require a Public Transportation and Highway Improvement Act Permit. This permit can involve either a building and land use permit when a structure is being constructed within a highway corridor control area (the control area varies by type of structure being built), or an encroachment permit when work must be completed within the highway right-of-way. The Ministry of Transportation may also dictate conditions of approval that apply to a site plan or draft plan of subdivision proposal.

Entrances, Access and Permits   **FOCUS ON ROADS**

The current description is merely an introduction to road issues as they relate to real property ownership. Both residential and commercial salespersons, particularly those involved in rural and cottage areas, should be aware of certain road-related topics including procedures for obtaining an entrance permit for access from a property to a highway, county road or municipal road, building set-back requirements, and matters relating to access roads, seasonal roads and shore allowance roads in cottage country.

Additional information is provided in subsequent chapters within this course, as well as in *The Residential Real Estate Transaction*.

Geographic Information Systems

Traditional mapping systems have sufficed for many years, but increasingly, complex ownership structures, road systems and other attributes of modern real estate have proven challenging. Fortunately, new digital technology addresses many of those challenges. A **geographic information system** (GIS) combines the best of mapping with databases outlining everything from road systems to land developments and environmentally-sensitive areas within a defined locale. GIS is a software tool that combines the user-friendly attributes of conventional maps with numerous databases which form the fabric (layers of information) including streets, buildings, parcels of land, natural geographic features, crime statistics, traffic counts and zoning requirements.

Public and private enterprises use GIS systems for better planning, lower administrative costs, fewer redundancies and better decision-making. Data is derived from three primary sources:

- Spatial data—mapping information including geographic features; e.g., buildings and streets.
- Tabular data—quantified information to complement a mapping feature; e.g., building permits issued by area.
- Image data—visual images; e.g., satellite images and aerial photographs.

Data can be displayed using either vector or raster modeling methods. Vector represents the mathematical expression of a feature; e.g., its location as a function of x, y co-ordinates, such as building lines, township lines, roads, etc. Raster represents the bit-mapped visual depiction of the feature; e.g., visual charting of rainfall statistics over a defined geographic area. At present, the worlds of surveying and GIS systems are converging. Ultimately, land descriptions and property information will be contained within one land description system.

GIS Fabric—Layers of Information

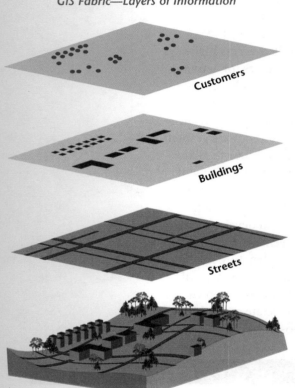

Customers

Buildings

Streets

WEB LINKS

Geographic Information Systems   Land Information Ontario (LIO) is the government agency most directly involved with geographic information systems. The LIO is primarily focused on geospatial database information to municipalities, government ministries, the Municipal Property Assessment Corporation, conservation authorities and others requiring information about individual property parcels and Crown parcels. Go to *www.lio.mnr.gov.on.ca*.

KNOWLEDGE INTEGRATION

- Practitioners should always rely on primary documents, not secondary documents, when obtaining a legal description.

- Historically, the legal description evolved from the orderly division of land into counties, townships, concessions and lots.

- Metes and bounds descriptions set out property boundaries including distance and direction.

- Directions within a metes and bounds description can vary from a survey as the former outlines the direction of travel, while the latter shows all bearings in relation to north.

- Metes and bounds descriptions must fully enclose the property beginning and ending at the point of commencement.

- Surveys contain four components: research, measurement, monumentation and a plan/report.

Notables

- The *Surveys Act* sets out requirements for the establishment and/or re-establishment of survey items such as lines, boundaries and corners.

- A Surveyor's Real Property Report contains two parts: Part 1—Plan of Survey and Part 2—Written Report.

- A reference plan (R-plan) is a graphic illustration of the land that is typically deposited (not registered) on title. Reference plans are not plans of subdivision.

- A plan of subdivision, prepared by an Ontario Land Surveyor, must be fully compliant with the *Planning Act* and registered in the appropriate land registry office.

- Condominium contains units and common elements. Condominium is a creature of statute brought into creation by the registration of a Declaration and a Description.

Glossary

Concession
Condominium
County
Declaration
Description
Double Front Township

Geographic Information System
Lot
Metes and Bounds
More or Less
Plan of Subdivision
Plan of Survey

Reference Plan
Sectional Township
Single Front Township
Survey
Surveyor's Real Property Report
Township

Web Links

Web links are included for general interest regarding selected chapter topics.

Land Surveyors For more information concerning the Association of Ontario Land Surveyors, go to the Association's web site at ***www.aols.org***.

Condominium The *Condominium Act* can be accessed at ***www.e-laws.gov.on.ca***.

Geographic Information Systems Land Information Ontario (LIO) is the government agency most directly involved with geographic information systems. The LIO is primarily focused on geospatial database information to municipalities, government ministries, the Municipal Property Assessment Corporation, conservation authorities and others requiring information about individual property parcels and Crown parcels. Go to ***www.lio.mnr.gov.on.ca***.

Strategic Thinking For Your Career

Questions are included to assist in developing your new career. No answers are provided.

1. What township system was used for land descriptions in my local marketplace?

2. How will I know if a property is located within a registered plan of subdivision, based on the legal description for that property?

3. What dangers might arise if I relied upon an old, out-of-date survey when listing a property?

4. Can I identify a reference plan and clearly distinguish it from a plan of subdivision?

5. If a seller produced a recent Surveyor's Real Property Report of his or her property, could I readily review the document and understand key factors affecting the property and improvements thereon?

6. Can I readily identify different types of roads within my local area?

Chapter Mini-Review

Solutions are located in the Appendix.

1. The single front township is the oldest of the township systems used in Ontario.

    ○ True   ○ False

2. A concession is a township roadway.

    ○ True   ○ False

3. The sectional township system in Ontario was based on 1,000 acres per section.

    ○ True   ○ False

4. In a double front township, farms were usually patented in half-lots of 100 acres.

    ○ True   ○ False

5. The number for a reference plan is always preceded by the number 99.

    ○ True   ○ False

6. Plans of subdivision are assigned numbers at the time when the developer acquires the property.

    ○ True   ○ False

7. A registered plan of subdivision must be prepared by an Ontario Land Surveyor.

    ○ True   ○ False

8. A condominium declaration includes a plan of survey, architectural building plans and structural plans (if there are any).

    ○ True   ○ False

9. Field survey standards for Ontario Land Surveyors are set out in the *Surveyors Act.*

    ○ True   ○ False

10. A Surveyor's Real Property Report typically includes the location of pertinent improvements on the property, but not easements on the property.

    ○ True   ○ False

11. A survey, according to the Association of Land Surveyors, includes four components two of which are research and measurement.

    ○ True   ○ False

12. A Surveyor's Real Property Report and a reference plan are essentially the same and used for the same purposes.

    ○ True   ○ False

13. A registered plan of subdivision creates a new geographic identity for the land.

    ○ True   ○ False

14. Direct access by adjacent property owners to 400-series highways in Ontario is permitted provided that the applicable permits are obtained.

    ○ True   ○ False

15. A permit issued by the Minister is required for various activities near a highway designated as the King's Highway; e.g., placing, erecting or altering buildings.

    ○ True   ○ False

16. A geographic information system is typically used instead of a survey to precisely locate property boundaries.

    ○ True   ○ False

17. Compiled plans are largely replacing reference plans within the land registry system.

    ○ True   ○ False

Active Learning Exercises

Solutions are located in the Appendix.

■ Exercise 1   Multiple Choice

1.1   For purposes of land description, most of Southern Ontario was originally divided into counties. Counties were then divided into rectangles called townships. Townships were in turn divided into strips of land running the entire length of the township. The areas between these strips of land were called:

a.   Road allowances.

b.   Lot lines.

c.   Concessions.

d.   Lots.

1.2   Which of the following statements are correct?

    i.   Land is described in a precise manner so that one piece of land cannot be mistaken for another.

    ii.   A description such as *the lot with two mature maples* or *43 Main Street* is not sufficient as a land description in a current legal document.

    iii.   When originally laid out, county boundaries might follow natural boundaries (e.g., a river or lake) but most often were straight lines through the bush.

    iv.   A concession is normally 66 feet in width.

a.   i., ii. and iv.

b.   i., ii. and iii.

c.   ii. and iii.

d.   i. and ii.

1.3   In a metes and bounds description, which of the following are correct?

    i.   Some measurements are said to be *more or less* to compensate for minor errors.

    ii.   The description must completely enclose the parcel of land.

    iii.   On a survey, straight lines are described in relationship to North.

    iv.   The directions are given in bearings within quadrants.

a.   i. and ii.

b.   i., ii. and iii.

c.   i., ii., iii. and iv.

d.   i. and iv. only.

1.4   Metes and bounds is a system of written land descriptions. Which of the following is correct?

a.   All boundary lines are described by the use of lot numbers.

b.   All boundary lines are described by the use of terminal points and angles.

c.   All boundary lines are described as whole lots or fractional parts of lots.

d.   None of the above.

1.5   Which of the following is NOT true with respect to a reference plan?

    a.   A reference plan is used for ease of description.

    b.   Reference plan numbers are always preceded by the letter R.

    c.   A reference plan is a plan of subdivision.

    d.   A reference plan describes areas that are identified as parts; e.g., PART 1, PART 2, etc.

1.6   Which of the following is one of the two Parts of a Surveyor's Real Property Report?

    a.   Part 1—Plan Sheet.

    b.   Part 2—Certification.

    c.   Part 1—Plan of Survey.

    d.   Part 2—Reference Plan.

1.7   Which of the following statements are true?

    i.   Surveyors are required to prepare field notes for every survey.

    ii.   The Association of Ontario Land Surveyors is the governing body for surveyors.

    iii.   The *Surveys Act* sets out requirements for establishment or re-establishment of lines, boundaries and corners.

    iv.   The *Surveys Act* sets out requirements for a valid survey.

    a.   i., ii., iii. and iv.

    b.   i., ii. and iii.

    c.   i. and ii.

    d.   ii., iii. and iv.

■ Exercise 2   Getting Your Bearings

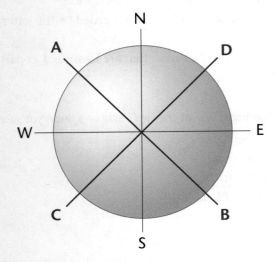

2.1   The line travelling in the direction from C to D has an approximate bearing of

....

2.2   What is the reverse (reciprocal) bearing of line C to D?

....

2.3   The line travelling in the direction from B to A has an approximate bearing of

....

■ Exercise 3   The Vacant Lot

Salesperson Lee of ABC Realty Inc. has inspected Owner Smith's vacant lot fronting on a concession road allowance. Smith is not certain of the exact property boundaries, but has a metes and bounds description. Assist by drawing a sketch based on this description. Make certain that your sketch has an arrow indicating north, contains all measurements and bearings as provided, and identifies the location of the road allowance. An excerpt from the original metes and bounds description follows.

The property fronts on the Northerly limit of a road allowance having a bearing of North 69 degrees East. Choose a point of commencement anywhere on the Northerly limit of the road allowance. The first measurement begins immediately after the point of commencement has been established on the side of the road allowance and the final measurement represents the lot frontage on the road allowance.

THENCE North 20 degrees West, a distance of 294.50 feet to a point;

THENCE South 69 degrees West, a distance of 354.50 feet to a point;

THENCE South 20 degrees East, a distance of 294.50 feet to a point;

THENCE North 69 degrees East, a distance of 354.50 feet more or less to the point of commencement.

NOTE: The final boundary line measurements include the phrases *more or less* and *to the point of commencement* to ensure that the description completely encloses the property.

◼ Exercise 4   The Reference Plan

Refer to the R-Plan illustrated in this chapter and answer the following questions.

4.1   What is the full legal description of Part 1?

4.2   When was the reference plan deposited in the land registry office?

4.3   Based on a review of the document and your knowledge of land descriptions, what appears to be the intended uses of Parts 1, 2 and 3?

4.4   Identify five key elements that differentiate this reference plan from a Surveyor's Real Property Report?

4.5   Briefly explain why this reference plan is not a plan of subdivision.

■ Exercise 5   The House on Northwood Crescent

Refer to the Surveyor's Real Property Report illustrated in this chapter and answer the following questions.

5.1   What potential problems may arise concerning the metal shed at the rear of the property?

5.2   On what date was this survey completed?

5.3   How many survey monuments were planted by the surveyor in completing this survey?

5.4   What is the legal description of the property?

CHAPTER 3

Land Registry and Title Registration

Introduction

Land registration systems provide for the orderly ownership of land in Ontario. Real estate salespeople require knowledge of the registration process including how registry and land titles systems operate, as well as what documentation is used. The emphasis in this chapter is on land titles and electronic registration (e-registration) as Ontario is rapidly moving towards a fully electronic system.

The conversion from the antiquated registry format to land titles is now over 90% complete. The conversion includes transferring registry records into land titles and, at the same time, automating these records and providing for electronic registration (e-registration). These online facilities now permit land registry users to retrieve real property information and conduct land transactions. Certain descriptive materials about paper-based systems and registry procedures are included in this chapter, as full conversion has not occurred at this point. Practitioners may encounter registry, paper-based documents in selected areas of the province.

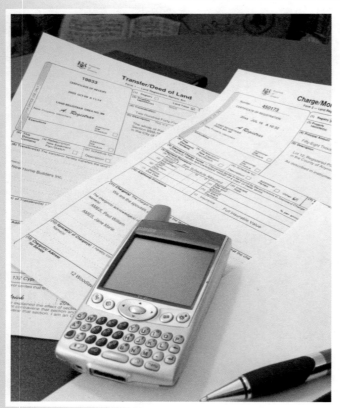

The process leading to full automation began in the mid-1980's. The key to automated registration lies in the parcelization process. Every property in Ontario is being identified geographically and assigned a parcel number. That number becomes the central reference for a host of property details. Most large urban centres are now fully automated.

While e-registration is the immediate goal, this new approach speaks to exciting opportunities in how properties are listed and marketed in the future. With a few mouse clicks, for example, practitioners can confirm who is the registered owner, determine what financing exists and identify various issues that might affect the selling of the property. Such information, when combined with assessment information and GIS data, will revolutionize the entire process.

Learning Outcomes

At the conclusion of this chapter, students will be able to:

- Outline basics of land registration procedures and differentiate between registry and land titles systems.
- Discuss procedures within a land registry office with particular emphasis on paper-based vs. electronic systems, title searching and other services offered.
- Detail fundamentals underlying the land titles conversion project now nearing completion within the province.
- Briefly outline the new system of automated records using POLARIS and e-registration procedures using the Teraview electronic gateway software.
- Identify and describe standard title registration documents (paper-based and online versions) including the transfer/deed of land, land transfer tax affidavit, charge/mortgage of land, discharge of charge/mortgage and document general.
- Briefly outline various miscellaneous registration-related topics including leasehold interests, crown lands, native lands, powers of attorney and properties of deceased persons.

LAND REGISTRATION SYSTEMS

Two land registration systems currently exist in Ontario under the *Registry Act* (registry system) and the *Land Titles Act* (land titles system). Land registration is administered by the Real Property Registration Branch, Ministry of Government Services (**www.mgs.gov.on.ca**). The **registry** system has traditionally prevailed in Southern Ontario with the majority of Northern Ontario under **land titles**.

Historically, both systems were paper-based but, as mentioned in the introduction, the conversion to an automated procedure is nearing completion. The process involves **POLARIS** (the mapping and property detail database of the Ontario government) and **Teranet** (responsible for implementation, operation and enhancement of POLARIS). Coincident with this change, records are also being gradually converted to land titles, officially referred to as the land titles conversion project. Ultimately, the registry system will disappear from the Ontario scene.

WEB LINKS

Ministry of Government Services   For more information concerning the Real Property Registration Branch of the Ministry of Government Services and land registration, go to the Ministry's web site at **www.mgs.gov.on.ca.**

The Recording Acts

The recording Acts (*Registry Act* and *Land Titles Act*) provide statutory rules affecting interests with respect to any particular plot of land and the priority of those interests. These Acts attempt to induce prompt registration and to indicate clearly what interests are claimed in the land, thus facilitating the sale of real property.

In Ontario, all land is registered under either the *Registry Act* or the *Land Titles Act*, but never under both. In the Registry system, the Land Registrar is an administrative official only, taking no responsibility for verifying title. In the land titles system, the Land Registrar maintains and guarantees title.

THE REGISTRY ACT

The registry system, dating back to 1795, records property interests on a geographic basis. All land within counties is registered at registry offices. The next largest division is the township. Accordingly, **abstract** books in the registry office are divided on a township basis. Townships are divided into concessions and lots. The basic recording books are the abstract books. Each book covers particular farm lots within each concession and within each township.

As urban areas developed and large subdivisions arose, the description of land (arrived at through metes and bounds descriptions consisting of parts of a farm lot) rapidly became unmanageable. Subdivision plans were developed and the legal description changed from a lot and concession reference to a plan number. Each parcel of land within the plan was assigned a number. New abstract books were opened to accommodate these plans. As time progressed, the shelves became filled with not only basic abstract books, but also many others to handle such things as condominiums, leasehold interests, wills, probates, highways and sundry lots.

The process of searching records became equally complex. A person wishing to search a particular lot would access the plan (abstract) book and look up the appropriate lot number. Title searches for a minimum 40-year period are typically necessary, therefore, searchers might have to go behind the plan (book) back to the abstract books that covered the original farm lot. Ultimately, the **chain of title** should go back to the original **Crown Patent** (i.e., the root of title).

Under this system, abstract books are indexed not under the people's names having interests in the land, but rather under the land description (referred to as tract indexing). Instruments (documents) affecting the land are summarized in chronological order within the abstract books thereby establishing priority. A title searcher obtains the document number from the abstracted information, presents it to the registrar and receives a copy.

LAND TITLES ACT

The *Land Titles Act* operates on the premise that the Land Titles Register (a book roughly comparable to the Abstract Book in Registry) is the sole information source for purchasers. Land titles is based on three principles: mirror principle, curtain principle and insurance principle.

The government is prepared to guarantee that no interests other than those set out in the register can affect the land. Consequently, the process of searching titles is significantly reduced. The register differs from the abstract book in that only existing and valid interests remain on the register. All prior interests that have ended are deleted. A detailed discussion of land titles follows.

Land Titles

The first *Land Titles Act* in Ontario was passed in 1885. With limited exceptions, all provincial Crown Patents must now be registered under the Act. In addition, all land to be subdivided by a registered plan of subdivision and all land on which condominiums are developed under the *Condominium Act* must be registered under the *Land Titles Act*, if that system of land registration is available in the applicable land registration office.

Land registered under the *Registry Act* may be brought under land titles by the owner through a process called first application. The large-scale conversion of registry records into land titles (commonly referred to as the administrative conversion) is now nearing completion. The land titles conversion project involves the conversion of registry records into land titles coincident with the move to electronic registration systems.

FEATURES/PRINCIPLES

While registry operates under a tract indexing system using geographic location, all land titles entries are by way of assigned parcel numbers. A separate parcel record is kept in a register of title for each unit of ownership. The actual title searching process involves identifying outstanding entries on the most recent parcel register for a specific property. The primary features of the land titles system are:

- A method of government registration of title to land in which the government, subject to certain limitations, guarantees the title and operates the registration process.

- All transactions must be registered against the title in the provincially-operated land titles office and are not valid in the form of mere instruments executed by parties as against other competing registered interests.

- The certificate of title is intended to be a complete and accurate reflection of the result of all preceding transactions affecting the property. Persons dealing with a registered property do not need to look elsewhere, except to search a few statutory exceptions to indefeasibility (that which cannot be annulled or terminated).

- An assurance fund is provided that is intended to provide compensation to those persons who suffer loss due to errors or omissions of the registrar in the operation of the system.
- No title to land registered under the Act that is adverse to the title of the registered owner can be acquired by any length of possession or prescription.
- Each parcel of land is recorded in the register at the land titles office as a unit of property. The land is surveyed and accurate boundaries in parceled descriptions are available that facilitate the recording of land dispositions.
- A land titles office is officially referred to as: The Land Registry Office for the Land Titles Division of the Regional Municipality [or county] of [name]. Each land titles division is overseen by a land registrar.

The land titles system operates in accordance with three principles (**mirror principle**, **curtain principle** and **insurance principle**):

THE MIRROR PRINCIPLE	THE CURTAIN PRINCIPLE	THE INSURANCE PRINCIPLE
The register of title is a mirror that accurately and completely reflects, beyond all argument, the current facts that are material to a person's title.	The register is the sole source of information for proposed buyers, who need not and indeed must not, concern themselves with trusts and equities that lie behind this curtain of information.	The mirror (register) is deemed to give the absolute correct reflection of title, but if through human error a flaw appears, anyone who suffers loss must be put in the same position, so far as money can do, that he would have been in had the reflection been a true one.

LEGISLATIVE STRUCTURE

The *Land Titles Act* is divided into several parts.

THE LAND TITLES ACT	
PART I	Preliminary (Definitions)
PART II	Organization and Administration
PART III	Jurisdiction of the Court
PART IV	Application for First Registration
PART V	Assurance Fund
PART VI	Part Owners
PART VII	Subsequent Registrations
PART VIII	Descriptions of Land and Registered Plans
PART IX	Fraud
PART X	Rectification of the Register
PART XI	Regulations and Procedure

Forms permitted for registration include the *Transfer/Deed of Land* (Form 1), *Charge/Mortgage of Land* (Form 2), *Discharge of Charge/Mortgage* (Form 3), *Document General* (Form 4) and *Schedule* (Form 5). (Note: Forms are analyzed later in this chapter.) The

Act provides that documents are effective on registration and that priority of registration prevails. The parcel register page is abstracted and, therefore, examining the actual registered documents is usually necessary to gain proper perspective on the extent of ownership.

The land registrar is empowered to make rulings as to the sufficiency of documents, subject to certain avenues of appeal. Detailed, uniform procedures must be followed in the preparation of all documents, either manually or electronically, for registration under land titles.

LAND TITLES ASSURANCE FUND

The Land Titles Assurance Fund, established under Part V of the *Land Titles Act*, provides that persons deprived of ownership through selected errors or fraud are entitled to compensation, provided such compensation cannot be obtained from other sources. (More specifically, the fund is designed to provide financial compensation for persons wrongfully deprived of land or some interest therein, due to the land being brought under this Act or by reason of some other person being registered as owner through fraud or, by reason of any misdescription, omission or other error in a certificate of ownership or charge, or in an entry on the register.) The compensation is subject to various qualifications.

The person claiming to be entitled to payment for compensation must apply to the Director of Titles. The amount of compensation will be determined by the Director of Titles, subject to certain rights by the claimant. The Land Titles Assurance Fund should not be confused with **title insurance** (see *Curiosity: Title Insurance*).

EXAMPLE   *Land Titles Assurance Fund*

Owner Smith owns a dilapidated home in the village of Westend and has not occupied the property for a considerable period of time. Jones, an individual unknown to Smith, forges various documents and successfully has the property registered in his own name. Following the forgery, he sells the property to an innocent buyer for fair market value.

The new owner tears down the dilapidated house and builds a new, modern two-storey home on the property. Smith ultimately uncovers the situation and legally pursues both Jones and the new owner.

The new owner may have no involvement, as the property was acquired in good faith at fair market value. Further, if Jones turns out to have no money or has disappeared in the process, Smith would then look to the Land Titles Assurance Fund for settlement. Smith has lost an interest in land, cannot recover that interest and has suffered loss as a consequence of fraud. An owner's success in dealing with the assurance fund would depend on specific circumstances.

Title Insurance   CURIOSITY

Title insurance has made significant strides in Canadian commercial and residential marketplaces. The attraction of this value-added product lies in additional title security extending to various risks (including fraud) and undisclosed interests that may or may not be covered through other legal investigative services leading to land registration.

Title policies are designed for two audiences: lenders and owners. Real estate practitioners should be fully aware of coverages provided and potential benefits concerning closing costs, hidden risks, need for surveys and problems at closing concerning property title. A detailed discussion of title policies is provided in *The Real Estate Transaction – General* when discussing title conveyancing.

LAND REGISTRY OFFICES

Land registry offices (LROs) were originally located at the county seat for each county in Ontario in which land within that county is registered. However, municipal consolidations and regional government structures have somewhat altered traditional county-based arrangements.

Members of the public access the land registry office during normal business hours to search titles and register documents. The need to physically attend the land registry office has diminished significantly with the advent of e-registration for land transactions and online search facilities provided through Teranet. Presently, both e-registration and paper-based systems co-exist in Ontario, but the vast majority of land registry offices are now automated.

Procedures: Paper-Based vs. Automated Offices

In the traditional paper-based land registry offices, real estate practitioners search property records by preparing a Request for Service form and paying the appropriate fee, if required. In such cases, the request form must first be presented to a cashier and then taken to the appropriate counter, where it is filled by registry office staff in order of receipt. In automated land registry locations, users access land information via computer using Teraview software that provides a secure information gateway (see subsequent topic).

Posted fees involve document registration, furnishing of selected information from title records, and provision of maps, large surveys, subdivision plans and other oversized documentation. Separate fee structures apply to registry and land titles. Fees are amended from time to time and published in a Tariff of Fees. Currently, record organization will vary based on available space and internal setup. E-registration will ultimately standardize land registry operations throughout the province.

Title Searching

Title searching refers to locating, organizing and condensing pertinent facts about documents and other related materials registered on title. The typical search normally involves a lawyer, or a title searcher on behalf of the lawyer, seeking out either paper or electronic documents concerning a real estate conveyance. However, many others search title documents; e.g., employees of lending institutions, government representatives, appraisers, private investors, developers, municipal authorities and law enforcement agencies. Organizations have traditionally retained the services of title searchers as freelancers.

Title information, once reviewed by legal counsel, leads to a conclusion as to whether or not the owner has good and marketable title. The title searcher provides no opinions on such issues. He or she merely condenses information, copies or electronically receives certain documents and summarizes relevant information (as the need arises) leading to an ultimate conclusion. The process of title searching, once a complex activity involving numerous documents and written notes, has become simple and straightforward in today's automated office through computer access to registry records either at off-site authorized user locations (e.g., legal offices using Teraview software) or on-site at land registry office computer terminals.

Other Services

The land registry office serves other functions besides its repository role for land registration documents. Some local offices provide access to other registration systems such as the Personal Property Registration System (PPRS). The PPRS involves registerable interests in equipment, inventory and consumer goods. Offices may also provide services for corporate, birth, marriage and death certificate registrations.

PERSONAL PROPERTY SECURITY REGISTRATION

The PPSR records and stores information concerning purchases of goods and other personal property used to secure loans regarding such purchases. Practitioners can search the Personal Property Security Registration (PPSR) system by means of a specific search (the first and last name plus middle initial of the person, along with date of birth) or a non-specific search (first and last name only). Personal property filed with the PPSR is referred to as a chattel.

Under the PPSR, the creditor (secured party) files a financing statement that includes the names and addresses of the debtors, classification of the chattel and a brief description, if applicable. Generally, registration of the financing statement must be done within 30 days following the signing of a security agreement. The actual security agreement can be in various forms, such as an equipment lease with an option to purchase (e.g., office computer equipment or photocopier), a conditional sale contract (e.g., appliances or a hot water tank) or a chattel mortgage. If changes are made to the information registered under the PPSR, a financing change statement must be recorded. This statement is also used when discharging the debt recorded on the financing statement.

LAND TITLES CONVERSION PROJECT

The land titles conversion project now nearing completion involves the conversion of registry documents to land titles coincident with a change to the automated POLARIS system. Under traditional procedures, a property would enter land titles through an investigation and subsequent certification by way of first application under the *Land Titles Act* (Part IV). The land titles conversion project provides streamlined procedures to accelerate the process and the access to land registration records by way of Teraview (operated by Teranet).

Land Titles Conversion Qualified

In the land titles conversion project, the first application process is replaced with a large-scale administrative conversion. A pre-established search procedure verifies existing titles within the registry. Certification of title is issued upon that investigation and the recommendation of representatives of the Ministry of Government Services. Properties so converted bear the initials LTCQ indicating land titles conversion qualified. The title to the property is insured with claims being settled under the Land Titles Assurance Fund.

Understandably, such a large scale conversion does not come without some qualifiers as to the extent of title guaranteed. A dispute mechanism is designed to handle a variety of unique circumstances; e.g., planning issues affecting adjoining properties, conflicting descriptions and disparate boundary lines.

Persons using the remaining registry offices that are scheduled for conversion should take time to read bulletins published by the Real Property Registration Branch of the Ministry regarding the rationale underlying the conversion, implications for owners and revised search procedures.

CONVERSION SEARCH PROCESS

The administrative conversion of registry to qualified land titles is an integral part of the POLARIS automation process. For land titles conversion, a search process was developed that would account for all claims outstanding during the 40-year search period and establish the owner of the parcel. Under this process, at least ten years of ownership or the last three deeds are searched, whichever is the greater, to establish ownership.

Interests and claims recorded on the parcel index for the 40-year search period are carried forward to the automated parcel register. The abbreviated search process assumes that any prior errors or omissions would have been detected by at least one of the law firms conducting the 40-year search necessary to transfer title properly. The record created is guaranteed by the registration system and any loss caused as a result of error or omission, if any occurs, will be compensated through the Land Titles Assurance Fund.

The search process does not involve applications by individual owners supported by current surveys. Individual notification is not given and no hearings are held to resolve disputes concerning the extent of title. Therefore, the boundaries of the land included in the application are not fixed, as would be the case with first registration. Consequently, the title statement given by the government varies from that provided under the existing first application conversion process. Title qualifications, in addition to those set out in the *Land Titles Act*, are modified and legal advice should be sought regarding such matters.

LAND TITLES CONVERTED QUALIFIED (LTCQ) VS. LAND TITLES ABSOLUTE

Land titles absolute is issued for parcels that are brought into land titles by way of first application. As such, these titles are subject to title qualifiers set out in Section 44 of the Act. The land titles converted qualified (LTCQ) involves parcels that are brought into land titles during the administrative conversion from registry records to a land titles parcel.

The land titles conversion project represented a special challenge given the mass administrative conversion from registry to land titles. Risk factors associated with the process had to be carefully examined. The Ministry of Government Services determined that the title for all properties issued under the land titles conversion would be given qualifications that differ slightly from the normal land titles qualifications. Most notably, title brought into land titles by conversion are subject to the rights of any person who would, but for the land title, be entitled to the land or any part of it through adverse possession, prescription, misdescription or boundaries settled by convention. Such matters, however, go beyond the scope of this current course.

As a further note, owners wishing to develop property by registering a plan of subdivision or condominium on an LTCQ parcel must make application for an absolute title in order to deal with removing qualifiers relating to such things as adverse possession and misdescription. The resolution of any problems regarding boundaries and adverse claims is required before such plans are registered in the automated system.

TITLE PROBLEMS

If a title-related problem is uncovered during the search process that cannot be resolved, the property will not be converted to land titles. It will be automated and maintained in the registry system. Any property that is not converted initially may be converted later, without a formal first application, as soon as the missing title evidence is supplied.

Problems with boundaries, encroachments and conflicting descriptions are more common than title-related problems and typically involve conflicting descriptions in deeds of adjoining properties. The search conducted for land titles conversion will often uncover such conflicts. Since the situation is so common, all printouts of the parcel register contain a note to advise the reader that he/she should search for inconsistencies in adjoining descriptions. In the case of properties containing serious conflicts (e.g., overlapping descriptions for major portions of the parcels), conversion will not proceed and the parcel is entered in the automated system as a registry parcel pending any possible further investigation.

AUTOMATED RECORDS AND E-REGISTRATION

The *Land Registration Reform Act*, consisting of three Parts, originally came into force on April 1, 1985, and was instrumental in the introduction of standardized records while paving the way for electronic registration. Part I of the *Land Registration Reform Act* (LRRA) was devoted primarily to the implementation of standard registration documents for both registry and land titles.

Part II authorized the automation of records and property mapping, including the storage and retrieval of such documentation.

Part III, outlined procedures for electronic registration including the use of electronic formats. Part III also set the stage for various regulations relating to the conversion of land registration records to an automated format. The Regulations provide detailed requirements concerning direct electronic transmissions to the land registration office and requirements regarding the content of electronic documents. Lastly, the Act provided the legislative authority for the land titles conversion project.

POLARIS

POLARIS is an acronym for **P**rovince of **O**ntario **LA**nd **R**egistration and **I**nformation **S**ystem. This automated land registration system operates based on a title index (description of property ownership) and property mapping (surveys and plans) databases.

POLARIS registers property under a parcel basis in much the same fashion as a land titles system. The guarantee of title normally associated with land titles does not accompany this parcelization process (parcelizing refers to the organization of property by land ownership, as opposed to geographic location in registry). By centralizing data electronically, search times are reduced, manual abstracting is eliminated given direct input of data through online terminals and access is provided to remotely search records, as well as mapping information.

IMPLEMENTATION

The implementation of POLARIS has proven costly and time consuming given the searching and reorganizing of documents and property data under individual parcels. This data forms the basis for the computerized title index. Secondly, the recording of mapping information forms the foundation for the property mapping database. POLARIS, as a

result, permits the user to find property by individual parcel (referenced by a property identification number (PIN)), by individual name or by street address within the title index. Further, property mapping allows the geographic pinpointing of described properties.

Activities concerning the automation of records under POLARIS are being carried out coincident with the land titles conversion project enabling the gradual move to full electronic facilities throughout the province.

MAPPING

As previously mentioned, POLARIS permits the user to access property by address, owner's name or property identification number (PIN). However, if the first two are unknown, the PIN can be quickly located through block and property index maps.

Block Index Map	Property Index Map
Large tracts of land within individual communities are organized in terms of blocks. The user first references the block index maps to find the general location of the property.	The user then views the property index map for the appropriate property. Each map is merely a detailed expansion of individual blocks identified in the block index maps.

PROPERTY IDENTIFICATION NUMBER (PIN)

A PIN number is assigned when properties are converted to land titles and automated under the POLARIS system. Properties can then be sourced by PIN number. A combination of block number and property index number form the property identification number (PIN). For example, if the block number is 00114, and the property number is 0051, the PIN is 00114–0051. With this information, the user can then access the online title index database.

Block Index Map & Property Index Map

Source: Teranet

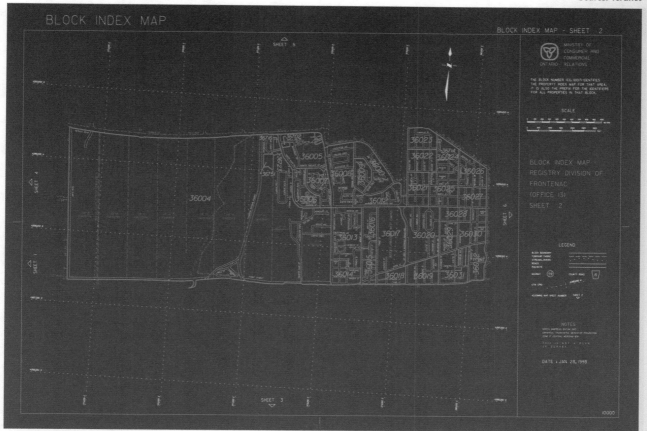

BLOCK INDEX MAP

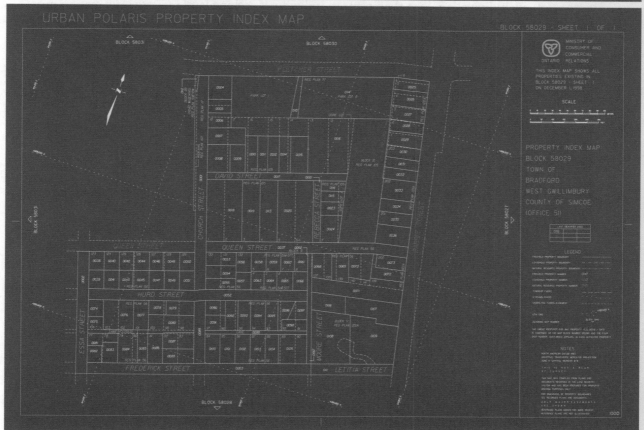

URBAN POLARIS PROPERTY INDEX MAP

Teranet

Teranet was originally described as a land information services company offering land-related data access, technology and expertise to private and public sector clients. However, the scope of e-services has significantly expanded to include web-based applications for the legal profession, spatial data-related programs, online payment of parking tickets and moving violations and e-service delivery mechanisms to facilitate government administration.

AUTOMATION OF LAND REGISTRY OFFICES

For real estate practitioners, Teranet is most closely associated with the automation of land registry offices. The process of adapting land registration records into POLARIS was combined with the conversion of those records to land titles. In 1991, Teranet began working in partnership with the Ontario government to revamp the land registry system. Teranet's objectives in this regard were to:

- automate and enhance the Province of Ontario's land registration system based on the POLARIS technology developed by the provincial government;
- develop an information utility to manage the land registration databases and other land-related information, and serve as the communications gateway for remote access; and
- market its expertise, systems and applications within Canada and internationally through creative solutions in information management and land-related information systems by way of in-house expertise along with the resources of various technology partners.

As mentioned previously, over 90% of all registry offices records are now automated including all major urban centres. Individuals seeking land registry information no longer have to visit the applicable land registry office to obtain information, but instead can access such details using Teraview software.

WEB LINKS

Teranet   Go to ***www.teranet.ca*** for details about the scope of services offered by Teranet over and above land registry automation. Current endeavours include geospatial services as well as security, transaction and risk management.

Teraview

This electronic gateway software, operated by Teranet, provides clients with online remote access to land information products and services, including the POLARIS land registration system. The gateway is designed to permit users (e.g., lawyers, real estate practitioners, municipal officials and appraisers) to perform selected search activities through online connections to land registry offices.

Real estate practitioners acquiring this software can access title information online, verify property identification numbers (PINs) and confirm legal descriptions as well as other ownership particulars. Detailed information can be searched such as property abstracts, transfers/deeds, charges/mortgages, liens and other registered encumbrances.

The legal profession uses **Teraview** software to perform **e-registration** (electronic registration) functions including searches, creating and submitting title documents for registration, viewing/printing instruments registered on title and accessing parcel registers and maps. The *WritSearch* feature allows lawyers to search both personal and company names regarding writes of execution.

Each user, under a Teranet account holder (e.g., law firm) has a Personal Security Package (PSP) that includes a removable storage device with encrypted information and a pass phrase. Packages are issued following completion of a Personal Security Licence Application to Teranet and the approval of that application both by Teranet and the Teranet account holder. The initial approval process, combined with a unique digital signature associated with each PSP, provides a secure electronic pathway and an effective electronic audit trail for transaction activity.

SEARCHING POLARIS

The Teraview software accesses three different databases within POLARIS:

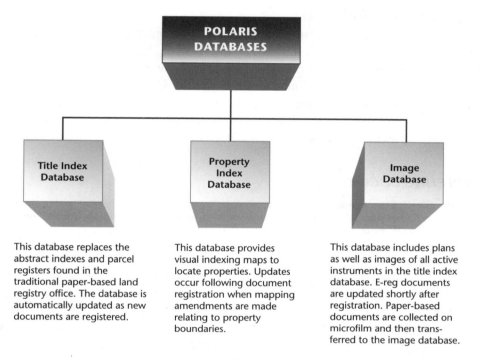

This database replaces the abstract indexes and parcel registers found in the traditional paper-based land registry office. The database is automatically updated as new documents are registered.

This database provides visual indexing maps to locate properties. Updates occur following document registration when mapping amendments are made relating to property boundaries.

This database includes plans as well as images of all active instruments in the title index database. E-reg documents are updated shortly after registration. Paper-based documents are collected on microfilm and then transferred to the image database.

PREPARING FOR E-REGISTRATION

The e-reg capability of Teraview allows the client to search parcel records within POLARIS by entering one of the following:

- Unique nine-digit property identification number (PIN)
- Municipal address
- Name
- Registered instrument number
- Map
- Condominium Plan
- Plan of Subdivision

A successful search will produce the full property description, the owner(s) of the property and a list of all current registered instruments. The printed result will contain the same information as would be received in person at the land registry office. The search can also be expanded to include the mapping interface in order to identify easements, rights-of-way or encroachments, search for *Planning Act* compliance and identify owners of nearby properties.

E-REGISTRATION METHODS

Individuals who are provided access to the system may register documents electronically from their offices, use a kiosk in the applicable land registry office or request assisted service by a staff member in the land registry office. Not all documents can be registered electronically. For example, certain types of documents such as Crown grants (see later discussion) and the Declaration and Description for the registration of a condominium must be registered using traditional, paper-based methods. Also, certain documents, given their size and number, may exceed limits within the electronic registration system. An example might involve a complex legal document that affects hundreds or thousands of properties.

E-REGISTRATION PROCEDURES

E-registration refers to title documents being created, submitted and maintained in electronic form. E-registration is initiated by means of dockets and messaging. A docket includes registration documents prepared by one lawyer with subsequent forwarding (messaging) by secure transmission to another user through the Teraview gateway software. An illustrated e-registration document flow is illustrated. Detailed discussions of closing procedures and registration of applicable documents involving real estate transactions are included in *The Real Estate Transaction – General*.

COMPLETING DOCUMENTS

NOTE: The following description briefly summarizes steps in creating a transfer/deed of land by the seller's lawyer, further steps taken by the buyer's lawyer, followed by electronic signing and electronic submission to the land registry office.

The seller's solicitor accesses the Teraview software and creates a transfer by inserting relevant information in successive data entry fields (which generally parallel those found in the paper-based *Transfer/Deed of Land*, Form 1); e.g., property details, transferor and transferee. This process would include *Planning Act* statements and other legal statements that are part of the document preparation process. After completing all necessary details, the seller's lawyer sends a message to the buyer's lawyer allowing access to the document.

The buyer's lawyer, upon receiving the message, can electronically accept access to the sent document (i.e., the transfer). He or she then checks for writs of execution against the seller. Assuming none, the buyer's lawyer adds the buyer's information to the document. As with the seller's lawyer, this process would include *Planning Act* statements and other legal statements that are part of the document preparation process. Next, the buyer's lawyer completes the land transfer tax statements (information found in the Land Transfer Tax Affidavit that accompanies the Transfer/Deed of Land).

The document, when completed by both lawyers, is ready for electronic signature. Two types of signatures are required: completeness and release. The completeness signature validates the accuracy of statements made and the release signature confirms that the document is ready for registration. With the documents now completed and signed, the electronic registration can occur. The system performs a sub search and searches for writs. Upon registration, a registration number is assigned to the transfer by the POLARIS database.

WEB LINKS

Teraview   The Teraview web site (*www.teraview.ca*) provides a wide range of information concerning the software, including full descriptions of functionalities and steps to follow in the e-registration process.

E-Registration Document Flow

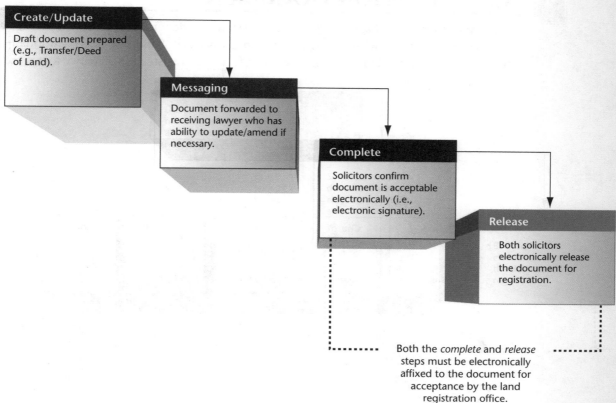

Create/Update
Draft document prepared (e.g., Transfer/Deed of Land).

Messaging
Document forwarded to receiving lawyer who has ability to update/amend if necessary.

Complete
Solicitors confirm document is acceptable electronically (i.e., electronic signature).

Release
Both solicitors electronically release the document for registration.

Both the *complete* and *release* steps must be electronically affixed to the document for acceptance by the land registration office.

Compliance with Law Statements

A document requiring compliance with law statements, can only be accepted by the land registration office from individuals authorized to practice law in Ontario. A compliance statement on an electronic document replaces supporting evidence that would normally be included in a paper-based system. Other solicitors can rely on, and need not look behind the compliance statement for verification. Proper evidence must be retained by the lawyer making the statement.

Practice Directives

The Law Society of Upper Canada (LSUC) has established and continues to refine detailed procedural guidelines for lawyers engaged in the e-registration process.

Client Authorization/Consent

As document registration occurs by means of lawyers' digital signatures, LSUC has developed two primary forms as evidence of client authorization and consent:

- Acknowledgment and Direction Report (authorization to proceed with a specific transaction); and

- Document Registration Agreement (authorization for electronic registration).

REGISTRATION DOCUMENTS

The *Land Registration Reform Act* sets out five standard documents. Until that point, registry was burdened with countless forms and schedules. Land titles has traditionally been more regimented in terms of acceptable forms for registration. The five forms are:

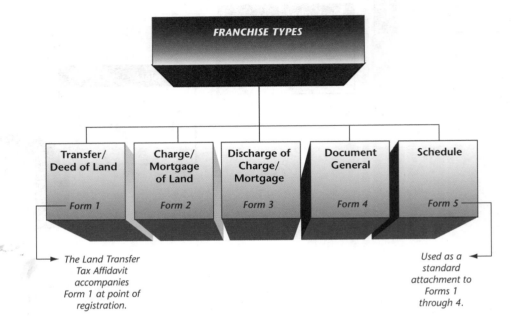

Paper-Based and Electronic Forms

Completed paper-based examples of the Transfer/Deed of Land (including the Land Transfer Tax Affidavit) and the Charge/Mortgage of Land are included for illustration purposes, as practitioners will most commonly encounter these forms when reviewing title documents. Selected electronic versions are also provided (at the end of this chapter). These include the Transfer (Transfer/Deed of Land), Land Transfer Tax Statements (in lieu of the Land Transfer Tax Affidavit), Charge/Mortgage (Charge/Mortgage of Land), Discharge of Charge (Discharge of Charge/Mortgage) and the applicable parcel register page. An electronic clear certificate regarding writs of execution is also included.

Content is generally the same for both paper-based and electronic versions. The most notable differences involve form layouts and the fact that no signatures are required in electronic versions. Under land titles, in addition to the five forms identified, other forms being attached either manually or electronically must meet prescribed standards established by the *Land Titles Act*. In registry, attached documents can vary but are subject to statutory formalities regarding registration.

Transfer/Deed of Land

Standard form (Form 1) for conveyance of a real estate interest.

Transfer/Deed Of Land (Paper-Based)

This standard form is used to register a **deed** under either the registry or the land titles system. Standardized forms were introduced to create uniformity in registry records. Prior to that time, various document formats were utilized. The **Transfer/Deed of Land** is normally registered along with the Land Transfer Tax Affidavit.

Sample Transfer/Deed of Land

Source: Dye & Durham Inc.

Province of Ontario

Transfer/Deed of Land

Form 1 — Land Registration Reform Act

DYE & DURHAM CO. INC.—Form No. 970
Amended NOV. 1992

A

19833	**(1)** Registry ☐ Land Titles ☑ **(2)** Page 1 of 2 pages **AR**
CERTIFICATE OF RECEIPT	**(3)** Property Identifier(s) Block Property Additional: See Schedule ☐
20XX OCT 09 A 11:14	**(4)** Consideration Two Hundred Forty-Five Thousand Dollars $ 245,000.00
LAND REGISTRAR OREA NO. 99	**(5)** Description This is a: Property Division ☐ Property Consolidation ☐
A. Registrar New Property Identifiers	The whole of Parcel 32-1 in the Register for Section 99M-165 being Lot 32 on Plan 99M-165 in the City of Anycity, County of Anycounty.

FOR OFFICE USE ONLY

Additional: See Schedule ☐

Executions Additional: See Schedule ☐

---

(6) This Document Contains (a) Redescription New Easement Plan/Sketch ☐ (b) Schedule for: Description ☐ Additional Parties ☐ Other ☐

(7) Interest/Estate Transferred Fee Simple

---

(8) Transferor(s) The transferor hereby transfers the land to the transferee and certifies that the transferor is at least eighteen years old and that

Name(s)	Signature(s)	Date of Signature Y M D
New Home Builders Inc.	*Raymond Patrick* President Raymond Patrick I have the authority to bind the corporation	20xx 10 09

(9) Spouse(s) of Transferor(s) I hereby consent to this transaction

Name(s)	Signature(s)	Date of Signature Y M D

(10) Transferor(s) Address for Service 1333 Dupont Street, Anycity, Ontario K7T 2X2

(11) Transferee(s)

		Date of Birth Y M D
HAINES, Paul Mark	*Paul Haines*	19xx 11 13
HAINES, Susan Gail	*Susan Haines*	19xx 02 05

as joint tenants and not as tenants-in-common

(12) Transferee(s) Address for Service 132 Cypress Circle, Anycity, Ontario K1K 3B3

---

(13) Transferor(s) The transferor verifies that to the best of the transferor's knowledge and belief, this transfer does not contravene section 50 of the Planning Act.

Signature. *Raymond Patrick* Date of Signature Y M D 20xx 10 09 Signature .... Date of Signature Y M D

Solicitor for Transferor(s) I have explained the effect of section 50 of the Planning Act to the transferor and I have made inquiries of the transferor to determine that this transfer does not contravene that section and based on the information supplied by the transferor, to the best of my knowledge and belief, this transfer does not contravene that section. I am an Ontario solicitor in good standing.

Name and Address of Solicitor Alice James, 136 King St. W. Anycity, Ontario K2E 1B4 Signature. *Alice James* Date of Signature Y M D 20xx 10 09

(14) Solicitor for Transferee(s) I have investigated the title to this land and to abutting land where relevant and I am satisfied that the title records reveal no contravention as set out in subclause 50 (22) (c) (ii) of the Planning Act and that to the best of my knowledge and belief this transfer does not contravene section 50 of the Planning Act. I act independently of the solicitor for the transferor(s) and I am an Ontario solicitor in good standing.

Name and Address of Solicitor Robert G. Wilson 387 Terrace Street Anycity, Ontario K3B 1Z2 Signature. *Robert Wilson* Date of Signature Y M D 20xx 10 09

Planning Act — OPTIONAL *Affix Statement by Solicitor for Transferee(s) here if necessary*

---

(15) Assessment Roll Number of Property

Cty.	Mun.	Map	Sub.	Par.
99	12	000	012	00432

Fees and Tax

Registration Fee	
Land Transfer Tax	*ILLUSTRATION ONLY FEE NOT SHOWN*
Total	

FOR OFFICE USE ONLY

(16) Municipal Address of Property 132 Cypress Circle Anycity, Ontario K1K 3B3

(17) Document Prepared by: Marshall and James 136 King Street West Anycity, Ontario K2E 1B4

This form is used to convey title or an interest in real property and includes the full names of both sellers (transferors) and buyers (transferees) along with birth dates. Any other person who has an interest in the estate being conveyed would also join in the document; e.g., third parties such as a life tenant, a spouse releasing matrimonial home possessory rights and heirs or beneficiaries of an estate.

IMPLIED COVENANTS

Section 5 of the *Land Registration Reform Act* sets out the implied covenants for a transfer of freehold or leasehold land by the transferor. Additional covenants can apply; e.g., a release by a trustee. Only freehold covenants are included for illustrative purposes:

- The seller's (transferor's) right to convey the land and the buyer's (transferee's) right to quiet enjoyment.
- The assurances that both seller and buyer will execute such further assurances and do such other acts as may be reasonably required.
- The assurance that the seller has not done, omitted or permitted anything whereby the land is, or could be, encumbered (other than as per the land registration records).
- The seller transfers to the buyer all existing claims that he/she has upon the land except as noted in the land registration records.

Implied covenants can be changed through an amending schedule or by setting out an appropriately amended covenant. When the deed or transfer is submitted for registration and accepted by the land registrar, the transaction is said to be closed or completed. Ownership normally changes at that time and typically possession and payment occur simultaneously, unless otherwise provided in the agreement of purchase and sale.

Land Transfer Tax Affidavit (Paper-Based)

Land Transfer Tax Affidavit

Standard form relating to land transfer tax for the conveyance of a real estate interest.

A **Land Transfer Tax Affidavit** (previously referred to as an Affidavit of Residence and of Value of the Consideration) must accompany every document being registered in Ontario land registry offices that transfers an interest in land. The affidavit is required by the *Land Transfer Tax Act* and the land registrar is required to collect land transfer tax when this document is presented for registration either at the land registry office or by electronic transmission.

The amount of tax is computed based on consideration declared on the affidavit (or Land Transfer Tax Statements in the case of electronic registration). This tax can also be paid directly to the Ministry of Finance. In the paper-based system, the payment is made to the Registrar at the applicable land registry office. With electronic registration, an automatic payment is taken out of the lawyer's account or the lawyer's Teranet account.

REAL ESTATE APPLICATION

Practitioners searching land registration records will find the Land Transfer Tax Affidavit useful in determining what constitutes total consideration for a particular sale. In addition to oaths concerning the disposition, property information and school support, the form addresses monies paid in cash as well as other financial information including, but not limited to, mortgage(s) assumed or seller take back financing, any property transferred in exchange, other valuable consideration and value of chattels. Affidavit information can prove useful in analyzing sale particulars from an appraisal perspective.

Sample Land Transfer Tax Affidavit   *Source: Dye & Durham Inc.*

DYE & DURHAM CO. INC. - Form No. 500
Printed August 2002

Property Identifier(s) No.
19833

Land Transfer Tax Affidavit
Land Transfer Tax Act

Refer to all instructions on reverse side.

IN THE MATTER OF THE CONVEYANCE OF *(insert brief description of land)*   Lot 32, Plan 99M-165 in the City of Anycity, County of Anycounty

BY *(print names of all transferors in full)*   New Home Builders Ltd.
TO *(print names of all transferees in full)*   Paul Mark Haines and Susan Gail Haines

I/We have personal knowledge of the facts herein deposed to and MAKE OATH AND SAY THAT:

1. I am/We are *(place a clear mark within the square opposite the following paragraph(s) that describe(s) the capacity of the deponent(s)):*
   - [x] (a) the transferee(s) named in the above-described conveyance;
   - [ ] (b) the authorized agent or solicitor acting in this transaction for the transferee(s);
   - [ ] (c) the President, Vice-President, Secretary, Treasurer, Director or Manager authorized to act for _____ (the transferee(s));
   - [ ] (d) a transferee and am making this affidavit on my own behalf and on behalf of *(insert name of spouse or same-sex partner)* _____ who is my spouse or same-sex partner.
   - [ ] (e) the transferor and [ ] I am tendering this document for registration and
     - [ ] no tax is payable on registration of this document.

2. **THE TOTAL CONSIDERATION FOR THIS TRANSACTION IS ALLOCATED AS FOLLOWS:**

   (a) Monies paid or to be paid in cash .... $ 245,000.00
   (b) Mortgages (i) Assumed *(principal and interest)* .... $ NIL
               (ii) Given back to vendor .... $ NIL
   (c) Property transferred in exchange *(detail below in para. 5)* ...... $ NIL
   (d) Other consideration subject to tax *(detail below)* .... $ NIL
   (e) Fair market value of the lands *(see instruction 2)* .... $ NIL
   (f) Value of land, building, fixtures and goodwill subject to
       Land Transfer Tax *(Total of (a) to (e))* .... $ 245,000.00 $ 245,000.00
   (g) Value of all chattels - items of tangible personal property
       which are taxable under the provisions of the
       Retail Sales Tax Act .... $ NIL
   (h) Other consideration for transaction not included in (f) or (g) above .... $ NIL
   (i) Total Consideration .... $ 245,000.00

   All Blanks must be filled in. Insert "Nil" where applicable.

3. To be completed where the value of the consideration for the conveyance exceeds $400,000.00
   I have read and considered the definition of "single family residence" set out in subsection 1(1) of the Act. The land conveyed in the above-described conveyance:
   - [ ] does not contain a single family residence or contains more than two single family residences.
   - [ ] contains at least one and not more than two single family residences.
   - [ ] contains at least one and not more than two single family residences and the lands are used for other than just residential purposes. The transferee has accordingly apportioned the value of consideration on the basis that the consideration for the single family residence is $_____ and the remainder of the lands are used for _____ purposes.

   Note: Subsection 2(1)(b) imposes an additional tax at the rate of one-half of one percent upon the value of consideration in excess of $400,000.00 where the conveyance contains at least one and not more than two single family residences and 2(2) allows an apportionment of the consideration where the lands are used for other than just residential purposes.

4. If consideration is nominal, is the land subject to any encumbrance?   [ ] Yes   [ ] No
5. Other remarks and explanations, if necessary. _____

Sworn before me at the   City of Anycity

in the   County of Anycounty

this   9th   day of   October   ,   20xx   .
(year)

A Commissioner
A Commissioner for taking Affidavits, etc.

Paul Haines
Signature(s)

Property Information Record

A. Describe nature of instrument: Transfer/Deed of Land
B. (i) Address of property being conveyed *(if available)*   132 Cypress Circle, Anycity, Ontario
    K1K 3B3
   (ii) Assessment Roll No. *(if available)*   99 12 000 012 00432
C. Mailing address(es) for future Notices of Assessment under the Assessment Act for property being conveyed
    Mr. & Mrs. Paul Haines, 132 Cypress Circle, Anycity, Ontario, K1K 3B3

D. (i) Registration number for last conveyance of property being conveyed *(if available)* _____
   (ii) Legal description of property conveyed: Same as in D.(i) above.   [x] Yes   [ ] No   [ ] Not known

E. Name(s) and address(es) of each transferee's solicitor
    Mr. Robert G. Wilson, 387 Terrace Road, Anycity, Ontario, K3B 1Z2

For Land Registry Office Use Only
Registration No.
Registration Date (Year/Month/Day)
Land Registry Office No.

School Support (Voluntary Election) (See reverse for explanation)	Yes	No
(a) Are all individual transferees Roman Catholic ?	[ ]	[x]
(b) If Yes, do all individual transferees wish to be Roman Catholic Separate School Supporters ?	[ ]	[ ]
(c) Do all individual transferees have French Language Education Rights ?	[ ]	[x]
(d) If Yes, do all individual transferees wish to support the French Language School Board (where established)?	[ ]	[ ]

NOTE: As to (c) and (d) the land being transferred will receive French Public School Board election unless otherwise directed in (a) and (b).   0449H (02-01)

This form also provides for explanatory comments if the consideration is nominal; e.g., a non-arm's length transaction involving natural love and affection. As a final note, consideration may not always be recorded. Buyers may elect to pay land transfer tax directly to the Ministry of Finance and, therefore, details would not appear on the affidavit.

Charge/Mortgage of Land

Charge/Mortgage of Land

Standard form (Form 2) for registering a charge/mortgage.

The **Charge/Mortgage of Land** (Form 2) is a standard form used to register a mortgage under either the registry or land titles system. This form provides important information to practitioners concerning mortgage financing on property being listed or sold. Salespeople and brokers will find the form relatively straightforward to analyze and extract relevant information. Selected portions of the paper-based form are briefly described.

- Box 4 sets out the principal amount of the mortgage that was originally placed on the property.
- Box 5 provides the legal description of the mortgaged property. Box 7 outlines the type of estate; e.g., fee simple, leasehold or life estate.
- Box 8 identifies the standard charge terms that apply between mortgagee and mortgagor. Standard charge terms provide detailed terms of the mortgage and are assigned a number in the land registry office when filed.
- Box 9 outlines the payment provisions including last payment. A balance due date is provided as Canadian mortgages typically have long amortization periods combined with short terms (often referred to as Canadian roll-over mortgages) resulting in a balance due amount and an appropriate balloon payment is required. Box 10 provides for any special provisions agreed between mortgagee and mortgagor; e.g., prepayment privileges. If insufficient space, a schedule is used.
- Boxes 11–13 set out details concerning the chargor (mortgagor) with Boxes 14–15 relating to the chargee.

The balance of the form involves property details including assessment roll number, who prepared the form and fees associated with the mortgage registration.

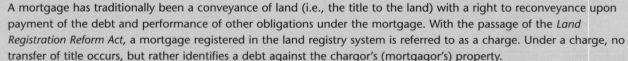

Mortgage vs. Charge   CURIOSITY

A mortgage has traditionally been a conveyance of land (i.e., the title to the land) with a right to reconveyance upon payment of the debt and performance of other obligations under the mortgage. With the passage of the *Land Registration Reform Act*, a mortgage registered in the land registry system is referred to as a charge. Under a charge, no transfer of title occurs, but rather identifies a debt against the chargor's (mortgagor's) property.

A charge creates a lien on the property with the term *discharge* referring to the removal of the lien, as opposed to the actual reconveyance of title following payment. However, consumers, real estate practitioners and lenders generally speak in terms of mortgages. Therefore, for descriptive purposes in this text, *mortgage* and *charge* are viewed as synonymous. All text references use the terms *mortgage*, *mortgagor* and *mortgagee*, unless context requires otherwise; e.g., when legislation using *charge*, *chargor* and *chargee* is directly quoted.

Sample Charge/Mortgage of Land   *Source: Dye & Durham Inc.*

Charge/Mortgage of Land
Form 2 — Land Registration Reform Act

Province of Ontario

Form No. 975   **B**

Number **450173**	(1) Registry ✔ Land Titles ☐ (2) Page 1 of 2 pages *AR*
CERTIFICATE OF REGISTRATION	(3) Property Identifier(s) Block Property Additional: See Schedule ☐
20xx JUL 16 A 10:32	(4) **Principal Amount** Fifty-Eight Thousand Dollars $ 58,000.00
A Registrar	(5) **Description**
LAND REGISTRAR OREA NO. 99	Lot 12, Registered Plan 88 in the Township of Anytownship, in the County of Anycounty.
New Property Identifiers Additional: See Schedule ☐	As described in instrument number 449639
Executions Additional: See Schedule ☐	

FOR OFFICE USE ONLY

(6) **This Document Contains** (a) Redescription New Easement Plan/Sketch ☐   (b) Schedule for: Description ☐ Additional Parties ☐ Other ✔   (7) **Interest/Estate Charged** Fee Simple

(8) **Standard Charge Terms** — The parties agree to be bound by the provisions in Standard Charge Terms filed as number **8461** and the Chargor(s) hereby acknowledge(s) receipt of a copy of these terms.

(9) **Payment Provisions**

(a) Principal Amount $	See Schedule Attached	(b) Interest Rate	% per annum	(c) Calculation Period	
(d) Interest Adjustment Date	Y M D	(e) Payment Date and Period		(f) First Payment Date	Y M D
(g) Last Payment Date		(h) Amount of Each Payment		Dollars $	
(i) Balance Due Date		(j) Insurance	Full Insurable Value	Dollars $	

(10) **Additional Provisions**

Continued on Schedule ☐

(11) **Chargor(s)** The chargor hereby charges the land to the chargee and certifies that the chargor is at least eighteen years old and that

.... We are the spouses of one another ....

The chargor(s) acknowledge(s) receipt of a true copy of this charge.

Name(s)	Signature(s)	Date of Signature Y M D
AMES, Paul William	*Paul W. Ames*	20xx 07 09
AMES, Jane Marie	*Jane Marie Ames*	20xx 07 09

(12) **Spouse(s) of Chargor(s)** I hereby consent to this transaction.

Name(s)	Signature(s)	Date of Signature Y M D

(13) **Chargor(s) Address for Service**   12 Woodlawn Street, Anycity, Ontario   K2K 1Y1

(14) **Chargee(s)**   Bank of Ontario

(15) **Chargee(s) Address for Service**   806 Westway Road, Anycity, Ontario   K2J 1X1

(16) Assessment Roll Number of Property	Cty. 99	Mun. 12	Map 000	Sub. 012	Par. 23912		Fees
							Registration Fee

(17) **Municipal Address of Property**

12 Woodlawn Street
R.R. #2
Anycity, Ontario K2K 1Y1

(18) **Document Prepared by:**

James E. Calvin
Barrister and Solicitor
176 King Street
Anycity, Ontario   K2Z 2R3

ILLUSTRATION ONLY FEE NOT SHOWN

Total

FOR OFFICE USE ONLY

IMPLIED COVENANTS

The *Land Registration Reform Act*, coincident with the introduction of standardized forms for registry and land titles, permitted the inclusion of standard charge terms. This provision was designed to ensure that certain covenants were included, which might otherwise be omitted from a mortgage (**charge**) document. In effect, a mortgage under land titles or registry could be registered with nothing more than the basic information included in the standard Charge/Mortgage of Land form. Consequently, certain covenants (originally implied in the *Mortgages Act*) were included in the *Land Registration Reform Act* and deemed to be implied upon registration of the mortgage document.

> **Charge**
>
> The name given to a mortgage document when title is registered under the *Land Titles Act*.

FIRST IMPLIED COVENANT

- The mortgagor will make payments including interest and also pay taxes.
- The mortgagor has the legal right to give the mortgage.
- The mortgagor will provide insurance on the buildings.
- The mortgagor has no other encumbrances other than those currently registered on the specific property.
- The mortgagee, when the mortgagor is in default, has the right to take possession, collect rents/profits or sell the land.
- The mortgagee in possession by default shall be granted quiet possession.
- Upon default, total monies due shall become payable.
- Interest in arrears may be collected.
- The mortgagor in default agrees to do such things as reasonably requested by the mortgagee in possession relating to the land.

SECOND IMPLIED COVENANT

- The mortgagor covenants that the land held in fee simple is owned with good title.

THIRD IMPLIED COVENANT (relates to leasehold property)

- The mortgagor covenants that the lease is valid and up-to-date and, further, that reimbursement to the mortgagee will be made by the mortgagor for non-payment or non-performance of other covenants under the lease.

EXAMPLE   *Implied Covenants*

Seller Smith and Buyer Jones are attempting to close a transaction without legal counsel. In preparing the *Charge/Mortgage of Land* (Form 2), Jones doesn't understand the reference to Standard Charge Terms (Box 8) and leaves it blank. Smith overlooks the missing information. As no set of standard charge terms is referenced, the document is registered lacking important provisos, remedies and procedural matters. Regardless, the implied covenants as set out in the *Land Registration Reform Act*, at minimum, assure Seller Smith that certain significant covenants are addressed.

Standard Charge Terms

Standard charge terms were also introduced under the *Land Registration Reform Act*. As such, a person or corporation had the right to file standard charge terms with the land registrar. Terms vary by lender. A few examples are included for illustrative purposes only regarding requirements by the borrower to:

- Promptly pay all amounts required.

> **Standard Charge Terms**
>
> A document containing mortgage terms and conditions registered by a mortgagee in land registry which can be referenced in a Charge/Mortgage of Land.

- Insure the building, along with any other structures or improvements.
- Pay all taxes and assessments.
- Keep the property in good repair.
- Provide assurances that all improvements to the property meet building codes and other applicable legislation.
- Abide by the declaration, by-laws and rules (in the case of a condominium).
- Pay the lender for all costs, expenses and charges paid by the lender when mortgage payments are not made in accordance with the mortgage.

Other provisions may include:

- Certain assurances that the borrower is the owner of the property and that there are no other encumbrances against the title, other than those disclosed to the lender.
- Circumstances in which someone else (other than the borrower) guarantees the loan and obligations related thereto.
- Procedures to be followed when the mortgage is discharged (paid in full).
- Payment of the mortgage amount (at the lender's option) should the property be sold.

PAPER-BASED

In a paper-based land registry system, the registrar assigns a number to this unique set of charge terms and circulates the set to all land registry offices. This number would then be included in a Charge/Mortgage of Land and the mortgage is deemed to automatically include that particular set of terms.

Standard charge terms can be amended by filing a new set with a new number. In reality, a mortgagee may have several sets of standard charge terms registered with the land registrar at any particular point in time, each with a unique reference number. Should any information within the set of standard charge terms conflict with the Charge/Mortgage of Land, then the latter will prevail. If specific prepayment or other privileges are inserted in the appropriate space provided on the charge form, these also preempt any terms outlined in the set of standard charge terms.

ELECTRONIC

The conversion to automated land registration in Ontario has eliminated the need for extensive paper documentation. Standard charge terms can now be attached electronically to mortgages as part of the registration process using Teraview software. Currently, most lenders provide PDF versions for that purpose. A number is assigned electronically for each unique set of charge terms.

WEB LINKS

Standard Charge Terms   Various lenders post standard charge terms on the Internet. For examples, use a search engine (e.g., *www.google.ca*) and search *set of standard charge terms* or *standard charge terms*.

Discharge of Charge/Mortgage

This standard form is used when discharging a mortgage under either registry or land titles systems. An electronic version is included at the end of the chapter. The **Discharge of Charge/Mortgage** is executed by the mortgagee and given to the mortgagor verifying that a mortgage loan has been repaid in full before, at or after the maturity date. This

Discharge of Charge/ Mortgage

Standard form (Form 3) relating to discharge of a charge/mortgage.

document is registered at the land registration office as a permanent record of the discharge. Merely paying off the debt is not sufficient for the mortgagor when discharging a mortgage. Since a document was originally registered to give evidence of the mortgage's existence, the discharge is registered as evidence of the removal of the claim. The mortgagee's solicitor normally prepares the discharge and a fee is charged for this service. The mortgagor or the respective solicitor should ensure that the discharge is properly registered.

Occasionally, a mortgagor will pay off a mortgage debt and fail to obtain a discharge. This situation may not be discovered until a future date when the owner attempts to refinance or sell the property. In some instances, a discharge cannot be obtained because the mortgagee has disappeared or, for some reason, is unable to sign. The mortgagor can pay any monies still owing on the mortgage to a court, or otherwise prove to the satisfaction of that court that the debt has been paid. An order discharging the mortgage is then obtained that can then be registered on title within the applicable land registration office.

Document General

Document General

Standard form (Form 4) relating to land registration process.

The **Document General** is essentially a blank form meeting prescribed standards that is used to register any documents that are not a transfer, charge or discharge; i.e., the *Transfer/ Deed of Land* (Form 1), *Charge/Mortgage of Land* (Form 2) and *Discharge of Charge/ Mortgage* (Form 3). Practitioners will encounter the *Document General* in a variety of circumstances associated with property titles; e.g., caution, notice of lien, discharge of lien, power of attorney, judgment and notice of survivorship.

A *Document General* registered on title should be carefully analyzed as the contents can significantly impact the title to the property and, consequently, buyers/sellers involved in that particular property. Caution is advised on all matters relating to title. Seek legal advice.

Schedule

The **Schedule** (the fifth of the prescribed forms under the *Land Registration Reform Act*) is used as an attachment with other paper-based or electronic forms. The schedule can accompany a transfer, charge, discharge or document general.

REGISTRATION—MISCELLANEOUS

Real estate practitioners may encounter certain registration-related matters when listing and selling residential or commercial properties both within rural and urban settings. Selected topics are included to advance general knowledge of registration within Ontario.

Leasehold Interests

Leasehold interests may be registered under both registry or land titles systems. As most titles are now being converted to land titles, practitioners should be aware of certain registration fundamentals under land titles. The lessee (tenant) holding a lease exceeding three years must register a notice of lease, using the prescribed form, in order to protect his or her interest. The actual notice sets out particulars of the lease including the parties, term and expiry date, and any rights (e.g., right to renew). Such registration can either involve a notice of the lease or a specific interest that an individual has relating to a lease (e.g., a sublease). Further, the lessor (landlord) can register an assignment of rents relating to a lease that has been registered; e.g., the lessor wants to borrow money based on future rents under the lease.

In instances where the unexpired lease term is 21 years or more (including any right to renew), the tenant may make application to the Registrar in the applicable land registry office to have a leasehold parcel opened that will reflect both the leasehold interest and any agreements, mortgages or other encumbrances affecting that interest.

Crown Lands

Crown lands refer to property vested in the Crown and administered under provincial legislation and procedures. In Ontario, all crown land falls under public land as defined in the *Public Lands Act*. Indian lands are an exception as they originate with the federal government and the Crown in Right of Canada. Accordingly, all registration documents are filed federally. Practitioners frequently encounter crown lands in two ways: title matters associated with the Crown Patent and disposition of crown lands.

CROWN PATENT

A Crown Patent is an original title deeded by the government and generally accepted as the root of all title. Most property in Canada commences the legal chain of title from the Crown Patent. The passing of title from the Crown is typically accompanied by certain reservations; e.g., save and except for mineral rights and/or trees. Further, a portion of land may be reserved for the purpose of future road construction. The extent of such reservations are set out in the original patents for such lands and can vary based on when the patent was issued. Practitioners, particularly those dealing with rural and recreational properties, should be aware of such limitations as property value can be directly impacted. Salespeople are not expected to decipher all the intricacies of Crown Patents and should seek legal advice.

DISPOSITION OF CROWN LAND

The method by which Crown lands are patented and sold goes beyond the scope of this introductory course. The method used is based on applicable legislation, procedures of the administrative body handling these lands and requirements of the land registration system. Patents are typically processed following research involving the appropriate government agency and subsequent issues of a patent that is registered in the appropriate land registry office. Practitioners most commonly encounter disposition of crown lands relating to cottage lots in remote locations.

Native Lands

Native lands refer to reserved lands held by the Crown for the use and benefit of native people, pursuant to the *Indian Act*. To convey such property to other persons, the land must be surrendered to the federal government. The government then, in turn, may convey titles by way of sale, or grant leases on the surrendered land.

Real estate practitioners marketing this type of property require an understanding of methods by which such lands are controlled, registered and developed. Certain complexities exist in negotiations concerning native lands.

INDIAN ACT: PROCEDURES AND ISSUES

Methods associated with the surrender and management of lands by the federal government have caused much debate. The *Indian Act* and various amendments dating from the mid-1800s have failed to adequately address various difficulties. Historically, all lands surrendered ceased to be viewed as lands for the use and benefit of native people. Control of such properties was vested in the Federal government once any surrender was undertaken. However, Subsection 38(2) of the *Indian Act* (1951 Revision) clearly states that a surrender may be absolute or qualified, conditional or unconditional. In light of this, much debate has centred on the more recent idea of conditional surrender. Various court decisions have found that conditional surrender, such as a lease, does not eradicate the basic premise that these lands are still reserved for native people.

The fundamental benefit of conditionally surrendered land lies in the native people being able to develop the property through leases to outside interests, while retaining underlying ownership. However, to effect meaningful ownership of the lands, native bands require control over the property for purposes of regulation, servicing, taxation and a host of other responsibilities usual to a municipal government.

Unfortunately, little guidance can be found in the *Indian Act*. As a result, individuals other than native people on leased property find themselves caught between an outdated federal Act, band councils that regulate affairs within the native lands (including the surrendered area), and provincial governments/local municipalities that seek to tax and otherwise control the endeavours of such persons and enforce land planning requirements.

NATIONAL REGISTRY

The real estate practitioner is cautioned as expert advice is essential, together with direct band council contact and proper guidance and documentation from Indian and Northern Affairs Canada. The government ministry has also maintained a national Indian lands registry since 1968. In essence, the system parallels provincial registry procedures and is generally modelled on the land titles system (although no guarantee of title is attached to ownership). The land registrar is required to maintain both a reserve land register and a surrendered land register.

EXAMPLE   *The Leased Cottage*

Salesperson Garcia has a buyer interested in leasing a cottage property currently located within the Lake District First Nation Reserve. Based on a conversation with Indian and Northern Affairs Canada, Garcia concludes that the buyer may have a seasonal recreational lease. Consent from both Band Council and the federal agency must be obtained. According to her research on the topic, leases are normally written on a five-year renewable basis, at fair market rent. In this instance, an assignment of the lease does not apply, but such is possible. The new lease in this Reserve must clearly state that the use is for seasonal occupation only (i.e., non-occupation from October 31 to May 1). Indian and Northern Affairs may require a site plan along with the lease agreement. If at some future point, the buyer wishes to assign the lease, an assignment of lease must be completed and approved by both the Band Council and Indian and Northern Affairs Canada.

Power of Attorney

Powers of attorney may be involved in the registration of property. A power of attorney is a delegated written authority to a person to act on behalf of another. For example, an individual owning property may grant a power of attorney to another to act on his or her behalf. More specifically, a power of attorney is an instrument in writing whereby one person (the donor) appoints another (the attorney) as his/her attorney and confers upon the attorney the authority to perform certain specified acts or kinds of acts on behalf of the donor.

- The donor is the person who grants the power of attorney.
- The attorney is the person who exercises the power of attorney.

Practitioners may encounter powers of attorney in signing various documents; e.g., listings and agreements of purchase and sale.

TYPES

Ontario recognizes three types of written authorization to sign and/or act on another's behalf.

A Power of Attorney For Personal Care	This power of attorney is pursuant to the *Substitute Decisions Act*, R.S.O. 1992 concerning medical/care decisions.
Continuing Power of Attorney for Property	Also under the *Substitute Decisions Act*, this power of attorney continues in force even during a subsequent Donor incapacity.
Power of Attorney	This older form of power of attorney (pursuant to the *Powers of Attorney Act*, R.S.O. 1990) was most commonly used prior to the enactment of the *Substitute Decisions Act*. This form deals with property and other matters, but is infrequently used as it does not continue in force during a subsequent donor incapacity.

REAL PROPERTY

Powers of attorney are of a general nature, but can be given for a specific purpose and time; i.e., dealing with a particular property. The Continuing Power of Attorney for Property is commonly used, given its continuance despite a subsequent donor incapacity.

Statutory provisions govern the giving of such power, effective date, limitations, revocation, who may act as the attorney, obligations of the attorney and other significant legal issues. Accordingly, donors should seek legal advice.

A Continuing Power of Attorney for Property dealing with real estate must be registered in the registry office showing both the donor and the attorney. Any document that is signed by the attorney, on behalf of the donor, should be in the donor's name. When the attorney signs a document pursuant to the power of attorney, that document should state that the donor was of age when the power of attorney was signed and that the power of attorney is in effect.

EXAMPLE *Power of Attorney*

Susan Smith has been appointed the attorney for William Smith to sell William Smith's home. The listing agreement, agreement of purchase and sale, deed and supporting documentation show "William Smith" as the seller. Documents would be signed by Susan Smith as follows:

> *Susan Smith,*
> *as Attorney for William Smith*

The documents would also contain a recital such as:

Continuing Power of Attorney for Property (or Power of Attorney) registered January 1, 2006 as Instrument No. LT 123456. To the best of my knowledge and belief the Continuing Power of Attorney for Property [or Power of Attorney] is still in full force and effect and the principal was at least 18 years of age when it was executed.

An attorney can only sign for the donor who granted the power of attorney. The attorney cannot sign documents for other parties, such as the donor's spouse or the donor's co-owner. Separate powers of attorney for those other parties would be necessary.

An attorney acting under a power of attorney has legal obligations, duties and liabilities. Salespersons and brokers are recommended not to act as attorneys for a client. One concern is whether the RECO insurance program would cover actions as an attorney under a power of attorney. Further, dual agency would be virtually impossible under a power of attorney (see subsequent chapter for a discussion of dual agency issues). The attorney effectively steps into the shoes of the donor/client. Legal advice should be sought given these and other potential complications.

Estate of Deceased Person (Registered Owner)

Lawyers must address certain complexities when dealing with conveyances and land registration involving the estate of a deceased person. Further, real estate practitioners dealing with such property must also be cautious under such circumstances regarding matters such as the authority of the person selling the deceased's property, the rights of a beneficiary to deal with the property, how the debts of the estate will be satisfied, whether the Will is valid and who may be entitled to any claims against the estate.

In Ontario, an estate of a deceased person is administered by an estate trustee. That trustee is the personal representative who signs on behalf of a deceased person. The individual is called an *Estate Trustee With a Will* (formerly an executor) if the deceased left a valid Will. If no Will, the person is referred to as an *Estate Trustee Without A Will* (formerly an administrator).

SIGNING OF DOCUMENTS

The estate solicitor should be involved at an early stage to resolve any potential concerns. Circumstances will dictate who can sign documents and whether the buyer will obtain good title. Typically, the Will is processed through the court and a *Certificate of Appointment of Estate Trustee With A Will* is issued. If no Will, the court will issue a *Certificate of Appointment of Estate Trustee Without a Will* to an individual.

Until such time as a Certificate is issued, no one can either sign a listing or enter into an agreement of purchase and sale. An exception does apply for property held in joint tenancy by the deceased and another individual. The application process to obtain a Certificate of Appointment can be lengthy. The nature and value of the estate assets must be determined, possibly requiring a valuation by a real estate registrant or other professional. The lawyer for the estate must make application for the certificate—typically issued six weeks following filing of necessary documents. Only at that point can a listing or an agreement of purchase and sale be lawfully signed by the estate trustee.

The Certificate of Appointment is registered at the land registry office and the appropriate recitals are inserted in the documents. Various legal statements must be included in the documents depending on the deceased's circumstances, nature of the property, spousal rights, rights/consents of beneficiaries, etc. Descriptive details are in summary form only, as estate administration can be complex. Salespersons and brokers are advised to seek guidance from the estate solicitor.

JOINT TENANCY

Property in joint tenancy is outside of the estate. Therefore, joint tenancy property can be dealt with before the Certificate of Appointment is issued. The surviving joint tenant can deal with the property as he/she wishes once the estate solicitor has registered the appropriate documentation on title to confirm that title is now in the name of the sole surviving joint tenant.

Sample Transfer/Deed of Land: Electronic Version   *Source: Teranet*

**** NOT VALID - TO BE USED FOR TRAINING PURPOSES ONLY ****

The applicant(s) hereby applies to the Land Registrar.		yyyy mm dd	Page 1 of 2
LRO # 20 **Transfer**		Receipted as HH198 on 2006 06 16	at 10:15

Properties

PIN	07014 - 0500 LT	Interest/Estate	Fee Simple
Description	LT 48 , PL 1361 ; HAMILTON		
Address	05000 IDLEWOOD CR HAMILTON		

Consideration

Consideration $ 259,000.00

Transferor(s)

The transferor(s) hereby transfers the land to the transferee(s).

Name	JONES, MARIANN JOYCE
Address for Service	123 Main St. Toronto, Ont M7T 5R4

I am at least 18 years of age.

JONES, JOHN WILLIAM and I are spouses of one another and are both parties to this document

This document is not authorized under Power of Attorney by this party.

Name	JONES, JOHN WILLIAM
Address for Service	123 Main St. Toronto, Ont M7T 5R4

I am at least 18 years of age.

JONES, MARIANN JOYCE and I are spouses of one another and are both parties to this document

This document is not authorized under Power of Attorney by this party.

Transferee(s)

		Capacity	Share
Name	SMITH, JOHN FRANKLIN	Joint Tenants	
Date of Birth	1969 06 04		
Address for Service	05000 IDLEWOOD CR HAMILTON, ON L8N 5R4		
Name	SMITH, ELEANOR JOYCE	Joint Tenants	
Date of Birth	1978 08 07		
Address for Service	05000 IDLEWOOD CR HAMILTON, ON L8N 5R4		

Signed By

Paul P. Lawyer(TCD)		acting for Transferor(s)	Signed	2006 06 16
Tel				
Fax				
Paul P. Lawyer(TCD)		acting for Transferee(s)	Signed	2006 06 16
Tel				
Fax				

Submitted By

TRAINING COMPANY D	2006 06 16
Tel	
Fax	

Fees/Taxes/Payment

Statutory Registration Fee	$60.00
Land Transfer Tax	$2,360.00
Total Paid	$2,420.00

**** NOT VALID - TO BE USED FOR TRAINING PURPOSES ONLY ****

LAND TRANSFER TAX STATEMENTS

In the matter of the conveyance of: 07014 - 0500 LT 48 , PL 1361 ; HAMILTON

BY:	JONES, MARIANN JOYCE		
	JONES, JOHN WILLIAM		
TO:	SMITH, JOHN FRANKLIN	Joint Tenants	%(all PINs)
	SMITH, ELEANOR JOYCE	Joint Tenants	%(all PINs)

1. SMITH, JOHN FRANKLIN AND SMITH, ELEANOR JOYCE

    I am

    ☐ (a) A person in trust for whom the land conveyed in the above-described conveyance is being conveyed;

    ☐ (b) A trustee named in the above-described conveyance to whom the land is being conveyed;

    ☑ (c) A transferee named in the above-described conveyance;

    ☐ (d) The authorized agent or solicitor acting in this transaction for _____ described in paragraph(s) (_) above.

    ☐ (e) The President, Vice-President, Manager, Secretary, Director, or Treasurer authorized to act for _____ described in paragraph(s) (_) above.

    ☐ (f) A transferee described in paragraph ( ) and am making these statements on my own behalf and on behalf of _____ who is my spouse described in paragraph (_) and as such, I have personal knowledge of the facts herein deposed to.

3. **The total consideration for this transaction is allocated as follows:**

(a) Monies paid or to be paid in cash	259,000.00
(b) Mortgages (i) assumed (show principal and interest to be credited against purchase price)	0.00
(ii) Given Back to Vendor	0.00
(c) Property transferred in exchange (detail below)	0.00
(d) Fair market value of the land(s)	0.00
(e) Liens, legacies, annuities and maintenance charges to which transfer is subject	0.00
(f) Other valuable consideration subject to land transfer tax (detail below)	0.00
(g) Value of land, building, fixtures and goodwill subject to land transfer tax (total of (a) to (f))	259,000.00
(h) VALUE OF ALL CHATTELS - items of tangible personal property	0.00
(i) Other considerations for transaction not included in (g) or (h) above	0.00
(j) Total consideration	259,000.00

PROPERTY Information Record

A. Nature of Instrument: Transfer

LRO 20   Registration No.   HH198   Date: 2006/06/16

B. Property(s):   PIN 07014 - 0500 Address 05000 IDLEWOOD CR   Assessment   2402090 - 91508900
                                                                    Roll No
                   HAMILTON

C. Address for Service: 05000 IDLEWOOD CR
                           HAMILTON, ON
                           L8N 5R4

D. (i) Last Conveyance(s): PIN 07014 - 0500 Registration No.   600000

   (ii) Legal Description for Property Conveyed : Same as in last conveyance? Yes ☑ No ☐ Not known ☐

E. Tax Statements Prepared By: Paul P. Lawyer(TCD)

Sample Sheriff's Certificate: Electronic Version   *Source: Teranet*

```
                                          CERTIFICATE #:
                                          NO DE CERTIFICAT:
                                          03488521-1810000B


                    CLEAR CERTIFICATE / CERTIFICAT LIBRE

    SHERIFF OF /
    SHERIF DE: *** NOT VALID - TO BE USED FOR TRAINING PURPOSES ONLY ****

    DATE OF CERTIFICATE /
    DATE DU CERTIFICAT  : 2006-06-16

    THIS CERTIFIES THAT THERE ARE NO WRITS OF EXECUTION, EXTENT OR
    CERTIFICATES OF LIEN IN MY HANDS AT THE TIME OF SEARCHING AGAINST
    THE REAL AND PERSONAL PROPERTY OF:

    JE CERTIFIE, PAR LA PRESENTE, NE PAS AVOIR DE BREF D'EXECUTION,
    NI DE CERTIFICAT DE PRIVILEGE, NI D'ORDONNANCE EN MA POSSESSION
    AU MOMENT DE LA RECHERCHE VISANT LES BIENS MEUBLES OU IMMEUBLES DE:

                  SURNAME / NOM      GIVEN NAME(S) / PRENOM(S)
    ==========================================================================

    (PERSON/PERSONNE) JONES, MARIANN JOYCE

    CAUTION TO PARTY REQUESTING SEARCH:
    ENSURE THAT THE ABOVE INDICATED NAME IS THE SAME AS THE NAME SEARCHED.
    THIS NAME WILL REMAIN CLEAR UNTIL THE CLOSE OF BUSINESS THIS DATE.

    AVERTISSEMENT A LA PARTIE QUI DEMANDE LA RECHERCHE:
    ASSUREZ-VOUS QUE LE NOM INDIQUE CI-DESSUS EST LE MEME QUE CELUI QUI
    EST RECHERCHE.  CET ETAT DEMEURE VALIDE JUSQU'A LA FIN DE LA JOURNEE
    DE TRAVAIL.

    CHARGE FOR THIS CERTIFICATE /
    FRAIS POUR CE CERTIFICAT    : $11.00

    SEARCHER REFERENCE /
    REFERENCE CONCERNANT L'AUTEUR DE LA DEMANDE:


                                          CERTIFICATE #:
                                          NO DE CERTIFICAT:
                                          03488523-4380000B


                    CLEAR CERTIFICATE / CERTIFICAT LIBRE

    SHERIFF OF /
    SHERIF DE: *** NOT VALID - TO BE USED FOR TRAINING PURPOSES ONLY ****

    DATE OF CERTIFICATE /
    DATE DU CERTIFICAT  : 2006-06-16

    THIS CERTIFIES THAT THERE ARE NO WRITS OF EXECUTION, EXTENT OR
    CERTIFICATES OF LIEN IN MY HANDS AT THE TIME OF SEARCHING AGAINST
    THE REAL AND PERSONAL PROPERTY OF:

    JE CERTIFIE, PAR LA PRESENTE, NE PAS AVOIR DE BREF D'EXECUTION,
    NI DE CERTIFICAT DE PRIVILEGE, NI D'ORDONNANCE EN MA POSSESSION
    AU MOMENT DE LA RECHERCHE VISANT LES BIENS MEUBLES OU IMMEUBLES DE:

                  SURNAME / NOM      GIVEN NAME(S) / PRENOM(S)
    ==========================================================================

    (PERSON/PERSONNE) JONES, JOHN WILLIAM

    CAUTION TO PARTY REQUESTING SEARCH:
    ENSURE THAT THE ABOVE INDICATED NAME IS THE SAME AS THE NAME SEARCHED.
    THIS NAME WILL REMAIN CLEAR UNTIL THE CLOSE OF BUSINESS THIS DATE.

    AVERTISSEMENT A LA PARTIE QUI DEMANDE LA RECHERCHE:
    ASSUREZ-VOUS QUE LE NOM INDIQUE CI-DESSUS EST LE MEME QUE CELUI QUI
    EST RECHERCHE.  CET ETAT DEMEURE VALIDE JUSQU'A LA FIN DE LA JOURNEE
    DE TRAVAIL.

    CHARGE FOR THIS CERTIFICATE /
    FRAIS POUR CE CERTIFICAT    : $11.00

    SEARCHER REFERENCE /
    REFERENCE CONCERNANT L'AUTEUR DE LA DEMANDE:
```

Sample Charge/Mortgage of Land: Electronic Version   *Source: Teranet*

**** NOT VALID - TO BE USED FOR TRAINING PURPOSES ONLY ****

The applicant(s) hereby applies to the Land Registrar.

LRO # 20   **Charge/Mortgage**

yyyy mm dd   Page 1 of 2

Receipted as **HH199** on 2006 06 16   at 10:55

Properties

PIN	07014 - 0500 LT	Interest/Estate Fee Simple
Description	LT 48 , PL 1361 ; HAMILTON	
Address	05000 IDLEWOOD CR	
	HAMILTON	

Chargor(s)

The chargor(s) hereby charges the land to the chargee(s). The chargor(s) acknowledges the receipt of the charge and the standard charge terms, if any.

Name	SMITH, JOHN FRANKLIN
Address for Service	05000 Idlewood Cr.
	Hamilton, ON
	L8N 5R4

I am at least 18 years of age.

Eleanor Joyce Smith and I are spouses of one another and are both parties to this document

This document is not authorized under Power of Attorney by this party.

Name	SMITH, ELEANOR JOYCE
Address for Service	05000 Idlewood Cr.
	Hamilton, ON
	L8N 5R4

I am at least 18 years of age.

John Franklin Smith and I are spouses of one another and are both parties to this document

This document is not authorized under Power of Attorney by this party.

Chargee(s)

		Capacity	Share
Name	MONEY BANK		
Address for Service	144 Constitutional Dr.		
	Burlington, ON		
	B9T 5R2		

Provisions

Principal	$ 259,000.00	Currency CDN
Calculation Period	half yearly, not in advance	
Balance Due Date	2010/11/01	
Payments	$ 1,681.00	
Interest Adjustment Date	2006 12 01	
Payment Date	first day of each month	
First Payment Date	2006 12 01	
Last Payment Date	2011 11 01	
Standard Charge Terms	9412	
Insurance Amount	full insurable value	
Guarantor		

Additional Provisions

The chargor shall have the privilege of prepaying, at any time, without notice, the whole or any part of the principal hereby secured without notice or bonus.

Signed By

Paul P. Lawyer(TCD)		acting for Chargor(s) Signed	2006 06 16
Tel			
Fax			

Submitted By

TRAINING COMPANY D	2006 06 16
Tel	
Fax	

Fees/Taxes/Payment

Statutory Registration Fee	$60.00
Total Paid	$60.00

Sample Discharge of Charge/Mortgage: Electronic Version   *Source: Teranet*

**** NOT VALID - TO BE USED FOR TRAINING PURPOSES ONLY ****

The applicant(s) hereby applies to the Land Registrar.

LRO # 20   **Discharge Of Charge**

yyyy mm dd   Page 1 of 1
Receipted as HH200 on 2006 06 16   at 11:10

Properties

PIN	07014 - 0500 LT
Description	LT 48 , PL 1361 ; HAMILTON
Address	05000 IDLEWOOD CR HAMILTON

Document to be Discharged

Registration No.	Date	Type of Instrument
HH199	2006 06 16	Charge/Mortgage

Discharging Party(s)

This discharge complies with the Planning Act. This discharge discharges the charge.

Name	MONEY BANK
Address for Service	4050 Eglinton Ave. Burlington, ON B9Y 7E8

I, Paul Johnson, have the authority to bind the corporation.

This document is not authorized under Power of Attorney by this party.

The party giving this discharge is the original chargee and is the party entitled to give an effective discharge

Signed By

Paul P. Lawyer(TCD)   acting for Applicant(s)   Signed   2006 06 16

Tel

Fax

Submitted By

TRAINING COMPANY D   2006 06 16

Tel

Fax

Fees/Taxes/Payment

Statutory Registration Fee	$60.00
Total Paid	$60.00

File Number

Discharging Party Client File Number :   2580-01

Sample Parcel Register: Electronic Version   *Source: Teranet*

| TRAINING | Ministry of Government Services | LAND REGISTRY OFFICE #20 | | | PARCEL REGISTER (ABBREVIATED) FOR PROPERTY IDENTIFIER 24910-0020 (LT) | PAGE 1 OF 1 PREPARED FOR pplawyer ON 2006/06/16 AT 11:43:56 |

**** NOT VALID - TO BE USED FOR TRAINING PURPOSES ONLY **** PCL 6-1, SEC 30M500 ; LT 6, PL 30M500 ; OAKVILLE

SUBJECT TO RESERVATIONS IN CROWN GRANT

PROPERTY DESCRIPTION:

PROPERTY REMARKS:

ESTATE/QUALIFIER:
FEE SIMPLE
ABSOLUTE

RECENTLY:
FIRST CONVERSION FROM BOOK

PIN CREATION DATE:
1995/12/20

OWNERS' NAMES
JOHNSON, TIM

CAPACITY   SHARE
BENO

REG. NUM.	DATE	INSTRUMENT TYPE	AMOUNT	PARTIES FROM	PARTIES TO	CERT/CHKD
EFFECTIVE 2000/07/29 THE NOTATION OF THE "BLOCK IMPLEMENTATION DATE" OF 1995/12/20 ON THIS PIN						
WAS REPLACED WITH THE "PIN CREATION DATE" OF 1995/12/20						
** PRINTOUT INCLUDES ALL DOCUMENT TYPES (DELETED INSTRUMENTS NOT INCLUDED) **						
H280000	1986/05/29	NOTICE AGREEMENT REMARKS: PRELIMINARY DEVELOPMENT			THE REGIONAL MUNICIPALITY OF HALTON	C
H260000	1986/07/15	NOTICE AGREEMENT			THE CORPORATION OF THE TOWN OF OAKVILLE	C
H350000	1987/10/07	NO SUB AGREEMENT			THE CORPORATION OF THE TOWN OF OAKVILLE	C
H360000	1988/01/22	TRANSFER	$221,900		JOHNSON, TIM	C
H630000	1996/07/24	CHARGE	$300,000	JOHNSON, TIM	HONGKONG BANK OF CANADA	C

NOTE: ADJOINING PROPERTIES SHOULD BE INVESTIGATED TO ASCERTAIN DESCRIPTIVE INCONSISTENCIES, IF ANY, WITH DESCRIPTION REPRESENTED FOR THIS PROPERTY.
NOTE: ENSURE THAT YOUR PRINTOUT STATES THE TOTAL NUMBER OF PAGES AND THAT YOU HAVE PICKED THEM ALL UP.

KNOWLEDGE INTEGRATION

Notables

- Land registration, through registry or land titles systems, provides for the orderly ownership of land in Ontario.

- The Land Registrar, under Land Titles, maintains and guarantees title; under Registry, he or she takes no responsibility for title.

- Registry requires a chain of title search, typically for a 40-year period.

- Land Titles operates under three principles: mirror, curtain and insurance.

- The automation of land registry records and conversion to e-registration is nearing completion within Ontario.

- E-registration involves the creation, submission and maintenance of property records in electronic format.

- E-registration involves Title Index and Property Index Databases under POLARIS.

- Automated records are accessed by Teranet's electronic gateway called Teraview, and initiated by means of dockets and messaging.

- The *Land Registration Reform Act* established five standard forms which are used in both paper-based and electronic registration processes.

- A Land Transfer Tax Affidavit accompanies the Transfer/Deed of Land. This affidavit provides details relating to land transfer tax and other property information; e.g., selected assessment and school support details.

- Leasehold interests can be registered under both Registry and Land Titles systems.

- A crown patent is an original title deeded by the government and generally accepted as the root of title.

- Matters relating to land registration for native lands are a federal responsibility.

- Three types of written powers of attorney are recognized in Ontario.

- Caution is advised on all matters concerning conveyances involving the estate of a deceased person.

Glossary

Abstract	Land Transfer Tax Affidavit
Chain of Title	Mirror Principle
Charge	POLARIS
Charge/Mortgage of Land	Registry
Crown Patent	Schedule
Curtain Principle	Standard Charge Terms
Deed	Teranet
Discharge of Charge/Mortgage	Teraview
Document General	Title Insurance
E-Registration	Transfer/Deed of Land
Insurance Principle	
Land Titles	

Web Links

Web links are included for general interest regarding selected chapter topics.

Ministry of Government and Consumer Services	For more information concerning the Real Property Registration Branch of the Ministry of Government and Consumer Services and land registration, go to the Ministry's web site at ***www.mgs.gov.on.ca***.
Teranet	Go to ***www.teranet.ca*** for details about the scope of services offered by Teranet over and above land registry automation. Current endeavours include geospatial services as well as security, transaction and risk management.
Teraview	The Teraview web site (***www.teraview.ca***) provides a wide range of information concerning the software, including full descriptions of functionalities and steps to follow in the e-registration process.
Standard Charge Terms	Various lenders post standard charge terms on the Internet. For examples, use a search engine (e.g., ***www.google.ca***) and search *set of standard charge terms* or *standard charge terms*.

Strategic Thinking For Your Career

Questions are included to assist in developing your new career. No answers are provided.

1. Where is the local registry office located for property records in my market area?

2. What personal land registry documents are available to review and better understand what is included in such documents?

3. Can I clearly differentiate between land titles and land registry systems, if asked to do so?

4. Have land registry records been automated in my local area? What additional information is available at the local registry office regarding this new process?

5. What products does Teranet provide that might be of interest to me in being more competitive in the marketplace?

6. If a seller provides any of the five standard forms used for land registration, can I confidently review and discuss basic information with him or her?

7. Are there Crown lands or native lands within my market area?

Chapter Mini-Review

Solutions are located in the Appendix.

1. An original title issued by the government (Crown) is generally referred to as root of title.

   ○ True   ○ False

2. The large-scale conversion of registry records into land titles is a process referred to as making first application.

   ○ True   ○ False

3. Chain of title is most commonly associated with land titles.

   ○ True   ○ False

4. Recording of property ownership by its geographic location is known as tract indexing.

   ○ True   ○ False

5. A parcel register is used under the registry system.

   ○ True   ○ False

6. Part II of the *Land Registration Reform Act* authorized the automation of property records.

   ○ True   ○ False

7. A combination of block index number and property index number form the PIN (Property Identification Number).

   ○ True   ○ False

8. Teranet is an electronic software operated by Teraview and provides online remote access to automated property records in Ontario land registry offices.

   ○ True   ○ False

9. A Land Transfer Tax Affidavit normally accompanies every Charge/Mortgage of Land at point of registration in a land registry office.

   ○ True   ○ False

10. An implied covenant under a Charge/Mortgage of Land is that the mortgagor will make payments (including interest) and pay taxes.

    ○ True   ○ False

11. A mortgagor must pay monies owing on a mortgage to a court in order to discharge a mortgage.

    ○ True   ○ False

12. The Document General is best described as a standard form used to register documents in a land registry office other than a transfer, charge or discharge.

    ○ True   ○ False

13. Leasehold interests can only be registered in land titles if the lease does not exceed three years.

    ○ True   ○ False

14. A Crown Patent is typically accompanied by certain reservations concerning title to the land.

    ○ True   ○ False

15. A national registry of Indian lands is maintained by the Federal government.

    ○ True   ○ False

16. A power of attorney cannot be involved in the registration of property.

    ○ True   ○ False

Active Learning Exercises

Solutions are located in the Appendix.

■ Exercise 1   Fill-in-the-Blanks

1.1   Properties in an automated land registry office can be searched using a nine-digit number referred to as the

                                       .

1.2   A sequence of conveyances and encumbrances affecting title over time under the registry system is commonly referred to as a (an)

                                       .

1.3   The estate of a deceased person is administered by a (an)

                                       .

1.4   Public lands under the *Public Lands Act* administered by the government are also known as   .

1.5   The   principle under land titles provides that information accurately and completely reflects the present status of land ownership.

1.6   The registration of goods, services and personal property is handled under a system referred to as   .

1.7   The Land Transfer Tax Affidavit involves the payment of land transfer tax to the Ministry of   .

1.8   Standard charge terms were introduced into the land registration process under legislation titled   .

1.9   A Discharge of Charge/Mortgage is executed by the   and given to the   verifying that the mortgage has been paid.

1.10   A lessee (tenant) having a lease exceeding 21 years may make application to the registrar in the applicable land registry office to have a (an)

                                   opened.

◼ Exercise 2   Multiple Choice

2.1   Teraview gateway software:

    a.   Provides for searching of automated records, but does not have e-registration functionality.

    b.   Only permits the user to search property by means of a nine-digit identification number.

    c.   Is designed for use by lawyers and not other individuals.

    d.   Accesses various databases within POLARIS.

2.2   Which of the following is a true statement about the discharge of charge/mortgage?

    a.   When a registered charge/mortgage is paid off, it is necessary to register this document to give evidence of the removal of the claim.

    b.   The discharge of a charge/mortgage is usually executed by the mortgagor.

    c.   Under land titles, a discharge of a charge/mortgage is typically registered by attaching the discharge to a Document General.

    d.   The form referred to as the *Discharge of Charge/Mortgage* is also referred to as Form 2.

2.3   Which of the following is a true statement about a set of standard charge terms?

    a.   The land registrar limits the number of sets of standard charge terms that can be filed in the land registry office.

    b.   The concept of standard charge terms was initiated by the *Registry Act*.

    c.   The land registrar assigns a number to each unique set of standard charge terms.

    d.   A provision stating that the mortgagor will abide by the declaration and all by-laws is required in all sets of standard charge terms.

2.4   In land titles, the parcel register is deemed to be the sole source of information. Which of the following principles best describes this fact?

    a.   Curtain principle.

    b.   Insurance principle.

    c.   Mirror principle.

    d.   Title principle.

2.5   The *Land Titles Act* is administered by:

    a.   The Ministry of Municipal Affairs and Housing.

    b.   The Ministry of Financial Institutions.

    c.   The Ministry of Government Services.

    d.   The Ministry of Titles.

2.6 The Land Titles Assurance Fund:

    a. Is designed to provide financial compensation for persons wrongfully deprived of land or some interest therein (subject to certain qualifications).

    b. Refers to a title insurance policy offered by added coverage from a private insurer in Ontario covering property title defects.

    c. Currently applies solely to paper-based and not automated land registry offices.

    d. Will not cover situations in which persons are wrongfully deprived of land due to fraud.

2.7 In a Transfer/Deed of Land, if the purchaser was acquiring the property and the interest/estate being transferred was other than fee simple, in which box on Form 1 would it appear?

    a. Box 3.

    b. Box 5.

    c. Box 7.

    d. Box 9.

2.8 In a Charge/Mortgage of Land, the principal amount of the mortgage could appear in two boxes within Form 2. Which are they?

    a. Boxes 4 and 10.

    b. Boxes 4 and 9.

    c. Boxes 9 and 13.

    d. The principal amount does not appear on this form.

2.9 Which of the following statements is correct?

    a. A power of attorney can only be of a general nature and not for a specific purpose or time period.

    b. A continuing power of attorney can be used in the conveyance of real property.

    c. A continuing power of attorney cannot be used if the donor (the person granting the power of attorney) is incapacitated.

    d. Four different powers of attorney are recognized in Ontario.

▣ Exercise 3   Analyzing the Transfer/Deed of Land and Charge/Mortgage of Land

3.1   A seller may produce certain title documents when listing a property and practitioners should be familiar with the formats. A fictitious Transfer/Deed of Land, along with the Land Transfer Tax Affidavit, is illustrated earlier in this chapter. Identify who is the buyer and seller, the sale amount, the ownership interest being conveyed and any other noteworthy items.

3.2   A fictitious Charge/Mortgage of Land is also illustrated. Identify the amount of the charge, who is borrowing the funds, who is lending the funds and any other noteworthy items.

■ Exercise 4   Smith's Legal Papers

Seller Smith is busy rummaging through legal papers attempting to locate his mortgage documents. After considerable effort, he pulls out the original reporting letter from his lawyer who acted on the purchase of the home approximately five years ago. The Charge/Mortgage of Land is attached with no reference to a set of standard charge terms or any other mortgage documentation. He insists on digging further in hopes of finding a fully detailed mortgage. Smith remembers the days when mortgages were ten or more pages long and contained all sorts of provisions, legal seals, etc.

4.1   Based on your knowledge of the Charge/Mortgage of Land, list six implied covenants that apply despite the fact that no set of standard charge terms exist.

4.2   If Smith had in fact paid off this charge/mortgage and could not find a copy of the discharge of charge/mortgage, what could be done to effect a discharge of the charge/mortgage?

SECTION II

PLANNING AND LAND USE

Broker William's car lurches over the last few boulder-strewn metres of construction road. Six years of effort are culminating on this cool May morning. Officials from the municipality, region and provincial ministries, as well as numerous stakeholders, will arrive shortly. Public meetings, amended zoning by-laws and development agreements are now in the past. All approvals are in place.

Complying with strict legislative requirements has proven costly, but worthwhile. This community will be a model for future environmentally-conscious developments in Ontario. Strict planning principles are being applied from initial land clearing to final tree planting.

Williams is poised to maximize the opportunity through an effective marketing program on behalf of the developer/builder. Real estate developments are complex. Williams quickly reflects on all the steps: flood plain requirements, wetland conservation, street pattern layout, building construction standards, housing density requirements and so on.

And now the time has arrived. Williams hurriedly unlocks the model home centre, does one final check of the banners, tests the PA system and mentally reviews the seating arrangements. A trail of dust confirms that the first guests are arriving.

CHAPTER 4

Municipal Planning

Introduction

Effective land planning provides a framework for orderly growth and development while protecting resources of provincial interest, public health and safety, and the quality of the natural environment. Land use planning and management is a modern day necessity. Every property owner is impacted in one way or another by such requirements that span federal, provincial and municipal government levels.

Practitioners most commonly encounter planning at a municipal level when inquiring about zoning restrictions, permitted land uses, minor variances, building permits and related topics. However, all salespersons and brokers require a broader awareness of land planning including policies that drive the process and procedures that must be followed.

Land use planning directly affects all of us, either as property owners or tenants. To most, the actual planning activity lies behind the scenes, as negotiations typically unfold between land owner, developer, and government ministries and agencies. Informed consumers are often aware of new development plans when notices are circulated and public meetings scheduled. For others, new developments are only noticed when construction equipment suddenly appears. But, the process usually began many months, if not years, before.

Planning policies and procedures are continuously refined to meet changing needs. In the past decade, provincial authorities have sought means to intensify land use within urban areas and discourage urban sprawl. At a local level, municipal zoning by-laws are probably the most visible examples of planning, but as this chapter reveals, the planning process is complex with responsibilities ranging from federal to local municipal authorities.

SECTION II

PLANNING AND LAND USE

Learning Outcomes

At the conclusion of this chapter, students will be able to:

- Describe the division of responsibilities and jurisdictional controls regarding planning and development in Ontario.
- Discuss the purpose and structure of the *Planning Act*, as the focal legislative framework for planning within the province.
- Detail the role of provincial interests, upper and lower-tier municipalities, provincial policy statements and one window planner service in the planning process.
- Discuss the scope of duties performed by the Ontario Municipal Board.
- Identify and describe the role of municipalities including their spheres of influence and the impact of such spheres on listing and selling activities.
- Outline the purpose underlying an official plan and the approval process including official plan amendments.
- Describe the operation of a committee of adjustment with particular reference to minor variances and non-conforming uses.
- Identify major steps involved in land division applications for both land severances and plans of subdivision.

PLANNING FUNDAMENTALS

The **planning** system established in Ontario came about largely through the **Planning Act** and related legislation. Planning is focal to real estate marketing, as permitted uses directly affect value. Further, accurate responses about a particular property can often make the difference between success and failure for that particular sale.

Responses to such questions, or at least an understanding of where to get such answers, requires a working knowledge of planning responsibilities, operational basics within the province, the names and functions of government organizations involved in planning and the scope of decisions made by such organizations.

Planning

The orderly development of land through a structured planning process.

Levels of Authority

Land planning and use in Ontario is governed by legislation at federal, provincial and local (municipal) levels. The federal government has selective involvement; e.g., airport facilities/lands and oceans/fisheries responsibilities (including fish habitat which impacts how shoreline property is used). The federal government, in particular, works with provincial ministries regarding lands adjacent to the Great Lakes and federal canal systems (e.g., Trent-Severn Waterway and the Rideau Canal). Participation, however, is best described as indirect, with the most direct controls at the provincial level or municipal level.

The provincial government established a policy framework for consistency, but delegates various powers to municipalities under the *Planning Act*, particularly regarding official plans and land use controls. In the past decade, notable downloading of responsibilities from the provincial government to municipalities has occurred. Municipal responsibilities are set out in the *Municipal Act, 2001*.

Federal Government

Selective involvement primarily concerning airport facilities/lands and oceans/fisheries *(including the Great Lakes and federal canals/waterways).*

Provincial Government

Responsibile for overall provincial planning. Establishes planning policies while delegating many responsibilities to municipalities.

Municipal Government

Various defined areas of responsibility. Responsibilities are set out in the *Municipal Act, 2001*. Increasing authority has been granted to municipalities over the past decade.

Provincial and Municipal Perspectives

The *Planning Act* provides the statutory framework for orderly land development. This Act is administered by the Ministry of Municipal Affairs and Housing (**www.mah.gov.on.ca**) which also broadly directs overall planning in the province by way of **provincial policy statements**. All planning bodies within the province must be consistent with such statements when applying planning policies. Further, the *Planning Act* sets out specific **provincial interests** to further delineate what is considered to be sound planning within the province.

The Act permits selected agencies to make decisions on various matters such as patterns of land use, road networks, schools, recreational facilities and water supply. The long range effect of such decisions has tremendous impact on salespersons and brokers.

Municipalities, empowered to enact local planning, are classified as either **upper tier** or **lower tier**, each having specific rights and responsibilities in the process. Most local planning is focused on the preparation, adoption and revision of **official plans** within respective planning areas, the adoption of zoning by-laws for land use control and strict controls over the process of dividing and developing land. Zoning and related land use restrictions are detailed in Chapter 5.

Official Plan

A formal projection of development of a planning area for a specified future period of time.

SECTION II   PLANNING AND LAND USE

At the municipal level, a **committee of adjustment** can be appointed with the power to grant **minor variances** from the provisions of zoning by-laws, to grant **consents** and to control the continuance of **non-conforming uses**. While the Ministry oversees planning matters and the *Planning Act*, the Ontario Municipal Board is most directly involved in appeals of planning decisions and provides a public forum for resolving planning-related disagreements.

Minor Variance

Small variations from the zoning by-laws.

Non-Conforming Use

A use that existed prior to the current zoning by-laws.

 WEB LINKS

Ministry of Municipal Affairs and Housing   The Ministry provides an informative site outlining various aspects of the planning process. Go to ***www.mah.gov.on.ca***.

The Planning Act

The *Planning Act*, including various Regulations, establishes the framework for an orderly planning system throughout the Province of Ontario. A general overview of the *Planning Act* is provided to better understand provincial and local planning roles.

THE PLANNING ACT	
PART I	Provincial Administration
PART II	Local Planning Administration
PART III	Official Plans
PART IV	Community Improvement
PART V	Land Use Controls and Related Administration
PART VI	Subdivision of Land
PART VII	General

ADMINISTRATION

The *Planning Act* gives general administrative control of the planning system in Ontario to the Minister of Municipal Affairs and Housing. The interests of the government, as identified in the Act, are protected through the approval of long-range planning documents by the Minister or a delegated representative. Divisions of the Ministry are responsible for specific administrative functions involving ministerial approvals under the Act; i.e., official plans or amendments, plans of subdivision and zoning orders.

The Ministry also supports the objectives of the *Planning Act* by the extension of municipal planning throughout the province and the ongoing improvement of its quality. Activities involve aiding municipal governments in their planning procedures, the provision of research and technical advice, grants, training and education, and publication of manuals and planning information.

The *Planning Act* also authorizes the Minister of Municipal Affairs and Housing to issue policy statements on matters relating to municipal planning, mineral aggregate resources, flood plains, housing and wetlands.

LOCAL PLANNING

The Act establishes parameters for the creation of local planning advisory committees, planning areas and the development of official plans. Planning involves a two-tiered structure for municipalities:

UPPER TIER (region, county or district)	LOWER TIER (municipality)
Preparation, adoption and revision of the official plan, and the process of dividing and developing land.	Preparation, adoption and revision of the official plan and the adoption of zoning by-laws, interim control by-laws and other by-laws.

Where an upper tier municipality exists, its council will often coordinate planning between the respective lower tier municipalities, as well as address matters for which it may be directly responsible, including roads and water/sewer systems. In some instances, the upper tier municipality may assume, by agreement, any of the planning responsibilities of the lower tier municipality. Otherwise the lower tier municipality will handle land-use matters within its jurisdiction, such as location, type and density of development.

The Act contains provisions of considerable force, flexibility and effect. Properly employed, these provisions enable municipalities to mount comprehensive planning programs tailored to particular needs, resources and inclinations. Although the actual process is carried out by municipal organizations, the provincial government maintains the function of approving proposals, following passage by municipal councils.

PROVINCIAL INTERESTS

The *Planning Act* sets out provincial interest matters that the Minister, municipalities, local planning boards and the Ontario Municipal Board (OMB) must *be consistent with* when carrying out their responsibilities. Sec. 2 of the Act highlights the following areas:

- Protection of ecological systems.
- Protection of provincial agricultural resources.
- Conservation/management of natural resources.
- Conservation of significant architectural, cultural, historical, archaeological and scientific interests.
- Supply, efficiency, and conservation of energy and water.
- Provision/efficient use of communication, transportation, sewage and water services, and waste management systems.
- Minimization of waste.
- Orderly development of safe and healthy communities.
- Accessibility for persons with disabilities to all facilities, services and matters to which the *Planning Act* applies.
- Adequate provision and distribution of educational, health, social, cultural and recreational facilities.
- Adequate provision of a full range of housing and employment opportunities.
- Protection of the provincial financial and economic well-being.
- Co-ordination of public planning activities and resolution of related public/private conflicts.
- Protection of public health and safety.
- Appropriate location of growth and development.

RECENT INITIATIVES

The *Planning Act* is undoubtedly one of the most complex pieces of legislation affecting property. During recent years, significant attempts have been made to simplify practices, reform various procedures and ensure that the Act (including associated planning tools) were effective. However, changing governments have somewhat complicated the process.

Selected changes were introduced in 1996 to modify the planning framework. Most notably, legislative amendments deleted the requirement that planning decisions *be consistent with* provincial policy statements. Such decisions would only *have regard to* provincial policies. This key wording change effectively gave local decision-makers the discretion and flexibility to implement the policy statement in ways that would meet their own community needs.

Interestingly, the wording was reversed with a new provincial policy statement announced effective March 1, 2005. This date coincided with the effective date of Section 2 of the *Strong Communities (Planning Amendment) Act, 2004*, which required that planning decisions on applications that are subject to the new provincial policy statement *shall be consistent with* the new policies.

This requirement *to be consistent with policy* goes to the heart of any decision made by a local planning board, a municipality, a commission or agency of the provincial government and others involved with planning-related matters. The present government is clearly committed to providing firm policy direction on all land-use planning in the province. The stated purpose of this policy-directed approach is to ensure strong communities, a clean and healthy environment, and a strong economy.

The planning emphasis is clearly moving in the direction of orderly development and large scale planning to ensure the wise utilization of land, heightened intensification within existing communities and more compact, efficient development. The scope of planning reforms not only involve the *Planning Act*, but also the operation of agencies including reforms to the Ontario Municipal Board to ensure that decisions and orders involving appeals are also consistent with the overall policy-directed approach to planning.

Recently, the government passed legislation for further reforms to improve accessiblity for residents interested in the local planning process and also strengthen the role of municipalities in ensuring that neighbourhood developments are well designed and properly integrated within the community. This legislation also introduced a new development permit system (DPS) to streamline the development process, promote stronger communities and enhance environmental protection.

PROVINCIAL PERSPECTIVE

Provincial Policy Statement

The provincial policy statement issued by the Minister of Municipal Affairs and Housing concerns land use planning issues of province-wide interest. Provincial policy statements, a key reference point for planning and development, contain major policy areas concerning the management of change, and promotion of efficient, cost-effective development and land use patterns that stimulate economic growth, while protecting the environment and public health.

Officials and approval bodies engaged in the planning process must *be consistent with* provincial policy statements. Individuals, committees, councils, planning bodies and others involved with planning must align with specific policy provisions when carrying out any planning responsibility. Such policy provisions are issued pursuant to Section 3 of the *Planning Act* and typically set out broad principles concerning the interplay of economic, environmental and social factors that come into play in the development of land.

Policy statements are presented in terms of overall principles, along with specific policies regarding the efficient, cost-effective development of land, agriculture, mineral resources, natural heritage, water quality and quantity, cultural/archaeological resources and lastly public health and safety. Broad guidelines are accompanied by interpretative materials and definitions. The provincial policy statement is reviewed every five years.

RECENT DEVELOPMENTS

The current provincial policy statement, issued under Section 3 of the *Planning Act*, came into effect March 1, 2005 replacing the previous statement issued on May 22, 1996 and amended on February 1, 1997. The document contains five parts:

PROVINCIAL POLICY STATEMENT

PART I	Preamble
PART II	Legislative Authority
PART III	How to Read the Provincial Policy Statement
PART IV	Vision for Ontario's Land Use Planning System
PART V	Policies

The new PPS includes policies that:

- Support long-term planning for alternative and renewable energy sources such as wind power;
- Discourage urban sprawl across Ontario by supporting intensification in appropriate areas and the efficient use of land and resources;
- Support the protection of Ontario's environment through enhanced policies, including stronger protection of the province's water resources consistent with recommendations of the Walkerton Enquiry in advance of upcoming source water protection;
- Protect more strongly the province's natural heritage resources including habitats, provincially significant wetlands on the Canadian Shield and coastal wetlands;
- Promote development of affordable housing by requiring municipal targets;
- Respond to concerns about the loss of farmland by prohibiting retirement lots and residential infilling on prime agricultural lands; and
- Support and protect rural areas, by allowing development that is in keeping with the unique character of rural Ontario.

Land use planning is increasingly focused on specific activities that should be of interest to every real estate practitioner seeking directions for the future. A major thrust in planning is centred on the development of property leading to higher densities than currently exist, whether that is achieved through redevelopment, development of under utilized lots and land, infill projects and expansion or conversion of existing buildings. Further, planning authorities want such activities located within existing urban and rural settlements (i.e., cities, towns, villages and hamlets).

Clearly, planners want to limit urban sprawl while taking advantage of existing infrastructure and under utilized property. Many new inner core residential and commercial developments have sprung up in Ontario urban settings. Undoubtedly, many more will appear.

One Window Planning Service

The Ministry of Municipal Affairs and Housing (MMAH) has a one-window planning service, when the Ministry is the approval body, to streamline the approval processes and provide a single point of contact for planning activities involving municipalities, planning boards, developers, builders and land owners. While other ministries may provide technical input, the single point of contact is the MMAH for both applicant and municipal activities. Other ministries that might provide input would include Environment, Natural Resources, Transportation, Citizenship and Immigration, Agriculture, Food and Rural Affairs, and Northern Development and Mines.

Municipalities and planning boards at the local level are responsible for land use applications and approvals, and are entrusted to protect provincial interests pursuant to the provincial policy statement. The provincial policy statement details overall guidelines concerning provincial interests. The provincial ministry assists in furnishing needed data, support and training, as required. Applicants deal directly with the municipality and complete appropriate application forms that include information required by the ministry, municipality and the approval authority.

The one-window planning service provides a co-ordinated approach that reduces duplication of effort, shortens approval times, and better serves municipalities, developers, practitioners and others involved in the planning process. Landowners will typically encounter the one window planning service when seeking approval for land use planning applications being reviewed by the applicable approval authority. As mentioned earlier, the government has recently introduced a new development permit system to further streamline the development process.

Practitioners should exercise caution regarding land use applications and related matters involving land owners in the local marketplace. The approval authority for such applications can vary depending on the particular municipality, as well as the specific type of application being submitted. Common applications involve changes to an official plan, zoning by-law amendments, severances and plans of subdivision. Persons contemplating such applications should contact local municipal staff to assess whether or not a contemplated change is possible and be directed to the appropriate approval authority.

ONTARIO MUNICIPAL BOARD

The Ontario Municipal Board (OMB) is an administrative tribunal that operates similar to a court of law, but with less overall formality. The OMB is governed by the rules of natural justice and requirements as set out in the *Statutory Powers Procedures Act*. The OMB addresses the concerns of individuals, public organizations and corporations that object to decisions of various public authorities. The board operates under the *Ontario Municipal Board Act*.

Scope of Duties

The OMB hears applications and appeals on:

- Land use planning under the *Planning Act* and other legislation;
- Financial issues related to development charges, land expropriation, municipal finance and other legislated financial areas;
- Municipal issues as legislated under the *Ontario Municipal Board Act* and other legislation; and
- Other issues assigned to the OMB by provincial statute. The Ontario Municipal Board is referred to in over 70 public statutes.

Source: Ontario Municipal Board, 2007.

For real estate purposes, relevant OMB activity typically focuses on objections to decisions made by local or regional councils, committees of adjustment and land division committees (see later discussion in this chapter). Such matters usually involve land use and planning issues; e.g., official plans, zoning by-laws, minor variances, subdivision plans and land severances. However, given its role in numerous statutes, the OMB can be involved in hearings with such diverse topics as development charges, compensation for expropriated land and applications for gravel pit licences.

OMB Reform

The provincial government recently passed legislation to reform Ontario's land use planning system and clarify the role of the Ontario Municipal Board relating to such matters, including making the Board more accessible and user-friendly. The legislation seeks to return the OMB to its original function as an appeal body on local planning matters, requiring the OMB to give greater weight to the decisions of local councils during the appeal process and limiting appeals to information and materials that were provided to council when making its original decision. Reforms are also aimed at facilitating increased participation by people in the planning process and in the OMB appeal process.

WEB LINKS
Ontario Municipal Board   Details concerning the role of the Ontario Municipal Board in land planning, as well as other activities, can be found on the OMB web site at *www.omb.gov.on.ca*.

MUNICIPAL PERSPECTIVE

The *Municipal Act, 2001* expanded spheres of responsibility for municipalities giving added powers and flexibility to organize and govern local affairs including planning-related matters. Subsequent amendments have generally been consistent with that overall direction.

Unlike its predecessor, this Act moves away from rigid controls on municipalities and now recognizes municipal governments as responsible and accountable. In doing so, municipalities can undertake necessary initiatives within defined spheres of influence without the need for lengthy, often complex legislative changes. Real estate practitioners will notice increasing responsibilities within municipalities for many service-related areas, and more particularly those impacting real property including everything from flood control to signs and fences.

Proponents of this legislation (the first major statutory change to the *Municipal Act* in 150 years) point to increased flexibility for both upper-tier and lower-tier municipalities in carrying out their roles, responding to local changes and meeting service delivery needs in innovative ways.

SPHERES OF INFLUENCE

The new legislation sets up ten spheres of influence over which municipal governments have authority, subject to certain limitations. These spheres encompass not only various powers under the preceding legislation, but also include new activities that can be carried out without the need for legislative changes. In other words, the municipality can now take action without the need for specific provisions in legislation, but rather can refer to a particular sphere of influence as sufficient authority for taking action.

IMPACT ON LISTING/SELLING ACTIVITIES

Real estate practitioners should be generally aware of municipal government responsibilities that affect day-to-day real estate marketplace activities. Examples include:

- Sign restrictions relating to the placement of signs, notices or advertising on property.
- Establishing provisions regarding flood control that affect properties in flood-prone areas.

- Requiring property owners to meet various standards in the control of noise, vibration, odour, dust and outdoor illumination; e.g., operation of commercial enterprises and noise bylaws relating to residential uses.
- Regulatory matters concerning the construction of fences; e.g., height and set-back requirements.
- The placing or removal of soil and grading; e.g., new home construction.
- Instituting energy conservation programs and incentives for commercial and residential property owners.
- The authority to enter private lands to inspect the discharge of waste into the municipal sewage system.

CURRENT INFORMATION

Descriptive materials in this text are provided for general guidance only. Practitioners should contact the local municipality for additional information on general spheres of influence and relevant municipal responsibilities/procedures. Further, the *Municipal Act* is reviewed on an ongoing basis. At time of publication, the most recent changes were included in the *Municipal Statute Law Amendment Act, 2006* and most sections were proclaimed into force on January 1, 2007. However, such amendments were introduced to refine the provincial/municipal relationship and complemented the underlying desire to provide municipalities with legislation that would offer flexibility and latitude in addressing the dynamic needs of today's growing Ontario municipalities.

WEB LINKS

Municipal E-Guide   Practitioners seeking detailed information about the *Municipal Act* should access the informative e-guide on the Ministry of Municipal Affairs and Housing web site (***www.mah.gov.on.ca***). The e-guide is a joint project of the Ministry and the Association of Municipalities of Ontario, in co-operation with the Ontario Municipal Administrators Association, the Association of Municipal Managers, Clerks and Treasurers of Ontario, the Municipal Finance Officers' Association of Ontario, the Ontario Good Roads Association and the Association Française des Municipalités de l'Ontario.

Official Plan

The official plan is a planning document, approved by the Minister of Municipal Affairs and Housing pursuant to the *Planning Act*, containing:

- Goals, objectives and policies concerning the management and direction of physical change with due regard to the effects such changes have on the social, economic and natural environment.
- A description of measures and procedures to attain these objectives and a description of such measures and procedures to inform the public and obtain views regarding amendments to the plan.

The official plan for a municipality is designed to provide a framework for future decision-making and to respond in an organized fashion to trends and influences currently experienced within that municipality or anticipated in the future. Part III of the *Planning Act* articulates detailed procedures for the development, approval and adoption of official plans as well as determining needs for revision to such plans. Regulation 198/96 sets out procedures for public meetings and notices for proposed official plans or plan amendments. The official plan normally extends for a period of ten to 15 years, based on growth projections and needs of the community.

More specifically, an official plan describes local, county or regional council's policies on how land in your community should be used. This plan for a municipality addresses matters such as where new residential and commercial developments will be located, what infrastructure (roads, sewers and watermains) will be required and what particular areas of the community are forecasted for growth in the foreseeable future. The plan also helps in setting various local regulations and standards; e.g., lot and building sizes within a municipality. A formal process is followed in the preparation of an official plan, including input from citizens, to help ensure that future planning and development properly meet the needs of the municipality.

APPROVAL

The plan typically requires provincial approval by the Ministry of Municipal Affairs and Housing before becoming official. However, certain official plans may not require such approval. For example, a regional government may be authorized by the Ministry to approve local official plans within that region. Once approved, no development can take place within a municipality unless it is in general conformity with the policies and designations established in the official plan. The municipality can acquire land for the purpose of developing any feature of the official plan, but it cannot physically undertake any public works unless such activities conform with the plan.

OFFICIAL PLAN AMENDMENT

An official plan amendment is a formal document that alters the current official plan usually due to new situations that have arisen in the municipality. Changes to a plan are handled in much the same way as the plan itself.

Committee Of Adjustment

A committee of adjustment is charged with responsibility for granting minor variances in keeping with planning principles and zoning by-laws (discussed in the next chapter). A municipal council or planning authority normally has the authority, under the *Planning Act*, to grant consents regarding land severance. The *Planning Act* provides that such a council or authority has the right to delegate this power.

Typically, a committee of adjustment is appointed, although a land division committee may also perform the function. In selected instances, the Ministry of Municipal Affairs and Housing may retain the right to grant consents; e.g., northern areas without municipal organization.

The three functions of a typical committee of adjustment are as follows:

- Empowered to grant minor variances from the provisions of zoning by-laws. The *Planning Act* leaves the determination of what is *minor* to the discretion of the committee of adjustment, as each application is reviewed on its own merits. Committees cannot add new uses to the zoning requirements, but where the permitted uses in the by-law are defined in general terms, they can approve a similar use if it conforms to the by-law and its intent.

- Control of any alteration to uses that does not conform to existing zoning by-laws, including the enlargement, alteration or modification of the non-conforming use.

- Usually empowered to grant consents to sever.

ADJUSTMENT PROCESS

Practitioners should be familiar with underlying processes involving both the operation of the committee of adjustment and associated appeal procedures.

EXAMPLE   *Minimum Lot Frontage*

The zoning by-law states the minimum lot frontage required to build a single-family dwelling is 60 feet. An owner of a vacant lot with a 59-foot frontage, although zoned for the use, would normally not be issued a building permit. He/she could make application to the local committee of adjustment for relief from the provisions of the zoning by-law. The decision of the committee would undoubtedly rest on whether a one-foot variance is judged minor in nature. The committee would typically rely on other comparable decisions to arrive at a conclusion.

Three additional scenarios are illustrated that involve a broader perspective of original committee decisions along with subsequent appeals.

VARIANCE

This circumstance involves an appeal by the original applicant against a decision of the committee of adjustment dismissing an application to permit the demolition of the existing structure and the erection instead of a two-storey masonry building, notwithstanding the following infringements to the zoning by-law: a minimum depth of approximately 125 feet, easterly and westerly side yards of approximately ten feet and an access lane to parking having a maximum depth of ten feet whereas the by-law requires a minimum lot depth of 200 feet, easterly and westerly side yards of 20 feet and an access to parking having a minimum of 20 feet.

The application was originally refused by the committee on the grounds that the variances requested were major and outside the jurisdiction of the committee. The appellant argued that the committee erred in considering that the 200-foot minimum depth for commercial properties set forth in By-law 7989 was applicable to this parcel of land, which consequently led to their refusal to permit 10-foot side yards rather than the required 20 feet. The appellant further submitted that the committee was in error in its interpretation of the provisions of the *Planning Act* in that the application as submitted was a minor variance in the light of pertinent legislation.

The appeal before the appeal board was vigorously opposed by two owners of commercial developments within the immediate area as follows:

> Consideration has been given to the rather interesting submission made by counsel for the appellant in which he makes reference to section 22.6.2 of By-law No. 7989 of the Township of Anytownship, which sets forth the requirements for registered lots in a commercial zone, possessing a depth of 125 feet or less. It is his contention that at the time the zoning by-law was passed, the council must have considered such undersized lots as that of his client as being capable of utilization since they were zoned commercially, and furthermore states that it is against this background of lesser requirement that the committee must determine the extent of the variances sought. It is his opinion that since a minor variance has never been actually defined by the courts that the determination of what is minor should be to a large extent dependent upon whether or not the proposal is in keeping with the spirit and intent of the zoning by-law and provide for the best use and development of the property rather than on the actual dimension of the variance sought.

The board was of the opinion that the appellant could not bring his lands within the scope of Section 22.6.2 of the By-law and further stated:

> While it is quite true that the courts and indeed this board have not as yet defined a minor variance in terms of feet and inches, it would appear that this exercise is not necessary to determine, in the light of any given case, what should constitute a minor variance. What remains to be determined in the light of the legislation cited above may be summed up as follows:
>
> - Is the variance requested desirable for the appropriate development of the land, building or structure?
> - Does it maintain the general intent and purpose of the by-law and official plan?

The board was of the opinion that the variance requested was not minor.

Appeal dismissed: *Advanced Southgate Projects Limited and the Committee of Adjustment, Township of Anytownship, OMB A-8921-00, 31, March, 20xx.*

SECTION II   PLANNING AND LAND USE

FRONT YARD SETBACK

This circumstance involves an appeal from a decision of the committee of adjustment who refused a variance of 4'3" in the front yard of the subject property on the grounds that the relief applied for was not a minor variance. The parcel is situated in an R-1, residential zone that, among other things, requires a front yard setback of 25 feet and a maximum building area occupancy of 35%. The existing building coverage is only 30.64%. Many of the actual set-backs of buildings in the area are less than 25 feet and various neighbouring property owners appeared and gave evidence in support of the appeal. The appellant contractor gave a reasonable explanation as to how the violation occurred.

The appeal board stated:

Since it is obvious that the building coverage is within the zoning by-law provisions, this cannot be a reason for dismissing the application. In this circumstance no one appears to be adversely affected.

Appeal allowed: *Jones, James J. and the Committee of Adjustment of the City of Anycity, O.M.B., A-8081-00, 29 June, 20xx.*

CONTINUANCE OF NON-CONFORMING USE

This is an appeal of a decision of the committee of adjustment granting the owner a request to enlarge or extend the larger of two buildings used as a nursing home by the erection of a two-storey addition at the rear of the larger building. The appeal board stated:

From the evidence adduced at the hearing, this Board finds as follows:

- *By-law 6593 of the City of Anycity was passed on July 25, 1997.*
- *That by-law designates an area that includes the subject property as a "C" zone and prohibits in such zone the use of land and the erection and use of a building for the purpose of a maternity hospital or a nursing home.*
- *On the day of the passing of the by-law, the building for which an extension is now proposed was in existence and in use as a maternity hospital.*
- *The subject property was vacant from October 20, 1997 until February 22, 1999.*
- *On March 14, 1999, the subject property was sold by registration of a transfer/deed of Land to William McKay.*
- *Since March 14th, 1999, the subject property has been used continuously for the purpose of a nursing home.*

The appeal board does not consider the change from a maternity home to a nursing home to have been a change of use, but regards both uses as types of activity of the same general purpose. Since the legal non-conforming use in question was interrupted from October 20, 1997 until February 22, 1999, the evidence before the board does not satisfy the statutory requirement that such use has continued until the date of the application to the committee of adjustment. Since satisfaction of that requirement is a condition of jurisdiction over the matter, this board must therefore allow the appeal and set aside the decision of the committee of adjustment.

Appeal allowed: *Anycity Retirement Centres Inc. and the Committee of Adjustment of the City of Anycity, O.M.B. A-291-00, 9th February, 20xx.*

MINOR VARIANCE

A minor variance, for planning purposes, is generally described as a small or insignificant variation concerning a particular property in relation to by-laws in force within a municipality. A committee of adjustment established by a municipal council may authorize minor variances deemed desirable for the appropriate development of a particular site and associated buildings/structures. Such a variance must be consistent with the general intent and purpose of applicable by-laws, as well as the official plan.

NON-CONFORMING USE

The powers of the committee of adjustment also extend to non-conforming uses. For example, an enlargement or extension may be permitted to a non-conforming property provided that the use has continued from the passing of the by-law until the application to the committee. A similar provision exists for an alteration of an existing use involving a non-conforming property provided that the amended use is more compatible with the by-law. In certain instances, uses defined in the zoning by-law may be sufficiently general and an applicant may apply for a specific use that is not directly referenced. The committee may approve such a use if it conforms with the uses permitted under the by-law.

EXAMPLE   *The Existing Business*

An operating business may reside within a residential zone owing to its existence on the day that the by-law concerning such zoning came into force. Although this business enterprise is not recognized in the by-law, the *Planning Act* does not forbid its continuance. However, should modifications, renovations or other alterations be considered, the owner must make an application to the committee of adjustment.

LAND DIVISION APPLICATIONS

As mentioned earlier, various land use applications can be made by landowners. Two of the most common, and most relevant to real estate practitioners, involve the subdividing of land. Land division is stringently regulated under the **subdivision** control provisions of the *Planning Act*.

In Ontario, land division applications can be viewed from two perspectives: **land severances (consents)** and **subdivision plans**. The consent granting authority in the local area determines whether a consent is appropriate or a subdivision plan is necessary for proper and orderly development.

> **Subdivision**
>
> From a planning perspective, the process of taking an individual piece of land and separating it into parts.
>
> **Land Severance**
>
> The division of land by means of a consent under the *Planning Act*.

Land Severance vs. Subdivision

If a landowner in Ontario is attempting to divide one parcel of land into two or three parcels, the process typically begins with an application to a local committee of adjustment. Councils of regions, counties, districts, etc., are given limited power to grant consents to sever.

- Power of consent is normally vested in a committee of adjustment.
- The power is sometimes granted to a land division committee at the county or regional level; e.g., if a local committee of adjustment exceeds limited authority to grant consents.
- Where neither exist, the Ministry of Municipal Affairs and Housing grants consents.

If a landowner is attempting to divide one parcel of land into many parcels, a plan of subdivision registration is required by completing necessary steps outlined in the *Planning Act*. Registration involves a two-stage process: **draft plan approval** and **final plan approval**.

> **Draft Plan Approval**
>
> Initial step in the subdivision approval process under the *Planning Act*.

Subdivision Control: Planning Act Compliance

At one time, subdivision of land went virtually unchecked in this province. Two hundred acre parcels could be divided into individual lots simply by surveying a subdivision and registering it on title. Now the authority rests in the subdivision and part-lot control sections of the *Planning Act*, which exercises real control by preventing any transfer of a portion of land unless the owner has received permission.

Under Section 50 of the Act, a person is not allowed to convey (sell) land or lease it to someone for more than 21 years unless:

- The person conveying does not retain ownership of any abutting land.
- The person conveying has received a consent to divide the land.
- The land is within a registered plan of subdivision (i.e., has gone through a subdivision approval process).
- The land is being sold or bought by the Crown, federally, provincially or municipally.
- The land is being acquired for transmission lines under the *Ontario Energy Board Act*.
- The land is being acquired to enforce flood plain control measures.

EXAMPLE   *Planning Act Compliance*

Two examples are provided to illustrate the application of Section 50 in the conveyance of real estate.

- An owner is selling a 25-acre parcel of land described by a metes and bounds description. His daughter is registered as the owner of an adjacent 25 acres. The seller does not own any other property in the immediate vicinity and will not be retaining any rights in lands abutting the parcel being sold. The conveyance should not contravene the *Planning Act*.

- An owner is selling a single-family, detached bungalow in an urban area described as Lot 42, Plan 634 and is also the owner of Lot 43 that abuts Lot 42. As the properties are described according to a registered plan of subdivision, the conveyance would not contravene the *Planning Act*.

Consent (Severance) Process

A land severance involves the separation of land into two adjoining properties. As mentioned, a plan of subdivision is normally required where more than two or three lots are to be created. However, no specific rule regulates this circumstance. The *Planning Act* provides that appropriate authorities may give a consent if satisfied that a plan of subdivision of the land is not necessary for the proper and orderly development of the municipality.

Standards concerning the number of lots to be created by severance can vary, as some municipalities may include a provision in the official plan regulating the number, while in others no policy exists. However, from a practical perspective, the municipality would undoubtedly object if the consent granting authority exceeded reasonableness in such decisions.

Drafting an Agreement of Purchase and Sale   MARKET PERSPECTIVE

Practitioners encounter matters relating to the *Planning Act* each time an agreement of purchase and sale is drafted for a buyer or seller. A clause in the OREA *Agreement of Purchase and Sale* form (Form 100) effectively makes the entire agreement conditional upon the seller complying with the *Planning Act* and its provisions for subdivision control; e.g., plans of subdivision and consents.

The *Planning Act* prevents the transfer of ownership of any portion of a larger parcel of land unless the owner has received permission. If a consent is necessary to legalize a conveyance, this requirement does not need to prevent the entering into of an agreement of purchase and sale. The Act permits agreements that are conditional upon the granting of a consent. The clause is constructed so that the agreement does not contravene the *Planning Act*. However, an agreement without such a clause would have no legal force, if a consent is required.

EXAMPLE

Salesperson Lee is asked to sell five acres of land, including a two-storey brick dwelling. The five acres are part of a 20-acre parcel described by metes and bounds. The owner of the land wishes to retain 15 acres and build a new dwelling. In this situation, the owner will be retaining ownership of a parcel of land that abuts the land being conveyed and the land being sold is not within a registered plan of subdivision.

This conveyance would contravene the *Planning Act*, however, the owner of the lands may apply for a consent to convey the five acres. Such a consent, usually obtained from a land division committee or an equivalent committee would make the conveyance legal, as long as the conveyance took place within the specified time limit and under the conditions specified when granted. When a severance is required, costs may be substantial and normally include application fees, dedication of land or monies, a survey or reference plan, legal costs and so on. The pre-printed wording in the agreement of purchase and sale form requires that the seller pay these costs.

OVERVIEW

Real estate practitioners are not normally involved in the severance process, but an overall understanding is appropriate for general discussions with buyers and sellers. Land severance methods vary throughout the province. The question of whether a plan of subdivision or merely a consent is required revolves around certain key factors; e.g., compliance with the official plan and zoning by-laws, suitability of land for proposed purposes, overall matters of provincial interest (e.g., protection of environmentally sensitive areas), availability of services and the public interest. Anyone contemplating a severance is strongly advised to seek prior consultation with the local planning department.

CONSENT APPLICATION

A Regulation under the *Planning Act* sets out rules of procedure for consent applications. A published schedule details information and materials that must be included with the application. For example:

- name and address of owner;
- type and purpose of proposed transaction;
- name of person to which an interest in land is to be transferred, charged or leased;
- description of the property;
- detailed information concerning the land being severed and the land being retained (e.g., dimensions, method of access, and provision of water and sewage);
- any previous application relating to the subject land;
- a sketch outlining boundaries of the land and any abutting lands owned by the applicant;

SECTION II   PLANNING AND LAND USE

- any previously severed lands from the parcel;
- natural (watercourses, slopes and banks) and artificial features (buildings, septic tanks, etc.);
- the use of adjoining land;
- location of road allowances, streets, private roads and rights-of-way; and
- the nature of any restrictive covenants or easements.

APPROVAL PROCESS

The approval body is typically a committee of adjustment or a land division committee (see *Curiosity: Land Division Committee*) delegated by the municipality. However, in some instances, it may be a committee of a council or an appointed individual. In others, the Minister of Municipal Affairs and Housing performs this function. A Regulation under the *Planning Act* sets out procedures for consent applications both to councils (or their delegates) and to the Minister. The following information, relating to consents by council, is provided for illustration purposes only.

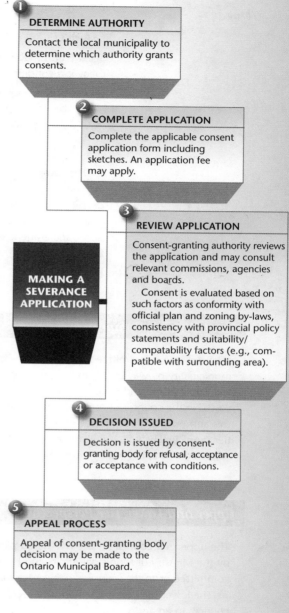

MAKING A SEVERANCE APPLICATION

1 DETERMINE AUTHORITY
Contact the local municipality to determine which authority grants consents.

2 COMPLETE APPLICATION
Complete the applicable consent application form including sketches. An application fee may apply.

3 REVIEW APPLICATION
Consent-granting authority reviews the application and may consult relevant commissions, agencies and boards.
Consent is evaluated based on such factors as conformity with official plan and zoning by-laws, consistency with provincial policy statements and suitability/compatability factors (e.g., compatible with surrounding area).

4 DECISION ISSUED
Decision is issued by consent-granting body for refusal, acceptance or acceptance with conditions.

5 APPEAL PROCESS
Appeal of consent-granting body decision may be made to the Ontario Municipal Board.

- Notices concerning the application must be made pursuant to Regulation 197/96, PART I under the *Planning Act*. Notices involve personal service or prepaid mail to land owners within a prescribed distance of the lands and the posting of signs on the land that are clearly visible from a public highway or other accessible point. A notice using a newspaper with circulation sufficient to provide reasonable notice to the public may be used in lieu of mailing if an official of the approval authority agrees. The notice includes a description of the proposal plan, a key map locating the property under proposal, a source for additional information, and statements concerning appeal and notification of a decision relating to the application.

- The approval authority also requires that notices (including the application) must be forwarded to various public bodies and others identified in the Regulation (e.g., clerks of the local municipality, county, region and/or district having jurisdiction for the area being considered and, as applicable, others including conservation authorities, TransCanada Pipelines, Niagara Escarpment Commission, park commissions and Chiefs of First Nation councils within one kilometre of the area covered by the application).

Upon completion of all requirements set out in the *Planning Act* and Regulation 197/96, the approval authority publishes its decision and forwards various documents to the Ministry of Municipal Affairs and Housing. Appeal procedures concerning consents go beyond the scope of this text and practitioners are encouraged to seek expert advice.

LAPSE OF CONSENT

In granting a consent, the approval authority may specify conditions that must be fulfilled including a time limit in which the consent can be exercised. The lapse of a consent occurs two years from the written notice of the conditional approval, unless the approving authority stipulates an alternative time period. The time period is often one year if conditions are imposed, subject to special rules if an appeal occurs pursuant to the *Planning Act*.

EXAMPLE   *Lapse of Consent*

Seller Smith made application to the local municipality and received a consent, subject to the following conditions:

- A parkland dedication amounting to 5% of the property, or cash equivalent based on market value.
- A widening of the existing roadway to 66 feet to meet township standards.
- Entering into a site plan agreement with the municipality.

The severance approval issued by the land division committee set out these conditions including the requirement for completion within one year immediately following the written notice of decision. Smith must forward a letter to the committee within that time limit acknowledging that all three conditions have been met, along with corroborating letters or approvals from appropriate agencies. If the conditions are not met within this specified period, the application for consent, along with the conditional approval, is deemed null and void unless appeal provisions apply.

Land Division Committee   CURIOSITY

A land division committee is a committee constituted by the council of a county or a regional, metropolitan or district municipality by way of by-law for the purposes of granting consents, pursuant to the *Planning Act*. The Minister of Municipal Affairs and Housing may also appoint such a committee. The power to grant consents to divide land is usually vested in the councils of regions, counties, districts and certain cities outside regions. These councils may, in turn, delegate this authority to a committee of the council, an appointed official, a land division committee or the council of a lower tier municipality, which in turn can delegate to a committee of adjustment. In everyday practice, most consents are reviewed and approved by either a land division committee or a committee of adjustment.

Upper and Lower Tier Perspectives   LABOUR FORCE FOCUS

The upper tier council (in the two-tiered planning system used in Ontario) may delegate the consent authority granted by the Ministry of Municipal Affairs and Housing to a committee of council, an appointed official, a land division committee or *to the council of a lower tier municipality*.

The lower tier council can, in turn, deal with consents or can delegate the responsibility to a committee of that council, to an appointed official or to a committee of adjustment. In practice, the majority of consents in Ontario are granted by an upper tier Land Division Committee or a lower tier Committee of Adjustment. In practice, most committees limit themselves to the creation of two or three parcels from the original land holding. This is not a limitation of law, but the *Planning Act* has a general limitation and official plan policies may further restrict their activities.

Assume that a salesperson is selling a 50-acre site for development into a residential subdivision. While two 25-acre parcels might be created by consent (assuming such severances are permitted), the further division into more than several lots would be beyond the power of the consent authority, because the development proposal for this 50 acres would have a major impact on the orderly municipal development. The only way for the developer to legally divide the land into numerous lots is to register a plan of subdivision.

Practitioners contemplating listing and selling activities involving land severances should contact the local planning authority for specific guidelines.

Plan of Subdivision

Land owners seeking to divide land by way of a plan of subdivision require approval by the appropriate approval authority. The formal process for subdividing land involves preparing the necessary application forms and associated documents provided by the applicable approval authority. Many of the same criteria (e.g., conformity with the official plan, compliance with zoning by-laws and suitability of the land for development purposes) are applied as was the case with consents. A detailed discussion is provided outlining the steps progressing from draft plan to final plan, and ultimately to a registered plan of subdivision.

SUBDIVISION—DRAFT PLAN

The draft plan is generally viewed as the first official step by a developer in the planning process leading to a plan of subdivision. The developer creates a draft plan in consultation with engineers, solicitors, surveyors and planning consultants. The resulting detailed plan of the proposed project is commonly referred to as the *draft plan.*

Practitioners should be aware of basic procedures involved in the preparation and approval of a draft plan. The following is summarized for general reference purposes only. The *Planning Act* should be consulted directly regarding specifics.

Content

The *Planning Act* sets out various requirements for a draft plan of subdivision including:

- Boundaries of the land proposed to be subdivided.
- Locations and names of proposed highways in the plan or highways abutting the property.
- Adjacent subdivisions and property in which the applicant has an interest.
- Proposed use, dimensions and layout of proposed lots and existing uses of adjoining lands.
- Natural and artificial features (e.g., buildings) within or adjacent to the proposed subdivision.
- Soil conditions and existing contours/elevations.
- Existing or planned municipal services.
- Nature and extent of restrictions affecting the land.

A Regulation under the *Planning Act* provides detailed information on materials that must accompany an application for a plan of subdivision. Recent planning reforms also expand the process to include such things as the supply, efficiency and conservation of energy when considering proposed subdivisions.

Approval Process

The approval body is typically an upper tier municipality (region or district), the council of a city or certain counties identified in the *Planning Act.* A variety of other situations (e.g., towns, townships and territorial districts) fall to the Minister of Municipal Affairs and Housing. In Northern Ontario, a planning board may be the delegated authority. (Note: The Minister also has the right under the Act, with written explanation, to revoke approval authority from approval bodies detailed above.)

The owner of the land applies to the approval body with the draft plan including other documentation as requested. Notification of persons and public bodies is accomplished through several means.

- Notices concerning the application must be made pursuant to Regulations under the *Planning Act*. As a general description, notices involve the use of personal service or prepaid mail to land owners within a prescribed distance of the land, and the posting of signs on the land that are clearly visible from a public highway or other accessible point. A notice in a newspaper with circulation sufficient to provide reasonable notice to the public may be used in lieu of mailing, if an official of the approval authority agrees. The notice includes a description of the proposal plan, a key map locating the property under proposal, a source of additional information, statements concerning appeal and notification of a decision relating to the application.

- The approval authority also requires, pursuant to the Regulations, that notices (including the application) must be forwarded to various public bodies and others identified in the Regulations. Examples include clerks of the local municipality, county, region and/or district having jurisdiction for the area being considered and, as applicable, conservation authorities, electric utilities, natural gas utilities, natural gas or oil pipeline companies, local architectural conservation advisory committees, the Niagara Escarpment Commission and federal parks commissions. Chiefs of First Nation councils within one kilometre of the area covered by the proposed plan of subdivision must also be included.

- A public meeting is also required if the proposed plan falls within a municipality or in the planning area of a planning board. The Regulations set out requirements concerning notices, as well as the timing of such meetings in relation to notices and records that must be compiled.

Upon completion of all requirements as set out in the *Planning Act* and Regulations, the approval authority forwards its decision along with various documents to the Provincial Planning Services Branch of the Ministry of Municipal Affairs and Housing. The legislation sets out procedures for appeals regarding the approval of the draft plan that go beyond the scope of this text. Practitioners are encouraged to seek expert advice on all planning matters.

WEB LINKS

Subdivision   Practitioners contemplating involvement in the planning process and subdivision registration are directed to the *Planning Act* (PART VI) and Regulation 196/96. Go to ***www.e-laws.gov.on.ca*** to review the legislation and contact your local municipal planning authority for full details.

SUBDIVISION—FINAL PLAN

Upon draft plan approval, the person making application may normally proceed with the construction of roads and lots in accordance with the *Surveys Act* and *Land Titles Act*. Subsequently, the approval authority will approve the plan of subdivision, assuming that the plan conforms with the approved draft plan and that any conditions imposed have been or will be fulfilled.

Conditions may be imposed that are judged reasonable and typically include requirements that land for park or other recreational purposes, roads and certain land abutting existing highways (i.e., for highway expansion) have been dedicated, and any required municipal agreements have been entered into. This process is usually referred to as final plan approval with the plan being referred to as the final plan. At that point, the plan of subdivision may be tendered for registration in the appropriate land registry office. If a final plan of subdivision is not registered within a specified time period, the approval authority may withdraw its approval.

SUBDIVISION—REGISTERED PLAN

The final step involves registration of the plan. The term *registered plan of subdivision* is not specifically defined in the *Planning Act* but generally is described as a plan prepared by an Ontario Land Surveyor showing lots, blocks or parcels of land intended to be dealt with separately and that such separation has been fully approved. The plan must be registered in the land registry office and be in full compliance with the *Planning Act*.

As discussed previously under land registration in a previous chapter, each plan is assigned a number at the time of registration. A subdivision plan number was traditionally preceded by the letter M, if initial registration was carried out in land titles. Recent conversion programs from registry to land titles are not utilizing the letter M. A plan of subdivision, upon registration, creates a new legal identity for the land. The land is no longer referred to as being part of a township lot (or similar legal description) and must be identified by reference to the numbered or named units.

Under the *Land Titles Act*, a new plan parcel register is created. A typical legal description of land shown on a registered plan of subdivision is as follows (omitting the preamble):

EXAMPLE   *Legal Description for Lot 11 in a Registered Plan*

Lot 11 according to a plan registered in the Land Registry Office for the Land Titles Division of West Region as number 99M-165 or simply Lot 11, Plan 99M-165.

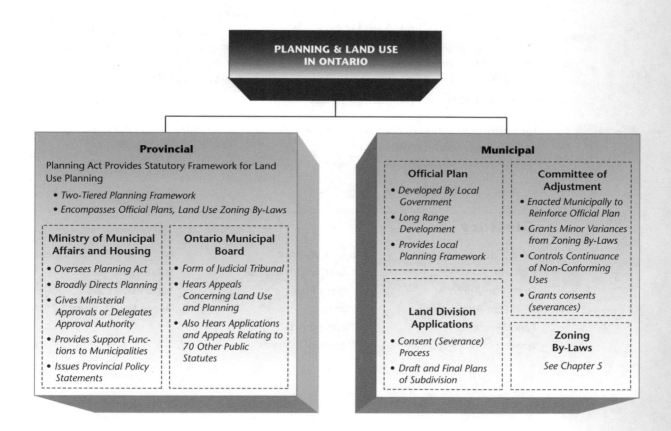

PLANNING & LAND USE IN ONTARIO

Provincial

Planning Act Provides Statutory Framework for Land Use Planning

- *Two-Tiered Planning Framework*
- *Encompasses Official Plans, Land Use Zoning By-Laws*

Ministry of Municipal Affairs and Housing

- *Oversees Planning Act*
- *Broadly Directs Planning*
- *Gives Ministerial Approvals or Delegates Approval Authority*
- *Provides Support Functions to Municipalities*
- *Issues Provincial Policy Statements*

Ontario Municipal Board

- *Form of Judicial Tribunal*
- *Hears Appeals Concerning Land Use and Planning*
- *Also Hears Applications and Appeals Relating to 70 Other Public Statutes*

Municipal

Official Plan

- *Developed By Local Government*
- *Long Range Development*
- *Provides Local Planning Framework*

Land Division Applications

- *Consent (Severance) Process*
- *Draft and Final Plans of Subdivision*

Committee of Adjustment

- *Enacted Municipally to Reinforce Official Plan*
- *Grants Minor Variances from Zoning By-Laws*
- *Controls Continuance of Non-Conforming Uses*
- *Grants consents (severances)*

Zoning By-Laws

See Chapter 5

KNOWLEDGE INTEGRATION

Notables

- Land planning and use are governed by federal, provincial and local (municipal) levels. The Ministry of Municipal Affairs and Housing, the Ontario Municipal Board and the local municipality are most directly involved in the process.

- Most activity impacting real estate practitioners centres on provisions of the *Planning Act* and its administration at a local municipal level.

- Local municipal planners must ensure that activities undertaken in land planning are consistent with the Provincial Policy Statement.

- The Ontario Municipal Board hears appeals relating to various applications including those relating to land uses.

- The official plan for a municipality is designed to provide a framework for future land planning decisions.

- The Committee of Adjustment typically has three functions: granting of consents, granting of minor variances in relation to zoning by-laws and matters concerning to non-conforming uses.

- Various types of applications can be submitted to approval bodies for consideration. Emphasis in this chapter is placed on consents (severances) and plans of subdivision.

- The consent granting authority at a local level generally determines whether a land severance (consent) can be granted or a plan of subdivision is required.

- Practitioners should be aware of significant steps in applying for and being granted a severance (consent).

- Subdivisions must meet stringent criteria for registration. A subdivision goes through two overall processes: draft plan and final plan.

- The *Planning Act* has various requirements with which conveyances of land must comply. Accordingly, the OREA Agreement of Purchase and Sale includes a clause requiring compliance with that Act.

Glossary

Committee of Adjustment	Minor Variance	Provincial Policy Statement
Consent	Non-Conforming Use	Subdivision
Draft Plan Approval	Official Plan	Subdivision Plan
Final Plan Approval	Planning	Upper Tier Municipality
Land Severance	Planning Act	
Lower Tier Municipality	Provincial Interests	

Web Links

Web links are included for general interest regarding selected chapter topics.

Ministry of Municipal Affairs and Housing
The Ministry provides an informative site outlining various aspects of the planning process. Go to ***www.mah.gov.on.ca.***

Ontario Municipal Board
Details concerning the role of the Ontario Municipal Board in land planning, as well as other activities, can be found on the OMB web site at ***www.omb.gov.on.ca.***

Municipal E-Guide
Practitioners seeking detailed information about the *Municipal Act* should access the informative e-guide on the Ministry of Municipal Affairs and Housing web site (***www.mah.gov.on.ca***). The e-guide is a joint project of the Ministry and the Association of Municipalities of Ontario, in co-operation with the Ontario Municipal Administrators Association , the Association of Municipal Managers, Clerks and Treasurers of Ontario, the Municipal Finance Officers' Association of Ontario, the Ontario Good Roads Association and the Association Française des Municipalités de l'Ontario.

Subdivision
Practitioners contemplating involvement in the planning process and sub division registration are directed to the *Planning Act* (PART VI) and Regulation 196/96. Go to ***www.e-laws.gov.on.ca*** to review the legislation and contact your local municipal planning authority for full details.

Strategic Thinking For Your Career

Questions are included to assist in developing your new career. No answers are provided.

1. Who has authority for planning activities within my local municipality?

2. How can I obtain a copy of the official plan in order to better understand planned developments within my community?

3. A seller approaches me regarding a land severance. While expert advice is clearly needed, am I able to generally describe the process and differentiate between severances and plans of subdivision?

4. What specific duties does the committee of adjustment carry out in my local market area?

5. What information, circulars and other materials are available at the local planning department that would assist in preparing for my new career?

6. What subdivisions are currently in draft planning stage that might provide opportunities for me once registered as a salesperson?

Chapter Mini-Review

Solutions are located in the Appendix.

1. Land planning in Ontario is governed by legislation at federal, provincial and local (municipal) levels.

   ○ True   ○ False

2. A region, county or district would typically be a lower-tier municipality in the two-tier structure found in many parts of Ontario.

   ○ True   ○ False

3. The provincial policy statement now in effect in Ontario generally discourages urban sprawl.

   ○ True   ○ False

4. The Ontario Municipal Board only hears matters concerning land planning and is not involved with other legislation.

   ○ True   ○ False

5. Committees of adjustment are rarely involved in issues concerning non-conforming uses.

   ○ True   ○ False

6. Municipalities use the official plan to assist in forecasting both the size and location of future development.

   ○ True   ○ False

7. The power to grant consents to convey is usually vested either in a committee of adjustment or a land division committee.

   ○ True   ○ False

8. The *Planning Act* permits the entering into of an Agreement of Purchase and Sale that is conditional upon the procuring of a consent to convey.

   ○ True   ○ False

9. A plan of subdivision is normally required where more than two or three lots are to be created.

   ○ True   ○ False

10. An individual seeking a consent to sever would rarely be required to include a sketch of property boundaries along with the application.

    ○ True   ○ False

11. The requirement to publish a notice in a newspaper is one aspect of the overall approval process for a plan of subdivision.

    ○ True   ○ False

12. A plan of subdivision must be registered in the applicable land registry office, as a final step in the approval process.

    ○ True   ○ False

Active Learning Exercises

Solutions are located in the Appendix.

◼ Exercise 1   Multiple Choice

1.1   An owner of a shoe repair store wishes to expand his operation. His store is located in the midst of a residential subdivision zoned for single family use. His commercial operation existed prior to the passage of current planning requirements for the community in question. Under normal circumstances, which of the following will the owner have to appear before in order to gain permission to enlarge his commercial operation?

   a.   Land Division Committee.
   b.   Municipal Council.
   c.   Ontario Municipal Board.
   d.   Committee of Adjustment.

1.2   Which of the following is a major function of the Ontario Municipal Board?

   a.   Administers the *Planning Act*.
   b.   Hears appeals involving decisions of local committees of adjustment.
   c.   Conducts studies and prepares official plans.
   d.   Conducts research and formulates overall provincial policy statements.

1.3   Smith owns a Southern Ontario home in an area where the by-law states that minimum side yard clearances are 7 feet, and he wants to build a carport that would extend to within 4 feet of the side yard lot line. Which of the following would Smith *typically* approach to receive approval for this construction?

   a.   Land Consent Application Committee.
   b.   Municipal Council.
   c.   Committee of Adjustment.
   d.   Ministry of Municipal Affairs and Housing.

1.4   The *Planning Act* addresses the fact that any conveyance of land affecting the right to the land for more than a 21-year period is invalid except for certain circumstances. Which of the following is NOT one of these circumstances?

   a.   Where the person granting does not retain the fee or the equity of redemption in or the power or right to grant any land abutting the land that is conveyed.
   b.   Where the land is being acquired for transmission lines under the *Ontario Energy Board Act*.
   c.   Where the land is being bought or sold by the Crown, federally, provincially or municipally.
   d.   Where the land is being acquired in the hopes of registering a plan of subdivision.

1.5   According to the *Planning Act*, committees of adjustment are entitled to grant consents. If a committee exceeds stated limitations in this consent authority, the Ministry of Municipal Affairs and Housing may take this power away and transfer it to a:

    a.   Municipal council.

    b.   Provincial arbitrator.

    c.   Land division committee.

    d.   Ontario Municipal Board.

1.6   The municipal government is responsible for various spheres of activities that can directly impact real estate practitioners. Which is NOT one of them?

    a.   Conducting hearings to settle land use disputes.

    b.   Flood control provisions that impact flood-prone properties.

    c.   Sign restrictions (e.g., placement of signs on properties).

    d.   Noise, odour, dust and outdoor illumination controls.

1.7   Which of the following statements most correctly describes how land could be severed by application for a consent instead of having to obtain approval for a plan of subdivision?

    a.   A Committee of Adjustment may approve a subdivision plan of no more than 5 lots.

    b.   You are limited by statutory law to no more than two lots in an application for a consent.

    c.   You will probably not need a subdivision plan for a project of 50 lots if the services are available to the site.

    d.   You may possibly obtain a consent to sever if you want to create a small number of lots and your project will not have a major impact on the orderly development of the municipality.

SECTION II

PLANNING AND LAND USE

■ Exercise 2 Planning Terminology (Matching)

Match the description in the left column with the appropriate phrase in the right column (not all phrases are used).

____	Airport Facilities	a. Ontario Municipal Board
____	Upper Tier	b. Minor Variance
____	Form of Judicial Tribunal	c. One Window Planning Service
____	Grants Spheres of Influence to Municipalities	d. Regional Government
____	Planning Period Usually Spanning 10 to 15 Years	e. Planning Act Compliance
____	Land Use Controls	f. Official Plan
____	Small or Insignificant Variation	g. Part V, Planning Act
____	Clause—Agreement of Purchase and Sale	h. Federal Government
		i. Provincial Interests
		j. Municipal Act

■ Exercise 3 The Smith Severance

Seller Smith wants to list and sell his recreational home, but wants to retain approximately one-half acre of land from the original two-acre parcel to build a smaller retirement home. Smith has asked that you list the property, with the understanding that his original home will be marketed subject to a pending severance. Apparently, the Planning Department for the local municipality would look favourably on a severance, provided that proper application is made. In this instance, the application will be considered by a land division committee.

3.1   Briefly detail the steps that must be taken to obtain a consent by the land division committee.

3.2 What problems, if any, do you anticipate in selling this property? What must be included in the Agreement of Purchase and Sale?

SECTION II

PLANNING AND LAND USE

3.3   When the proposed lot was surveyed in preparation for the severance, the measurements were 108.9 feet (frontage) x 200 feet (depth). The land division committee required that the rear half of the lot be filled with 18 inches of soil for improved drainage. A contractor has quoted the job at $4.85 per cubic yard. What is the cost and what must Smith do regarding this requirement to be granted the severance?

CHAPTER 5

Land Use Restrictions

Introduction

Land use restrictions and related controls are complex given interwoven responsibilities involving various levels of government including local municipalities, provincial ministries and federal control over selected waterways. Chapter 5 focuses on three perspectives involving municipal controls, agencies/ministries involved with waterway/flood restrictions and the expanding role of provincial environmental legislation impacting land owners.

Local municipal requirements centre on property uses and zoning stipulations, building standards concerning existing or planned construction and fire/safety regulations. In recent years, site plan control has also been introduced to better ensure that new construction and renovations meet increasingly rigid municipal requirements. Municipalities are also involved in issuing various permits, most notably building permits.

Watercourses, wetlands and flood-prone areas warrant special attention. Property near water can significantly restrict owner's plans relating to construction, grade alterations and uses. Real estate practitioners must exercise caution and be fully informed of various agencies and legislation that impact such lands.

In recent years, other environmental legislation beyond water-related issues has taken an increasingly central role. Selected initiatives are discussed along with their impact on real estate uses.

Learning Outcomes

At the conclusion of this chapter, students will be able to:

- Describe the impact of zoning by-laws on land usage including typical provisions found in those by-laws.
- Discuss the role of site plan control agreements during the planning and development process including application and review/approval processes.
- Identify key provisions in the Ontario Building Code including fire protection/ occupant safety and sewage systems.
- Briefly outline the typical steps involved in a building permit and the role of building inspectors in the approval process.
- Identify and describe how the Fire Code impacts existing structures including the retrofitting of such structures.
- Describe the primary watercourse controls and restrictions with particular emphasis on activities of conservation authorities in regard to flood plains and flood controls.
- Briefly outline how wetlands are classified within the province, including those identified as Areas of Natural and Scientific Interest (ANSIs).
- Identify the range of watercourse-related controls that can be imposed by various agencies and ministries on land owners, over and above those discussed in relation to conservation authorities.
- Briefly outline selected environmental initiatives that affect property owners and practitioners.
- Discuss the role of federal and provincial legislation relating to environmental controls and briefly discuss environmental protection involving the Greenbelt, the Niagara Escarpment and the Oak Ridges Moraine.

MUNICIPAL CONTROLS/RESTRICTIONS

Primary land use control rests with zoning at the local municipal level. An underlying premise of such controls is orderly property development and assurance of compatibility with specific areas (zones). Zoning is key to most property negotiations, as the scope of uses typically translates directly into value.

Zoning Overview

Zoning by-laws are enacted by municipalities setting out permitted uses, building structure standards (e.g., minimum setbacks and coverage) and other necessary regulations (e.g., signage, noise and parking). Zones are further broken into classifications (e.g., residential) and sub-classifications (e.g., single-family), each with its own detailed standards.

Flexibility is permitted within the by-laws. As discussed in the previous chapter, owners may seek **minor variances** when property does not specifically meet requirements. In other words, the rules may be bent slightly to accommodate the owner and not unnecessarily restrict his or her uses. Further, owners may also fall under **non-conforming use** status if a usage predates the passage of a specific zoning by-law or a **non-conforming structure** in the case of a building.

Communities may also have **site-specific exemptions** and special policy areas of the community designated for distinctive zoning treatment. The *Planning Act* sets out parameters as to how zoning controls are imposed at the municipal level.

> **Zoning By-laws**
>
> A by-law that defines zones for various types of uses and sets selected standards for erecting buildings.

> **Non-Conforming Structure**
>
> A structure that lawfully existed prior to the current zoning by-law.

TYPICAL ZONING BY-LAW

SECTION	CONTENT
1	Definitions and Interpretations
2	Compliance with the By-Laws
3	Administration, Enforcement and Enactment
4	Zone Boundaries
5	General Provisions for All Zones
6	Residential Zones
7	Commercial Zones
8	Industrial Zones
9	Development Zones
10	Other Zones
11	Detailed Zoning Map

> **Site-Specific Exemptions**
>
> Properties that are specifically exempted under a zoning by-law.

Individual zones (Sections 6–10) normally detail permitted uses; regulations for uses (e.g., minimum lot coverage, front, side and rear yard requirements, enlargement of existing dwellings); and regulations concerning accessory buildings.

Zoning By-Law

A zoning bylaw is a document having the legal status of an ordinance or subsidiary law used by municipalities to regulate the use of land. Terminologies differ in various Ontario municipalities, but the overall intent remains the same. By-laws may restrict or prohibit the use of land, the erecting, locating and use of buildings, and the utilization of marshy, rocky, steep sloping, hazardous land or related circumstances for building purposes.

The parameters for zoning by-laws typically extend to prohibitions over use or construction in relation to contaminated lands or sensitive areas, natural features and significant archaeological resources. By-laws may also regulate the type of construction, minimum elevation of doors, windows or openings, loading or parking facilities and minimum area/density provisions. Matters concerning zoning by-laws in Ontario fall under Part V Land Use Controls and Related Administration of the *Planning Act*.

Practitioners commonly encounter zoning by-laws in relation to restrictions imposed on residential, commercial and industrial properties. Municipalities provide detailed maps (usually for a fee) along with zoning categories or classifications for guidance.

PLANNING ACT PROVISIONS

The *Planning Act* details restrictive provisions that must be addressed by local municipalities in passing and enforcing zoning by-laws. The legislation also provides detailed appeal procedures for a person or public body objecting to the passage of proposed by-laws.

Non-Conforming	Provides for unique circumstances by specifically addressing properties that are used in a certain manner at the point of passing a by-law. In such instances, the existing use is permitted, as long as it continues to be used for that purpose.
Residential Restrictions	Provides that municipalities may not distinguish between persons who are related and persons who are unrelated in respect to the occupancy and use of a building or structure.
Holding Provision	Provides a holding provision in which the symbol 'H' may be affixed to land specifying a future use that can subsequently be removed by amendment to the by-law.
Increased Density Provision	Provides for an increase in height or density of development in return for the provision of facilities, services or matters set out in the by-law.
Interim Control Provision	Provides the right to pass a by-law for a study of a specific area over a period of no more than one year in relation to land use planning policies.
Temporary Use Provision	Provides the right to pass a by-law authorizing temporary use of land, buildings or structures; e.g., temporary placement of a garden suite. **NOTE:** Maximum length of temporary use is ten years for a garden suite and three years for any other use.

Regulation 199/96 sets out detailed procedures for proposed zoning, holding provisions and interim control provisions.

BY-LAW STRUCTURE

The official plan details general policies for future land use, while zoning by-laws put the plan into practice. A zoning by-law is legally enforceable and directly relates to the everyday administration of land use and associated activities. Municipalities commonly have comprehensive policies under one by-law for the entire jurisdiction detailing permitted uses along with required standards. The by-law normally divides the municipality into land use zones and specifies the permitted uses (e.g., commercial or residential) along with required standards (e.g., building size and location) in each zone. No uniform format exists for a zoning by-law, but most follow a more or less standard classification system outlined below.

Interpretation and Administration	Includes definitions applicable to the by-law (e.g., floor and landscaped areas, lot frontage and lot line), classification of zones and associated symbols (e.g., R1—residential single-family), zone boundaries, summary of site-specific exceptions and non-conforming uses, and other applicable by-laws that may impact land use and building standards.
General Regulations *Applicable to All Zones*	Uses that are either permitted or prohibited in all zones, special regulations concerning flood plain or hazard lands including special policy areas, accessory uses involving buildings and structures, off-street parking and fencing.
Zone Regulations	Specific requirements relating to classes of use and sub-classes (zones) within the municipality. Permitted uses are fully detailed along with site development specifications.
Site-Specific Exceptions	Exceptions within zoning areas that have been formally approved by way of amending zoning by-laws, or that existed prior to the passage of the current by-law; i.e., non-conforming uses. Site specific exceptions frequently involve distinct requirements to meet unique developments or uses. Exceptions might involve allowance for such things as limited parking facilities and unique setbacks that differ from standard requirements.
Zoning Maps	Includes detailed zoning maps presented in numeric order based on a grid system for the entire municipality.
Special Area Zoning Maps	Geographic areas in which specific use or building standard requirements apply; e.g., height restrictions near an airport and special policy areas relating to the regulatory flood plain that impose restrictions on new construction or renovation of existing structures.

CLASSIFICATION

The zoning by-law typically divides the entire municipality into a minimum of six general uses (**zoning classifications**): residential, commercial, industrial, institutional, open space and agricultural. Each class is further subdivided into sub-classes or zones along with appropriate symbols. Classification systems will vary throughout the province. An example is provided illustrating typical residential classifications.

| *Zoning Classifications*
Specific property divisions within a zoning by-law (e.g., residential, and commercial), along with further sub-classifications (e.g., single-family and duplex).

ZONE CLASS	ZONE SYMBOL	MINIMUM CLEARANCE (M)
R	R1	Detached single-family dwellings.
	R2 to R5	To accommodate varying urban densities in detached single-family developments.
RS	RS1	Semi-detached single-family dwellings.
RM	RM1	Multiple-unit residential buildings.
	RM2, RM3	To accommodate varying urban densities in multiple-unit residential buildings.
RR	RR1	Rural non-farm dwelling units within rural settlement areas.
	RR2	Rural non-farm dwelling units outside of rural settlement areas.

ZONING AMENDMENTS

Property owners may want to use property in a manner not permitted in the zoning by-law and must make application to amend the zoning by-law. The council of a municipality will only consider a zoning by-law amendment if the proposed use is in keeping with the official plan. Buyers and sellers are well advised to contact the appropriate municipal planning authority prior to making an application.

If the proposed change does not conform exactly to the zoning, but does generally conform with its overall intent, an application can be made for a minor variance. The committee of adjustment normally deals with such matters.

Building Restrictions   CURIOSITY

Practitioners in the marketplace may refer to building restrictions, which can include restrictions concerning the construction and location of buildings and services *either* registered against the land *or* required through municipal restrictions in the form of zoning and land use control. The focus at present is on zoning-related restrictions.

Such restrictions either directly refer to the structure (e.g., minimum gross floor area, height of structure, type of structure based on use and construction of accessory buildings) or indirectly limit it (e.g., various setback requirements dictating overall building size and shape). Residential zoning requirements typically set out restrictions relating to front, rear and side yards, maximum lot coverage, minimum landscaped open space, parking needs and various requirements concerning buildings located on the same lot. Commercial properties may also be restricted in terms of minimum setback requirements relating to lands abutting major highways, railway lines and residential areas; specifics regarding storage areas, store size limitations within regional shopping malls and power centres; and limitations on gross floor area in neighbourhood, community, sub-regional and regional shopping centres.

Restrictions can also arise by way of specific requirements applicable to a particular development or defined area, over and above those stated in general zoning by-laws; e.g., a larger minimum size of building or site. Such restrictions typically arise by agreement with the municipality at the time of development. Restrictions may also be imposed by the seller as part of an overall design strategy relating to development lands owned by that individual; e.g., architectural standards established for all residential units within a specific housing development.

Site Plan Control

This method of development control is imposed by a municipality (or by the appropriate planning approval body) during the planning and development process. Site plan approval is authorized under the *Planning Act*, thereby exerting influence over building design and site amenities in addition to requirements set out in zoning by-laws and the Ontario Building Code (see subsequent discussion).

Site Plan Control Area

An agreement setting out terms for property development within a site plan control area.

Real estate practitioners most commonly encounter **site plan control area** provisions in relation to commercial and industrial properties. In actual fact, site plan control typically applies to all structures within a municipality. Detached single-family, duplex and triplex properties including accessory buildings are usually excluded, as adequate control provisions are included within the zoning by-laws. In rural areas, farm buildings are not normally included under such provisions, but recreational properties are often subject to site plan control and, in particular, cottages on or near the water.

APPLICATION PROCEDURES

Individuals making application should contact the local planning department for exact procedures. In most instances, the applicant must provide legible, original blueprints of the following:

- site plan;
- landscape plan;
- grading and servicing plan;
- a perspective rendering of the completed structure and other improvements;
- elevation drawings of the completed structure and other improvements; and
- floor plans and cross-sectional drawings.

REVIEW/APPROVAL PROCESS

The site plan approval process allows the municipality to review the overall design of planned structures and assess developmental impact on surrounding land uses. Typically, the municipality will consider facts such as adequate landscaping and buffering from adjacent properties, grading and lot considerations and the need for any widening of roads abutting the site including provision of curbs, signs, walkways and storm, surface and water runoff facilities.

The review process also involves assessment of vehicular traffic flows, parking requirements, emergency vehicle access, lighting requirements, perimeter fencing needs or enclosure of selected areas and storage areas. The application is also circulated to appropriate agencies who may provide input, as well as the municipality, prior to final site approval. Additional approvals may be required from various agencies and ministries; e.g., a local **conservation authority**, the Ministry of Transportation and the building department pursuant to the **Ontario Building Code**.

Conservation Authority

An agency authorized under conservation legislation to oversee regulated areas.

On completion of the review process and assuming that all requirements have been met, the final drawings are stamped and recommended for approval. Typically, the owner of the land is then required to enter into a site plan control agreement with the municipality. The actual time required will vary depending on the accuracy/completeness of the application, complexity of the project and impact on adjoining properties or community infrastructure. Once site plan approval is obtained, the applicant is responsible for carrying out the development in accordance with the approval plans and any conditions imposed by the municipality.

Site Plan Control Agreement

An agreement setting out terms for property development within a site plan control area.

SITE PLAN CONTROL AGREEMENT

The exact format of a **site plan control agreement** or similar document will vary by municipality. Typically, the agreement contains covenants by the owner that the property will be developed and used in accordance with stipulations set out in the site plan approval process. A site plan control agreement for a recreational property is illustrated.

THE CORPORATION OF THE TOWNSHIP OF NORTHSIDE
SITE PLAN AGREEMENT

THIS AGREEMENT made in triplicate this _____ day of _____ ,20xx.

BETWEEN: _____
hereinafter called the "OWNER" OF THE FIRST PART,

–and–

THE CORPORATION OF THE TOWNSHIP OF NORTHSIDE, hereinafter called the "TOWNSHIP" OF THE SECOND PART.

WHEREAS the OWNER is the owner in fee simple of these lands and premises in the Township of Northside in Lake District being more particularly described in Schedule 'A' attached hereto;

AND WHEREAS the OWNER has applied to the TOWNSHIP to permit development on the OWNER'S lands;

AND WHEREAS the OWNER has agreed with the TOWNSHIP to furnish and perform the works, material, matters and things required to be done, furnished and performed in the manner hereinafter described in connection with the proposed use of the subject lands;

AND WHEREAS the said lands have been designated by the Council of the TOWNSHIP as being within a site plan control area as provided for by the Planning Act as amended;

NOW THEREFORE witnesseth that in consideration of other good and valuable consideration and the sum of ONE_____($1.00)_____DOLLAR of lawful money of Canada now paid by the TOWNSHIP to the OWNER, the receipt whereof is hereby acknowledged, the OWNER and the TOWNSHIP covenant, declare and agree as follows:

SECTION I—LANDS TO BE BOUND

1) The lands to be bound by the terms and conditions of this Agreement (sometimes referred to as "the subject lands"), are located in the _____Ward of the TOWNSHIP, and are more particularly described in Schedule "A" hereto.

SECTION II—COMPONENTS OF THE AGREEMENT

1) The text consisting of Sections I through V, and the following Schedules, which are annexed hereto, constitute the components of this Agreement.

> Schedule "A"—Legal Description of the Lands being developed
>
> Schedule "B"—Site Plan
>
> Schedule "C"—Architectural Drawings
>
> Schedule "D"—Drainage Plan

SECTION III—REGISTRATION OF AGREEMENT

1) This Agreement shall be registered on title to the said lands as provided by the Planning Act as amended, at the expense of the OWNER;

2) The OWNER agrees that all documents required herein shall be submitted in a form suitable to the TOWNSHIP and suitable for registration, as required;

3) The PARTIES agree that this Agreement must be registered against the OWNER'S lands within thirty (30) days of the execution thereof by the TOWNSHIP.

SECTION IV—BUILDING PERMITS

1) The OWNER agrees to not request the Chief Building official to issue a building permit to carry out the development until this Agreement has been registered on title to the lands described in Schedule "A" attached hereto and a registered copy of same has been provided to the_____ TOWNSHIP.

2) It is agreed that if the OWNER fails to apply for any building permit or permits to implement this Agreement within 12 months from the date upon which such building permit would be available, then the TOWNSHIP, at its option has the right to terminate the said Agreement and require that a new Site Plan Agreement be submitted for approval and execution.

SECTION V—PROVISIONS

1) The OWNER further covenants and agrees to develop the subject lands in accordance with the Site Plan, being Schedule "B" attached hereto, and that no work will be performed on the subject lands except in conformity to all provisions of the Agreement.

2) The OWNER agrees that parking of all highway vehicles on the subject lands shall be restricted to the parking areas illustrated on Schedule "B". The OWNER agrees to restrict the location of entrance ways and of parking to those locations marked on Schedule "B".

3) The OWNER further agrees to take such action as may be necessary from time to time to ensure that dust emanations, if any, from parking areas and walkways do not create any nuisance to adjacent property owners.

4) The OWNER further agrees that external lighting facilities on the subject lands and buildings will be designed and constructed so as to avoid, wherever possible, the illumination of adjacent properties and provide a level of illumination that is consistent with the natural beauty of the surrounding properties and waterbody.

5) The OWNER further agrees to provide for the storage of garbage and other waste material at its sole risk and expense in the location as shown on Schedule "B".

6) The OWNER further agrees to provide for the removal of snow from access ramps, driveways, parking areas, and walkways at its sole risk and expense, in order to permit the passage of emergency vehicles.

7) The OWNER further agrees to preserve and maintain the mature, healthy trees located on the subject lands and beyond the building sites, as shown on Schedule "B".

8) The OWNER further agrees to preserve all healthy trees in areas designated as buffer areas on Schedule "B".

9) The OWNER agrees to complete all landscaping in these areas designated for such on Schedule "B" and detailed on Schedule_____.

10) The OWNER hereby acknowledges that the lands described in Schedule "B" attached hereto, are considered significant deer wintering habitat by the Ministry of Natural Resources. As a result of this, and for the protection of adjoining lands, the OWNER hereby agrees that no existing trees or other vegetation shall be removed or diminished from the lands described in Schedule "B" without prior written consent from the Lake District Office of the Ministry of Natural Resources. It is understood that approval will be given for the removal of vegetation to provide for a building envelope, a septic system location, access and removal of dead trees.

11) The OWNER further agrees to provide for the grading or change in elevation or contour of the land and the disposal of storm, surface and waste water from the land and from any buildings or structures thereon as shown on Schedule____, and will ensure that the natural drainage is not altered in any way that will cause damage to any adjacent lands or to any public highway. The installation of storm water management works and the final grading of the OWNER'S lands, including any and all necessary ditching and culverts, shall be provided by the OWNER.

12) The OWNER further agrees to construct all buildings in accordance with the provisions of Schedule_____, illustrating the massing and conceptual design, and the general elevations and typical cross-sections of the buildings to be erected by the OWNER. The Site Plan, Schedule "B", shows the building envelopes and locations in which buildings are to be erected. Except for minor deviations necessitated by soil conditions, topography, the requirements of the Ministry of the Environment to preserve mature standing trees, and deviations for structural orientation, no building will be located on the subject lands except in accordance with Schedule "B".

SECTION VI—BINDING PARTIES, ALTERATION, AMENDMENT, EFFECT, NOTICE, PENALTY

1) This Agreement may only be amended or varied by a written document of equal formality herewith duly executed by the parties hereto and registered against the title to the subject lands.

2) The OWNER further agrees to complete the items detailed on Schedules_____ within one (1) year of the date of registration of this Agreement.

3) Following completion of the works, the OWNER shall maintain to the satisfaction of the TOWNSHIP, and at the sole expense of the OWNER, all the facilities or works (including landscaping) described on Schedule____.

4) This Agreement shall enure to the benefit of and be binding upon the respective successors and assigns of each of the PARTIES hereto.

5) The Agreement shall come into effect on the date of execution by the Municipality.

Northside Site Plan Agreement, Page 3

6) The OWNER acknowledges that this Agreement is entered into under the provisions of the Planning Act as amended, and that the expenses of the TOWNSHIP arising out of the enforcement of this Agreement may be recovered as taxes pursuant to the Municipal Act, as amended.

7) Section V 10 of this Agreement will not be amended or removed from the title of the lands described in Schedule "A", hereto, except where the Ministry of Natural Resources has given prior written consent.

8) Any notice required to be given pursuant to the terms hereto shall be in writing and mailed or delivered to the other at the following address:

To the OWNER:

To the AREA MUNICIPALITY: Clerk Administrator, Township of Northside, County of Lake District.

IN WITNESS WHEREOF the OWNER and the TOWNSHIP have caused their corporate seals to be affixed over the signatures of their respective signing officers.

SIGNED, SEALED AND DELIVERED

in the presence of: _____

_____   Per:_____
Witness

_____   Per:_____
Witness

THE CORPORATION OF THE
TOWNSHIP OF NORTHSIDE,

_____
Mayor

_____
Clerk Administrator

BUILDING AND FIRE CODES

Building Codes

Real estate practitioners will encounter building code requirements and minimum construction standards in both the residential and commercial fields. Building codes are based to a large extent on provisions of the National Building Code of Canada (NBC) and are statutorily established through an applicable provincial act; e.g., the Ontario Building Code. The codes do not function as authoritative textbooks on building design, but rather set out requirements in regard to safety, fire protection and structural sufficiency. Codes generally address:

- Specific uses and related occupancy requirements including acceptable fire and safety standards, means of exit, accessibility, service facilities and loads.
- Structural loads, foundations and design requirements for structural materials.
- Wind, water and vapour protection including vapour barriers, air barriers, control of groundwater and rain penetration, and material specifications.
- Heating, ventilating and air-conditioning including air duct systems, heating appliances, piping, refrigeration systems and chimneys/venting equipment.
- Plumbing including materials, equipment and specific requirements concerning piping, drainage and venting, along with stipulations regarding the use of potable and non-potable water systems.
- Requirements for housing and small buildings.
- Change of use requirements and renovations.

Ontario Building Code

ONTARIO BUILDING CODE

PART 1	Scope and Definitions
PART 2	General Requirements
PART 3	Fire Protection, Occupant Safety and Accessibility
PART 4	Structural Design
PART 5	Wind, Water and Vapour Penetration
PART 6	Heating, Ventilating and Air-Conditioning
PART 7	Plumbing
PART 8	Sewage Systems
PART 9	Housing and Small Buildings
PART 10	Change of Use
PART 11	Renovation
PART 12	Transition, Revocation and Commencement
APPENDICES	Explanatory Materials
INDEX	

The Ontario Building Code is made by Regulation under the *Building Code Act* that generally follows the National Building Code of Canada. The Ontario Building Code sets out minimum standards for building design as well as provisions in regard to safety in buildings, fire protection and structural sufficiency.

The current code is referred to as a consolidated version as it consists of the 1997 Ontario Building Code together with a range of Regulations and amendments to the present time. This consolidated addition includes significant changes, the most notable for practitioners being the introduction of sewage systems (Part 8) as a result of the transfer of various regulations from the *Environmental Protection Act* to the *Building Code Act*. The Code is administered by the Ministry of Municipal Affairs and Housing.

Practitioners are not typically involved with the building, installation, extension or alteration of buildings, but nevertheless are indirectly impacted by the Ontario Building Code in numerous situations involving new construction and renovations.

FIRE PROTECTION/OCCUPANT SAFETY

Part 3 of the Ontario Building Code sets out requirements concerning fire protection, occupant safety and accessibility in the construction of new buildings or the renovation of existing ones. The Code provides detailed minimum standards for various types of buildings and occupancy requirements and addresses such issues as fire resistance, fire separations and closures, firewalls and flame-spread ratings for finishes and coverings.

The Code also details fire safety provisions involving fire alarm and detection systems, provision for fire fighting equipment, additional requirements for selected types of buildings, safety within floor areas by type of occupancy, exits and a range of other standards designed to maximize occupant safety.

Practitioners should note that, effective August 6, 2001, carbon monoxide (CO) detectors became mandatory in all new residential buildings and garages that contain fuel-burning appliances. This Code amendment established uniform provincial standards for consistency across municipalities. In advance of this change, various municipalities had passed local carbon monoxide detector by-laws.

SEWAGE SYSTEMS

Sewage system inspectors are approved pursuant to qualifications established in Part 8 of the Ontario Building Code. A board of health or conservation authority may be responsible for enforcement of provisions relating to sewage systems in designated municipalities and territories without municipal organization. A sewage system inspector has powers and duties in relation to sewage systems as does the chief building official in relation to buildings.

The Code sets out qualifications for sewage system inspectors as well as for persons engaged in the on-site construction, installation, repair, servicing, and cleaning or emptying of sewage systems. The Code details design standards and general requirements for Class 1, 2, 3, 4 and 5 sewage systems together with specifications regarding general operation and maintenance. Sewage systems are discussed in more detail in a subsequent chapter detailing residential structural components.

RECENT CODE CHANGES

On June 19, 2002, the *Building Code Statute Law Amendment Act* was passed by the Ontario Legislature. This Act, amending the *Building Code Act* and the *Planning Act*, includes several significant amendments that have been introduced in the period 2003–2006:

- Enhance public safety by requiring that designers and building inspectors meet qualifications regarding building code knowledge.
- Streamline the building approvals process and remove red tape.
- Align building permit fees to enforcement costs.
- Allow municipalities to outsource plan review and construction inspection functions.
- Encourage innovation in design and construction.
- Enhance accountability among building practitioners through insurance requirements.

More recently, Ontario Regulation 350/06 was filed introducing the 2006 Building Code, which includes over 700 technical changes from the previous Code. Most of these are being phased in over the next few years.

WEB LINKS

Ontario Building Code   Go to *www.obc.mah.gov.on.ca* for information on how to obtain copies of Building Code publications, recent Code developments and related information concerning how the Ministry of Municipal Affairs and Housing works with municipalities in the ongoing enforcement of the Code.

Building Permits

The council of each municipality appoints a chief building official and a number of building inspectors necessary to enforce the provisions of the Code. In some instances, two or more municipalities may, by agreement, establish an arrangement for joint enforcement. The chief building official issues permits for proposed construction or demolition unless the proposal is contrary to the *Building Code Act*, the Ontario Building Code or any other applicable law; e.g., a builder as defined under the *Ontario New Home Warranties Plan Act* who is not registered under that Act. A person cannot construct or demolish a building as defined in the Code unless a **building permit** (sometimes referred to as a *construction permit*) is issued.

Example of a Typical Building Permit Process

ANYCITY BUILDING PERMIT PROCESS*

STEP 1 Application
Submit permit application to Building Department, along with plans, property survey (or site plan) and fee.

STEP 2 Review
Building Department reviews documentation. Drawings must conform to zoning by-laws, and comply with mechanical (e.g., HVAC and plumbing) and architectural/structural Building Code Requirements.

STEP 3 Permit
Legal permission granted to start construction. Permit must be posted prominently on the site and building plans must be kept on site. Any changes require review and approval as per Step 1 and 2.

STEP 4 Inspections
Requests for inspections must be made 24 hours before work proceeds beyond stages set out in the permit. Failure can result in work stoppage until remedies made.

*Check your local municipality as procedures will vary.

PERMIT APPLICATION

Sellers and buyers considering any type of construction on a specific property are well advised to seek assistance from the local building department and/or building inspector prior to the start of any construction. If a permit is required, the building department requires an application outlining the planned work including plans, building sketches and related documents.

Municipal staff will review the application to ensure that the planned construction meets with the applicable building codes, local zoning by-laws for the area in which the construction is taking place and other relevant regulations; e.g., special requirements for properties located in or near flood prone areas of a community.

Requirements for new construction, additions, alterations, renovations, relocations, and repairs or rehabilitation of a building or structure will vary. Building permits are typically required for a variety of projects.

- Finishing previously unfinished spaces such as family rooms, recreation rooms or attics.
- Repair and underpinning of foundations.
- Installation of pools.
- Construction of decks in excess of a specific height above the ground.
- Construction of accessory buildings in excess of a specified square footage.
- Construction of attached and detached garages.

INSPECTOR

A **building inspector** is permitted to enter onto the lands subject to a building permit at any reasonable time to inspect the building. If a contravention is found, the inspector is authorized to make an order that corrective action must be taken immediately or within a specified period of time. If work is not completed pursuant to the order, a stop work order may be issued.

Inspectors are also authorized to enter upon land and into buildings at any reasonable time without a warrant to inspect for unsafe conditions. An order can then be issued requiring that remedial steps be taken, once again within a specified time period. The order may require immediate repairs in the case of an emergency situation. Building permits

SECTION II

PLANNING AND LAND USE

detail the project location, scope of work, conditions imposed regarding the work and the building inspections required, depending on the project size.

OCCUPANCY PERMIT

An **occupancy permit** is issued for the structure once all inspections are completed and Ontario Building Code requirements are met. Individuals are not permitted to occupy the premises until the permit is issued.

Occupancy Permit

A municipal permit issued following final inspection permitting occupancy of a structure.

Entrance Permits

CURIOSITY

Practitioners should also be aware of other permits that may be required when involved with new construction. For example, an entrance permit is needed to provide access to lands that were not previously accessible from an adjacent road. Such entrances can involve a permanent entrance to a farm, residential or commercial/industrial property, a temporary entrance (usually for a period of not more than one year for purposes of construction, repairs or related improvements) or a public entrance (e.g., from a registered plan of subdivision to a municipal or county road).

Approval of an entrance will take into consideration such factors as the safe movement of public traffic, favourable grade and alignment considerations and minimum sight distances. The approval may be granted subject to specific requirements regarding grading, surfacing materials, culverts, curbs and gutters. Contact the local municipality for additional details.

Fire Code

The National Fire Code of Canada (NFC) establishes levels of fire safety for both new and existing buildings related to both occupants and emergency responders. The national fire code is published by the Institute for Research in Construction (IRC), an organization within the National Research Council. The NFC complements the National Building Code in the construction, renovation or maintenance of buildings. Each province has a fire code establishing specific requirements that apply within provincial jurisdictions. Fire codes are continuously evolving, particularly in the areas of fire prevention, fire protection and public safety.

FIRE MARSHALL

The fire marshall is an individual appointed by the Lieutenant Governor in Council pursuant to Part III of the *Fire Prevention and Protection Act*. The Act sets out general powers and duties of the fire marshal along with the right to delegate responsibilities to assistants, namely, the fire chief of every fire department, the clerk of every municipality that does not have a fire department, any member of a fire prevention bureau established by a municipality and anyone designated by the fire marshal as an assistant to the fire marshal.

Ontario Fire Code

A provincial code setting out compliance criteria for fire safety.

The *Fire Protection and Prevention Act* is an enabling statute under which the **Ontario Fire Code** (Reg. 388/97 as amended) was enacted. From a real estate practitioner's point of view, the Ontario Fire Code is most relevant as it directly impacts residential and commercial structures.

WEB LINKS
Ontario Fire Code   The Office of the Fire Marshal of Ontario provides detailed information concerning fire-related topics and applicable legislation including the Ontario Fire Code. Go to *www.ofm.gov.on.ca.*

ONTARIO FIRE CODE

The Ontario Fire Code provides for the safety of occupants in existing buildings, through the elimination or control of fire hazards in and around buildings, the maintenance of life safety systems in buildings, and the establishing of a fire safety plan in those buildings where necessary.

The *Fire Protection and Prevention Act*, in addition to providing the enabling legislation for the Ontario Fire Code, sets out responsibilities for fire protection services, the duties and powers of the fire marshal and those appointed by the fire marshal, rights of entry in emergencies and fire investigations, inspections and related orders, offences and enforcement, recovery of costs, and employment and labour relations issues.

ONTARIO FIRE CODE

PART 1	Application and Definitions
PART 2	Building and Occupant Fire Safety
PART 3	Property Protection for Industrial and Commercial Occupancies
PART 4	Flammable and Combustible Liquids
PART 5	Hazardous Materials, Processes and Operations
PART 6	Fire Protection Equipment
PART 7	Inspection, Testing and Maintenance of Fire Emergency Systems in High Buildings
PART 8	Demolition
PART 9	Retrofit
APPENDIX	Building Code References
COMMENTARY	Commentary on Changes to the Ontario Fire Code
AUDIT GUIDES	
INDEX	

RETROFIT PROVISIONS

Part 9 is most relevant to real estate practitioners as various sections specifically address retrofit provisions affecting a broad range of occupancies, most notably Sections 9.5, 9.6 and 9.8. Part 9 is divided as follows:

Section 9.1
General Information

Section 9.2
Assembly Occupancies
(e.g., clubs, bingo halls and lecture halls)

Section 9.3
Boarding, Lodging and Rooming Houses

Section 9.4
Health Care Facilities

Section 9.5
Buildings Up to and Including Six Storeys in Building Height with Residential Occupancies

Section 9.6
Buildings Higher than Six Storeys in Building Height with Residential Occupancies

Section 9.7
Reserved

Section 9.8
Two Unit Residential Occupancies

Section 9.9
Hotels

SECTION II   PLANNING AND LAND USE

Part 9 of the Ontario Fire Code addresses a broad range of property types including retrofit provisions for existing buildings, which goes beyond the scope of this course. Practitioners should gain familiarity with regulations impacting their particular areas of expertise.

- Section 9.8 of the Ontario Fire Code (Ontario Regulation 385/94) placed minimum standards for fire safety in existing buildings with two units effective July 14, 1994. These retrofit requirements should not be confused with the compliance deadline of October 9, 1994 set for high and low rise residential apartment buildings (Fire Code, Section 9.5 and 9.6, Reg. 454/90). The provisions came into effect two years earlier on October 9, 1992.

Accessory Apartments   CAUTION

An **accessory apartment** is a self-contained unit within a house, making it a house with two residential units. Legislation commonly refers to such properties as two-unit houses, although various terminologies are found in the marketplace. The retrofit provisions of the Ontario Fire Code concerning two-unit residential properties (Section 9.8) address various considerations regarding occupant safety including fire separation and containment provisions for each dwelling unit, escape (egress) from each dwelling unit, fire alarm and detection, suppression and electrical safety. Owners are provided various options to comply with the regulations. Approval requires two separate inspections, an electrical inspection and an inspection by the local fire department. The electrical inspection is in accordance with the Electrical Safety Code enacted under the *Power Corporation Act*. Homeowners may face significant fines for failing to comply with the fire safety standards. Each municipal fire department is bound by legislation to ensure specific code compliance.

Practitioners should exercise caution in all matters concerning accessory apartments. The key issue typically centres on whether an existing unit is 'legal or not'; i.e., meets all current requirements. Several questions that can come into play when determining if an existing accessory apartment can be legally used include:

- When was the unit constructed?
- When was it occupied?
- Was a building permit issued at the time of construction?
- Did the unit meet fire code provisions at time of construction/occupancy?
- Did the unit meet zoning requirements at time of construction/occupancy?
- Did the unit meet electrical requirements at time of construction/occupancy?
- Were all necessary inspections completed to ensure compliance?

Salespeople and sellers need to consult with the local municipality regarding all existing accessory apartments. Requirements concerning accessory apartments can vary by municipality. Also, salespeople need to be aware of current zoning, building code and fire code specifics impacting the construction of accessory apartments, when involved with such matters. Buyers should be strongly encouraged to include a condition in an agreement of purchase and sale to provide sufficient time to consult with appropriate experts when considering the purchase of a home with an accessory apartment or contemplating constructing an accessory apartment within a residential structure.

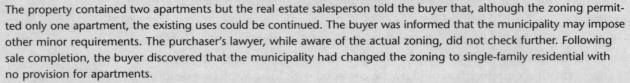

The property contained two apartments but the real estate salesperson told the buyer that, although the zoning permitted only one apartment, the existing uses could be continued. The buyer was informed that the municipality may impose other minor requirements. The purchaser's lawyer, while aware of the actual zoning, did not check further. Following sale completion, the buyer discovered that the municipality had changed the zoning to single-family residential with no provision for apartments.

The buyer sued the salesperson for misrepresentation and the lawyer for negligence. The trial Judge determined the salesperson was fully responsible for the buyer's losses, and the lawyer was not liable as his conduct was not a causative factor in the buyer's loss. A key matter in this determination was that the lawyer was not retained until after the agreement of purchase and sale was signed.

On appeal, the Appeal Court decided the lawyer was responsible along with the salesperson, as he should have enquired about zoning and advised the buyer that the agreement could be rescinded due to the agent's misrepresentations. The court found that although real estate professionals may not be required to possess expertise as to zoning matters, they are liable for any false representations made. The lawyer and salesperson were equally responsible for the losses.

Reference   Redmond v. Densmore (Nfld).

BUILDING CODE VS. FIRE CODE

Fire safety requirements are regulated under one of two provincial regulations, the Ontario Building Code or the Ontario Fire Code. Noting differences between safety regulations established in these codes is important.

- The Ontario Building Code applies to construction of new buildings, alterations, additions and changes in use within existing buildings.
- The Ontario Fire Code regulates fire safety in existing structures (including two-unit residential occupancies; see *Caution: Accessory Apartments* on a previous page).

FIRE CLASSIFICATIONS

CLASS A FIRES

Start in ordinary materials which burn easily, such as paper, wood, cloth, rubber and many plastics. Such fires can usually be extinguished with water.

CLASS B FIRES

Involve grease or flammable liquids that burn rapidly, such as gasoline, oil, lacquers, paints, mineral spirits, alcohol, fats and greases. A smothering or blanketing effect is needed to stop them.

CLASS C FIRES

Start in energized electrical equipment, such as air-conditioning compressors, motors, transformers, generators and electrical wiring. The use of water or a chemical that carries an electrical charge may result in death or injury for the person trying to stop such a fire and should therefore not be used.

CLASS D FIRES

Start in combustible metals such as aluminum, magnesium, titanium, zirconium, sodium and potassium.

DEFINITIONS

Real estate practitioners encounter various terminologies relating to the practical application of provincial fire codes in regard to residential occupancies. Following are a few, frequently encountered definitions included for illustration purposes only.

SECTION II   PLANNING AND LAND USE

Access to Exit	That part of a means of egress within a floor area that provides access to an exit serving the floor area.
Alarm Signal	An audible signal transmitted throughout a zone or zones or throughout a building to advise occupants that a fire emergency exists.
Closure	A device or assembly for closing an opening through a fire separation such as a door, shutter, wired glass or glass block assembly, and includes all components, such as hardware, closing devices, frames and anchors.
Dwelling Unit	A room or suite of rooms operated as a housekeeping unit used or intended to be used as a domicile by one or more persons and that may contain cooking, eating, living, sleeping and sanitary facilities.
Exit	That part of a means of egress that leads from the floor area it serves and includes any doorway leading directly from a floor area to a public thoroughfare or to an approved open space.
Fire-Protection Rating	The time in hours, or fraction thereof, that a closure, window assembly or glass block assembly will withstand the passage of flame when exposed to fire under specified conditions of test and performance criteria, or as otherwise prescribed in a provincial building code.
Fire-Resistance Rating	The time in hours, or fraction thereof, that a material or assembly of materials will withstand the passage of flame and the transmission of heat when exposed to fire under specified conditions of test and performance criteria, or as determined by extension or interpretations of information derived therefrom as prescribed in a provincial building code. The actual rating assigned to a material, assembly of materials or structural members of a building, is based on test results conducted according to the Standard Methods of Fire Endurance Tests of Building Construction and Materials. Fire resistance ratings provide the basis for assessing types of material and establishing required minimums for their use in exterior walls, supporting construction, floor, ceiling and roof assemblies, fire separations, firewalls, exit corridors, and partition walls.
Fire Separation	A construction assembly that acts as a barrier against the spread of fire and may or may not have a fire-resistance rating or a fire-protection rating.
Firewall	A fire separation of noncombustible construction that subdivides a building or separates adjoining buildings to resist the spread of fire that has a fire-resistance rating as prescribed in a provincial building code and the structural stability to remain intact under fire conditions for the required fire-rated time.
Floor Area	The space on any storey of a building between exterior walls and required firewalls and includes the space occupied by interior walls and partitions, but does not include exits and vertical service spaces that pierce the storey.

Means of Egress	A continuous path of travel provided by a doorway, hallway, corridor, exterior passageway, balcony, lobby, stair, ramp or other egress facility, or combination thereof, for the escape of persons from any point in a building, floor area, room or contained open space to a public thoroughfare, or other approved open space and includes exits and access to exits.

SMOKE ALARMS

A combined smoke detector and audible device is designed to sound an alarm within the room or suite in which it is found, when smoke is detected. Effective March 1, 2006, an amendment to the Ontario Fire Code requires homes to have working smoke alarms on every storey. This requirement is in addition to the existing requirement that smoke alarms must be installed outside all sleeping areas.

The amendment applies to all single-family, semi-detached and town homes, whether owner-occupied or rented. Both homeowners and landlords who do not meet smoke alarm requirements are subject to fines. Penalties to landlords can be up to $50,000. An illustration is provided showing the proper smoke alarm placement. Additional specifics are located in the Ontario Fire Code.

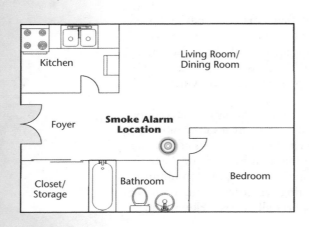

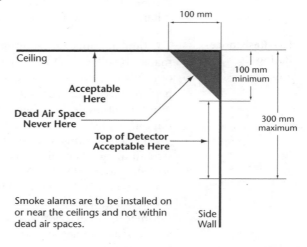

WATERCOURSE CONTROLS/RESTRICTIONS

Flood Plains

Area along a stream or watercourse that is subject to flood hazard.

Practitioners listing and selling properties abutting or in close proximity to watercourses can have difficulty determining which legislation and/or government agency to contact. All three levels of government are involved and authorities may be overlapping and/or not clearly defined. Two key areas involving **flood plains** and **wetlands** are highlighted. In addition, a detailed summary of major responsibilities and jurisdictional controls of governing bodies is included later under this topic. Other matters concerning waterways (e.g., legal disputes and **riparian rights**) fall to common law enforcement by the Courts.

Flood Plains

Properties located within flood plains typically fall under regulation of the Conservation Authorities (**www.conservation-ontario.on.ca**) who are directly involved in administration of flood plains (regulated areas). Regulated areas refer to lands adjacent to watercourses that require special consideration. Typically, jurisdictional controls extend into valley and stream corridors and associated watersheds.

Municipalities include either **one zone flood plain** or a **two zone flood plain** within official plans and consequently site uses and the ability to construct buildings or other structures are impacted by **flood proofing** and related activities.

A conservation authority is granted powers under the *Conservation Act* and approvals involve building construction, fill placement and watercourse alterations in regulated areas. Development applications are reviewed to prevent, eliminate or reduce the risk to life and property from flooding, erosion of river banks and slope instability.

One Zone Flood Plain

A regulated area in which the entire area is considered to be a floodway.

Flood Proofing

Structural or related methods that minimize flooding for a flood-prone property.

Conservation Authority

Thirty-six conservation authorities operate across Ontario, the oldest dating from 1946. Conservation authorities, established under the *Conservation Authorities Act*, administer resource conservation, watershed management and related programs. The most visible activity involves regulation of flood plains (regulated areas) and associated requirements including permits for specified activities within those regulated areas. Regulated areas are defined as lands adjacent to a watercourse that require special consideration because of potential for flood, erosion or pollution problems.

From a real estate perspective, conservation authorities are most commonly associated with restrictions that impact buyers and sellers of properties within regulated areas. The conservation authority's primary mandate is to reduce risk to life and property from flooding or erosion. Consequently, new construction or alterations to existing housing is often regulated and subject to permit issuance. In areas susceptible to flooding, work may be totally prohibited.

AUTHORITY/SCOPE

Conservation authorities must give approval within regulated areas for watercourse alterations, placement of fill and building construction.

Approvals: Watercourse Alteration/Fill/Construction   Conservation authorities are primarily concerned with the adverse effect that an altered watercourse has on neighbouring properties, flow and direction of floodwaters, and erosion. In terms of fill placement, approval is required in designated areas of the watershed, specifically described as the fill line. Detailed maps of both the fill and flood lines are available for individual municipalities. In the case of building construction, the Ontario Building Code does not permit the issuance of a municipal permit if it contravenes any applicable regulatory requirements, including those of a local conservation authority.

The *Conservation Act* gives conservation authorities the right to make regulations applicable to the area under its jurisdiction:

- To prohibit, regulate or require permission of a conservation authority for the construction of any building or structure in or on a pond or swamp, or in any area susceptible to flooding during a regional storm.

- To prohibit, regulate or require permission of the conservation authority for the placing or dumping of fill of any kind in any defined part of the area over which the authority has jurisdiction, where the control of flooding or pollution or the conservation of land may be affected by the placing or dumping of fill.
- To prohibit, regulate or require the permission of the conservation authority for the straightening, changing, diverting or interfering in any way with the existing channel of a river, creek, stream or watercourse.

Review of Planning Documents   The Conservation Authority is required under the *Planning Act* to review the following:

- Official plans and amendments thereto.
- Zoning by-laws.
- Consents to severance applications.
- Minor variances.
- Subdivision and condominium applications.
- Site plan control.

To accomplish such reviews, the following information is typically required:

- Location of which the document deals.
- Location of watercourses and slopes on or adjacent to the area.
- Existing and proposed use(s) of land.
- Location of new structures or fill.

Many planning documents circulated to other government agencies by applicants contain the information requested.

Storm Water Management   Flood control provisions typically focus on large-scale developments. The conservation authority is primarily concerned with post-development flows to ensure that no adverse downstream results occur. The evaluation of any project includes a review of flood lines (if applicable), comparison of pre- and post-development flows and percent changes in flow, method and location of discharging storm water from the site, and method and location of erosion control.

WEB LINKS
Conservation Authorities   For additional information about conservation authorities and the specific authority within particular areas of Ontario, go to *www.conservation-ontario.on.ca.*

Flood Controls

Conservation authorities may designate areas where the control of flooding or conservation of land can be affected by placing or dumping fill. Any proposals for placing or dumping fill within such areas are reviewed to assess impact. Scheduled areas are often identified based on several criteria that may be interrelated; e.g., location of ponds and wetlands, susceptibility to pollution and stability of sloping areas. Criteria for establishing scheduled areas are set out according to provincial standards.

FISH HABITAT

Recently, conservation authorities in Ontario are taking a larger role in reviewing water-related activities including the impact on fish habitat. The Ministry of Fisheries and Oceans (federal) now frequently uses local conservation authorities to ensure compliance with requirements of the *Fisheries Act*. The extent of involvement varies by specific conservation authority but, ultimately, citizens will encounter a more co-ordinated approach to the review and approval of projects on or near the water.

FLOOD PROOFING

Techniques involving a combination of structural changes and/or adjustments incorporated into individual buildings, structures or properties subject to flooding that would reduce or eliminate flood damage.

Conservation authorities refer to flood proofing as either active or passive and as wet or dry protection. Active flood proofing involves some form of action taken at the time of an advance warning to flood proof the property; e.g., firmly closing and sealing watertight doors and preparing sandbanking around the perimeter of the structure. Passive flood proofing includes construction activity such as floodwalls, stone gabions at shorelines and elevated improvements on the property. These changes are designed to flood proof without any action being taken.

Dry flood proofing refers to various activities designed to keep the property and buildings dry and is normally passive. The most common form of dry flood proofing is the elevation of structures by means of fill. Wet flood proofing, on the other hand, anticipates that water may infiltrate the area, but that such flooding will not cause any structural damage to the property. A good example would be a football stadium in which all portions of the structure below a pre-determined level are left unfinished (painted only) and all equipment (e.g., electrical circuitry and mechanical components) is placed on higher levels to minimize clean-up, if a flood occurs.

EXAMPLE   *Garage Renovation*

Buyer Jones wants to renovate a small repair garage in a flood-prone area near the downtown. Currently, the main office levels meet all requirements as set out by the municipality and the conservation authority, given flood possibilities throughout the central core. However, Jones wishes to renovate a basement area for storage and incidental repair work relating to company vehicles.

The mortgage company is concerned about flood risk and the potential for water damage. Accordingly, an engineer is contracted to work with the conservation authority and arrives at an acceptable wet flood proofing scheme that will ensure structural integrity, minimize flood damage and clean-up, and accommodate requirements as set out for this special policy area. The final requirements are as follows:

- Basement to remain unfurnished and contain non-habitable space only.

- Mechanical, electrical, heating and storage facilities to be located above the regulatory flood plain level.

- Four opening windows to be installed on opposite sides of the building, along with two full-size garage doors and two sump pumps.

EXAMPLE   *The Addition*

Seller Smith wants to add a small addition to his property that is located in a regulated area under the control of the local conservation authority. While Smith's property could be generally described as a low risk area both in terms of velocity and depth of any potential flood, it is necessary that certain passive flood proofing measures be undertaken.

The conservation authority requires that the addition be placed on an elevated slab, raising the structure approximately four feet from existing ground level. Given the size of the addition and the compaction required for fill, Smith will have to employ an engineer for design, review and inspection. The authority also informs Smith that columns, piles or piers can be used to accomplish the same result. Given that the required elevation is less than six feet, the authority will permit the use of brick piers, but strongly recommends reinforced concrete masonry or poured-in-place concrete piers.

FLOOD TERMINOLOGY

A knowledge of selected flood terms is important in understanding the activities of conservation authorities. Descriptions are summarized from formal definitions. Precise wordings and further descriptive materials are available through brochures provided by local conservation authorities.

Flood Fringe	The outer portion of the flood plain between the floodway and the limit of the regulatory flood level (flood hazard level). Flood depths and velocities are generally less severe in the flood fringe than those experienced in the floodway.
Flood Hazard	An inundation of water under specified conditions.
Flood Line	The extent of a flood plain subject to flood hazard including the floodway and the flood fringe.
Flood Plain	The area along a stream or watercourse that is subject to flood hazard and has been or could be flooded.
Floodway	The channel of a watercourse and that inner portion of the flood plain where flood depths and velocities are generally higher than those experienced in the flood fringe. The floodway represents that area required for the safe passage of flood flow and/or that area where flood depths and velocities are considered to pose a potential threat to life and possibly result in property damage.
One Hundred Year Flood Level	A flood, based on an analysis of precipitation, snow melt or a combination thereof, having a return period of 100 years on average or having a 1% chance of occurring or being exceeded in any given year. The one hundred year flood level is used to assess flooding hazards along waterways. The flooding hazard is the greater of the one hundred year flood level, actually experienced during a major storm (e.g., Hurricane Hazel, 1954), or a flood that was greater than either of these and specifically approved as a standard by the Ministry of Natural Resources.
Watershed	All the land that drains into a river, stream or similar waterbody.

SECTION II   PLANNING AND LAND USE

REGULATED AREAS

Conservation authorities have jurisdiction over regulated areas. A regulated area is broadly described as lands adjacent to a watercourse that require special consideration because of the potential for flood or erosion damage and pollution problems. The regulated area generally involves the total area of a flood plain that is subject to flood hazard given the worst case scenario for a storm occurring within a specific region.

Conservation authorities in conjunction with municipalities provide flood plain maps indicating regulated areas. These maps are for general reference only. Buyers and sellers should contact the local municipality and applicable conservation authority for precise locations of regulated areas, along with appropriate procedures for properties located within such areas.

EXAMPLE   *The Riverfront Home*

Seller Smith has a property fronting on a river. He has confirmed that the property is located within the regulatory flood plain and falls under restrictions established by the local conservation authority. Smith must make application and obtain a permit if he wishes to do any of the following:

- place, remove or grade fill from any source, including material now on the property;
- construct or add to an existing building of any type; or
- alter the waterfront on his property.

Smith must call the conservation authority for assistance and obtain a copy of the appropriate application. The application will be reviewed by staff to assess if the planned activity adversely affects the regulated area. Depending on the scope of the project, the process may also include a formal review by the executive committee at their regularly scheduled meeting.

SLOPE STABILITY/EROSION

Steep slopes to floodways and flood fringes are frequently subject to erosion and are typically found throughout watershed areas. Conservation authorities are actively involved in ensuring that any developments near such slopes do not affect stability or cause erosion. The development of such lands may concentrate run-off, accelerate erosion through the removal of vegetation and affect stability by the dumping of fill over such slopes. New developments are typically restricted by reasonable set backs to preserve these areas.

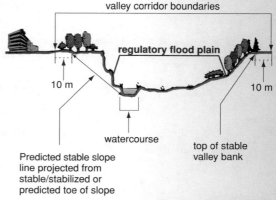

Source: Toronto Conservation Authority

VALLEY AND STREAM CORRIDORS

Traditionally, conservation authorities have concentrated on floodways and flood fringe areas within the regulatory flood plain. However, these agencies have consistently recognized that entire valley and stream corridors within watershed areas are very important. The Metropolitan Toronto Region Conservation Authority (MTRCA), for example, has developed an extensive valley and stream management program that goes beyond traditional regulated areas.

The extent of involvement with valley corridors will often depend on the stability of such slopes. Valley and stream corridors are differentiated in that valley corridors may or may not have a defined watercourse channel. Stream corridors will typically have a defined watercourse channel, except at the upper limit of the corridor, that is, the source area. An illustration is provided showing the traditional regulatory flood plain along with adjacent significant area arising from the valley and stream corridors under the new management program. The MTRCA encourages the public and private use of valley and stream corridors only for activities that are compatible with their land form, features and functions. Practices will vary by conservation authority. Practitioners should investigate the scope of valley and stream corridor management programs in the local area.

Source: Toronto Conservation Authority

WATERWAYS

Conservation authorities are also responsible to review and issue permits concerning any alteration to waterways. As a general guideline, conservation authorities promote natural channel design as opposed to the straightening or ditching of watercourses. Such actions are viewed as counterproductive to natural waterway characteristics, fish habitat and overall aesthetics. Alterations to waterways include culverts, bridges, pipeline and cable crossings, and bank protection programs.

FLOOD PLAINS

One Zone Flood Plain	An area in which the entire flood plain is considered to be a floodway. Typically, all development is prohibited except for such items as passive parkland areas, flood control structures, marinas, agriculture or public works facilities that require proximity to the water. Small accessory buildings may be permitted to service existing structures provided that they do not impede the flow of water in a flood situation. Also, minor alterations may be permitted to first floor levels in existing structures.

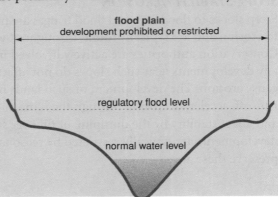

Two Zone Flood Plain	Two areas (zones) within a flood plain in recognition of the fact that certain parts of the flood plain are considered less hazardous and development could occur safely, subject to certain restrictions. The two-zone concept applies to areas of land, located within a flood plain, that forms an integral part of an existing flood prone community. This approach is used when adherence to one zone policy is not practical and a more reasonable approach is required, given current development within that community.

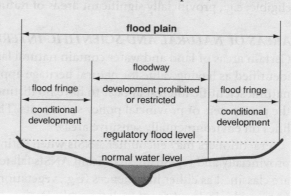

Special policy areas are also sometimes created within communities, or portions thereof, that have historically existed in the flood plain and where strict adherence to province-wide policies concerning new developments would result in social or economic hardships for the community and where requirements as set out in one and two zone classifications are not feasible.

Prudent Steps	CAUTION

Real estate practitioners should contact local conservation authorities and familiarize themselves with regulated areas, scope of conservation activities and local procedures involving development, renovations and other matters affecting real estate. Maps from local conservation authorities (if available) are useful for general reference. The district office of the Ministry of Natural Resources may also provide mapping suitable for practitioners involved in rural/recreational areas. Copies of official plans within municipalities can also be helpful when locating flood plains.

In the listing process, always enquire of the seller if the property is located in a flood plain and verify as necessary. Be particularly wary of properties near permanent or seasonal watercourses. Don't make any unverified representations and have the appropriate parties make direct contact with the local conservation authority. At all times, insert appropriate clauses in any agreement to ensure that the document properly reflects the understanding of the parties regarding flood plains and related issues.

Wetlands

Wetlands involve areas covered, either seasonally or permanently, by shallow water or where the water table is at or near the surface. Five major types of wetlands are swamps, bogs, fens, marshes and open water less than two metres in depth. The goal of conservation authorities is to protect and conserve wetland areas wherever possible.

Wetlands are classified as provincially or regionally significant. Generally, no new development is permitted in provincially significant wetlands. In the case of regionally or locally significant wetlands, environmental impact studies are required to assess overall effect and appropriate action must be taken to ensure that the wetland function is maintained or enhanced.

Practitioners should exercise caution with any wetlands on or immediately adjacent to properties being marketed. The Ministry of Natural Resources (MNR) (**www.mnr.gov.on.ca**)

Conservation Land Tax Incentive Program (CLTIP)

A provincial program providing tax exemption for conservation lands.

has evaluated many wetlands that are more than two hectares (approx. five acres) in size. Provincially significant wetlands are eligible for the **Conservation Land Tax Incentive Program** (CLTIP) tax exemption (see Curiosity: Areas of Natural Scientific Interest). CLTIP promotes private stewardship of wetlands in the province. Other defined areas are also eligible; e.g., provincially significant **areas of natural and scientific interest** (ANSIs).

AREAS OF NATURAL AND SCIENTIFIC INTEREST

Certain areas of land and water contain natural landscapes or features that have been identified as having value for natural heritage appreciation or study. Currently, areas of natural scientific interest appear to have no distinct legal status, but generally fall under the parameters of provincial policy statements. These statements furnish general guidelines on environmentally sensitive areas.

Practitioners may encounter ANSIs when listing or selling property. In Ontario, provincially and regionally significant ANSIs fall to the Ministry of Natural Resources and are classified as either life sciences (e.g., vegetation, marshes, forests) or earth sciences (e.g., geological and geomorphological). Designation of ANSIs is currently an MNR responsibility with input from regional governments and other environmental stakeholders. The MNR protects all ANSIs on public lands. On private land, the MNR seeks the owner's co-operation in protecting such features.

The Ministry provides mapping for various districts identifying both regionally and provincially significant ANSIs. While the legal status of such areas may be under negotiations, their impact on land use appears established. Real estate practitioners should take the initiative to locate ANSIs within the local trading area by contacting the appropriate MNR district office. Exercise caution when dealing with property in or near such designated areas.

WEB LINKS

Ministry of Natural Resources   The Ministry of Natural Resources is involved in various aspects of environmental control within the province. For information concerning its activities, go to: *www.mnr.gov.on.ca.*

Conservation Land Tax Incentive Program   CURIOSITY

This program involves owners of conservation lands that are at least 1/5 hectare (½ acre) in size who may be eligible for tax incentives, subject to guidelines established by the Ministry of Natural Resources (MNR). The tax incentive is in recognition of individuals who agree to protect natural heritage aspects of their property.

Eligible land must be considered highly significant by the Ministry and includes provincially significant wetlands, significant areas of natural scientific interest (ANSIs), habitats of endangered species, lands designated as escarpment natural area in the Niagara Escarpment Plan and community conservation land.

Land owners with eligible land must apply each year to take part in the program and must agree to maintain the property as conservation land. The local office of the MNR can provide additional information concerning appropriate activities and uses on the land.

SECTION II   PLANNING AND LAND USE

Who's Who in Water Control
PERSPECTIVE

A summary of key authorities involved with water control is provided. This is for general educational and informational purposes only. Contact the local municipality and applicable Ministries for current information.

GOVERNING BODY	ROLE/RESPONSIBILITY/JURISDICTION
Local Municipality	• Zoning by-laws detail property uses near or abutting water.
Conservation Authority www.conservation-ontario.on.ca	• Regulations controlling construction and placement of fill (*Conservation Authorities Act*), in relation to flood plains and watersheds.
Ministry of the Environment www.ene.gov.on.ca	• Contaminants are not permitted to flow into watercourses (*Environmental Protection Act*). • Prohibitions regarding the discharging of pollutants on the surface or to groundwater. Individuals taking large quantities of water must obtain a permit (*Ontario Water Resources Act*). • Property owners involved in the application of pesticides that may impact both surface and ground water must adhere to Regulation 914 under the *Pesticides Act*.
Ministry of Natural Resources www.mnr.gov.on.ca	• Protection of fish habitat including control of pollutant discharges into watercourses and stream alterations that could adversely affect such habitat (*Fisheries Act*). These activities are performed on behalf of the Department of Fisheries and Oceans, Government of Canada. • Approvals required for diverting, holding back, or other activities affecting water flow and levels for other users (*Lakes and Rivers Improvement Act*). • Permits required for work or other activity on shorelands adjacent to navigable waterways. The bed of these waterways (below the high water mark) is public land (*Public Lands Act*).
Ministry of Municipal Affairs and Housing www.mah.gov.on.ca	• Minimum set-back requirements relating to structures which are enforced at the municipal level (*Planning Act*). • Wetlands policy statements (*Planning Act*) and protection of wetlands in conjunction with the Ministry of Natural Resources.
Ministry of Government Services www.mgs.gov.on.ca	• Requirements for fuel tanks (aboveground and underground) to minimize threat of ground water pollution.
Ministry of Agriculture, Food and Rural Affairs www.omafra.gov.on.ca	• Prohibition regarding discharge of contaminants into drainage systems, control of surface drainage and financial assistance for drain construction/maintenance (*Drainage Act*).
Ministry of Health www.health.gov.on.ca	• Regulatory control if landowner creates a health hazard that impacts quality of water (*Health Protection and Promotion Act*).

ENVIRONMENTAL CONTROLS

Practitioners face increasingly complex and comprehensive environmental legislation when listing and selling both residential and commercial properties. Regulatory controls have expanded beyond basic land use measures into diverse areas such as noise control, air quality monitoring, reclamation of environmentally hazardous land and limitations on commercial business practices. Both federal and provincial ministries are involved.

The **Canadian Environmental Protection Act** sets a national framework for environmental controls, but real estate practitioners commonly encounter restrictions and regulations through the provincial Ministry of the Environment who oversees the **Environmental Protection Act**. The MOE is empowered to investigate waste-related violations and issue **orders** to property owners to prevent, remediate or stop pollution. However, many other provincial ministries are also involved in environment-related activities.

Canadian Environmental Protection Act

The *Canadian Environmental Protection Act* (CEPA), administered by Environment Canada, concerns various regulatory matters involving environmental issues in Canada. The CEPA is referred to as enabling legislation in that rules and regulations can be enacted through authority granted under this statute. The Act, enacted in 1988, was designed to provide a legislative framework for increasing standards, to assure citizens of certain rights concerning the environment and to set out minimum standards for provincial environmental initiatives.

The Act consolidates various pieces of federal legislation while addressing a broad range of environmental viewpoints involving most toxic substances used in the marketplace and their control throughout specific life cycles, whether in water, on land or in the air. In addition to Environment Canada, other federal agencies are involved in the environmental process through selected statutes; e.g., *Transportation of Dangerous Goods Act* and the *Clean Air Act*. The federal government is also involved in environmental concerns through the *Fisheries Act*.

Real estate practitioners have little involvement with federal agencies as most environmental land use regulations and activities concerning hazardous materials are provincially oriented. One notable exception involves waterfront property fronting on canals administered by Parks Canada (with input from the appropriate provincial authority responsible for fish habitat matters and shoreline regulations).

Environmental Protection Act

The *Environmental Protection Act* (EPA) is the primary environmental legislation impacting the ownership and use of real property within the Province of Ontario. Since 1971, this Act has gradually expanded both in terms of jurisdictional authority as well as degree of control/enforcement over environmental issues. The Ministry of the Environment (MOE), as the major force behind the EPA, is empowered to investigate matters concerning pollution, waste management, waste disposal and litter management/disposal. The MOE exercises a wide range of powers including search and seizure provisions to ensure adherence to environmental regulations.

Practitioners should be aware of the mandate and role of the MOE in the trading of real estate. The Ministry of the Environment has demonstrated its desire to aggressively pursue polluters by powers vested in the *Environmental Protection Act*, as well as through the judicial process. The Ministry has the ability to exercise broad powers granted under the EPA relating to search and seizure. The Act empowers officers to enter and search premises, interview individuals and examine documents to ensure that violations of the EPA are dealt with expediently. The *Environmental Protection Act* covers a broad array of topics. A limited number are summarized for descriptive purposes.

APPROVALS

The Ministry of the Environment is empowered to issue various licences, permits and certificates of approval concerning a wide range of activities that impact the environment; e.g., permits relating to private water wells, approvals concerning herbicide use by cottage owners to control aquatic plant life, remediation of contaminated lands, land development and associated sewage works, haulage of septic waste and air quality including the control of emissions.

ORDERS

The Act provides for various types of orders that can be invoked by either the Minister or the Director of the MOE. Five types of orders most directly impact real estate practitioners.

Remedial Order	The MOE can require a party (including a corporation) to remedy a situation in which a discharge is involved.
Preventative Order	The MOE can require a party (including a corporation) to take preventative measures; e.g., equipment, personnel and monitoring apparatus.
Waste Removal Order	The MOE can require a party (including a corporation) to remove hazardous waste from a site.
Control Order	The MOE can require a party (including a corporation) to control or eliminate the source of pollution.
Stop Order	The MOE can require a party (including a corporation) to stop the discharge of a contaminant that is an immediate threat to human health or life.

The range of parties (individuals and corporations) subject to orders can vary considerably; e.g., former owners, persons in possession, present owners or personnel managing, in control or in charge. If an administrative order is not followed, the MOE can undertake the work and charge the costs back (referred to as a cost recovery order) to the person originally receiving the order. The *Environment Protection Act* should be consulted directly for detailed information and procedures.

SPILLS

Part X of the EPA, enacted in the mid-1980s (often referred to as the spills bill), introduced the concept of no fault liability; i.e., liability regardless of negligence or fault. Liability for spills rests with those who had ownership or control of the pollutants at the time of the spill, even where these individuals had not caused or participated in the spill themselves. If an individual in control is unable, unwilling or unlocated, the Ministry will take over and seek compensation for work completed. The individual responsible has strict liability to injured third parties in regard to spills.

For real estate purposes, environmental issues surrounding spills normally focus on soil or water pollution. This portion of the Act has important ramifications particularly for industrial or commercial lands that involve the use of hazardous substances. Regulatory issues concerning spills go beyond the normal scope of real estate activities, however, practitioners should exercise appropriate caution in the listing and selling of such properties and seek expert advice as required.

Environmental Protection: Land Use

The provincial government advances sound environmental planning in many aspects of land use and development. Three significant initiatives involving the protection of environmentally sensitive and agricultural lands in this province are highlighted in this chapter. Specialized environmental legislation impacting specific marketplaces and property types (e.g., hazardous materials in residential and commercial properties, redevelopment of brownfields, underground storage tanks, recreational property restrictions and farm practices concerning nutrient management) are covered in *The Residential Real Estate Transaction* and *The Commercial Real Estate Transaction*.

THE GREENBELT

The *Greenbelt Act, 2005* established a greenbelt area protecting about 1.8 million acres (723,400 hectares) of environmentally sensitive and agricultural land in the Golden Horseshoe. This legislation significantly impacts both residential and commercial developments within the defined boundaries of the Greenbelt Plan. This plan, which includes the Niagara Escarpment Plan and the Oak Ridges Moraine Conservation Plan (see subsequent discussions), calls for the following three broad categories of protected countryside.

ENVIRONMENTALLY SENSITIVE LAND	PRIME AGRICULTURAL LAND/ SPECIALTY CROP	RURAL AREAS
Excluded uses include residential subdivisions, commercial activity and industrial/manufacturing plants.	Agricultural land protected for agriculture and supporting agri-related businesses.	Towns and villages may expand boundaries every 10 years subject to available water/sewer services. Recreational, leisure and tourism uses are permitted.

The objectives of the Greenbelt Plan are:

- To establish a network of countryside and open space areas which supports the Oak Ridges Moraine and the Niagara Escarpment;
- To sustain the countryside, rural and small towns and contribute to the economic viability of farming communities;
- To preserve agricultural land as a continuing commercial source of food and employment;
- To recognize the critical importance of the agriculture sector to the regional economy;
- To provide protection to the land base needed to maintain, restore and improve the ecological and hydrological functions of the Greenbelt Area;
- To promote connections between lakes and the Oak Ridges Moraine and Niagara Escarpment;
- To provide open space and recreational, tourism and cultural heritage opportunities to support the social needs of a rapidly expanding and increasingly urbanized population;
- To promote linkages between ecosystems and provincial parks or public lands;
- To control urbanization of the lands to which the Greenbelt Plan applies;
- To ensure that the development of transportation and infrastructure proceeds in an environmentally sensitive manner; and
- To promote sustainable resource use.

Source: Greenbelt Act, 2005, Sec. 5

Practitioners listing and selling property within identified areas, particularly those involved with land development projects, should seek appropriate guidance from the Ministry of Municipal Affairs and Housing and the local municipality.

Greenbelt Plan Area

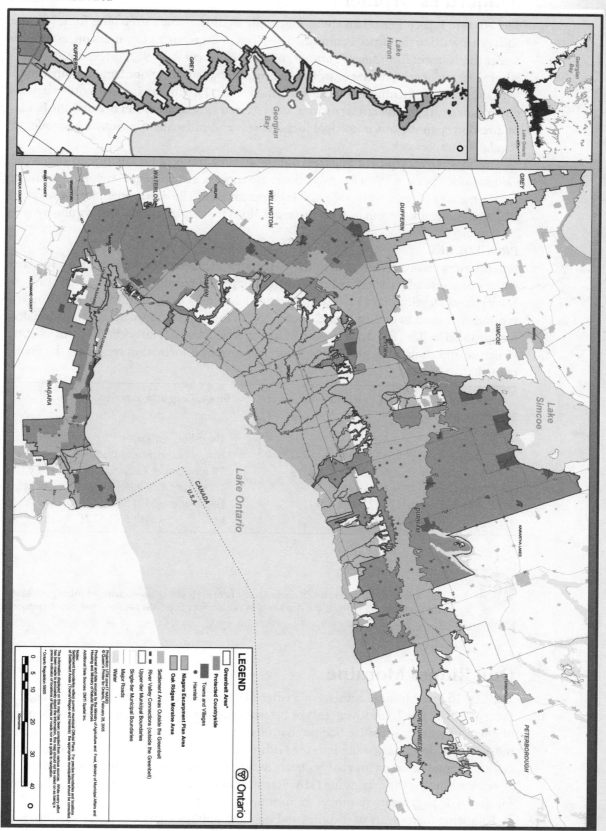

PLANNING AND LAND USE   **SECTION II**

Niagara Escarpment

The Niagara Escarpment is an environmentally significant area stretching from Niagara Falls northward to the Bruce Peninsula. The Niagara Escarpment Commission, established under the *Niagara Escarpment Planning and Development Act,* 1973, is responsible for administering development control and ensuring that any development is compatible with the natural environment in the identified territory. This area, as with other large environmentally significant territories, has received special attention because the lands in question span various municipal jurisdictions and consequently require a broader regulatory framework.

The Niagara Escarpment Plan sets out the specific limits of jurisdiction in which the Commission operates. With few exceptions, the Niagara Escarpment Development Control Area is the area covered by the Niagara Escarpment Plan. The development control concept is actually a flexible system of land-use regulations that replace municipal zoning by-laws.

PROCEDURES

Practitioners involved with land in the Niagara Escarpment Development Control Area should be aware of basic procedures. Any development requires a permit (Niagara Escarpment Development Permit Application) issued by the Commission. A permit is typically required to build a house, cottage, or an industrial, commercial, recreational, or institutional building, change the use of a property, construct an addition to an existing structure and change the grading of a site. For current information regarding the Plan, contact:

For County of Dufferin, City of Hamilton and Regional Municipalities of Halton, Peel and Niagara:	For Bruce, Grey and Simcoe Counties:
Georgetown Office 232 Guelph Street Georgetown, ON L7G 4B1 Telephone: (905) 877-5191 Fax: (905) 873-7452	Thornbury Office Niagara Escarpment Commission 99 King Street East, Thornbury, ON N0H 2P0 Telephone: (519) 599-3340 Fax: (519) 599-6326

WEB LINKS

For more information, access the Niagara Escarpment web site at *www.escarpment.org*. Detailed procedures regarding permits are described in the booklet titled *Do I Need a Niagara Escarpment Permit?*

Oak Ridges Moraine

The Oak Ridges Moraine consists of a ridge of sandy hills, stretching from the Niagara Escarpment to the Trent River (east of Peterborough) and includes a 160-kilometre tract of environmentally-sensitive habitat that serves as the source of numerous headwaters, most notably streams flowing into the Greater Toronto Area (GTA). Development and environmental interests inevitably clash given that 65% of the moraine is situated in close proximity to the expanding GTA. To compound matters, the moraine has abundant, much-needed aggregate resources to meet urban growth demands.

Following many years of disputes and ongoing public debate, the *Oak Ridges Moraine Protection Act, 2001*, received royal assent on May 29, 2001. This statute effectively froze

SECTION II

development in the moraine for six months pending the development of a comprehensive, long term plan. On December 14, 2001, the *Oak Ridges Moraine Conservation Act* received royal assent followed by the creation of a regulation titled The Oak Ridges Moraine Conservation Plan.

The comprehensive provincial plan is intended to protect the moraine in perpetuity, including all natural and water resource features, agricultural land preservation and to focus development within approved settlement areas. Coincident with the plan, the government announced the resolution of various development applications relating to sites within the moraine. Through land donations and land exchanges for other development properties, many acres of sensitive land are being secured for protection of natural areas.

Practitioners listing and selling property impacted by the Oak Ridges Moraine Conservation Plan should exercise caution given legislative restrictions imposed and be generally aware of such restrictions. For additional information, contact the local municipality and/or the Ministry of Municipal Affairs and Housing.

KNOWLEDGE INTEGRATION

Notables

- Zoning is the primary land use control method utilized at the Ontario municipal level. Flexibility is achieved through various methods including minor variances, non-conforming uses, non-conforming structures and site-specific exemptions.

- Site plan control agreements typically impact building design and site amenities, over and above restrictions imposed by zoning by-law requirements and building code standards.

- The Ontario Building Code regulates building standards by establishing minimum provisions for safety and structural sufficiency.

- Municipalities issue and collect fees for various permits, the most relevant for practitioners are the building permit (sometimes referred to as the construction permit) and the occupancy permit.

- The Ontario Fire Code provides for occupant safety in existing buildings. Fire and safety provisions for new construction are found in the Ontario Building Code.

- Caution is advised on all matters concerning accessory apartments. Contact the local municipality for guidance.

- Conservation authorities take a lead role in watercourse controls through regulated land (flood plain) administration.

- Practitioners should consult local municipal officials concerning water control roles and responsibilities. The local municipality, the conservation authority and various ministries are involved.

- Environmental controls are generally provincial in nature with primary responsibility resting with the Ministry of the Environment who may issue orders affecting property owners to prevent, remediate or stop pollution.

- Broad-based environmental land use plans are highlighted in this chapter with detailed discussions impacting specific types of property provided in *The Residential Real Estate Transaction* and *The Commercial Real Estate Transaction*.

Glossary

Accessory Apartment

Areas of Natural and
    Scientific Interest

Building Inspector

Building Permit

*Canadian Environmental
    Protection Act*

Conservation Authority

Conservation Land Tax
    Incentive Program

Environmental Protection Act

Flood Plain

Flood Proofing

Minor Variances

Non-Conforming Structure

Non-Conforming Use

Occupancy Permit

One Zone Flood Plain

Ontario Building Code

Ontario Fire Code

Order

Riparian Rights

Site Plan Control Agreement

Site Plan Control Area

Site-Specific Exemptions

Two Zone Flood Plain

Wetland

Zoning By-law

Zoning Classification

Web Links

Web links are included for general interest regarding selected chapter topics.

Ontario Building Code Go to *www.obc.mah.gov.on.ca* for information on how to obtain copies of Building Code publications, recent Code developments and related information concerning how the Ministry of Municipal Affairs and Housing works with municipalities in the ongoing enforcement of the Code.

Ontario Fire Code The Office of the Fire Marshal of Ontario provides detailed information concerning fire-related topics and applicable legislation including the Ontario Fire Code. Go to *www.ofm.gov.on.ca*.

Conservation Authorities For additional information and the specific authority within particular areas of Ontario, go to *www.conservation-ontario.on.ca*.

Ministry of Natural Resources The Ministry of Natural Resources is involved in various aspects of environmental control within the province. For information concerning its activities, go to *www.mnr.gov.on.ca*.

Niagara Escarpment Access the Niagara Escarpment web site at *www.escarpment.org* for more information. Detailed procedures regarding permits are described in the booklet titled *Do I Need a Niagara Escarpment Permit?*

Strategic Thinking For Your Career

Questions are included to assist in developing your new career. No answers are provided.

1. What local zoning information and mapping are available that will assist in my listing and selling activities?

2. What specific procedures are followed regarding site plan control agreements in the local marketplace?

3. What procedures are in place locally for issuing building permits?

4. What information is available at the local municipality to assist me in dealing with accessory apartments in resale homes?

5. Are flood plain maps available to purchase and where is the local conservation authority located that regulates flood areas in my marketplace?

Chapter Mini-Review

Solutions are located in the Appendix.

1. Minimum setbacks and building coverages are most commonly found in a zoning by-law.

    ◯ True   ◯ False

2. Requirements concerning non-conforming structures and non-conforming uses are outlined in the Ontario Building Code.

    ◯ True   ◯ False

3. An inspector is permitted to enter onto the lands subject to a building permit at reasonable times for inspections.

    ◯ True   ◯ False

4. The Ontario Fire Code applies only to new residential construction.

    ◯ True   ◯ False

5. A regulated area, for purposes of a conservation authority, can be generally described as lands adjacent to a watercourse that require special attention owing to various matters including the potential for flooding.

    ◯ True   ◯ False

6. Flood proofing can be described as either active or passive.

    ◯ True   ◯ False

7. A two-zone flood plain is sometimes used when certain parts of the flood plain are considered less hazardous and development is possible subject to conditions.

    ◯ True   ◯ False

8. Wetlands may be eligible for the Conservation Land Tax Incentive Program.

    ◯ True   ◯ False

9. The *Environmental Protection Act* (EPA) is a federal statute administered by the Ministry of Fisheries and Oceans.

    ◯ True   ◯ False

10. The *Greenbelt Act* protects environmentally sensitive land in Northern Ontario.

    ◯ True   ◯ False

11. A permit is usually required to build a house within rural areas that are part of the Niagara Escarpment Development Control Area.

    ◯ True   ◯ False

12. The Oak Ridges Moraine is a low-lying wetland located near Peterborough.

    ◯ True   ◯ False

Active Learning Exercises

Solutions are located in the Appendix.

■ **Exercise 1   Land Use Restrictions and Codes (Fill-in-the-Blanks)**

1.1   The _____ has authority regarding permission to dump fill within a regulated area.

1.2   The continued lawful use of a building that existed prior to an adoption of a local zoning by-law is referred to as a (an) _____ .

1.3   The _____ addresses, among other things, retrofit standards for occupancy of various building types including accessory apartments.

1.4   A regulated area in which the entire flood plain is considered to be a floodway is called a _____ .

1.5   Responsibility for inspecting a new residential structure within a municipality falls to inspectors operating under the _____ .

1.6   A fire that involves grease or flammable liquids is classified as a Class _____ Fire.

1.7   One of the main objectives underlying a (an) _____ is to ensure that adjacent lands have compatible uses.

1.8   Owners of eligible conservation land may receive a (an) _____ under a program administered by the Ministry of Natural Resources.

1.9   Land identified for a future use that can be subsequently amended within a zoning by-law is commonly referred to as a (an) _____ provision.

1.10   The conservation authority uses a period of [...........] years in assessing flooding hazards along waterways.

1.11   The *Greenbelt Act* protects approximately 1.8 million acres of environmentally sensitive land and also prime [...........................] .

1.12   Protection of fish habitat is primarily the responsibility of the provincial Ministry of [...........................] .

■ Exercise 2   Matching

Match the description in the left column with the appropriate phrase/word in the right column (not all phrases/words are used).

____	Temporary Use Provision	*a.* Ontario Fire Code
____	Preventative Order	*b.* Entrance Permit
____	Part 9: Retrofit	*c.* Ministry of the Environment
____	Grade Requirements and Sight Distances	*d.* Watershed
____	Land Draining into a Stream or River	*e.* Greenbelt Act
____	Withstand Passage of Flame	*f.* Zoning By-Law
____	Canadian Environmental Protection Act	*g.* Federal Legislation
		h. Fire Resistance Rating
		i. Oak Ridges Moraine

SECTION II   PLANNING AND LAND USE

■ Exercise 3   The Smith Property in Northside

Buyer Smith is contemplating a vacant land purchase on a county road zoned RR1 in Northside. The lot measures 40 metres (frontage) x 60 metres (depth). Zoning information for the Township of Northside is illustrated below:

ZONING BY-LAWS FOR THE TOWNSHIP OF NORTHSIDE

Section 4.4—Rural Residential 1
Permitted Uses

No person shall within a Rural Residential 1 (RR1) zone use any land or erect, alter or use any building or structure except as specified hereunder.

a.	Minimum Lot Area Requirement:	2,320 square metres
b.	Minimum Lot Frontage Requirement:	38 metres
c.	Minimum Yard Requirements:	
	i) Front Yard	10 metres
	ii) Side Yard	10 metres
	iii) Rear Yard	10 metres
d.	Minimum Dwelling Unit Area Requirement:	100 square metres
e.	Maximum Lot Coverage: (All buildings and structures)	15 percent
f.	Minimum Setback from Street Centreline:	
	i) County Road	23 metres
	ii) Township Road	20 metres
g.	Minimum Landscaped Open Space Requirement	30 percent

Based on the zoning information illustrated, complete the following:

3.1   Does the 40 metre frontage x 60 metre depth meet minimum zoning standards?

3.2   What is the maximum house size (including all outbuildings) permitted on the lot?

3.3   Based on the requirements, draw the outline of a bungalow on the diagram provided that comprises 245 square metres of total living area and an attached garage (63 square metres) to correctly fit on the property, while meeting all the zoning requirements. Once the diagram is completed, insert all necessary measurements to illustrate that the shape selected complies with prescribed setbacks. Assume that the county road allowance at the front of the property is 66 feet.

NOTE: 66 × .3048 = 20.12 m (use 20 metres for approximate width of road allowance).

County Road

3.4   Could Smith build a storage/workshop measuring 8m x 6m? If so, place the structure on the diagram noting prescribed setbacks.

■ Exercise 4   The Severed Property

This exercise consolidates learning based on topics addressed in both Chapter 4 and Chapter 5.

Jones lists his home in the Township of Northside with ABC Realty Inc. and Mr. and Mrs. Williams appear interested. Jones originally owned two acres, but severed ½ acre for his daughter three years ago. He intends to sever another lot, coincident with the sale, leaving the listed property with the remaining 120 foot frontage x 200 foot depth. A reference plan has been completed for the planned severance. The property is zoned Rural Residential 1 as described in Exercise 3.

Two other circumstances are noteworthy. First, a small lower level accessory apartment is rented to students. Secondly, an outbuilding used for a small motor repair business (lawnmowers and outboard motors) is directly behind the house. You are confident that Williams will want to continue this business.

Identify and describe four major issues that you should consider as the selling salesperson. Reference legislative, zoning compliance, fire code and building code matters.

■ Exercise 5   The Accessory Apartment

Buyer Jefferson recently acquired an Anycity bungalow which included an existing accessory basement apartment, occupied until a few weeks prior to closing. Jefferson wants to re-rent the vacant unit, but this may prove awkward as the tenants must access the unit through the main level kitchen.

This exercise is included for instructional purposes only. Extreme caution is advised in all matters concerning accessory apartments. Contact the local municipality for specific requirements involving existing and new residential structures, as requirements vary. Seek appropriate expert advice as needed.

5.1   Briefly detail primary issues that should be of concern to Jefferson from the perspective of zoning by-laws, the building code, the fire code and electrical safety.

5.2   Jefferson calls following the inspection saying that the fire department has noted certain deficiencies in the property and remedial action is necessary:

- a 30 minute fire resistant rating for the fire separation wall between the accessory apartment and adjoining rooms is required;
- two means of egress are required (only one exists at present); the existing egress must not be shared and both means of egress must have proper exits; and
- any exits to adjoining rooms require closures (45 mm solid core wood).

Explain in your own words what the fire department specifically requires.

SECTION III

STRUCTURAL TYPES AND COMPONENTS

The average salesperson is not expected to possess the knowledge of a builder or engineer. However, practitioners should have sufficient understanding of basic structural designs and construction components/materials. Keep in mind, however, that expert advice should always be sought regarding such matters.

Building component knowledge, in particular, has become increasingly important given buyer representation. The buyer representative has a fiduciary duty to promote the client's best interests and building deficiencies can understandably be a focal concern. Buyers want to make informed decisions. The fact that a roof has a predictable life expectancy or that leaks often occur at certain vulnerable points in the roof can be valid and relevant discussion points. Salespeople may encounter basements where leakage or dampness is present and knowledge of typical contributing factors may be of assistance.

While ultimate responsibility rests with the buyer or other professionals relied upon in the home buying process, a sound knowledge in basic housing components can prove invaluable in a real estate career.

CHAPTER 6

Structures and Components

Introduction

Chapter 6 describes major types of residential and commercial structures found in Ontario. Various illustrations are provided including structures from differing time periods. Commercial structures included are based on common structural configurations found in the marketplace, while acknowledging that many specialized designs exist given the variety of intended uses.

Illustrations are accompanied by basic descriptions of each structural type. Design information is limited to basic details only. Students are encouraged to pursue advanced courses in exterior designs and trends in Ontario architectural styles to augment information provided in this introductory course.

This chapter also highlights major structural components contained in residential housing. Some components also apply to certain commercial structures. Students pursuing a career in commercial sales will find additional details on such construction components as sprinkler systems, loading docks, floor loads and HVAC (heating, ventilation and air conditioning) in *The Commercial Real Estate Transaction*.

Chapter topics are centred on structural integrity considerations with particular emphasis on footings, foundation, wall systems and roofing. Particular emphasis is placed on drainage and damp-proofing issues when discussing the foundation. Students will also analyze floor systems including associated components such as beams, joists, bridging/blocking and subfloors. Framing techniques (platform and balloon framing) are highlighted including structural components in wood frame walls. Additional information concerning exterior walls, roofing materials and other finishings are contained in a subsequent chapter.

Learning Outcomes

At the conclusion of this chapter, students will be able to:

- Identify various residential detached and attached structures commonly found in the Ontario marketplace.
- Identify and differentiate between common residential detached structures including bungalows, one and one-half storey, two storey and split level homes.
- Identify and differentiate between common residential attached structures including semi-detached, town (row) houses and multi-family.
- Identify and differentiate between various commercial industrial structures broadly grouped under office, retail, industrial and agricultural classifications.
- Describe major components of a foundation, a floor system and a wall system in a residential structure.
- Discuss key issues concerning basement leakage including damp-proofing methods and proper drainage techniques.
- Describe major components of floor and framing systems.
- Describe major components of a roof system in a residential structure.
- Apply knowledge of foundations, floors, walls and roofs to identify selected current or potential flaws in residential structures.
- Identify and describe non-structural issues that can affect wood-structured buildings.

RESIDENTIAL STRUCTURES—DETACHED

Residential structures can be broadly grouped by category. For descriptive purposes, this chapter classifies residential structures in terms of single-family detached and attached homes. A detached home typically refers to a residential structure on a specific plot of land, whereas attached homes range from semi-detached (commonly built in the 1970's and 1980's) to various forms of townhomes and other multi-unit residential properties (e.g., high rise structures).

Residential condominium does provide certain complications given the fact that the owner has title to a unit, but shares the common elements with other owners within the condominium corporation. For example, a condominium may initially appear to be a single-family detached home but, in fact, the owner holds title only to the structure (the unit) with the land held as a common element owned by all unit owners. Of course, the land immediately adjacent to the structure may be an exclusive use common area (i.e., available for the exclusive use of that unit owner). Additional discussion of condominium, as well as rental properties, are addressed in *The Residential Real Estate Transaction* and *The Commercial Real Estate Transaction*.

Bungalows

The bungalow has traditionally been a highly popular housing style given the lack of stairways with the primary living area contained on one floor. The bungalow design in Ontario dates from the early 1900's, but gained its greatest popularity during the post-war years of the late 1940's.

Bungalows remain popular, particularly for empty nesters, but 2 storey houses now dominate the residential market in most urban areas given high land costs and the ability to maximize living area on two or more floors on the same lot size. Given that the cost of the land, foundation and roof represent a sizeable component of total housing cost, the addition of a second floor is a relatively small additional cost to gain significant size advantages.

VARIATION: RANCH STYLE

The bungalow has proven highly adaptable to consumer needs over the years. The ranch style bungalow offered extensive space typically with an attached double garage. These extended bungalows often contained 2000 square feet or more on one floor. A side benefit was an extremely large basement for additional living and entertainment rooms, and storage areas.

During the past few decades, the ranch bungalow has all but disappeared from new urban construction projects given the large lot sizes required with the two-storey representing a far more efficient use of land. However, variations on ranch bungalows are still popular in rural areas where large lots are more readily available.

VARIATION: BI-LEVEL/SPLIT ENTRANCE

The bi-level or split entrance bungalow gained popularity in the 1970's as consumers wanted to make more effective use of lower basement areas. The typical split entrance bungalow has the front door foyer located as a 'split level' between the upper main areas and the lower area. As such, the basement area is higher than the traditional bungalow allowing for larger windows for greater sunlight access and ventilation.

Bungalow Circa 1960

Bungalow Circa 1970

Ranch Style Bungalow Circa 1970–1980

Bungalow Circa 2000

Bi-Level (Split Entrance) Bungalow Circa 2000

One and One-Half Storey

The one and one-half storey was particularly attractive during the post war years (1940 and 1950) and the baby boom. Typically, about 60% of the total living area is contained on the first floor. From a cost perspective, this style is more cost effective than the bungalow, by providing more square footage on the same building coverage (or foot print) on the land.

The one and one-half storey provides a high pitched roof for additional living area. Dormers were added as the design became more popular emulating the Cape Cod design popularized in the north eastern United States. Both one and one-half storey and Cape Cod designs remain popular.

One and One-Half Story Circa 1950

One and One-Half Storey With Dormers Circa 1960

One and One-Half Storey With Modified Dormer Circa 2000

One and One-Half Storey—Cape Cod Circa 1990

One and One-Half Storey—Cape Cod Circa 2000

SECTION III   STRUCTURAL TYPES AND COMPONENTS

Two-Storey

The two-storey home has been the most popular design of choice during the 1980's to the present time. This plan provides an attractive blend of large living area combined with a separate level for sleeping areas. Unlike the one and one-half storey, rooms on the upper level do not have the angled ceilings on the upper level and can be very spacious. Two storey designs in the marketplace offer tremendous variety in terms of exterior shape, roof design and floor layouts. A few of many possibilities are highlighted.

Two-Storey Circa 1960

Two-Storey Circa 1980

Two-Storey Circa 1990

Two-Storey Circa 2000

Split Level

The split level home, a variation on the bungalow, split entrance bungalow and the two-storey, attempts to provide ease of movement from one area of the home to another with minimal steps. Split levels were first introduced in the 1960's and gained their widest popularity during the 1970's and early 1980's. The most common split levels built at that time were the side split and the back split.

Side and back splits can involve three or more levels of living area depending on size; e.g., lower family room, main level living room, dining room and kitchen, and upper level bedrooms. Elaborate split level homes can typically involve as many as five levels. Proponents point to the ease of accessing different levels (few stairs between levels). Critics argue that stairs are everywhere, thus impacting ease of movement from various levels in the house.

Side Split Circa 1960

Side Split Circa 1970–1980

Back Split Circa 1970–1980

Back Split Circa 2000

Back Split (Variation) Circa 2000

SECTION III   STRUCTURAL TYPES AND COMPONENTS

Specialty Homes

Creative design is uppermost for many Ontario homes. Builders achieve a distinctive flair through the use of creative roof slopes and pitches, along with unique front elevations and window designs. Two examples are provided for illustration purposes only.

Two and One-Half Storey with Tudor Design

One and One-Half Storey with Stone/Shake Features

RESIDENTIAL STRUCTURES—ATTACHED

Attached homes have gained popularity in Ontario, undoubtedly driven in part by price considerations given the rising cost of detached homes on individual lots. Attached homes have two primary advantages from a cost savings point of view. First, they share one or more common (party) walls which reduces overall building cost and, secondly, higher densities can be achieved than with detached homes on specific plots of land. An added factor in the growing popularity of attached homes is the aging Ontario population in which empty nesters seek out smaller living quarters.

Semi-Detached

Semi-detached homes gained popularity in England many years ago (as did row housing) in order to meet housing needs on limited land areas. Semi-detached (units side-by-side having a common party wall) have proven popular over the past forty years as they provide many features associated with detached homes (i.e., size and individual title to the land) while offering certain price advantages, particularly for young families.

Semi-Detached Circa 1970–1980

Semi-Detached Circa 1970–1980

Semi-Detached Circa 2000

Town (Row) Houses

Row housing has also become a popular alternative in which three or more units are joined together by common party walls. Each town house unit typically contains a full basement, main level living area and upper level for bedrooms. Many variations exist in the marketplace. Town houses are attractive from a developer's perspective given higher densities available. Two examples are illustrated. Town houses are normally grouped in sets of three to six units.

Town houses are either offered as freehold (the owner holds title to the structure and the land) or condominium (the unit owner owns the structure as defined in the condominium documentation) and shares the land as a common element with other unit owners.

Town (Row) House Circa 2000

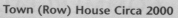

Town (Row) House Circa 2000

Multi-Family

Many variations of multi-family exist in today's marketplace ranging from low density walk-up units to mid (4 storey to 12 storey) and high rise (more than 12 stories buildings). Various examples are included for illustration purposes.

Duplex Circa 1970–1980

Triplex Circa 1970–1980

Mid-Rise Circa 1980

High Rise Circa 2000

COMMERCIAL/INDUSTRIAL

Office

Commercial office buildings can range from free-standing small offices and retail operations to low and high rise office complexes. Office parks with attractive office suites are typically found in suburban areas on one or two floor buildings with landscaped areas. These facilities are often targeted to professional tenants. Further, many commercial buildings are classified as mixed use in which office, retail and/or residential are combined in one complex.

Mid Rise Office Building

High Rise Office Building

Office Park

Retail

Retail commercial operations also range from single, standalone buildings and groupings of retail stores on a downtown street to neighbourhood malls and large indoor shopping centres that serve local and or regional markets. In recent years, big box stores and outlet malls have also gained prominence.

In addition to retail stores, many service type businesses operate that do not fall directly under retail, but represent a significant commercial market. For example, professional medical and dental businesses often locate in free-standing buildings. Other service-related businesses between commercial retail operations and industrial groupings include such activities as heating/air conditioning services, parts/supply operations and repair facilities.

Neighbourhood Mall

Community/Regional Shopping Centre

Outlet Stores

Industrial

Industrial structures can be broadly grouped under three categories. General purpose buildings offer features and facilities for a wide range of operations. Special purpose buildings offer selected features (e.g., a custom built manufacturing plant or a distribution centre with numerous loading docks) but could be used for alternative purposes. Lastly, single purpose buildings are designed for a specific use with little or no potential for conversion to other purposes.

General Purpose

Single Purpose

Special Purpose

Agricultural

The agri-business is a significant component in the provincial economic picture. Large scale farm operations require special purpose buildings for livestock and crops. Ontario boasts a rich diversity in crop production ranging from cereal crops to tender fruit, vegetable and greenhouse/nursery crops.

Farm Buildings and Silos

Agri-Business

STRUCTURAL COMPONENTS

The safety and usability of a building relies on structural integrity. The structure is the skeleton, including the foundations and footings as well as the floors, walls and roof. Structures are evaluated based on their stability.

Since many components are buried below grade or behind finishes, structural inspection is necessarily performed by looking for resultant movement. Where no movement has occurred, structural imperfections may well go undetected. Also, new interior and exterior finishes and patching work may conceal imperfections over the short term. In such instances, identification of problems is often impossible.

Regardless, real estate salespeople require an understanding of such components. Through a knowledge of basic structures, practitioners can be more aware of potential problems and external indicators that might point to less than obvious defects.

ROOF
- Transfers Roof Loads to Rafters, Trusses and Joists
- Ultimately Transfers Loads to Bearing Walls and Framing
- Roof Covering Protects the Roof Sheathing

FRAMING/FLOORS
- Balloon or Platform Construction
- Floor Provides Continuous Pad for Framing

WALLS
- Carry Weight of Roof and Floors to the Foundation
- Wall Structure Varies Based on Type of Framing

FOOTINGS/FOUNDATION
- Transmits the Weight of the Structure to the Soil

NOTE: Salespeople are cautioned not to make representations, but rather refer consumers to appropriate experts.

Footing

The **footing** is identified as a widened section, usually concrete, at the base or bottom of a **foundation** wall, pier or column. The footing transmits the weight of the structure to the soil, without allowing the structure to sink. Footings are typically 16 to 24 inches wide and 6 to 16 inches thick. Generally, the heavier the building and the weaker the soil, the larger the footing required.

When the footings fail, the entire structure moves causing a situation that can be expensive and sometimes impossible to correct. Since the footings are located below grade and under the basement floor, the cause of the failure is often difficult to ascertain. The failure may be restricted to a single area and not be uniform below the entire structure. Consequently, the building may not sink straight down but rather lean to one side or another. Frequently, one part of the structure will pull away from the rest, leading to cracking of interior and exterior wall surfaces. The illustration provided demonstrates the distribution of load from beams and joists down to wall and column footings.

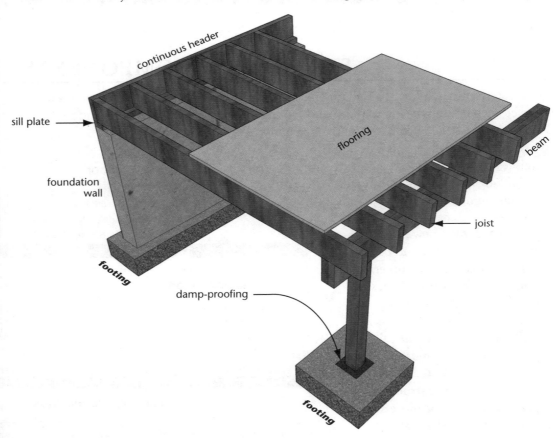

Foundation

The foundation, the base upon which a structure is built, has three basic functions.

- To transmit the weight of the structure from the above-grade walls and floors down to the footings.
- To resist the lateral pressure of the soil on the outside of the basement and act as a retaining wall.
- To carry the weight of the structure below the frost line to prevent frost heaving.

Typical materials include stone, brick, poured concrete, concrete block, cinder block, clay tile and wood. Most of these materials behave in similar fashion, with wood foundations being the exception.

POTENTIAL PROBLEM AREAS

Practitioners should be aware of certain problems that can arise with foundations. Foundations that do not provide enough lateral support will deflect inwards. This can be a result of:

- Mechanical forces exerted during backfilling;
- Backfilling with frozen soil;
- Unusual frost development in the soil immediately outside the building;
- Foundation walls that are too thin or do not have adequate reinforcement; or
- The floor system does not provide adequate bracing for the top of the foundation wall.

This last problem is common on the high side wall on a sloping lot. Both unit masonry walls and poured concrete walls can fail if not properly built.

Foundation walls that move inward can be repaired by tying them back from the outside, using ties and anchors common in conventional retaining wall construction. Alternatively, buttresses can be provided on the interior that often consist of concrete or concrete block structures built against basement walls. A third choice is to build a new foundation wall inside the old. Occasionally, replacing the foundation is necessary. Fortunately, many innovative products are now available for insulating and damp-proofing foundations.

Foundation Innovations   FOCUS

Foundations have traditionally been constructed with poured concrete or concrete block. Polystyrene building components have been recently added resulting in a stronger, more energy efficient basement wall system.

These systems, typically referred to as insulated concrete forms (ICFs), provide a permanent interlocking interior/ exterior form into which the concrete is poured. Such systems can extend beyond basements to replace all exterior walls currently using traditional wood framing systems.

Proponents point to ease of use, added insulation value, increased damp-proofing and fire hazard reduction (as compared to traditional framing). Opponents focus on high labour costs in assembling numerous interlocking forms and shipping/storage expense (as opposed to traditional form boards which are reused).

WOOD FOUNDATION

Wood foundations were introduced in the early 1960's. The life expectancies of below grade wood foundations are estimated in the 50 to 100-year range, considerably less than many traditional building foundation materials. Some manufacturers offer 60-year limited warranties. The wood is chemically treated to retard rot. Chemical treatment for wood used in foundations is more intensive than that typically used in wood for decks and fencing.

Wood foundations may rest on concrete. Special care must be taken to ensure that the foundation can perform its retaining wall function (adequately resisting lateral forces) as it is not known whether rot and termites will become a major problem. If this were to occur, masonry or poured concrete foundations could be retrofitted.

WALL CONSTRUCTION

Basement walls are normally built using poured concrete or concrete block, however, insulated variations have been introduced in the marketplace to address potential damp-

ness problems while also increasing insulation values. The walls are the load-bearing component of the structure and transfer the weight of the roof and floors down to the footing. Building codes set out requirements concerning damp-proofing and water-proofing of exterior walls below ground level (or any slab in contact with the ground).

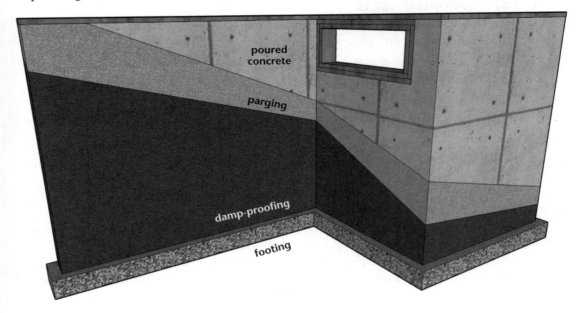

poured concrete

parging

damp-proofing

footing

INSULATION

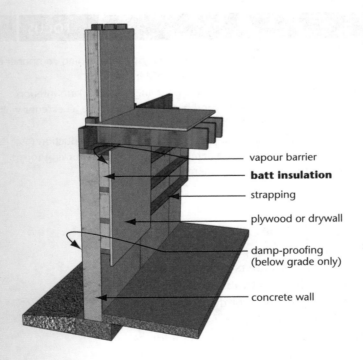

vapour barrier

batt insulation

strapping

plywood or drywall

damp-proofing (below grade only)

concrete wall

The typical insulated wall consists of below grade damp-proofing, batt insulation, a vapour barrier and a finished interior wall usually consisting of drywall or panelling.

Building codes establish insulation requirements for basement walls in new homes. Insulation in older homes is relatively inexpensive, easy to do and cost effective, but certain risks exist. If the basement has chronic moisture areas, correction of the external problem must be completed. Second, interior insulation could cause frost damage to the foundation walls, as the walls will be significantly colder after installing the insulation. Third, obstructions such as electrical panels and plumbing must be accommodated. An illustration is provided depicting a typical, poured concrete insulated basement wall including a vapour barrier and possible finishings; e.g., plywood or drywall.

CONCRETE FLOOR
In residential construction, these floors are usually not structural but rather rest on the ground. Modern building practices use three-inch thick slabs, although older ones can be as thin as two inches. Building codes set out requirements concerning slabs-on-ground in

regard to the amount of granular fill required, sloping of floor surface to accommodate floor drains, thickness and compression strength. Floor systems used for structural purposes; e.g., multi-level concrete building, fall under building code design requirements that detail sufficient structural capacity and integrity to effectively and safely carry specified dead and live loads.

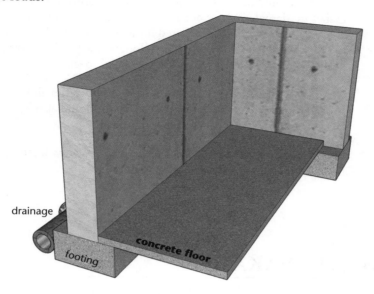

drainage

footing

concrete floor

Posts/Columns

A post (often referred to as a column) is a structural component to carry the load of a beam vertically down to the footings. Occasionally, a post or column is introduced to carry a concentrated load (a large piano, for example) straight down to the footings without benefit of a beam. Typical materials include brick, concrete block, poured concrete, wood or steel. Every post or column should have a footing, typically concrete.

Practitioners should be aware of various problems that can arise in the use of posts/columns.

Moisture	Masonry posts may deteriorate due to moisture or poor mortar. Rising dampness, a common problem with brick columns, is characterized by deteriorated mortar and efflorescence (white salty deposits) on the bottom of the post.
Out of Plumb	Posts that are built (or have been pushed) out of plumb lose their strength. Generally, if the amount by which the column or post is out of plumb approaches one-third of the thickness of the column, structural integrity may be a concern.
Rust	A serious problem, often found in a chronically flooding basement, which will quickly reduce the load-carrying capacity of a steel post.
Footing	A sinking post is usually the result of an absent or inadequately-sized footing.

Undersized	Column collapse is unusual, but is normally the result of an undersized column or one that has suffered mechanical damage. A brick column should be at least 12 inches by 12 inches or 10 inches by 15 inches. Rectangular concrete columns should be at least 8 inches by 8 inches. Circular concrete columns should be no less than 9 inches in diameter. Steel posts are 3 inches in diameter under normal circumstances. A top and bottom plate at least 4 inches square is required if the beam is wood. With a steel beam, the four-inch plate is not needed, as long as the post is secured to the beam. Consult building codes for provincial specifics.
Secured to Beam	A post that is not well secured to the beam above can allow the structure to shift during wind uplift forces. The beam should also be supported laterally to prevent it from moving sideways.
Fire	Fire will damage wood and steel posts. A steel post will fail much earlier than a solid wood post, although it will not burn.

BASEMENT LEAKAGE

Building codes set out requirements for structural components, including basements, to ensure sufficient structural capacity and integrity that will effectively handle anticipated loads and influences. Most building codes specifically refer to the foundation. Generally, the foundation is intended to be sufficiently strong so that failure will occur first in the superstructure, unless the design of a particular building provides otherwise.

Basement leakage is an issue routinely addressed by real estate practitioners, as this problem is often found at some point in the life of a basement. In the vast majority of cases, the leakage is not structurally significant and can be controlled relatively inexpensively. Most basement leaks tend to be intermittent—it may only be wet during or after periods of rain or melting snow. Homeowners must monitor the situation and take action based on the frequency and extent of the leakage.

Basement leakage can often be identified by repairs on interior or exterior walls. Repairs may include patching, cement parging or the use of various water-proofing products. A freshly excavated area or new sod along the edge of a house may indicate that remedial work has been undertaken. Efflorescence, a whitish mineral deposit, on interior walls is also an indication as it remains after water has evaporated. Many other signs may be present: rusty nails in baseboards; rusted electrical boxes near floor level; rusted support posts on appliances; mould or mildew; crumbling plaster or drywall at floor level; peeling paint; water stains; warped boards; or sagging cardboard boxes stored on the floor.

Most leakage problems can be corrected or eliminated by improvements to exterior grading and proper performance of eavestroughs and downspouts. The ground immediately adjacent to the foundation should slope away from the structure at a rate of one inch per foot, for at least the first six feet. If the general topography is such that water is directed toward the structure, further measures to divert water may be required. Practitioners are always cautioned regarding basement leakage. While many situations can be addressed and resolved, certain properties may have water problems that require significant modifications, and even then, may not be successfully resolved. At all times, direct buyers and sellers to appropriate experts for guidance on leakage matters.

Tell-Tale Signs   CAUTION

Basement foundations can be problematic, particularly as homes age. Prudent buyers should be aware of tell-tale signs including:

- peeling floor tiles or moisture under carpets;
- rust on posts, furnace equipment, baseboard nails or other metal objects in or near walls;
- stains/discoloration on panelling, drywall or other interior-side finishes;
- musty odours and dampness (e.g., carpets);
- mould/mildew forming on walls;
- improper exterior drainage;
- leaky window wells;
- cracks in basement walls; and
- dampness forming on exterior concrete walls.

DAMP-PROOFING

Most buyers think in terms of visible cracks in walls and floors. However, water vapour can enter basement areas given the porous nature of concrete. Concrete blocks are even more porous than poured walls. Without proper damp-proofing, water enters in a gaseous form, condensing on inner services given high indoor temperatures. The lower air pressure within structures compounds the problem by increasing water vapour flow as nature seeks to equalize indoor and outdoor pressures.

Basement walls are covered with coatings or membranes to hinder the process. However, construction damage, cracks and general deterioration over time can render such products less than fully effective. Various sealants impact the concrete's inherent porous quality, can be readily applied to both interior and exterior surfaces at point of construction and are also possible for unpainted interior concrete surfaces in resales. Serious water problems may require a combination of remedies including window well covers, altered surface drainage, exterior and interior basement drainage systems and sump pumps.

Damp-proofing exterior walls in a residential property normally requires coating with a waterproof bituminous material and parging with a one-quarter inch layer of mortar, which ideally extends down to the footing. The foundation/footing joint is also covered to improve the seal and direct water into the drainage tile. Tar is applied from grade level to the footing for protection against moisture.

Experts may recommend exterior basement insulation. Rigid glass fibre insulation board designed for use below grade provides good insulation and helps keep the basement dry. Water, entering the insulation, flows down to the drainage tile.

Efflorescence is a whitish mineral deposit sometimes seen on the interior of foundation walls. The presence of efflorescence suggests moisture penetration, although its existence does not tell a great deal about severity or whether the problem is active. Water passing from the outside through the wall dissolves salts in the masonry, concrete or mortar, and arrives on the inner surface with various minerals. A crystalline salt deposit is left as water evaporates from the surface of the wall. Efflorescence can pose certain problems for real estate practitioners both in listing and selling property.

EXAMPLE 1   *The Listing*

Salesperson Lee is completing an exclusive listing agreement on Smith's property. Accompanied by the seller, Lee enters the basement to take various measurements of the improved areas, namely a family room and a finished three-piece bath. In one corner of the basement, a whitish substance is evident on the interior of the block wall next to the gas furnace.

The salesperson makes a point of discussing the potential moisture problem with Smith, however, the seller is concerned that this information will affect the home's saleability and wants the situation ignored. Lee explains that water leakage is a significant fact and that both he and the seller could be liable if this information was not shared with prospective buyers. Smith, now with a better understanding of the situation, agrees to remedy the problem before marketing his property.

EXAMPLE 2   *The Offer*

Buyer Jones completed an inspection of a residential property at 110 Main Street. While seriously interested, he noticed efflorescence in the corner of the basement. The salesperson, noting this concern, suggested that a home inspector view the property. Accordingly, the following clause was inserted in the agreement/contract.

This offer is conditional upon the inspection of the subject property by a qualified home inspector and the obtaining of a report satisfactory to the buyer at the buyer's own expense. Unless the buyer gives notice in writing delivered to the seller by 12:00 P.M. on the 1st day of May, 20xx that this condition is fulfilled, this offer shall be null and void and the deposit shall be returned to the buyer in full without deduction. The seller agrees to co-operate in providing access to the structure for the purpose of this inspection. This condition is included for the sole benefit of the buyer and may be waived at the buyer's option by notice in writing to the seller within the time period stated herein.

Drainage

Proper drainage is an important consideration in relation to basements. Draining can be broadly described as a system of drains, either artificial or natural, used for the removal of liquid. Drainage is most commonly associated with a system of piping, conduits, ditches, or similar drainage devices for the run off of water on land and/or near building structures on surface or sub-surface levels. Provincial building codes establish drainage requirements including tile pipe standards as well as minimum size requirements related thereto.

EXTERNAL

Practitioners most commonly encounter drainage requirements in relation to foundations. Building codes set out sub-surface specifications concerning the type of granular materials needed to drain the bottom of the foundation, and the location of drainage disposal piping including drainage tile, sump pits and dry wells.

Surface drainage requirements typically necessitate site grading to prevent the accumulation of water at or near the building. Such drainage must also ensure that adjacent properties are not adversely affected. Requirements also apply to wells and septic disposal beds, the use of catch basins where required for runoff water, and the proper installation of downspouts.

SECTION III   STRUCTURAL TYPES AND COMPONENTS

INTERNAL

Internal systems are often installed by property owners to remedy dampness or the influx of ground water into a basement. Drainage is accomplished by installing tile inside the footings below basement floor level leading to a sump pump or waste sewage system. This approach is less desirable than the external approach, since water has no natural inclination to find this drainage tile.

Water may accumulate on the outside of the foundation for some time and could leak through the exterior walls before it is carried away by the drainage system on the inside. The water must pass through the foundation or footing system, or go under the footing to reach this tile. Also, with no exterior excavation, damp-proofing or waterproofing the outside of the foundation wall is not possible. Occasionally, holes are drilled through the foundation wall just above the footing to allow water to drain into the internal tile system.

Water Damage   LEGAL FOCUS

Water seepage has caused considerable litigation over the years. Real estate practitioners now rely heavily on property disclosure forms and home inspections to investigate this as well as other flaws within structures.

Property disclosure documents, (referred to as a Seller Property Information Statement (SPIS) in Ontario), are used in selected provincial jurisdictions and in various real estate boards within Ontario.

The statement is typically completed by the seller and then verified by the salesperson. A recent court case involving a property disclosure should point to the benefits of proper documentation and the need for prudence. Property disclosure statements are more fully discussed in *The Real Estate Transaction – General.*

Water Damage Not Disclosed in Statement

The sellers signed a property information statement and answered no to the question concerning their awareness of any damage to the residence due to water problems. The buyers, accepting statements made in the document, subsequently closed the sale. Water damage was discovered following closing. Evidence revealed that the sellers had, in fact, applied caulking to the exterior in the exact area identified as the point of penetration of water. Water stains were found on all three inside windows and behind curtains. An engineer gave evidence that the damage to the foundation was ongoing for some two years. The Judge found that their no statement to the question: Are you aware of any moisture and/or water problems in the basement or crawl space?, was made without regard to the truth.

The buyers stated that they relied on the information statement for the property and that, although the offer was conditional on a home inspection, they waived that condition because they were relying on the truthfulness of the sellers. The property information statement had been given to the buyers.

The Judge said, It is the opinion of this court that a disclosure statement is an integral part of the purchase and sale process. Although there is no legal obligation upon the vendors to complete and supply such a statement, once a decision is made to complete it, the obligation is on the vendors to do so with accurate information. The vendors must also be aware that purchasers will rely on the contents of such statement in drawing conclusions as to whether to submit an offer to purchase. The sellers were found liable for the repair costs.

Reference   Lewis v. Peladeau, Unreported Case—Digested from Full Text Judgment

---

Although an extensive condition regarding a home inspection was inserted in the agreement, the buyers decided not to proceed with the inspection. The action taken by the buyers may be a combination of believing the sellers, not wanting to spend the money and trusting everyone.

The sellers relied extensively on the argument that the buyers should not succeed because they waived their right to an inspection. Although that is an important fact, the buyers were lulled into a false sense of security by the sellers' misrepresentations. The result would undoubtedly be different if the buyers were told the truth regarding the water problem and went ahead without a home inspection despite the problems.

FLOOR AND FRAMING SYSTEMS

The floor system starts with sills providing a continuous pad between the foundation top and the bottom of the framing system. The **joists**, resting on the sills, provide the structure on which subflooring is attached.

Bridging/bracing is used to restrain the joists from twisting and to help the transmission of loads from one joist to the next. The subfloor transmits live loads of people and furnishings to the joists. The wood **framing** is built on this base through a technique known as **platform framing**. **Balloon framing** was often used in older construction.

Bridging/Bracing

Cross members between joists facilitating weight transfer and minimizing joist twisting.

Framing Systems

Balloon framing was common in the late 19th and early 20th centuries. This wood frame construction technique used conventional wood studs and floor joists. The principal difference was that the wall studs were built before the floor systems, and the wall studs were continuous from the foundation up to the roof line. Simply put, the walls are constructed first and the floor systems are hung from the walls.

In modern day platform framing, a different approach is taken. A wood floor joist and subfloor system is provided on top of the foundation and studs are erected over this system, that are one-storey high. In other words, platforms (floors) are constructed for each level of the structure with wall framing for each floor placed on the respective platform. For example, if the house is two-storeys, a second floor platform is assembled on top of the studs and then a second set of studs is put on top of this platform.

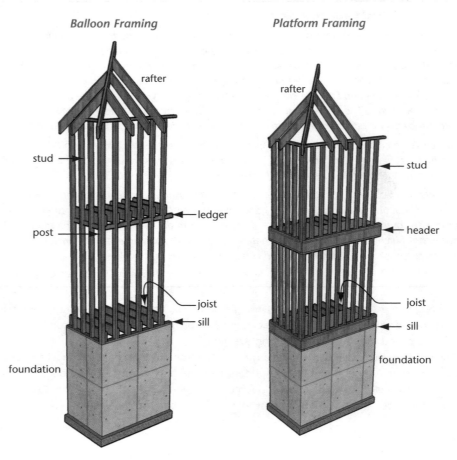

Balloon Framing

Platform Framing

WOOD FRAME WALLS

The wood frame walls in the framing system are load-bearing and carry the weight of the roof and floors down to the foundation. These may be either interior or exterior walls. Studs provide space for insulation and surfaces to secure interior and exterior finishes. Some studs are load bearing, others are not. Bearing stud walls should have a double top plate. Non-bearing stud walls may only have a single top plate. A single bottom or sole plate is provided in either case.

Typical materials have been two-by-four studs spaced sixteen inches on centre, although more recently, two-by-six exterior studs have become common in energy efficient homes, as they provide additional space for insulation. Metal studs are not used extensively in single-family homes, although they are common in commercial construction. Metal studs are normally non-load bearing.

In addition, wood frame walls typically contain door and window openings. The horizontal framing members over these openings are referred to as lintels.

Problem Areas

Practitioners should be aware of certain problems that can arise with wood frame walls.

Nailings and Openings	Inadequate nailing can lead to difficulties. Openings in walls may not be correctly framed. Wall sections above large openings for picture windows, for example, can sag if the openings are not bridged with appropriate lintels.
Condensation	Condensation damage to studs in exterior walls is a concern, especially where insulation is being upgraded in older houses, and good interior vapour barriers on the warm side of the insulation are not provided. Since the process is largely concealed, it is difficult to spot during a visual inspection and may exist for a long time before the damage is noticed. Occasionally, peeling exterior paint is one indication that wall condensation is a problem. Condensation is typically a seasonal problem occurring during the winter months. Warm moist air enters the wall from the house. As it passes through, the air cools. Cool air cannot hold as much water as warm air and condensation forms inside the wall as the air cools and gives off its water.
Low Quality Lumber	Poor quality studs or studs that warp and bow shortly after construction can lead to unsightly wall surfaces in new construction. No easy answer to this problem exists–the bowed or twisted studs have to be removed and replaced.

Framing Components

BEAM

A beam is a long structural component, typically made of wood (solid or built-up), plywood or steel designed to carry floor and wall loads horizontally to the foundation. The structural integrity of beams is important in any building. Undersized or over-spanned beams may sag or crack and lead to the ultimate failure of an entire framing system. Over-spanned wood beams can be readily identified and are usually remedied with the addition of posts, enlarged beams or effected through some type of load reduction.

Problem Areas

Beams can suffer mechanical damage and be weakened by notching, cutting or drilling. The amount of weakening is a function of where the damage occurs on the beam, how significant the damage is and how far it is from the supports. Steel beams can be much stronger than wood beams and are more resistant to rot, termites and mechanical damage, but are more expensive, heavier, difficult to handle and are susceptible to rust.

Fire is an obvious concern with both wood and steel beams. Interestingly, a steel beam will lose its strength in a fire earlier than a wood beam, although a wood beam actually burns. Steel loses its strength after being exposed to temperatures of 1,000° F for about four minutes.

Built-Up Beam

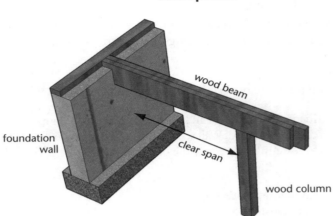

JOIST

A **joist** is one of a series of horizontal wood members, usually of 2-inch nominal thickness, used to support a floor, ceiling or roof. Joists are laid on edge and derive their strength largely by their depth. The adding of a joist, by putting another of the same size beside it, will double its resistance to bending. Doubling the depth of a joist increases its deflection resistance eight times. Typical joist materials include wood, and more recently, metal, plywood and wafer board.

Joists Supported on Top of Wood Beam

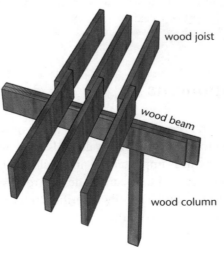

The deflection of a floor and joist system in modern construction may be quite surprising. A typical code allows a floor to deflect 1/360th of its length under normal live loading, if there is a finished ceiling below. For example, the following situation is acceptable by current code: 2 x 10 inch floor joists spaced 16 inches on a centre span of 15 feet. When the room is empty, there should be no perceptible deflection. When the room is occupied with furniture and people, the centre part of the floor can be ½ inch lower than the floor edges. A ½ inch drop in the floor over a distance of 7½ feet is certainly noticeable. While this is permitted by modern codes, it may not be satisfactory to some home owners. It should be noted that codes are intended as minimum standards. Further, a very brittle floor finishing material such as ceramic tile, would not tolerate this degree of flex.

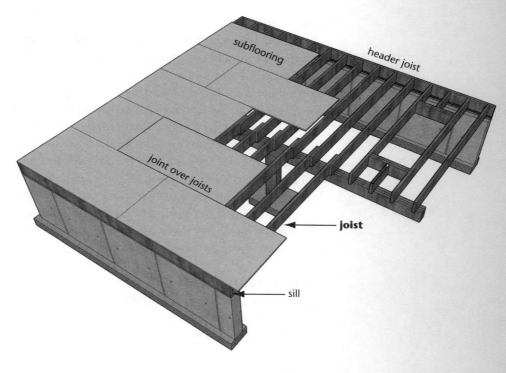

EXAMPLE   *The Older Resale Property*

Buyer Jones has viewed and is now seriously considering the purchase of an older resale property. Following the first visit, Jones has retained a home inspector to accompany him on a subsequent trip to the property. Jones notices that the living room floor has a springiness and asks the inspector to comment. The inspector explains the building code standards including permitted deflection on a floor in relation to span. However, he wants to personally inspect the floor joists, citing four significant problems that can arise.

- Floor joists that are over spanned (undersized) are prone to excessive sagging. The acceptable span is determined by load, species and grade of lumber used, and joist depth/spacing. Usually, over spanning can be readily corrected by adding joists or a beam below the joists.

- Mechanical damage to joists is also common. Joists are notched, drilled and even cut through to accommodate heating, plumbing and electrical systems. Joists are sometimes notched at the end to rest on a beam or foundation wall. This can weaken the joist considerably. The joist usually cracks horizontally from the top of the notch toward the midpoint of the span.

- Joists may be prone to crushing at the ends and/or slipping off the beam or foundation where less than 1½ inch end bearing is provided.

- Joists below partitions are subject to concentrated loads and are more prone to sagging. Beams or walls, as opposed to joists, should be used below load-bearing partitions.

Offset Bearing Wall

One of the problems often unfairly blamed on joists is that of an offset bearing wall. In houses with a beam and post configuration or a bearing wall in the basement, there is usually a wood-frame bearing wall above. Ideally the wall above is directly over the beam or basement wall. In practice this is rarely the case. If the wall is offset enough (sometimes 12 inches is sufficient) the floor joists under the first floor wall will be deflected. This will lead to a low spot and a hump on the floor immediately above the basement beam or bearing wall. This can be arrested by running a second beam and post system or bearing wall in the basement under the offset wall.

BRIDGING/BLOCKING

Bridging and blocking are building components that restrain the joists from twisting and helps transmit loads from one joist to adjacent joists, thereby reducing the springiness in the floor.

Diagonal bridging is most commonly found in residential construction where two-inch by two-inch pieces of wood are used to restrain the floor joists from springing. An alternative, referred to as solid blocking, uses wood with the same dimensions as the floor joists, excepting length. Traditionally, one set of diagonal bridging or solid blocking is provided for each joist span. Depending on the configuration and building code requirements, more or less may be required.

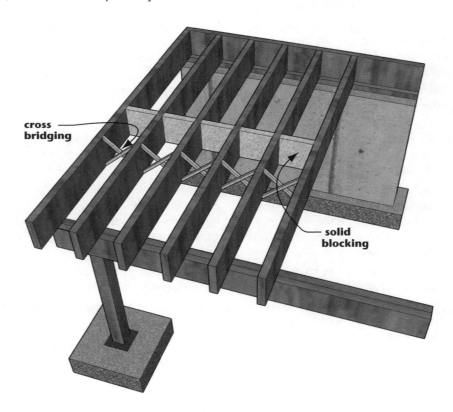

cross bridging

solid blocking

SILL

A sill is a level, continuous pad between the foundation top and the bottom of the framing system. Typically, the floor joists rest directly on and are secured to the sill. These sills should be anchored to the foundation using bolts fitted into the top of the foundation wall, passing through the sill, and secured with a washer and nut.

In new construction, the sill is usually a 2 inch x 4 inch piece of wood laid flat. In older construction, it may be a substantial wood beam, for example, 8 inch x 8 inch. Wood sills support wood framing members, but not masonry, that is, a brick veneer wall sits directly on the foundation, not on a wood sill.

Problem Areas

Practitioners should be aware of certain problems associated with sills.

Rot and Termites	Wood sills very close to grade level are subject to rot and termite attack. In some older houses, the sills are actually below grade level and may be in constant contact with the soil. Soil contact will undoubtedly lead to rot and the sills can be expected to crush under the weight of the framing system as the rot advances. This phenomenon also applies to beams, posts and joists.
Point Loads	Sills may be crushed as a result of concentrated loads, for example, steel posts built into walls.
Anchoring	Where the sills are not secured to the foundations, a danger of the building shifting exists during high winds as significant upward and lateral forces are generated.
End Bearing	If the joists are too short, and only the ends rest on the sill (less than one inch, for example), then the concentrated loads may lead to crushing of the sill or joist.

Any wood component in a house is also vulnerable to fire and mechanical damage. Damaged wood sills can usually be replaced readily. Where at or below grade, a material such as concrete would be more suitable. Poorly anchored sills can be secured using bolts.

SUBFLOOR

This building component transmits live loads of people and furnishings to the floor joists. Subflooring may be covered with a finish or may serve as a finished flooring. Historically, one inch thick wood boards were used. More recently, plywood and wafer board have been used. Current standards call for plywood or wafer board to be at least $5/8$ inch thick when the floor joists are 16 inches apart.

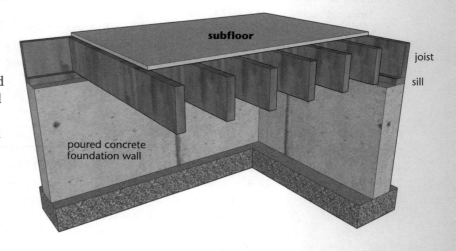

poured concrete foundation wall

subfloor

joist

sill

Problem Areas

Practitioners should be aware of selected problems with subflooring.

Springy Floors	Wood subflooring (usually found in residential construction) that is too thin will be springy and may fail under concentrated loads such as that of a piano. An overlay is normally required to provide a stiffer subfloor; e.g., the installation of ceramic floor tile.
Squeaky Floors	Subflooring not adequately secured to the floor joists is likely to be squeaky and may be springy. Most floor squeaks are the result of poor contact between the subflooring and joists. The weight of someone walking on a floor will temporarily push the subfloor down onto the joist. When the foot is removed, the subfloor will lift off slightly again. The noise usually results from the wood moving against the nail. Solutions include re-nailing, screwing and gluing the subfloor to the joists. Shims can also be used between the subfloor and joists.
Water Damage	Wafer board subflooring can be damaged by relatively small amounts of water. The board tends to swell, resulting in floor unevenness. The swelling also pulls the nails out of the joists or through the wafer board. Ultimately, of course, the board can lose its strength.
Uneven	Uneven subflooring can be irritating, although it is rarely a structural problem. Uneven joist installation is a common cause, as is debris on the top of the joists when the subfloor is laid. Swelled wafer board or delaminating plywood can also result in unevenness. Careless joining of tongue and groove sheets can lead to surface irregularity.

Wood Rot   CAUTION

While the chapter emphasizes structural components and weaknesses, many problems can arise due to natural forces at work in the environment. Rot, for example, is a form of deterioration that occurs in wood under combined conditions concerning temperature, moisture and oxygen. The decay is caused by fungus that attacks the wood cells, causing the cells and the wood as a whole to collapse. The fungus that causes rot requires a temperature of roughly 40 to 115 degrees Fahrenheit. Above that temperature, the fungus can be killed and below that temperature the fungus becomes dormant, but can be reactivated once the temperature increases.

   Sufficient moisture is required for rot to occur. When the moisture content of the wood exceeds approximately 20%, fungus spores that are naturally present in the atmosphere can be sustained and grow within the wood. Once the rot forming fungus is established, it will continue to grow and decay the wood, while the wood remains wet. If the lumber is dried to below 20% moisture content, the rot will spread no further and become dormant.

 # ROOF

The primary purpose of a roof is to keep the building and its occupants protected from rain, snow, sun, wind and all combinations thereof. Roofs may also add to or detract from the appearance of a building. Roofs provide some protection against falling objects, although anyone who has seen the damage done by a large tree falling on a house knows that the strength of the roof is limited. Roof coverings are not intended to keep out the cold and the majority of roofs are extremely poor insulators.

SECTION III   STRUCTURAL TYPES AND COMPONENTS

Problem Areas

The most vulnerable areas of a roof are where it changes direction, or where a change in materials occurs, such as the roof meeting a chimney or a wall. These areas are flashed on a properly installed roof. In addition to flashings, areas where television antennas or satellite dishes and their supporting wires are attached are potential trouble spots. Areas that have already been repaired are also vulnerable. As a general rule, a roof with a low slope tends to be more vulnerable to wear and leakage.

| Ice Damming | Some roofing configurations are more prone to ice damming problems than others. Ice damming occurs when snow and ice collect in a certain area of the roof, often the eaves. Melting snow on the upper portion of the roof cannot drain properly as it is trapped behind the ice dam. If the dam is large enough and enough water collects, it will back up under the shingles and leak into the eaves or worse, into the exterior walls or the building interior.

Ice damming problems do not necessarily occur every winter. They normally occur after periods of heavy snow when day time temperatures are at or slightly above freezing while night time temperatures are below freezing. Effective solutions to ice damming problems are increased attic insulation and ventilation. These two measures reduce the air temperature in the attic to minimize snow melt over the heated portions of the house. |
| Tree Branches Touching Roof | Trees should be kept trimmed away from roof and wall surfaces. The abrasive action of branches rubbing against the roof can damage the roof system and shorten its life expectancy. Also, tree limbs touching buildings provide easy access to the home for pests, such as squirrels. |

Flashings

Flashings are designed to keep water out and are used where dissimilar materials meet, where a material changes direction or at joints in materials. Most flashings are galvanized steel; however, they can also be tin, aluminum or copper.

Pitch

Roofing systems can be divided into two main categories: sloped roofs and flat roofs. Sloped roofing systems are not watertight per se and shed water much like a pyramid of umbrellas. Flat roofs, on the other hand, are watertight membranes designed to be impervious to water penetration. Flat roofing is actually a misnomer as these roofing systems should never be perfectly flat. They should slope enough to allow water to drain properly, since water standing on the roof for long periods of time will accelerate deterioration of the membrane.

The pitch of a roof is really the slope of the roof. Convention dictates that the slope is defined as a ratio of rise over run. For uniformity, the run is always defined as twelve feet. Therefore, a six in twelve roof would have a vertical rise of six feet, over a horizontal distance of 12 feet. Roofs with a pitch greater than four in twelve are considered conventional roof systems. Roofs with a slope between four in twelve and two in twelve are considered low slope roofs, and roofs with a pitch less than two in twelve are considered flat roofs.

Single ply membranes used for flat roof applications have gained increasing popularity since the early 1980's. Some are a modified bitumen (asphalt) base while others are plastic (primarily PVC) or synthetic rubber. The membranes may be glued, tarred down, or mechanically fastened with strips or buttons. Others are laid loose and held in place with gravel.

Sheathing

Roof **sheathing**, most commonly wood plank and plywood dating before 1970, has now been largely replaced by wafer board panels. This sheathing performs two functions by supporting the roof covering and transmitting the load of this material as well as the live loads due to snow, ice and wind to the **rafters**, trusses or roof joists.

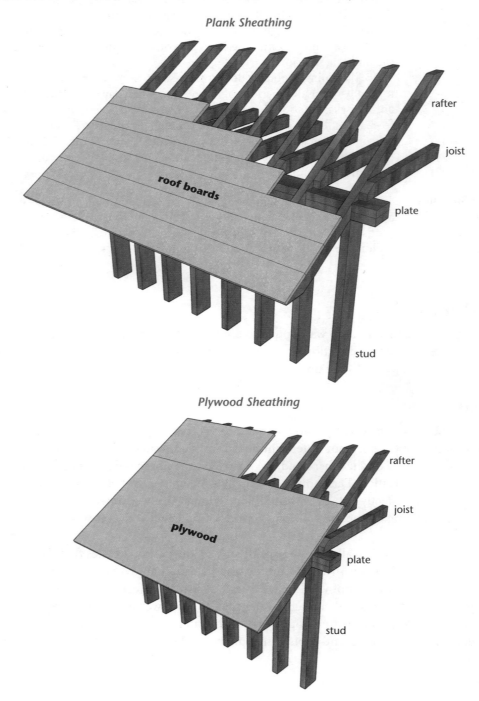

Plank Sheathing

roof boards

rafter

joist

plate

stud

Plywood Sheathing

plywood

rafter

joist

plate

stud

PROBLEM AREAS

Practitioners should be aware of certain problems that can arise with roof sheathing.

Condensation	Moisture in an attic can cause considerable problems. Plywood roof sheathing will delaminate and wafer board sheathing will swell. This can cause loss of strength in the sheathing and render the nailing of the sheathing ineffective, as nails are pulled out of the rafters, or through the sheathing. In severe cases, the roof covering has to be removed and the sheathing replaced.
Too Thin	Sheathing that is too thin for the application will deflect under load and result in sagging of the roof line. Aesthetically, this is considered unacceptable although sagging to the point of failure would be unusual.
Edge Support	Unsupported edges of roof sheathing may lead to differential movement between two panels. This can lead to horizontal ridges appearing in the roofing. Seams parallel to rafters in panel roof sheathing should occur only over the rafters and should be staggered. If the sheathing is unusually thick, edge support is not necessary.

Trusses

Roof **trusses** perform the same function as rafters, collar ties, knee walls and ceiling joists. The roof truss holds up the roof sheathing and shingles, transferring the roof loads to the outside or bearing walls. The bottom of the truss also supports the ceiling finish, upon which the insulation rests.

Most trusses used in residential construction are made up of wood components. The top and bottom members of the truss are referred to as chords, the interior members are called webs. Individual wood members are secured with gusset plates and may be made of plywood or steel. Various configurations of trusses have different strengths, and engineers can use the shape and component size that best suits them. Trusses are typically pre-engineered systems and are normally spaced 24 inches apart, but can vary, depending on spans and depth of the desired truss.

Two common types of trusses are used residentially. The Fink Truss has web members that form a W. The Howe truss can be identified by vertical web members, including a vertical web running up to the peak. The Howe Truss is stronger, however if long spans are within the capabilities of the truss, either will perform well.

Fink Truss

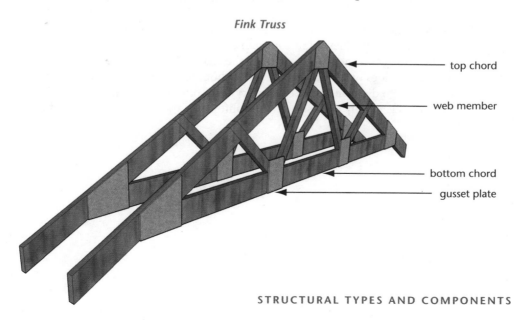

top chord

web member

bottom chord

gusset plate

Howe Truss

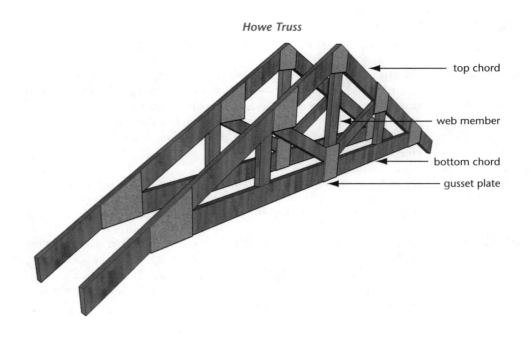

top chord

web member

bottom chord

gusset plate

PROBLEM AREAS

Practitioners should be aware of specific problems that can arise with trusses.

Cut	Individual chords or webs that are cut or damaged can be a serious problem. Cutting a truss in one spot may seriously compromise the entire truss structure. Special engineering consideration should be given where trusses have to be cut to accommodate chimneys or other interruptions in the roof line.
Truss Uplift	A phenomenon known as truss uplift is relatively common in new houses and involves the bottom member (chord) of the truss deflecting upward during winter weather. Apparently, the temperature and humidity changes in the attic during the winter months affect the sections of the truss above the insulation level differently than the bottom chord buried in the insulation. This results in an upward bowing of the bottom chord.
	The result of truss uplift is that the centre section of the bottom chord moves upward and gaps as large as ½ inch appear at the top of the interior walls, where they join the ceiling. The ceiling is picked up by the truss. It is less common but also possible, that the entire wall below will be lifted up, and separation will occur between the bottom of the wall and the floor. At present, a good solution is not known for this problem, and common corrective action is to secure a moulding to the ceiling (but not to the wall). As the ceiling moves up and down, the moulding slides up and down the wall although no gap will appear. Another solution is to disconnect the ceiling drywall from the truss. Alternate ceiling support is generally necessary. Trust uplift is not a serious structural problem.

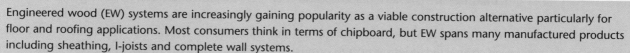

Manufactured Wood

CURIOSITY

Engineered wood (EW) systems are increasingly gaining popularity as a viable construction alternative particularly for floor and roofing applications. Most consumers think in terms of chipboard, but EW spans many manufactured products including sheathing, I-joists and complete wall systems.

Current research is now focused on mixing plastics with wood. New products are expected to further enhance EW advantages; i.e., light-weight, more environmentally friendly (less wood consumed in house construction), straightness and smoothness (as compared to traditional lumber products), handle higher weight loads and an ability to span larger areas and consequently fewer column supports.

Rafter

A rafter is a roof component commonly associated with sloped roofs, whereas a similar member under a flat roof is referred to as a roof joist. The rafter supports the roof sheathing and transmits the roof loads to bearing walls and beams below. Some rafters support finished ceilings such as cathedral ceilings. In this case, insulation is often fitted between the rafters.

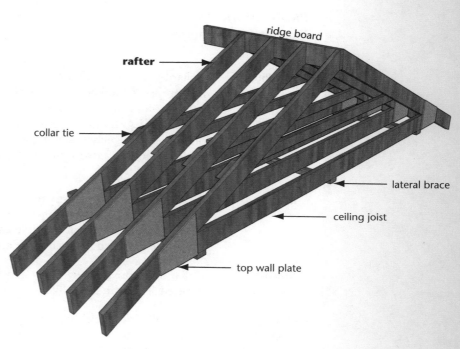

PROBLEM AREAS

Real estate practitioners should be aware of certain problems that can occur with rafters.

Over Spanned	Wood rafters are susceptible to rot, termite and fire damage. Further, the roof will sag if rafters are over spanned or spaced too far apart.
Rafter Spread	Rafters may spread if not adequately secured to the walls at the bottom edge. This is a common problem on older houses, particularly those with gable roofs. Rafter spread is often noted at the soffits, as they will pull away from the wall when the spreading occurs. In other cases, the rafters may push the top of the wall outward, causing serious problems.
Condensation	Attics with good insulation but poor ventilation may be susceptible to condensation problems. Condensation will attack roof sheathing and rafters. Left unchecked, this problem can lead to structural failure. Corrective action includes improved ventilation and replacing damaged wood.

Collar Tie

Collar ties are laterally-placed, wood members installed between opposing rafters approximately halfway up the attic space. These ties are designed to prevent rafters from sagging inward and provide the same job as knee walls. Collar ties, two-by-fours or two-by-sixes, are connected at either end to opposing rafters, and act as stiffeners to prevent the rafters from sagging.

One collar tie should be placed for each pair of opposing rafters. If more than eight feet long, a rat-tail or other sort of bracing should be attached to the midpoint of the collar ties to prevent them from buckling in the middle. See the illustration provided for placement of collar ties in relation to other roof and ceiling components.

PROBLEM AREAS

Practitioners require awareness of certain problems that can arise regarding collar ties.

Buckling	Collar ties are susceptible to buckling and discovering that the use of an inappropriate lumber size has been used is not uncommon. For example, a two-by-four makes an adequate collar tie, but a one-by-eight does not. Because of its very thin one-inch dimension, pushing on either end of a one-by-eight, which is what rafters do, will likely cause bending in the middle. Bending a two-by-four by pushing from either end is much more difficult.
Missing	Securing collar ties on every third rafter was very common on older houses. However, such arrangements have proven inadequate particularly with the added weight of multiple layers of roof shingles. Collar ties should be provided for each rafter and can be readily added.
Bracing	Collar ties more than eight feet may buckle if lateral bracing has been omitted. They can be easily installed.
Wrong Location	Often collar ties are either too high or too low. Ideally, their placement should be near the midpoint of the rafter span.
Low Slope Roof	Collar ties are only effective when the roof slope is four in twelve inches or greater. Larger rafters, or knee walls, are typically used on lower slopes on a retrofit basis to strengthen a roof.

Knee Wall

A knee wall is a small wall, typically built with two-by-four wood studs in the attic, that prevents rafter sag. Knee walls in 1½ or 2½ storey houses sometimes form the walls of a room on the upper floor as they run from the attic floor up to the underside of the rafters near their midpoint. Upper rooms created by this approach often have partly sloped ceilings as a result.

PROBLEM AREAS

Certain problems can arise concerning knee walls.

Poorly Secured and Weak Floor	As with any wood component, knee walls are subject to rot, termites, mechanical damage and fire damage. These walls will also move if not adequately secured to the rafters or to the joists. If the floor joist system below is not strong enough, the knee wall can cause deflection in the ceiling below with resulting damage to the ceiling finish.
Location	The knee wall may not be effective in preventing rafter sag if not located at the mid span of the rafters. Typically, where the roof line is fairly long, a knee wall is used on the lower end of the rafter to provide immediate support and a collar tie is used higher up. Where both a collar tie and a knee wall are used, their placement should provide for equally-sized rafter spans.

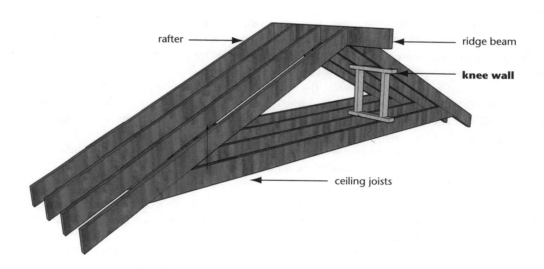

Termites feed on wood and are found chiefly in tropical climates but have been known to exist in North America for more than 50 years. Termites live in sophisticated social colonies in the soil, not in the wood. In colder climates, their colonies are usually located below the level of frost penetration, and are typically close to some moisture source. When termites travel, they do so by moving through wood, soil or shelter tubes that they construct. Termites will not expose themselves to the open air, as their bodies can dry out very quickly.

Shelter tubes are small tunnels that the termites build across any open surface they want to traverse. The shelter tubes are made of earth, debris and a material they excrete which acts as a binder to hold the tubes together. These tubes are typically sandy in colour and can be readily broken open by hand. An initial tube may be less than one quarter inch in width, although several tubes can be built together over time and the entire grouping may be one or two inches wide. Since the termites do not like to be exposed to the air, they will typically eat through the inside of a piece of wood, often following the grain. They tend to eat in parallel galleries and leave a smooth honey-combed appearance on the inside of the wood. Termites will eat any kind of wood, although damp or rotted wood is easier for them to break down. Termites need a regular supply of moisture, and workers return to the colony every 24 to 48 hours.

Detection

The shelter tubes are usually the first indication of infestation. The second indication is typically damaged wood, although often the wood has to be probed to identify damage. An infestation can develop unnoticed behind finished basement floors or walls where shelter tubes are not visible. A small amount of frass is usually found inside the damaged wood consisting of small grey flecks, differing from the powdery wood (sawdust) generated by carpenter ants. Carpenter ants will tend to push the wood debris out of the tunnels, while termites consume the material.

Wherever termite activity or termite treatment is in evidence, the question is raised as to whether any structural damage has occurred. If none is visible, it may be difficult to know whether damage is concealed or has been repaired. While direct verification can be difficult without disassembling the house, the building should be monitored for sagging structural components, floor springiness or other signs of structural weakness. It is not unusual for termites to attack a house, passing through the floor and wall systems up into the attic. Wood damage may occur a considerable distance from the point of attack in the basement as the termites move to the centre of wood members.

Treatment

Licensed pest control specialists can eliminate or prevent subterranean termites from attacking a building by employing chemicals, which are believed to be effective over a 20–30 year period. The chemical is injected into the soil around the building, through the basement floor and foundations, and through any posts or other penetrations in the basement floor. The objective is to create a chemical envelope around the house. Termites live in a colony in the soil and chemical treatment does not kill the colony, but simply prevents the colony from sending its workers into the building to collect wood to feed the colony. It is also necessary to treat all attached buildings to ensure effectiveness of the treatment. An envelope created around one-half of a semi-detached building will not prevent infestation to the other half and entry of the termites into the treated half through the upper levels. Government grants are available in certain areas for chemical treatment as well as elimination of wood/soil contact.

Detection—Existing Treatment

Plugged holes roughly the size of a quarter, spaced from 12 to 24 inches apart in sidewalks or driveways around the house is usually evidence of chemical treatment. Similar holes may also be found on the exterior foundation walls above grade, on the interior foundation walls, on the basement floor just inside the exterior walls and on interior walls around the base of columns. Occasionally, the treatment is also injected directly into the columns. Another sign that chemical treatment may have been undertaken is the obvious breakage of wood/soil contact. A wood post with a relatively new concrete base and a concrete pad at the bottom of an old wood basement staircase are typical signs.

SECTION III   STRUCTURAL TYPES AND COMPONENTS

KNOWLEDGE INTEGRATION

Notables

- The footing transmits the weight of the structure to the soil. When a footing fails, the shifting of the structure can result in expensive repairs.

- Many basement leakage problems can be remedied with exterior grading improvements and properly performing eaves-troughs and downspouts.

- Building codes set out requirements for damp-proofing and water-proofing of below-grade exterior walls.

- Foundations perform three functions involving support of the structure's weight, preventing frost heaving and resisting lateral pressure of the soil.

- A joist is laid on edge, derives strength primarily from its depth and is used to support a floor, ceiling or roof.

- Bridging/blocking helps prevent joists from twisting and helps transfer weight load between joists.

- Two framing types are used in residential construction: balloon framing and, more recently, platform framing.

- The most vulnerable roof areas are located where it changes direction or where a change in material occurs.

- Residential roof trusses, typically made of wood components, hold up the roof sheathing and shingles.

- Roof trusses perform the same function as rafters/ceiling joists. Roof sheathing is now commonly wafer board panels.

- The term flat in regard to a flat roof is actually a misnomer. Such systems are never perfectly flat, but are designed to be impervious to water penetration.

Glossary

Balloon Framing	Foundation	Platform Framing
Bridging/Bracing	Framing	Rafter
Footing	Joist	Sheathing
		Truss

Strategic Thinking For Your Career

Questions are included to assist in developing your new career. No answers are provided.

1. What local information sources are available to expand my construction knowledge concerning foundation, wall and roofing systems?

2. What types of materials are being used locally to construct foundations, walls and roofing systems?

3. Are there any new innovations being used in building construction within my marketplace?

4. How can I improve my knowledge of residential construction in a practical manner, meet people involved in new construction and expand my career potential?

Chapter Mini-Review

Solutions are located in the Appendix.

1. The ranch style bungalow is currently widely used in new urban residential construction projects in Ontario.

    ◯ True   ◯ False

2. The typical split entrance bungalow has bedroom areas on a higher level than the kitchen, dining room and living room.

    ◯ True   ◯ False

3. Industrial buildings can be broadly grouped under three categories: general purpose, unique purpose and retail purpose.

    ◯ True   ◯ False

4. In wood frame construction, wooden sills are placed on the rim of the foundation walls and are attached by bolts embedded in the foundation wall.

    ◯ True   ◯ False

5. Efflorescence is the result of water carrying dissolved salts to the surface of masonry, then evaporating and leaving salt stains on the surface.

    ◯ True   ◯ False

6. Bridging is only used in roofing areas and acts to restrain the roof rafters from twisting and also helps to transmit loads from one rafter to another.

    ◯ True   ◯ False

7. The subfloor may cause squeaks if not properly secured to joists.

    ◯ True   ◯ False

8. Vapour barriers are rarely used in the construction of new home basements.

    ◯ True   ◯ False

9. Concrete block basement walls are typically covered with parging then damp-proofing.

    ◯ True   ◯ False

10. A post or column typically carries the load of a beam down to the footings.

    ◯ True   ◯ False

11. Collar ties are used to connect joists in order to avoid joist twisting.

    ◯ True   ◯ False

12. Shelter tubes are used for drainage in and around basement areas.

    ◯ True   ◯ False

13. Wood rot is caused by a fungus that attacks the wood.

    ◯ True   ◯ False

14. Drainage tile can either be found in internal or external drainage systems.

    ◯ True   ◯ False

15. Platform framing is differentiated from balloon framing in that trusses are used instead of rafters.

    ◯ True   ◯ False

Active Learning Exercises

Solutions are located in the Appendix.

■ Exercise 1   Matching

Match the phrase/word in the left column with the appropriate description in the right column (not all descriptions are used).

____ Efflorescence	a. Balloon Framing
____ Floor Support	b. Rafter Spread
____ Floor Flexibility	c. Roof Pitch
____ Continuous Wall Studs	d. Knee Wall
____ Chords/Webs	e. Whitish Mineral Deposit
____ Sloped Roof	f. Deflection
____ Small Wall	g. Roof Trusses
	h. Joist
	i. Subfloor

■ Exercise 2   Multiple Choice

2.1   In a typical one and one-half storey house, what percentage of the total living area is usually contained on the first floor?

a.   60%

b.   90%

c.   40%

d.   75%

2.2   Split level homes:

a.   Have few stairways.

b.   Can involve as many as five levels.

c.   Are most commonly classified as either backsplits or front splits.

d.   None of the above.

2.3   In the construction of a new home, the purpose of installing footings is:

a.   To provide a solid base for installation of roof trusses.

b.   To provide extra strength for the overlapping of floor joists.

c.   To transmit the weight of the house to soil without allowing the house to the sink.

d.   To prevent moisture damage when water seeps down exterior finishes and is trapped next to the foundation.

2.4   Which of the following is NOT one of the functions of a foundation?

a.   To carry the weight of the house below the frost line to prevent heaving.

b.   To transmit the weight from the above grade walls and floors down to the footings.

c.   To act as a retaining wall to resist lateral pressure of the soil on the outside of the foundation.

d.   To provide a base for installation of roof trusses.

2.5   Which of the following correctly identifies the vertical wall framing members to which wall sheathing and cladding are attached?

a.   Beams.

b.   Joists.

c.   Studs.

d.   Sills.

2.6   What are the horizontal framing members over door and window openings?

a.   Lintels.

b.   Studs.

c.   Sills.

d.   Knee Walls.

2.7   Which of the following would NOT be a sign of termite infestation?

a.   The presence of frass inside damaged wood.

b.   The presence of shelter tubes.

c.   Signs of wood debris.

d.   Indications of damaged wood when probed.

2.8   The presence of efflorescence in a concrete basement:

a. Indicates that moisture was present.

b. Clearly indicates the severity and extent of a moisture problem.

c. Occurs typically in the summer due to humidity.

d. Is found with poured concrete walls, but not concrete block walls.

2.9   What component of a structure could be most directly affected if a top chord is cut or damaged?

a.   Joist.

b.   Roof truss.

c.   Roof sheathing.

d.   None of the above.

SECTION III   STRUCTURAL TYPES AND COMPONENTS

■ Exercise 3 Fill-in-the-Blanks

You have decided to specialize in new home sales and want to gain familiarity with housing construction lingo. While speaking with Jim Anderson (a local builder) several tradespeople interrupt. Based on the brief conversations below, identify what structural component is being discussed and insert your answer in the space provided.

3.1. Jim, we're having trouble with the gusset plates and web members on that recent shipment. They are separating during installation.

3.2 Have you seen that bag of metal "H" clips? We want to install the panels by the end of the day.

3.3 Once Bill's crew has installed the sills and joists, we'll start laying it.

3.4 Jim, do you want both solid blocking and cross bridging?

3.5 We've just finished the expansion joints and are ready to pour.

3.6 We've only got enough studs to complete the first level on Lot 18, then we'll build the floor system for the second level and proceed with the second floor studs tomorrow.

3.7 What size of lintel do you want to use above the bow in the living room on Lot 21?

3.8 Jim, can you ask one of the other guys to help? I'm having trouble installing the collar ties and lateral braces.

■ Exercise 4   The Riverside Drive Property

Salesperson Martin decided to preview 48 Riverside Drive, as he has a buyer client interested in that type of property. The home, vacant for six months, is an older ranch style bungalow backing onto the river. The property requires considerable updating, particularly decorating in main floor areas and bathroom/kitchen renovations.

The largely, unfinished basement has an unmistakable musty smell and whitish material can be seen on concrete blocks near the furnace, directly under one of several small basement windows. While no water damage is directly visible, it is clear that the house has a dampness problem. Martin also notes rusty nails in baseboards in a small finished office near the stairway leading upstairs.

Martin wants to investigate further, prior to calling the client. Assist Martin by briefly listing five possible causes of the dampness.

■ Exercise 5   The Renovated House

Mr. and Mrs. Jones are seriously weighing their options. While originally seeking a bungalow, a two-storey has caught their undivided attention. Mrs. Jones is mentally placing furniture in the living room while Mr. Jones is patiently inspecting the structural aspects of this house. The home, built in 1970, has three bedrooms on the upper level, one of which is a huge 21' x 26' master bedroom with an adjoining five-piece washroom. The large bedroom was only one of several modifications made by the current owner when he purchased the property approximately ten years ago. On the main level, the seller removed two walls and made necessary structural changes to create an open concept design encompassing the kitchen, dining room and family room. Immediately above, the master bedroom originally consisted of two bedrooms until the middle wall was removed.

The Joneses are impressed with the bright, open appearance of the house. However, just when all the buying signals are clear and a decision is apparent, they decide to make a re-tour. Apparently, they have a king-sized waterbed and a grand piano to be placed in the master bedroom. Mr. Jones stands in the middle of the bedroom and suddenly jumps in the air. His 240 pounds come crashing back to the floor and everything in the room shakes. His curiosity aroused, he now is testing various parts of the floor only to discover a number of squeaks.

Mr. Jones turns to his wife and states: *This floor will never support the waterbed and piano. The owner must have structurally weakened it when he renovated. Besides, there's all sorts of squeaks. That proves that something is wrong.* While Jones will undoubtedly want a home inspector or other expert to look at the home, provide insight by answering the following:

5.1   What type of structural damage might have been caused by the modifications? Comment on whether the floor squeaks are relevant. Be specific.

5.2   Jones, now concentrating on potential defects, notes a long hairline crack that runs along the top of the bedroom wall where it joins the ceiling. While an expert would need to be consulted on this matter, do you think that this hairline crack could be part of an overall structural problem? What other explanation is possible? Be specific.

■ Exercise 6   An Exterior Viewpoint

Mr. and Mrs. Jones are now intensely scrutinizing the house. After all, if the master bedroom floor shakes and squeaks, the problem probably doesn't end there. Mr. Jones bolts from the room, down the stairs and outside to look at the roof. While it appears normal given the age of the property, Jones is certain that there is sagging. Once again, a home inspector is qualified to deal with such matters, but Jones wants some insight into what types of problems might cause this.

6.1   While not certain whether this roof is supported by rafters or a roof truss system, list typical structural weaknesses leading to a sagging roof. Be specific.

SECTION III   STRUCTURAL TYPES AND COMPONENTS

6.2   Beyond structural considerations, briefly list other factors that might explain a sagging roof.

CHAPTER 7

Finishes and Features

Introduction

An increasing array of new processes and products greet consumers selecting finishes and features in the marketplace. As with the previous chapter on structural issues, practitioners should be aware of general descriptions and potential problem areas, while leaving specifics to appropriate experts.

Chapter 7 begins with basic roofing styles and coverings along with detailed information about roof materials including options such as asphalt, metal, wood, slate and concrete. Particular emphasis is placed on new innovative methods to improve efficiency through the use of green roofs, as well as the key role played by eavestroughs and downspouts in ensuring that proper drainage is achieved.

Course content is then focused on exterior wall finishes with detailed descriptions of brick veneer, brick masonry (solid brick) and siding exterior wall surfaces. Fortunately, today's consumers can choose from siding products that are moisture, mould and insect resistant due to recent advances in engineered wood or fibre cement panels.

Discussion of interior finishes focuses on drywall and important environmental and health considerations when selecting building materials and finishes. Lastly, the chapter ends with an overview of door components and detailed discussion of window components, styles and energy efficiency standards and ratings.

Learning Outcomes

At the conclusion of this chapter, students will be able to:

- Identify and describe major roofing styles used in residential and commercial construction including sloped and flat roofs along with key problem areas concerning roof leakage.

- Identify and describe various common roofing materials used in Ontario including asphalt, metal, wood shingle, slate and concrete/clay tile.

- Discuss the role of eavestroughs, types typically used in Ontario and significant problem areas encountered with eavestroughs.

- Outline common types of exterior wall finishes including brick veneer walls, brick masonry walls, stucco and the use of siding materials, along with typical problem areas encountered with each type.

- Discuss the basics of drywall installation and key considerations from an environmental and health perspective when selecting building materials and finishes for both residential and commercial construction.

- Outline common types of doors and describe the components of a door frame.

- Outline significant window features and components with special emphasis on methods to analyze and improve energy efficiency.

- Describe standards and efficiency ratings applied to windows, along with new innovations that have increased overall window efficiency.

ROOFING

Sloped and Flat Roofs

Two basic roofing styles are found on structures (*sloped* and *flat*) along with various types of roof coverings—each with its own benefits, drawbacks and life expectancy. Sloped **shingle** roofs with various **pitches** dominate residential construction. Structural issues concerning sloped roofs were discussed in the previous chapter.

Built-up roofs are most commonly identified with industrial/commercial. This multi-ply roofing system, commonly referred to as a *tar and gravel* roof, is particularly popular in industrial buildings. The roof usually consists of two to five plies of roofing felts with a mopping of asphalt between layers. A flood coat of asphalt is then applied over the top and covered with gravel to reflect ultraviolet light and protect the roof from damage. Some roofers use roll roofing rather than gravel to protect and hold down the membrane.

Roof Leaks

In roof design, **flashing** is used where dissimilar materials meet, where material changes direction or at joints in materials. Eavestroughs and downspouts protect the walls of a building from water and contribute toward a dry basement. Common sources of water damage include condensation in attic areas, leaks in the roof, flashing and skylight(s), and leakage due to ice damming. Most roof leaks are localized with the source often located at an intersection or a flashing.

Roof leaks can be difficult to trace because the water does not always appear on the interior immediately below the defective area. Water may run along framing members or vapour barriers and alter the flow to other locations. For example, many roof leaks appear first around ceiling light fixtures. Five key questions underlie any leak found in a structure.

- What is the source of the damage?
- Is the leak still active?
- Is there any concealed damage?
- What is the cost to cure the problem?
- What is the cost to repair the damaged building materials?

Roofing Materials

While roofing structures were discussed in the previous chapter, practitioners should also be aware of various roofing materials used in Ontario and other provinces in Canada.

ASPHALT SHINGLES

Asphalt shingles are the most common roofing material. Shingles consist of asphalt impregnated felt paper, coated with an additional layer of asphalt, and covered with granular material.

Asphalt shingles are classified by weight. The most common type of shingles used today weigh 210 pounds per square (a square represents the amount of shingles required to cover 100 square feet) and have a life expectancy of 12–15 years (225's, 235's and 320's are also available with corresponding higher life expectancies; e.g., 320's typically have a life expectancy exceeding 25 years).

Shingle

A relatively thin and small unit of roofing, laid in overlapping layers as a roof covering or as cladding on the sides of buildings.

Pitch

The roof slope defined as a ratio of rise over run.

Flashing

Tin, aluminum, copper or galvanized steel sheets used as part of a roofing system.

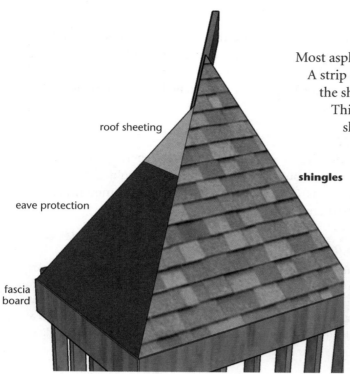

roof sheeting

eave protection

fascia board

shingles

Most asphalt shingles are self-sealing. A strip of tar is put on the surface of the shingles by the manufacturer. This strip is covered by the shingle installed immediately above. When the sun warms the roof surface, the two shingles stick together. Shingles installed in the late fall or winter do not normally seal themselves until spring.

METAL

Metal roofs have gained popularity in Ontario, particularly during the past two decades. Metal roofs can effectively withstand weather influences, most notably high winds. Further, appropriately coated metal roofs reflect solar rays thereby enhancing energy savings. Advantages to homeowners also include low maintenance, resistance to decay and long lasting durability, complemented by a wide variety of designs and colours. Consumers will find various styles of metal roofing including vertical rib, seam and tile configurations.

WOOD SHINGLES AND SHAKES

Wood shingles are machine cut, while wood shakes are hand split or mechanically split. Wood shakes are thicker and have a much more uneven surface. Most wood shingles are cedar; however, some are redwood. The life expectancy of wood shingles is generally 30 to 40 years.

The rate of wear depends largely on exposure (the amount of shingle which is exposed to the weather), the pitch (the steeper the better), the grade of shingle and the amount of sun and shade. Too much sunlight dehydrates the shingles, causing them to become brittle. Too much shade and moisture causes rot and moss to grow.

SLATE

Slate shingles, a sedimentary rock, can have average life expectancies of 60–100 years. Slate roofs weigh three to five times as much as conventional asphalt shingles.

CONCRETE/CLAY TILE

Concrete/clay tile roof systems are rare in Canada, but are high quality roofing systems with life expectancies of 50–100 years. Like slate, these roofs are heavy, weighing four to five times as much as asphalt shingles. However, clay shingles are brittle, subject to mechanical damage and also somewhat prone to failure of fastenings (e.g., nails).

ROLL ROOFING

Roll roofing, sometimes referred to as selvage roofing, consists of materials similar to asphalt shingles but is manufactured in 18-inch or 36-inch wide rolls. The surface can be completely covered with granules or only 50 percent covered in the case of two-ply applications. Roll roofing is most appropriate for low pitched roofs and typically has a life expectancy of five to ten years.

CORRUGATED PLASTIC TILE

Corrugated plastic tile is a single-ply, translucent roof surface generally used over patios and light structures. Such roofing is considered low quality and is subject to fading/discolouring and leakage at the joints. Corrugated plastic tile is most commonly associated with accessory buildings and structures.

EXAMPLE   *The Cottage Deck Roof*

Buyer Jones, lacking sufficient funds to install a fully winterized addition to the lakeside portion of the cottage, elects to build a wooden deck with an overhanging roof attached to the main roof. To minimize weight on the structure, Jones uses a wooden grid arrangement for the roofed area and installs corrugated plastic tile. This material provides additional light (opposed to a solid roof), protection from rain and is relatively inexpensive until a more substantial addition can be built.

Green Roofs   **FOCUS**

A **green roof** structure has a waterproofing membrane and drainage system covered with landscape cloth that serves as the base for soil and/or specialized growing medium and plants. Green roofs have long been recognized in Europe for their positive environmental impact.

Green roof systems, well suited to urban settings, provide building shade, moderate heat gain/loss, retain stormwater runoff, improve air quality and positively impact rising urban temperatures–referred to as urban heat island effect. This effect results from traditional construction that relied on reflective roof and building surfaces.

Green roof size and sophistication can vary significantly from thin soil installations containing limited plant selection to deep soil, irrigated roof-top projects providing extensive gardens and plant diversity, superior insulating quality and the possibility of planned green recreational areas; i.e., when downtown open space is at a premium.

Green roofs are typically categorized as extensive (relatively low cost basic designs) or intensive (complex, high capital cost designs complete with irrigation systems). Both accessible (allowing individuals to utilize the area) and non-accessible versions are found in the Canadian marketplace.

Notable projects can be found in most major Canadian cities. In particular, Toronto boasts several excellent examples. At present, most involve public buildings, institutions and co-operatives. However, private entrepreneurs are becoming involved given other environmental and economic considerations. Interestingly, roof gardens are also attractive from a renovation/repair perspective. As an example, a high-rise condominium corporation faced with extensive roof leakage can solve the problem by installing a durable waterproof membrane and then constructing an intensive roof garden, as an added amenity for unit owner enjoyment.

Eavestrough/Downspouts

These building components have two major functions in residential and commercial structures:

- Protect against wall damage and localized ground level erosion caused by roof runoff.
- Assist in keeping basement areas dry by directing water away from the foundation.

SECTION III   STRUCTURAL TYPES AND COMPONENTS

Regardless of the type of foundation wall, the possibility of water penetration always exists. The less water in the soil near the foundation wall, the less likelihood of water penetration into the basement. Eavestroughs should collect all water runoff, and downspouts should discharge the water into proper drains or onto the ground a safe distance away from foundation walls.

The two most common sizes of eavestroughs are four and five inch widths and are normally either attached to the fascia board or form an integral part of the eaves. Four inch is acceptable for small roof areas, while five inch is usual on larger, as well as steeply pitched roofs owing to greater capacity.

Eavestroughs are typically aluminum, galvanized steel, plastic or copper.

ALUMINUM	GALVANIZED	PLASTIC	COPPER
Does not rust, but dents easily. The number of joints required is less than other systems as it is often fabricated on the site. Aluminum is pre-finished thereby offering low maintenance and a life expectancy of 20 to 25 years.	Requires periodic painting and has a life expectancy of 20 to 25 years.	Generally designed for do-it-yourself activities, with limited colour selection.	Very expensive but considered the best, with a life expectancy of between 50 and 100 years.

PROBLEM AREAS

Leakage	The most common problem is that galvanized eavestroughs rust and holes can develop in copper eavestroughs as well. All types are prone to leakage at the joints. Missing end caps are another source of leakage.
Loose	This type of problem is normally due to improper fastening during original installation or damage caused by ice during winter months.
Damage	Ladders and tree limbs frequently cause mechanical damage.
Slope	Lacking proper slope, eavestroughs will collect and hold water resulting in accelerated deterioration.
Debris	Screens can be installed to prevent clogging from twigs and leaves, however, they often come loose, fall out and can make proper cleaning difficult.

Malfunctioning eavestroughs can result in serious problems. The water leaking out of the troughs usually ends up in the structure, causing rot and other damage.

Downspout Discharge

Downspouts take the water from the eavestrough and discharge it into drains or onto the ground. Underground drains (usually made of clay tile, cast iron or plastic) can plug or break. Often, this problem cannot be determined from a visual inspection. If an underground drain malfunctions, localized water problems will likely develop in the basement area adjacent to the downspout. If this occurs, two options exist: exterior digging and repair, or disconnect the downspout and redirect the discharge away from the house.

All downspouts that discharge onto the ground should be directed a good distance from the house: six feet or more, if possible. The slope of the ground in this area should direct water away from the basement. On pre-1950 homes, downspout drains are often connected to floor drains in the basement. A significant amount of debris in the discharge from the downspouts can plug the basement floor drains and cause backup.

EXTERIOR WALL FINISHES

Brick Veneer

A wood frame wall with an exterior layer of brick.

Exterior wall finishes protect the building's skeleton and exterior from damage. Many different wall finishes are used in today's marketplace with **brick veneer**, **vinyl siding** and **metal siding** being traditional favourites. Recently, compressed wood fibre combined with weather resistant adhesives are gaining popularity. Vinyl siding, made of polyvinyl chloride, has proven particularly effective in Canadian environments. Other siding materials include redwood or cedar shingles, stucco and various veneers; e.g., stone and mortarless brick veneers (made of concrete).

Creative exterior insulation and finishing systems (EIFS) have found their way into both residential and commercial marketplaces. EIFS provide an attractive, continuous exterior surface (excepting doors and windows) consisting of several component layers. The outermost layer is a sprayed-on acrylic/stone finish. The finish is applied over mesh and insulation attaching to the building structure. This method has proven effective in expelling moisture, limiting air leakage and providing an effective building envelope. EIFS can minimize thermal loss found in traditional structures due to thermal bridges created by studs and other wall components that permit conduction from inside to outside and vice versa.

Brick Veneer Walls

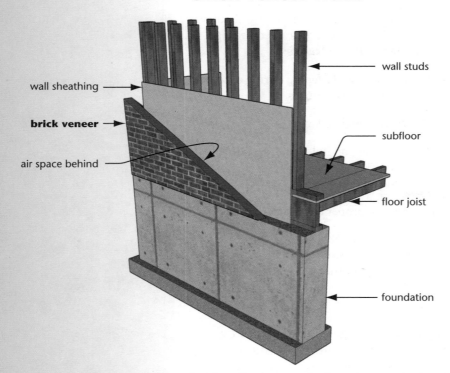

wall studs

wall sheathing

brick veneer

air space behind

subfloor

floor joist

foundation

Brick veneer wall construction has, and continues to, be a popular choice for home buyers. A brick veneer wall is a wood frame wall with an exterior single width of brick. The wood framing transmits the roof and floor loads down to the foundation and employs a structural wood frame inner wall, and a four-inch thick masonry outer section (veneer) which does not have any load bearing responsibility. Typically, metal ties are used to secure the brickwork to exterior sheathing and, consequently, no header courses are employed in the brickwork. This usually enables practitioners to visually differentiate between a brick masonry wall and a brick veneer wall.

Brick veneer walls have been used as long as builders have been building with brick and, in fact, are the only type of brick walls commonly found in single-family homes after about 1970. Other exterior finishes involving exterior walls are discussed in a subsequent chapter.

The rain screen construction principle involves the dispersal of rain relating to brick veneer walls. The rain screen provides for such dispersal through air space and weep holes (every 24 inches). The underlying principle acknowledges that a wind driven rain will pass through the brick wall. A one inch air space is left behind the brick, between the inner face of the brick and the sheathing on the wood studs. Water is allowed to pass through the wall and run down the inner face of the brick, or the outer surface of the sheathing paper, and through the weep holes.

Brick Masonry Wall

In residential construction, a solid brick wall is typically eight inches thick not including the interior wall finish. The inner wythe (layer) is most often brick, concrete block or cinder block (stone, clay tile or glass block can also be used). The outer wythe is usually weather-resistant brick or stone. Construction of brick masonry walls in commercial properties will vary based on the type of structure.

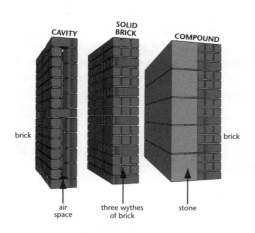

A wall is a load-bearing component of the building that transfers the weight of the roof and floors to the foundation. Brick masonry walls are identified by the header courses (brick rows turned endwise to tie the inner and outer wythes of the wall together) every five to seven courses (rows) up the wall. Occasionally every brick in the course is turned endwise, every other brick is turned or the entire pattern is random. In most cases, however, there are at least some units that are turned every fifth, sixth or seventh course.

If metal ties or specially sized bricks are used to join inner and outer wythes, then no header courses will be present. Masonry walls, with few exceptions, have not been used on single family homes since the early 1970's.

PROBLEM AREAS

Real estate practitioners should have a general awareness of potential problems associated with brick masonry walls.

Lean or Bow	Where the inner and outer wythes are not adequately secured together, the outer wythes can lean or bow outwards. This also occurs during foundation settlement or when the wall is too thin to carry its load. The ultimate danger is that it may fall, but the more immediate danger is that the rafters and joists resting on the wall can slip as the wall moves away from the building. If the ends of joists are resting on the wall by only an inch or two, a relatively small lean can create an unsafe situation. If floor or roof joists slip off their supports, the framing system will collapse.
Rafter Spread	Spreading roof rafters may push the top of the walls out, resulting in an unstable condition.
Out of Plumb	The wall may be built out of plumb, or be pushed out of plumb by mechanical forces (such as being struck by an automobile), or failure of another component in the building.

Wavy	A less than smooth appearance when looking up the wall, with waves often having crests every five to seven courses. Wavy walls may be the result of building too quickly, as bricks are laid on top of mortar that has not had time to set and strengthen. This situation was particularly problematic with old lime mortars that took longer to set. Another theory to explain waviness is not placing a full bed of mortar between each course of brick. If ties or headers were used every five to seven courses, a full mortar bed would be used on these courses only. If the mason skimped on mortar, only the front edge of the brick would get mortar causing the back to come together and create a bulge at the front.
Deterioration	The structure of the wall can be compromised if the masonry units, or the mortar between them, deteriorate. Mortar strength should be similar to, but not stronger than, the brick.
On Side	Hollow bricks or concrete blocks are weak if laid on their sides and should not be expected to carry any type of load.
Cracks	Cracks should be used as clues, with their size, location, direction and rate of growth as important indicators of problems. Generally, cracks through the mortar joints are less serious than cracks through the brick or block, but exceptions do exist.
When Correction Needed	A masonry wall may be unsound if bowed out of plumb by approximately one-sixth of its thickness (typically measured halfway up the wall). Joists may pull out of wall pockets before the wall actually falls, causing collapse of the framing system. A wall may also be unsound if leaning out of plumb by one-third of its thickness (measured from the top to bottom). In some cases, the brick wall can be tied back into the building using anchors and steel rods or cables. If the movement results from foundation difficulties, a rebuilding of the wall may be required following the underpinning of the foundation.

Establishing the appropriate action may require a structural engineer. Repairs should only be undertaken once the cause of the movement is fully understood.

Siding

External siding (e.g., wood, metal and vinyl) is frequently used in Canadian residential housing. Siding is installed on top of building paper and over flashings on the exterior walls and is butted against exterior trim. Siding normally has a minimum 6-inch clearance at the bottom above finished grade level.

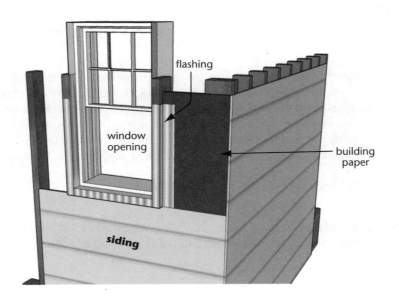

PROBLEM AREAS

Practitioners should be aware of problems associated with various types of external siding. In the case of wood siding, rot and water penetration occur most commonly at joints in the siding. Many wood systems require trim to be installed over the joints. Wood-soil contact should be avoided as it promotes rot and provides an ideal environment for wood-boring insects such as termites.

Metal and vinyl sidings have gained the widest popularity in residential construction owing primarily to the low maintenance factor. A variety of metal sidings are available for vertical and horizontal installation. The prevalent materials are aluminum and steel, aluminum being the most common. Metal siding should be ventilated to allow air and moisture pressures to equalize on either side of the metal.

Vinyl sidings are similar to metal in that the majority of problems are associated with installation, as opposed to the material itself. A lack of proper securing, and improper detail work at edges and corners are the most common deficiencies. Some vinyl sidings discolour with age. Most come in a limited colour selection. Vinyl siding can become brittle during cold weather, and can be punctured or cracked.

Stucco

The term *stucco* generally refers to any cement-like material typically used as an exterior covering for walls that is put on wet and dries hard and durable. Stucco is really the exterior equivalent of plaster, made of cement, lime, aggregate and water. Stucco can be thought of as a thin coat of concrete, with the cement and lime acting as binders, the aggregate providing the bulk and strength, with the water initiating the chemical reaction.

PROBLEM AREAS

As with all exterior finishes, practitioners should be aware of common problems encountered. Much like plaster, stucco requires periodic maintenance as cracks develop. The amount of maintenance required depends largely on the mix of the stucco, the lath used (if any) and the surface to which the stucco is applied.

Stucco over masonry walls tends to stand up significantly better than stucco over wood-frame construction. The rigidity of a masonry structure allows for virtually no flexing of the stucco, and consequently less cracking and surface separation is likely to occur.

The Vertical Garden   CURIOSITY

This environmental counterpart to the green roof consists of a perpendicular garden utilizing perennial vining plants growing up the building facades. As with green roofs, vertical gardens have become increasingly popular in Europe for energy-savings, ecological considerations and the overall improvement of urban environments. In recent years, the concept has gained increasing popularity in the Canadian marketplace as more proponents advocate the benefits of improved air quality, the positive impact on heating/cooling systems in urban structures and the reduction of urban heat.

INTERNAL FINISHES

Floors provide a durable surface for foot traffic and furniture. Properly constructed floors are level, have an even surface and require minimal maintenance if correctly installed. Popular floor finishes include carpeting, hardwood, vinyl, ceramic or porcelain tile and slate.

Wall finishes, typically **drywall** in residential construction, provide a decorative skin to conceal building components. Wall finishes also hide structural members, insulation, duct work, pipes and wires. Plaster walls, once widely found in residential structures, have been largely replaced by drywall installations with the exception of certain custom home builders typically offering products in the higher price ranges.

> *Drywall*
> Pre-manufactured wallboard typically built using gypsum.

Drywall

Drywall and plaster are basically the same material (usually gypsum) except that drywall is pre-manufactured while plaster is mixed and applied by trowel on-site. Occasionally, aggregate or fibres are added to the gypsum as stabilizers and strengtheners. Drywall now dominates the residential marketplace in the finishing of interior areas. Illustrations are provided relating to the installation process.

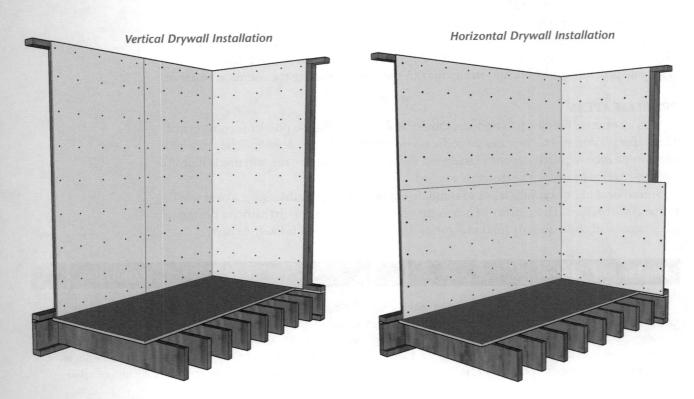

Vertical Drywall Installation

Horizontal Drywall Installation

Building Materials, Finishes and VOC's

Buyers increasingly focus on environmental issues. Those concerns impact how houses are built and what materials are used for both structure, as well as internal and external finishes. The issue of environmental safety and indoor air quality are particularly important from a real estate perspective given concerns regarding sick building syndrome and the effects of some products on occupants (e.g., allergic reactions, illness, nausea, etc.).

Building materials often contain adhesives, resins, caulking, fillers and finishes that produce **volatile organic compounds** (VOC's) which off-gas emissions into the interior of structures. Given concerns, considerable progress has been made in green building by lowering VOC omissions or, in some instances, creating Zero-VOC products:

- Medium density fibreboard (MDF) containing urea-formaldehyde or phenol-formaldehyde, has traditionally been the mainstay of house construction. In recent years, both formaldehyde-free and low emission MDF are available.

- Adhesives used in flooring and related applications have also been targeted given off-gas potential, particularly owing to the use of plastic resins. Water-based adhesives or the use of plant resins have dramatically reduced the incidence of toxicity resulting from VOC emissions.

- Various zero or low emission VOC painting and finishing products are now available on the market and considerable advances are being made in others (e.g., cabinets, countertops, caulking, fillers, plumbing products and housing envelope barriers).

> **Volatile Organic Compounds**
>
> Products that have gas emissions which can impact indoor air quality.

VOLATILE ORGANIC COMPOUNDS (VOC'S)

Volatile organic compounds can be toxic; i.e., cause harmful health effects to occupants of buildings, particularly those individuals who are hypersensitive to various chemicals and gases. The term *volatile* refers to the ability of a substance to evaporate.

VOCs have received extensive attention given that numerous gases emitted from building materials (referred to as off-gasing) can relate directly to flu-like symptoms, headaches and nausea whether at work or at home. VOCs can be found in such products as carpeting, paints, stains, varnishes and cleaning supplies.

Often such gases are most noticeable at point of installation, but then begin to dissipate. However, that process can take an extensive period of time. Given that Canadians are purported to spend up to 90% of their time in buildings, the effects on health standards can be significant. Individuals exposed to such gases may have an immediate reaction, but research also indicates that people can fall victim to sensitization. In other words, an individual may over a period of time develop a serious allergic reaction to a chemical that initially only caused minor discomfort.

Organizations such as the Canada Mortgage and Housing Corporation and green building advocates have developed material guides to assist consumers in selecting non-VOC or VOC-reduced products. While total avoidance of VOC products may be not be feasible, significant limitation of such compounds, the selection of lowest-possible VOC emission rates and the introduction of a proper filtration/ventilation system strategy are key steps to minimize possible problems.

 WEB LINKS

For additional information concerning volatile organic compounds, search the Internet using your favourite search engine (e.g., *www.google.ca*). Information is also available by searching on the Canada Mortgage and Housing Corporation web site (*www.cmhc.ca*).

SICK BUILDING SYNDROME (SBS)

Sick building syndrome generally involves circumstances under which building occupants experience health-related problems apparently arising from time spent in part or all of a structure. The term *syndrome* refers to symptoms that, in combination, characterize a certain type of illness.

Conditions associated with SBS can be temporary such as fumes entering a structure or long-term resulting from air pollutants, mould, spores or other particulate affecting indoor air quality. Poor indoor air quality can arise from various circumstances ranging from building design/construction to specific activities being carried out (e.g., manufacturing processes).

SBS symptoms can be diverse, but typically centre on dizziness, nausea, lack of concentration, allergic reactions, throat irritations, headaches and asthma. Typical causes of sick building syndrome include inadequate building ventilation, lack of proper air filtration to limit external entry of contaminants, inappropriate measures to control moisture which can give rise to bacteria and moulds, and building products that emit volatile organic compounds (VOCs).

DOORS

A door is a solid barrier for opening or closing an entrance-way including associated framing materials. Solid wood doors have been the traditional exterior door as wood has certain natural insulating properties, although weather tightness is always enhanced with the addition of a storm door. However, the heaviest wood door does not provide as much insulation value as a poorly insulated wall.

Practitioners should be familiar with basic facts regarding doors. Solid wood doors provide reasonable security depending on the amount of glass area, the hardware used and the quality of installation. Hollow wood doors are generally not for exterior use and are inferior to solid wood doors regarding insulation, security and durability. Deterioration of the wood veneer on the surface exposed to the exterior is a common problem.

Metal doors, often having decorative plastic mouldings on the surface, are commonly used as exterior doors in modern construction and typically have a metal exterior skin together with an internal insulating material (usually polystyrene or polyurethane). Magnetic weatherstripping can be used to create a proper air seal. Problems have occurred when a storm door is added to an insulated metal door. The space between the doors may become overheated, the plastic mouldings can be affected, and in some instances, the metal door panel may even buckle. Many manufacturers do not recommend the use of storm doors for this type of metal door.

Door Frame

The framework, upon which a door is hung, is made of wood or hollow metal and includes the following:

Head	The horizontal top portion of the door frame.
Jamb	Either the left or right vertical portion of the frame.
Sill	The bottom of the door at floor level.
Stop	A continuous projection around the frame to resist the door from travelling beyond a closing point.
Buck	The sub-frame of wood or pressed metal to which the door case is fixed.

Sliding Glass Door

The sliding glass door has been a popular feature in residential property since the 1950's. Early models were made of metal that often resulted in condensation and ice on inside surfaces. The introduction of thermal breaks between the inner and outer halves, closing/locking hardware and improved framing have greatly improved the product over the past four decades. In particular, the thermal break was effective in keeping the inside metal part of the frame warmer, thereby reducing condensation and icing problems.

Sliding doors typically have two thicknesses of glass. Each pane can be in a separate sliding door component, or there may be one door sash with a double-glazed or even triple-glazed pane. Better quality sliding glass doors are distinguished by more expensive hardware and sophisticated means of adjustment.

Why a Lintel is Needed

CURIOSITY

The lintel is a horizontal structural member (beam) that supports the load over an opening, such as a door or window. The lintel performs the same function as an arch. Typically flat, it relies on the inherent strength of the material used to transmit the load, as opposed to the arch principle. The area that the lintel supports can safely be thought of as a triangle above the lintel. The height of the triangle is roughly half the width of the opening. Accordingly, a window with twenty stories of brick above requires the same lintel as a window with six feet of brick above. Lintels are typically constructed of steel, wood, stone or concrete. Typical problems include undersizing in relation to load requirements, improper end bearings and general deterioration.

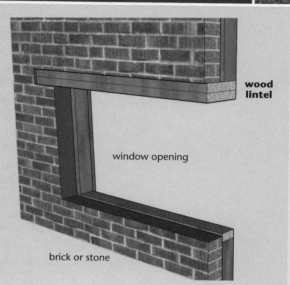

wood lintel

window opening

brick or stone

WINDOWS

A window can be broadly defined for real estate purposes as an opening in the wall of a building, typically providing light and ventilation. Various window types are marketed in Canada with most containing more or less common components.

- The pieces of glass are called panes or lites.
- The panes are held in a sash that may move as the window is opened.
- The sides of the sash are called the stiles.
- The top and bottom pieces are the rails.
- When the window within the sash is divided into several small panes, the dividing pieces are muntins.
- The sides of the window frame are the jambs, the sill is the bottom assembly of the frame and the head is the top.
- The casing or trim (exterior and interior) covers the frame edge to finish the window edges in relation to wall finishes.

Conventional window glass is $3/32$ inch to $1/8$ inch with thicker glass used where increased thermal insulating value is desired. Glass can be strengthened by tempering, tinted to reduce glare or absorb heat, coated to reflect heat, installed with wire to provide additional fire resistance or laminated (made up of two or more layers of glass and a plastic film between the layers) to improve strength, safety and/or sound insulation.

Glazing

The term glazing refers to the act of furnishing and/or fitting panes or sheets of glass as in the case of windows and doors. Prior to 1950, all windows were single-glazed (one pane of glass). The insulation value of a single conventional pane of glass is approximately R-1. Presently, double-glazing is either factory sealed or vented. The factory sealed, double-glazing is designed to have no air infiltration or exfiltration between the two panes. Vented double glazing allows for outside air movement to the space between the two panes.

Optimum air space between the panes is widely debated but is usually considered to be roughly to ¾ inch. Typical double-glazed windows have an approximate R-value of 2. The triple-glazed window provides for two air spaces between three panes of glass with an R-3 or slightly higher insulating value.

EXAMPLE   *The Factory Windows*

Buyer Jones is concerned about energy loss from windows. The industrial property under consideration lacks factory sealed, double-glazed windows. Admittedly, the two front windows are factory sealed with double-glazing, but all remaining windows consist of a primary (inner) window and a separate storm (outer) window. Jones calls in an energy expert to review the situation.

The expert explains that the value of a primary plus a storm window is not significantly more than a primary window. Therefore, the single pane of glass on all but the front windows translates into roughly R-1 whereas double-glazing produces R-2 and triple, R-3. The expert explains that energy costs relate not only to the R-value, but also the amount of air leaks given the primary/storm arrangement. In summary, Jones must address two issues: first, the loss of energy by heat conduction owing to a low R-value in the primary/storm window combinations, and second, outside air infiltration due to leakage in and around the frames of those windows.

Casement Window

A casement window is hinged at the side and can open either inward or outward. A handle is located on the side of the window opposite the hinge along with a crank, and in some cases, a guide bar along the bottom of the window. An operating crank is often included at the bottom of modern casement windows. Glazing may be single, double or triple. Manufacturing materials include wood, metal, vinyl or a combination thereof. Muntins may be used to separate the glass into smaller panes (usually done on older, traditional style homes).

Casement windows are popular as replacement windows owing to proper ventilation and degree of air tightness. Larger casement windows require quality hardware to ensure smooth operation.

lintel

frame

muntin

stop

sash

sill

Double Hung Window

A double hung window is constructed with two moving parts: an outer part in the top half of the opening and an inner part on the bottom half of the opening. Both halves can be moved up and down in their guides.

Early versions of double-hung windows were held open by using a counterweight system. Some modern double-hung windows use a spring loaded mechanism concealed in the side of the sash. Certain high quality versions are pivoted so that the external glass area can be swung inside for cleaning. Double-hung windows can be wood, metal, vinyl or a combination thereof.

Slider

A type of window normally identified by single panes of glass sliding on a wood or vinyl track with a simple locking device and pull knobs attached to the surface of the glass. The slider window was popular during the 1960's and is generally regarded as a poor quality window. If properly constructed, however, this type of window can perform as well as any other normal household design.

Lower quality sliders have given this style of window a somewhat tarnished reputation, as they suffer from air and water leakage. Better sliders are provided with sashes (metal, vinyl or wood) around the glass. Sliders are relatively inexpensive and typically have very simple locking hardware. If well made, their performance can be as good as any other type of window. Glazing may be single, double or triple.

PROBLEM AREAS

Problems include low quality hardware, tracks at the bottom that do not drain water to the outside, poorly fitted slides and improper joints at corners of the frames. Leaks often result in water damage to wall finishes below the windows, most often at the corners. Exterior caulking may help in some cases; in others, storm windows added to the outside improve weather tightness. Where the problem is chronic, replacement windows may be the best answer.

Skylight

A skylight, frequently installed both in new construction and resale homes, is typically made of tempered glass or plastic (flat or bubble shaped). These materials have better resistance to breakage than conventional glass, although they are subject to scratching. Abrasive cleaners should not be used.

PROBLEM AREAS

Practitioners should be aware of selected problems that can arise. Poorly installed skylights can create a leakage problem due to incorrect flashing. Manufactured skylights should be carefully installed following the manufacturer's recommendations. Flashing kits available from the factory should be used, where appropriate.

Most skylights are not operable and are often installed after the house is built. The installation can be tricky, given the need to cut a hole in the roof (and structural considerations related thereto) and ensure that leakage does not occur. This can be difficult, as the skylight usually presents a curb that will collect water. The skylight requires flashing detail that makes a good watertight connection between the roof and the skylight.

Window Standards and Efficiency Ratings

Windows can contribute up to 25% of overall heat loss in a residential structure and, consequently, any strategy to improve energy efficiency must closely address this issue. Significantly improved technologies during the past few years have resulted in appreciable gains in overall efficiency and durability. Windows are primarily rated according to the following two standards.

CSA STANDARDS (CSA–A440)

CSA standards provide for window ratings using three primary criteria:

AIR TIGHTNESS (A CRITERIA)	WATER TIGHTNESS (B CRITERIA)	WIND RESISTANCE (C CRITERIA)
Air tightness refers to leakage based on a 40 km/h (25 mph) wind. A1 represents the maximum acceptable standard, with A2 being 60% of A1 and A3 being 20% of A1.	Water tightness is a test involving a constant stream of water against the window plus varying levels of windload. B1 represents 57 km/h (35 mph) wind/load with progressive levels up to B7 which represents 123 km/h (76 mph).	Windload and blow-out ratings range from C1 to C5. In the case of windload deflection, 104 km/h (64 mph) is C1 with the highest load (C5) at 329 km/h (204 mph).

The CSA standard also addresses condensation resistance, forced entry resistance and ease of operation. In addition, components related to the window system (e.g., screens) are tested.

EFFICIENCY RATING (ER)

The ER represents the heating required for a window during the heating season based on the combined analysis of solar heat gain, heat loss (through frames, spacers and glass) and air leakage. The efficiency rating measures thermal performance in which a positive number indicates that the window generates more solar heat gain than heat loss. A

negative number indicates that more heat is lost than gained. Value ranges are from a low of -80 (very poor) to +12 (excellent). To place the ratings in perspective, a rating of -8 to +12 would roughly correspond to an R-value of 5 and a window between -15 and +5 would represent an R-value of 4.

ER Ratings   CAUTION

Caution is necessary when interpreting efficiency ratings. For example, frame to glass ratio can impact results, despite the fact that similarly-sized windows are being tested. A fixed window typically has reduced framing as compared with an operable window and altered ratings may result given differing glass sizes. Also, rating variations are possible given that operable sash windows have additional framing in comparison to its fixed version counterpart. The Model National Energy Code for Houses provides acceptable minimums for efficiency ratings based on various locales across Canada.

WEB LINKS

The Model National Energy Code for Houses is more fully detailed on the National Research Council Canada site. Go to *www.nationalcodes.ca*.

WEB LINKS

The Insulating Glass Manufacturers Alliance (IGMA) sets product certification for insulating glass. Go to *www.igmaonline.org*.

Efficiency: Window Features

LOW-E

Low-e (low emissivity) refers to the ability of a surface to reflect long-wave radiation. Low emissivity glass contains a thin metallic layer that allows sunlight into the structure during winter months. This layer retards the outward flow of internally-generated furnace heat. In summer, this same glazing allows sunlight into rooms, but significantly reduces unwanted heat (long-wave radiation) that is absorbed by reflective surfaces; e.g., driveways, adjacent structures, decks, sidewalks and other materials near the building and radiated upwards to windows.

As a result, a significant portion of this heat fails to enter the building, which typically translates into lower cooling costs. New low-e coatings can now limit both short-wave and long-wave infrared solar radiation, as well as ultraviolet rays that can damage draperies, furnishings and carpeting.

U-VALUE

U-value is a measure of heat flow through an object (e.g., window glazing), often referred to as the heat transfer coefficient. The U-value is the reciprocal of the R-value commonly associated with insulation; i.e., if the U-value decreases, the R-value increases. U-value is a component in establishing the efficiency rating (ER) of windows.

Inert Gas Fills
Gas, such as argon or krypton, inserted between glass panes in windows.

INERT GAS FILL

Inert gases such as argon and krypton are currently used as fill between glazings given their ability to reduce window heat transfer and cold spots at the window base between the panes. Both **inert gas fills** are non-toxic and colourless. Argon is most common, given the more expensive krypton option.

OTHER FEATURES/CONSIDERATIONS

High efficiency windows also boast other features; e.g., double and triple glazing and low conductivity spacers between window panes. However, the single most important factor to consider involves installation. Window system efficiency hinges on how well windows are fitted and insulated. The best ER value can be effectively nullified without prudent attention to installation details.

Homeowners should also carefully review the merits of a partial replacement (retrofit of window components) versus a full tearout. While costs associated with a tearout and full replacement using high performance windows can be substantially higher, long term benefits in terms of comfort, energy-efficiency and durability are usually realized.

KNOWLEDGE INTEGRATION

Notables

- Sloped shingle roofs dominate residential markets with built-up roofs being most popular in commercial and industrial applications.

- Common roof leakage problems involve flashings, skylight leaks and ice damming.

- Roof materials include asphalt, metal, wood shingles, slate and concrete/clay tile.

- Eavestroughs and downspouts are vital building components that protect against damage due to runoff and assist in keep basement areas dry.

- Various exterior wall finishes are used in Ontario including brick veneer, vinyl siding and stucco.

- Solid masonry walls are rarely found in today's residential construction, but were popular in homes dating back to the early part of the twentieth century.

- Drywall and plaster are essentially the same material, except that drywall is pre-manufactured.

- Environmental issues and indoor air quality have become an increasingly important concern when selecting building materials and wall finishes.

- Indoor air quality can be impacted by finishes used given the existence of volatile organic compounds. Poor air quality has been associated with sick building syndrome.

- Doors can be broadly categorized as either solid or hollow; the former most commonly used for exterior doors and the latter for interior purposes.

- Windows can contribute up to 25% of over-all heat loss in a residential structure.

- Windows are currently rated on CSA Standards (including air tightness, water tightness and wind resistance) and also by means of efficiency ratings.

- Low-e glass and inert gas fill have improved window efficiency.

Glossary

Only selected items are listed given the scope of construction terms.

Brick Veneer	Low-E	Vinyl Siding
Drywall	Metal Siding	Volatile Organic Compounds
Flashing	Pitch	
Green Roof	Shingle	
Inert Gas Fill	Sick Building Syndrome	

Web Links

Web links are included for general interest regarding selected chapter topics.

Volatile Organic Compounds
For additional information concerning volatile organic compounds, search the Internet using your favourite search engine (e.g., **www.google.ca**). Information is also available by searching on the Canada Mortgage and Housing Corporation web site (**www.cmhc.ca**).

Energy Code
The Model National Energy Code for Houses is more fully detailed on the National Research Council Canada site. Go to **www.nationalcodes.ca**.

Glass Standards
The Insulating Glass Manufacturers Alliance (IGMA) sets product certification for insulating glass. Go to **www.igmaonline.org**.

Strategic Thinking For Your Career

Questions are included to assist in developing your new career. No answers are provided.

1. What roofing materials are most commonly used for residential and commercial structures in the local marketplace?

2. What local information sources are available to expand my construction knowledge concerning roofing, finishes, doors and windows?

3. What types of energy efficient components in windows are marketed locally?

4. Are there new innovations being used in building finishes within my marketplace?

5. How can I improve my knowledge of interior finishes and features to be in a better position to assist buyer clients looking for new homes?

SECTION III   STRUCTURAL TYPES AND COMPONENTS

Chapter Mini-Review

Solutions are located in the Appendix.

1. The most common type of asphalt shingle used today weighs 210 pounds per square.

   ⦿ True   ⦿ False

2. Most asphalt shingles are self-sealing and classified by weight.

   ⦿ True   ⦿ False

3. The life expectancy of wood shingles can extend to 40 years, depending on the shingle quality.

   ⦿ True   ⦿ False

4. The pitch of a roof has little or no impact on how long asphalt shingles will last before having to be replaced.

   ⦿ True   ⦿ False

5. Roof leaks can be difficult to trace because the water does not always appear on the interior immediately below the source of the leak.

   ⦿ True   ⦿ False

6. A window sash is basically the frame that holds the pane of glass.

   ⦿ True   ⦿ False

7. Glazing is the process of tempering glass to increase its strength.

   ⦿ True   ⦿ False

8. Brick masonry walls are commonly used when constructing new residential structures in Ontario.

   ⦿ True   ⦿ False

9. Drywall in residential structures is usually installed over a base coat of plaster.

   ⦿ True   ⦿ False

10. Low-e glass produces greater energy efficiency in windows due to its ability to reflect long-wave radiation.

    ⦿ True   ⦿ False

11. An ER of -80 represents an excellent efficiency rating for a window.

    ⦿ True   ⦿ False

12. Volatile organic compounds can be toxic.

    ⦿ True   ⦿ False

13. A lintel might be found above a door or a window in a typical residential structure.

    ⦿ True   ⦿ False

14. A double hung window is constructed with two moving parts.

    ⦿ True   ⦿ False

Active Learning Exercises

Solutions are located in the Appendix.

▣ Exercise 1   Fill-in-the-Blanks

1.1   In a solid masonry brick wall, a wythe is a [   ] of brick.

1.2   [   ] eavestroughs are considered the best, with a life expectancy of between 50 and 100 years.

1.3   A built-up roof is commonly called a [   ] and [   ] roof.

1.4   Roll roofing normally has a life expectancy of [   ] to [   ] years.

1.5   A slider window typically travels in a wood or [   ] track.

1.6   Early glass sliding doors made with [   ] were very poor insulators.

1.7   On most houses, the eavestrough is attached to the [   ] board.

1.8   A downspout should have a minimum discharge distance of [   ] feet.

■ Exercise 2   Multiple Choice

2.1   Which of the following is the most appropriate description of a casement window?

   a.   Hinged at the top to swing out.

   b.   Windows which move up and down in their guides.

   c.   Hinged at the side and opens inward or outward.

   d.   Two panes of glass sliding on a wooden track.

2.2   Which of the following is NOT correct?

   a.   Most skylights have leaked or will leak at some point.

   b.   Triple glazing is becoming more common as energy costs increase.

   c.   Most doors are a source of heat loss.

   d.   Most manufacturers recommend the use of storm doors with insulated core metal doors.

2.3   Most roof flashings are galvanized steel and are designed to keep water out. In which of the following circumstances are flashings usually necessary?

   a.   At changes of direction.

   b.   At joints in material.

   c.   Where dissimilar materials meet.

   d.   All of the above.

2.4   Which of the following statements is NOT true with respect to eavestroughs and downspouts?

   a.   Downspouts should discharge water into proper drains or onto the ground a good distance away from foundation walls.

   b.   An important function of eavestroughs and downspouts is to collect leaves from the roof areas and discharge them away from the foundation.

   c.   The proper function of eavestroughs and downspouts should contribute toward a dry basement.

   d.   Eavestroughs and downspouts will help protect the walls of buildings from water ordinarily running off the roof.

2.5   Volatile organic compounds:

   a.   Are essential in the glazing process in window production.

   b.   May be found in building materials which off-gas emissions into the interior of a structure.

   c.   Are only identified as a problem involving off-gasing within commercial and not residential structures.

   d.   Are no longer a health-related issue.

2.6   A green roof has many benefits. Which is NOT one of them?

    a.   Improves the reflective quality of the roof.

    b.   Improves stormwater runoff in and around the building.

    c.   Improves the shade factor thereby reducing heat gain/loss.

    d.   Improves air quality.

2.7   Which of the following statements is NOT true with respect to windows?

    a.   Windows provide light and ventilation for homes, at the expense of some heat loss.

    b.   As energy costs have increased, double and triple glazed windows have become more popular.

    c.   The rain screen principle refers to water drainage techniques specifically involving window installations.

    d.   Windows may include low emissivity technology to improve energy efficiency.

2.8   Which of the following statements is correct with respect to roofing?

    a.   Most roofing materials are excellent insulators.

    b.   Asphalt shingles have a life expectancy of at least 50 years.

    c.   While wind may cause shingle roof deterioration, sunlight does not affect the wear factor.

    d.   Corrugated plastic tile is typically used for roofs over patios and light structures.

2.9   Which of the following statements is correct?

    a.   The steeper the roof pitch, the longer the shingled roof will typically last.

    b.   Built-up roofs are designed primarily for residential structures.

    c.   Inert gas fills are now used in all residential and commercial windows.

    d.   A solid masonry wall requires an interior wooden framework for support.

2.10   Building components that assist in keeping basement areas dry by directing water away from the foundation are the:

    a.   Fibreboard.

    b.   Lintels.

    c.   Eavestrough/Downspouts.

    d.   Exterior Insulation and Finishing System.

SECTION III   STRUCTURAL TYPES AND COMPONENTS

■ **Exercise 3   Water Stains**

Mr. and Mrs. Jones are carefully inspecting a 1970's bungalow with brick veneer on the front elevation and brick veneer/aluminum combination on the remaining three sides. The structure is original with the exception of updated kitchen cupboards and a hallway skylight. The Joneses are viewing the property in the afternoon following an early morning thunderstorm in the area.

3.1   The Joneses detect water stains immediately above a window frame in the master bedroom. It appears to have been patched recently. Identify three possible causes.

3.2   Mr. Jones notes that small amounts of water are leaking from small holes between the bricks on the front brick veneer wall. Why is this happening? Be specific.

3.3   Mr. and Mrs. Jones removed their shoes when inspecting the house. While walking on the broadloom in the recreation room, Mrs. Jones suddenly noticed carpet dampness near the basement wall facing the backyard. What could be the possible cause(s)?

CHAPTER 8

Mechanical Systems and Insulation

Introduction

Chapter 8 concludes the section focused on structural and building components. Basic mechanical systems in both residential and commercial structures include electrical, heating and plumbing systems. Insulation systems are also detailed given their direct relevance to heating systems. As with previous topics, emphasis is placed on residential structures with further details concerning commercial buildings included in applicable, subsequent courses.

Salespeople are expected to have a general familiarity with mechanical systems and insulation, but are not required to demonstrate detailed technical knowledge. Further, practitioners should be cautioned not to make representations regarding such matters, but rather to refer consumers to appropriate experts.

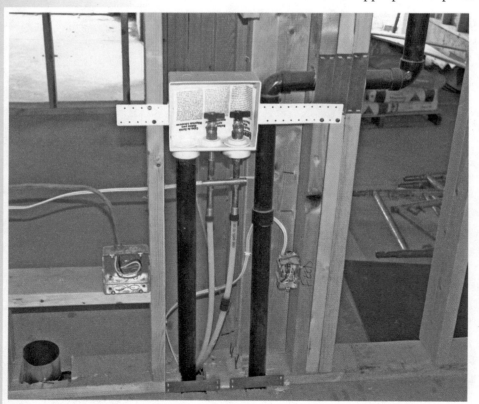

This chapter seeks to provide sufficient information to ensure a general familiarity with terms and basic operational concepts that can prove helpful when working with buyers and sellers. Buyers, whether as clients or customers, may look to salespeople for insight into such topics.

Topics include major electrical components found in residential properties, various types of heating systems commonly used in Ontario and plumbing distribution systems, along with a detailed discussion of water well and sewage systems facing rural practitioners. Information concerning insulation places appropriate emphasis on new techniques to improve energy efficiency and promote general energy conservation.

Learning Outcomes

At the conclusion of this chapter, students will be able to:

- Identify and describe major components of an electrical system including electrical service size, entrance cable, main disconnect, distribution panel and outlets.
- Identify and describe a heating system including types of systems, furnaces, boiler systems, HVAC, fireplaces, chimneys and flues.
- Briefly outline new heating/cooling innovations including the use of ground source heat pumps.
- Identify and describe a plumbing system including major components involving water distribution and drainage/venting, as well as hot water heaters.
- Describe well water analysis from both chemical and bacteriological (microbiological) perspectives.
- Discuss installation, maintenance and supply/measurement considerations in relation to water wells.
- Discuss sewage systems with particular emphasis relating to on-site systems including approvals, permits, inspections, classes of systems and records.
- Explain briefly the operation of Class 4 and Class 5 sewage systems.
- Identify and describe heat/gain loss, R-values, insulation and energy efficiency considerations in structures.

MECHANICAL SYSTEMS

Mechanical systems in residential properties are broadly grouped under electrical, heating and plumbing. New homes have either 100 or 200 amp services, 100-amp services are most frequently found in resales dating from the 1960's, with 60-amp in earlier years. Two hundred amp services have now become commonplace, given increasingly larger homes and greater electrical demands in today's society.

Residential heating systems include forced air, hot water, radiant and electrical baseboard (or comparable). In commercial properties, heating systems are more commonly referred to as HVAC systems (heating, ventilation and air conditioning).

Plumbing systems involve both supply and waste components. Practitioners must pay special attention to private systems involving water wells and septic tanks.

ELECTRICAL

Overview

Electrical systems are generally expanded and upgraded over the life of a house, rather than taken out and replaced on a regular basis. **Electrical service size**, ranging from 60 amps in old homes to 200 amps in new, larger homes, is dictated by the service entrance cable entering the property.

Electrical Service Size

The number of amps provided to a structure(s) through a primary service wire.

Current, measured in amps, is the electricity flow resulting when voltage is applied across a given resistance. Voltage is the potential energy of the electrical system. The resistance of any given material to the movement of electricity through it is measured in ohms. The power is measured in watts and is calculated by multiplying the voltage by the current. The amount of electricity a wire can carry in amps is determined largely by its diameter.

The **distribution panel** distributes electricity through individual circuits into various parts of the house. While older systems can handle low energy appliances, upgrading is required for modern appliances such as dryers, room air conditioners and the like. Consequently, real estate practitioners may find dated distribution panels replaced with updated circuit breaker systems to accommodate these appliances.

Distribution Panel

An electrical panel between the service entrance wires and power distribution within a structure.

Hydro One oversees electrical standards for residential property. In an earlier chapter, the need for **electrical inspections** of accessory apartments was emphasized. In new construction, electrical requirements are set out in the Ontario Building Code. No retroactive provisions exist concerning dated electrical installations in existing houses. For that reason, real estate practitioners may encounter systems that are inadequate and may not perform safely. Expert advice is required.

WEB LINKS

Hydro One is most commonly associated with managing the electricity transmission and distribution systems in Ontario, but has other subsidiary companies including Hydro One Remotes that provides electrical services to distant communities in Ontario. For more information, go to *www.hydroone.ca*.

Electrical Current

Current, measured in amps, is the flow of electricity that results when a voltage is applied across a given resistance. Voltage is the potential energy of the electrical system. A large

electrical voltage means that a significant potential electric force is available. Most houses are equipped with a 240-volt system that provides 240 or 120 volts.

The resistance of any given material to the movement of electricity through it is measured in ohms. When there is no electrical flow, the resistance is considered to be infinitely large and is referred to as an open circuit. When effectively no resistance exists, the current load is very large and is referred to as a short circuit. This is usually unsafe and will blow a fuse.

The current flowing through the electrical system is what electrocutes individuals. Generally, a current of less than one amp is capable of killing someone. A 60-watt light bulb normally draws about 0.5 amps, however, the amount of current depends on resistance. Water in close proximity to a live electrical wire is extremely dangerous and must be avoided.

> **EXAMPLE**   *Electricity Flow*
>
> When an appliance is turned on, the flow of electricity generates heat—the more amps flowing through a circuit, the hotter the wire becomes. Since the voltage is fixed at roughly 120 volts, the amount of current that flows will be the result of the resistance in the circuit. If an appliance malfunctions or too many appliances are plugged in, the amount of electric current flowing through the wire will be more than can be safely handled and will begin to overheat. The purpose of a fuse or circuit breaker is to shut off the electricity at the point when overheating may occur.

Electrical Service Size

The size of the electrical service (amps) is provided from the primary line to the building. As the power enters the house, it travels into a main disconnect with two fuses or two circuit breakers, sometimes connected together to look like one big breaker. One fuse is for the black wire and one fuse is for the red. No fuse is necessary for the neutral wire. The fuse is rated by the amperage that the wire can safely carry (60 amps, 100 amps, etc.).

Service entrance cable size will determine service size, however, the two fuse ratings on the main panel are normally reliable in determining that size. Two 100 amp fuses in that main disconnect, for example, would normally indicate a 100 amp service—the two fuses are NOT added together. However, certain exceptions apply and caution is recommended. Real estate practitioners can also encounter 60 amp services in older residences. While this service size is adequate for normal household lighting and small appliances, heavy appliances in conjunction with the operation of normal appliances can exceed the maximum load. Many institutional lenders are unwilling to finance a home with 60 amp service, unless the electrical service is upgraded.

Again, it is important to emphasize that one cannot add the two fuse ratings together to get the house service. Increasing the service size means replacing the wires coming from the street to the house and providing a new main disconnect. If the wires run overhead, the conversion is not normally a major undertaking. However, if the wires are underground, a problem may present itself if the conduit through which the wires are passed is not large enough to hold a larger set of wires. This would mean excavation and replacement of the conduit. The appropriate utilities office should be contacted.

Electrical services in rural areas are impacted by unique circumstances owing to geographic distances and isolated locations. Consequently, certain additional costing factors must be considered.

Provincial utilities, in servicing rural areas, will install primary lines along dedicated/accepted road allowances for properties such as seasonal cottages up to a pre-determined distance. Any additional costs are normally borne by the customer. The utility company also typically provides secondary lines on the customer's property for a pre-determined distance (referred to as free wire) with additional costs borne by the customer.

Certain costs may be reduced if electrical and telephone services are installed at the same time. For marine cables, the user must obtain a separate quotation. However, the use of marine cables has been dramatically curtailed owing to environmental considerations.

Questions concerning procedures and quotations for the provision of electrical services in rural areas should be directed to the appropriate utilities office.

Electrical Service Entrance Cable

The electrical entrance cable provides electrical service by overhead or underground wires from the street supply to the structure. A typical house has 240 volts brought in through overhead or underground wires from the street supply. A normal system is composed of three wires. The black and red wires are live, and the white wire is neutral. The potential between the black and white wire is 120 volts, as well as between the red and white wires, however, between the black and red, the potential is 240 volts. Incidentally, the red wire often has black sheathing.

The size of the service entrance cable determines how much electricity is available. Either copper or aluminum cable may be used. Aluminum connections should be coated with an anti-oxidant, grease-like material, to prevent rusting.

Electrical Main Disconnect

A disconnect switch is used to provide or shut off all power in a structure. Switch handles are located on the outside and main fuses or breakers are inside. Hydro authorities often seal the cover on the main disconnect.

The main disconnect is frequently incorporated into the distribution panel. In some structures, the main disconnect is simply a box that stands alone. In either case, the rating on the main disconnect box itself must be at least as large as the service entrance cables and fuses inside. For example, if a house has a 100-amp service, a main disconnect box rated for only 60 amps is not acceptable. More than 60 amps passing through this main disconnect may lead to overheating.

Distribution Panel

The distribution panel is an electrical panel providing the interface between the service entrance wires to a structure and the wires for dispersing power throughout that structure.

The distribution panel, as an interface, is connected by service wires from the main disconnect. The black and red wires are each connected to a live busbar (a current carrying metal bar with several connection points) and the white wire is connected to the neutral busbar. Each household circuit fuse (or breaker) is directly connected to either the red or black busbar.

The distribution panel typically has several 120-volt circuits (10 are required for most homes) and one or more 240-volt circuits for large electric appliances. Many codes now require a panel with room for 24 120-volt circuits. Real estate practitioners may also encounter auxiliary panels which do not bring additional power into the house, but simply allow for more branch circuits to carry electricity to various areas of the home. An illustration is provided showing a typical distribution panel found in residential structures.

Outlets

An outlet is a receptacle into which electric appliances can be plugged. Prior to 1950, all electrical appliances were ungrounded, with two slots, or two slots of different sizes (polarized) so that only polarized appliances could be installed in the proper orientation. The convention is that the smaller slot is for the black wire and the larger for the white.

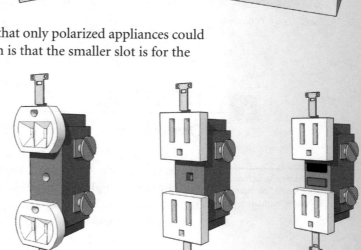

Grounding of electrical outlets became popular after 1960, as the third ground wire affords additional protection. Grounded outlets have a third ground wire that normally conducts no electricity, providing a safety escape route in case something goes wrong with the appliance or receptacle. Live electricity may be brought to a point where it could be touched by a person, leading to electric shock when an appliance malfunctions, a cord is damaged or a receptacle is faulty.

The purpose of the ground wire is to provide a path that the electricity will follow. It should be understood that grounded receptacles are only of value where appliances with ground plugs are used. Typical outlets found in residential properties are illustrated.

Ground Fault Circuit Interrupter

A ground fault circuit interrupter is a device specifically designed to shut the power off to a circuit when as little as .005 amps are leaking. If there is a flaw in the system, some electricity may be flowing to a dangerous spot, but not enough to blow a fuse or trip a breaker. The ground fault circuit compares the electricity flowing from both the white wire and black wire. If the difference is more than .005, the system will be shut off.

If a nail has inadvertently been driven through an electrical cable and is barely touching the black wire, there may be a small current of less than one amp flowing from the black wire into the nail. Under normal circumstances, this would not be detected and since the nail presents a high resistance (not connected to a good conductor), electricity leaking out of the system would probably not be noticed. However, this can become very dangerous if a person (particularly if not well insulated with rubber gloves or shoes or is perhaps wet) touches the nail. The resistance is lowered and a very large electrical current can flow through the person to the ground thus creating an electrical shock hazard. Ground fault circuit interrupters are normally used for bathroom circuits and exterior outlets, but could be utilized in various situations.

Knob-and-Tube Wiring   CAUTION

Knob-and-tube wiring was used in residential construction during the early part of the last century (pre-1950). The wiring set derives its name from the ceramic knobs by which the wire is secured and the ceramic tubes used where it passes through wood-framing members such as joists. Insulation breakdown is the most frequent reason for replacement.

Real estate practitioners must be aware of recent concerns regarding knob-and-tube electrical systems. In particular, insurance companies are increasingly cautious both about 60-amp services and older buildings with knob-and-tube wiring. While some insurers will renew existing policies on such properties, a change of ownership and/or selection of a new insurer can lead to a refusal. Older systems may not be inherently dangerous, but problems can arise with over-loading due to new appliances and other modernization within houses.

Buyers and sellers should be aware that an inspection of an older home may result in expenditures on the electrical system. For example, knob-and-tube in the basement area (next to heat ducts and copper plumbing pipes) will probably have to be replaced.

HEATING

Overview

Heating System

A system used to warm structures including but not limited to warm air, steam, hot water, radiant and electrical.

The **heating system** generates heat for disbursement to various parts of a structure. **Furnaces** are central heating systems in that the heat is generated in one location and distributed through the house. **Boilers** are also central heating systems, as heat generated in one location is disbursed via piping to the various rooms.

Capacity refers to the amount of heat the system can generate. Capacity readings are given as BTU's per hour. Heating systems should be:

- Large enough to provide adequate heat on the coldest day;
- Reliable and safe;
- Inexpensive to install and operate efficiently; and
- Capable of heating all parts of the home equally or differentially, as the occupants desire.

No one heating system performs all these functions perfectly. Every heating system is a compromise in one way or another, with initial low cost often as the predominant criteria for selection. Often wood burning **fireplaces** or wood stoves are used requiring substantial flues and chimneys. Alternatively, gas fireplaces offer various options including inserts, zero-clearance units and free-standing designs. Direct vent (venting as apposed to flue and chimney) models are the most popular.

Heating Systems

Convection or radiant systems, or a combination of both are typically used to heat structures. Hot air, hot water and steam are the most common heating systems in residential and commercial structures.

Warm Air	Heat is distributed to the various rooms of the house through metal hot air ducts with cool air returned through returning cold air ducts. The temperature is controlled by a thermostat. The air flow may be by gravity or forced by means of a blower fan that is placed at the entrance of the cool-air passage into the furnace. Forced air systems are the most common.
Steam	Heat is distributed by means of steam from the boiler to cast iron radiators. Steam gives up its heat to the radiator, becomes cool, condenses into water and returns by gravity to the boiler.
Hot Water	This type of system can operate by gravity, or water may be forced through the system by motor-operated impellers or circulators. The system may have either a one-pipe or a two-pipe configuration. In the one-pipe system containing a single main, the hot water passes through each radiator, returns to the main and mixes with the hot water travelling to the next radiator. The cooler water returning from the radiator reduces the temperature of the water in the main. The two-pipe system has a separate pipe for the return of the cooler water from the radiator to the boiler. Hot water heating, in addition to quiet operation, provides steady, even heat. Hot water heating systems are fairly common in older homes.
Radiant	Most systems are not entirely radiant as convection is also used. In panel heating, for example, the direct heating units are sections of the floor, ceiling or wall. Heat is obtained by circulating water through copper pipes embedded in the concrete floor of houses without basements.
Electric	Two main types of electric heating systems are found in homes: baseboard resistance heater and radiant heating cables or coils that are placed in the ceiling or floor. Electric heat has several advantages such as quiet operation, cleanliness, elimination of chimneys, thermostatic control for each room and cheaper installation cost.

Furnace

A furnace is a central heating system in which heat is generated in one location and then distributed through the structure, typically through sheet metal ductwork. With the exception of electric furnaces, all furnaces have three major components: heat exchanger, burner and blower.

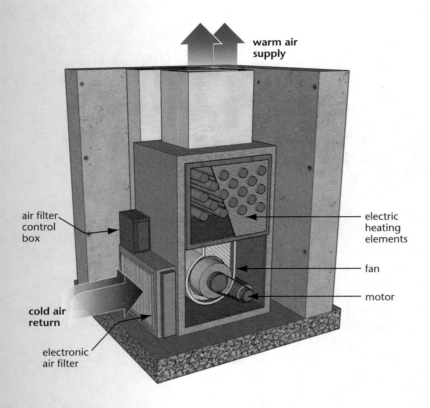

warm air
supply

air filter
control
box

electric
heating
elements

fan

motor

cold air
return

electronic
air filter

ELECTRIC FURNACE

An electric furnace has no actual combustion and consequently no need for a heat exchanger, burner or a chimney. These components are replaced by electric heating elements sitting directly in the air stream. The blower simply forces air across the heating elements and the warmed air returns to the rooms via ductwork. An illustration depicts the movement of air from point of entry through to the exit.

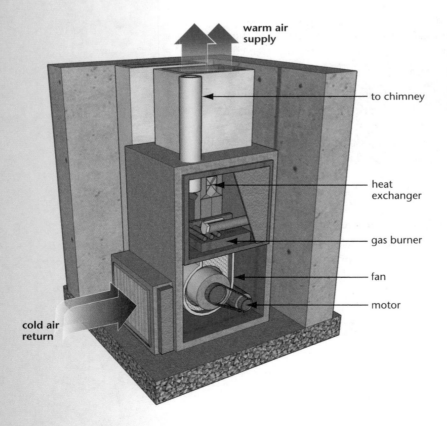

warm air
supply

to chimney

heat
exchanger

gas burner

fan

motor

cold air
return

GAS FURNACE

Gas furnaces can generally be divided into four levels for purposes of residential and commercial usage in the Canadian marketplace:

- Conventional;
- Mid-efficiency;
- High efficiency; and
- High efficiency pulse.

GRAVITY FURNACE

The gravity furnace, often referred to as the octopus furnace, operates similarly to a conventional furnace except that no fan exists to draw house air to the furnace, blow it through the furnace and push it out of the air registers. Instead, the system works on gravity (convection), relying on warm air to rise through the supply ducts and cool air to settle back through the return ducts to the furnace. Gravity furnaces are now viewed as obsolete due primarily to their inefficiency. A typical gravity furnace is illustrated showing a large return air inlet to accommodate convection and an outlet at floor level for warm air leading from the furnace.

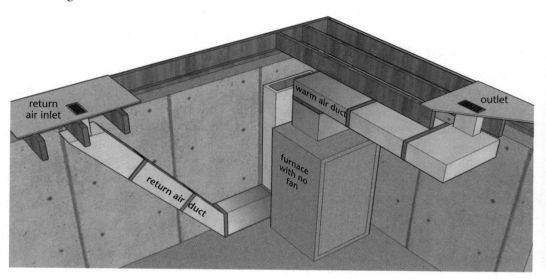

Capacity and Efficiency   FOCUS

CAPACITY

Capacity refers to the amount of heat that a system can generate. The output rating is a percentage of the input rating and will depend on whether it is a conventional, mid-efficiency or high-efficiency system. Ratings are given as BTU's per hour. A BTU is a British Thermal Unit representing the amount of heat required to raise the temperature of one pound of water, one Fahrenheit degree. Electric heaters are rated in kilowatts.

EFFICIENCY

Furnaces and boilers are classified by their efficiency. Most systems, until the mid-1970s, had an operating (steady state) efficiency of approximately 80%. However, this rating only applies to continuous operation. Given losses, particularly when the unit is starting up and shutting down, the actual efficiency is about 55 to 65%.

Mid-efficiency furnaces using devices such as vent dampers (to prevent heat from escaping up the chimney when the unit is shut down) and the replacement of continuously operating pilot lights by spark ignited pilots, now provide a seasonal efficiency in the eighty percent range. High efficiency furnaces and boilers go a step further as mid-efficiency furnaces are limited due to condensation. High efficiency furnaces are commonly referred to as condensing units. A condensing unit typically uses a second heat exchanger (and sometimes a third) to extract additional heat contained within water vapour in the heated air. Condensing units have a drainage system to expel condensate and are designed to withstand corrosion.

Some manufacturers also employ a pulse process for improved combustion. This system relies on pressure waves to force products of combustion out of the combustion chamber, the pressure wave is then reflected back and ignites the next gas/air mixture to continue the pulse process that becomes self perpetuating. The hot gases, forced out of the combustion chamber, pass across a heat exchanger where the heat is transferred These systems tend to be noisier than most high efficiency systems. High efficiency furnaces incorporate features (as do mid-efficiency systems) to limit off-cycle losses. High efficiency furnaces have a seasonal efficiency in the mid to high 90 percent range.

OIL FURNACE

Oil-fired forced air heating systems, operating in similar fashion to gas furnaces, have a burner, combustion chamber, with exhaust through flue pipe and chimney. A significant difference with oil is the need for on-site storage either within the structure or adjacent to it. Regulations concerning storage tank specifications, acceptable locations and maintenance requirements will vary by provincial jurisdiction.

Conventional oil furnaces have traditionally demonstrated low efficiency rates; i.e., 50 to 60%. However, recent improvements to burner technology have produced mid-efficiency products raising efficiency levels to 80–89%. Given higher efficiency, venting can sometimes be installed through a side wall, rather than a chimney.

Boiler (Hot Water System)

A boiler is a central heating system where heat is generated in one location and distributed via piping to various other locations. The term boiler is somewhat confusing in that hot water systems do not actually boil the water, but rather heat it to 160°F maximum.

Hot water boilers consist of closed and open systems. Real estate practitioners will normally encounter only closed systems in which water in the boiler, piping and heat source within individual rooms is under pressure. Pressure within the system is normally a few pounds higher than what is required to force water up to the highest level within the structure. Closed systems typically have a circulating pump to force the water through the system.

Closed Boiler System

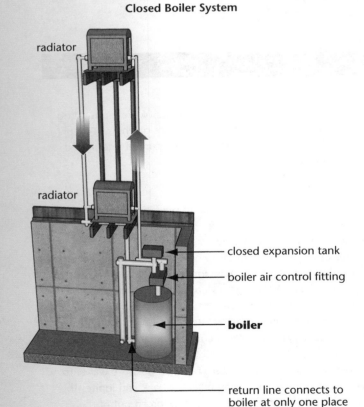

radiator

radiator

closed expansion tank

boiler air control fitting

boiler

return line connects to boiler at only one place

Open Boiler System

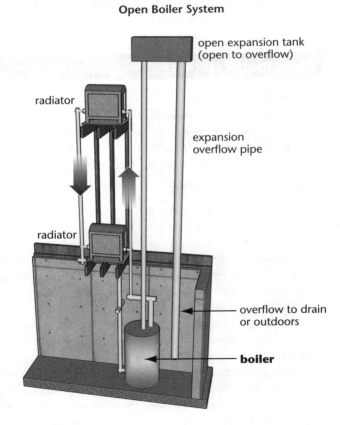

open expansion tank (open to overflow)

radiator

expansion overflow pipe

radiator

overflow to drain or outdoors

boiler

Open systems, common prior to the introduction of the closed system, utilizes an expansion tank located above the highest radiator in the structure. This tank provides for expansion when water is heated and comes equipped with an overflow pipe. Open systems do not utilize circulating pumps as gravity moves the water.

Boiler systems are most commonly associated with commercial properties, although hot water systems were popular in residential property during the early and mid portions of the twentieth century. All boiler systems, with the exception of electric boilers, have two major components: a heat exchanger and a burner. The heat exchanger contains the burning fuel on one side and the water to be heated on the other. The most common fuels are natural gas and oil. Burners on hot water systems are very similar to those on warm-air furnaces.

Two illustrations are provided showing simplified boiler systems and the flow of heated water. Convectors and radiant heating are viable alternatives to radiators. Hot water convectors are either cast iron or tubing (usually copper) with aluminum fins normally less than 12 inches high. Some hot water heating systems employ piping buried in the floor or ceiling that in turn radiates heat to the room.

Heating, Ventilation and Air Conditioning (HVAC)

HVAC systems, commonly associated with commercial applications, regulate the even distribution of heating, cooling and fresh air throughout a building. A broad range of HVAC systems are used in the marketplace. These commercial systems are commonly mounted above suspended ceilings with supply air diffusers strategically placed within that ceiling along with return air ducts. Following are selected components:

- **Air Handler**   The blower or series of fans within an HVAC system used to move heated or conditioned air through the structure, normally by means of duct work.

- **Condensing Unit**   Normally situated outside the structure, the condensing unit contains a compressor that compresses freon, thereby providing the cooling effect within an air-conditioning unit.

- **Ductwork**   A series of ducts used for the distribution of warm or cool air throughout a structure to various rooms, offices and work areas. The ducted system permits the return flow of air back from various portions of the structure to the HVAC unit.

- **Roof Top HVAC**   A large HVAC unit mounted on the roof of a structure that provides cooling and heating for the structure.

- **Unit Heater**   A large interior, roof-hung unit that heats open areas.

Fireplace

A traditional wood fireplace is generally viewed as recreational, as opposed to functional, in that most take more heat away from a structure than they generate. Fireplaces provide radiant heat into a room but use the warmed house air for combustion. The air that goes up the chimney typically represents more heat loss than the radiant heat gained from the flames.

A roaring fire can draw three to four hundred cubic feet of air out of a structure every minute. Heatilators, glass doors and outside combustion air intakes help reduce heat loss. Provincial building codes set out detailed specifications for fireplace inserts and hearth mounted stoves.

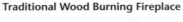

Traditional Wood Burning Fireplace

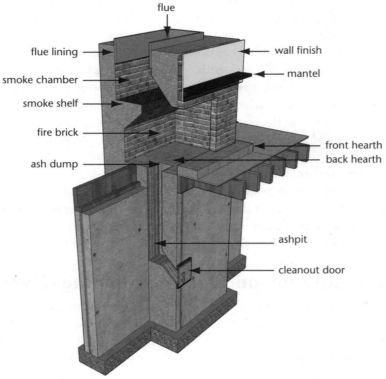

EXAMPLE   *Constructing the Fireplace*

Owner Smith is contemplating the construction of a traditional fireplace with the following specifications.

- A footing and foundation system (usually of the same material as the house foundation).
- A hearth (floor of the fireplace) constructed of poured concrete and one inch of slate, firebrick, stone or tile, and extends at least sixteen inches beyond the front of the fireplace and at least eight inches beyond either side.
- Firebox walls (usually brick, stone or concrete) with a firebrick liner giving a total wall thickness of eight inches.
- A mantel lever or inside firebox control damper to be installed. The damper should be firebox width, at least six inches above the fireplace opening and closer to the front than the back.
- A smoke shelf behind the damper that provides for deflection of downdrafts and rain/snow.
- A smoke chamber located above the damper and below the chimney, typically brick, stone or concrete block, and is often specially parged for smoothness to allow better smoke movement.
- A chimney made of the same masonry as the fireplace with a clay liner.
- Fire mantle having no combustible materials within six inches of the fireplace opening.

SECTION III   STRUCTURAL TYPES AND COMPONENTS

FLUE

A flue is a separate and distinct channel for the discharge of smoke on the inside of the chimney. Each appliance, requiring a flue, must have a separate flue with certain exceptions. For example, a gas furnace and a gas hot water heater on the same level may share one flue. Some flues are unlined; i.e., exposed masonry on the inside of the flue. This type of flue is commonly found in pre-Second World War houses constructed for fireplaces and oil-fired furnaces.

Real estate practitioners should direct all inquiries concerning flues to appropriate experts. Detailed requirements concerning flues can be found in the Ontario Building Code.

CHIMNEY

A chimney, typically a vertical structure, contains one or more flues for the discharge of smoke and/or gases from a fire or furnace. The most common materials used in chimney construction are masonry and steel. Masonry chimneys can be brick, block or stone and are sometimes stuccoed or parged.

Chimney Cap

The chimney cap prevents water from penetrating the top of a masonry chimney. This cap should not be confused with rain caps that sometimes cover the tops of chimney flues to prevent the entry of rain water. A chimney cap is usually constructed of concrete, however, some are made from stone or metal. A good quality cap normally overhangs the sides of the chimney at least one inch to provide some protection for the chimney from rainwater dripping off the cap.

Removal

Many chimneys that are no longer required are removed to a point below roof level during re-roofing. This eliminates the need to maintain the upper section and reduces the risk of water leakage through the chimney flashing, a common source of problems. This is appropriate provided nothing is connected to the chimney that might be used inadvertently. Occasionally, abandoned chimneys are knocked down part way, but still protrude above the roof line. In some cases, the flue is sealed with concrete.

PROBLEM AREAS

Practitioners should be aware that chimney deterioration is a common problem in both residential and commercial structures. Most often, water is the culprit. Metal chimneys corrode and masonry chimneys can suffer deterioration to the mortar, brick and stucco. The source of the water can sometimes be wind driven rain, but often results from condensation within the chimney. One of the by-products of burning fossil fuels is water vapour. Exhaust gases, travelling up the chimney, cool and sometimes reach the dew point, thereby forming condensation. The water droplets are absorbed into masonry chimneys or sit on the interior of metal chimneys. These droplets are somewhat acidic due to their formation from combustible products and can cause corrosion in metal flues and deterioration within masonry flues.

The problem is compounded in masonry chimneys by use of cyclical heating. Chimneys are forever heating up and cooling down as furnaces, boilers, hot water heaters and fireplaces are only operated intermittently. The moisture that has been absorbed into masonry chimneys freezes as the temperature drops, causing mortar to deteriorate, bricks to spall and parging or stucco to loosen. This is a natural phenomenon with all chimneys and deterioration should be anticipated.

Certain masonry chimneys are lined with clay tile. The top flue tile should protrude at least two inches beyond the top of the chimney. If the top section of clay tile was too short to protrude, some brick masons simply raised the top tile, leaving a gap between the top two tiles in the flue. A ring of more rapid deterioration normally shows up on the exterior of the chimney, corresponding to the gap in the clay tile liner. The amount of deterioration dictates whether chimneys require repair or rebuilding. On tall chimneys or chimneys situated on steeply pitched roofs, building scaffolding is often required to facilitate repairs adding to the cost of repair.

Other Heating Options	LABOUR FORCE FOCUS

Many fireplace and alternative heating appliances are available including stoves and fireplace inserts (inserted in the hearth of a traditional fireplace). In the case of wood-burning fireplaces, consumers can now choose traditional masonry structures or factory-built caste iron, plate steel or even lighter materials (e.g., aluminum). Gas fireplaces are popular as they provide the convenient *instant on* feature and can be readily installed with an exterior wall vent pipe. These fireplaces, commonly referred to as zero clearance, are insulated metal units that are light in comparison to traditional masonry fireplaces. Some zero clearance models can have efficiency ratings up to 70%.

Notable changes are occurring particularly regarding heating systems for both residential and commercial structures. Technology is driving innovations that promise increased energy efficiency and heightened comfort levels. Two of many examples are highlighted.

New Innovations

ZONED HEATING/COOLING SYSTEMS

Computers and the digital revolution are transforming residential heating/cooling systems. Remember the days when one floor or a particular room was cold and everywhere else was hot...or the reverse? Welcome to the zoned system.

For years, Ontarians have lived with a single-zone approach (i.e., one ductwork system fits all) but many new homes are opting for a centralized furnace controller, motorized dampers (or valves in a hot water system) to disperse heat/cooling and multiple zones for personal preference settings. Owners can have 23-degree Celsius comfort in the family room, with 16-degree Celsius in the unused storage room and other settings for bedrooms, home office and finished basement areas.

Zoned systems use sensors, communicating with the controller, dampers and furnace, to direct air as required. Remember those frustrating times when the afternoon sun turned the kitchen into a hot house, while the other side was cold? Sophisticated zoned systems can handle the problem with ease. Just add a high-efficiency furnace for the complete energy-saving package. New upscale homes increasingly boast this feature.

GROUND SOURCE HEAT PUMPS

The ground source heat pump, often referred to as a geothermal system, uses the earth's temperature as a heat source in the winter and a heat sink (removal of heat) in the summer. Liquid (typically an antifreeze solution) circulates through a loop extending into the ground (vertical loop extending downwards) or a horizontal loop (a few feet below ground level, but paralleling the surface). Some loops are laid at the bottom of ponds or other water courses.

Increasingly used in Western Canada for both residential and commercial applications, this cost-efficient method of heating/cooling homes is gaining popularity in eastern portions of the country. The attraction lies in minimum maintenance, quiet operation and significant yearly energy savings.

SECTION III STRUCTURAL TYPES AND COMPONENTS

PLUMBING

The **plumbing system** of piping and associated fittings is designed for two basic purposes: the supply of water for drinking, washing and cooking to appropriate areas of a structure and the disposal of water and waste from that structure. An illustration is provided detailing a typical house waste portion of a plumbing system. Standards concerning water distribution and drainage systems are set out in provincial building codes.

Water Distribution (Residential)

Galvanized steel piping was used almost exclusively until approximately 1950. Depending on the pipe diameter, the water composition and the amount of use, this piping usually lasts 40 to 60 years. Copper pipes have been in use residentially since approximately 1900. Following the mid-1950s, copper became the predominately used material.

In the 1970s plastic supply piping was approved and is now reasonably prevalent in new home construction. Recently, polyethylene, PVC, CPVC and polybutylene pipes and fillings have appeared. Plumbers still appear to prefer working with copper and, although the plastic pipe is less expensive than copper, the fittings are expensive. Some codes do not allow plastic pipes and some types of plastic pipe are only suitable for waste, underground or cold water piping. In particular, building codes set out certification standards concerning piping and cement types allowed for hot and/or cold water systems. The water distribution system for a typical two-storey residential structure is illustrated.

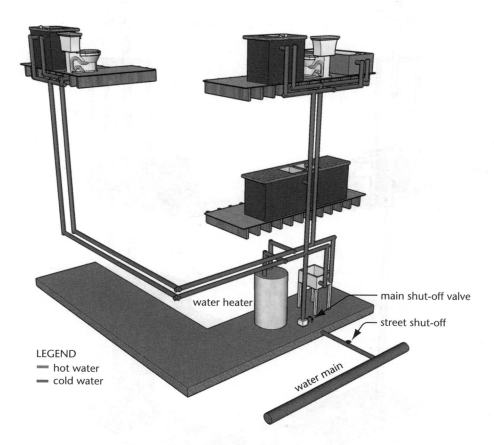

water heater

main shut-off valve

street shut-off

water main

LEGEND
— hot water
— cold water

Drainage (Waste) and Venting

Copper plumbing was used commonly after World War II until the mid 1960's for drain lines, main stacks and vent piping but has become rare in single-family residential homes, as plastic plumbing is much less expensive. In multi-family construction, copper waste plumbing is used where authorities will not allow plastic piping.

Galvanized steel plumbing is used only for purposes of venting. Cast iron (for main stack venting) and lead pipes were both prevalent in the 1950s, but have fallen largely into disuse. ABS plastic piping has become practically the exclusive waste plumbing material. Its only noticeable disadvantage is the noise factor when water is passing through it. Efforts to control the noise include wrapping the pipes with fibre glass insulation.

In order for water to drain freely out of a house waste system, adequate venting must be provided. Venting performs three functions.

- Allows air in front of the water rushing through the waste pipe to be pushed out of the way.
- Allows air to be re-introduced to the piping after the water has passed. If a system is not properly vented, the water passing through the drain line will siphon the water from the various fixture traps. The trap at each plumbing fixture provides a water seal that prevents sewer odours from entering the house.
- Allows sewer gases to escape outside through a vent stack.

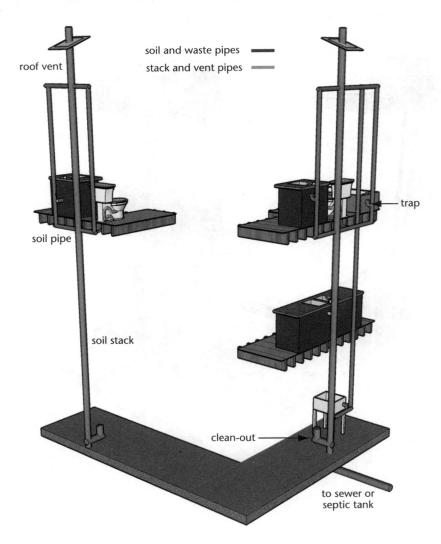

Hot Water Heater

The **hot water heater** is typically a tank or reservoir used for heating water in commercial or residential structures. Hot water heaters, regardless of heat source (i.e., gas, oil or electric) operate in essentially the same way. Cold water is pumped into the heater from a supply source and heated water is discharged from the other end of the tank. The temperature of the tank water is typically maintained at approximately 140°F. When hot water is removed by opening a faucet, cold water is introduced to the tank, triggering the thermostat. If enough hot water is removed from the tank, the tank will cool down. Therefore, the larger the holding tank (40 to 60 gallons), the greater the supply of hot water available. A diagram is provided illustrating the components of a typical electric hot water heater.

Recovery rate is an important consideration. Oil has the fastest rate of recovery, followed by gas and then electricity. The rate ultimately depends on the size of the burner or element provided. The faster the recovery rate, the more water can be drawn off without depleting the hot water supply. Hot water tanks are now insulated to ensure higher energy efficiency. In many cases, hot water supply pipes are also insulated to minimize heat loss.

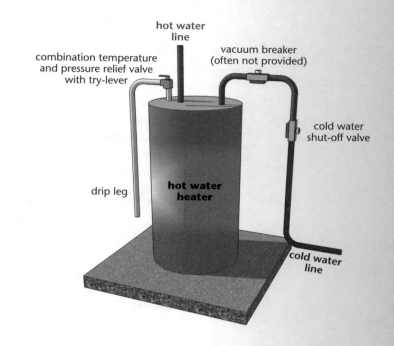

hot water line

vacuum breaker (often not provided)

combination temperature and pressure relief valve with try-lever

cold water shut-off valve

drip leg

hot water heater

cold water line

WATER WELLS

Drilled, bored or dug **water wells** are subject to legislative control. The protection of water quantity and quality falls to the *Ontario Water Resources Act* administered by the Ministry of the Environment. Practitioners commonly encounter issues surrounding private well systems in the listing and selling of property and should be aware of associated legislative requirements and procedures concerning the testing of private well water.

Water Testing—Overview

Water quality testing can involve a wide array of water sources such as:

- well water;
- dugouts, springs and gravel pits;
- lakes and rivers;
- municipal systems and chlorinated water;
- cisterns and other holding tanks;
- effluent (sewage, industrial waste, etc.); and
- swimming pools, whirlpools and jacuzzis.

Activities of real estate practitioners are generally focused on drinking water and the testing of private well systems when homes are offered for sale. If a supply of drinking water comes from a well or other non-municipal source, then the issue of the quality and safety of the water from that source is an important consideration in both the listing and selling process. Further, every owner should be aware of the quality of water and test it on a regular basis.

Water testing is best viewed from two perspectives: chemical analysis and microbiological analysis (bacteriological). Both are relevant to water testing, but the latter is most frequently addressed in the sale of property supplied by private wells.

CHEMICAL ANALYSIS

Chemicals in water come from a number of sources, including the geological formations around the well and the leaching of materials that may have been applied to the soils. It is very important for well-owners to be aware of the chemical quality of their water, as the presence of contaminants may not be apparent by taste or appearance.

Some typical situations are identified. Generally, most chemical-related, water quality problems can be resolved using treatment systems specifically designed to remove the contaminants.

Metals	Metals such as lead, cadmium, mercury or arsenic are harmful to health. They may be present naturally in the water or result from the leaching of metals from pipes.
Fluoride	Fluoride can be naturally present in the water of wells. If too high a level exists, mottling of tooth enamel in young children can occur.
Hardness	Often evidenced as mineral scale on kettles and water heaters. Although not a health hazard, hardness can create aesthetic concerns when using soaps.
Red or Black Staining	This type of staining is indicative of the presence of excessive iron or manganese in the water.
Organic Contaminants/ Pesticides	The list of organic contaminants that can be present in drinking water is quite extensive. Their presence will depend on the proximity of the well to potential sources of these compounds.

BACTERIOLOGICAL (MICROBIOLOGICAL) ANALYSIS

Bacteriological testing of well water in private well systems typically falls to local health authorities. The quality of well water and the existence of any contamination is generally due to two factors:

- Well construction; e.g., drainage, depth and proper seals at the well cap.
- Any potential ground contamination that affects the water quality at the source.

All wells in Ontario must be constructed using licensed water well contractors or well technicians approved by the Ministry of the Environment.

The Ministry of the Environment and the public health authority provide a variety of information concerning water testing, including procedures and guidelines in the testing of well water and interpretation of bacteriological reports. When testing well water, three separate samples are recommended and should be collected one to three weeks apart. Following initial testing, one or two tests per year appear adequate, unless some occurrence has taken place that would affect the water supply to the property. For cottages, two or three samples are recommended during any particular season. The first should be conducted at the start of the season when the cottage is initially opened.

Bacteriological Testing

Testing of water to assess water quality and existence of contamination.

SECTION III   STRUCTURAL TYPES AND COMPONENTS

Tests establish the existence of two groups of bacteria: namely, coliform and fecal coliform. The presence of coliform bacteria indicates the existence of pollution and the presence of other harmful bacteria must be assumed until proven otherwise. The existence of fecal coliform immediately renders the water unsafe. Fecal coliform breaks down quickly in the environment, therefore, any presence indicates relatively recent sewage contamination.

Bacteriological results provided by the laboratory do not imply anything about the chemical quality of the water supply, as these tests relate solely to the presence or absence of coliform. Guidelines are provided regarding the interpretation of bacteriological reports. Further, the request form used to obtain a bacteriological test provides additional instructions concerning the process.

Unacceptable tests on any water supply should be taken very seriously. While chlorination accomplishes immediate well disinfection in certain instances, this technique is only a temporary measure. Long-term pollution problems such as seepage can still exist and expert advice is required. Water treatment devices such as reverse osmosis systems are designed to remove various contaminants and are available through private suppliers.

HOW TO INTERPRET A BACTERIOLOGICAL REPORT

Remember that strict numerical limits for safety are difficult to establish and that as the number of coliform bacteria increases so does the risk of disease agents being present in the water.

Coliform Bacteria per 100 mL		Interpretation
Total	Fecal	
>160	>60	Unsafe for drinking. This water is contaminated and should not be used for drinking under any circumstances. Do not attempt to apply these standards and interpretations to surface waters used for swimming.
10–160	1–60	Unsafe for drinking. Pollution source may be some distance from the water source, diluted with large volumes of pure water, or the sample may not have been received within 48 hours of being taken. Samples older than 48 hours cannot provide reliable results.
10–160	0	Unsafe for drinking. Contamination is not likely to be of sewage origin unless far removed from the water source or unless there has been a delay in receipt of sample. Common with new wells before disinfection and shallow dug wells which are not properly sealed.
2–10	0	Doubtful for a single sample, but safe for drinking if condition remains stable and supply is protected and located at least 30–40 metres from any source of human or animal wastes.
<2	0	Safe for drinking. Repeat samples may not show exactly the same results because bacteria are not distributed uniformly in water. Contamination tends to enter intermittently and numbers can change during sample transit time.
Est		Unsafe for drinking. Number has been estimated due to some interference with the test. Exact number is not really critical, especially if in excess of limits shown above, for judging safety.
O/G		Doubtful condition and not recommended for drinking. No coliform bacteria could be detected because of "overgrowth" by other bacteria. This condition frequently occurs with new wells, dug wells receiving soil drainage or wells which have been idle for some time. Collect another sample and identify clearly "REPEAT SAMPLE".

Well systems have caused many litigation problems. Real estate practitioners are advised to avoid any representations concerning the quality of water. Buyers and sellers must be fully informed regarding water test procedures. In terms of bacteriological testing, ensure that the parties:

- Clearly understand the need for such testing;
- Are aware that three samples are recommended in line with appropriate time frames; and
- Are aware of the importance of a suitable condition in an agreement of purchase and sale.

Installation

The Ministry of the Environment licenses well contractors and their employees pursuant to Regulations of the *Ontario Water Resources Act*. Under provincial law, all well contractors and technicians must be licensed and their work must meet minimum well construction requirements. Persons seeking a licence as a well contractor must pass an examination involving applicable legislation, the structure, design and hydraulic operation of a well and the installation and operation of pumping equipment.

A Well Technician Licence Class 4, is awarded on successful completion of the examination and the demonstration of appropriate work experience. Three other levels of licensing are available: Class 1: drilling; Class 2: digging and boring; and Class 3: special. Only Class 4 can be involved in the installation of pumps.

The well contractor is required to test new wells by means of a bailer or pump for one hour and measure the rate at which water is withdrawn from the well and measure the water levels in the well during pumping or recovery after pumping. A water well record is used to record the rate. The contractor must provide the owner with a copy of the water well record. This record, including additional information about well location and construction, is filed with the Ministry of the Environment.

Once the well is constructed, the well owner is responsible for monitoring and maintaining the well and preventing contamination of the well or the aquifer. Section 20 (Regulation 903) under the *Ontario Water Resources Act* states:

Well Maintenance

20. (1) The well owner shall maintain the well at all times after the completion of the well's structural stage in a manner sufficient to prevent the entry into the well of surface water and other foreign materials. O. Reg. 372/07, s. 19.

(2) If the casing of a well extends above the ground surface, no person shall,

    (a) reduce the height of the casing, if the casing of the well extends to a height of less than 40 centimetres above the ground surface; or

    (b) reduce the height of the casing to a height of less than 40 centimetres above the ground surface, if the casing extends to a height of 40 centimetres or more above the ground surface. O. Reg. 372/07, s. 19.

(3) Subsection (2) does not apply to a well described in subsection 13 (10) or a test hole or dewatering well described in subsection 13 (11). O. Reg. 372/07, s. 19.

SECTION III   STRUCTURAL TYPES AND COMPONENTS

Standards

Recent regulatory requirements now impose much tougher standards for well construction and higher performance standards for well contractors and technicians. Education and training requirements have been increased along with more extensive technical specifications and procedures for well construction, methods for sealing space between the well casing and surrounding soil, improved casings and more effective well caps.

Further, the Regulations contain rules for the closing (decommissioning) of wells. Also, anyone who constructs a new cased well in Ontario (except for oil and gas wells) must affix a permanent stainless steel identification tag, issued by the Ministry of the Environment. The tag provides an alpha-numeric identifying code for the well. The well tag requirement helps both local and provincial officials monitor water quality and respond quickly to potential problems.

What is a Water Well Record?	CURIOSITY

Water well records for the initial installation of water wells installed in Ontario are maintained by the Ministry of the Environment. Practitioners can receive a copy for one or more properties by calling 1–888–396–9355 to obtain the necessary water well record request form. The caller is prompted to leave a fax number or return address so that the form can be mailed.

Real estate practitioners should note that a water well record provided through the centralized resource represents circumstances surrounding the original well installation only and does not address the current status of the well. Prospective buyers of properties serviced by a private well system should fully investigate matters concerning the operation of the well and water quality/quantity.

Maintenance

Proper care and maintenance is fundamental to continuous, good quality water.

Avoid Contamination	Homeowners must be careful not to undertake any activity near a well that could result in contamination, including the storage or disposal of potential contaminants such as gasoline, salt, pesticides and garbage.
Control Surface Drainage	Surface drainage in outside yard areas should be directed away from the well location. If the area in which the well is located is susceptible to flooding or lacks proper drainage, the area surrounding the well cap should be raised to provide sufficient runoff slope. At all times, keep the well pit free of groundwater seepage and surface water.
Ensure Proper Well Cap and Seal	The sanitary well seal and well cap must be firmly situated and watertight. Cracks or other damage to the well cap can provide ready access for contaminants to flow into the well pit. Any openings to the well should be carefully sealed from the outside using durable sealing materials.
Check Vent Pipes and Connections	Well vent pipes must be appropriately screened or otherwise protected from entry of foreign matter. Connections at the well casing involving electrical lines, water lines and pumps must be watertight and properly sealed.
Have a Raised Casing	The well casing should be visible to ensure easy access if repair work is required. If the existing well is below ground level, it is advisable to have the casing raised to a minimum of 40 cm above ground surface.

Be Responsible	Well owners are required to maintain all wells on their respective properties. If a well is not being used, it must be sealed (plugged) in accordance with appropriate regulations under the *Ontario Water Resources Act*.
Seek Expert Advice	If any uncertainty exists as to the condition of the well cap, drainage arrangements, water tightness of the casing or other components, appropriate qualified personnel should be contacted. The Ministry of the Environment provides instructions concerning the construction, maintenance and abandonment of wells.

Supply/Measurement

The matter of water supply and appropriate measurement is an ongoing consideration. Homeowners should measure the depth of water on a periodic basis and keep appropriate records. Measuring the static water level is relatively straightforward through the use of a survey tape or electrical measuring device. Sufficient tests should be done to ensure that identical readings are being obtained. Make certain that no water is pumped for several hours prior to testing in order to obtain an accurate reading.

Homeowners may also wish to re-test the capacity of the well (often traditionally referred to as a gallonage test). This test, completed when the well was first installed, provides a good benchmark for subsequent assessment under differing conditions.

WATER SHORTAGE

The issue of water shortage must also be addressed. Water shortages are due to any number of reasons including insufficient ground water, increased usage due to new construction and climatic conditions. Faced with such situations, water conservation may be the only available solution. However, homeowners seeking to improve water supply may increase pump size without regard to other factors at play. For example, if the current system is incorrectly installed, an increase in pumping ability may exceed the well capacity and also cause damage, particularly in the case of small-diameter drilled wells.

Property owners sometimes increase well depth to augment water supply. Caution is advised as high quality water supply may only extend to a certain depth. Below that level, poorer quality water can flow upwards and contaminate the entire water supply. This contamination may make the water unusable, require a special water treatment facility and potentially affect other wells in the area if the supplying aquifer is contaminated.

The aquifer is a geological formation consisting typically of sand and gravel that naturally filters water. Contamination could have a significant impact on adjoining properties depending on the size of the aquifer and the proximity of neighbouring wells.

Owners should also consider other alternatives including increasing the storage capacity within the pressure system to offset dry periods and ensuring that the bottom of the existing well is not in some way plugged, thereby affecting water flow. Alternatively, a new well, installed by a qualified licensed well contractor, may be required.

WEB LINKS
Practitioners marketing residential and commercial properties that rely on water wells, should keep up to date on water quality and water well requirements as set out in provincial legislation. Go to the Ministry of the Environment web site at *www.ene.gov.on.ca*

SECTION III   STRUCTURAL TYPES AND COMPONENTS

Complaints

Ministry of the Environment staff investigate well water complaints. Priority is placed on cases involving possible health-related issues or aquifer contamination. Where warranted, the ministry conducts investigations that may lead to charges being laid. If a buyer or seller is concerned about water quality, he/she should contact the local heath authority and obtain a bacteriological test involving the sampling and testing of the well water supply.

Some water quality problems are detectable by taste, odour or colour. Routine monitoring by the well owner should help detect water quality problems. Ministry of the Environment publications provide more information regarding well maintenance.

SEWAGE SYSTEMS

Municipal

Most houses in built-up areas are connected to a municipal sewer system that allows waste from a house to flow by gravity into sewer piping. The waste is carried to a treatment facility where it is cleaned before being released.

Practitioners should be aware of different systems found within urban areas. In older neighbourhoods, a combination of storm and sanitary sewers was employed. In modern areas, where sewer pipes have been replaced, a sanitary sewer carries house waste and a separate storm sewer handles rain and snow run off. Where the street sewers are not deep enough, the main drain pipe from a house must leave the house above the basement floor. This means that plumbing fixtures cannot be put in the basement without the waste being pumped up to the main drain level. A basement floor drain in this situation would also require special attention.

A street with a storm sewer and sanitary sewer is more desirable than a combination sewer. Basement flooding as a result of storm sewer back-up is less likely in a house with separate sewers. With combination sewers, a large volume of storm water may overload the sewers and water (including raw sewage) can back up through basement floor drains. In some areas, this problem is common and some homeowners install one-way valves in their floor drain that allows water down into the drain, but prevents water from coming back up. If pressures are high enough, sewage may back up through basement plumbing fixtures. With separate sewers, floor drains should connect to the sanitary sewer and eavestroughs and downspouts to the storm sewer, or onto the ground several feet away from the building.

On-Site

Real estate practitioners, particularly those involved with rural/recreational property, require knowledge regarding approval procedures, types of systems and related details concerning **sewage systems (on-site)**. The following is for general information only, contact the local municipality for specifics.

Sewage Systems (On-Site)

A private system, identified by various classes, for the disposal of waste.

APPROVALS/PERMITS/INSPECTIONS

As a general guideline, municipalities are responsible for issuing permits, collecting fees, making inspections and storing various documents concerning septic tank installations. Municipalities must follow detailed guidelines as set out in Part 8 of the Ontario Building Code concerning design standards and system requirements. However, not all municipalities perform all functions in regard to on-site sewage systems.

The Code provides that a municipality may enter into an agreement with other municipalities or the county (or region) for enforcement of Part 8. Further, in the absence of an agreement, a municipality may delegate the authority to a health unit or conservation authority having jurisdiction in that particular municipality. Practitioners should contact the local municipality to determine specific arrangements within their trading area(s).

CLASSES

Private onsite sewage systems are classified by the Ministry of the Environment according to type.

CLASS 1

Includes various waterless toilets involving pit, privy vaults, portable privies, chemical toilets and composting toilets. Privy vaults refer to a latrine in which the receptacle consists of a constructed vault from which waste is periodically removed.

CLASS 2

A soak or leaching pit that may only be used for non-human waste; in other words, a grey water system. The Ontario Building Code sets out a maximum sewage flow for such systems.

CLASS 3

A cesspool, similar to a Class 2 System, but is used to receive human waste.

CLASS 4

A septic tank and leaching bed system. The Class 4 system is most widely encountered by practitioners in the marketplace.

CLASS 5

A system that uses a holding tank for the retention of hauled sewage at the site where it is produced, prior to its collection by a hauled sewage system.

RECORDS

Historically, records for septic systems would in most cases be located in the public health unit. With the transition to municipal control, municipalities now maintain septic tank records along with other permits and documents by individual property, unless the municipality has delegated the authority.

This move to centralized records by specific property is a further attempt to consolidate information under a one-stop window approach when developing property within a municipality. For installations prior to record conversion, historical documents must be accessed at the previous location, typically the public health unit.

Septic tank records normally include design drawings and field review reports completed at time of installation. Further, any changes to the system will also be filed, if a permit was obtained at time of alteration. Real estate practitioners should be aware that such reports only reflect circumstances at the time of installation (or alteration, if applicable) and do not address current circumstances. Buyers should have existing systems inspected to ensure that they meet standards and are functioning properly.

Check with the Experts   CAUTION

Practitioners must exercise caution in all matters concerning sewage systems. Contact the local municipality concerning current requirements. Subsequent discussions in *The Residential Real Estate Transaction* focus on appropriate clauses concerning both water wells and septic systems when drafting agreements of purchase and sale.

SECTION III   STRUCTURAL TYPES AND COMPONENTS

Class 4 Sewage System

Class 4 is the most common form of private onsite waste sewage systems. This sewage system (often referred to as a *septic system*) operates through the use of both aerobic and anaerobic bacteria and consists of a tank, along with a leaching (absorption) bed. The term *anaerobic* refers to the ability of bacteria to survive without oxygen.

System design is dictated by the total daily sanitary sewage flow as set out in the Ontario Building Code. For example, in a residential dwelling, the system is designed based on the number of bedrooms within the household. A four-bedroom house has an estimated volume flow of 2,000 litres and a five-bedroom has a flow of 2,500. Additional flow is added for more bedrooms at the rate of 500 litres per bedroom and 50 litres for each ten square metres above 200 square metres of total finished area within the residence.

The Ontario Building Code requires that a site evaluation be conducted for both new and replacement sewage system installations. Septic and leaching bed location is dictated by percolation time relating to soil, which is measured by either a percolation test or by soil classification according to accepted standards. Percolation testing requires a minimum of three possible locations on the site with the area having the highest percolation time being used.

TREATMENT UNIT

Septic tanks must meet requirements as set out in the Ontario Building Code including detailed specification documents for prefabricated septic tanks and sewage holding tanks. The minimum working capacity of a septic tank for residential purposes is the greater of 3,600 litres and the daily design sanitary sewage flow previously referenced.

The Code also details requirements concerning non-residential uses, the installation of multiple tanks and specifications involving compartments within septic tanks. A typical septic tank is illustrated along with minimum clearances as set out in the building code. Practitioners should also be aware that clearances can be affected by specific soil conditions and other factors impacting the effective operation of the sewage system. Contact the municipality for current requirements.

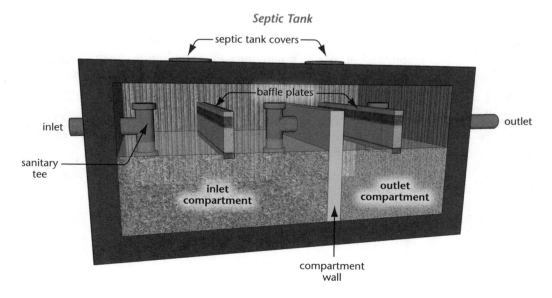

Septic Tank

MINIMUM CLEARANCES—TREATMENT UNITS	
	MINIMUM CLEARANCE (m)
Structure	1.5
Well	15
Lake	15
Pond	15
Reservoir	15
River	15
Spring	15
Stream	15
Property Line	3

Source: Ontario Building Code 1997, Table 8.2.1.6.A

LEACHING (ABSORPTION) BED

The leaching bed containing distribution piping is most commonly associated with Class 4 sewage systems. The leaching bed and septic tank (referred to in the Ontario Building Code as a treatment tank) make up the complete system.

The bed is an arrangement of pipes with holes surrounded by various filter materials. Liquid exiting the septic tank passes through the holes into the filter material, where bacterial action (oxygen-using aerobic bacteria) breaks down impurities. Filtering materials remove contaminants so that ultimately fluid reaching the water table has little or no contaminants. Nutrients and some amount of liquid move upwards toward surface grass areas. Three types of leaching beds are commonly used.

Conventional	The conventional bed, the most common type, is installed where land is well drained and the bed can work with stone-filled dug trenches below ground level.
Raised	The raised bed, the second most common, is used where the topography and/or soils do not permit sufficient filtering and drainage. Approved sand and soil filtering materials are brought to the site to create a raised bed for the stone-filled trenches.
Filter	The filter bed is used when space is limited. The entire bed area is excavated and filled with special filtering sand to permit the closer placement of pipes within the bed.

The Ontario Building Code sets out minimum acceptance clearances for distribution piping contained in a leaching system. An excerpt from the Code is provided for information purposes only. In the case of slow percolation times, the clearances may be increased. Clearances can also be affected by the type of bed required given specific soil conditions and other factors impacting the effective operation of the sewage system. Contact the municipality for current requirements.

MINIMUM CLEARANCES—LEACHING BEDS

	MINIMUM CLEARANCE (m)
Structure	5
Well with a Watertight Casing to a Depth of 6m	15
Any Other Well	30
Lake	15
Pond	15
Reservoir	15
River	15
A Spring Not Used as a Source of *Potable* Water	15
Stream	15
Property Line	3

Source: Ontario Building Code 1997, Table 8.2.1.6.B

OPERATION

The septic system will last for many years when properly designed, operated and maintained. Contrary to popular belief, only a small amount of treatment occurs in the septic tank; the majority occurs in the soils below the leaching bed. The tank acts as a storage area for the sewage. Solid material either settles down to the bottom (sludge) or floats to the top (scum) and accumulates until the tank is pumped out. Effluent from the tank flows to the leaching bed either by gravity or through a pump.

A leaching bed usually consists of a network of pipes with holes equally spaced along the length of the pipe. The total length of this pipe will vary depending upon the size of the house and the type of soil. The holes in the pipe allow the wastewater to seep into the soil where it is treated. The soil traps and holds most of the fine solids that escape from the septic tank. These solids are then digested by bacteria, fungi, insects and worms living in the soil. If wastewater isn't fully treated, contaminants can leach into the groundwater that supplies the home's well or it can drain into adjacent lakes, streams or even the home's backyard.

COMMON PROBLEMS

The most common reason for an improperly functioning septic system is misuse, often due to the homeowner's misunderstandings as to how the septic system works. A septic system is designed for existing soil conditions and the estimated number of toilets, tubs, showers and sinks that drain into it. Many people will add additional plumbing fixtures without considering how this affects the septic system. The increased sewage load often results in the plugging of pipes in the leaching bed and sewage rising to the ground surface.

Other activities that can damage a septic system include parking a car over the leaching bed, placing a pool or tennis court over the leaching bed, excessive cultivation, or planting trees and plants or trees with extensive root systems on the leaching bed. Typically, a malfunctioning septic system is noticed only when grey or black water surfaces in the yard, but other warning signs can include unusually green grass, spongy sections in the yard, dead spots where no grass will grow and drains slowing down or backing up frequently. If any of these signs are evident, the septic system should be inspected by a qualified contractor. A septic system that is not performing properly can pose a health hazard and should be treated as a high priority problem.

Maintaining a Class 4 System

TIPS/GUIDELINES

- Have the tank pumped every three to five years, including an inspection of the entire system.

- Keep a map of the location of the system along with maintenance records.

- Periodically check the system with particular attention to the existence of sewer gases and raw sewage.

- Conserve water. Use low flush toilets, along with water saving faucets and shower heads. Use dishwashers and washing machines only when full.

- Take hazardous wastes to approved disposal centres.

- Plant grass on the drain field instead of trees or shrubs.

- Divert roof, patio and driveway runoff away from the drain field. Keep sump pumps, hillside runoff and foundation drains away from the system.

- Ensure that the system is large enough for needs.

DON'T

- Put nondegradable; e.g., cigarettes, diapers, hair, grease, litter and coffee grounds down sinks or toilets.

- Use excessive amounts of bleach or solvents.

- Pour harmful chemicals down drains as they can leach into groundwater and poison the environment.

- Discharge water softening devices into the system.

- Park or drive on the drain field. Buildings, patios or pools can also compact the soil, crush pipes and reduce the oxygen supply to the drain field.

- Over water grass covering the drain field.

- Pack snow over the drain field as snow acts as an insulator.

Class 5 Sewage System (Holding Tank)

Holding tanks must meet minimum working capacity and be of acceptable construction to allow the complete removal of solid matter that settles in the tank. A person is permitted to install a Class 5 sewage system only under specific situations outlined in the Ontario Building Code. For example, a Class 5 would be permitted to remedy an unsafe sewage system where the installation of a Class 4 system is impractical, or to upgrade a sewage system on an existing lot where a Class 4 is not possible due to lot size or clearance limitations. Other provisions relate to interim measures and temporary operations.

The person installing a Class 5 system must, in all instances, obtain a written agreement for the disposal of sanitary sewage from the sewage system by a hauled sewage system operator. Minimum clearances are provided for illustration purposes only. Clearances can be affected by specific soil conditions and other factors impacting the effective operation of the sewage system. Contact the local municipality for additional information and current specifications.

MINIMUM CLEARANCES—HOLDING TANKS

	MINIMUM CLEARANCE (m)
Structure	1.5
Well with a Watertight Casing to a Depth of 6m	15
Any Other Well	15
A Spring	15
Property Line	3

Source: Ontario Building Code 1997, Table 8.2.1.6.B

INSULATION

The control of heat loss from a structure is as important as the heating system. Thermal insulation is typically discussed in terms of **R-Value**: the higher the number, the greater the resistance to heat transfer. Differing types of insulation have different R-values per inch of thickness. An R-value is a numerical representation of thermal resistance, the higher the number, the greater resistance to heat transfer. The RSI-Value is the metric equivalent of an R-value (divide the R-value by 5.6).

The Ontario Building Code establishes minimum requirements for new structures based on R-values; i.e., minimum thermal resistance of insulation to be installed in building elements exposed to exterior or unheated spaces, such as ceilings below attics, foundation walls and floors.

Heat Gain/Heat Loss

However, to understand the broader insulation picture and energy efficiency, heat gain/loss must be viewed in terms of three processes: convection, conduction and radiation. In combination, their effective use heightens energy efficiency and ultimately reduces energy consumption.

CONDUCTION

Conduction is the conveyance or transferral of a substance through a solid material. For real estate purposes, conduction commonly occurs with energy transferral through solid objects such as basements, walls and ceiling components. Conduction is effectively minimized through the introduction of non-conductive insulation materials in exterior structures.

Conduction is often accelerated through thermal bridges that exist in most structures. For example, while walls may be fully insulated, hot or cold energy travels through highly conductive window frames or structural components; i.e., metal supports that span the distance between inside and outside walls. Elimination or minimizing thermal bridges is an important element in energy-efficient design.

Typical Insulation R-Values

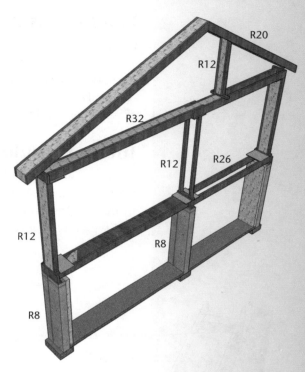

CONVECTION

Convection involves the movement of a gas or liquid given changes in density (e.g., heating of air causes the air to expand and rise with cooler air falling, thereby producing a convection loop). From a real estate perspective, convection is commonly controlled by minimizing air leakage and air flow between a structure's interior and exterior surfaces.

For most structures, leakage around doorways and windows represents a major heat loss source. An air leakage test is typically performed as part of an energy audit. Mass insulation products, proper sealing techniques and energy-efficient building components (e.g., windows) are most effective in limiting convection (e.g., drafts and cold floors).

RADIATION

Radiation involves the transmission of energy through space via a straight line between the source and the absorber (e.g., roof, walls and windows of a structure). Radiation is an important factor in both residential and commercial construction. Radiant heat travels at the speed of light. Intensity depends on transmission angle and absorption quality of the receiving material.

The best example of radiant heat is the warmth generated by sunlight entering a room on a cold winter's day. Despite the fact that the outside temperature may be –10°C, the room can be passively heated to 20°C or higher. Radiated heat, which can either be absorbed or reflected, is an important consideration when installing insulation and windows.

Exterior Insulation

Exterior insulation is a beneficial modernization in older homes, provided that window and door modifications are made, along with care in installing new insulating materials. If not done properly, old uninsulated cavities may short circuit much of the effectiveness. Normally, external insulation is not cost-effective unless the exterior of the building, for example new siding, is also installed.

Interior Insulation

Insulation involves limiting the movement of air through techniques including air barriers, vapour barriers, caulking and weather stripping, and various types of batt or similar insulation. Insulation is rated based on its R-value. An illustration is provided showing batt type wall insulation.

Insulation Types

Different types of insulation have correspondingly different R-values. In fact, even the form of individual types will affect R-value (glass fibre insulation in the form of batts has a higher value than if in loose form). Six insulation types are illustrated along with corresponding R-values.

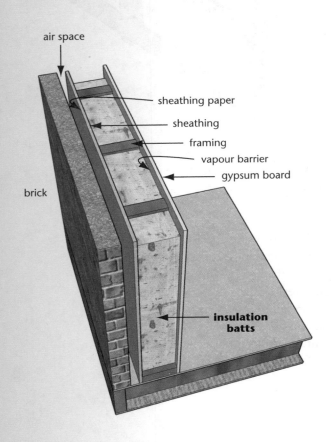

air space

sheathing paper

sheathing

framing

vapour barrier

gypsum board

brick

insulation batts

TYPE	R-VALUE
Glass Fibre Insulation	2.9–4.2 per inch
Mineral Wool/Rock Wool	3.0–3.2 per inch
Cellulose Fibre	3.4–3.6 per inch
Vermiculite	2.3 per inch
Wood Shavings (treated with fire retardant/moisture resistant materials)	2.4 per inch
Plastic Board	3.7–6.0 per inch

ENERGY EFFICIENCY

Energy efficiency, along with the prudent use of resources, is increasingly focal in residential and commercial construction, as well as real estate negotiations. Residential buyers seek energy savings through well-built homes and commercial investors search out energy-efficient structures to reduce costs and maximize returns. Practitioners are increasingly encountering energy efficiency standards and rating systems in both residential and commercial construction.

Emphasis in this course is placed on the **R-2000** house and energy audits associated with resale residential properties. Further expansion regarding energy efficiency issues is provided in the advanced component of *The Residential Real Estate Transaction* relating to important trends in residential and commercial real estate.

R-2000

R-2000 is an energy efficiency program, launched in the 1980s, to encourage energy efficient and environmentally responsible home construction. The R-2000 program, managed by the Office of Energy Efficiency (Natural Resources Canada), includes technical performance standards exceeding energy efficiency requirements set out in building codes.

R-2000

An energy efficiency program relating to new residential construction.

TECHNICAL STANDARDS

An R-2000 house is certified based on continuously updated technical requirements; e.g., ventilation, minimum air leakage and insulation material selection. Builders are trained and certified to meet R-2000 design and construction standards. On average, buyers can expect to pay between two and six percent more for such houses, but can potentially realize significant savings in energy usage. An R-2000 Registration Certificate is issued by Natural Resources Canada upon the completion and inspection of an R-2000 home to ensure that the entire building meets R-2000 standards.

R-2000 standards have expanded to include water consumption targets through the use of water-saving devices (e.g., toilets, shower heads and faucets). Increased emphasis is also being placed on green building materials that reduce indoor air pollutants (e.g., various finishes, adhesives and carpet materials) and more reliance on recycled materials in building construction.

THE PROCESS

Real estate practitioners should be conversant with basic processes underlying the R-2000 home, as energy efficiency is an increasingly focal issue in both new and resale markets. Every R-2000 home must meet stringent quality control standards. Home plans are first computer analyzed to ensure program compliance. During construction, the home is inspected by R-2000 experts, in addition to normal building code inspections. Technicians installing the ventilation system must also be trained and certified. As the home nears completion, an air leakage test is performed to ensure that the structure meets comfort, as well as, energy efficiency, standards. A certificate is issued upon successful completion of all tests and standards compliance.

The R-2000 home promotes a systems approach to house construction; i.e., components work in concert to advance energy efficiency, promote quality construction techniques and advance sound environmental practices. Conversely, a change in one component of a house can impact the others. The secret lies in properly co-ordinating various elements, while achieving heightened standards in all aspects of house construction. Key components include:

- Whole-house continuous ventilation system;
- Advanced energy-efficient heating and cooling systems;
- Energy efficient windows;
- Tighter exterior wall and roof construction to reduce air leakage and drafts, and high levels of insulation;
- Construction and finishing products (e.g., water fixtures, paints, adhesives, flooring) are all selected to reduce waste, maximize use of recycled content and minimize negative environmental effects;
- A heat recovery ventilator replaces indoor air with fresh filtered outside air approximately eight times a day; and
- Overall design minimizes temperature fluctuations, while helping to reduce outdoor noise and dust from entering the house.

QUALITY ASSURANCE

R-2000 builders are provided ongoing training; i.e., current technologies and new product availability. Further, design evaluators use a computer modeling program to analyze the builder's blueprints to ensure R-2000 standard compliance including energy reduction levels in line with prescribed energy targets. Each R-2000 home is thoroughly inspected upon completion and lastly, the home is registered with Natural Resources Canada to allow future purchasers to verify certification. Since 1982, over 8,000 homes have been certified.

FACTORY-BUILT HOMES

The controlled environment within a manufacturing operation is ideally suited to R-2000 standards. Home production is undertaken in climate-stable conditions rarely attained with site-built houses. Certified R-2000 factory-built homes are inspected by an independent, licensed third party and tested prior to delivery to ensure compliance with all R-2000 standards. As with other R-2000 homes, a Registration Certificate is provided and the home is registered with Natural Resources Canada.

Energy Audit

Energy Audit
An analysis of energy loss in a structure, typically including recommendations.

An **energy audit** is an analysis of a residential or commercial building, typically provided by an energy consultant, to identify energy loss sources. Audits are increasingly popular with buyers tuned into energy efficiency issues. An audit commonly involves a full property inspection by a professional, often complemented with a computer-driven analysis program, to identify:

- Air leakage and general condition of insulation within walls and ceilings;
- Humidity levels and any indication of moisture that can result in mould formation;
- Windows and other openings and assess contribution to heating/cooling loss;
- Furnace and duct distribution systems; and
- Water heater system.

Audits typically furnish recommendations for increased energy performance, with particular emphasis on windows, doors and mechanical systems. Passive technologies may also be highlighted including sun control devices, high efficiency appliances and natural sunlight diffusion techniques for daytime energy conservation. The scope and focus of audits will vary by provider. Local utilities are often involved in such projects. Information can also be obtained from the Office of Energy Efficiency, Natural Resources Canada.

Energy Savings and Grants   FOCUS

Natural Resources Canada offers the ecoENERGY program through its Office of Energy Efficiency. Currently, the ecoENERGY program provides financial support to homeowners, small and medium-sized businesses, and industrial facilities. Residential property owners of single-family, detached, semi-detached and low density multi-unit residential buildings) can qualify for grants when improving energy efficiency. Commercial and industrial facilities can receive incentives (based on annual energy savings). Current program details are available at the Office of Energy Efficiency. See the following Web Link.

 WEB LINKS

For more information concerning energy efficiency grants and incentives, as well as various programs offered by the Government of Canada, go to the Office of Energy Efficiency (Natural Resources Canada) web site at *www.oee.nrcan.gc.ca.*

KNOWLEDGE INTEGRATION

Notables

- Basic mechanical components in residential and commercial structures include electrical, heating and plumbing systems.

- Be cautious regarding electrical distribution panels. Size is dictated by the service entrance cable.

- The heating system, typically a furnace or boiler system, generates heat for disbursement to various parts of the structure.

- Capacity and efficiency are key considerations in a heating system.

- Boiler (hot water) systems can be either open or closed.

- HVAC units are commonly associated with commercial applications.

- Chimney deterioration is a common problem in both residential and commercial structures.

- Plumbing systems are best described from two perspectives: supply and waste.

- Exercise caution with all matters concerning private water wells and water quality including issues regarding bacteriological testing.

- Installation of water wells are falling under increasingly strict regulatory controls.

- Water well records are maintained by the Ministry of the Environment.

- Approvals and inspections of onsite sewage systems is administered by local municipalities.

- Practitioners typically encounter Class 4 sewage systems in rural areas, but other types are also used; e.g., Class 5 (holding tank).

- Builders are trained and certified to build R-2000 houses. An R-2000 Registration Certificate is issued upon the completion and inspection of R-2000 homes.

- Energy audits are increasingly popular in both residential and commercial structures.

Glossary

Bacteriological Testing	Fireplace	R-2000
Boiler	Furnace	R-Value
Distribution Panel	Heating System	Sewage System (On-Site)
Electrical Inspection	Hot Water Heater	Water Well
Electrical Service Size	HVAC System	Water Well Record
Energy Audit	Plumbing System	

Web Links

Web links are included for general interest regarding selected chapter topics.

Hydro One   Hydro One is most commonly associated with managing the electricity transmission and distribution systems in Ontario, but has other subsidiary companies including Hydro One Remotes that provides electrical services to distant communities in Ontario. For more information, go to *www.hydroone.ca*.

Water Wells   Practitioners marketing residential and commercial properties that rely on water wells, should keep up to date on water quality and water well requirements as set out in provincial legislation. Go to the Ministry of the Environment web site at *www.ene.gov.on.ca*.

Office of Energy Efficiency   For more information concerning energy efficiency grants and incentives, as well as various programs offered by the Government of Canada, go to the Office of Energy Efficiency (Natural Resources Canada) web site at *www.oee.nrcan.gc.ca*.

Strategic Thinking For Your Career

Questions are included to assist in developing your new career. No answers are provided.

1. Are older electrical service sizes typically found in my market area (e.g., knob-and-tube wiring) as well as other related issues (e.g., inadequate service size due to an accessory apartment, large home with 60 amp service, etc)?

2. What new innovative technologies are being used for heating systems for residential and commercial structures in the local marketplace?

3. How is bacteriological testing for water wells handled in the local area?

4. What is the approval process at the local municipal level to install an onsite sewage system?

5. Which local builders are building R-2000 houses? What additional features are other builders including in their new homes to improve energy efficiency?

6. Is the local utility (or other energy experts) providing energy audits for residential and/or commercial property and what is included in a typical analysis?

Chapter Mini-Review

Solutions are located in the Appendix.

1. Ground fault circuit interrupters are used for certain bathroom outlets and installations near water; e.g., swimming pools.

    ⚪ True   ⚪ False

2. Hot water tanks are typically insulated to prevent water leakage during operation.

    ⚪ True   ⚪ False

3. Plumbing repairs or improvements are typically costly owing to the fact that most plumbing components are enclosed within structures.

    ⚪ True   ⚪ False

4. A traditional open wood fireplace can take more heat away from a structure than it generates.

    ⚪ True   ⚪ False

5. RSI-Value is the metric equivalent of R-Value.

    ⚪ True   ⚪ False

6. Knob-and-tube wiring in a residential structure does not typically pose problems when attempting to obtain home insurance.

    ⚪ True   ⚪ False

7. Water testing is mandatory for all residential water wells in Ontario within six months of purchasing the property.

    ⚪ True   ⚪ False

8. Class 5 sewage systems can only be used for residential cottage purposes.

    ⚪ True   ⚪ False

9. A leaching (absorption) bed is most commonly associated with a Class 4 system.

    ⚪ True   ⚪ False

10. A raised absorption bed is typically used where topography/soils does not permit sufficient filtering and/or drainage.

    ⚪ True   ⚪ False

11. Standards concerning R-2000 houses are developed and enforced by the Ministry of Housing in Ontario.

    ⚪ True   ⚪ False

12. Convection refers to the conveyance or transferral of a substance thorough a solid material.

    ⚪ True   ⚪ False

Active Learning Exercises

Solutions are located in the Appendix.

■ Exercise 1   Technical Terms (Fill-in-the-Blanks)

1.1   The size of the service entrance cable determines how much
[   ] is available to the house.

1.2   An R-value is a numerical representation of [   ]
[   ] .

1.3   Of wood shavings insulation, mineral wool or cellulose fibre, [   ]
[   ] has the highest R-value.

1.4   Two 100-amp fuses in the main disconnect would normally indicate
[   ] amp service.

1.5   An octopus furnace is normally referred to as a [   ] furnace.

1.6   High efficiency furnaces have an efficiency in the mid to high [   ] %
range.

1.7   There must be adequate venting in a plumbing system to permit
[   ] .
(phrase)

1.8   Modern boilers are normally [   ] systems.

1.9   Grounded outlets have one major difference from ungrounded outlets, that
being the [   ] .
(phrase)

1.10   In a hot water tank, the more water that can be drawn off without depleting the
hot water supply is referred to as the [   ]
[   ] .

■ Exercise 2　Multiple Choice

2.1　Which of the following statements is true with respect to the electrical service supplied to a house?

a. The resistance of any material to the flow of electricity is measured in amps.

b. Distribution panels are used in large commercial structures, but are not used in residential homes.

c. Electrical power entering the typical house goes into a main disconnect, which has two fuses or two circuit breakers.

d. Both a. and c. are correct.

2.2　Which of the following statements is NOT correct with respect to knob-and-tube wiring systems?

a. Knob-and-tube systems must be replaced in existing residential property.

b. The system gets its name from the ceramic knobs by which the wire is secured and the tubes that are used where wires pass through wood framing members.

c. Breakdown of the insulation on knob-and-tube wiring is most often the reason it has to be replaced.

d. Knob-and-tube wiring was used residentially until approximately 1950.

2.3　Which of the following statements is NOT correct with respect to the seasonal efficiency of heating systems?

a. A conventional system is about 55–60% seasonally efficient.

b. A mid efficiency system operates optimally at approximately 80% efficiency.

c. A high efficiency system operates above the 90% range.

d. A gravity furnace operates at the same level as a high efficiency system.

2.4　Which of the following statements is correct with respect to a septic tank system?

a. The septic tank is a water tight container usually made of fiberglass, concrete or steel.

b. The septic tank serves as a holding tank which allows heavy solids to settle to the bottom.

c. Liquids are ultimately discharged from the tank into a tile bed.

d. All of the above.

2.5　Which of the following statements is NOT correct?

a. Galvanized steel piping was used in plumbing systems up to approximately 1950.

b. Plastic supply piping has gained considerable popularity in recent years.

c. Adequate venting is required to minimize noise factor when water is passing through piping.

d. A pressure tank provides relatively even water pressure to the house.

2.6   Convection:

    a.   Involves the movement of a gas or liquid given changes in the density of that medium.

    b.   Is dramatically accelerated when heat travels through highly conductive materials such as window frames.

    c.   Is the transmission of energy through space via a straight line.

    d.   Is a process used when conducting a bacteriological analysis of well water.

2.7   Which of the following is NOT typically analyzed in an energy audit?

    a.   Sources of air leakage and general condition of insulation.

    b.   Furnace and duct distribution system.

    c.   Electrical distribution panel.

    d.   Water heater.

■ Exercise 3   Commentary

Four statements made by salespeople are provided. In each instance, comment upon each with direct reference to chapter materials.

3.1   *A buyer called me [the salesperson] saying that the bathroom outlets were not working in his newly-constructed house. I told him the wiring must not be connected properly. That's the only possible reason!*

3.2   *The buyer called about minimum septic system requirements. I told him that size requirements are based on lot size and to go directly to the municipality who has all the details. I also mentioned that he should be asking for information about a Class 3 system.*

3.3 *In new construction, the R-value is normally higher in basement areas because the walls are directly abutting outside cold ground areas.*

3.4 *The only chance of having a sewer backup into a house on municipal services is if the property is situated in a low lying area of the city.*

SECTION III   STRUCTURAL TYPES AND COMPONENTS

SECTION IV

PROPERTY VALUATION

Early daylight is often best for photos. Broker Reynolds adjusts the car visor, blocking the morning sun as she nears the downtown. A quick right, a short left and the property is just three blocks . The owner will be anxiously waiting. They always are when it's a corporate move.

Every couple of weeks, Reynolds completes an appraisal report for a Toronto-based relocation company. She has an unmistakable air of confidence, backed by numerous appraisal courses and years of experience. While her appraisals number in the hundreds, every one is unique and must be carefully planned and executed.

Some research has already been done. Historical MLS® data, assessment information and a zoning check confirmed seller details obtained by telephone. Comparable sales and accompanying photos lay on the car seat, along with the appraisal report form, camera and the trusty city map.

Reynolds believes in taking what she calls the roundabout way to the subject property. What's happening in the neighbourhood is key. It's all about trends. Neighbourhood analysis is just one in many important steps in the appraisal process.

Reynolds makes the final left turn looking for the subject property. Her trained eye critically scans adjacent properties and then focuses on the job at hand. Third house on the right… there it is. She abruptly stops, grabs the camera, checks the sun angle and click… another appraisal is underway.

CHAPTER 9

The Appraisal Process

Introduction

Real estate salespeople are routinely involved in appraisal activities, but not in a formalized sense. Typically, discussions with buyers and sellers centre on value issues, but the emphasis is focused on probable listing and selling prices. However, the appraisal fundamentals are present, even if detailed forms are not always completed.

Chapter 9 focuses on the formal appraisal process including a detailed description of eight steps that begin with defining the problem and planning the work, to data collection and analysis, applying approaches to value, arriving at a final estimate and, lastly, writing the appraisal report.

The Comparative Market Analysis (CMA) is then discussed in relation to appraisals. The CMA is not designed to establish market value, but rather is used to assist a seller in establishing a listing price. Fundamental components of the CMA are discussed. The practical application of the CMA in the real estate marketplace is addressed in *The Real Estate Transaction – General.*

Lastly, the link between valuation and assessment in Ontario is highlighted. The role of the Municipal Property Assessment Corporation is discussed, along with fundamental processes including determining assessed values, preparing assessment roles and issuing notices of property assessment.

Chapter 9 establishes the groundwork for detailed analysis of the three approaches to value in subsequent chapters. While many practitioners will not seek professional appraiser status, knowledge of the appraisal process is vital. Real estate salespersons must fully understand the sound basics underlying property valuation to be in a better position to competently serve the needs of consumers. Those same basics pave the way for advanced courses in appraisal that benefit any professional real estate career.

Learning Outcomes

At the conclusion of this chapter, students will be able to:

- Define appraisal and discuss the relevance of the appraisal date and appraisal purpose.
- Identify five primary purposes for a real estate appraisal.
- Differentiate between narrative and form appraisal reports and briefly highlight why letters of opinion are no longer used.
- Detail activities required in the eight steps to the appraisal process.
- Discuss activities involved in Step 3: Data Collection and Analysis with particular emphasis on neighbourhood, site and site improvement analysis and additional resources available to appraisers.
- Discuss differing perspectives when conducting a neighbourhood analysis when addressing single family, multi-residential, retail and farm properties.
- Describe key steps involved in the reconciliation process leading to a final estimate of value and the inclusion of limiting conditions and certification when writing the appraisal report.
- Differentiate between an appraisal and a comparative market analysis and briefly discuss major components within the Residential Market Comparison Guide.
- Explain how appraisal activity is related to property assessment and discuss key elements in the property assessment process including assessed value, property classes, valuation date, assessment roles, property improvements and notice of property assessment.

REAL ESTATE APPRAISAL

Appraisal can be broadly described as the act or process of estimating value. The resulting opinion of value derived from the appraisal may be informal, transmitted verbally, or it may be formal, presented in written form. Usually, it is a written statement setting forth an opinion of the value of an adequately described property as of a specified date, supported by the presentation and analysis of relevant data.

Real estate appraisal has undergone dramatic changes over the past several decades. Professional appraisers, often referred to as **fee appraisers**, have faced the onslaught of fast-track mortgage approval systems that sometimes places more emphasis on buyer financial stability and personal covenant than on the property being mortgaged.

While many homes are still rigorously inspected, lenders increasingly rely on sophisticated databases and automated approval processes. Lenders may rely solely on drive-by property inspections, depending on the buyer's covenant and related considerations.

Have the Right Credentials	CAUTION

Formal appraisals are usually handled by individuals with appropriate credentials and expertise. Once registered, check with your employing brokerage if requested to complete an appraisal. Persons interested in pursuing a professional career in appraisal can obtain additional information from the Appraisal Institute of Canada web site at **www.aicanada.ca.**

WEB LINKS

Appraisal Institute   Persons interested in pursuing a professional career in appraisal can obtain additional information from the Appraisal Institute of Canada web site at ***www.aicanada.ca***.

Appraisal Date

The appraisal date is the date to which the valuation applies, sometimes referred to as the effective date of the appraisal.

> **EXAMPLE**   *Appraisal Date*
>
> An appraiser, when preparing an appraisal report, will identify the appraisal date when discussing the purpose of the appraisal; e.g., *This appraisal is to estimate the market value of the subject property as of November 30th, 20xx for sale purposes.*
>
> The appraisal date is also found in the final estimate of value, as illustrated below.
>
> *Based on the above data and analysis, it is my opinion that the estimated market value of the subject property, as described in this report, is $225,000 as of November 30th, 20xx.*

Appraisal Purpose

The purpose of the appraisal refers to the use that will be made of the value estimate. Five major purposes or reasons are outlined for which an appraisal may be required.

Transfer of Ownership	Involves the buying, selling and exchanging of real estate.
Extension of Credit	Normally relates to mortgage lending or other financing and an estimate of value to establish the loan amount.

Compensation for Damage or Loss	Usually involves insurance claims or expropriation.
Taxation	Includes municipal assessment for property taxes and income tax on capital gains.
Land Use Studies or Feasibility Studies	Largely carried out for developers and investors interested in establishing the highest and best use of a particular parcel of land. This process typically involves a number of estimates of value for different forms of development; e.g., freehold detached homes as compared to condominium townhouses.

The purpose must be established at the very beginning of the assignment and be clearly stated in the appraisal report. The purpose is often simply stated as follows:

> *This appraisal is to estimate the market value of the subject property as of November 30th, 20xx, for sale purposes.*

Historical Appraisals CAUTION

The effective date of an appraisal is the date on which the value estimate applies, sometimes referred to as the 'as of' date. This date is critical, as it defines the specific point in time when value is estimated based on the then current market forces and conditions.

Sellers may request a property valuation for some past date; e.g., for purposes of establishing capital gains tax. Extreme caution is advised. Such valuations require retrospective analysis. While past knowledge of the marketplace may assist, complications can arise.

As an example, the subject property and comparable sales may have been renovated or otherwise modified since the effective appraisal date. Consequently, accurate historical data is required. Practitioners are strongly advised to refer such requests to appropriate appraisal experts.

Appraisal Reports

Most appraisals are either **narrative reports** or **form reports**. Form reports range from two or three page mortgage appraisal forms to multi-page relocation forms (often 10+ pages). Narratives vary from short versions detailing primary research and approaches to value (e.g., used in a divorce action) to detailed 60+ page products for litigation and expropriation, etc.

NARRATIVE REPORT

A narrative report can vary substantially in size based on the property type and appraisal purpose. This comprehensive report provides a logical and systematic presentation of pertinent facts, theoretical premises and explanations leading to a final opinion of value. Narrative reports tend to be lengthy, fully documented and time consuming to prepare. A residential appraisal using the narrative format provides a full description of full description of the appraisal process so that the reader can follow the logic leading to a final estimate of value.

Narrative Report

A detailed appraisal report typically prepared by a fee appraiser.

Form Report

A standardized appraisal report format typically associated with property valuations for residential property; e.g., mortgage applications.

EXAMPLE   *Preparing the Narrative Report*

Anne Appraiser is preparing a detailed narrative report on a residential property owned by Smith. Smith requires the appraisal for pending expropriation plans concerning new highway construction. Anne carefully details the main topic areas within the planned narrative report.

- Appraisal Summary
  (important facts and conclusions)
- Letter of Transmittal
  (summary letter to the client)
- Title Page
- Table of Contents
- Taxes and Assessment
  (specific information regarding taxes on the property, taxation trends and impact on value)
- Area and Neighbourhood Analysis
  (description of external factors impacting value)
- Site and Improvement Analysis
  (exterior and interior description of the property)
- Approaches to Value
  (application of the market data, cost and income approaches to value)
- Reconciliation
  (details how the value estimate was determined)

FORM REPORT

The form report is used frequently by appraisers when providing appraisal reports for financial institutions, relocation companies and government agencies. This type of report consists mainly of preprinted information that must be checked off where relevant. Space is also available for additional comments and supporting details.

The form report allows for a brief, systematic presentation while providing clients with an easy-to-follow consistent approach. Many lending institutions have developed their own unique form reports. Recently, the trend in appraisal activity is toward more standardized form reports. The Appraisal Institute of Canada (AIC) has a standard form report called the *Uniform Appraisal Report Form*.

As background information to the AIC form, during the late 1980s, Uniform Standards of Professional Appraisal Practice (USPAP) were established by the Appraisal Standards Board (a division of the Appraisal Institute in the United States). These standards have been generally accepted by most fee appraisers throughout North America. Appraisers can use either complete or limited use appraisals, along with three acceptable forms: self-contained, summary and restricted reports. Accordingly, USPAP provides today's appraiser with six different combinations.

Complete appraisals have the necessary materials for a credible analysis and do not exclude any of the three approaches to value. Limited-use appraisals are allowed to vary from a fully detailed narrative report. Such variations are referred to as departures. The most common departure is the exclusion of one or more of the approaches to value.

Limited use appraisals provide a level of reliability for selected situations; e.g., internal valuations or reports to lenders, or when a value must be reported quickly. Without delving into each type of report, these recent changes reflect the need for shorter, summarized reports with associated lower fees and turnaround times. At present, many lenders now want the direct comparison approach only for residential property and may give only cursory, if any, consideration to the cost approach.

LETTER OF OPINION

A **letter of opinion** is a brief, unsubstantiated statement of an appraiser's opinion of value or value range that is not recommended as a method of appraisal reporting. Although only limited information is given in the letter of opinion, the individual providing such an opinion should understand that a complete appraisal process must still be conducted and all relevant data, analysis and conclusions kept within the appraiser's files. Indeed, completion of a full appraisal report may be required at some future date to substantiate the opinion.

While clients may expect a large reduction in the fee charged (assuming that a letter of opinion is a timesaving method of appraisal), a form report can usually be completed more quickly and easily. Also, given the vagueness of the letter of opinion, it often tends to create confusion and problems between the client and appraiser, resulting in both parties being dissatisfied. Letters of opinion are usually not accepted by lending institutions.

Historically, real estate brokers provided letters of opinion that limited information to salient property details and a value estimate. This practice is now generally discouraged given liability issues. It should also be noted that the letter of opinion failed to meet USPAP standards for fee appraisers. Brokers have since gravitated to standardized forms that resemble mortgage appraisal forms or relocation reports. For example, the Ontario Real Estate Association provides two standard report formats: *Standard Appraisal Report–Single* (Form 700) and *Standard Appraisal Report–Condominium* (Form 701).

APPRAISAL ASSIGNMENTS

Salespersons may receive client requests for appraisals when involved with normal listing and selling activities. Check with the brokerage for guidance. While comparative market analysis (CMA) and related activities are encouraged, formal appraisals are typically handled by those with appropriate credentials and experience. Liability and proper insurance coverage are two primary concerns. The use of a comparative market analysis is discussed in more detail later in this chapter.

THE APPRAISAL PROCESS

The appraisal process represents a systematic analysis of factors that bear upon the value of real estate. This is an orderly process by which the task (e.g., estimating market value as at a specified date) is established, the work necessary to solve the problem is planned and the data involved is acquired, classified, analyzed and interpreted into an estimate of value. The appraisal process involves eight sequential steps.

THE APPRAISAL PROCESS

STEP 1
Define the Problem
Identify the property to be appraised, the property rights involved, the purpose of the appraisal, type of value required, the date of the appraisal, identify any assumptions and limiting conditions, and reach an agreement with the client.

STEP 2
Preliminary Inspection and Planning the Work
A preliminary survey determines the highest and best use, type and sources of data needed to support the analysis, determines the value approaches to be used, provides the design for the research program and outlines the appraisal report. An appraisal plan is then established.

STEP 3
Data Collection and Analysis
Involves the acquisition of relevant data concerning market trends, neighbourhood and site analysis, and the inspection/analysis of the property's improvements.

STEP 4
Apply the Cost Approach
Estimate the site value through an acceptable method, estimate reproduction or replacement cost for the improvements, estimate accrued depreciation and complete the necessary calculations to arrive at value by the cost approach.

STEP 5
Apply the Direct Comparison Approach
Detail the five steps in this approach consisting of selection of comparables, data collection, analysis of relevant data, comparisons with subject property together with appropriate adjustments and reconciliation to arrive at value estimate.

STEP 6
Apply the Income Approach
Estimate the annual gross income, total annual operating expenses and the net operating income (or cash flow), select the appropriate capitalization rate and convert the income into a value estimate.

STEP 7
Reconciliation and Final Estimate
Provide final reconciliation by reviewing the approaches to value and arriving at a final estimate.

STEP 8
Write the Appraisal Report
Prepare the final report (narrative, form or letter of opinion), along with certification and necessary appendices.

Online Innovations   FOCUS

Computers and the Internet are simplifying various appraisal complexities. For example, updated assessment records are now readily available online for appraisers. Similarly, other property details once delegated to dusty land registry books can be accessed online.

Most recently, the AVM (**automated valuation model**) has taken centre stage. Fee appraisers, property assessors and others involved with property valuation have entered the high tech world of automated valuation. This computer-based valuation methodology, formally referred to as an automated valuation model (AVM) derives a value estimate based on subject property attributes, recent sales and various trends compiled for neighbouring properties, as well as the local/regional markets.

SECTION IV   PROPERTY VALUATION

AVMs are proving increasingly popular, particularly in assessment and mortgage financing sectors. Virtually instantaneous results are possible in a web-based system by inputting a property address. The AVM database can track hundreds of property features for quick comparison between a subject property and recent comparable sales. Advanced systems not only provide an estimate (typically including a high/low range and confidence level regarding the estimate; e.g., low, medium or high level) but also key factors affecting the property's value.

The automated valuation model is typically driven by location-oriented data. In other words, the system groups properties within a defined neighbourhood affected by similar market trends and/or external influences. As with any system, the AVM is limited by the volume and accuracy of input data.

While originally designed strictly for valuation purposes, AVMs are being creatively linked to other spatially-defined data found in geographic information systems (GIS). For example, detailed reports can include a value estimate, together with demographics, local/regional price increase/decrease trends and other local/regional statistics furnishing a broad property profile. Alternatively, GIS's are provided greatly enhanced information to complement existing data layers; e.g., physical property details (soil type, terrain, etc.), land registration data, survey details, structural descriptions, adjacent road systems, zoning and census data.

AVMs are growing increasingly sophisticated providing market trends, key neighbourhood benefits/features, price increases/decreases, comparisons with adjacent neighbourhoods and even photos of comparable properties. Links to geographic information systems will broaden online resources to include zoning, land-use, assessment, property boundaries, utilities and structures.

ANALYZING THE EIGHT-STEP PROCESS

The typical narrative report provides detailed descriptions of all eight steps in the appraisal process. Form reports and other summary appraisals also broadly adhere to these steps. Students need not understand the intricacies of each step, but should understand the grand design. The appraisal process flows logically from definitions and principles of value studied in *Real Estate as a Professional Career.*

STEP 1   Define the Problem

The appraiser requires terms of reference: what must be done and why. Any ambiguity regarding the assignment must be eliminated through the following seven items:

PROPERTY TO BE APPRAISED	PROPERTY RIGHTS	PURPOSE OF THE APPRAISAL	SPECIFIC TYPE OF VALUE	EFFECTIVE DATE	LIMITING CONDITIONS & ASSUMPTIONS	REACH AGREEMENT WITH CLIENT
Municipal address and legal description to determine property boundaries.	Fee simple or a lesser interest such as a leasehold interest.	Transfer of ownership, extension of credit, compensation for loss or damage, taxation, or land use studies.	If market value, then the definition of market value should be included.	The date on which the value estimate applies.	Identification of circumstances under which the appraisal is being carried out.	Establish agreement to avoid any misunderstandings.

STEP 2   Preliminary Inspection and Planning the Work

Six factors must be considered in developing an appraisal plan.

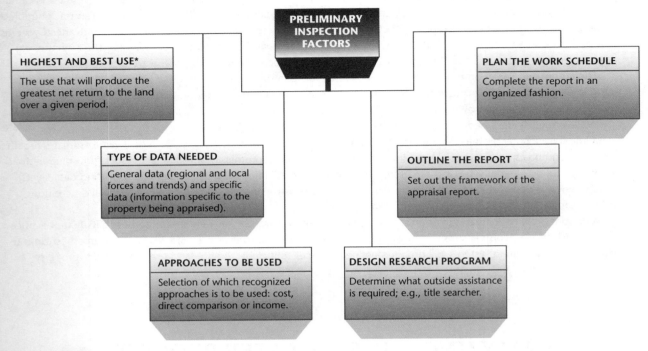

PRELIMINARY INSPECTION FACTORS

HIGHEST AND BEST USE*

The use that will produce the greatest net return to the land over a given period.

PLAN THE WORK SCHEDULE

Complete the report in an organized fashion.

TYPE OF DATA NEEDED

General data (regional and local forces and trends) and specific data (information specific to the property being appraised).

OUTLINE THE REPORT

Set out the framework of the appraisal report.

APPROACHES TO BE USED

Selection of which recognized approaches is to be used: cost, direct comparison or income.

DESIGN RESEARCH PROGRAM

Determine what outside assistance is required; e.g., title searcher.

* Three factors normally determine highest and best use:

    (1) Is the use legal in light of deed restrictions and zoning requirements?

    (2) Is the property physically suitable for the use intended?

    (3) Does demand exist for the intended use?

STEP 3   Data Collection and Analysis

Data collection involves general information (i.e., economic, political, social and physical forces/trends) impacting value) and specifics about the subject and comparable properties.

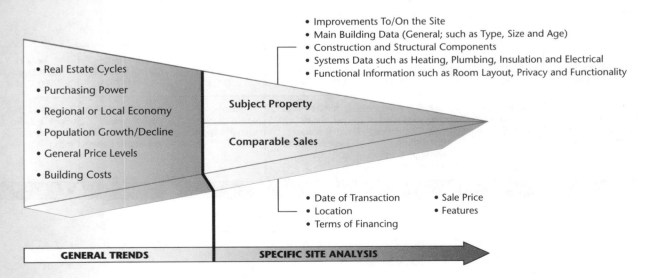

- Improvements To/On the Site
- Main Building Data (General; such as Type, Size and Age)
- Construction and Structural Components
- Systems Data such as Heating, Plumbing, Insulation and Electrical
- Functional Information such as Room Layout, Privacy and Functionality

- Real Estate Cycles
- Purchasing Power
- Regional or Local Economy
- Population Growth/Decline
- General Price Levels
- Building Costs

Subject Property

Comparable Sales

- Date of Transaction
- Location
- Terms of Financing
- Sale Price
- Features

GENERAL TRENDS   **SPECIFIC SITE ANALYSIS**

Data collection and analysis includes various stages ranging from general overall trends to more specific research focused on the neighbourhood, the site and the improvements (structures). Emphasis is placed on neighbourhood, site and site improvement analysis. Further detail on valuation considerations relating to this factors is addressed in subsequent chapters.

NEIGHBOURHOOD ANALYSIS

A neighbourhood, for purposes of appraisals, refers to a portion of a larger community, or an entire community, in which there is a homogeneous grouping of inhabitants, buildings or business enterprises. Inhabitants of a neighbourhood usually have a more than casual community of interest and a similarity of economic level or cultural background. Neighbourhood boundaries may consist of well-defined natural or man-made barriers, or may be more or less well defined by a distinct change in land use or in the character of the inhabitants.

Age (Life) Cycle

An age or life cycle refers to the economic lifespan of a highly similar grouping of structures within a naturally defined or man-made area known as a neighbourhood. The age cycle of any neighbourhood is composed of three distinct phases:

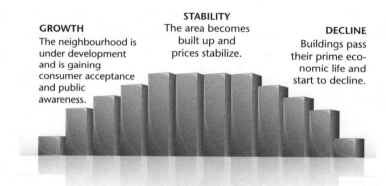

GROWTH
The neighbourhood is under development and is gaining consumer acceptance and public awareness.

STABILITY
The area becomes built up and prices stabilize.

DECLINE
Buildings pass their prime economic life and start to decline.

Various programs and initiatives may tend to extend cycles, particularly during the decline stage. Renewed interest in declining neighbourhoods can give way to new forms of growth and promotion of higher and better use of the land, such as larger houses following demolition of original homes within specific areas and demolition of older residential property in favour of new office and retail complexes.

EXAMPLE   *Neighbourhood Age (Life) Cycle*

Salesperson Lee has been asked to establish fair market value for a home at 13 Main Street. The subject property is approximately 40 years old and has been extremely well maintained. However, the general vicinity, while once primarily single-family housing, has changed particularly during the past five-year period. While the property being reviewed would be worth approximately $360,000 in a more stable neighbourhood, the broker must make adjustments for the deteriorating neighbourhood. In particular, adjacent houses on the street are in a poor state of repair. Lee identifies the neighbourhood as declining, makes a note in his appraisal report and, after detailed research, establishes a fair market value of $326,000.

Differing Perspectives

In viewing a neighbourhood, the appraiser will assess its age cycle in terms of growth, stability or decline, boundaries and any factors or forces affecting that neighbourhood. A neighbourhood analysis requires reliable and accurate data. **Appraisers** are normally reasonably familiar with the neighbourhood and consequently, their own files provide much of the required information. Understandably, the exact approach will vary, based on the type of use; e.g., low density, apartments, industrial, commercial or rural. Examples are provided illustrating differing appraisal perspectives on neighbourhood factors.

SINGLE FAMILY

Salesperson Ward has been asked to provide an appraisal for a single-family home in a low density neighbourhood. Ward describes the neighbourhood in terms of four factors:

Physical   First and foremost, Ward will assess the property's location. Poor location can offset many other factors that would otherwise enhance its value. Besides location, Salesperson Ward will consider proximity of public transportation, parks, schools, churches, retail and service outlets, topography, landscape and availability/quality of utilities. Her checklist also includes nuisances or hazards such as smoke, noise, pollution and heavy traffic.

Economic   Ward will also give regard to stability of uses, property values, vacancies, new construction, personal and family income levels, degree of maintenance (pride of ownership), stage in the neighbourhood age (life) cycle, amount of undeveloped land available, mortgage lending policies, interest rates, sale price trends and rate of turnover.

Political or Governmental   Ward must be aware of legal factors affecting low density residential values, such as zoning regulations, building codes, property taxes, local improvement taxes, official plans, site plan control agreements and deed restrictions.

Social   Significant social factors include population trends with respect to growth or decline, trends to larger or smaller family sizes, harmony or lack of harmony of ethnic or economic groupings, educational attitudes, level of prestige, crime rates, age groupings and population densities.

FARM

Salesperson Ward is considering a farm appraisal. In analyzing farm areas, various factors discussed under residential and commercial areas can apply, but there are others of which Ward specifically makes note.

- Distance to market.
- Types of soils and crops grown in the area.
- Typical farm properties, including their size and scope of operations.
- Services, including roads, power, mail delivery and school transportation.

MULTI-RESIDENTIAL

Anne Appraiser has been asked to establish the fair market value of an apartment building. Skilled in this type of appraisal work, Anne will consider various factors that impact the estimate of value.

Transportation
Located near public transportation.

Major Thoroughfares
Close to major traffic arteries so that apartment tenants need not pass through residential areas to access these arteries.

Services
Proximity to shopping, schools, churches and other services.

Amenities/Recreational Facilities (Physical)
Proximity to parks, playgrounds or other related features adds to desirability and reduces the effects of possible future competition.

Vacancies
Assessment of short-term apartment vacancies, resulting from boom construction, in conjunction with the possible future market for apartment units in the neighbourhood; i.e., concern with possible long-term vacancies throughout the economic life of the building.

RETAIL

Anne Appraiser is preparing for a commercial appraisal. In analyzing commercial neighbourhoods, she developed a list of key factors.

- Extent, population, incomes and demand of the trading area.
- Major traffic thoroughfares and accessibility.
- Ample, easy to find, affordable parking facilities.
- Pull of competition from other areas and its effect on the subject property.
- Degree of comparability with other uses in the area.
- Degree to which the subject property is located within the general direction of growth for the community.
- Vacancy factors for both commercial buildings and available development sites.

SECTION IV   PROPERTY VALUATION

Boundaries

The boundaries or limits of a neighbourhood relate to the grouping of inhabitants, buildings or business enterprises. Several characteristics set a specific neighbourhood apart from surrounding areas and make boundaries easier to delineate:

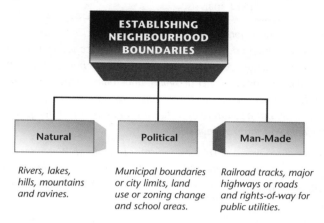

Factors

There are significant items that impact the nature, design, composition and overall make-up of a neighbourhood. Appraisers view most neighbourhoods in terms of four characteristics:

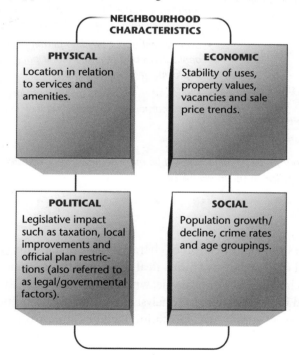

In apartment neighbourhoods, important factors tend to centre on transportation, major thoroughfares, social and recreational facilities, services and vacancy rates. Retail neighbourhoods are usually analyzed in terms of access, parking facilities, compatibility of uses, growth trends, vacancy factors and competitive position (in relation to other retail areas). Industrial sites, in addition to selected factors referred to above, must consider specific services required (rail, utilities, etc.), labour pool and access to raw materials. Farm appraisers analyze distance to market, soil types, crops/yields, typical size of farm units and services.

A Hands-On Viewpoint   MARKET PERSPECTIVE

A professional appraiser visiting Broker William's office made a short presentation at a recent sales meeting. This practical discussion should help in better understanding neighbourhood analysis.

When I complete a detailed narrative report, extensive information concerning general and specific trends is provided. However, most form reports focus solely on neighbourhood information and site improvements. Let me concentrate on neighbourhood issues. As you know, value is impacted by many external factors beyond the property itself. No house sits in isolation. Carefully scrutinize the neighbourhood. I like to think of neighbourhoods as either declining, undergoing some form of renewal, growing or stable. All neighbourhoods go through this cycle. In inner core areas, the pattern may have been repeated several times. Such trends are vital not only concerning current value, but also future expectations. I have a list of things to watch for regarding declining neighbourhoods...these may help you sharpen your skills:

- *Look for neglect, dated housing styles and lack of repairs.*

- *Take particular note of any commercial properties. Are there any vacant stores? Have low-end, transient retail outlets replaced better shops and facilities?*

- *What about the rental/owned composition? Are more and more houses being converted to rentals?*

- *Check with average price trends. Are prices, even though they may be moving upwards, increasing at a slower pace than adjacent neighbourhoods? Are prices falling?*

- *Does the neighbourhood look well maintained including parks, boulevards and streetscapes?*

- *What is the average time to sell a property, in comparison to adjacent neighbourhoods?*

- *What other factors may be impacting housing in that area; i.e., employment trends? What signs suggest a renewal in a neighbourhood? This topic can be more challenging.*

- *The best indicator is demand. Watch for renewed interest. If the smart money is moving in that direction, you can usually bet that some form of renewal is underway.*

- *Are more and more older homes being torn down and replaced by larger homes? Even one or two on a residential street may indicate that something significant is happening.*

- *Are new facades being installed on neighbourhood commercial space? What about the types of tenants and owners moving in? Is the clientele changing?*

- *Don't forget about building permit activity, re-zoning applications and renewed municipal interest in improving services/facilities.*

- *Check out assessments and recent price trends. Are neighbourhood prices reflecting new demand?*

In short, become a neighbourhood sleuth. Your property valuations will be more accurate, your knowledge more complete and your expertise will be sought by buyers and sellers in the marketplace.

SITE ANALYSIS

Site analysis involves the identification of characteristics that create, enhance or detract from the utility and marketability of a site. Real estate practitioners encounter site analysis within specific specialty fields. For example, with an industrial site, the principal physical elements considered in site selection and analysis are usually soil conditions, drainage facilities, water supply, power supply, transportation facilities and proximity to major centres.

Factors

A comprehensive analysis is basic to valuation and normally involves identifying the highest and best use of the property after examining the site's locational, physical, legal-governmental and economic attributes; all of which must be analyzed separately. However, before the highest and best use of the site can be estimated and subsequently valued, regional and neighbourhood data are considered. Conclusions drawn from this data are then related to the site analysis and highest and best use can be estimated.

Locational Factors	For example, land use patterns, access, corner influences, hazards and nuisances. See *Example: Locational Impact on Value* for additional discussion.
Physical Factors	For example, site dimensions (frontage, depth, width, shape and area), soils, topography, plottage, excess land and assembly, climatic conditions, services and utilities, road and street patterns, and landscaping.
Legal/ Governmental Factors	For example, legal description, title data, easements, zoning, assessment and taxes, and private restrictions. These factors can be generally described as dealing with the lawful and restrictive uses of the property.
Economic Factors	For example, prices of comparable sites, tax burden, utility costs and service costs.

EXAMPLE   *Locational Impact on Value*

Seller Smith is having his residential property appraised for mortgage purposes. The appraiser is particularly interested in locational factors affecting value. Smith inquires about just what types of locational factors might impact his property. The appraiser provides the following explanation:

> *Location is always expressed in terms of the relationship of the site to surrounding and nearby facilities and nuisances. In looking at your property, I will probably consider the following four major factors.*
>
> ❶ *Land Use Pattern in the Area*   *The location of various types of land uses within a city or neighbourhood is not determined at random. Uses come about in response to market demand and are effectively controlled by zoning by-laws. Your home is not adversely affected as most properties in the area are similar in size, structure and overall condition.*
>
> ❷ *Access*   *Proximity to desired facilities such as schools, shopping centres, workplaces, recreational centres and other civic facilities is a plus factor. While your home is located somewhat distant from the main shopping areas, a small shopping complex is only two blocks away. Public transportation facilities are just down the street, as is a small park. Overall, these locational factors are a positive force in establishing your value.*
>
> ❸ *Corner Influence*   *The effect of a corner location on value depends on the type of land use. Commercial corners provide the site with additional access and exposure for advertising purposes. Corners for single-family residential properties may have an adverse effect on value. Residential corners often lack private rear yards, an amenity usually sought by the buyer. Corner properties may also cause the owner additional maintenance; e.g., snow removal and side yard upkeep. The fact that your home is located on a corner will have a negative impact on the value.*
>
> ❹ *Hazards and Nuisances*   *The existence of nearby hazards and nuisances such as non-conforming land uses, noise, odour and traffic have a detrimental effect. There are no such deficiencies impacting your property or its value.*

Dimensions

The dimensions of a parcel of land include the frontage, depth and width. Site dimensions and resulting shape and area create the ultimate desirability, utility and value of any site. Frontage is that side of a site that abuts a public street or highway. Depth is the distance(s) between the front and rear lot lines. Width is the distance between the side lines of a lot. The shape of a site is determined by its frontage, depth and width. Area is the size of the site typically measured in square metres, square feet, hectares and acres.

Site vs. Raw Land

A site is a parcel of land improved to the extent that it is ready for its intended purpose and should be clearly distinguished from raw land. Land includes the surface of the earth, supra surface air space and sub-surface area and is typically referred to as raw acreage, raw land or unimproved land because it is unused or in a natural state. A site, on the other hand, is a parcel of land that has been subdivided and serviced to some degree so that it can be used for some purpose, usually as a building site. Generally, the land will have been cleared, graded for drainage and provided with access to a street or road, together with storm and sanitary sewers, gas, water, electricity and telephone service. Usually arrangements have been made to ensure that the intended use is legally permitted.

SITE IMPROVEMENT ANALYSIS

While no precise definition exists to differentiate *improvements on-site* from *improvements to site*, improvements on-site are generally limited to enclosed structures such as buildings, garages and sheds, situated on a site so that the land can be used for a specific purpose. In a residential appraisal, the improvements on-site (also referred to as improvements on land) are normally restricted to the main building and any significant accessory buildings, such as a detached garage or permanent garden shed.

Improvements to site include items that either add to or detract from the outside enjoyment of the property. Examples include fencing, landscaping, paved driveway, patio, deck, outdoor swimming pool, parking areas and exterior lighting. An outdoor pool is an improvement *to site*, an indoor pool within an enclosed structure is an improvement on-site. Improvements to site are also referred to as improvements to land.

Both improvements on-site and improvements to site are detailed for appraisal purposes and taken into consideration when establishing value. Typically, the main structure is described in terms of building type, exterior finish, roof materials and foundation. The appraiser also takes into consideration construction quality and exterior condition/appeal. Interior analysis includes details of rooms, room sizes, evaluation of interior components (e.g., modern, average or outdated), equipment and special features. The amount of descriptive detail for other improvements will vary depending on their size and relevance to the overall appraisal process.

ADDITIONAL RESOURCES

Appraisers may have additional resources to assist in better understanding the property and associated improvements. Surveys and home inspections are two excellent examples.

Survey

Surveys provide important information about the extent of ownership and related information. The Surveyor's Real Property Report shows the dimensions and bearings of all property boundaries, adjacent properties, road and lands, location and description of all pertinent improvements on the property, along with setbacks to the property boundaries, the location of any easements or rights-of-way and any visible encroachments that can affect the extent of ownership.

Home Inspection

The home inspection contains details of the physical structure and mechanical systems within the structure. Descriptions and details regarding overall condition specifically relate to the roof, attic areas, walls, floors, ceilings, windows, doors, insulation and other visible components. Also, the home inspection provides information about the condition of mechanical aspects including electrical, plumbing and heating systems.

Title Insurance and Appraised Value   CURIOSITY

Title insurance is designed to insure for potential loss due to the invalidity of title or a defect relating to that title. Interestingly, title insurance can come into play with real estate appraisal. For example, title insurance can insure over a potential problem area that would negatively impact value and, therefore, could be viewed as an additional resource in the valuation process. An encroachment might exist that does not directly affect the intended use of the property, but nevertheless creates a negative impact from a valuation perspective. A title company might insure over this issue, thereby effectively neutralizing any negative consequences relating to the valuation.

STEPS 4, 5 AND 6   Approaches to Value

Three approaches to value are used in the marketplace. Residential appraisals typically involve the cost approach and direct comparison approach. The income approach most commonly applies to income producing properties. Detailed discussions of all three approaches are included in subsequent chapters.

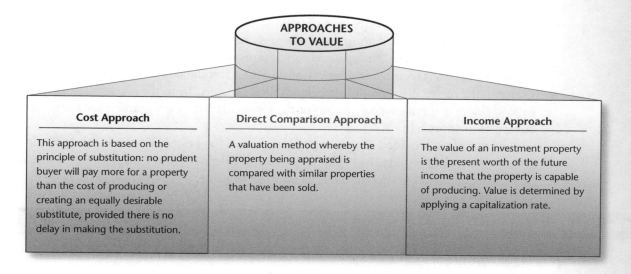

APPROACHES TO VALUE

Cost Approach

This approach is based on the principle of substitution: no prudent buyer will pay more for a property than the cost of producing or creating an equally desirable substitute, provided there is no delay in making the substitution.

Direct Comparison Approach

A valuation method whereby the property being appraised is compared with similar properties that have been sold.

Income Approach

The value of an investment property is the present worth of the future income that the property is capable of producing. Value is determined by applying a capitalization rate.

STEP 7   Reconciliation and Final Estimate

The appraiser arrives at a **final estimate of value** through **reconciliation** of estimates arrived at in Steps 4, 5 and 6.

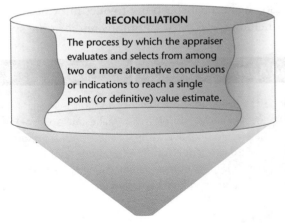

RECONCILIATION

The process by which the appraiser evaluates and selects from among two or more alternative conclusions or indications to reach a single point (or definitive) value estimate.

FINAL RECONCILIATION

The process of arriving at a final estimate of value that is convincing and defensible, by making a choice between the alternative value conclusions, while giving due consideration to and fully reviewing the whole appraisal.

RECONCILIATION PROCESS

The appraiser, when applying the reconciliation process, evaluates and selects from two or more alternative conclusions or indications, to reach a single-value estimate. It is important, during reconciliation, to review and check all calculations and the reliability and relevance of the data, analysis and conclusions used to reach the required estimate.

Reconciliation is required in a variety of situations throughout the appraisal process, for example, the reconciliation of capitalization rates obtained from the market (as discussed in *Real Estate as a Professional Career*) or the reconciliation of comparables in the direct comparison approach.

An example is provided illustrating a hypothetical final estimate of value for a single-family residential property. Two value estimates were derived from the appraiser's research and subsequently reconciled to the final estimate of value.

Not Simply a Math Calculation   CAUTION

Reconciliation requires careful analysis and judgement and the appraiser should not substitute this for a mathematical or mechanical process such as averaging or calculating the median. Generally, two approaches to value are used in an appraisal. In the majority of cases, each approach will result in a slightly different value estimate of the subject. The object of the final reconciliation is to arrive at a single point of value that is defensible and convincing.

In considering which of the approaches to value should be given the most weight, the final reconciliation process will include identifying the strengths and weaknesses of each approach.

EXAMPLE   *Reconciliation*

Value Indicated by Cost Approach
$185,000

The cost approach required three separate value estimates (i.e., site value, current building and site improvement costs, and depreciation) and as a result required a significant number of adjustments. In addition, estimating the current reproduction costs and accrued depreciation of a 25-year old building, such as the subject, was found difficult to measure and support. Apart from these difficulties, a typical buyer would likely find it hard to think of a 25-year old building in terms of reproduction cost new less accrued depreciation. As a result, less weight has been given to this approach, although its use tends to support the value indicated by the direct comparison approach.

Value Indicated by Direct Comparison Approach
$180,000

The direct comparison approach was found to reflect market behaviour and is most widely used and understood by a typical buyer for the subject property. Furthermore, this approach required far fewer adjustments with the comparables being relatively recent sales. In addition, the quality of the data left no doubts as to its reliability. Accordingly, bearing in mind the purpose of this appraisal and the type of value required, most weight was given to this approach.

Final Estimate of Value
Therefore, the market value of the subject property as of (the effective date of appraisal), is estimated to be:

ONE HUNDRED AND EIGHTY THOUSAND DOLLARS ($180,000.00)

FINAL ESTIMATE OF VALUE

The final estimate of value is an estimate of value made in the appraisal process following the selection of the most appropriate approach to value for the property being appraised and the completion of the reconciliation.

The final estimate can be given as a single point estimate or range of value. Usually, clients will ask for a single point estimate. However, if a range is requested, it should be realistic as a wide range will not be of practical use. The final estimate of value should be given in rounded, as opposed to exact terms, since the appraisal process uses judgement and experience and the value given is an estimate only.

STEP 8   Writing the Appraisal Report

Lastly, the appraiser must convey information by way of a written report; i.e., form or narrative. The written report typically contains **limiting conditions** and a certification.

LIMITING CONDITIONS

Limiting conditions represent a series of qualifying statements and assumptions commonly associated with appraisal reports in which the appraiser sets out items that define, limit and/or restrict the scope of the appraisal and inform the client accordingly. Limiting conditions are usually grouped under *Assumptions and Limiting Conditions* that may be included in a letter of transmittal, but more commonly at the end of the appraisal report.

Limiting conditions normally relate to such issues as legal title (no warranty by the appraiser concerning title validity), the appraiser's reliance on information furnished by others is deemed to be correct, the improvements on the property assumed to be confined within the property boundaries, a disclaimer that the appraiser does not have expertise concerning the existence of hazardous materials or their impact on value, and other matters that the appraiser feels should be specifically highlighted to the person requesting the report.

Appraisers will vary the scope of assumptions and limiting conditions based on circumstance. Consequently, no standard can be identified in the marketplace. Professional appraisal organizations do publish typical wordings for the assistance of their respective memberships.

CERTIFICATION

Certification generally refers to the process of attesting to something as being certain, the truth or fact. In an appraisal, a signed and dated certification may state that the appraiser has made a personal inspection, reviewed relevant factors and has no interest, present or contemplated, in the property. The certification may also state that facts being used are believed to be true and factual and have been verified where possible; that the findings are subject only to assumptions and limiting conditions stated in the report; and that the valuation is not in any way contingent on the compensation received. An example is provided for general information purposes only. Significant wording variations are found in the marketplace.

CERTIFICATION OF APPRAISER

I, Anne Appraiser, hereby certify that, to the best of my knowledge and belief:

- The statements of fact contained in this report are true and correct;

- The analysis, opinions and conclusions are limited only by the reported assumptions and limiting conditions and are my personal unbiased professional analysis, opinions and conclusions;

- I have no present or prospective interest in the property that is the subject of this report and I have no personal interest or bias with respect to the parties involved;

- My compensation is not contingent upon the reporting of a predetermined value or direction in value that favours the cause of the client, the amount of the value estimate, the attainment of a stipulated result or the occurrence of a subsequent event;

- I have made a personal inspection of the property that is the subject of this report;

- No one provided significant professional assistance to the person signing this report.

The subject property was inspected as of November 28th, 20xx. Having regard to all of the information contained in this appraisal, it is my professional and considered opinion that the market value as of November 29th, 20xx was:

Two Hundred and Forty Thousand Dollars ($240,000.00)

Anne Appraiser   *November 30, 20xx*
Anne Appraiser   Date

Form 700   *Standard Appraisal Report—Single Family, Page 1 of 6*

OREA Ontario Real Estate Association

Standard Appraisal Report
Single Family

Form 700
for use in the Province of Ontario

CLIENT: .... Client Ref No: ....

Client: Phone No: (............)................................... Fax No: (............).................................. E-mail: ....

Client's Customer: .... Appraiser: .... Appraiser's Ref No: ....

GENERAL APPRAISAL AND PROPERTY INFORMATION

Property Address: ....

Municipality: ....

Full Legal Description: ....

Owner: .... Assessment: Total .... Taxes $ .... Year ....

This Appraisal is to estimate **MARKET VALUE** for a: ☐ Sale ☐ Financing ☐ Other ....

Effective Date of Appraisal: .... Date of Inspection: ....

Highest and Best Use is: ☐ Current ☐ Other (*) ....

Zoning: .... Occupancy: ☐ Homeowner ☐ Tenant ☐ Vacant

SUBJECT & MARKET HISTORY

Subject Last Sold	**Subject Currently Listed**	**Property Values**	**Demand/Supply**
Date:	☐ Yes ☐ No	☐ Stable	☐ In Balance
Sale Price: $	Current List Price $	☐ Increasing	☐ Under Supply
Days on Market:	Days On Market	☐ Decreasing	☐ Over Supply

Typical Exposure Time Required for Properties to Sell in Subject Neighborhood is: ....

Typical Exposure Time Required for Properties to Sell on Subject Street is: ....

NEIGHBOURHOOD INFORMATION

Type		**Trend**	**Subject For Area is**	**Adjoining Homes**
☐ Rural	☐ Prestige	☐ Improving	☐ Comparable	☐ Comparable
☐ Residential	☐ Average	☐ Stable	☐ Superior *	☐ Superior
☐ Commercial	☐ Starter	☐ Declining	☐ Inferior	☐ Inferior
☐ Industrial				

Neighbourhood is: ....% Developed

Distance to

Elementary School	....
Secondary School	....
Public Transit	....
Shopping	....
Downtown	....
Recreational Facilities	....

Age Range of Typical Property in Neighbourhood: .... to .... Years

Age Range of Typical Property on Subject Street: .... to .... Years

Price Range of Properties on Subject Street: $................................. to $...........................

Price Range of Properties in Neighbourhood: $................................. to $...........................

Comments: (include any positive or negative factors that will have a measurable impact on the subject's marketability and value - items with an * should be discussed) ....
....
....
....

SITE INFORMATION
Utilities & Services

Street
- [ ] Paved
- [ ] Municipal
- [ ] Sidewalks
- [ ] Street Lighting
- [ ] Underground Wiring
- [ ] Aboveground Wiring
- [ ] Gravel
- [ ] Private
- [ ] Curbs

Drainage
- [ ] Open Ditch
- [ ] Sanitary Sewer
- [ ] Other ....
....
- [ ] Storm Sewer
- [ ] Septic Tank

Water
- [ ] Municipal
- [ ] Cistern
- [ ] Other ....
- [ ] Private Well
- [ ] Shared Well

Utilities
- [ ] Hydro
- [ ] Gas
- [ ] Telephone
- [ ] Cable

Site Dimensions: ....

Encroachments: [ ] Yes*   [ ] No

Total Site Area: ....

Easements: [ ] Yes*   [ ] No

Site Shape: ....

Topography: Lot in relation to street grade: [ ] Even   [ ] Above   [ ] Below

Parking
Driveway
- [ ] Laneway
- [ ] Private
- [ ] Mutual
- [ ] Other ....
- [ ] None
- [ ] Paved
- [ ] Gravel

Garage (Indicate # of cars):
- [ ] Attached # ....
- [ ] Detached # ....
- [ ] Built In # ....
- [ ] Carport # ....

Site Appeal
- [ ] Excellent
- [ ] Good
- [ ] Average
- [ ] Fair*
- [ ] Poor*

Landscaping Includes: ....
....
....

Comments: (include any positive or negative factors that will have a measurable impact on the subject's marketability and value - items with an * should be discussed) ....
....
....

INFORMATION ON IMPROVEMENTS (BUILDINGS)

Building Type:
- [ ] Detached
- [ ] Semi-detached
- [ ] Attached Row
- [ ] Other ....
- [ ] High Ranch
- [ ] Apartment
- [ ] Split
- [ ] 1 Storey
- [ ] 1 1/2 Storey
- [ ] 2 Storey
- [ ] 3 Storey

Sq. Ft. (Above Grade)

Level 1	Level 4 ....
Level 2	Level 5 ....
Level 3	
Total	

Actual Age ....Years   Effective Age ....Years   Total Economic Life ....Years

Exterior Finish
- [ ] Brick Veneer
- [ ] Solid Brick
- [ ] Stucco
- [ ] Alum. Siding
- [ ] Other ....
- [ ] Vinyl Siding
- [ ] Wood Siding
- [ ] Solid Stone
- [ ] Artificial Stone

Roof Material
- [ ] Asphalt Shingle
- [ ] Cedar Shake
- [ ] Metal
- [ ] Other ....
- [ ] Wood Shingle
- [ ] Slate
- [ ] Tar & Gravel

Foundation
- [ ] Poured Concrete
- [ ] Concrete Block
- [ ] Brick
- [ ] Stone
- [ ] Preserved Wood
- [ ] Other ....

Window Type
- [ ] Single
- [ ] Other: ....
- [ ] Thermal
- [ ] Wood Frame
- [ ] Aluminum
- [ ] Vinyl

Evidence of UFFI   [ ] Yes *   [ ] No

Construction Quality   [ ] Excellent   [ ] Good   [ ] Average   [ ] Fair   [ ] Poor*

Exterior Condition/Appeal   [ ] Excellent   [ ] Good   [ ] Average   [ ] Fair   [ ] Poor*

Form 700   2008   **Page 2 of 6**

SECTION IV   PROPERTY VALUATION

Form 700   *Standard Appraisal Report—Single Family, Page 3 of 6*

INFORMATION ON IMPROVEMENTS (INTERIOR)

Rooms	Living	Dining	Kitchen	Family	Beds	Bath	Wash	Rec	Other
Basement									
Main									
Second									
Third									

Room Sizes   ☐ Large   ☐ Medium   ☐ Small

Additional Information on Room Sizes ("Optional"): ....
....
....

Kitchen
☐ Modern
☐ Average
☐ Outdated

Bathrooms
☐ Modern
☐ Average
☐ Outdated

Closets/Storage
☐ Excellent
☐ Adequate
☐ Inadequate

Basement
☐ None
☐ Full
☐ Partial

☐ Crawl Space
% Finished ....

Floors
☐ Carpet
☐ Hardwood
☐ Vinyl Tile
☐ Ceramic
☐ Other ....

Walls/Ceilings
☐ Drywall
☐ Plaster
☐ Panelling
☐ Tile
☐ Other ....

Heating
☐ Forced Air
☐ Hot Water
☐ Baseboard
☐ Other ....
....

Fuel
☐ Gas
☐ Oil
☐ Electricity
☐ Other ....
....

Plumbing
☐ Copper
☐ Plastic
☐ Lead
☐ Galvanized
☐ Other ....

Electrical
☐ Fuses
☐ Circuit Breakers
Amps ....

Floor Plan
☐ Excellent   ☐ Good   ☐ Average   ☐ Fair   ☐ Poor*

Interior Condition
☐ Excellent   ☐ Good   ☐ Average   ☐ Fair   ☐ Poor*

Equipment/Built-Ins/Chattels Remaining With Property:
☐ HWT   ☐ Fridge   ☐ Central Vac   ☐ Wood Stove   ☐ Elect Air Cleaner
☐ Central Air   ☐ Washer   ☐ Humidifier   ☐ Hood   ☐ Garburator
☐ Heat Pump   ☐ Dryer   ☐ Security System ☐ Oven   ☐ Water Purifier/Filter
☐ Stove   ☐ Dishwasher   ☐ Dehumidifier   ☐ Range   ☐ Central Intercom
☐ Fireplace(s)
☐ Other: ....
....

Equipment/Chattels Leased or Rented
....
....

Special Features
....
....

Comments: (include any positive or negative factors that will have a measurable impact on the subject's marketability and value - items with an * should be discussed) ....
....
....
....

COST APPROACH TO VALUE

Land Value .... $............................

Improvements	Cost New	Depreciation	Current Value
Building	$............................	$............................	$............................
Garage	$............................	$............................	$............................
....	$............................	$............................	$............................
....	$............................	$............................	$............................
....	$............................	$............................	$............................

Total Current Value of All Improvements $............................ $............................

Indicated Value by the Cost Approach $............................

Value Rounded to $............................

DIRECT COMPARISON APPROACH
Competitive Listings

Item	Subject	Listing #1	Listing #2	Listing #3
Address				
Distance To Subject				
Original List Price				
Current List Price				
Original List Date				
Date Price Last Revised				
House Style				
Lot Size				
Building Size				
Age				
Condition				
Beds				
Baths				
Listing is: Inferior/Similar/Superior				

Comments:...
....
....
....
....

Form 700   *Standard Appraisal Report—Single Family, Page 5 of 6*

Sales Analysis

Item	Subject	Comparable 1	Comparable 2	Comparable 3
Address				
Distance To Subject				
Date Sold				
Sale Price				
Days On Market				
Time Adjustment				
Time Adjusted Price				
Location				
Lot Size				
House Style				
Age of House				
Total Sq. Footage				
Family Room				
Bedrooms				
Bathrooms				
Basement/% Finished				
Rec Room				
Garage/Parking				
Interior Condition				
Exterior Condition				
Total Adjustments				
Totally Adj. Sale Price				

Comments, Reconciliation And Estimate Of Value By The Direct Comparison Approach

....
....
....
....
....
....
....

Based on the above information and analysis, a value by the Direct Comparison Approach is estimated to be: ($..)

    Form 700   2008   **Page 5 of 6**

FINAL RECONCILIATION, CERTIFICATION AND FINAL ESTIMATE OF VALUE

Given the nature of the subject property, the level and quality of information, the reliability of the necessary adjustments, and the actions of typical buyers in the subject neighbourhood, most weight has been given to the value arrived at by the .... Approach.

- This valuation and report is subject to the attached assumptions and limiting conditions.
- This valuation and report has been completed in accordance with the Canadian Real Estate Association's Code of Ethics and Standard of Business Practice, as well as the Code of Ethics of the Real Estate and Business Brokers Act.
- I confirm that I personally inspected the subject property and that I have no current or contemplated interest or bias (positive or negative) towards the subject property.
- Unless otherwise detailed in writing within this report, I can confirm that I have no personal relationship or bias (positive or negative) towards any of the parties using or affected by this valuation and report.
- I can confirm that my being employed and paid to complete this valuation is not conditional on the amount of the valuation or on any specific information being included or excluded in this appraisal report.

Therefore, based on a .... day marketing period, a reasonable market value for the subject property as at

................................., 20............. is estimated to be:

.... Dollars ($....................................)

Appraiser's Signature: ....   Date of Signature: ....

Appraiser's Name: ....   Company: ....
Appraiser's Address: ....   Phone No: ....
....   Fax No: ....
....   E-mail: ....

ATTACHMENTS

☐ Neighbourhood Map   ☐ Additional Information/Analysis: ....
☐ Copies of MLS Listing/Sales   ☐ Additional Assumptions/Limiting Conditions: ....
☐ Site/Building Sketch   ....
☐ Photos   ☐ Other: ....
☐ Survey   ....

ASSUMPTIONS AND LIMITING CONDITIONS

1. This report may not be read or used by anyone other than the client without the written authorization of the appraiser. This report should only be used for the property and purpose identified within it. The appraiser accepts no responsibility or liability should the information contained within this report be used by anyone other than the client (or other authorized user) or for any other purpose or property other than that specified within this report.

2. Values are subject to varying and continual changes in market conditions and neighbourhood factors. Accordingly, the value presented in this report can only be relied on as the value estimated as of the effective date of appraisal specified in this report. Should the user of this report wish to know the value of the subject property as of another date, the appraiser will need to complete an update or a new appraisal report.

3. A search on title and ownership has not been performed. A good title with respect to the subject property has been assumed. Therefore, other than what is noted in this report, the appraiser assumes no responsibility for matters legal in nature that may affect the subject property's title, ownership, marketing or value.

4. Any sketches in this report are included solely for the purpose of assisting the reader in visualizing the property.

5. The appraiser has carried out a visual cosmetic inspection of the subject property only. This inspection and the ensuing appraisal report is not and should not be considered a structural, environmental or mechanical inspection and report. Accordingly, unless stated otherwise in this appraisal report, the appraiser is unaware of any hidden or not apparent structural, environmental or mechanical defects or problems and assumes for the purposes of this report and valuation that there are none. Therefore, should it subsequently become known that there is a structural, mechanical or environmental problem or defect, then the appraiser reserves the right to alter the value given in this appraisal report.

6. This appraisal has been based on the assumption that the subject property is in compliance with the applicable zoning, building codes, by-laws, and environmental regulations. Should this in fact turn out not to be so, the appraiser reserves the right to make any necessary changes to the final estimate of value.

7. This valuation has been based on the assumption that the information collected from industry recognized sources and professionals is in fact correct and can be relied upon for the purpose of this appraisal.

    Form 700   2008   **Page 6 of 6**

COMPARATIVE MARKET ANALYSIS

A comparative market analysis (CMA) should be clearly differentiated from an appraisal. The CMA, commonly used by real estate practitioners, assists the seller in comparing his/her property with others in the marketplace in order to establish a listing price. The comparative market analysis is not designed to establish market value, as is the case with an appraisal.

The CMA form typically includes homes that are currently for sale, have recently sold or on which listings have expired or did not sell in a defined time period. This information provides the seller with an indication as to what buyers are prepared to pay, given current market conditions. The CMA is a valuable tool for salespeople when properly informing sellers regarding market conditions and obtaining saleable listings. In Ontario, the most widely used comparative market analysis form is referred to as a Residential Market Comparison Guide (see form on the following page).

Guide Description

Form preparation is relatively straightforward. The form has space for a description of comparable properties for sale now, comparable properties sold within the past 12 months and comparable properties that expired during that same period. The form and its preparation parallel, in certain limited ways, the direct comparison approach used in appraisals. However, this form is intended only as a general guide for the competitive pricing of property with no exact adjustments, as would be the case in an appraisal report.

❶ Comparables for Sale Now

The competitive position of the seller's house is extremely important. The selection of properties should be made with careful consideration to overall comparability with the subject property. Under *Features/Comments*, highlight significant differences and/or similarities. The *available for sale* market provides the seller with an overall perspective in assessing his/her likelihood of selling and in what general price range. Properties should be listed in order of highest comparability based on type, location and features.

❷ Comparables Sold Past 12 Months

This category represents what the buyers paid. The more recent the comparables, the more relevant the information, assuming that most properties selected are more or less comparable with the seller's house. The order should start with the most comparable and proceed sequentially.

❸ Comparables Expired Past 12 Months

This category outlines properties that did not sell. While the precise reasons for a *no sale* situation will vary, this information provides valuable insight concerning the *top of the market* for a particular type of property. Again, list as much detail as possible.

The form provides space for recommendations concerning both maximum list price and probable selling price and expenses leading to an estimate of net proceeds. Completion of any/all of these, including the salesperson's signature, is optional. Often salespeople complete information on comparables only and then use this form as a guide for general discussions with the seller. If the net proceeds portion is completed, practitioners must ensure that details regarding mortgage balance and selling costs are accurate. Additional information regarding comparative market analysis and the use of the Residential Market Comparison Guide is included in *The Real Estate Transaction – General* when discussing the preparation of representation agreements.

OREA Ontario Real Estate Association

Residential Market Comparison Guide

Form 260
for use in the Province of Ontario

Subject Property: ....

Prepared for: ....

Prepared by: ....   **Date:** ....

COMPARABLES FOR SALE NOW:

Address	Price	Features/Comments

(Use back of form for additional features/comments if required)

COMPARABLES SOLD PAST 12 MONTHS:

Address	Price	Features/Comments

(Use back of form for additional features/comments if required)

COMPARABLES EXPIRED PAST 12 MONTHS:

Address	Price	Features/Comments

(Use back of form for additional features/comments if required)

ESTIMATED SELLING COSTS:

Brokerage Fee:	$ ....
Mortgage Payout Penalty	$ ....
Mortgage Discount	$ ....
Approximate Legal Costs	$ ....
Miscellaneous	$ ....
Total	$ ....

Recommendations: as of ....

I recommend a maximum list price of: $ ....

With estimated selling price of: $ ....

With estimated outstanding mortgage balance of $ ....

With estimated selling costs of: $ ....

Anticipated net proceeds would be: $ ....

Signature: ....

N.B. The above information is NOT an appraisal and is to be used for marketing purposes only.

SECTION IV   PROPERTY VALUATION

APPRAISAL AND PROPERTY ASSESSMENT

Assessment broadly refers to the process of establishing value for purposes of taxation. Property assessment in Ontario has undergone various reforms in an effort to create a fair, consistent approach based on current value. As such, assessments can prove useful to real estate practitioners seeking additional input when assisting sellers in establishing listing prices.

Property is assessed to provide a basis for taxation and the funding of local and/or regional education and municipal services including, but not limited to, police and fire protection, garbage and snow removal, road maintenance, public health and welfare.

Municipal Property Assessment Corporation (MPAC)

The Municipal Property Assessment Corporation (MPAC) assesses all property in Ontario. Every municipality is a member of MPAC. MPAC's primary responsibility is to determine assessed values and provide these values on annual assessment rolls to the municipalities. The municipalities and the provincial government, in turn, apply these values when calculating property taxes and education taxes.

The Municipal Property Assessment Corporation (MPAC) is a corporation established pursuant to the *Municipal Property Assessment Corporation Act* as of December, 1998. MPAC has responsibility for assessment delivery services throughout Ontario, oversees the uniform, province-wide system based on current value assessment and provides various services to municipalities including the preparation of the annual assessment role used to calculate property taxes. MPAC offices generally align with county, region or district boundaries.

WEB LINKS

For more information concerning MPAC operations, assessment procedures, the property assessment reconsideration process and assessment appeals, access the Municipal Property Assessment Corporation web site at *www.mpac.on.ca*.

Assessed Value

For assessment purposes, assessed value is synonymous with current value. Current value is defined as the amount of money a property would realize if sold at arm's length by a willing seller to a willing buyer. Assessors use the three traditional approaches to estimate current value in much the same fashion as appraisers, subject to certain legislative requirements.

DIRECT COMPARISON APPROACH

The direct comparison approach attempts to mirror the behaviour of the market by comparing the property being appraised (subject property) with similar properties that have recently sold (comparables). Comparable properties are selected based on their similarity to the subject property with sale prices being adjusted for differences in comparison to the subject property. Finally, a current value of the subject is estimated based on the reconciliation of adjusted sale prices of the comparable properties.

COST APPROACH

The cost approach is based on the theory that the market value of an improved parcel can be estimated as the sum of the land value and the depreciated value of the improvements. The cost approach is justified in part by the principle of substitution. This principle implies that an informed buyer will pay no more for an improved property than the price of acquiring a vacant site and constructing a substitute building of equal utility, assuming no costly delays in construction.

The cost approach requires estimates of land value, the current cost of constructing the improvements and accrued depreciation. Depreciation is subtracted from current construction costs to obtain an estimate of improvement value. A land value, reflecting the value of the site as if vacant and available to be developed to its highest and best use, is added to the value of the improvement.

The cost approach is most effective with newer buildings that have less depreciation and more easily estimated construction costs. The cost approach is particularly useful for appraisal of property types for which sales and income data are scarce, such as industrial and special purpose properties. Even when values from the other approaches are relied upon in assessment valuation, cost approach calculations are recommended for corroboration purposes.

INCOME APPROACH

The income approach is based on the principle of anticipation; i.e., present value is a function of anticipated future benefits. With investment properties, anticipated future benefits in terms of cash flow can be analyzed through either direct (income) capitalization or discounted cash flows, and yield capitalization to arrive at an estimate of value.

Some properties seldom trade in the marketplace or are unique and, therefore, require special treatment. In such instances, regulated rates are established and assigned by the Province of Ontario. Examples might include power generating stations and gas/electrical rights-of-way.

Farm valuation also poses some complexities. As a general rule, those farms used solely for farming are valued based on farmer-to-farmer sales in the marketplace. However, circumstances can arise where the farm land is used for agricultural purposes, but the house is rented to a non-farming tenant or farm buildings are used for other purposes. In such instances, assessment is established analyzing each component; e.g., the farm land being based on productivity, with the house assessed as a residential.

Property Classes

The assessment system establishes seven standard property classes for assessment and taxation purposes:

CLASS 1:	Residential/Farm
CLASS 2:	Multi-Residential
CLASS 3:	Commercial
CLASS 4:	Industrial
CLASS 5:	Pipeline
CLASS 6:	Farmlands
CLASS 7:	Managed Forests

Various optional classes are available to municipalities including:

CLASS 8:	New Multi-Residential
CLASS 9:	Office Building
CLASS 10:	Shopping Centre
CLASS 11:	Parking Lots and Vacant Land
CLASS 12:	Large Industrial
CLASS 13:	Professional Sports Facilities

These classes, in turn, may be further refined through sub-classes that more clearly articulate uses and provide for special tax treatment.

Valuation Date

The valuation date is the day on which all Ontario properties are valued for assessment purposes. This value is used by municipalities when setting property taxes. In 2006, for example, the valuation date was January 1, 2005. Value changes to the property are then reflected in the current value established for the subsequent period. The valuation date of January 1, 2005 has applied to the taxation years 2006 and 2007, and will also apply to the 2008 taxation year. The next province-wide assessment is scheduled for 2008, which will then impact the 2009 taxation year.

Assessment Rolls

Assessed values of all properties are listed on assessment rolls delivered to municipalities. The assessment roll is an official record of real property assessments subject to revision on an annual basis. Assessment rolls are available for public viewing at local municipal offices. The rolls are organized by street address and list the current value assessment, property classification, the names of registered owners and the legal description of the property. The total assessed value of all properties on the roll provides the base for property taxation. Assessment rolls can be a valuable source of information for real estate practitioners.

Notice of Property Assessment

Property owners receive a notice of property assessment setting out a description of the property, the property classification for assessment purposes, the estimated current value and school support particulars, if applicable. The assessment notice is not a demand for payment of taxes, but merely a notification of the assessed value for purposes of subsequent tax calculations.

This notice sets out procedures for assessment appeal. As an initial step, the property owner may immediately request a reconsideration through the regional assessment office. If a change is warranted, the assessment office will recommend that change to the assessment review board. Property owners, as a second step, have the right to appeal assessments directly to the assessment review board within a specified time period. The decision of the board is final, however, the property owner may appeal to the Divisional Court of Ontario on a question of law.

Property Improvements

One of the anomalies of a tax on real property, according to critics, is that the assessment system tends to discourage the improvement of property. In theory, if improvements increase value then the current value assessment will rise accordingly, resulting in higher taxes. New additions or renovations will affect property assessment to the extent such changes increase the fair market value of the property as calculated by the assessor; e.g., addition of a sunroom or an outdoor swimming pool, addition or enlargement of a carport or garage, extensive remodeling or modernization, or creation of additional living space such as a basement recreation room.

Assessors routinely monitor building permits to determine where renovations and new construction are taking place. Not all improvements to a property are assessed for taxation purposes. However, as a practical guideline, the owner of a property contemplating improvements is well advised to anticipate not only the costs of such improvements but also their impact on future taxation.

Appraisal Complexities   MARKET PERSPECTIVE

From Stigmas to Waterfront Views

Technology may be simplifying the appraisal process for fee appraisers, property assessors and real estate practitioners, but increasingly complex factors impacting value can challenge even the most experienced individual.

- **Stigma**   Stigmas are a hot topic. Going well beyond the physical, stigmas reside in the unsettling world of perception. As an extreme example, what about the haunted house? The perception may increase value (if someone perceives commercial value in promoting a haunted property) or a loss in value (restriction concerning marketability of the house). What if a murder occurred in the property? How long is the value affected? What happens when contaminated property is cleaned up? Does perception out-live the cleanup date and, if so, for how long?

- **Detrimental Conditions**   How much loss of value can be attributed to noise? What about environmental problems; e.g., existence of asbestos, lead, radon or underground storage tanks? What about smells emanating from a nearby agricultural operation? What impact does an industrial stack spewing out contaminates have on surrounding properties? To compound matters, detrimental conditions can be temporary or long lasting.

- **Direct/Indirect Damage**   Stigmas and detrimental conditions have led to more sophisticated appraisal analysis. Take contamination for example. Assessment of direct remediation costs is not enough, what about other factors; e.g., additional loss if further contamination is found, uncertainty about the thoroughness of the cleanup, the chance that contamination may have migrated to adjacent properties and legislative restrictions that may now or in the future be placed on the property to restrict its long term use?

- **The Good Things**   Lots of positive forces also come under scrutiny. Each requires careful analysis. How much value should be attributed to a waterfront view versus a partially obstructed view? How much more will the buyer pay if the property is landscaped? What is the value of a well-placed shade tree given the added beauty and possible energy savings (shade that reduces summer air conditioning)? How much does green space add to adjacent residential properties? What about the value of privacy? The list goes on and on.

SECTION IV   PROPERTY VALUATION

Notice of Property Assessment

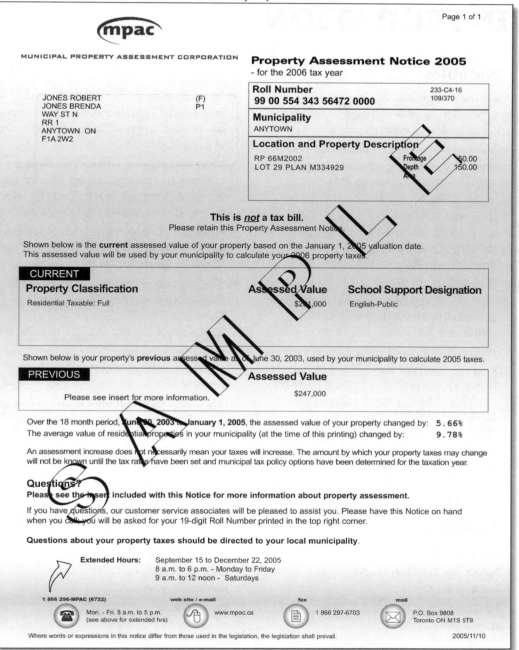

Source: Municipal Property Assessment Corporation

KNOWLEDGE INTEGRATION

Notables

- Caution is advised. Appraisals should be conducted by persons having appropriate credentials and experience.

- Most appraisal reports are either form reports or narrative reports. Letters of opinion are now discouraged given liability issues.

- Real estate brokerages have gradually adopted standardized form reports; e.g., the OREA *Standard Appraisal Report– Single Family* (Form 700) rather than using letters of opinion.

- The appraisal process involves eight steps culminating in the preparation of a written report.

- Data collection and analysis, along with reconciliation are emphasized in chapter materials. Subsequent chapters focus on applying the three approaches to value (Steps 4, 5 and 6).

- Data collection and analysis includes neighbourhood, site and site improvement analysis.

- Reconciliation in an appraisal report involves the appraiser selecting between two or more approaches to value to arrive at a single value estimate.

- Most salespersons restrict valuation discussions and concentrate on determining probable listing price for property by using a comparative market analysis form.

- Assessment in regard to properties generally refers to the process of establishing value of real property for taxation purposes.

- The Municipal Property Assessment Corporation assesses all property in Ontario.

- Assessed value is determined in much the same fashion as market value in an appraisal, subject to certain legislative provisions.

- The assessment roll for a municipality is the official record of property assessments.

Glossary

Appraiser

Automated Valuation Model

Fee Appraiser

Final Estimate of Value

Form Report

Letter of Opinion

Limiting Conditions

Narrative Report

Reconciliation

Web Links

Web links are included for general interest regarding selected chapter topics.

Appraisal Institute   Persons interested in pursuing a professional career in appraisal can obtain additional information from the Appraisal Institute of Canada web site at *www.aicanada.ca*.

Municipal Property Assessment Corporation   For more information concerning MPAC operations, assessment procedures, the property assessment reconsideration process and assessment appeals, access the Municipal Property Assessment Corporation web site at *www.mpac.on.ca*.

Strategic Thinking For Your Career

Questions are included to assist in developing your new career. No answers are provided.

1. What types of appraisal form reports are used by local lenders?

2. What policies does my intended employing brokerage have in place regarding property valuations completed by salespersons?

3. If a seller requests that I complete a letter of opinion merely setting out an estimate of value, how will I handle this situation?

4. What types of detrimental conditions exist in my local marketplace that may affect residential and/or commercial values?

5. How would my local neighbourhood be classified in terms of age cycle? What factors point to that conclusion?

6. Which neighbourhoods in the local marketplace are in growth or decline stages and why? Will this impact my decision as to which areas to concentrate my efforts and what strategies I will develop to market my services?

Chapter Mini-Review

Solutions are located in the Appendix.

1. Two purposes of an appraisal involve the transfer of ownership and the extension of credit.

   ◯ True   ◯ False

2. Form reports in Ontario can only be completed by fee appraisers.

   ◯ True   ◯ False

3. Narrative reports tend to be lengthy.

   ◯ True   ◯ False

4. A letter of opinion is best described as a brief, unsubstantiated estimate of value.

   ◯ True   ◯ False

5. The effective date of an appraisal can differ from the inspection date of that appraisal.

   ◯ True   ◯ False

6. Step 1 in the appraisal process involves establishing an appraisal plan.

   ◯ True   ◯ False

7. The age cycle of a neighbourhood consists of four phases.

   ◯ True   ◯ False

8. The factors taken into consideration when analyzing a neighbourhood in relation to a single family home appraisal will typically differ from those for a retail or a farm operation.

   ◯ True   ◯ False

9. Site analysis normally involves assessing various factors including locational and physical considerations.

   ◯ True   ◯ False

10. Analysis of site improvements only includes improvements on the site.

    ◯ True   ◯ False

11. Reconciliation typically involves taking estimates derived from two or more approaches to value and averaging these amounts to arrive at a final estimate of value.

    ◯ True   ◯ False

12. An appraiser's certification can involve various statements such as: *the appraiser has no present or contemplated interest in the property* and *that a personal inspection of the property has been made.*

    ◯ True   ◯ False

13. A comparative market analysis is a form of appraisal.

    ◯ True   ◯ False

14. The *Residential Market Comparison Guide* (OREA Form 260) provides space for recommendations concerning both maximum list price and probable selling price.

    ◯ True   ◯ False

15. Assessors use the traditional three approaches to value in much the same fashion as appraisers when estimating value.

    ◯ True   ◯ False

16. The assessment notice includes a property's assessment and the taxes payable arising from that assessment.

    ◯ True   ◯ False

Active Learning Exercises

Solutions are located in the Appendix.

◼ Exercise 1   Multiple Choice

1.1 The estimation of value for an insurance claim or expropriation is best described as:

   a.   The purpose of the appraisal.

   b.   A limiting condition in an appraisal.

   c.   Step Four in the appraisal process.

   d.   The certification signed by the appraiser.

1.2 The appraisal report (OREA Form 700) illustrated in this chapter:

   a.   Does not require the personal inspection of the subject property by the appraiser.

   b.   Includes a limiting condition that refers to environmental defects.

   c.   Is designed specifically for use with residential condominiums.

   d.   Includes provisions for using the income approach to value.

1.3 A loss of value that arises from the perception of a problem:

   a.   Does not apply for residential appraisals, only commercial valuations.

   b.   Is most commonly referred to as a detrimental condition.

   c.   Is most commonly referred to as a stigma.

   d.   Is only considered in narrative reports and not form reports.

1.4 The date to which an appraisal applies is referred to as the:

   a.   Inspection date.

   b.   Effective date.

   c.   Market value date.

   d.   Data collection date.

1.5 The term typically used to describe when a neighbourhood becomes built up and prices stabilize is:

   a.   Growth.

   b.   Decline.

   c.   Prosperity.

   d.   Stability.

1.6 A step in the appraisal process that necessitates obtaining information about general area trends as well as site and improvement specifics is described as:

   a.   Step 1.

   b.   Step 2.

   c.   Step 3.

   d.   Step 4.

1.7   A statistical method to establish value through computer searching of extensive property files in a database is commonly referred to as a (an):

    a.   Automated market review.

    b.   Automated valuation model.

    c.   Computer-enabled browser.

    d.   Comparative market analysis.

1.8   The process by which an appraiser evaluates and selects from two or more alternative conclusions or indications to arrive at a single-value estimate is normally referred to as:

    a.   Approach to estimate value.

    b.   Limiting condition.

    c.   Final estimate of value.

    d.   Reconciliation.

1.9   Assessors use three traditional approaches to valuation. Which is NOT one of them?

    a.   Direct Assessment Approach

    b.   Cost Approach

    c.   Direct Comparison Approach

    d.   Income Approach

1.10   When conducting a site analysis, patterns of land use and access to transportation are commonly referred to as:

    a.   Legal/governmental factors.

    b.   Economic factors.

    c.   Physical factors.

    d.   Locational factors.

■ Exercise 2   Appraisal Form

Using the OREA *Standard Appraisal Report–Single Family* (Form 700) reprinted in this chapter, answer the following:

2.1   In the General Appraisal and Property Information section, the form provides for an *Effective Date of Appraisal* and a *Date of Inspection*. Why might the dates be different and what cautions should be emphasized in that regard?

SECTION IV   PROPERTY VALUATION

SECTION IV

2.2   Under both *Neighbourhood Information* and *Site Information*, the report asks for positive or negative factors that affect the subject property's marketability and value. List seven possible factors.

2.3   Under *Information on Improvements (Interior)*, the report asks for positive or negative factors that affect the subject property's marketability and value. List seven possible factors.

■ Exercise 3   Assessment (True/False)

1. MPAC has responsibility for assessment delivery services throughout Ontario.

   ◯ True   ◯ False

2. The assessment system establishes four standard property classes, but also provides for various optional classes.

   ◯ True   ◯ False

3. The valuation date is the day on which all Ontario properties are valued for assessment purposes.

   ◯ True   ◯ False

4. Assessment rolls do not list the current value established by assessors for specific properties, as such information is confidential.

   ◯ True   ◯ False

5. The Notice of Property Assessment does not include procedures for assessment appeal.

   ◯ True   ◯ False

6. Assessors routinely monitor building permits to determine where renovations and new construction are taking place.

   ◯ True   ◯ False

CHAPTER 10

Direct Comparison Approach

Introduction

Direct comparison is a straightforward, verifiable method of estimating value, which is particularly popular in residential markets. The appraiser compares the subject property to other recently-sold, similar properties, making adjustments for differences between the properties.

The elements used for comparison include all discernible differences that affect value, typically centering on structural variations, time adjustments and location. The challenge involves making accurate adjustments in value for such differences.

The procedure is then straightforward. An adjusted sale price is calculated for each comparable. The process, in effect, makes the comparables more or less similar to the subject. The appraiser reconciles differences in these adjusted sale prices to arrive at the estimate. However, as with most professional activities, experience, careful judgement and skill are uppermost.

Chapter contents include various examples illustrating how adjustments are made to comparable properties and the calculation of corresponding adjusted sale prices. Three detailed exercises are provided to ensure understanding of the entire process.

Learning Outcomes

At the conclusion of this chapter, students will be able to:

- Outline the basic procedural steps and sources of information required when using the direct comparison approach.
- Describe how comparisons are made with reference to comparability, time, significant characteristics and sum vs. parts.
- Name the four steps involved when applying the direct comparison approach and describe factors to consider under each approach.
- Delineate what constitutes a good comparable that can be used in relation to the subject property being appraised.
- Explain how adjustments are made in relation to time, location, lot size and physical characteristics.
- Describe and perform calculations involving typical adjustments made to comparable properties when arriving at adjusted sale prices.
- Analyze adjusted sale prices to arrive at a single-point estimate of value.
- Describe limitations and summarize strengths and weaknesses regarding the direct comparison approach.

NOTE: Exercises contain both metric and imperial measurements.

OVERVIEW

The direct comparison approach (also sometimes referred to as the sales comparison approach) is based on the proposition that an informed buyer will pay no more for a property than the cost of acquiring an existing property with the same utility. This approach has widespread popularity, particularly in residential appraisals. Practitioners routinely apply this approach in Ontario.

Little wonder this methodology is the most popular. Direct comparison is widely accepted by the courts, understood by the general public and, given reliable comparable sales, a proven, time-tested approach.

Procedural Steps

The direct comparison approach follows certain logical steps to arrive at a value estimate:

- Locate and select all available comparable sales and listings. Look for four primary qualities in selecting a good comparable sale:
  - Within the local market area;
  - At or near the date of the appraisal;
  - Truly comparable in that it will appeal to the same type of buyer who would consider buying the subject property being appraised; e.g., if the appraisal is for a single-family home, then a duplex would not normally be a good comparable; and
  - A bona fide arm's length transaction.

Based on the selections made, the appraiser would:

Obtain Information	Collect pertinent information on each comparable to make meaningful adjustments and gain a true understanding of the comparable properties. Direct inspection of comparables is an advantage in that regard.
Analyze Data	Analyze all relevant data, including differences that exist between the comparable and subject; e.g., time of sale and features.
Compare with Subject Property	Compare each property with the subject property, making the necessary adjustments. Adjustments can be either dollar amounts or percentages. Real estate practitioners typically use dollar adjustments.
Reconcile/Final Estimate	Reconcile the data and arrive at a reasonable value estimate.

Sources of Information

A variety of sources exist for sales data to use in the direct comparison approach. The best resources are the brokerage's files and the real estate board's Multiple Listing Service®. Selected data can also be obtained from registry or land titles offices. Banks, lending institutions and insurance companies may supply information regarding mortgage financing and details of mortgaged property. Other sources of information are newspapers, as well as legal and other professional publications.

MAKING COMPARISONS

The most acceptable method of comparison in residential properties is a physical one. Consideration is given to various characteristics such as number of rooms, physical condition of the building, number of garages, bathrooms and fireplaces, and a finished or semi-finished basement. If these and many other factors are taken into consideration separately and a dollar factor allocated to each, then a proper comparison can be made.

Various factors must be considered in making comparisons of residential property.

Comparability

The single most important factor is the selection of truly comparable properties. One-storey houses cannot be compared with one and one-half storey or two-storey ones, new houses cannot be compared with old houses, 50-acre fruit farms cannot be compared with 100-acre vegetable or dairy farms and large lots to small ones. The best test of comparability lies in the size of the individual adjustments that are necessary. Big adjustments indicate poor comparability. Small adjustments indicate proper selection of comparable properties.

Time

The time element is also important in comparative analysis. The general economic conditions that existed at the time of sale of the comparable property may be quite different from those existing at the time or date of the appraisal. The appraiser must understand and recognize the significance of changing conditions and make appropriate adjustments.

Practitioners typically rely on MLS® statistics to obtain price trends within local market areas. The **time resale method** is also used. Under this approach, appraisers seek comparable properties that have sold and then resold within a short period of time to gauge changes in market conditions.

Significant Characteristics

Adjustments should be made for significant and pertinent characteristics only. Each lump sum adjustment should be defensible by market data. For example, the market may indicate that the difference in price paid for a house with an attached garage as compared with one without a garage is $20,000, notwithstanding that the cost of adding the garage may be greater than that amount.

Most significant characteristics are grouped under location, lot size and physical characteristics. Practitioners typically rely on new home development data for location adjustments; e.g., views and differing lot prices for selected neighbourhoods. Appraisers have also traditionally used the paired sales approach; i.e., comparable properties that have sold in different neighbourhoods (one being near the subject property being appraised). By pairing these sales, reasonably accurate location adjustments can be made. Lot sizes are typically adjusted either by the front foot/metre or on a *per lot* basis. Lastly, physical characteristics are broken down into components along with appropriate value adjustments.

Value Not Cost		CAUTION

Adjustments are made on the basis of value, not cost. The cost of the garage is not the issue; its value is. The assumption made is that the presence or absence of factors being considered will make a difference to the price paid for a property. Therefore, any adjustment has to be made in consideration of a typical buyer's actions.

Sum Versus Parts

A buyer purchasing a residence acquires an entire package that includes land and improvements at a given price. If the house was separated into parts such as the garage, recreation room or extra washroom and a cost assigned to each, a higher value would probably be derived than what a typical buyer would pay. As a parallel, consider assembling an automobile using individual parts bought at retail prices from a dealership. The cost of the finished product would be prohibitive compared to that of a new car off the assembly line. While not a perfect analogy, the appraiser must always remember that adjusted amounts must reflect the contribution of the parts to the whole.

ADJUSTMENTS AND RECONCILIATION

Adjustments are required to effectively make comparable properties similar to the subject property, so that a valid comparison can be made.

Comparable Better Than Subject Property	Comparable Worse Than Subject Property
If a feature in the comparable is better than the subject property, a minus adjustment is made to the sale price of that comparable. For example, if the comparable has two baths and the subject has one, the comparable is better in this respect and a minus (negative) adjustment is required.	If the feature in the comparable is poorer or less desirable than the subject, a plus adjustment is required to the sale price of that comparable; e.g., the comparable has an old kitchen and the subject a modern one. The comparable is inferior, consequently a plus or positive adjustment is required.

Dollar vs. Percentage Adjustments

While percentage adjustments are possible, dollar amounts are preferred because the direct comparison approach is market oriented. This approach reflects the reaction of a typical buyer who, in comparing property with another, consciously or subconsciously adds or subtracts sums for differences in properties. Under each heading in an adjustment chart, plus and minus amounts appear reflecting what a typical buyer would allow.

Rounding the Final Estimate

Practitioners are reminded that an appraisal is only an opinion of value and cannot be accurate within a few hundred dollars, usually the final estimate is rounded to the nearest five hundred dollars. In some cases, a value range might be quoted as opposed to a single figure.

An illustration is provided showing three comparable properties being adjusted to arrive at adjusted sale prices.

Adjusted Sale Price

Sale price of a comparable property under the direct comparison approach following all adjustments in comparison with the subject property being appraised.

The Reconciliation

As discussed in the previous chapter, the **reconciliation** is a logical reasoning process used to narrow down the value range to a final estimate of value. When all adjustments have been made, each comparable sale will provide a different **adjusted sale price** (original sale price plus or minus total adjustments). If three comparable properties are used, the adjustment process will likely result in three different figures.

Subject Address: 31 Hazel Lane

	Comparable 1	Comparable 2	Comparable 3
Address	42 Centre St.	200 Avenue Rd.	77 Walton Blvd.
Distance from Subject	1 Block	½ Block	2 Blocks
Date Sold	Oct. 18, 20xx	Dec. 10, 20xx	Nov. 15, 20xx
Sale Price	$266,000	$282,000	$283,000

Direct Comparison Approach

	Subject	Comparable 1		Comparable 2		Comparable 3	
	Description	Description	Adj.	Description	Adj.	Description	Adj.
Time	Dec. 31, 20x1	Inferior Market	+ 5,000	Similar	0	Inferior Market	+ 2,000
Location	Quiet Street	Similar	0	Similar	0	Similar	0
Lot Size	30 x 150	31 x 150	0	29 x 148	0	31 x 155	0
Age of House	45 Years	42 Years	0	45 Years	0	43 Years	0
House Style	Detached Bungalow	Detached Bungalow	0	Detached Bungalow	0	Detached Bungalow	0
Total Sq. Ft.	1000 sq. ft	992 sq. ft.	0	988 sq. ft.	0	1004 sq. ft.	0
Bedrooms	2 + 1	2 + 1	0	2 + 1	0	2 + 1	0
Bathrooms (pieces)	1 ½	1	+ 2,000	2	– 2,000	2	– 2,000
Sep. Dining Room	Yes	Yes	0	Yes	0	Yes	0
Family Room	No	No	0	No	0	No	0
Recreation Room	Yes	Yes	0	Yes	0	Yes	0
Garage	No	Single	– 3,000	No	0	Single	– 3,000
Construction Quality	Above Average	Above Average	0	Above Average	0	Above Average	0
Fireplace(s)	One	One	0	One	0	None	+ 2,000
Central Air	Yes	No	+ 2,000	Yes	0	Yes	0
Condition	Modernized Very Good	Well Maintained Good	+ 5,000	Modernized Very Good	0	Modernized Very Good	0
Total Adjustments			**+ 11,000**		**– 2,000**		**– 1,000**
Adjusted Sale Price			**$277,000**		**$280,000**		**$282,000**

Value by Direct Comparison Approach   **$280,000**

Comments & Explanations: The adjusted sale prices range from a low of $277,000 to a high of $282,000. The most weight was given to Comparable #2, as it had the least amount of adjustments when reviewing all other comparables. Therefore the value assigned to the subject property by the Direct Comparison Approach as of the date of this Appraisal is estimated at:

Two Hundred and Eighty Thousand Dollars $280,000.00

The appraiser must examine all information used in arriving at the reconciliation. A properly completed reconciliation will include the final estimate, along with written justification. No two appraisers will necessarily approach the reconciliation in precisely the same manner. The overall objective is to give the most weight to the best evidence, least weight to the poorest evidence and look for any overall trends that indicate the value of the subject property.

In preparing a reconciliation, the appraiser should:

- Check all calculations;
- Review the comparability of each sale;
- Give less weight to sales requiring extreme adjustments;
- Give more weight to sales with the highest degree of comparability; and
- Make a final value estimate.

USING THE FOUR-STEP APPROACH

The direct comparison approach involves four basic steps leading to a final estimate of value:

Direct Comparison Approach: 4 Steps

STEP 1	**Select Comparables** Determined based on time, location, size and other physical characteristics.
STEP 2	**Make Adjustments** Plus or minus value adjustments made to comparables.
STEP 3	**Establish Adjusted Sale Price** Original sale price plus or minus total adjustments.
STEP 4	**Complete Reconciliation** Value estimate based on adjusted sale prices.

STEP 1   Select Comparables

Comparable properties are carefully selected based on the following factors:

Time/Market Conditions	Close to the effective date of the appraisal; i.e., the older the sale, the less reliable the result. Historical sales may have occurred under differing market conditions and adjustments are required.
Market Value	The sale must be at arm's length reflecting the definition of market value; i.e., informed buyer and seller, prudent behavior, no undue pressure and reasonable time. Non-arm's length can result in flawed adjusted sale prices and an inaccurate final estimate of value.
Similarity	A good comparable should be physically similar so that minimum adjustments are required.
Proximity	A good comparable should be located on the same street or in close proximity to the subject property; e.g., the same neighbourhood.

STEP 2 Make Adjustments

Comparable sale prices are adjusted based on differences between the comparable property and the subject property. The objective is to remove the effect of the differences so the two properties can be compared directly based on a common set of characteristics. Adjustments are commonly separated into four areas:

Time	Comparable sales are historical facts and, consequently, time of sale must be adjusted (brought forward) to coincide with the appraisal date of the subject property. The adjustment should reflect changes in market conditions. Typically, increases and decreases are expressed in percentage terms and then translated into dollar amounts.
Location	Location adjustments relate to general location (i.e., a particular locale or neighbourhood) as well as specific attributes (e.g., adjacent to parkland).
Lot Size	Lot size adjustments are often calculated based on a per front foot/metre (e.g., residential and waterfront recreational) with little regard to minor differences in depth (assuming that the lots have equal utility). Depending on circumstances, a summary adjustment, such as adjustment per lot, is more appropriate if per lot values are widely used in a particular marketplace. Industrial/commercial properties are often adjusted on a square foot/metre basis, as area coverage is often more important than frontage.
Physical Characteristics	The OREA *Standard Appraisal Report–Single Family* (Form 700) includes selected physical characteristics (e.g., total square footage and differences in dining room, living room and garage) with additional blank lines. This facilitates improved accuracy in breaking down individual components and achieving more pinpointed adjustments. *Reminder:* Adjustments are made based on value, not cost. For example, while a fireplace may cost $9,000 to build, its adjustment value might only be $6,000.

Establishing Component Value   CURIOSITY

Some appraisers rely on **payback** data for further input on the value of specific components; i.e., what percentage of original cost is retained as value. As an example, payback analysis attempts to determine what value is retained when a new furnace or a new shingle roof is installed. Typically, the focus is on whether or not such an investment will repay in terms of resale dollars, assuming that the property is offered for sale within a reasonable time following installation of the particular component.

As a point of interest, bathroom and kitchen renovations seemingly have the highest payback (i.e., 75 to 100%) according to a 2004 survey of appraisers conducted by the Appraisal Institute of Canada. Of course, whether or not such a payback can be realized will depend on many factors including the current market conditions, locale and workmanship. Interestingly, building a fence, adding a swimming pool and installing a skylight had low payback potential, ranging from 0 to 50%. (*Source:* Appraisal Institute of Canada, 2004 Home Renovation Survey.)

The issue of payback in establishing value is not without critics. For example, while professionals may estimate that an aging improvement has value, buyers may not be willing to pay extra. Further, the amount of payback often appears directly hinged to the strength of the market. As with many techniques, professional judgement is a key factor. Fortunately, practitioners typically rely on their extensive experience with resales when establishing value versus cost. Appraisers also attempt to establish the value of various components using the **paired sales** approach (discussed subsequently in this chapter).

STEP 3 Establish Adjusted Sale Price

All adjustments are summed to arrive at an adjusted sale price for each comparable used in the analysis. Note: When using the OREA *Standard Appraisal Report–Single Family* (Form 700), any unusual circumstances surrounding adjustments should be highlighted by way of written comment.

STEP 4 Complete Reconciliation

Typically, three adjusted sale prices for the most comparable properties are included in a form report. Factors to consider during the reconciliation process include:

- The most recent sale is normally the best indicator of value, assuming that minimal adjustments have been made.
- The sale requiring the least number of adjustments is the most comparable to the subject property and should be given appropriate weighting.
- The range of adjusted sale prices is a good measure of comparability between the subject property and the comparables.

As a general rule, give the most weight to the best evidence and the least weight to the poorest.

ADJUSTMENT CALCULATIONS

Three simple rules apply when using the direct comparison approach:

PLUS ADJUSTMENT TO COMPARABLE

COMPARABLE PROPERTY POORER

If the feature in the comparable is poorer than the subject property, a **plus** adjustment is made.

- Subject property has garage; comparable does not. Value of a double garage is $32,000. Plus adjustment of $32,000 made to comparable (to make it similar to subject property).
- Subject property has double garage (value: $32,000); comparable property has single garage (value: $18,000). Plus adjustment of $14,000 made to comparable (to make it similar to subject property).

COMPARABLE PROPERTY BETTER

MINUS ADJUSTMENT TO COMPARABLE

If the feature in the comparable property is better than the subject property, a **minus** adjustment is made.

- Subject property does not have fireplace; comparable does. Value of fireplace is $9,000. Minus adjustment of $9,000 made to comparable (to make it similar to subject property).
- Subject property has small family room; comparable has large family room. Difference in value is $10,000. Minus adjustment of $10,000 made to comparable (to make it similar to subject property).

NO ADJUSTMENT

COMPARABLE PROPERTY SAME

If the feature in the comparable property is the same as the subject property, **no** adjustment is made.

- Subject property has 60' x 100' lot backing onto green space; comparable has same size lot backing onto comparable green space. *No adjustment made.*

Time Adjustments

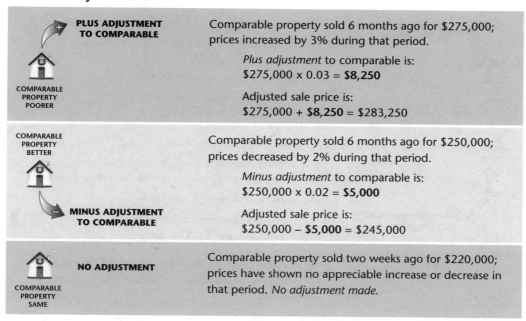

PLUS ADJUSTMENT TO COMPARABLE — COMPARABLE PROPERTY POORER	Comparable property sold 6 months ago for $275,000; prices increased by 3% during that period.
	Plus adjustment to comparable is: $275,000 x 0.03 = **$8,250**
	Adjusted sale price is: $275,000 + **$8,250** = $283,250
COMPARABLE PROPERTY BETTER — **MINUS ADJUSTMENT TO COMPARABLE**	Comparable property sold 6 months ago for $250,000; prices decreased by 2% during that period.
	Minus adjustment to comparable is: $250,000 x 0.02 = **$5,000**
	Adjusted sale price is: $250,000 – **$5,000** = $245,000
NO ADJUSTMENT — COMPARABLE PROPERTY SAME	Comparable property sold two weeks ago for $220,000; prices have shown no appreciable increase or decrease in that period. *No adjustment made.*

MARKET TREND ANALYSIS

Practitioners typically obtain price trends by analyzing MLS statistics (or other market trend data either developed by or acquired by the brokerage) for average sale prices within the particular market area. Assume that MLS average sale price in an area increased from $239,950 to $244,149 in the past four months. The estimated increase would be:

$$(244,149 - 239,950) \div 239,950 = \textbf{1.75\%}$$

Caution is advised as different property types making up the average can vary at differing rates. Further, the average may be based on a small number of sales. Lastly, MLS statistics may be too general (includes various types of housing), and not provide reliable area/house style-specific data.

TIME RESALE ANALYSIS

Practitioners performing appraisals may search out comparable properties that have sold and resold within a short time period. For example, Property A sold 6 months ago for $250,000 and resold two months ago for $260,000. Using the time resale method, the increase per month is:

$$(260,000 - 250,000) \div 4 \text{ months} = \textbf{\$2,500}$$

Based on the original selling price, this increase is:

$$2,500 \div 250,000 = \textbf{0.01 or 1\%}$$

If two other comparables produced a similar result, the appraiser would undoubtedly conclude that 1% per month was a reliable estimate and make appropriate time adjustments. The reliability of this approach is directly tied to how closely the comparables match the subject property. Further, sale/re-sale activities can be very small and an accurate estimate difficult to obtain.

Location Adjustments

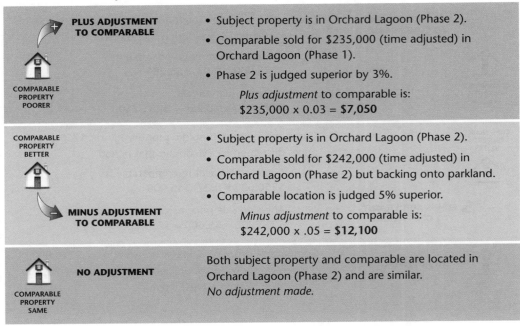

PLUS ADJUSTMENT TO COMPARABLE	COMPARABLE PROPERTY POORER	• Subject property is in Orchard Lagoon (Phase 2). • Comparable sold for $235,000 (time adjusted) in Orchard Lagoon (Phase 1). • Phase 2 is judged superior by 3%. *Plus adjustment* to comparable is: $235,000 x 0.03 = **$7,050**
COMPARABLE PROPERTY BETTER	**MINUS ADJUSTMENT TO COMPARABLE**	• Subject property is in Orchard Lagoon (Phase 2). • Comparable sold for $242,000 (time adjusted) in Orchard Lagoon (Phase 2) but backing onto parkland. • Comparable location is judged 5% superior. *Minus adjustment* to comparable is: $242,000 x .05 = **$12,100**
NO ADJUSTMENT	COMPARABLE PROPERTY SAME	Both subject property and comparable are located in Orchard Lagoon (Phase 2) and are similar. *No adjustment made.*

Two methods are commonly used to make percentage increases/decreases for location adjustments:

PAIRED SALES ANALYSIS

To make location adjustments, appraisers have traditionally sought out two comparable properties in differing locations (locations that match the comparable and subject properties, and are identical to each other save and except for location), and have sold recently. While theoretically sound, the paired sales approach proves difficult in practice given obvious scarcity of such sales, particularly in smaller and/or low activity markets.

NEW HOUSE STATISTICS

Practitioners often rely on data from new house developments to estimate location adjustments; e.g., premiums paid for views, locations abutting green space, and specific areas or conversely, incentives (discounted prices) for homes on busy arterial streets or adjacent to commercial enterprises.

Lot Size Adjustments

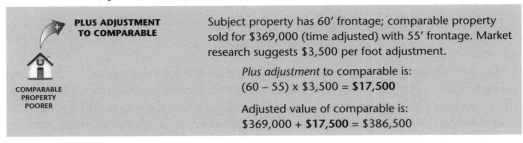

PLUS ADJUSTMENT TO COMPARABLE	COMPARABLE PROPERTY POORER	Subject property has 60' frontage; comparable property sold for $369,000 (time adjusted) with 55' frontage. Market research suggests $3,500 per foot adjustment. *Plus adjustment* to comparable is: (60 – 55) x $3,500 = **$17,500** Adjusted value of comparable is: $369,000 + **$17,500** = $386,500

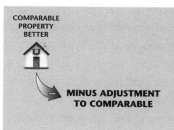

Subject property has 55' frontage, comparable property sold for $229,000 (time adjusted) with 60' frontage. Market research suggests $2,000 per foot adjustment.

Minus adjustment to comparable is:

(60 – 55) x $2,000 = **$10,000**

Adjusted value of comparable is:

$229,000 – **$10,000** = $219,000

Physical Characteristic Adjustments

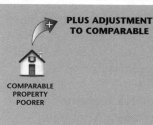

Comparable property sold six months ago for $175,000 (time adjusted) without fireplace. Subject property has fireplace. Value (not cost) of fireplace is $7,500.

Plus adjustment to comparable is:

$7,500

Adjusted value of comparable is:

$175,000 + **$7,500** = $182,500

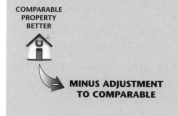

Comparable property sold six months ago for $250,000 (time adjusted) with large deck. Subject property has no deck. Value (not cost) of deck is $11,500.

Minus adjustment to comparable is:

$11,500

Adjusted value of comparable is:

$250,000 – **$11,500** = $238,500

Other Adjustments

Other adjustments are possible, which go beyond the scope of this course. For example, financing terms may impact value; i.e., the comparable sold at a higher price owing to attractive financing being assumed and an adjustment would be required for that fact. A similar situation might arise regarding the motivation of the buyer and/or seller. For example, the comparable property may represent a distress sale in which the seller did not truly receive market value. Once again, an adjustment is required. Caution is advised as the adjustment process can be complex. Seek advice from your brokerage.

LIMITATIONS

The direct comparison approach, while popular particularly in residential appraisals, is not without certain potential drawbacks.

- Lack of recent, comparable sales can limit reliability of value estimates.
- Direct comparison is reliant on timely information. Sales involve past events and must be carefully adjusted to reflect present reality. Extremely active markets only serve to compound the problem.

- Investors may find the approach limiting, as they often place more weight on economic performance than on comparable sales. Hence, the income approach and capitalization rates are often favoured. Interestingly, the capitalization rates used are typically established by the comparison approach.
- Special purpose commercial/industrial structures also pose challenges. Current, comparable sales may be limited or non-existent.
- Lastly, all practitioners must be prudent in selecting comparables that reflect valid, arm's length transactions. Reliance on unverified information that proves incorrect can have disastrous results.

Lack of Comparables   CAUTION

What happens if good comparables are not available or limited to one or two in the immediate vicinity due to slowed market activity or property uniqueness? Appraisers will typically broaden the search area and relax search criteria somewhat.

In doing so, the aim is to select comparables that would appeal to the same person who would ultimately buy the subject property. Often, this broadened search will produce comparables that require more adjustments than ideally desired. The individual requesting the appraisal should be informed of this situation.

Occasionally, appraisers will consider listed property within the area for additional insight. While not part of the formal analysis, adjusting such properties can establish the upper limit; i.e., what the subject property is not worth (assuming that selected properties have been on the market for a reasonable period of time).

Summary: Strengths/Weaknesses

The direct comparison approach is applicable when an active market provides sufficient quantities of reliable data that can be verified from authoritative sources. While being the most popular approach, particularly in residential markets, it can be somewhat unreliable in an inactive market or in estimating the value of properties for which no real comparable sales data is available.

This approach also falls under close scrutiny when sales data cannot be accurately verified with parties to the transaction. For example, the sale price may not be at arm's length, but rather a disposition involving family members. Fortunately for real estate practitioners, the abundance of real estate data provided through MLS® systems proves invaluable in obtaining comparable properties for appraisal purposes. Despite any short-comings, the direct comparison approach remains the most popular appraisal method.

KNOWLEDGE INTEGRATION

Notables

- The direct comparison approach, the most widely used valuation method, involves four steps: selecting comparables, making adjustments, establishing adjusted sale prices and completing the reconciliation.

- Comparables are selected based on comparability, time, significant characteristics (e.g., location, lot size, physical characteristics and sum vs. parts).

- Adjustments to comparable properties consist of plus and minus amounts depending on whether a feature in the comparable is poorer or better than that in the subject property.

- Percentage adjustments are possible, but dollar amounts are preferred and most commonly found in today's appraisals.

- Four important factors determine the best comparables; time/market conditions, market value, similarity and proximity.

- Adjustments are commonly separated into four categories: time, location, lot size and physical characteristics.

- In order to make time adjustments, practitioners should seek out MLS® statistics, other internally acquired or developed brokerage data and/or utilize the time resale method.

- With location adjustments, paired sales can be used and/or relevant new home data.

- Physical characteristics adjustments are based on value not cost. Nothing replaces extensive experience and supporting data when making such adjustments.

- The direct comparison approach, while popular, has certain limitations.

Glossary

Adjusted Sale Price

Paired Sales

Payback

Reconciliation

Time Resale Method

Strategic Thinking For Your Career

Questions are included to assist in developing your new career. No answers are provided.

1. What range of information is available in the local marketplace to assist in making accurate time, location, lot size and physical characteristics adjustments?

2. Is it realistic to apply the time resale method in the local marketplace or do market size/activity levels make this highly unlikely?

3. How are lot size adjustments typically made and what information is available at my intended employing brokerage to assist?

4. What data is available to help me with establishing cost versus value when making adjustments for physical characteristics?

5. If a seller or buyer asked me about the pros and cons of using the direct comparison approach, could I fully describe both strengths and weaknesses?

Chapter Mini-Review

Solutions are located in the Appendix.

1. Certain information can be obtained from a land titles office regarding comparable sales in the marketplace.

   ◯ True   ◯ False

2. A key to the successful use of the direct comparison approach is the selection of highly comparable property sales for comparison purposes.

   ◯ True   ◯ False

3. If the feature in the comparable is poorer than the subject property, a minus adjustment is made.

   ◯ True   ◯ False

4. If the subject property has a fireplace (valued at $9,000 but costs $11,500) and the comparable does not have a fireplace, a plus adjustment of $11,500 is made to the comparable.

   ◯ True   ◯ False

5. Beneficial financing associated with a comparable property may have to be adjusted, if the subject property does not have similar financing.

   ◯ True   ◯ False

6. If both the subject property and a comparable back onto the same golf course, but are located on different areas of the course, an adjustment to location may be required.

   ◯ True   ◯ False

7. The time resale method used in time adjustments relies on finding comparable properties that have sold and then resold within a short period of time.

   ◯ True   ◯ False

8. If construction quality in the subject property is significantly better than that found in a comparable, a minus adjustment to the comparable would normally be required.

   ◯ True   ◯ False

9. If a local market was experiencing rising prices and a recently constructed home (typical of homes which are increasing in price) was selected as a comparable, any adjustment to that comparable for time would be a minus amount.

   ◯ True   ◯ False

10. Lot size adjustments are always calculated on a per front foot/metre basis.

    ◯ True   ◯ False

11. Estimating value for a unique property can be difficult using the direct comparison approach, as few comparables may be available.

    ◯ True   ◯ False

12. The fact that some information is sometimes difficult to obtain regarding a comparable property (e.g., the motivation of the seller), can be a weakness when applying the direct comparison approach.

    ◯ True   ◯ False

Active Learning Exercises

Solutions are located in the Appendix.

■ Exercise 1 Direct Comparison Approach: 13 Maple Street

You, as a salesperson with ABC Realty Inc., are preparing a fully reconciled direct comparison approach appraisal of the Smith property. Salesperson Lee has accompanied you to assist.

SUBJECT PROPERTY

The Smith property at 13 Maple Street is a four-year old brick veneer bungalow located on a 55' x 120' lot in a residential subdivision. Upon personal inspection, you ascertain that the building size is 1,205 square feet. The living room fireplace adds $2,000 to value. The property has been reasonably well maintained, has three bedrooms, a finished recreation room, one 4-piece bathroom and no garage.

MARKET FACTS

An analysis of sales in the area indicates that a 2-piece washroom adds $1,500 to value, recreation rooms add $5,000 and sale prices have risen, gradually and evenly, by 10% over the last year. Lots in the area sell for $1,975 per front foot and present construction costs for this dwelling type are $92.75 per square foot.

COMPARABLE SALES

COMPARABLE 1 *42 Main Street*	Sold 6 months ago for $208,500, building size 1,140 square feet, style, location, age and general condition similar to subject property but lacking a finished recreation room. The home, 2 blocks from the subject property, has a fireplace in the living room, lot size is 50' x 120', one 4-piece and one 2-piece washroom and single-car garage. This type of garage adds $4,000 to value.
COMPARABLE 2 *36 Reid Street*	Sold last week for $222,000, lot size 60' x 115', similar in all respects to subject except having no fireplace or recreation room. The property, located three blocks away, has central air conditioning, which adds a value of $2,000. Building size is 1,260 square feet.
COMPARABLE 3 *239 Apple Cres.*	Sold during the past two weeks for $223,800. No time adjustment is required. The location, four blocks away, is on a ravine lot judged to be $7,000 superior to the subject, lot size is 55' x 125'. The home contains one 4-piece and one 2-piece washroom. The home has neither a recreation room or garage, but boasts a walkout from the master bedroom which you estimate adds $1,500 to value. Same as subject in all other respects.

Using the form provided, record details for comparable sales, make appropriate adjustments, determine the adjusted sale prices and prepare a reconciliation and value estimate.

Sales Analysis

Item	Subject	Comparable 1	Comparable 2	Comparable 3
Address				
Distance To Subject				
Date Sold				
Sale Price				
Days On Market				
Time Adjustment				
Time Adjusted Price				
Location				
Lot Size				
House Style				
Age of House				
Total Sq. Footage				
Family Room				
Bedrooms				
Bathrooms				
Basement/% Finished				
Rec Room				
Garage/Parking				
Interior Condition				
Exterior Condition				
Total Adjustments				
Totally Adj. Sale Price				

Comments, Reconciliation And Estimate Of Value By The Direct Comparison Approach

....
....
....
....
....
....

Based on the above information and analysis, a value by the Direct Comparison Approach is estimated to be: ($..)

Form 700 2008 **Page 5 of 6**

Exercise 2   New Comparables

Having completed Exercise 1, you prepare to meet with Broker of Record Johnson to review your findings and conclusion. However, Salesperson Lee interrupts with three new comparables beyond those already selected. Complete another analysis using his information.

NOTE: For convenience purposes, the Subject Property description and Market Facts are reprinted from Exercise 1. Comparable sales are different.

SUBJECT PROPERTY

The Smith property at 13 Maple Street is a four-year old brick veneer bungalow located on a 55' x 120' lot in a residential subdivision. Upon personal inspection, you ascertain that the building size is 1,205 square feet. The living room fireplace adds $2,000 to value. The property has been reasonably well maintained, has three bedrooms, a finished recreation room, one 4-piece bathroom and no garage.

MARKET FACTS

An analysis of area sales indicates that a 2-piece washroom adds $1,500 to value, recreation rooms add $5,000 and sale prices have risen, gradually and evenly, by 10% over the last year. Lots in the area sell for $1,975 per front foot and present construction costs for this dwelling type are $92.75 per square foot.

COMPARABLE SALES

COMPARABLE 1 *193 Westway*	Sold 6 months ago for $226,500, building size 1,290 square feet, location, age and general condition similar to subject property, but lacking a finished recreation room. The home, 3 blocks distant, has a living room fireplace, lot size is 60' x 120', one 4-piece and one 2-piece washroom and 1½ car garage. This type of garage adds $6,000 to value. A large deck adds $2,500 to value.
COMPARABLE 2 *38 Weller Street*	Sold 1 year ago for $209,000, this property is situated approximately five blocks from the subject and has a recreation room similar to subject, but no fireplace. It has a single car garage on a lot 65' x 110'. The corner lot location negatively affects value in the amount of $4,000. The house is similar in all other ways to the subject including building size.
COMPARABLE 3 *202 Glendon Ave.*	Sold 1 year ago for $221,000, location is same as subject (one block away) and there is a recreation room but no fireplace. Building size is 1,325 square feet, with a lot size of 57.5' x 120', one 4-piece and one 2-piece washroom. The single car garage adds $4,000 to value.

2.1   Using the form provided on the following page, record details for comparable sales, make appropriate adjustments, determine the adjusted sale prices and prepare a reconciliation and estimate of value.

2.2   After completing your estimate of value, briefly state your opinion as to which of the two reports (Exercise 1 or Exercise 2) provides the best and most reliable value estimate.

Sales Analysis

Item	Subject	Comparable 1		Comparable 2		Comparable 3	
Address							
Distance To Subject							
Date Sold							
Sale Price							
Days On Market							
Time Adjustment							
Time Adjusted Price							
Location							
Lot Size							
House Style							
Age of House							
Total Sq. Footage							
Family Room							
Bedrooms							
Bathrooms							
Basement/% Finished							
Rec Room							
Garage/Parking							
Interior Condition							
Exterior Condition							
Total Adjustments							
Totally Adj. Sale Price							

Comments, Reconciliation And Estimate Of Value By The Direct Comparison Approach

....
....
....
....
....
....
....

Based on the above information and analysis, a value by the Direct Comparison Approach is estimated to be: ($...)

Form 700   2008   **Page 5 of 6**

■ Exercise 3   The Older Three Bedroom Sidesplit

Seller Anderson has asked you to list his older three bedroom sidesplit located in a mid-sized Ontario town. He intends on constructing a much larger home and has requested a value estimate.

SUBJECT PROPERTY

The subject property, 29 Brock Street, is situated in a good location close to shopping. The structure is 123 square metres in size, built on a lot 60' x 115', with a single-car garage but no fireplace.

MARKET FACTS

Prices have risen during the last year, with the entire increase occurring in the first six months with no appreciation during the last six month period.

- Excellent locations are $6,000 better and fair locations are $6,000 worse than good locations. Building costs for this type of property are $700 per square metre. Lots sell for $900 per front foot.
- Fireplaces add $2,000 to value.
- Single garages cost $12,000, double garages cost $22,000; however, each respectively adds $10,000 and $20,000 to value.

COMPARABLE SALES

COMPARABLE 1 38 Elgin Ave.	Three bedroom backsplit with a fireplace, double garage and 120 square metres in size. The property has a fair location four blocks from the subject property, with a lot size of 55' x 110' and sold 5 months ago for $152,300.
COMPARABLE 2 128 Maple Lane	Three bedroom sidesplit with lot size 60' by 120' and a building size of 112 square metres. The property, located approximately two blocks from the subject property, has no fireplace but does have a two-car garage and sold last week for $156,500.
COMPARABLE 3 218 Maxwell Ave.	This property, two blocks from the subject property, has an excellent location, building size of 123 square metres, a lot 64' x 110' with no garage. The property does not have a fireplace. This three bedroom backsplit sold 3 weeks ago for $162,900.
COMPARABLE 4 121 West Street	Three bedroom backsplit located five blocks from the subject property with a lot 57' x 120' in a fair neighbourhood, with a building size of 127 square metres. This home, sold 1 year ago for $149,000 and has a double-car garage.

From the four sales provided, select the three most comparable. Using the form provided, record details for comparable sales, make appropriate adjustments, determine the adjusted sale prices and prepare a reconciliation and estimate of value.

Sales Analysis

Item	Subject	Comparable 1	Comparable 2	Comparable 3
Address				
Distance To Subject				
Date Sold				
Sale Price				
Days On Market				
Time Adjustment				
Time Adjusted Price				
Location				
Lot Size				
House Style				
Age of House				
Total Sq. Footage				
Family Room				
Bedrooms				
Bathrooms				
Basement/% Finished				
Rec Room				
Garage/Parking				
Interior Condition				
Exterior Condition				
Total Adjustments				
Totally Adj. Sale Price				

Comments, Reconciliation And Estimate Of Value By The Direct Comparison Approach

....
....
....
....
....
....
....

Based on the above information and analysis, a value by the Direct Comparison Approach is estimated to be: ($..)

   Form 700   2008   **Page 5 of 6**

CHAPTER 11

The Cost Approach

Introduction

Appraisal is not just limited to professionals—at one time or another everyone estimates value—the difference is expertise. Ironically, some say the best appraiser in town is an informed, motivated buyer. He or she may intuitively apply more than one approach when attempting to establish value (e.g., the direct comparison and cost approaches) without fully understanding the underlying processes. While such skills can't be dismissed, professionals need proven methods for estimates and defense of valuations. That's where knowledge and skill come in.

Real estate practitioners must not only understand value estimates, but also delve into everyday market specifics. Can we compare a new house and a resale and see which is the better deal? Do renovations make sense for this older home? What is the lot cost as distinct from total cost? How much should we allow for depreciation?

Salespersons and brokers must have other tools beyond the direct comparison approach to address certain valuations. The cost approach may initially seem complex, but the technique involves straightforward steps. Practitioners, to properly understand its use, must be able to apply replacement costs, scrutinize cost vs. value and quantify depreciation. The cost approach, as an alternate to direct comparison, represents a time-tested, logical approach and proven method to analyze both residential and commercial values.

Learning Outcomes

At the conclusion of this chapter, students will be able to:

- Briefly describe how the cost approach method operates and outline key strengths and weaknesses.
- Detail five steps in arriving at an estimate of value using the cost approach.
- Discuss why both objective and subjective values are used in the cost approach.
- Differentiate between reproduction cost and replacement cost.
- Explain and apply procedures to estimate site value using the comparative sales method and briefly outline alternative methods to arrive at site valuation.
- Explain and apply procedures to estimate replacement or reproduction cost based on the comparative square metre/foot method and briefly outline alternative methods to arrive at these costs.
- Describe how to estimate accrued depreciation with particular reference to terminology including physical deterioration and obsolescence.
- Discuss how actual age, effective age and economic life apply when determining depreciation.
- Explain and apply procedures to estimate accrued depreciation by the flat depreciation and economic age-life depreciation methods and briefly outline alternative methods including the economic age-life depreciation method (modified) and the observed condition (breakdown) method.
- Explain and apply procedures to estimate total depreciated cost and arrive at an estimate of the value of the property.

COST APPROACH VALUATION

The cost approach used in the appraisal of real property is *primarily* focused on objective value. Objective value affirms that the *cost to create* is the main criterion in estimating value and is guided by the principle of substitution, which maintains that a prudent buyer will pay no more for a property than the cost of producing or creating an equally desirable property, providing no delay occurs in making the substitution.

Advantages/Disadvantages

The cost approach is generally understood by consumers who appreciate the fundamental notion of costing and the inevitable depreciation that occurs in improvements. Further, this approach may be the only one applicable to special purpose buildings given the lack of comparables. Lastly, the cost approach involves easy to make calculations, assuming that complex depreciation techniques are not being applied.

In terms of disadvantages, depreciation calculations can prove challenging, particularly when valuing older structures. Also, construction costs are an integral part of the process and can be difficult to obtain and analysis using different methodologies can yield varying costs, thereby affecting the final estimate.

Five Steps

The cost approach uses five sequential steps.

STEP 1	STEP 2	STEP 3	STEP 4	STEP 5
Estimate the value of the site.	Estimate the replacement cost on the effective date of the appraisal. Reproduction cost may be used in selected circumstances.	Estimate the accrued depreciation suffered by the improvements from all causes.	Estimate total depreciated cost by subtracting the accrued depreciation from the reproduction cost new (or replacement cost, if applicable) of the improvements.	Estimate the value of the property by adding the value of the site to the total depreciated cost.

The cost approach is particularly applicable when the property involves relatively new improvements that represent the highest and best use of the land, or when the site possesses unique or specialized improvements, for which there are no comparable properties on the market. An example is provided based on an industrial building to illustrate the five key steps.

Objective and Subjective Values

Interestingly, the cost approach actually relies on an intricate interplay of both objective value and subjective value. Cost to create calculations are typically based on objective costing measures. However, procedures used for site valuation, an integral component in the five-step process, favours subjective data and comparative analysis.

The cost approach and its unique combination of subjective and objective values, however, is often the only method available when valuing certain special-purpose buildings and other unique structures in markets lacking comparable sales. Practitioners should be aware that the cost approach is not only heavily based on *number crunching*, but that each of the alternative costing and depreciation techniques can yield significantly different results. Given the introductory nature of this program, selected popular methods are highlighted given their relatively straightforward methodologies.

EXAMPLE   *Cost Approach—Industrial Property*

An industrial site is being valued. Improvements include a small main building and attached storage area. Three comparable sites have been found. Prices for properties have been increasing at an even rate of 0.4% per month. For depreciation purposes, both structures have an effective age of ten years and a remaining economic life of 30 years. The square footage for each site is: Sale 1–8,312 square feet; Sale 2–7,770 square feet; and Sale 3–7,976 square feet. The subject site has 8,000 square feet.

SITE VALUATION	SALE 1	SALE 2	SALE 3
Sale Date	6 months ago	2 months ago	1 month ago
Sale Price	$103,900	$101,750	$103,275
Time Adjustment	2.4%	0.8%	0.4%
Time Adjustment Calculation	0.024 x 103,900	.008 x 101,750	.004 x 103,275
Adjusted Sale Price	$106,394	$102,564	$103,688
Adjusted Sale Price psf	$12.80	$13.20	$13.00

SITE VALUATION $104,000

(based on comparables and the appraiser's judgement of $13.00 psf)

REPLACEMENT COST	MAIN BUILDING	STORAGE
Measurement	30 x 66	18 x 32
Total Square Footage	1,980	576
Replacement Cost (psf)	$34.50	$21.00
Replacement Cost	$68,310	$12,096

TOTAL REPLACEMENT COST $80,406

ACCRUED DEPRECIATION ESTIMATION	MAIN BUILDING	STORAGE
Effective Age ÷ Economic Life	10 ÷ 40	10 ÷ 40
Replacement Cost	$68,310	$12,096
Depreciation	$17,078	$3,024

TOTAL ACCRUED DEPRECIATION $20,102

DEPRECIATED COST OF IMPROVEMENTS

Total Replacement Cost	$80,406
Accrued Depreciation	−20,102
DEPRECIATED COST OF IMPROVEMENTS	**$60,304**

INDICATION OF VALUE

Site Value	$104,000
Depreciated Cost of Improvements	+60,304
INDICATION OF VALUE	**$164,304**

(rounded to $164,300)

Older vs. Newer Structures   CAUTION

Practitioners should clearly understand that the cost approach provides valid and accurate value estimates of new or reasonably new properties, but loses much of its relevance when applied to older structures. The problem centres on accurately establishing accrued depreciation.

Reproduction vs. Replacement Cost

Historically, the cost approach relied on **reproduction cost**; i.e., the cost to produce an exact replica. Now, appraisers strongly favour **replacement cost** which represents the replacement of a structure with one of equal utility using current building materials and techniques. If building cost is estimated using reproduction cost and replacement cost, the former will always be higher. This factor may also have to be considered when calculating depreciation.

Replacement cost estimating is easier as various cost services manuals are readily available in the marketplace. Further, major economic sectors (most notably insurance and banking) have adopted replacement cost as the preferred method; i.e., in the event of an insurance claim.

REPRODUCTION COST

Reproduction cost can be defined as the cost of construction, at current prices, of an exact duplicate or replica, using the same materials, construction standards, design, layout and quality of workmanship, while embodying all the deficiencies (components which are less than needed), superadequacies (components which are more than needed) and obsolescence of the subject building (components which are no longer wanted, yet still may be in working order).

Replacement cost calculations are less complex, some forms of functional obsolescence do not have to be calculated and supporting data is more readily available in the marketplace. For example, when using reproduction cost, many non-standard and/or obsolete components would be included with offsetting deductions required for functional obsolescence. Similarly, outdated standards would have to be applied; e.g., mechanical systems that do not meet today's standards.

An Historical Debate   CURIOSITY

Appraisers traditionally preferred reproduction cost since it involved a costing of the actual building to be appraised. However, problems arose in older buildings where materials used were no longer available and/or when buildings suffered from severe forms of obsolescence, such as excessive foundation walls or ceiling heights. In this instance, replacement cost was found to more easily handle the difficulty of estimating the current costs of materials no longer available and eliminated the need for estimating the obsolescence due to these superadequacies.

In reality, the decision to use reproduction or replacement cost is the appraiser's responsibility. However, keep in mind that:

> *The older the building, the more effective the replacement cost estimate.*
>
> *The newer the building, the more effective the reproduction cost estimate.*

Notwithstanding such criticisms, reproduction cost remains an option for appraisers which can be established using the following techniques:

- Comparative Square Metre/Foot Method ;
- Quantity Survey Method;
- Unit-In-Place Method; and
- Cost Services Method.

REPLACEMENT COST

Replacement cost is defined as the cost of construction, at current prices, of a building having utility equivalent to the building being appraised, but built with modern materials and according to current standards, design and layout. Practitioners typically encounter replacement cost when performing value estimates under the cost approach.

As mentioned previously, reproduction cost (i.e., the cost of building an exact replica) had traditionally been the mainstay of appraisers and is included in professional appraisal texts. However, practical difficulties have brought replacement cost to the forefront. Complex calculations are inevitable and often compounded when encountering older structures. Reliable costing data on historical building components is also difficult to locate. Consequently, replacement cost has replaced reproduction cost in costing manuals found in the marketplace.

Cost vs. Value

The cost approach emphasizes objective value; i.e., the cost of an item. However, the subjective value can be substantially different. For example, a consumer may add an extra washroom that costs $3,100 and yet may improve the market value of the property by $4,000. Conversely, a swimming pool installed at substantial cost may not appeal to buyers.

However, is there ever a time when cost and value are equal? For appraisal purposes, four factors must be in place for cost to closely approximate value:

- the improvement must be new;
- the improvement must represent the highest and best use;
- the improvement is not affected by functional or locational obsolescence; and
- the expected return from the improvement justifies its cost.

STEP 1 ESTIMATE THE SITE VALUE

Four common site valuation methods are found in the marketplace. The **comparative sales method** is recommended, as it is readily understood by practitioners. This technique requires steps already introduced in the direct comparison approach; i.e., use of comparable sites recently sold, making adjustments (as required), determining adjusted sale prices based on those adjustments and completing a reconciliation.

Comparative Sales Method

A procedure used by appraisers to establish site values under the cost approach.

Comparative Sales Method—Site Valuation
(Recommended Basic Approach)

This method of estimating site value is based on the most recent sales data available on similar sites, preferably in the same neighbourhood. The assumption is made that, if the subject site had been vacant and offered for sale, it would have competed with the comparable sales and appealed to the same type of buyer. Six adjustment elements are considered when comparing sites to the subject property:

- rights conveyed by the transaction;
- financing terms;
- motivation of the parties;
- market conditions (time);
- location; and
- physical characteristics.

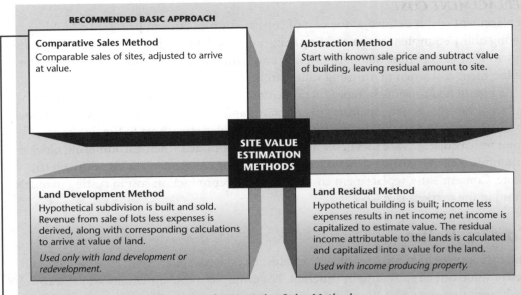

RECOMMENDED BASIC APPROACH

Comparative Sales Method
Comparable sales of sites, adjusted to arrive at value.

Abstraction Method
Start with known sale price and subtract value of building, leaving residual amount to site.

SITE VALUE ESTIMATION METHODS

Land Development Method
Hypothetical subdivision is built and sold. Revenue from sale of lots less expenses is derived, along with corresponding calculations to arrive at value of land.

Used only with land development or redevelopment.

Land Residual Method
Hypothetical building is built; income less expenses results in net income; net income is capitalized to estimate value. The residual income attributable to the lands is calculated and capitalized into a value for the land.

Used with income producing property.

EXAMPLE   *Site Valuation—Comparative Sales Method*

Anne Appraiser is estimating the site value. Of the highly comparable sites selected, Site #3 is most comparable to the subject property. Site prices in Anycity have been increasing at an even rate of 0.4% per month.

SALE	SALE DATE	SALE PRICE	TIME ADJUSTMENT	ADJUSTED SALE PRICE
1	6 months ago	$102,500	.024 x $102,500 = $2,460	$104,960
2	2 months ago	$103,500	.008 x $103,500 = $828	$104,328
3	1 month ago	$104,200	.004 x $104,200 = $417	$104,617
			SITE VALUATION	**$104,600**

(Site #3 is the most recent sale and the best comparable based on the appraiser's judgement.)

NOTE   Students should note that time adjustments are non-compounding to simplify calculations. For example, the compounded adjustment for Sale 2 would be:

Sale 2	Time Adjustment	Adjusted Sale Price
Sale 2 – 1st Month	.004 x $103,500 = $414	$103,500 + 414 =103,914
Sale 2 – 2nd Month	.004 x $103,914 = $416	$103,914 + 416 =104,330

The compounding has minimal effect ($2.00 in this instance). In fact, such differences are lost as time adjustments are typically rounded.

The most common adjustments relate to the final three items. The process of making adjustments under the comparative sales method is essentially the same as used in the direct comparison approach.

Select Comparables	Select a sufficient number of good comparable sites that have recently sold in the area. Gather all necessary data on these sites to make a proper comparison.
Make Adjustments	Compare each of the sales with the subject for differences that may exist.
Establish Adjusted Sale Price	Make the necessary adjustments to the sale price of each comparable based on those differences.
Complete Reconciliation	Reconcile the adjusted sale price of the comparables into an indication of value of the subject property.

Abstraction Method—Site Valuation

This method of appraising involves separating the value of structures and other physical improvements from the total value of the property to arrive at a site value. This approach is often used in establishing the value of a specific site when vacant comparable sites cannot be obtained (also referred to as the *allocation* or *extraction* method).

EXAMPLE   *Abstraction Method—New Home*

A developer is marketing new homes as a package that includes both the lot and improvements. The buyer is interested in establishing how much the lot represents in terms of value in relation to the complete package. The site value could be determined as follows:

Total Purchase Price	$392,700
– Value of Improvements	167,382 (includes structure, landscaping, etc.)
Site Value	$225,318

Land Residual Method—Site Valuation

The land residual method is based on the principle of surplus productivity. This principle affirms that the net income remaining after satisfying the requirements of labour, coordinating services and capital is attributed to land and sets its value through the capitalization process.

   The land residual technique is used to find a value estimate of a site that is readily adaptable for use as the location for an income producing property. The process is generally described, but specific calculations go beyond the scope of this course.

Construct Hypothetical Structure	A hypothetical building, that will develop the site to its highest and best use, is projected for the site and the cost of erecting the structure is calculated based on current building cost.
Estimate Gross Income	Potential annual gross income is estimated based on current rental rates. From this, an allowance for vacancy and bad debts is subtracted to arrive at the effective gross income.
Estimate Net Income	Expenses to operate the building are then deducted, resulting in a net income attributable to the property. This net income figure already takes the cost for labour and coordination into consideration, as they are part of the operating expenses of the building.
Deduct Income Attributable to the Structure	To satisfy capital requirements, an amount equal to the building value, multiplied by the combination of the interest rate plus the recapture rate, is deducted from this net income.
Capitalize Residual Income Attributable to the Land	The resulting residual income is attributable to the land value as detailed in the principle of surplus productivity. The actual conversion of income into value is achieved by capitalizing this residual income by an appropriate rate.

Land Development Method—Site Valuation

This appraisal method is normally applied when the comparative sales method cannot be used given a lack of comparable sales. This method is a variation on the land residual method. The appraiser must construct a hypothetical plan of subdivision or a building design based on the highest and best use.

He or she must then determine the sale price of the eventual development, evaluate costs associated with time delays (e.g., debt service, servicing costs and marketing costs) and arrive at a final estimate of the price that a developer would pay in light of such future anticipated gains. Given the wide range of assumptions, this approach has limited use, but may be the only method to arrive at a value or range of value for specific properties.

STEP 2   ESTIMATE REPLACEMENT COST

The cost of recently completed buildings is established using the comparative square metre/foot method and divided by the number of square metres/feet. This approach provides a price per square metre/foot to build the structure being appraised. While quick, straightforward and generally adequate for basic cost estimates, this approach lacks finesse when considering complex buildings, particularly those with significant structural variations.

Alternatively, appraisers in the marketplace typically opt for the cost services method. Various companies provide costing manuals setting out basic unit costs for residential and commercial structures. Many variations exist, but typically unit costs are grouped according to structure type. The appraiser selects the most comparable structure and associated component costs are fully detailed.

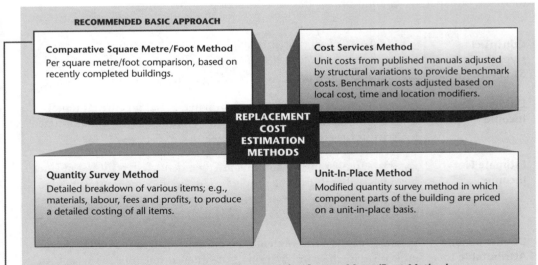

RECOMMENDED BASIC APPROACH

Comparative Square Metre/Foot Method
Per square metre/foot comparison, based on recently completed buildings.

Cost Services Method
Unit costs from published manuals adjusted by structural variations to provide benchmark costs. Benchmark costs adjusted based on local cost, time and location modifiers.

REPLACEMENT COST ESTIMATION METHODS

Quantity Survey Method
Detailed breakdown of various items; e.g., materials, labour, fees and profits, to produce a detailed costing of all items.

Unit-In-Place Method
Modified quantity survey method in which component parts of the building are priced on a unit-in-place basis.

EXAMPLE   *Replacement Cost—Comparative Square Metre/Foot Method*

Anne Appraiser has been asked to determine the replacement cost (RC) of a home located on Main Street. Her investigation of building prices results in a replacement cost of $108.50 per square foot for the house and $37.00 per square foot for the garage. The following calculations are based on measurements taken at the subject property.

STRUCTURE	MEASUREMENT	TOTAL SQ. FOOTAGE	REPLACEMENT COST ($ PER SQ. FT.)	TOTAL REPLACEMENT COST
Main Building	27 x 40 feet	1,080	108.50	$117,180
Detached Garage	20 x 25 feet	500	37.00	18,500
			TOTAL	$135,680

Comparative Square Metre/Foot Method
(Recommended Basic Approach)

This method involves calculating the known cost per square metre (or its imperial equivalent) of a newly-constructed building similar to the subject, and then multiplying this unit cost by the number of square metres in the subject structure. The accuracy of the **comparative square metre/foot method** depends on the refinements made by the appraiser to cover the differences between the properties from which the unit cost is derived and the property being appraised.

For example, it would be incorrect to ascertain the square metre cost of a two-storey house and apply this unit cost as a basis for estimating the cost of a bungalow. It would also be incorrect to apply the square metre cost of an odd shaped one-storey house to estimate the cost of a more conventional structure. To prevent these inaccuracies, the appraiser must ensure that the properties from which a cost estimate is derived are truly comparable to the property being appraised and that all cost estimates are current and apply as of the effective date of the appraisal.

This method is practical, particularly with new construction, provided that site values (which must be deducted from the sale price of the property) can be accurately estimated.

EXAMPLE	Comparative Square Metre/Foot Method		
	SALE #1	SALE #2	SALE #3
Sale Price of Property	$200,000	$218,000	$208,000
Site Value	−90,000	−96,000	−90,000
Value of Outside Improvements	−4,000	−6,000	−3,000
Building Cost	106,000	116,000	115,000
Building Time Adjustment	+ 4,000	+ 0	+ 0
Time Adjusted Building Cost	110,000	116,000	115,000
Bathroom Adjustment	−3,000	−3,000	−3,000
Quality of Materials Adjustment	−3,000	+ 0	+ 0
Recreation Room Adjustment	+ 0	−5,000	+ 0
Total Net Adjustment	−6,000	−8,000	−3,000
Fully Adjusted Building Cost	104,000	108,000	112,000
Size (m²)	208 m²	215 m²	225 m²
Indicated Cost per Square Metre	$500.00	$502.33	$497.78

Reconciliation

A value range of between $497.78/m² and $502.33/m² has emerged from this analysis. Within this range, most weight has been given to Sale 3, since it requires the fewest adjustments and is a recent sale with no time adjustment. Accordingly, the estimated reproduction cost new of the subject building (with an area of 210 m²), as of the effective date of the appraisal, is calculated as follows:

$$\$497.78 \times 210 = \mathbf{\$104,533}$$

Cost Services Method

This method relies on dollar costs provided in a cost services manual. Costing manuals provide basic unit costs for various building structures with specific categories detailing varying degrees of quality. Relevant component costs are also included; e.g., for residential purposes, these might include fireplaces, finished basement areas, along with cost difference considerations based on the shape/size of the structure.

Cost service manuals typically provide relevant photographs, charts and tables with supplements offered by the supplier on a periodic basis. These supplements furnish the necessary time and geographic location adjustments, by way of multipliers, which are then applied to the basic costing manual.

The appraiser's job is to select a structure within the chosen manual that is most similar to the subject property. Differences between the subject and the manual's benchmark structure must be adjusted based on amounts obtained from the manual.

The cost services method can be an effective method of estimating building costs provided that the appraiser selects the most comparable building and appropriate adjustments are made. A detailed illustration is provided for a one storey, detached home. The appraiser has selected an adjusted cost base taken from a cost services manual and then added cost factors for the basement area, fireplace and garage. A deduction has been made given the lack of a bathroom on the lower level.

Unit-In-Place Method

This method of estimating cost involves determining the unit cost of component sections of the structure installed or in place. The unit cost, in this case, includes both materials and labour. The unit-in-place method (also referred to as the *modified quantity survey method)* involves pricing of the various units (by area or volume in the structure) such as walls, openings (doors and windows), partitions and rooms. For example, the average cost of a wall may be a certain amount per square metre of wall surface (the rate applies to one side only) and includes the studs, interior drywall (or lath and plaster in higher end custom homes) painting, assembly and installation.

The unit-in-place method can also be used in greater detail to estimate the cost-in-place of such items as concrete foundation walls, cement block walls, footings, exterior brickwork, rough framing, roofing, plastering and wiring.

Quantity Survey Method

In its strictest application, this method parallels the original contractor's procedure used in the structures when estimating labour hours required and applying costs to material and labour quantities, with additional allowance for indirect costs such as overhead, labour, insurance and contractor's profit.

The quantity survey, although still an estimate, is the most accurate and provable method. However, this approach is time consuming to prepare and its general use is confined to contractors and to the valuation of public utility and special purpose properties. The unit-in-place method (i.e., the *modified* quantity survey approach) is more frequently used in appraisal calculations.

EXAMPLE   *Cost Services Method*

Purpose   To estimate the replacement cost of the subject structure as at Oct. 21st, 20xx

Subject Property One storey, detached residence of average quality and rectangular shape.

Area   Ground floor: 77.66 square metres
Perimeter: 35.62 metres (building)

Construction   Average quality with solid brick exterior walls.

Extras   Finished basement with forced air heating; fireplace; garage containing 18.56 square metres.

Deductions   Lacks a two-piece washroom in basement.

Location   Toronto, Ontario

Cost Estimate Calculation
(Class—C; Quality—Average; Shape—Rectangular)

	CALCULATION	COST ESTIMATE
1. Ground Floor Living Area	77.66 m² x $462.85 per m²	35,944.93
ADJUSTED BASE COST (Area x Area-Shape Multiplier)	$35,944.93 x 1.063	38,209.46
2. Add: Basement area (Unfinished/Unheated)	54.06 m² x $107.10 per m²	+ 5,789.83
3. Add: Basement area (Finished/Unheated)	23.60 m² x $192.68 per m²	+ 4,547.25
4. Add: Basement forced air heating (Moderate Climate)	77.66 m² x $20.45 per m²	+ 1,588.15
5. Add: Fireplace (One storey average)		+ 1,775.00
6 Deduct: Lack of ½ Bathroom in finished basement	Two fixtures at $425.00 each	– 850.00
7. Add: Garage (Class D; Type—Low Cost)	18.56 m² x $159.85 per m²	+ 2,966.82
TOTAL REPLACEMENT COST OF IMPROVEMENT		= $54,026.51

Local Multiplier for Anycity is 1.43
Cost Multiplier (Time) as at October, 20xx is 0.9865

REPRODUCTION COST NEW $54,026.51 x 1.43 x 0.9865 $76,214.93

In conclusion, based on the above, the current replacement cost of the subject property, including finished basement and garage, as at date of appraisal is $76,214.93 (rounded to $76,215.00).

UNDERSTANDING DEPRECIATION

Prior to discussing *Step 3: Estimate Accrued Depreciation*, certain depreciation concepts and terminology must be understood. Depreciation is broadly defined as a loss in value due to any cause. In real estate appraisal, depreciation refers to any decline in the value of a physical asset resulting from physical deterioration (ordinary wear and tear) as well as functional/external obsolescence. Appraisers rely on two perspectives regarding depreciation. In the cost approach to value, accrued depreciation is calculated, while in the income approach to value, accruals for depreciation are used.

This loss of value, measured as of the date of appraisal, indicates the difference between *reproduction cost new* or *replacement cost* of improvements, and the present worth of those improvements. Accrued depreciation is sometimes referred to as *diminished utility*. This loss of value or diminished utility of the improvements to real property can be caused by many different factors.

Depreciation

Curable depreciation generally refers to those items that are economically feasible to cure and therefore customarily repaired or replaced by a prudent property owner. The term *curable* is used as it would be economically sound for an owner to correct the physical situation based on repair costs. Curable depreciation can arise either through physical deterioration or functional obsolescence.

> **EXAMPLE**   *Curable Depreciation—Interior Painting*
>
> The cost to repaint the interior of a particular residential structure is $3,900, but the actual depreciation (loss in value) due to the current paint condition is $6,500. The curing of this deterioration makes economic sense. This situation should be contrasted with incurable depreciation in which items are not economically sound to cure since the cost of correcting the condition is greater than the anticipated benefit.

Incurable depreciation results from physical deterioration or functional obsolescence that either cannot be corrected, or can only be corrected at a cost greater than its contribution to the value of the property. More specifically, incurable depreciation applies to items in a structure that are not yet ready to be cured, that cannot be cured, or for which it is not economically sound to cure at this time since the cost of correcting the condition or effecting a cure is greater than the anticipated increase in value.

While the correction of a condition may well be physically or technically possible, the criterion is whether or not it is economically sound to cure.

> **EXAMPLE**   *Incurable Depreciation—Floor Layout*
>
> An older residential home has a poor overall floor layout that directly affects value. An appraiser estimates that this poor layout has an approximate $25,000 negative impact on value. However, the cost to cure this layout problem would be in excess of $150,000. As such, while the cure might be technically possible, the cost is prohibitive and not economically sound to cure.

While the term depreciation is widely used, appraisers typically categorize different types of loss in value based on the cause; i.e., physical breakdown (i.e., physical deterioration) and functional loss of value (i.e., obsolescence). Note: The following discussion highlights terminology associated with the Observed Condition (Breakdown) Method described later under *Step 3: Estimate Accrued Depreciation.*

Physical Deterioration

Physical deterioration generally refers to a reduction in utility and consequently a loss in value resulting from an impairment of physical condition. The amount of physical deterioration ultimately translates into depreciation (the cost to cure) resulting from the actual breakdown of structures and their components.

For purposes of appraisal, physical deterioration is most commonly categorized as curable and incurable; i.e., *physical deterioration–curable* and *physical deterioration–incurable.*

PHYSICAL DETERIORATION—CURABLE

Curable deterioration involves the physical breakdown of structures and their components that the prudent owner would anticipate correcting immediately. The cost of effecting the correction or cure is typically less than the anticipated addition to utility and hence,

---

Physical Deterioration

Depreciation resulting from physical condition of an improvement due to wear and tear, decay and structural defects.

---

ultimately, to value associated with the cure. Curable physical deterioration is frequently referred to as *deferred maintenance* or *rehabilitation*, because these terms reflect the type of activity typically associated with correcting the condition.

PHYSICAL DETERIORATION—INCURABLE

Incurable deterioration involves the physical breakdown of structures and their components that are not feasible to correct, based on market conditions as of the date of the appraisal. The cost of correcting the condition or effecting a cure is estimated to be greater than the anticipated increase in utility and, ultimately, in value of the property that will result from correcting or curing the condition.

The correction of the condition may be physically or technically possible; however, the criterion is whether it is economically sound to cure. All components of the structure not accounted for, or measured for depreciation under physical deterioration–curable, must be measured under physical deterioration–incurable. Incurable physical deterioration may be divided into short-lived and long-lived elements.

- **Short-Lived Items**   Those components that are not yet ready to be replaced but that will require replacement sometime before the end of the remaining economic life of the structure. In other words, their life expectancy is less than the remaining economic life of the building. The depreciation is measured by taking the ratio of the **effective age** (by observation) of the component to its life expectancy, and applying it to the reproduction or replacement cost of the item. Actual age in lieu of effective age could be used for certain components whose ages are more readily discernible than effective age.

- **Long-Lived Items**   Components that have suffered some physical deterioration but will not require replacement during the **economic life** of the structure. Depreciation is measured by taking the ratio of the effective age of the structure as a whole to its economic life, and applying it to the balance of the reproduction or replacement cost; i.e., the total cost less the reproduction or replacement cost of the items considered under curable physical deterioration and incurable physical deterioration short-lived.

> **Effective Age**
>
> The age of a structure based on its condition and utility, as opposed to its chronological age.

EXAMPLE   *Effective Age and Economic Life*

Salesperson Lee is attempting to establish the value of a property by the cost approach. The economic life of the structure, a brick veneer bungalow with an actual age of 20 years, is estimated to be 35 years. In other words, 35 years represents the life span of the bungalow in terms of viable economic contribution to the overall value of the property. Upon inspection, the structure reveals an effective age of 15 years given various improvements made to the structure. Accordingly, Lee will apply a depreciation rate of:

15 years (effective age) ÷ 35 years (economic life) x 100= .4286 or 42.86%

The remaining economic life of this structure is 20 years (35-year economic life minus the 15-year effective age).

Actual Age

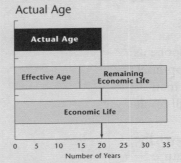

The actual number of years that have passed since a structure was built; also referred to as the *chronological age*. The actual age of a structure must be differentiated from its effective age for appraisal purposes.

Effective Age

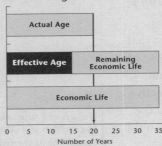

The estimated age in years as indicated by the condition and utility of a structure based on the age of structures of equivalent utility, condition and remaining life expectancy, as distinct from chronological age.

If a building has had better than average maintenance, its effective age may be less than its actual age. If there has been inadequate maintenance, it may be greater. A 40-year-old building may have an effective age of 20 years due to rehabilitation or modernization. The effective age is an important consideration in appraisal, as it affects the amount of depreciation deducted when estimating value by the cost approach.

Economic Life

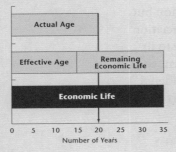

The period over which improvements to real estate contribute to the value of the property. Economic life is used to establish the capital recovery period for improvements in the residual technique of income capitalization. It is also used when estimating accrued depreciation (diminished utility) under the cost approach.

Remaining economic life is the estimated number of years remaining in the economic life of the structure (or structural component, if applicable) as of the date of appraisal as is determined by subtracting the effective age from the estimated economic life.

Obsolescence

Obsolescence involves the impairment of desirability and usefulness caused by new inventions, changes in design, improved processes for production or by external influencing factors. Obsolescence makes a property less desirable and less valuable for continued use in the marketplace. Obsolescence is generally discussed under two categories:

- Functional obsolescence (curable or incurable); and
- External (economic or locational) obsolescence.

FUNCTIONAL OBSOLESCENCE

Functional obsolescence is the impairment of functional capacity or efficiency and reflects the loss in value brought about by such factors as overcapacity, inadequacy, and changes in technology that affect the property item itself or its relation with other items comprising a larger property. A structure is said to be functionally obsolete when it cannot adequately perform the function for which it is currently employed. The method used to estimate loss of value varies based on the form of functional obsolescence.

Curable

This loss of value is due to deficiencies or superadequacies that the prudent owner or buyer would be justified in replacing, adding or removing because the cost of effecting a cure would be at least offset by the anticipated increase in utility, and ultimately in market value.

Deficiency refers to an inability to perform to today's standards owing to some missing item (requiring an addition); e.g., installation of smart building technology for energy conservation including software, hardware and communication links, or inadequacy regarding certain improvements (requiring a substitution or updating/modernization); e.g., a 100 amp electrical service that can be easily converted to 200 amp for a cost that is less than the value that would accrue to the property by its addition. A curable super-adequacy could involve costly upgrades that were installed at point of construction, but offer no real benefit and can be readily removed from the structure.

> **EXAMPLE**   *Functional Obsolescence Curable—Deficiency*
>
> Practitioners commonly encounter functional obsolescence resulting from lack of modernization. The cost to cure from an appraiser's perspective is the cost of the new item, plus its installation, less the present value of the old item currently in the building. Assume that the subject building has older-style kitchen cupboards that were no longer popular and buyers would, on moving in, replace them with modern cabinets as the value would be increased by the cost of the cupboards.

Incurable

This loss in value is due to deficiencies or superadequacies that the prudent buyer or owner would not be justified in replacing, adding or removing because the cost of effecting a cure would be greater than the anticipated increase in utility or market value resulting from the replacement, addition or removal.

While the correction of the problem may be physically or technically possible, such a change is termed *incurable* because the typical buyer would not make the correction given that the cost would be greater than the anticipated increase in value. In other words, it would not make economic sense to correct the obsolescence and most buyers would not do so.

As with curable functional obsolescence, the two types of obsolescence are: deficiency and superadequacy. A deficiency might relate to the lack of internal air-conditioning and associated duct work with no cost effective method to remedy. Superadequacy might involve an over improvement that does not realize any economic benefit; e.g., excess number of parking spaces that were not required and the areas consumed negatively impact overall building size given the small commercial lot.

> **EXAMPLE**   *Functional Obsolescence Incurable—Deficiency*
>
> Anne Appraiser is attempting to measure the rental loss from an income property arising out of incurable functional obsolescence and more particularly, deficiencies within that rental property. The subject property has a poor floor plan and insufficient closet space. As a result of this deficiency, the building would rent for less than a similar rental property that did not suffer from this problem and, accordingly, a loss in value is attributable arising from functional obsolescence.

Superadequacy and the Last Home   CURIOSITY

Superadequacy represents a greater capacity or quality in the structure, or one of its components, than the typical buyer or owner would include, or would pay for, in that type of structure under current market conditions. A superadequacy does not contribute to value in relation to its cost, as the following example highlights.

Smith is confident that his new home will be the last residence for the remainder of his lifetime. He insists that various components be upgraded well beyond normal requirements. For example, while specifications call for a 3" poured concrete slab for the garage floor, Smith insisted that it be 8" in depth. Further, all footings were doubled in size from those in the plans.

The architectural design called for a two-ton air-conditioner. In true form, Smith doubled the capacity to four. In terms of joists, while most residential specifications require 12 to 24 inch spacing, Smith insisted that all joists be placed 6" apart. His insistence on virtually doubling all building code requirements extended to practically all components of the structure.

To the casual observer, the interior and exterior of the house looked quite similar to other properties in the area. Smith's cost of construction was almost 50% higher that of comparable homes in the area. Unfortunately, less than one year following construction, Smith had to relocate given health problems and placed the home up for sale. Smith wanted to recoup his total investment of $525,000 while comparable properties were selling for approximately $370,000.

The appraiser, while attributing some additional value due to superior construction, placed the value at $395,000. This figure fell well short of Smith's investment, given superadequacy and the unwillingness of other buyers to pay for the greater quality and building standards within the home.

EXTERNAL OBSOLESCENCE

External obsolescence represents a loss of value arising from external factors that influence the property either by affecting the marketability of the property and/or its utility. External obsolescence is commonly grouped under two types: economic obsolescence relating generally to factors in close proximity to the subject property and locational obsolescence regarding more generalized conditions in the community that affect the property.

Economic Obsolescence

This form of obsolescence concerns the impairment of desirability or useful life or loss in the use and value of property arising from economic forces outside the building or property. Economic obsolescence can result from changes in optimum land use, altered economic circumstances within the community; e.g., loss of a major employer, legislative enactments that restrict or impair property rights, or other changes affecting supply/demand relationships.

Economic obsolescence should be distinguished from locational obsolescence which refers to localized factors adjacent to the property that impact that property. Economic obsolescence involves broader economic issues within the overall area that affect properties. These forms of obsolescence are grouped by appraisers under the general category of external obsolescence.

> **EXAMPLE** *The Declining Neighbourhood*
>
> When Seller Smith originally built his ranch style bungalow in the east end of Anycity approximately 30 years ago, Eastern Heights was very popular with young families. However, in the past several years, the neighbourhood has been changing. Recent plant closings have affected economic prospects for the community, various homes on neighbouring streets currently sit vacant, and generally, the entire area is in a state of decline. While redevelopment will undoubtedly occur in the future, immediate prospects are anything but encouraging. From an appraisal perspective, Smith's property is being negatively affected by economic obsolescence.

Locational Obsolescence

Locational obsolescence involves the loss in value that a structure incurs as a result of negative environmental forces beyond the boundaries of the property. Depreciation due to locational obsolescence is normally calculated based on paired sales data or capitalization of income loss.

- With paired sales data, appraisers isolate the impact of locational obsolescence through analysis of comparable properties. The amount of depreciation may be attributable to the building and land, to the land only or to the building only, depending on circumstances surrounding the subject property.
- With capitalization of rent loss, depreciation is determined by capitalizing the rent loss attributable to locational factors. The resulting capitalized value will represent the loss to both the land and building. The appraiser must make the determination of whether the loss in value is attributable to both land and building, or otherwise.

> **EXAMPLE** *Locational Obsolescence—Building*
>
> The subject property is located next to a gas station. As a result, the appraiser estimates that the rental loss will be $10,800 per year. Analysis of overall capitalization rates suggests a rate of 9%. For illustration purposes, the ratio of the value of land to buildings is 1 to 3 or 25% of value to land and 75% of value to building.
>
> | | |
> |---|---|
> | **Depreciation** | = Annual Rental Loss ÷ Overall Cap Rate |
> | | = $10,800 ÷ .09 = $120,000 |
> | **Ratio of Land to Building** | 1:3 *(or .25/.75 expressed as a decimal)* |
> | **Building Depreciation** | = $120,000 x .75 |
> | | = $90,000 |

Summary

The following estimate of value using the cost approach is provided to illustrate typical calculations for a small commercial building. This example is based on reproduction cost new (RCN) rather than replacement cost, as the building is relatively new; i.e., an effective age of 10 years.

ESTIMATE OF VALUE

Estimated Value of Site $177,000

Estimated Reproduction Cost New $71,750

Less Estimated Accrued Depreciation:

1. PHYSICAL DETERIORATION

Curable Physical Deterioration	RCN	Cost to Cure
Painting Interior	1,600	1,700
Eaves & Downspouts	500	650
Doors	400	450
	2,500	2,800
Curable Physical Deterioration		$ 2,800

Incurable Physical Deterioration	RCN	Eff. Age	Life Exp.	Dep. $
Short-Lived				
Heating	1,400	15	20	1,050
Kitchen Built-In	1,500	15	20	1,125
Tiled Floors	400	9	12	300
Hardwood Floors	800	15	20	600
Exterior Painting	1,000	1	4	250
Roof Covering	1,000	15	20	750
Electric Fixtures	600	15	20	450
Hot Water Heater	350	15	20	263
	7,050			4,788
Short-Lived Incurable Physical Deterioration				+4,788

Long-Lived	
RCN	71,750
Less Physical Curable RCN	−2,500
Less Physical Incurable (short-lived) RCN	−7,050
Total Long-Lived	62,200
Long-Lived Incurable Physical Deterioration	
[Eff. Age 10 yrs; Economic Life 50 yrs. (10 ÷ 50 x 62,200)] 12,440	+12,440

TOTAL PHYSICAL DETERIORATION   20,028

2. FUNCTIONAL OBSOLESCENCE

Curable Functional Obsolescence		
Modernization of Cupboards	2,000	
Less Depreciated Cost of Existing Cupboards	−685	
Curable Functional Obsolescence	1,315	1,315

Incurable Functional Obsolescence		
Monthly Rent Loss x Monthly Rental Factor ($10 X 180)	1,800	1,800

TOTAL FUNCTIONAL OBSOLESCENCE   +3,115

3. EXTERNAL (LOCATIONAL) OBSOLESCENCE

Monthly Rent Loss x Monthly Rental Factor: $5 X 180 = 900
Ratio of Land to Building: 1:3

TOTAL EXTERNAL (LOCATIONAL) OBSOLESCENCE (3/4 of $900)   +675

Total Depreciation (All Causes)   −23,818

Depreciated Cost of Building   47,932

Plus Depreciated Cost of Outside Improvements   +1,800

Total Depreciated Cost of All Improvements   +49,732

ESTIMATED VALUE BY COST APPROACH   **$226,732**

STEP 3   ESTIMATE ACCRUED DEPRECIATION

Two methods (**flat depreciation method** and **economic age-life depreciation method**) are illustrated. Caution is advised as both are aptly described as rules of thumb and can render differing results.

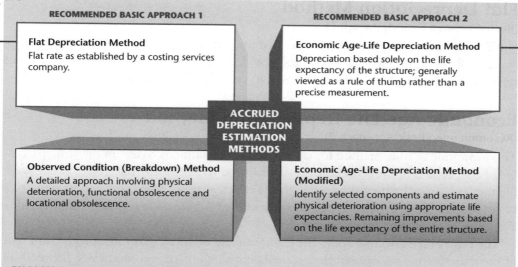

RECOMMENDED BASIC APPROACH 1

Flat Depreciation Method
Flat rate as established by a costing services company.

RECOMMENDED BASIC APPROACH 2

Economic Age-Life Depreciation Method
Depreciation based solely on the life expectancy of the structure; generally viewed as a rule of thumb rather than a precise measurement.

ACCRUED DEPRECIATION ESTIMATION METHODS

Observed Condition (Breakdown) Method
A detailed approach involving physical deterioration, functional obsolescence and locational obsolescence.

Economic Age-Life Depreciation Method (Modified)
Identify selected components and estimate physical deterioration using appropriate life expectancies. Remaining improvements based on the life expectancy of the entire structure.

EXAMPLE   *Accrued Depreciation—Flat Depreciation Method*

Costing service companies provide flat annual depreciation rates for various structures. A rule of thumb for residential structures (including attached garages) is 1% per year during the first 25 years of economic life. A single-family residence has an actual age of 20 years and a replacement cost of $147,300.

The flat depreciation based on a 1% rate is   .01 x 20 years x $147,300 = **29,460**

EXAMPLE   *Accrued Depreciation—Economic Age-Life Depreciation Method*

This approach takes into account a structure's effective age and its remaining economic life.

Example 1: Main Building

A single-family residence has an actual age of 15 years, an estimated effective age of 10 years and a remaining economic life of 30 years. The replacement cost is $83,500. The accrued depreciation is:

STRUCTURE	TOTAL REPLACEMENT COST	DEPRECIATION RATE EFF. AGE ÷ TOTAL ECONOMIC LIFE	DEPRECIATION
Main Building	$83,500	10 ÷ 40 or 25%	$20,875

Example 2: Main Building (Home) and Accessory Building (Garage)

A single-family residence has an actual age of 15 years, with an estimated 10-year effective age and a remaining economic life of 30 years. The replacement cost is $83,500. A frame garage was added to the property ten years ago and has an effective age of 10 years with a remaining economic life of 15 years. The replacement cost is $15,500. The accrued depreciation for both main and accessory structures is:

STRUCTURE	TOTAL REPLACEMENT COST	DEPRECIATION RATE EFF. AGE ÷ TOTAL ECONOMIC LIFE	DEPRECIATION
Main Building	$83,500	10 ÷ 40 or 25%	$20,875
Detached Garage	15,500	10 ÷ 25 or 40%	6,200
		TOTAL	$27,075

Fee appraisers typically use complex variations to ensure higher accuracy. The observed condition (breakdown) method, for example, addresses physical deterioration, functional obsolescence and external obsolescence. Flat depreciation and economic age-life depreciation methods only address physical deterioration.

Flat Depreciation Method
(Recommended Basic Approach 1)

Flat depreciation rates have gained increased popularity, particularly in the residential appraisal field. Costing service companies provide flat annual depreciation rates for various types of structures, which can then be used to establish depreciation.

Economic Age-Life Depreciation Method
(Recommended Basic Approach 2)

This economic age-life method for calculating depreciation is based on the anticipated life of a structure. In the economic age-life method (traditionally referred to as the age-life method) an estimate is made of both the effective age of a building and its remaining economic life. The effective age and remaining economic life together comprise the economic life of the building.

The ratio of the effective age to the economic life multiplied by the reproduction cost of the structure is a measure of the accrued depreciation. The economic age-life method takes physical deterioration into account but does not measure loss in value due to functional and/or external causes. Accordingly, this approach is often viewed solely as a rule of thumb or cross check for more complex methods.

EXAMPLE   *Calculating Accrued Depreciation*

Assume that a building has an actual age of 15 years, an estimated effective age of ten years, a remaining economic life of 40 years and a reproduction cost on the date of the appraisal of $71,150. The accrued depreciation estimated by the age-life method would be as follows:

Effective Age ÷ Economic Life   = 10 ÷ 50
                                      = 20% or .20

Accrued Depreciation   = .20 x $71,150
                                     = $14,230

Calculating Accrued Depreciation   **FORMULA FOCUS**

Reminder: Following are formulae used in the age-life depreciation method:

- Estimate Effective Age and Remaining Economic Life

- Calculate Economic Life of Structure and Accrued Depreciation:

    Economic Life of Structure =   Effective Age + Remaining Economic Life

    Accrued Depreciation   =   Effective Age ÷ Economic Life of Structure x Replacement Cost

Notes:

- Reproduction cost calculations are possible, but not used in the workbook.

- Effective age may or may not reflect actual age, as maintenance/upgrades typically affect aging.

- Effective age and economic life may vary for various parts of a structure and other improvements.

SECTION IV   PROPERTY VALUATION

Economic Age-Life Depreciation Method (Modified)

This modified measure of depreciation is based on the anticipated life of a structure using the economic age-life method. However, this modified approach breaks down and measures the depreciation of the physical components of the building structure based on two categories:

- Physical Deterioration—Curable; and
- Physical Deterioration—Incurable: Short-Lived and Long-Lived.

However, as with economic age-life depreciation, the modified method does not take into account either functional and/or external obsolescence. Consequently, appraisers normally use this approach only when it is apparent that the property being appraised is not affected by such factors; or when this method is combined with other techniques that do account for functional and/or external obsolescence.

Observed Condition (Breakdown) Method

This method of estimating accrued depreciation is the most complex, given that estimates are developed for the deduction of physical deterioration, functional obsolescence and economic obsolescence. These estimates are then added to provide a lump sum deduction.

Under this method, accrued depreciation is broken down and measured under the following classifications, as illustrated earlier in this chapter:

- Physical deterioration—curable;
- Physical deterioration (short lived and long lived)—incurable;
- Functional obsolescence—curable;
- Functional obsolescence—incurable; and
- External (economic or locational) obsolescence.

STEP 4
ESTIMATE TOTAL DEPRECIATED COST

The fourth step involves totalling the estimated depreciation (Step 3) and deducting this from the replacement (or reproduction cost) calculated in Step 2.

EXAMPLE   *Step 4: Estimate Total Depreciated Cost*

Appraiser Williams has determined that the replacement cost for a large industrial structure (including ancillary buildings) is $1,347,500. Total depreciation is $268,700 based on a detailed analysis of physical deterioration and obsolescence using the observed condition (breakdown) method. Williams makes the following calculation to arrive at total depreciated cost.

Replacement Cost	$1,347,500
Depreciation	268,700
Total Depreciated Cost	**1,078,800**

STEP 5
ESTIMATE THE VALUE OF THE PROPERTY

The fifth step involves adding the total depreciated cost (Step 4) to the site value (Step 1) and arrive at an estimated value by the cost approach.

EXAMPLE   *Estimate the Value of the Property*

Appraiser Williams has determined that the total depreciated cost for the industrial structure (Step 4) is $1,078,800. The site value (Step 1) was determined by analyzing four comparable industrial sites to arrive at a value of 975,000. Accordingly, his estimate of value is calculated as follows:

STEP 1	Site Value		$975,000
STEP 2	Replacement Cost	1,347,000	
STEP 3	Depreciation	268,700	
STEP 4	Total Depreciated Cost		1,078,300
STEP 5	Estimate of Value by the Cost Approach		**$2,053,300**

A Helpful Viewpoint   PERSPECTIVE

Looking for another person's perspective on depreciation terminology. Here's how one person described physical deterioration and obsolescence.

Physical Deterioration

Deterioration is as it sounds–things are gradually falling apart. Appraisers group these items into:

- curable; and
- incurable.

Curable makes sense to correct; e.g., a paint job or replacing a damaged door. Incurable ones don't make financial sense to correct, but nevertheless impact value. Incurable depreciation can be further divided under:

- short-lived; and
- long lived.

Think of short-lived in terms of out-of-date features; e.g., aging built-in appliances. They still work but ideally should be replaced. A buyer isn't going to pay much for them, hence a loss in value. Longer term deterioration typically addresses structural matters and associated aging.

Functional Obsolescence

Everyone knows about obsolescence, but most don't apply a mathematical formula to it. Think of the buyer who walks into the kitchen and says: Now this place needs work, I haven't seen cupboards like these in 20 years. That's functional obsolescence. Bang your head on a low ceiling joist in the basement, put your hand against the window and feel a draft, try to park your new van in an antiquated garage (built in the 1930s) or add some new appliances in a kitchen served by a 60-amp service. Some things can be easily remedied—others can't. Appraisers group them under curable and incurable.

External Obsolescence

This last category is probably the easiest to understand. Loss doesn't just relate to the actual property, but also to things around it. As mentioned earlier, the adjacent gas station affects value. Appraisers broadly group such loss into:

- locational (what's nearby the property); and
- economic (what's impacting all properties in the area).

A home might suffer from both if situated at a busy intersection and also impacted by economic conditions in the area. What about a home abutting a 24-hour self-serve gas station with bright lights illuminating adjacent residential properties? Interestingly, external obsolescence can even impact new houses. Consider a situation in which too many houses are built and the market slows at the same time. The price of new homes may be reduced to attract buyers. The loss in value is attributed to economic obsolescence.

Using The Cost Approach: From Start to Finish

STEP 1   Estimate the Site Value

Three sites comparable to the subject property have been selected. Values for vacant lots have been increasing at the rate of 0.3% per month.

Sale	Sale Date	Sale Price	Time Adjustment	Adjusted Sale Price
1	6 months ago	$100,000	.018 x $100,000 = $1,800	101,800
2	4 months ago	$102,000	.012 x $102,000 = $1,224	103,224
3	2 months ago	$102,400	.006 x $102,400 = $614	103,014
			Site Valuation	**$103,000** ①

(most weight placed on Sale #3 and appraiser's judgement)

STEP 2   Estimate Replacement Cost

Salesperson Smith has researched the market and found that typical new homes cost approximately $115 per square foot to build with garages at $27.

Structure	Measurement	Sq. Footage	Replacement Cost ($ Per Sq. Ft)	Total Replacement Cost
Main Building	26 x 44	1,144	115	$131,560
Detached Garage	20 x 24	480	27	12,960
			Total	**$144,520** ②

STEP 3   Estimate Accrued Depreciation

This type of structure has an economic life of 60 years with an effective age of 12 years.

Structure	Total Replacement Cost	Depreciation Rate	Depreciation
Age-Life Depreciation Method			
Main Building	$131,560	12 ÷ 60 or 20%	$26,312
Detached Garage	12,960	12 ÷ 60 or 20%	2,592
		Total	$28,904
Flat Depreciation Method (most widely used method)			
Main Building	$131,560	1% x 12 = 12%	$15,787
Detached Garage	12,960	1% x 12 = 12%	1,555
		Total	**$17,342**

Depreciation $17,342 ③

Note: The flat depreciation method typically uses a lower rate of depreciation for the first 25 years of the economic life of the structure.

STEP 4   Estimate Total Depreciated Cost

Replacement Cost	$144,520	②
Less: Depreciation	–17,342	③
Total Depreciated Cost	**$127,178**	④

STEP 5   Estimate The Value of the Property

Site Value	$103,000	①
Add: Depreciated Cost	+127,178	④
Estimated Value by Cost Approach	**$230,178**	
(rounded to $230,000)		

KNOWLEDGE INTEGRATION

Notables

- The cost approach is best analyzed in terms of five steps leading to an estimate of value.

- The cost approach, as with the direct comparison approach, has certain strengths and limitations.

- Historically, reproduction cost was used in the cost approach, but in recent years appraisers now favour replacement cost given ready access to costing information.

- Site value is typically arrived at using the comparative sales method.

- While the comparative sales method is recommended for participants in this course when estimating the value of a site (Step 1), other approaches to site valuation include the abstraction method, land residual method and the land development method.

- The second step in the cost method involves estimating replacement cost.

- While the comparative approach is recommended for participants in this course when estimating replacement cost, other approaches when determining replacement cost (or reproduction cost) are the cost services method, unit in place method and quantity survey method.

- Depreciation can result from physical deterioration, functional obsolescence and/or external obsolescence.

- Physical deterioration can be either curable or incurable.

- Obsolescence can be grouped under functional (curable or incurable) and economic or external (economic or locational).

- Actual age, effective age and economic life are key terms when using the age-life depreciation method establishing the depreciation rate.

- While the flat depreciation method and the economic age-life depreciation method are recommended for students in this course when estimating depreciation, other approaches include the economic age-life depreciation method (modified) and the observed condition (breakdown) method.

- The final steps (Steps 4 and 5) in the cost approach are estimating the total depreciated cost and estimating the value of the property.

Glossary

Comparative Sales Method

Comparative Square Metre/Foot Method

Economic Age-Life Depreciation Method

Economic Life

Effective Age

External Obsolescence

Flat Depreciation Method

Functional Obsolescence

Locational Obsolescence

Physical Deterioration

Replacement Cost

Reproduction Cost

Strategic Thinking For Your Career

Questions are included to assist in developing your new career. No answers are provided.

1. How widely is the cost approach used in my local marketplace and for what types of property?

2. Are there situations in which reproduction cost might be used in lieu of replacement cost and do I clearly understand the difference?

3. Various examples of functional obsolescence are included in this chapter. What examples currently exist in the house, condominium, rental building or other property type that I currently occupy?

4. What sources of external obsolescence impact the property that I currently occupy?

5. A salesperson comments to you that the only valid means to estimate value is the direct comparison approach. What arguments can you put forward in support of the cost approach?

6. What local information sources are available to assist in understanding costs and depreciation rates?

Chapter Mini-Review

Solutions are located in the Appendix.

1. The cost approach is most suitable to situations in which various highly comparable property sales are available to compare with the subject property being appraised.

   ◯ True   ◯ False

2. The estimated age in years as indicated by the condition and utility of a structure is referred to as its effective age for purposes of calculating depreciation.

   ◯ True   ◯ False

3. Replacement cost is generally preferred to reproduction cost when appraising older structures.

   ◯ True   ◯ False

4. Physical deterioration can be broadly grouped under *functional* and *external* for purposes of calculating depreciation.

   ◯ True   ◯ False

5. A weak real estate market can potentially be viewed as economic obsolescence for purposes of calculating depreciation.

   ◯ True   ◯ False

6. If the replacement cost of a building is $187,500, its effective age is 15 years, its actual age is 10 years and its economic life is 60 years, the depreciation using the age-life method would be $44,550.

   ◯ True   ◯ False

7. Incurable items under physical deterioration may be physically or technically possible to remedy, but normally not economically sound to do so.

   ◯ True   ◯ False

8. A 100-amp service that may be easily converted to a 200-amp service might be viewed as a curable item under functional obsolescence.

   ◯ True   ◯ False

9. The term superadequacy refers to an overimprovement that does not realize any economic benefit, such as excess structural reinforcement in walls and ceilings that accrues no benefit to the property or its value.

   ○ True   ○ False

10. The cost approach is highly reliable, regardless of the age of the structure.

    ○ True   ○ False

11. Depreciation, in one form or another, can result in loss of value even if a house is not occupied.

    ○ True   ○ False

12. A furnace has an effective age of 15 years, an economic life of 25 years and a replacement cost of $2,290. Based on this information, the depreciation would be $1,174.

    ○ True   ○ False

13. Locational obsolescence involves the loss in value attributed to forces beyond the property's boundaries.

    ○ True   ○ False

14. The observed condition (breakdown) method is the simplest method of estimating accrued depreciation.

    ○ True   ○ False

15. If the replacement cost is $377,500, the site value is $244,000 and the accrued depreciation is $63,400, the estimated value of this property would be $621,500.

    ○ True   ○ False

Active Learning Exercises

Solutions are located in the Appendix.

■ Exercise 1   Multiple Choice

1.1   If site values have been increasing by 1% per month, what time adjustments should be made for two lots, one selling 3 months ago for $155,000 and the other for $150,000 6 months ago?

   a. $4,650 and $9,000

   b. $6,169 and $9,000

   c. $4,437 and 8,358

   d.   −$4,437 and −$8,358

1.2   If site values have been decreasing by 1% per month and a comparable sale for $140,000 four months ago is judged 3% superior to the subject property, what associated adjustments should be applied to that comparable in arriving at an adjusted price?

   a.   −$5,400 and −$4,000

   b. $1,400 and $4,200

   c.   −$5,600 and −$4,200

   d.   −$5,600 and $4,000

1.3   A lot sold 8 months ago for $240,000 and resold 4 months ago for $284,000. What monthly percentage increase in value applies to that sale?

   a.   2.33% per month.

   b.   4.58% per month.

   c.   5.46% per month.

   d.   6.05% per month.

1.4   A lot sold 6 months ago for $326,000 and resold last month for $385,690. What monthly percentage increase in value applies to that sale?

   a.   3.45%

   b.   2.95%

   c.   3.66%

   d.   5.02%

1.5   In the economic age-life method, the effective age and the remaining economic life, when combined, comprise the:

   a.   Accrued depreciation.

   b.   Economic life.

   c.   Actual age.

   d.   Replacement cost.

1.6 Small, curable items are those items that:

   a. A typical buyer would probably repair or replace when taking possession of a property.

   b. Would not be replaced during the economic life of the building.

   c. Would not be economically sound to cure.

   d. Relate solely to economic obsolescence.

1.7 Costing manuals:

   a. Typically provide residential costs only.

   b. Typically include unit costs for a range of building structures.

   c. Include only figures for reproduction cost.

   d. None of the above.

1.8 Locational obsolescence:

   a. Is one of two sub-categories under external obsolescence.

   b. Relates primarily to economic conditions in the general vicinity of the subject property.

   c. Does not apply in the case of new houses.

   d. Is always calculated using the economic age-life depreciation method.

1.9 An appraiser details various metric measurements concerning improvements located on a property at 154 Main Street. What is the total replacement cost if the main structure measures 16.32 x 12.50 metres and replacement cost is $978.32 per square metre?

   a. $193,429

   b. $199,577

   c. $207,682

   d. $197,622

1.10 Based on the following information, what is the accrued depreciation using the economic age-life depreciation method?

   • *Residential Structure*: actual age: 15 years; effective age: 10 years; remaining economic life: 30 years; and replacement cost $183,482.

   • *Single-Car Garage*: actual age: 10 years; effective age: 10 years; remaining economic life: 15 years; and replacement cost of $24,580.

   • *Swimming Pool*: actual age: 5 years; effective age: 5 years; remaining economic life: 10 years; replacement cost $29,585.

   a. $51,582

   b. $88,682

   c. $58,392

   d. $65,564

■ Exercise 2   Matching

Match the phrase/word in the left column with the appropriate description in the right column (not all descriptions are used).

____ Objective Value	a. Breakdown—Structures/Components
____ Site Value	b. Economic Life
____ Incurable	c. Abstraction Method
____ Replacement Cost	d. No Contribution to Value
____ Superadequacy	e. Not Economically Sound to Cure
____ Physical Deterioration	f. Exact Replica
____ Reproduction Cost	g. Comparative Square Metre/Foot Method
	h. Long-Lived
	i. Cost to Create

■ Exercise 3   Site Valuation (Time Adjustment)

Assume that site values have been increasing by .5% per month during the past year. All selected sites are the same size as the subject property and are comparable to the subject property. Sale #4 is judged the most comparable to the subject property. Provide an estimate of site value, based on the following information.

SALE	SALE DATE	SALE PRICE	TIME ADJUSTMENT	ADJUSTED SALE PRICE
1	8 months ago	$211,000		
2	6 months ago	$212,800		
3	4 months ago	$217,000		
4	2 months ago	$218,600		

Estimate of Value:

■ Exercise 4   Replacement Cost

Mr. and Mrs. Smith own a bungalow in Anycity. Based on the information provided, complete the following and calculate the replacement cost.

STRUCTURE	MEASUREMENT	TOTAL SQ. FT.	REPLACEMENT COST	TOTAL COST
Main Building	26 x 42 ft.		$180.00/sq.ft.	
Addition	14 x 26 ft.		$120.00/sq.ft.	
Garage	16 x 21 ft.		$47.00/sq.ft.	
Other Improvements:				
Storage Shed			$9,000	
Total Replacement Cost				

■ Exercise 5   Accrued Depreciation

A recreational cottage has an actual age of 10 years, an estimated effective age of 5 years and a remaining economic life of 30 years. The replacement cost new is $97,700. A frame boat house was added to the property 5 years ago and has an effective age of 3 years with a remaining economic life of 17 years. The replacement cost new is $27,500. The accrued depreciation for both main and accessory structures is:

STRUCTURE	EFFECTIVE AGE ÷ ECONOMIC LIFE	REPLACEMENT COST	DEPRECIATION
House			
Boat House			
Total Accrued Depreciation			

CHAPTER 12

The Income Approach

Introduction

The income approach is based on the theory that the value of an investment property is the present worth of the future benefits (i.e., income) which the property is capable of producing. This approach involves capitalizing the net income of the property, by an appropriate rate, into an indication of value.

The income approach is based on the assumption that the value of income-producing properties is related, in one degree or another, to their income-producing potential. Therefore, the higher the potential income, the higher price that the property will command on the market. However, real estate practitioners need to appreciate that each investor will have his or her own personal reasons for buying an investment property. While the majority of investors will be interested in achieving the greatest income or capital gain within the confines of generally accepted risk levels, other considerations, for instance, might be prestige or tax savings.

Investors can have many factors underlying their decisions such as security of income, security of invested capital and ability to liquidate the investment if needed and related risk tolerance issues. All these factors have a bearing on the value of any income producing property. However, when assuming that all these factors are equal, the general rule applies: the higher the potential income, the higher the value.

Learning Outcomes

At the conclusion of this chapter, students will be able to:

- Outline the six steps involved in the income approach and differentiate between the use of direct capitalization and yield capitalization when estimating value.
- Describe how a reconstructed operating statement is prepared and identify key steps required when analyzing an owner's operating statement including appropriate adjustments to that statement.
- Explain how potential gross (rental) income is estimated with particular reference to the establishment of market rent.
- Discuss the calculation of effective gross income with particular reference to vacancy and credit losses, and other income.
- Describe how to calculate gross operating expenses and net operating income.
- Differentiate between rate of return *on an investment* and *of the investment* when arriving at a blended capitalization rate.
- Apply the equation relating to value, income and capitalization in arriving at an estimate of value by the income approach.
- Apply the income approach to situations involving commercial property to arrive at estimates of value.

OVERVIEW

The **income approach** is an appraisal procedure consisting of six steps, which converts anticipated benefits (dollar income) to be derived from property ownership into a value estimate. The income approach is widely applied in the appraisal of income producing properties through the use of either direct or yield capitalization processes. The use of capitalization in estimating value by the income approach assumes a relationship between the income that a property is capable of earning and its value at any given time.

Steps in the Income Approach

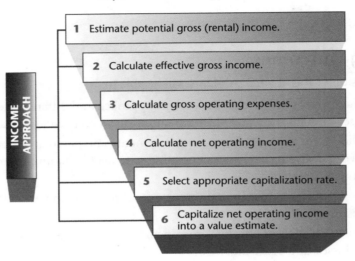

The Process

The appraiser, when applying capitalization, estimates the potential rental income for the current year. Where feasible, potential income is established using a reconstructed operating statement. A market-derived vacancy and bad debt loss allowance is then subtracted from this potential income to arrive at effective rental income. Typical operating expenses (also derived from the reconstructed operating statement, where feasible) are then deducted leaving net operating income. The appraiser selects and applies a capitalization rate converting the net operating income into value using the mathematical process called *capitalization*.

DIRECT VS. YIELD CAPITALIZATION

Direct Capitalization

The process of converting the income generated by a property into capital value by means of a capitalization rate, as opposed to discounting future cash flows through yield capitalization.

Yield Capitalization

The conversion of a projected income stream into an estimate of value by analyzing forecasted operations and sale proceeds over a specified holding period.

Direct capitalization is clearly distinguished from **yield capitalization** as it is based on a single year's projected income and expenses in arriving at value. This method involves the straightforward division of net operating income by an appropriate capitalization rate. Direct capitalization is generally preferred by appraisers (assuming sufficient market data to establish a capitalization rate) as it is market driven and has limited assumptions.

The yield method of capitalization, while utilizing Steps 1 through 4, requires alternate steps in the determination of operational cash flows (before or after tax) for a specified holding period including the reversionary value at point of sale (sale proceeds before or after tax). The result is discounted at an appropriate discount rate to arrive at present value. Yield capitalization is not discussed given complexities that go beyond the scope of this current course, but is analyzed in the articling course titled *Real Estate Investment Analysis*.

Direct capitalization was covered in *Real Estate as a Professional Career*. Students are expected to know how to establish an overall capitalization rate by way of investor analysis or market research, and apply the overall capitalization rate when estimating value. See *Real Estate as a Professional Career, Chapter 9: Capitalization, Taxation and Closing Adjustments*.

The Reconstructed Operating Statement

This statement is key when developing income and expense figures required for the six steps in the income approach. The **reconstructed operating statement** typically represents a one-year analysis of income and expenses and is derived from an owner's statement for an investment property with adjustments to properly reflect typical revenues and expenses. Adjustments are made based on research involving comparable properties. The reconstructed operating statement can also provide the basis of extended cash flow forecasts typically for a five-year to ten-year period. One-year reconstructed statements lead to estimates of value based on direct capitalization. Longer cash flow forecasts are applied when estimating value by means of yield capitalization.

> **Reconstructed Operating Statement**
>
> A statement used in the income approach to value, typically representing a one-year analysis of income expenses, derived from an owner's statement with adjustment to reflect typical income and expenses.

The reconstructed operating statement consists of two primary sections: income and expenses. The appraiser must reconstruct actual operating statements by first adjusting income to reflect market rental rates (subject to vacancy and collection losses) and then reconstruct expenses in relation to reasonable ranges found in the marketplace. This activity will include stabilizing certain fluctuating expense items, properly amortizing selected costs and making adjustments for other items based on prevailing ranges within comparable properties.

DETAILED ANALYSIS

A step-by-step example of an appraiser's reconstructed operating statement is illustrated on the following page, which includes:

- The owner's three-year operating statement;
- The appraiser's reconstructed statement; and
- An explanation of each adjustment in the reconstructed statement.

Estimating Operating Expenses

The process of estimating operating expenses within a reconstructed operating statement can be complex, particularly in the case of larger, multi-residential properties and commercial enterprises.

In establishing an estimate of total expenses, the appraiser must:

- Include only the expenses that are necessary to maintain the flow of rental income estimated as of the date of appraisal;
- Base the nature and level of expenses on typical management and should be consistent with market expenses; and
- Stabilize or smooth out expenses on an annual basis, since some expenses are concentrated in a particular year and not in others. For example, if a building is painted every five years at a cost of $10,000, then the expenses for painting should be shown as $2,000 per year. If this is not done, a buyer/investor might be lulled into paying more for the property during a year when the painting expense was not shown.

OWNER'S THREE-YEAR OPERATING STATEMENT

	3 yrs ago	2 yrs ago	1 yr ago	Ref.
REVENUE				
Rent Collections	$372,761	$379,964	$385,630	1
Parking/Laundry Income	33,975	35,375	35,450	2
Total Revenue	**406,736**	**415,339**	**421,080**	4
EXPENSES				
Realty Taxes	50,940	52,375	53,642	5
Superintendent—salary, etc.	9,500	10,500	11,500	6
Janitor—salary, etc.	4,800	5,280	5,808	7
Water	8,450	8,720	8,950	8
Electricity	974	1,135	1,217	9
Fuel	3,700	5,150	7,200	10
Insurance	2,000	2,000	2,000	11
Maintenance and repairs	5,800	6,800	4,000	12
Painting and decorating	16,400	10,500	18,400	13
Supplies	850	1,020	1,224	14
Legal and Audit	1,000	1,650	1,250	15
Elevator Maintenance	1,200	1,200	1,200	16
Depreciation	42,000	57,000	54,150	17
Mortgage Payments	206,750	206,750	206,750	18
Total Expenses	**354,364**	**370,080**	**377,291**	
NET INCOME	**$52,372**	**$45,259**	**$43,789**	

APPRAISER'S RECONSTRUCTED STATEMENT

		Ref.
POTENTIAL GROSS INCOME		
Rent Collections:		
18 1-bedroom units x $300/month x 12	$ 64,800	
78 2-bedroom units x $375/month x 12	351,000	
	415,800	1
ADDITIONAL INCOME		
Parking—96 spaces x $20 x 12	23,040	
Laundry—96 x $10 x 12	11,520	
	34,560	2
Total Gross Income Potential	450,360	
Less Vacancy and Credit Losses (5%)	−22,518	3
Effective Gross Income	427,842	4
OPERATING EXPENSES		
Realty taxes	$ 54,100	5
Superintendent	17,000	6
Janitor	9,989	7
Water	9,216	8
Electricity	1,320	9
Fuel	9,000	10
Insurance	2,700	11
Maintenance & repairs	4,000	12
Painting & decorating	18,000	13
Supplies	1,469	14
Legal and audit	1,300	15
Elevator maintenance	1,500	16
Management (3%)	12,835	19
Total Operating Expenses	142,429	
NET ANNUAL OPERATING INCOME	**$285,413**	

EXPLANATION

1. The potential annual gross income from rental collections is based on the market rent for each apartment with all suites fully rented. This amount would include the rental income collected for the suites presently occupied as well as those suites provided rent free for the superintendent and janitor.

2. In addition to normal rent, each tenant must pay $20 per month for parking and $10 per month for laundry facilities.

3. A vacancy and credit losses allowance of 5% of both rental and additional income is based on current competitive conditions as indicated by a survey of comparable properties in the area. Whether or not this factor applies to both gross income and additional income will depend on circumstances.

4. The effective gross income represents the total potential gross income less an allowance for vacancy and bad debts.

5. The current year's taxes as shown in the reconstructed operating statement were derived by multiplying the present assessment by this year's tax rate.

6. The superintendent's salary was adjusted upwards from last year's at the same rate of increase as previous years. Allowance of the free two-bedroom suite is also added.

7. The janitor's salary was adjusted upwards at the same rate as previous years. The allowance of a free one-bedroom suite occupied by the janitor was also added.

8. Water costs based on present consumption worked out to an average of $8.00 per suite per month. This checked out very closely to published figures for water consumption costs in this general area.

9. Electricity expenses pertain only to the public areas and to the equipment. The average current cost is estimated at $110 per month. Tenants are responsible for their own consumption, individually metered to each suite.

10. Fuel costs have been rising rapidly over the last three years. The estimate for the current year is based on the average consumption for the last three years at a rate quoted by the gas company for this year's heating season.

11. The annual insurance premium has now increased from $2,000 to a new rate for the current year of $2,700.

12. As a result of the property rehabilitation program undertaken almost two years ago, it is expected that expenses for maintenance and repairs will remain the same as last year's expense for at least the next two or three years.

13. The current year's painting and decorating expense is based on the cost of $500 per suite once every three years, and a total cost of $10,000 to paint the public areas and exterior trim once every five years.

14. Expenses for supplies have been increasing steadily by 20% per year. The current year's expenses are projected on this basis.

15. Legal and audit expenses for the current year are an average of the last three years.

16. Elevator maintenance expenses are based on a new three-year contract for $1,500 per year.

17. Depreciation is not a deductible expense for the purpose of deriving net operating income for appraisal purposes.

18. Mortgage payments of principal and/or interest are not a deductible expense in arriving at net operating income.

19. No management costs were reported in the owner's statements. The typical management cost for this type of property and operation in this area is 3% of the effective gross income.

The appraiser will reconstruct the operating expenses to fairly reflect reasonable expenses for the subject property based on:

- The prior operating experience of the subject property over the past three or more years;
- Market data available on comparable properties; and
- Published studies or reports concerning expenses of comparable properties.

Reconstructed Operating Statement: Excluded Items   FOCUS

In reconstructing the operating statement, appraisers will exclude certain items that might otherwise be included when preparing an operating statement for income tax purposes. The appraiser focuses on those expenses that directly relate to the property and not the owner.

Excluded items usually include business tax, depreciation or capital cost allowance, interest on mortgage or loan and capital improvements.

The only time the appraiser may be justified in including a reserve for replacement of such short-life components in the operating expense statement is when the market indicates that this is normal practice adopted by property owners in the area, and when the overall capitalization rate used by the appraiser in capitalizing the resulting net income has been extracted from comparable properties treated in the same way; i.e., provision was also made for reserves for replacement in arriving at their net operating income.

As a further description, an example is provided on the following page in which various operating expenses are detailed as well as items that would not be included; e.g., business tax and interest on a mortgage.

STEP 1
ESTIMATE POTENTIAL GROSS (RENTAL) INCOME

Potential gross income (sometimes referred to as potential rental income) represents the income that a property will produce with 100% occupancy at market rent, assuming typically competent and prudent management. This income is generally derived by multiplying the rental value per unit by the number of units in the building.

Potential gross (rental) income should be clearly differentiated from effective gross income (sometimes referred to as gross operating income). See *Step 2*.

EXAMPLE   *Potential Gross (Rental) Income—Apartment Building*

Anne Appraiser is reconstructing the owner's operating statement for a 96-unit apartment building to arrive at fair market value by the income approach. In doing so, she includes all apartment rentals at 100% occupancy, using current market rent. Following are the calculations:

> **Potential Gross (Rental) Income**
>
> | | |
> |---|---:|
> | 18 1-bedroom units x 800 per month x 12 | $ 172,800 |
> | 78 2-bedroom units x 1,175 per month x 12 | +1,099,800 |
> | | **1,272,600** |

EXAMPLE   *Reconstructed Operating Statement—Estimating Operating Expenses*

Anne Appraiser is analyzing the operating statements of a rental property and is attempting to reconstruct the statement. As a preliminary step, she has isolated selected expense categories for in-depth analysis in the reconstruction process.

Taxes	*The annual realty taxes are calculated by multiplying the total assessed value of the property, land and buildings, by the current tax rate. Local improvement charges would be included in the operating statement.*
Insurance	*Insurance normally includes fire and extended coverage, landlord's liability, boiler coverage and plate glass insurance. Only premiums relating to the functioning of the property should be included, not the cost of the owner's business insurance.*
Management	*The fee is usually calculated as a percentage of the effective gross income. A charge must be inserted in the statement if the owner is the manager and has not charged a fee.*
Utilities	*Usually includes heating, electricity, gas and water if paid by the owner.*
Superintendent/ Janitor	*If a free suite is provided, then market rent must be included in gross income and then deducted as an operating expense. Wages are included along with employer's portion of CPP and EI.*
Supplies	*Annual amount sufficient to pay for consumable supplies such as light bulbs and cleaning items.*
Repairs/ Maintenance	*Those repairs that are consistent with typically competent management; e.g., exterior/interior painting, caulking and repairs to mechanical and electrical systems.*
Site Maintenance	*Expenses usual to exterior maintenance such as gardening and snow removal.*
Professional Fees	*Legal, accounting and leasing services.*

EXCLUDED ITEMS

Business Tax	*This tax applies to the business and not the real property.*
Depreciation or Capital Cost Allowance	*Depreciation is omitted in a reconstructed statement, but normally appears in an owner's statement. The capitalization rate chosen to determine value by direct capitalization (one of two methods under the income approach) allows for the recapture of capital invested. Consequently, if depreciation were included, it would amount to a double entry.*
Interest on Mortgage	*Not a direct cost of calculating net operating income.*
Capital Improvements	*These expenditures, which enhance the property's value, are really designed to increase its income potential. Consequently, they are not operating expenses necessary to maintain the potential gross income. If items such as alterations, mechanical equipment and chattels cannot be legitimately charged as expenses for repairs or maintenance, then the full amount of these capital cost expenditures must be added to the remaining capital cost of the structure and not included as an operating expense.*

Terminology/Form Differences   CAUTION

Over the past few decades, custom worksheets have evolved both within real estate brokerages and appraisal companies for the reconstruction of operating statements. Further, while terminology is becoming more standardized regarding these worksheets, significant variations can still be found in the marketplace, along with differing techniques.

SECTION IV   PROPERTY VALUATION

Market rent, for purposes of calculating potential gross (rental) income, is the rental income that a property would most probably command on the open market, as indicated by current rentals being paid for comparable space as of the effective date of the analysis. The term *market rent* is synonymous with *economic rent* in appraisal terminology.

| Residential Tenancies Act | CAUTION |

The *Residential Tenancies Act* contains legislative provisions that impact the rent that can be charged for residential premises in Ontario. As such, market rent estimates can be affected and appropriate caution is advised when estimating potential gross (rental) income. Additional discussion of residential tenancy legislation is addressed in *The Residential Real Estate Transaction*.

EXAMPLE   *Market Rent—Office Space*

Broker/Owner Johnson of ABC Realty Inc. is estimating market rent for office space in a high rise Class A office complex. While competitive space in adjacent buildings is offered with various incentives such as rent free periods and other landlord concessions, Johnson has adjusted the base rents of five comparable office leases that contain approximately the same square footage as the subject property. All five leases were drafted within the past four-month period and involved Class A or Class B buildings.

For purposes of illustration, assume that all additional rents payable are generally the same. Based on this information and other factors concerning these leases, Johnson determines that the market rent (base rent) is $12.80 per square foot (PSF). Therefore, the subject property, consisting of 1,740 square feet of rentable area would probably have a base rent of approximately $22,300 (rounded):

1,740 sq. ft. x $12.80 = $22,272

LEASE	DATE	RENTABLE AREA	CLASS	BASE RENT PSF
Lease #1	Jan. 20xx	1650	A	$12.80
Lease #2	Jan. 20xx	1950	A	$12.50
Lease #3	Feb. 20xx	1750	B	$10.70
Lease #4	Mar. 20xx	1850	A	$12.30
Lease #5	Apr. 20xx	1700	B	$11.10

STEP 2
CALCULATE EFFECTIVE GROSS INCOME

Effective gross income (also sometimes referred to as gross operating income) is the potential gross (rental) income estimated in *Step 1* plus other income (e.g., parking and laundry), less an allowance for vacancy and credit losses.

The vacancy and credit losses allowance (sometimes referred to as *vacancy and bad debts*) will vary by specific locale, market conditions and/or type of property and refers to revenue lost due to vacancies in rental units and uncollectible rents from tenants. In the below example, vacancy and credit losses were calculated at five percent of both potential rental income and other income, but the percentage used would vary based on market conditions.

EXAMPLE   *Effective Gross Income—Apartment Building*

As a continuation of a previous illustration involving Anne Appraiser, the effective gross income was then estimated based on other income, as well as an allowance for vacancy and credit losses.

Potential Gross (Rental) Income	
18 1-bedroom units x 800 per month x 12	$ 172,800
78 2-bedroom units x 1,175 per month x 12	+1,099,800
	1,272,600
Add: Other Income	
Parking—96 spaces x $20 x 12	+23,040
Laundry—96 x $10 x 12	+11,520
	1,307,160
Less: Vacancy and Credit Losses	–65,358
(5% of Potential Gross (Rental) Income and Other Income)	
EFFECTIVE GROSS INCOME *(Gross Operating Income)*	**$1,241,802**

The assumption in this instance is that vacancy factors and credit issues would impact both revenue generated from the units, as well as ancillary income that is either directly or indirectly tied to that revenue stream. Appraisers may elect to deduct vacancy and credit losses for the potential gross (rental) income only, if circumstances warrant. For example, other rental income may involve an independent revenue source not directly impacted by unit rentals, such as rental income involving a cell phone tower located on the building.

STEP 3
CALCULATE GROSS OPERATING EXPENSES

See the detailed analysis provided earlier in this chapter under *Reconstructed Operating Statement*. When estimating expenses leading to gross operating expenses, ensure that only expenses necessary to maintain the flow of rental income are included. Annualize those expenses that span more than a one-year period and make certain that all expenses reflect typical costs found in the marketplace.

STEP 4
CALCULATE NET OPERATING INCOME (NOI)

Net operating income (NOI) represents the net income after deducting all expenses from gross operating income, but before deducting annual debt service (e.g., mortgage payments) and any tax liability associated with the income. Net operating income derived from a reconstructed operating statement for a single year's operation is then capitalized (i.e., conversion of future income into a single capital value) using the direct capitalization method to arrive at market value.

EXAMPLE   *Net Operating Income—Apartment Building*

Using the previous example, net operating income is calculated as follows:

Potential Gross (Rental) Income

18 1-bedroom units x 800 per month x 12	$ 172,800
78 2-bedroom units x 1,175 per month x 12	+1,099,800
	1,272,600

Add: Other Income

Parking—96 spaces x $20 x 12	+23,040
Laundry—96 x $10 x 12	+11,520
	1,307,160

Less: Vacancy and Credit Losses	–65,358
Effective Gross Income (Gross Operating Income)	$1,241,802
Less: Gross Operating Expenses	–891,060
(Expenses would be listed in an actual reconstructed statement)	
NET OPERATING INCOME	$350,742

STEP 5
SELECT APPROPRIATE CAPITALIZATION RATE

Two methods are used to establish an overall capitalization rate: investor analysis and market research (see *Real Estate as a Professional Career, Chapter 9* for a detailed discussion). The overall capitalization rate used in direct capitalization is made up of two rates:

- The rate of return **on** the investment (discount rate).
- The rate of return **of** the investment (recapture rate).

An investor seeks a return *on* invested capital and a return *of* invested capital. The overall capitalization rate selected is said to be blended; i.e., has two components.

- The rate of return *on* the money invested in both the land and the building (discount rate); and
- A rate of return *of* the money invested in the building which is a wasting asset (recapture rate).

This overall capitalization rate:

- Expresses the relationship between the current year's income and value; and
- Represents a blend of the rate of return *on* the investment and the rate of return *of* the investment.

The equation for value calculations using the overall capitalization rate is :

Net Operating Income ÷ Overall Capitalization Rate = Value of Property

$$\text{I} \qquad ÷ \qquad \text{R} \qquad = \qquad \text{V}$$

EXAMPLE   *Estimate of Value—Apartment Building*

Anne Appraiser establishes an overall capitalization rate of 10.5% based on the following market research. She arrives at the cap rate using the formula: I ÷ V = R.

SALE #	SALE PRICE	NET OPERATING INCOME	OVERALL CAPITALIZATION RATE
1.	3,400,000	360,500	10.6
2.	3,700,000	380,000	10.3
3.	4,200,000	441,000	10.5

Using this cap rate, she arrives at the following value estimate:

Potential Gross (Rental) Income

18 1-bedroom units x 800 per month x 12	$ 172,800	
78 2-bedroom units x 1,175 per month x 12	+1,099,800	
	1,272,600	

Add: Other Income

Parking—96 spaces x $20 x 12	+23,040	
Laundry—96 x $10 x 12	+11,520	
	1,307,160	

Less: Vacancy and Credit Losses   –65,358

Effective Gross Income (Gross Operating Income) $1,241,802

Less: Gross Operating Expenses   –891,060
(Expenses would be listed in an actual reconstructed statement)

Net Operating Income $350,742

Estimate of Value: I ÷ R = V
                350,742 ÷ .105 (10.5%)
                = $3,340,400 rounded to $3,300,000.

Reminder: When using capitalization rates, be aware that small changes in the cap rate used can result in substantial differences in value.

Important Reminders

1. *ESTIMATING POTENTIAL GROSS (RENTAL) INCOME*

- Use of market rent, not actual rent.
- Be careful with all residential investment properties. The *Residential Tenancies Act* contains provisions and guidelines concerning the lawful rent that may be charged and directly affects potential gross income.
- Occupancy at 100% with inclusion of any ancillary income.
- Use of typically competent management.
- Income based on highest and best use.

2. *CALCULATING OPERATING EXPENSES*

- Include all expenses necessary to maintain income flow.
- Assume that typically competent management is being used.
- Expenses are most often recorded on a cash basis (i.e., recorded when paid) whereas appraisers look at expenses on an accrued basis. For example, in a twenty suite apartment building, all suites might be painted at a cost of $2,000 per suite during a five-year period. While the painting may be completed at one time ($2,000 x 20 = $40,000), the expense is pro-rated equally over that period; i.e., four suites each year or $8,000 per year. This process is often referred to as annualizing.
- Typical expenses must be included even if not itemized in the owner's operating statement; e.g., superintendent receiving a free suite instead of salary, the free suite must be included at market rent; owner manages the property with no charge, a reasonable management fee must be charged.

3. *WORKING WITH CAP RATES*

- To estimate value:

$$\frac{\text{Income}}{\text{Rate}} = \text{Value}$$

- To estimate net operating income:

$$\text{Value} \times \text{Rate} = \text{Income}$$

- To estimate capitalization rate:

$$\frac{\text{Income}}{\text{Value}} = \text{Rate}$$

Cap Rate Limitations   PERSPECTIVE

Capitalization rates and commercial property go hand in hand. Unfortunately, many fail to realize uncertainties that can underlie caps. The prudent salesperson is wise to understand important limitations. An excerpt of a speech given recently by Broker/Owner Johnson, of ABC Realty Inc., to the Quarterly Luncheon of the Commercial Council, Anycity Real Estate Board has been reprinted.

Excerpt From Broker/Owner Johnson's speech

...and last, ladies and gentlemen, let me take a few moments to discuss the use of capitalization rates. Cap rates are invaluable to our profession, but caution is always advised.

FIRST, a small upward or downward change in a cap rate can have a dramatic impact on indicated value. For example, a one point differential from a 9.0 to 10.0 cap rate when capitalizing a net operating income of $40,000 can affect indicated value by over $44,000.

SECOND, cap rates are often quoted by investors as gospel. They will pay no more than the value obtained by a 10.25 cap rate on net operating income, not realizing the danger associated with such a statement. Two properties may have net operating incomes of $30,000 but their respective values can be substantially different from the $293,000 value indicated by the cap rate ($30,000 ÷ 0.1025 = $292,683). Important considerations might be ignored, such as building depreciation and recapture, debt service, tax liabilities and unique features.

THIRD, how accurate is the cap rate, given unknowns about income and expenses? Prudent developers do not construct industrial plants on weak foundations and real estate practitioners should not build extensive value indications based only on cap rates. We all know how difficult it is to get accurate financial information about operating income and expenses. Why then should we place our confidence in a calculated rate based heavily on such elusive information?

FOURTH, often too few sales are available to provide a proper cross-sectional analysis for particular classes of property. How can a reliable and accurate capitalization rate result? Last year, only three industrial plants with more than 20,000 square feet sold and each was unique. How can anyone assign a cap rate of 10.21 to those events? Two decimal point accuracy from three divergent sales...really!

FIFTH, capitalization rates are not nearly as accurate as internal rates of return. If we are seeking true precision, let's get down to yields and discounted cash flows rather than relying solely on cap rates. Several years' cash flow should be the basis for comparing properties where investors are concerned.

Now back to cap reality. It is a valuable tool, but only one of many. I have three suggestions:

FIRST, when providing indications of value, concentrate on a range of values rather than a specific one, unless extensive data can support our cap rate. Commercial properties are highly diversified both in function, structure and appearance. Make certain the client understands that selling price is driven by professional service, complete and accurate presentation of the property, selection of the right target audience(s) and proper exposure in the marketplace.

SECOND, when analyzing data for cap rates, make certain that you are not building your mathematical precision on too few or too diversified property sales. A solid cap rate is built on many sales. Further, it is always in flux, requiring constant research attention. More important, make certain that sales being used are truly at arms' length and that financial information leading to net operating incomes (NOIs) meets accepted criteria for reconstructed worksheets.

THIRD, when establishing values, remember that the cap rate provides only one indication of value. The cost approach and direct comparison approach must also be considered. Together, they provide the necessary perspective to arrive at an informed decision about an estimate of value. Even then, a range of values may be the best approach with the seller.

In conclusion, capitalization rates are an integral part of commercial analysis and can be very effective. Simply treat them with respect. Thank you.

SUMMARY

This concludes Section 4 containing four chapters devoted to appraisal procedures and application of the direct comparison, cost and income approaches to value. Significant emphasis is placed on this subject given the focal role of values in the marketplace. Practitioners are cautioned that advanced courses and experience are essential in arriving at value estimates and that buyers and sellers should consult appropriate professionals regarding such matters.

	ADVANTAGES	DISADVANTAGES
THE COST APPROACH	• People understand it. • Often the only method to use in the appraisal of special-purpose properties. • Relatively easy to make a cost calculation.	• Difficult to estimate depreciation, particularly in older buildings. • While the cost of construction appears relatively easy to estimate, no exact cost figure can be given as several methods yield varying costs. • Construction costs are constantly changing.
THE INCOME APPROACH	• Applicable in estimating the value of investment properties by means of cash flow analysis.	• Difficulty in selecting an appropriate capitalization for direct capitalization (or a discount rate in the case of yield capitalization). • Estimating income and operating expenses can sometimes prove difficult, and a slight error in either estimate is magnified on capitalization. • Of limited use in the appraisal of owner-occupied and/or special-purpose properties.
THE DIRECT COMPARISON APPROACH	• Consumers generally understand and use it. • Avoids various problems associated with estimating and forecasting; e.g., building costs, depreciation, revenues, expenses and cash flows. • Generally accepted by courts and the general public.	• Sometimes difficult to obtain good comparable sales. • Making adjustments for differences in properties requires careful judgement and experience. In some instances, such adjustments are often difficult to support and explain satisfactorily. • Difficult to obtain relevant information relating to each sale, particularly with reference to seller or buyer motivation. • The data is historical in nature.

KNOWLEDGE INTEGRATION

Notables

- The income approach is based on the theory that the value of an investment property is the present worth of the future benefits (i.e., income) which the property is capable of producing.

- The income approach involves capitalizing the net income of the property, by an appropriate rate, into an indication of value.

- An appraiser must reconstruct actual operating statements to properly reflect typical income and expenses.

- Important exclusions apply when reconstructing an operating statement such as business taxes, depreciation, interest of mortgages and capital improvements.

- Potential gross (rental) income is based on market rent, not actual rent. Caution is advised as legislative provisions of the *Residential Tenancies Act* impact rent that can be charged for residential rental premises.

- Net operating income (NOI) represents the net income after deducting expenses from gross operating income.

- The capitalization rate formula can be used in several ways to estimate value, net operating income or capitalization rate.

- Certain uncertainties and limitations underlie capitalization rates.

- Small changes in capitalization rates can result in substantial differences in value.

Glossary

Direct Capitalization

Effective Gross Income

Income Approach

Net Operating Income

Potential Gross (Rental) Income

Reconstructed Operating Statement

Yield Capitalization

Strategic Thinking For Your Career

Questions are included to assist in developing your new career. No answers are provided.

1. What expertise does my intended employing brokerage have in regard to using the income approach to valuation?

2. What information is available in the local marketplace regarding capitalization rates used in valuing commercial property?

3. What career opportunities are there in the local marketplace that involve valuation of income-producing properties?

4. What are the range of current market rents for various types of residential and commercial income-producing properties in my local marketplace?

Chapter Mini-Review

Solutions are located in the Appendix.

1. The appraisal procedure for the income approach consists of five steps.

   ○ True   ○ False

2. Direct capitalization involves the determination of operating cash flows for a specified holding period plus the reversionary value at point of sale.

   ○ True   ○ False

3. An appraiser, when reviewing the owner's operating statements, must stabilize expenses on an annual basis for purposes of a reconstructed operating statement.

   ○ True   ○ False

4. Business tax should be included as an operating expense within a reconstructed operating statement.

   ○ True   ○ False

5. If a free suite is provided to a superintendent or a janitor, market rent for that unit must be included in potential gross (rental) income.

   ○ True   ○ False

6. A deduction for vacancy and credit losses must apply both to potential gross (rental) income and to other income.

   ○ True   ○ False

7. If the effective gross income is $489,092, the gross operating expenses are $397,000 and the capitalization rate is 9.27%, the estimate of value calculation is $993,441.

   ○ True   ○ False

8. When estimating the potential gross (rental) income of a commercial property, the appraiser should use actual rent, not market rent.

   ○ True   ○ False

9. A relatively small upward or downward movement (e.g., 1%) in the cap rate can have a significant impact on the estimate of value.

   ○ True   ○ False

10. A disadvantage of the income approach is the difficulty of selecting an appropriate capitalization rate.

    ○ True   ○ False

11. The income approach is best suited to income-producing properties that are owner occupied.

    ○ True   ○ False

12. Gross operating expense is subtracted from effective gross income to arrive at net operating income.

    ○ True   ○ False

Active Learning Exercises

Solutions are located in the Appendix.

■ Exercise 1   Cap Rate: Thirty-Unit Apartment Building

Broker/Owner Johnson, of ABC Realty Inc., is undertaking an appraisal involving a 30-unit apartment building. He has asked for your assistance in determining the cap rate based on comparable sales. Following are six comparable properties that have sold in the past two months. Johnson has provided the sale price and the net operating income (based on reconstructed operating statements) for each.

SALE	SALE PRICE	NET OPERATING INCOME (NOI)	CAPITALIZATION RATE
1	2,100,000	196,300	
2	1,980,000	193,450	
3	1,700,000	164,050	
4	1,863,000	172,550	
5	1,986,000	184,490	
6	2,150,000	183,600	

1.1   In the space provided above, calculate the capitalization rate for all six properties. Cap rates are typically rounded to two decimal places for course discussion purposes.

1.2   If Sales #1 and #4 were most comparable, what capitalization rate would you select and why?

1.3   If the subject property has a net operating income of $187,000, what is its estimated value? Show all calculations.

■ Exercise 2   Cap Rate Calculations

2.1   Investor McKay owns an industrial property containing several rental units with an effective gross income of $393,000 and operating expenses of $303,500. Based on a capitalization rate of 10.25%, what is the estimated value of this property?

2.2   What capitalization rate is indicated if a property sells for $897,000 and the net operating income is $72,600?

2.3   Investor McKay sets objectives when purchasing industrial property. The property must reflect a cap rate of at least 9.75%. If the effective gross income is $293,000 and the annual expenses are $244,900 for a specific property that contains 12,000 square feet, what is the maximum he would pay per square foot for that property?

2.4   Salesperson Lane, of ABC Realty Inc., is attempting to establish a capitalization rate for commercial retail units less than 2,000 square feet. Fortunately, she has obtained data from seven properties that are reasonably comparable. Calculate the cap rate for each and provide an indicated cap rate as a result of your calculations. Degree of Comparability has three levels: *High* indicates highly comparable, *Medium* indicates selective comparability and *Low* indicates least comparability.

ADDRESS	SALE PRICE	NOI	DEGREE OF COMPARABILITY	CAP RATE
136 West St.	193,500	18,965	High	
210 Westcott St.	186,000	21,050	Low	
13821 Main	189,500	14,861	Low	
336 Perimeter Rd.	202,500	17,500	Medium	
98 Walkers Lane	201,600	19,300	High	
971 River Road	186,000	19,943	Medium	
2 Express Pkwy.	200,600	19,694	High	

2.5   Salesperson Jamieson, of XYZ Real Estate Ltd., has only found three properties that closely compare, given the uniqueness of the building at 138 Industrial Way. The results of his research follow.

ADDRESS	SALE PRICE	NOI	DEGREE OF COMPARABILITY	CAP RATE
298 East Ave.	193,500	24,328	Low	
89 Foundry Road	189,330	21,050	Low	
336 Gateway Park	210,300	20,300	Low	

His dilemma is simple. With three poor comparables, it is difficult to establish an indicated value of the property at 138 Industrial Way based on the income approach. While the 89 Foundry Road property is probably slightly more comparable owing to its similar structure, the problem remains. A range of values is undoubtedly the most appropriate route for Jamieson. Given that the subject property has a net operating income of $22,565 and a total building area of 12,500 square feet, provide an indicated value range (upper and lower values). Calculate total property value and value per square foot, along with an explanation for your decision.

■ Exercise 3   The Retail Store

You have recently joined the ABC Realty Inc. Commercial Division as a salesperson. Yesterday, a potential client called regarding the listing of a small retail store in an older part of Anycity. The owner claims that the NOI is $20,000. As preparation for a marketing proposal, you discover that little current research is available in the brokerage database regarding this type of operation. Fortunately, Salesperson Jamieson comes to the rescue…or does he?

JAMIESON   *I know that old building, it's really run down. The main tenant is a small discount operation, with a small shoe repair business accessed by a side entrance.*

Listen! If you want cap rates; I can help. A couple of guys from the regional government office gave me a bunch of rates. Here they are! Let's see…small building cap at 10.20%. You might want to adjust it upwards a little (to lower the estimated value) given the condition, risk and things like that; let's say to 11.5.

What's the NOI? Okay, let's get the price. Divide $20,000 by .115, there… $173,913 rounded to say $175,000.

That was easy. Good luck.

Critically analyze this conversation identifying potential problem areas when relying on the information provided by Jamieson. Ensure that your answer gives detailed support along with a conclusion about whether you would use this information with your potential client.

▣ Exercise 4   1287 Western Avenue

Salesperson Miller, of ABC Realty Inc., has asked for your assistance in restructuring the income and expenses for 1287 Main Street. This older 24-unit apartment building will be listed for sale and the owner has requested an estimate of its current value prior to listing the property.

INCOME

Investor McKay purchased the building approximately five years ago. The current rent is $234,982. Market rent (average) for all units should be $835.00 per unit per month. Additional income is derived from laundry room charges (estimated at $20.00 per unit per month). Each unit is provided with one free parking space. Eighteen additional parking spaces are rented at $30.00 per month. Vacancy factor and credit losses amount to 4% of potential gross (rental) income, which is deducted prior to adding other income.

OPERATING EXPENSES

Payment Type	Annual Payment
Property Tax	9,300
Water	3,800
Fire Insurance	9,300
Minor Repairs and Maintenance	12,570
Electricity for Common Areas	6,590
Landscaping Contract	5,300
Janitor's Salary	39,800

While Investor McKay manages the building himself, typical management fees for this type of building are 2.5% of the effective gross income.

The following expenses must be annualized:

- Every four years, halls are repainted at a cost of $9,800.
- Every eight years, exterior trim is repainted at a cost of $7,600.
- Once every six years, all suites must be painted and decorated. Three suites cost $2,887.50.
- Every ten years the main lobby is decorated at a cost of $8,700.

SALE	SALE PRICE	NOI	CAP RATE
1	1,496,660	149,870	
2	1,522,600	157,500	
3	1,621,400	164,840	

Determine the market value of the subject property using the format located on the following page. Round calculations to the nearest dollar.

SECTION IV

Potential Gross (Rental) Income

Less: Vacancy and Credit Losses   –

Add: Other Income   +

Effective Gross Income   =

Less: Operating Expenses   –

Net Operating Income   =

Indicated Value by the Income Approach

SECTION V

PROPERTY FINANCING

Financing is a necessity for most buyers given rising real estate prices over the years. Inevitably, salespeople are involved as either an advisor or resource person in the process.

Staying in step with the market is vital. Today's varied mortgage products and financing options offer many consumer choices. Awareness of current rates, approval processes, costs and product features/benefits is essential.

Active professionals must be knowledgeable about mortgagee and mortgagor rights/responsibilities, as well as financing sources, practices and procedures. What is the difference between a legal and an equitable mortgage? How are mortgage priorities established? What legislation impacts mortgages? What financing package best suits the buyer? Does the property meet lender underwriting requirements? Can the seller participate to get a faster sale while still meeting his/her financial objectives? Skilled negotiators are well armed with facts, carefully weigh the alternatives and set strategies in motion that result in successful sales. Don't let the mortgage market pass you by. Discover everything you can. Section 5 prepares prospective registrants for advanced mortgage discussions in the articling course titled *Principles of Mortgage Financing*.

CHAPTER 13

Mortgage Fundamentals

Introduction

A solid understanding of mortgage basics and funding sources is an essential step in building real estate knowledge. Mortgage financing is a critical element in most real estate transactions. Mortgages, from an historical perspective, have gradually evolved over time to provide a better balance between mortgagee and mortgagor. While today's financing procedures are becoming more streamlined through new procedures and innovative online facilities, underlying rights and responsibilities are more complex, particularly when addressing legal rights and mortgagor/mortgagee responsibilities.

Chapter 13 delves into registration priorities and important exceptions to 'time of registration' priority involving encumbrances such as conditional sales liens, judgments and real property taxes. Covenants, rights and privileges are detailed followed by both non-legal and legal remedies available to the mortgagee when the mortgagor is in default. Basics concerning foreclosure, judicial sale, quit claim deed, suing for payment (personal covenant), possession by mortgagee and power of sale are discussed.

The discussion then focuses on the underlying dynamics of the mortgage market and operation of both the primary and secondary (often referred to as the sub-prime) market. A discussion of key mortgage sources and factors relating to conventional and high ratio mortgages conclude this chapter.

Learning Outcomes

At the conclusion of this chapter, students will be able to:

- Describe significant historical developments regarding mortgages.
- Describe and differentiate among the three types of mortgages discussed in this chapter; i.e., legal, equitable and chattel.
- Outline how mortgage priorities are established and discuss important exceptions to *priority by time of registration*.
- Discuss various implied covenants associated with registered mortgages and identify rights of a mortgagee and a mortgagor.
- Identify four typical privileges that may be granted by a mortgagee to a mortgagor.
- Identify and briefly discuss key features of legal remedies for default including foreclosure, judicial sale, quit claim deed, payment (personal covenant), possession and power of sale.
- Describe the operation of the mortgage market including primary and secondary markets.
- Identify and describe primary mortgage sources and briefly highlight the role of mortgage brokers in the mortgage funding process.
- Identify the provinces legislation impacting mortgages and discuss the five parts of this legislation.
- Differentiate between conventional and high ratio mortgages and briefly discuss the roles of Genworth Financial Canada and Canada Mortgage and Housing Corporation in relation to high ratio financing.

MORTGAGE—BACKGROUND

A mortgage is a claim or encumbrance upon the real property given by the owner of the property to the lender as security for money borrowed and typically registered in the land registry office.

The two parties to a mortgage transaction are referred to as the **mortgagor** (borrower) and the **mortgagee** (lender). The lender *gives* or lends the money and registers the mortgage against the property. In return, the borrower gives the mortgage as security for the loan, receives the funds, makes the required payments and maintains possession of the property. The borrower has a right to have the mortgage discharged from the title once the debt is paid off.

> **Mortgagor**
>
> The one who gives the mortgage; i.e., the borrower or debtor.

> **Mortgagee**
>
> The one to whom property is given as security for the payment of a mortgage debt; i.e., the lender or creditor.

Historical Perspective

In Medieval England, borrowed funds were traditionally secured by the lender taking physical possession of the property. The property reverted back to the original owner on a specified date, assuming the loan was paid with interest. Otherwise, the property was lost forever due to lack of payments on agreed dates. No court action was required, as the property was already in the mortgagee's possession.

Over the years, the intent underlying a mortgage changed. The borrower came to retain possession of the land, but pledged it to the lender as security. If a default occurred, the mortgagee could obtain a court order for eviction purposes. The position of the common law courts was straightforward: *pay on time or lose your land.* No consideration was given if the default occurred by just a single day or that the land lost was considerably more valuable than the debt owed.

COURTS OF EQUITY

The Courts of Equity radically transformed the nature of mortgages. In the late Middle Ages, the King appointed Courts of Equity to remedy wrongs that had taken place with the Courts of Law. In the fifteenth century, this function was taken over by the Chancellor of England and the Court of Chancery. This Court's primary function was to alleviate harshness of common law that had arisen since medieval times.

Initially, intervention occurred in only the most outrageous cases. As time passed, the Court of Chancery took a more aggressive role. By the reign of Elizabeth I, the Court was readily giving a mortgagor, who had lost land, an additional opportunity to redeem the property by paying the mortgage debt. This right ultimately formed the modern day concept of equity of redemption.

EQUITY OF REDEMPTION

> **Equity of Redemption**
>
> The right of the mortgagor to reclaim clear title to the property upon full repayment of the debt.

By the sixteenth century, the **equity of redemption** was officially recognized as a legal estate in land with the owner having an equitable position in the property. Equity effectively brought the mortgage concept full circle. The mortgagor's rights shifted from virtually no rights to possession and even property redemption after default.

RULES OF EQUITY

In 1881, the Ontario Courts of Law merged the concept of common law and equity. The principles of equity, therefore, lie within all mortgage documentation. In fact, the *Judicature Act* which merged the two legal perspectives is quite specific regarding equity. When a conflict arises between the rules of law and the rules of equity, the rules of equity shall always prevail.

CHARGE VS. MORTGAGE

With the passage of the *Land Registration Reform Act, 1984*, a mortgage registered in the land registry system is now referred to as a **charge**. Under a charge, no transfer of title occurs. The charge identifies a debt against the chargor's (mortgagor's) property. The chargor has the same rights and remedies as a mortgagor for purposes of the *Mortgages Act* including power of sale and foreclosure actions. Rights for the chargee (mortgagee) have also remained unchanged. The term *mortgage* and associated terminology is used throughout this text, given its wide, continued use in the marketplace.

> **Charge**
>
> The name given to a mortgage document when title is registered under the *Land Titles Act*.

Types of Mortgages

LEGAL MORTGAGE

The **legal mortgage** in land registry historically transferred the estate or interest in land or other property for securing the repayment of debt. Since the legal title can only be transferred once by the current owner (mortgagor) to a mortgagee, it follows that only the first mortgage can hold this distinct status. A legal mortgage is therefore a document in which the direct conveyance of title is involved subject to the repayment of a debt.

NOTE The legal mortgage is also sometimes referred to as the senior mortgage, as distinct from junior (equitable) mortgage.

EQUITABLE MORTGAGE

The most common form of **equitable mortgage** from a real estate perspective is a mortgage of the equity of redemption. If an owner mortgages a property, he/she retains the right to the equity of redemption. This right, as an *interest* or *estate*, can be dealt with as any other interest. More importantly, this interest can be transferred to a mortgagee in return for funds. The subsequent mortgage gives way to a further equity of redemption that can again be mortgaged, and so on.

> **Equitable Mortgage**
>
> An historical term differentiating a mortgage against equity from a legal mortgage against title.

Equitable mortgages are sometimes used when a mortgagor requires additional funding but does not want to disturb the existing legal (first) mortgage or the mortgagee does not want added risk by increasing the first mortgage, but is agreeable to another secondary lender assuming that risk. The secondary lender is content with this added risk if he or she feels that the property and mortgagor's covenant are acceptable and usually requires a higher rate of return to offset the increased risk.

Blurred Lines: Legal vs. Equitable   CURIOSITY

In today's mortgage marketplace, the distinction between legal and equitable mortgages is not as distinct given that title no longer transfers upon registration of the legal (charge) mortgage. Instead, most people simply refer to mortgages based upon their order of priority; e.g., first mortgage, second mortgage and so forth.

Legally, numerous successive equitable mortgages can exist on the same property with the owner retaining a final equity of redemption to the last mortgage given. From a practical perspective, the giving of equitable mortgages will ultimately be limited by the amount of equity available to mortgage.

If the first mortgage is a legal mortgage, the second is against the equity. The second mortgagee, therefore, has a desire to see his/her interest protected. Two rights associated with this subsequent mortgage holder are addressed under *Priority* below.

CHATTEL MORTGAGE

A **chattel mortgage** is given on moveable possessions (e.g., vehicles, boats and trailers) or personal property (e.g., appliances, televisions and stereos) that may be removed without injury to the freehold estate. The chattel mortgage is one of three common methods of taking security on moveable possessions, the other two being a conditional sales contract or a lease with an option to purchase (e.g., photocopiers and computers). In Ontario, the *Personal Property Security Act* governs methods of taking security and establishes priority by means of a system of registration of security interests.

PRIORITY

As a general rule, **mortgage priority** is determined by time of registration under the *Registry Act* or the *Land Titles Act*. The standard form (Charge/Mortgage of Land) is used for mortgage registration. Additional provisions are included by way of standard charge terms, which are also filed in the land registry office. A mortgage is discharged by registering a Discharge of Charge/Mortgage. See *Chapter 3: Land Registry and Title Registration* to review contents of the Charge/Mortgage of Land, standard charge terms and registration practices/procedures.

Subsequent Encumbrances

In a typical mortgage situation, the holder of the first mortgage has first position with subsequent (equitable) mortgages having priority positions that would be ranked second, third and so forth. Accordingly, subsequent mortgagees have an interest in ensuring that their positions are protected. These mortgages are referred to as subsequent encumbrances. Two basic rights are associated with subsequent encumbrances:

Right To Prevent Default	Right To Be Notified
The best illustration of this right is explained using an example of a property with two mortgages. Should the mortgagor fail to make payments, insure the property, pay taxes or maintain the property, the second mortgagee may make such payments to stave off action by the first mortgagee. If such payments are required, then the second mortgagee merely adds these amounts to the debt of the second mortgage. Action can then be taken on the initial amount advanced, as well as all overdue payments and expenses.	If a mortgagee takes foreclosure action, he/she must sue not only the mortgagor, but all subsequent encumbrances to successfully foreclose all equities. The subsequent encumbrances are made aware of the action and given the opportunity to protect their respective interests. If the mortgagee proposes to sell under power of sale, all subsequent encumbrances must also be notified.

Priority Exceptions

While priority of registration generally prevails, many encumbrances can have legitimate claims that disrupt this principle. Interestingly, certain encumbrances can have legitimate claims and priority even though no registration of such claims has taken place in the applicable land registration office. Real estate practitioners should understand the range of such encumbrances that might affect title and their relative significance. However, issues concerning exact title priority can be complex and go beyond the scope of this text. Expert advice is required on all such matters.

NOTE   Seven encumbrances are listed in alphabetical order and do not in any way represent the priority of these encumbrances in relation to a registered mortgage. Such priority is largely dictated by circumstances.

COMMON EXPENSES (CONDOMINIUM)

A lien registered against title of a unit by a condominium corporation for the non-payment of common expenses takes priority over all other registered and unregistered encumbrances, with certain exceptions; e.g., taxes, a claim of the Crown (other than by way of mortgage) and a lien or claim that is prescribed.

CONDITIONAL SALES LIENS

Conditional sales liens (e.g., liens against a hot water tank or furnace), if registered on title, protect the seller from losing his/her security. Regardless of whether the registration takes place before or after the registration of a mortgage, the seller retains the right, in case of non-payment, to remove the chattel. Security is not on the land but on the chattel. The mortgagee does not receive priority provided that the lien is registered before the mortgagee forecloses.

CONSTRUCTION LIENS

The *Construction Lien Act* permits the registration of a lien by any person involved in effecting improvements to the value of a property. Wage earners, workers, material contractors and sub-trades involved in such work have lien rights. These rights have not been substantially altered from the older *Mechanics' Lien Act*, which preceded this legislation. A lien claimant can only register a claim for the value of services and/or materials supplied.

The Act provides for two types of liens: individual and general. An individual lien applies to persons providing services or materials when an owner enters into a single contract for improvements concerning one premise. A general lien applies when the work is conducted in several premises under one general contract and associated subcontracts.

The priority of construction liens is complex. As a general guideline, construction liens normally have priority over advances made under a mortgage. For example, a mortgagee may advance predetermined percentages of the total mortgage amount at specific points during new construction. However, such liens are not commonly encountered in the marketplace given the fact that holdbacks are legislated under the *Construction Lien Act*. The Act provides for two different types of holdbacks: basic and finishing.

The concept of holdbacks is important to real estate practitioners involved with new homes or renovations concerning existing homes. The Act requires that a basic holdback of 10% of the price of all services/materials provided under contract or a subcontract be withheld by the owner. This amount is retained until the time frame for all liens that can be claimed under the Act has expired. A similar finishing holdback applies following the date of substantial completion. In advancing funds under construction mortgages (e.g., the building of a new home) the mortgagee will typically withhold 10% of amounts advanced to ensure that all contractors and suppliers have been paid and the time limit for liens has expired.

JUDGMENTS

Judgments against the owner of land are encumbrances on that land and, under default, the property could be sold to satisfy these judgments. The mortgagee's lawyer always searches for judgment executions before registering a mortgage, as an existing judgment may have priority over the mortgage. Judgment executions against the mortgagor, which arise after mortgage registration, do not have priority over the mortgage.

LEASES

Generally, a lease that is entered into prior to the registration of a mortgage has priority over that mortgage. In other words, the mortgagee cannot alter the terms or the possession of the property given the tenant's leasehold interest. Upon mortgagor default, the mortgagee may take steps to be the mortgagee in possession and would in effect become the landlord for purposes of the landlord/tenant relationship. If a lease is granted subsequent to the registration of a mortgage, the relationship between the tenant and the mortgagee is altered.

Usually, a mortgagee is not bound by a lease that is entered into after a mortgage has been registered on the property. Notwithstanding that statement, two factors must also be considered. First, the lease may contain a clause that might in some way alter this arrangement; e.g., a non-disturbance clause (assuming mortgagee approval) in which the tenant's rights are respected even if default occurred . Secondly, the property may be residential and fall under special provisions under the *Mortgages Act*.

REAL PROPERTY TAXES

Property taxes *always* take priority over mortgages on title, even if the property is assessed subsequent to the registration of a mortgage.

OTHER ENCUMBRANCES

A range of other liens and encumbrances go beyond the scope of this text. Legal disputes as to the precise order of priority involving several encumbrances can be complex and only resolved through judicial process.

COVENANTS, RIGHTS AND PRIVILEGES

A mortgagor makes various promises (i.e., covenants) under the mortgage document. These are spelled out in standard charge terms or statutorily set out in provincial legislation. The *Mortgages Act* historically provided for implied covenants in mortgages.

However, the *Land Registration Reform Act* (LRRA) superceded these with three **implied covenants** for mortgages registered after April 1, 1985—the date on which all Ontario lands were included under Part 1 of the LRRA. Accordingly, a prescribed form (Charge/Mortgage of Land) was required for mortgage registration within a land registry office. The following has been reprinted from a previous chapter. For complete details, see *Chapter 3: Land Registry and Title Registration*.

Implied Covenants

Obligations of a mortgagor as set out in the *Land Registration Reform Act,* which apply to a Charge/Mortgage of Land registered in land titles or registry.

First Implied Covenant Often referred to as the *usual covenants*.	• Mortgagor will make payments including interest and also pay taxes. • Mortgagor has the legal right to give the mortgage. • Mortgagor will provide insurance on the buildings. • Mortgagor has no other encumbrances other than those registered on the specific property. • Mortgagee, when the mortgagor is in default, has the right to take possession, collect rents from tenants and sell the land. • Mortgagee in possession by default shall be granted quiet possession. • Upon default, total monies owing shall become due and payable. • Interest in arrears may be collected. • Mortgagor in default agrees to do such things as reasonably requested by the mortgagee in possession relating to the land.
Second Implied Covenant	• The mortgagor covenants that the land held in fee simple is owned with good title.
Third Implied Covenant	• The mortgagor covenants that the lease, in the case of leasehold property, is valid and up-to-date, and that reimbursement to the mortgagee will be made by the mortgagor for non-payment or non-performance of other covenants under the lease.

Practitioners should note that certain commonly-found provisions are not included in the three covenants; e.g., the mortgagor's obligation to maintain the property in good repair. The wording might also allow the chargee (mortgagee) to enter the lands, make an inspection, carry out such repairs if necessary and add reasonable costs associated with the repairs to the principal amount. Other covenants found in mortgages could include a promise to pay the property taxes or ensure the improvements to their full insurable value. Covenants and wordings will vary.

Additional mortgage terms can be added either by way of inserting the details in the Charge/Mortgage of Land or attaching a schedule to that form.

Mortgagee Rights

Rights of a mortgagee can be generally grouped under two headings:

RIGHT TO ASSIGN THE MORTGAGE

The mortgage, as an interest in land, can be sold, transferred or assigned without the consent of the mortgagor. The mortgagor must be notified of the assignment. The assignee acquires the rights of the mortgagee. This individual acquires only the rights that the mortgagee had and no agreement between the mortgagee and the assignee changes any right that the mortgagor already has, or imposes any additional burden on the mortgagor. In some instances, the new assignee may require an indemnification agreement from the mortgagee in the event that the mortgagor defaults.

The assignee takes the mortgage subject to the state of accounts between the mortgagee and mortgagor. If an additional payment off the principal had been made, of which the assignee was unaware, the assignee would have no claim against the mortgagor. If after notification, the mortgagor continues to pay the original mortgagee, the assignee can take legal action against the mortgagor to collect the money.

EXAMPLE   *Mortgage Assignment*

Investor Thompson holds a mortgage on the property owned by Jones. Thompson assigns the mortgage as of February 1, 20xx to XYZ Investment Ltd. and notifies Jones:

Amount of mortgage	$175,512 (as at February 1, 20xx)
Mortgage payment date	15th of each month

Thompson's interest as a mortgagee of $175,512 is transferred to XYZ. Jones' February payment is apportioned using the February 1 date. All future payments should be made to XYZ. Jones is liable to XYZ following that date if payments are inadvertently forwarded to Thompson.

RIGHT TO BE PAID

The mortgagee also has the right to be paid the principal sum advanced and interest thereon based on arrangements spelled out in the mortgage document. Failure on the part of the mortgagor to pay on those terms, to fulfill covenants or to observe the provisions of the mortgage will give rise to a number of remedies that can be exercised by the mortgagee including power of sale and foreclosure. If all covenants are fulfilled, a discharge is provided to the mortgagor.

Mortgagor Rights

Mortgagor rights are grouped under three headings.

RIGHT TO QUIET POSSESSION

The mortgagor has the right to quiet uninterrupted possession when not in default. He/she has the right to use the property and is not responsible to the mortgagee for ordinary wear and tear on the structures, but must exercise reasonable care and maintain the property.

RIGHT TO REDEEM THE PROPERTY FREE OF THE MORTGAGE

The mortgagor retains the right to sell or mortgage his/her interest, and to deal with it in the same manner as any interest in property. This right is extremely important. Any provision inserted in the mortgage document that attempts to prevent the mortgagor from exercising this right will be struck down as invalid. For example, if a mortgage contained a provision that the mortgagee had an option to purchase the property, it would be invalidated, as the mortgagor must never be prevented from redeeming the property free of the debt.

RIGHT TO DISCHARGE THE MORTGAGE

When the loan is paid off, the mortgagor obtains a discharge signed by the mortgagee. The discharge fee is normally paid by the mortgagor. If a discharge cannot be obtained, the provincial statute relating to mortgages typically provides for the mortgagor to make application through the courts to obtain a court order based on supporting evidence.

EXAMPLE   *Mortgage Discharge*

Smith, when purchasing his property five years ago, obtained a new first mortgage for $154,500, 25-year amortization and paid a monthly PIT amount of $1386.94. At the end of the term, Smith was able to discharge the mortgage. The lender, based on the 60-month payment schedule, informed Smith that the payout figure was $147,887.41. Nominal discharge fees applied. At the end of the term, Smith remitted the full payout to the mortgagee and obtained a discharge that was registered in the land registration office.

Privileges

In addition to rights, mortgagors may have certain privileges granted by the mortgagee. Currently, the marketplace abounds with numerous variations, particularly concerning prepayment. Most privileges can be grouped under four main categories:

PREPAYMENT PRIVILEGE

Prepayment is not a right under the mortgage document, but a privilege. Unless otherwise specified, the mortgagor has agreed to make payments according to a specified schedule and the contract is written to run for a specified period. No additional payments (i.e., prepayments) are permitted unless provided for in the mortgage document.

RENEWAL PRIVILEGE

Some mortgages have a built-in renewal privilege. However, this is an exception to the general rule. Most Canadian mortgages do not specifically spell out the opportunity to renew and, consequently, this opportunity does not exist. Normally, lenders prefer to reserve the right to renew based on financial circumstances of the borrower at the end of the mortgage term.

TRANSFER PRIVILEGE

The ability to transfer a mortgage again depends on the wording of the mortgage document. Generally, three different approaches exist in the Canadian mortgage marketplace:

- The mortgagor may be able to transfer without the consent of the mortgagee, but he/she may remain liable through the personal covenant.
- The mortgagee may insert sale/approval clauses requiring approval of any person who will be assuming the mortgage at the point of property sale.
- The mortgagee may insist on non-transferability; e.g., in the instance where a borrower has mortgaged his/her property with a lender as security for business loans, or in the case of a credit union who mortgaged a member's property and does not wish to continue financing the property after the member sells.

POSTPONEMENT PRIVILEGE

An existing mortgagee, if provided with a reasonable degree of security, may agree to postpone the priority of his/her mortgage in favour of a prior mortgage being replaced or another mortgage being created.

DEFAULT

Default is defined as a failure to fulfill a promise or obligation. A mortgagor would be in default if he/she failed to satisfy any of the covenants in the mortgage. However, most defaults specifically arise from failure to make the mortgage payments. When in default, the mortgagee will often rely on an acceleration clause in the mortgage document in which the full mortgage amount becomes due and payable upon default.

When default does occur, it is uncommon for the mortgagee to seek legal action immediately. The mortgagee will normally weigh practical considerations and attempt to remedy the situation through personal contact with the mortgagor. Normally, once these personal negotiations have broken down, the mortgagee will seek legal action.

In such instances, when the default situation has become untenable and all practical alternatives have been explored, a mortgagee will normally seek professional counselling, as a variety of possible remedies are available to him or her. Some remedies require court action, while others are authorized by the mortgage agreement. That said, it is important to emphasize that the mortgagee is under no requirement to seek non-legal remedies and may pursue legal action immediately. Specifically, the mortgagee has legal rights that can be involved in accordance with the *Mortgages Act.*

As a further qualifier, legal remedies are available assuming that the mortgagee has direct control over the loan and can act at will to enforce the document. If Canada Mortgage and Housing Corporation insures the loan, procedures must be in accordance with that organization. Insured loans are discussed more fully in the next chapter.

Non-Legal Remedies

The failure to fulfill obligations under a mortgage is often addressed by non-legal means. As mentioned, while the most common form of default is failure to make payments as specified in the mortgage document, the default can relate to other obligations under the mortgage; e.g., payment of taxes or common element expenses in a condominium.

Often practical considerations are the driving force behind non-legal remedies. An attempt is made to remedy the situation through correspondence and/or personal contact with the mortgagor, given certain practical realities. For most mortgagees (particularly larger lenders) the advantages of immediate direct negotiations are evident.

A wide range of non-legal actions can be taken to remedy default. Creativity in this regard rests solely with individual lenders; e.g., restructuring loan payments and extended amortization.

LACK OF EXPERTISE/SYSTEMS	*COST*	*ALTERNATIVE SOLUTIONS*
The lender is primarily motivated by advancing funds and obtaining a return. Often, lending institutions lack the personnel and default management systems to oversee income-producing properties; e.g., rent collection, tenant administration and property maintenance. Simply put, lenders would prefer that the property be maintained by the owner with suitable arrangements made to resolve any default issues.	Legal disputes can be costly and legal action can result in adverse publicity, thereby affecting the public image of the lender.	Problems with payments may be indicative of other financial difficulties that may be addressed by creative financial alternatives.

Legal Remedies

The failure to fulfill obligations under a mortgage can lead to selected legal remedies. Mortgagees typically proceed with legal action for default by mortgagors as a last resort. Six courses of action are available against a mortgagor in the Ontario marketplace, assuming that the mortgagee has direct control over the loan and can proceed to enforce the mortgage document:

- foreclosure;
- judicial sale;
- quit claim deed;
- payment (personal covenant);
- possession (by mortgagee); and/or
- power of sale.

The use of these remedies can indirectly involve real estate practitioners. Salespersons and brokers may be called upon to sell property on behalf of a mortgagee or be otherwise involved with property in default.

EXAMPLE   *Legal Remedy—The Smith Property*

Owner Smith is in default on a mortgage held by Investor Thompson. Following all reasonable attempts to settle the matter, Thompson elects to proceed with power of sale (contractual) as Smith is planning to vacate the property. Because the mortgagor has been in default well over the minimum 15-day period, the notice of default and the intention to sell is given to Smith and all subsequent encumbrances through Thompson's lawyer.

The notice gives Smith and/or other subsequent encumbrances 35 days to pay the mortgage. After 35 days, Thompson may sell the property privately, by auction or through a brokerage. Upon completion of the sale, Thompson is entitled to take whatever money is owing plus costs. Any excess goes to the next encumbrance in priority.

To use this remedy, Thompson must already have possession either by court order or by taking possession after Smith vacates the property. In fact, it is common to sue only for possession, get judgment, evict the mortgagor and then sell under the power of sale clause. Thompson's lawyer advises that a buyer purchasing the property under such circumstances will receive a deed in which all the steps of the power of sale are set out. Also, an affidavit of service of the notice to sell is registered on title. The new buyer then has good title, without a court order.

Seek Professional Guidance   CAUTION

This legal perspective on mortgages is summary in nature. Students seeking additional information, particularly concerning default procedures, should enroll in advanced mortgage courses. The articling course titled *Principles of Mortgage Financing* is recommended as a first step in further education for those wishing to find out more about mortgages. Salespersons and brokers in the marketplace should direct buyers and sellers to appropriate expertise in all such matters.

LEGAL REMEDY QUICK REFERENCE

FORECLOSURE

A remedial court action taken by a mortgagee, when default occurs on a mortgage, to cause forfeiture of the equity of redemption of the mortgagor and also subsequent encumbrancers' equities of redemption.

Foreclosure, in effect, places a specific time limit within which the mortgagor can redeem, failing which the mortgagee forecloses on the mortgagor's equity of redemption, that is, the equitable right to redeem and *the mortgagor forfeits any equity that he or she may have in the property*.

The right to foreclose arises only when repayment of the entire mortgage debt becomes due.

The process of foreclosure is governed by procedures set out in the Rules of Civil Procedure and can be expensive, time-consuming and subject to a number of requirements.

JUDICIAL SALE

Legal remedy involving the disposition of mortgaged property by court action. A mortgagee facing a default by a mortgagor may elect a judicial sale by the court with the proceeds applied to the mortgage debt.

If a deficiency occurs, the mortgagee can obtain judgment against the mortgagor under the personal covenant. This remedy is infrequently used as a judicial sale may net less than a private sale, given the mechanics of the process and the fact that it is frequently accomplished through an auction rather than marketing through a brokerage.

Judicial involvement provides a measure of objectivity, thereby shielding the mortgagee from criticisms and/or legal action by the mortgagor; e.g., improprieties concerning the disposition of property.

The proceeds of the sale are typically paid into court with funds applied to amounts owed to encumbrances according to priority. Any surplus would be awarded to the mortgagor.

QUIT CLAIM DEED

A legal document wherein a person agrees to release any right that he/she may possess in a parcel of land. In a mortgage, the quit claim deed would involve the mortgagor's release of his or her equity of redemption.

A quit claim deed can be an expedient, inexpensive process when mortgagee and mortgagor arrive at the conclusion that no practical way exists by which the mortgagor can keep the property.

If equity exists, the mortgagor could potentially bargain with the mortgagee for a payment to satisfy equity in return for giving the quit claim deed.

Important: The mortgagee, in accepting a quit claim deed, not only acquires rights concerning the property but also any problems associated with it and has no further recourse against the mortgagor.

PAYMENT (PERSONAL COVENANT)

The property serves as the basis for security of the mortgagor, however, the fundamental relationship between mortgagor and mortgagee is one of debtor and creditor. This relationship involves a covenant to pay and, consequently, any remedy available to an ordinary creditor is also available to the mortgagee.

The personal covenant is much like a personal commitment on a promissory note. The mortgagee is perfectly within his/her legal rights to sue for payment based on the strength of that personal covenant.

A suit for payment is normally combined with other concurrent remedies; e.g., the mortgagee sues not only for the personal covenant, but also for possession and foreclosure.

The *Mortgages Act* provides that the mortgagee can sue either the original mortgagor or the person who has been assigned the equity of redemption; e.g., the new purchaser who acquired the property from the original mortgagor. However, action can only be taken against one person by the mortgagee.

One important qualification should be noted. A personal covenant of a builder under a building mortgage, who assigns the mortgage to the purchaser of the new home, expires after one year.

POSSESSION BY MORTGAGEE

The actual holding and legal occupancy of a property by a mortgagee due to default by the mortgagor, typically undertaken coincident with some other action; e.g., foreclosure.

The action is taken against the mortgagor and anyone else occupying the property; e.g., a tenant. The tenancy must be respected by the mortgagee, however, the precise manner in which the tenant is dealt with will depend on such matters as when the tenancy agreement was completed in relation to the mortgage and whether the property is residential or otherwise.

The *Mortgages Act* sets out various requirements and limitations in regard to possession by the mortgagee. For example, the mortgagee can take on certain responsibilities for its upkeep and collect rents.

The mortgagee may also hire agents to carry out the maintenance and upkeep of the property, but must be careful not to incur expenses that are not directly linked to such maintenance and general good standing of the property.

SECTION V   PROPERTY FINANCING

LEGAL REMEDY QUICK REFERENCE

POWER OF SALE

The legal right of the mortgagee to force the sale of a property without judicial proceedings should default occur. Power of sale is the most frequently used method by which a mortgagee remedies a default by a mortgagor.

The power of sale can often be the fairest, most inexpensive method to deal with an unpleasant financial circumstance, as it allows the mortgagee to retrieve only what he/she is entitled to and no more. If a surplus occurs, then the owner/mortgagor will benefit.

The mortgagee, when marketing property under power of sale, must ensure that the property is actively promoted to the public in order to obtain fair market value. Although no statutory requirement exists for a formal appraisal, a prudent mortgagee will attempt to avoid the possibility of litigation by obtaining at least two appraisals.

The *Mortgages Act* contemplates two approaches to a power of sale with somewhat differing procedures. If a mortgage contains a power of sale provision, then a power of sale proceeding is governed by Part III of the *Mortgages Act* and is commonly referred to as a contractual power of sale. Statutory power of sale arises if no power of sale provision is contained in the mortgage document.

MORTGAGE FUNDING

The **mortgage market** is one of many components making up the Canadian capital market. The **capital market** is a trading forum in which savers (those accumulating wealth) and borrowers (those needing the use of such wealth) meet to arrange financial transactions.

Savers scrutinize investment options, as many competing investments operate in the capital market. While some direct trading occurs between savers and borrowers, most take place through interim agents; e.g., banking institutions. Capital markets are commonly associated with longer term investments; i.e., one year's duration or more. Shorter term borrowing is typically associated with the **money market**.

Primary and Secondary Markets

Mortgage markets consist of two segments:

- **Primary Market**   New loans for property financing, new construction and rehabilitation of existing structures.

- **Secondary Market**   Existing mortgage instruments are traded based on future cash flows; e.g., sale of a mortgage portfolio by a primary lender to an investment company or pension fund.

> *Money Market*
>
> A sector of the financial market dealing with short-term investments (usually one year or less), as distinct from longer term investments in the capital market.

PRIMARY MARKET (PRIME AND SUB-PRIME BORROWERS)

The primary market is most relevant to practitioners, as its dynamics largely determine mortgage funding costs and availability. This market relies on the free interplay of borrower and saver in the search for, and provision of, funds for property financing, new construction and renovations. Typically, strength in the primary market parallels strong performance in either or both the residential housing and the commercial/industrial markets.

The primary market consists of both prime and sub-prime markets. Prime markets are focused on borrowers who have A or A+ credit (i.e., high credit scores and no credit problems). Further, properties must meet acceptable standards concerning construction, finishes and location. Sub-prime markets involve lenders who entertain higher risk levels involving borrowers with B and C level credit (ranging from marginal credit scores and delinquency problems to discharged bankrupts and no credit ratings).

SECONDARY MARKET

The secondary market involves trading of existing mortgages. Primary market lenders sell mortgage portfolios to investment companies or pension funds in this market. Of particular note is the expanding secondary market involving securitization. Mortgages are pooled and converted into securities that can be purchased in pre-set dollar amounts; e.g., $5,000 per unit.

National Housing Act mortgage-backed securities have proven particularly attractive given guarantees both for the full principal amount in the event of default on the entire mortgage, as well as timely payment guarantees should mortgagors fall behind in individual mortgage payments.

Market Growth

The Canadian mortgage market has grown dramatically over the past decades. Federal legislation liberalizing mortgage policies has been a major factor. Easing of restrictions and increased lending limits positively impacted economic growth, capital availability and expansion of residential and commercial mortgage markets.

Today's mortgage policies have also opened the doors to more lender competition in products and rate offerings. However, a trend to shorter mortgage terms has generated concern. Increased consumer reliance on higher debt levels is now compounded by the need for borrowers to continuously return to the capital market for renewals and refinancing. Canadians are consequently more vulnerable to market swings. Any dramatic move in interest rates could have far-reaching consequences.

Interest Rates

Interest rates are largely determined by supply and demand forces, but other factors intervene. In the simplest scenario, when demand increases and supply remains constant, rates will rise. Abundant supply generally lowers rates, assuming all other factors remain constant.

However, savers are not restricted to a single market and may be swayed by other investment options including commodities, term deposits, business ventures, government securities, foreign currencies and bond issues.

An outflow from the mortgage market occurs when other options prove more attractive. A corresponding rise in mortgage rates is required to increase market appeal.

Many other variables are also at work. The government exerts tremendous influence on mortgage rates. The Bank of Canada, for example, can impact mortgage markets when setting monetary policies, controlling money availability and setting prime interest rates.

Traditionally, mortgage rates have been higher than other investments such as bonds and guaranteed investment certificates. The premium rates associated with mortgages reflects relative inflexibility associated with long term financing, inability to readily convert such investments to cash and legal expenses should default occur. Further, savers have come to expect not only higher general rates, but also added risk premiums given property specifics and borrower covenants.

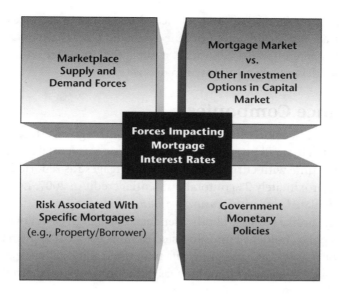

MORTGAGE SOURCES

The Canadian mortgage market relies on both regulated and unregulated capital sources to fund residential and commercial mortgages. Most mortgage transactions involve large regulated lending institutions acting as intermediaries for individual, corporate and foreign investors who have sought out investment opportunities in the capital market.

Chartered Banks

Banks, governed under the *Bank Act,* have a dominant position in residential mortgage lending. Positive legislative changes to that Act in 1967 opened the way by removing the ceiling on bank lending rates (previously set at 6%) and the authority to lend on conventional mortgages.

Banks are classified under the *Bank Act* as Schedule I (shares are widely held with no shareholder permitted to control more than 10%) and Schedule II (shares are closely held). A third schedule under the Act lists foreign banks and authorized names under which they may operate. Banks have a significant market share of residential mortgage credit. In 2007, their share represented slightly less than 60% of the total, as reported in by the Bank of Canada.

WEB LINKS

Bank Act   For a current listing of bank schedules, go to ***http://canada.justice.gc.ca*** and search *Bank Act* under *Laws* (located in upper portion of the web site banner).

Bank of Canada   Mortgage statistics published for various mortgage sources are available in the Weekly Financial Statistics report published by the Bank of Canada. For more information concerning credit measures, go to ***www.bankofcanada.ca***.

Trust and Loan Companies

Trust companies offer many services traditionally provided by chartered banks, but differ in one important aspect—the ability to act as a trustee. Trust companies aggressively pursued mortgages during the 1960s and 1970s, but now represent little more than 1%

of all residential mortgage outstanding balances. Loan companies, once distinct from trust operations, are now regulated under the *Trust and Loan Companies Act*. Unlike trust companies, loan companies cannot act as an agent or trustee and obtain funding primarily through debentures as opposed to deposits.

Life Insurance Companies

Life companies, once heavily involved as mortgage lenders given attractive yields, now account for a relatively small proportion of outstanding residential loans. Total volumes have declined over time with current residential mortgages (as reported by the Bank of Canada) being approximately 2% of total residential credit in 2007. Life insurance companies are regulated under the *Insurance Companies Act*.

Life companies, unlike banks and other lenders, must align cash flows with long-term commitments to policy holders. Funds invested in mortgages come primarily from policy premiums paid on whole, term and group life policies. Traditionally, the 25-year mortgage term proved attractive, as lack of liquidity was not a prime concern given life policy commitments with a similar time frame.

Today's emphasis on shorter mortgage terms, along with increased lender competition, largely account for the life insurance company move to other investment vehicles; e.g., equity participation in real estate ventures and longer term commercial financing. Interestingly, selected life insurance companies have diversified into subsidiary banking and trust operations.

That said, life insurance companies remain actively involved in both residential and commercial mortgages through subsidiary operations in banking and mortgage brokerage.

Pension Funds

Pension funds account for slightly less than 2% of all residential mortgage balances outstanding in 2007, according to Bank of Canada statistics. Pension fund managers continuously seek an asset mix that maximizes yields while ensuring that pension commitments are fulfilled. These funds typically favour bonds and equities, but mortgages and real estate factor into the mix.

The Pension Investment Association of Canada (PIAC) reports that members committed 1.6% of total assets to mortgages. PIAC consists of approximately 350 members administering $1/2 Trillion in assets.

Source: *PIAC Composite Asset Mix Report* as at Dec. 31, 2006.

Credit Unions/Caisses Populaires

Credit unions and caisses populaires now account for more than 13% of residential and approximately 20% of non-residential mortgages, as reported by the Bank of Canada in 2007. In Ontario, these organizations are incorporated and regulated under the *Credit Unions and Caisses Populaires Act*, administered by the Financial Services Commission of Ontario (FSCO).

A caisse populaire is a credit union conducting business primarily in the French language. Credit unions must conduct business only with members. Larger unions offer similar services as banks including chequing, savings, RRSP, mutual funds and ATM options.

WEB LINKS
Credit Unions   Many credit unions in Ontario are members of the Credit Union Central of Ontario (CUCO). CUCO provides operational and financial services to member credit unions. For additional information about credit unions, go to ***www.cuco.on***.

Mortgage Brokers

A mortgage broker generally brings together borrowers who need mortgage loans and companies and/or individuals with money to lend (as a representative of the mortgage brokerage) and negotiates on behalf of the borrower to get the best possible financing deal with the lender. Mortgage brokers are regulated by the Financial Services Commission of Ontario (FSCO) pursuant to the *Mortgage Brokerages, Lenders and Administrators Act, 2006*, which came into effect on July 1, 2008 to replace the *Mortgage Brokers Act*. This Act sets out various licence classifications including mortgage brokerage, mortgage broker, mortgage agent and mortgage administrator.

Mortgage brokers are assuming an increasingly focal role in residential financing. A surge in consumer reliance on mortgage brokers for residential financing generally coincided with heightened competition and product diversification in the mortgage market. The mortgage broker is aptly positioned to provide up-to-date information on loan policies and requirements, shop the market for the best rates and determine the optimum financial fit.

The mortgage broker, as an advisor, packages financial arrangements, obtains approvals, ensures that mortgage instructions are carried through and tracks funds for the closing. On a practical level, mortgage brokers assist consumers by handling the paperwork, explaining fees and lender requirements, informing borrowers of special offerings, screening products and assisting in the approval process. While many concentrate on the residential mortgage, specialty fields also exist regarding interim financing for large projects, commercial and industrial lending, and sale of mortgages in the secondary market.

Mortgage brokers can represent either the lender or borrower in securing mortgage financing. Typically, fees are paid by the lending institution for residential funds placement. However, borrowers may have to pay for broker services to secure financing given special needs or circumstances.

WEB LINKS
For more information concerning regulation of mortgage brokers, go to the Financial Services Commission of Ontario web site at ***www.fsco.gov.on.ca***.

Private Sources

Private investor sources include non-deposit taking entities including individuals and corporations who provide mortgage financing, but are not constrained by underwriting policies typically associated with major regulated lenders.

Real estate practitioners may use private financing sources, particularly when dealing with unique properties or clients/customers that have specific needs. Private sources are difficult to quantify as they can range from the local builder assisting in the sale of his/ her homes to the anxious seller taking back a mortgage to facilitate the sale. On a larger scale, an investment group may provide mortgage funding for local commercial projects.

Private investors are not limited in their lending scope, remain largely unregulated and need not address loan-to-value ratios followed by regulated lenders. Consequently, private sources tend to concentrate on market opportunities not currently serviced by banks or similar institutions. However, the degree of lender sophistication will vary significantly. Application forms, letters of commitment and policies/procedures may be scant or non-existent. Buyers should be made aware of the lack of legislation imposed on such individuals and corporations. As such, caution is advised and all parties involved with private financing should seek appropriate legal counsel.

Practitioners seeking private sources need to scrutinize the marketplace. Many local developers get involved with investment groups. Lawyers can be excellent sources, as they may act on behalf of private individuals and estates willing to place funds in the real estate market. In the case of specialty properties, private investors often advertise in appropriate trade journals/magazines (e.g., mobile homes, cottage properties, golf courses and time-share vacation properties).

A Moving Target	MARKET MEMO

At one time, lending was highly structured and everyone knew his/her place. Customers waited patiently for the clock to strike ten. Dutifully, a clerk would swing open the massive steel and glass doors and the bank would open for business. Pillars of the financial community—the trust companies, the insurance companies, the investment brokerages, the banks and so on, confidently presided over their respective turf.

Canadians understood the role of each. A bank was a place for personal accounts, loans and safety deposit boxes. Conversely, one would never ask for a chequing account in a trust company...that was the place for wills, savings certificates and estate management. The insurance company did what it did best: issued and managed policies for those seeking family or business protection in the event of untimely death. The finance company was a place of high interest rates, debt consolidation and chattel mortgages.

Today, the picture is blurred. Online lenders offer 24/7 service, insurance companies boast mortgage lending divisions, banks are heavily involved in retirement policies and mortgage-related insurance, and finance companies are pursuing prime real estate mortgages. Today's consumer faces a barrage of lenders and funding sources seeking their undivided attention and commitment.

At the same time, the staid, predictable mortgage business has all but abandoned traditional long-term financing. The 25-year mortgage, once the dominant force, is largely relegated to history. Consumers ride the renewal market, checking daily papers and online sources for interest rate blips. The big question: When to lock in...when not? We live in a growing world of debt where Bank of Canada interest rate announcements routinely capture headline status.

Today's e-financial world is now turning traditional banking upside down. Now consumers and businesses alike routinely transfer funds online, pay bills, move money between chequing accounts in search of greater frequent flyer miles and refinance houses online to service credit card debt.

MORTGAGE LEGISLATION

The *Mortgages Act* is the key provincial legislation impacting mortgages in Ontario. The Act is divided into five Parts. Part I is primarily focused on rights and obligations of mortgagors and mortgagees with Parts II, III and IV detailing specifics about default procedures. Part V details provisions relating to mortgagees in possession. Selected topics are highlighted, but the Act should be consulted directly for specifics.

PART I:
Rights and Obligations of Mortgagors and Mortgagees

Part I contains twenty-two provisions covering a broad range of topics. Four are highlighted for illustrative purposes only.

COPY OF MORTGAGE

The mortgagor (or his designated agent) must receive a copy of the mortgage within 30 days of signing. A penalty applies if a true copy is not delivered within that time frame.

INSURANCE

Insurance received from a claim involving mortgaged property must be applied in making good the mortgaged property, if the mortgagee so requires.

EXECUTORS

Executors are given certain authorities regarding how mortgages are handled in the event of death, as well as situations in which the mortgagee cannot be located. These authorities extend to preparing appropriate registration documents; e.g., registering a mortgage discharge.

PERSONAL JUDGMENT

The mortgagee can recover losses from either the original mortgagor or the grantee (i.e., a new buyer). However, if action is taken against one, the mortgagee ceases to have any rights against the other. As mentioned earlier under default remedies, a mortgagee may take no action against a mortgagor under a building mortgage (i.e., a builder constructing a home) after one year from the time that the mortgage documents are executed (assuming an arm's length transaction involving a third party).

PART II:
Statutory Powers

Part II of the *Mortgages Act*, R.S.O. 1990 details statutory powers associated with mortgage default and, more specifically, the statutory rights afforded mortgagees to take certain steps under power of sale such as selling the mortgaged property, insuring the buildings if required and adding associated insurance premiums to the debt. Section 27 is of particular note, as it fully details the order for disbursing funds under a power of sale:

- Payment of all expenses incurred in any sale or attempted sale.
- Discharge of all interest and costs relating to the mortgage.
- Discharge of all principal money due relating to the mortgage.
- Payment of amounts to subsequent encumbrances based on their priority.
- Payment to the tenants of rent deposits made pursuant to the *Residential Tenancies Act* where the rent deposit was not applied in payment for the last rent period and the residue shall be paid to the mortgagor.

Power of Sale	CAUTION

As discussed previously, two power of sale procedures can be used by a mortgagee. Various provisions set out in Part II apply to a statutory power of sale. However, such provisions do not apply where a mortgage contains a contractual power of sale provision. Lastly, no provisions of Part II apply to a mortgage that contains a declaration that Part II does not apply.

PART III:
Notice of Exercising Power of Sale

Part III of the *Mortgages Act*, R.S.O. 1990 outlines notices and related matters concerning power of sale proceedings. Notice must be given to all persons appearing on records of either registry or land titles systems, statutory liens in favour of the Crown or any other public authority where the mortgagee has written notice of the liens, and where the mortgagee has actual notice from other parties that are received prior to the notice exercising the power of sale.

Detailed procedures are set out in Sections 32 to 39 regarding notices, notice periods and general rules regarding the manner of giving notices. Part III of the Act does not apply to a mortgage given by a corporation to secure bonds or debentures.

PART IV:
General Provisions as to Power of Sale

This Part sets out additional power of sale requirements limiting other actions that might be taken by a mortgagee, outlining how payments must be accepted once a demand is made and a mechanism for handling disputes concerning costs under a power of sale.

PART V:
Mortgagees in Possession of Residential Premises

The final Part details provisions relating to mortgagees in possession of residential rental premises. A person who becomes the mortgagee in possession of a mortgaged residential complex that is subject to a tenancy agreement between the mortgagor and the tenant, or who obtains title to a residential complex by foreclosure or power of sale shall be deemed to be the landlord under the tenancy agreement and be subject to requirements set out both under the *Mortgages Act* and the *Residential Tenancies Act*. Detailed discussion of these provisions goes beyond the scope of this introductory text, but additional details are provided in the advanced articling course titled *Principles of Mortgage Financing*.

CONVENTIONAL VS. HIGH RATIO MORTGAGES

A high ratio mortgage is a mortgage loan that exceeds the normal limit for a conventional first mortgage and is insured through a mortgage loan insurance program. Currently, high ratio mortgages involve loans in which lender participation exceeds 80%. The loan is insured through either a private source (e.g., Genworth Financial Canada) or a government source (Canada Mortgage and Housing Corporation). The number of default insurance providers has varied over the years.

Deposit-taking lending institutions are not permitted to lend mortgage money above 80% of appraised lending value or sale price (whichever is less), commonly referred to as the loan-to-value (LTV) ratio. Conventional mortgages (80% or less) afford lenders a high level of equity protection. However, they may set more restrictive limits; e.g., 50% or 60% based on individual property considerations and associated risk.

Note: Lenders may require mortgage loan insurance on mortgages with LTVs less than 80% given risks associated with particular applications.

Fees associated with high ratio mortgages are addressed in *Chapter 14: Mortgage LendingPractices*.

EXAMPLE   *The New House Purchase*

Buyer Jones requires a mortgage for a new house purchase of $347,500. Genworth Financial is prepared to insure a high ratio mortgage for 85% of the total purchase price being $295,375. Jones will have to pay an insurance premium that can be either paid in cash or added to the mortgage amount. The rate for the high ratio insurance is calculated based on the loan-to-value ratio.

Mortgage Default Insurance Providers

Canada Mortgage and Housing Corporation (CMHC) has provided default insurance since high ratio financing was first introduced in Canada in 1954. During the 1970's three private providers of insurance were also active, but later merged and ultimately became GE Mortgage Insurance in the mid-1990's and then underwent a name change to Genworth Financial Canada.

Genworth Financial Canada and CMHC are the major suppliers of mortgage default insurance and are highlighted in this text. In 2006, AIG United Guaranty entered the Canadian market followed by PMI Canada in 2007.

GENWORTH FINANCIAL CANADA

Genworth Financial Canada is a private mortgage default insurer. Genworth provides a wide range of flexible products for the purchase, renovation or financing of homes. During 1995, GE Mortgage Insurance Canada acquired the residential lending insurance portfolio previously owned by the Mortgage Insurance Company of Canada (MICC). MICC was originally created to provide mortgage insurance that reduced the lender's risk in the event of default. In 2005, GE Capital was renamed Genworth Financial Canada.

Under the Genworth Financial Canada program the insurance fee is normally paid by the borrower. The majority of loans insured are high ratio mortgages, however, insurance can be provided on conventional financing. To qualify, the mortgagor must meet requirements as set out by the insuring company and the lending institution. In addition, the financial organization providing the monies must adhere to specific lending policies as set out by that insuring organization.

Genworth Financial Canada now offers a fully automated delivery and decision system that electronically receives customer applications, processes requests and approves applications within minutes. The system combines a scoring process with property information and underwriting guidelines to ensure not only fast, but consistent decisions.

WEB LINKS

For additional details regarding programs offered by Genworth Financial Canada, go to **www.genworth.ca**.

CANADA MORTGAGE AND HOUSING CORPORATION (CMHC)

As the housing agency for the Government of Canada, CMHC has a mandate to encourage:

- Construction of new houses;
- Repair and modernization of existing houses; and
- Improvement of living conditions and housing for Canadians throughout the country.

CMHC provides a range of publications and acts as a resource centre for both private and public organizations related to the housing industry. CMHC advises the government on housing matters and designs, as well as overseeing various federal housing programs. Canada Mortgage and Housing Corporation, through provision of mortgage loan insured products, is instrumental in increasing access to the housing market, financing rental accommodation construction, assisting in social housing projects and generally furthering access of Canadians to a wide range of housing choices.

Mortgage loan insurance guarantees that the lender will be repaid if the homeowner fails to keep up the payments. In return for that guarantee, lenders will provide mortgages on housing purchases with a 5% downpayment, compared with 20% normally required for conventional mortgages. The *National Housing Act (*NHA*)* and the *National Housing Loan Regulations* set out CMHC underwriting procedures and operating guidelines.

Part I of the Regulations detail guidelines for processing and approving residential mortgages and defines the maximum loans permissible as well as term and amortization periods. Details about construction loans, inspections, progress advances and holdbacks are outlined. The Regulations address procedures regarding gross debt service (GDS) and total debt service (TDS) ratios. Part I provides extensive documentation on internal procedures, overall loan administration and claims procedures for lenders using CMHC mortgage facilities.

WEB LINKS

Go to the CMHC web site (*www.cmhc.ca*) for detailed information regarding the mortgage loan insurance program and other programs offered by this government agency.

MORTGAGE DEFAULT INSURANCE VS. CREDITOR LIFE INSURANCE

Consumers may become confused about these two types of insurance. Mortgage default insurance provides default protection for the lender should the borrower fail to meet obligations set out in the mortgage. This type of insurance should be clearly differentiated from creditor life insurance, which provides protection for the borrower in the case of disability, critical illness and death. Creditor life insurance is often offered by mortgage brokers and lenders to prospective borrowers at point of arranging a mortgage.

Practitioners should be aware that creditor life insurance is not the only option when seeking such protection. Borrowers may also avail themselves of term insurance offered through a life insurance company.

High Ratio Mortgages: An Historical Overview

PERSPECTIVE

As early as 1886, the *Dominion Insurance Act* provided for mortgage investment, but set no limitations as to the ratio of loan to lending value. It was not until 1910 that the *Insurance Act* set conventional mortgage maximums at 60% of the value of the property. The introduction of the *Dominion Housing Act* during 1935 was a milestone in mortgage financing. This first major piece of housing legislation was designed to stimulate housing construction throughout the country.

The *Dominion Housing Act* had no reference to an insurable mortgage. Instead, the Act provided government funds for new home building based on a joint loans system. The conventional lender would advance a loan up to 60% of the value of the property. The balance (to a total loan maximum of 80%) was accessed from federal funds. The *Dominion Housing Act* also extended mortgage terms from 5 to 10 years along with corresponding amortization periods.

In 1938, the *National Housing Act* was introduced to replace the *Dominion Housing Act*. This new Act was designed to accomplish three objectives:

- Reduce the amount of unemployment within the housing industry;

- Improve general housing conditions throughout Canada; and

- Encourage the development of individual home ownership through better financial programs.

The year 1954 brought major changes that are with us today. During that year, chartered banks were approved as lenders under the *National Housing Act* (NHA) to meet the high demand for mortgage funding within residential markets. At the same time, an insurance fund was set up to change the NHA scheme from one of joint lending policy to that of insured loans. This major change saw Central Mortgage and Housing Corporation (CMHC) limit activity as a direct lender of mortgage funds and switch to providing the insurance for approved lending institutions. The name was subsequently changed to Canada Mortgage and Housing Corporation.

Major changes took place in 1970. The *Canadian and British Insurance Companies Act* was amended to permit institutional lenders to become involved in high ratio financing. This allowed mortgage investment above the 75% level provided that such loans were insured by private mortgage insurance firms. Prior to this time, investors had been able to participate in high ratio financing solely through the *National Housing Act*. With this amendment, high ratio financing found its way into nearly every sector in the housing market through combinations of government approved facilities and private market institutions. In 2006, the loan-to-value ratio for high ratio mortgages was increased from 75% to 80%.

KNOWLEDGE INTEGRATION

Notables

- The two parties to a mortgage are the mortgagee (lends the money) and the mortgagor (owes the money).
- Under land registry, a mortgage is now officially referred to as a charge which identifies the debt against the mortgagor's property, but no transfer of title takes place.
- Three types of mortgages are discussed in this chapter: legal, equitable and chattel.
- Mortgage priority is generally determined by time of registration under the *Registry Act* and the *Land Titles Act*, but important exceptions exist.
- A mortgagor makes various promises (covenants) in a mortgage document; three additional implied covenants are set out in the *Land Registration Reform Act*.
- Mortgagee rights include the right to assign and the right to be paid.
- Mortgagor rights include the right to quiet possession, right to redeem and right to discharge.

- Certain privileges may be granted by the mortgagee.
- Both legal and non-legal remedies can be pursued by a mortgagee when a mortgagor is in default.
- Six legal remedies are detailed with the power of sale being most commonly used in Ontario.
- The mortgage market is made up of a primary and secondary market.
- The primary mortgage market consists of two general categories: prime and sub-prime.
- Mortgage sources include chartered banks, trust and loan companies, life insurance companies, pension funds, credit unions/caisses populaires, mortgage brokers and private sources.
- Mortgages can be divided into two categories from a loan-to-value perspective: conventional and high ratio.
- Several mortgage default insurers offer default insurance in Ontario. Current major suppliers of default insurance are Canada Mortgage and Housing Corporation and Genworth Financial Canada.

Glossary

Capital Market

Charge

Chattel Mortgage

Equitable Mortgage

Equity of Redemption

Implied Covenants

Legal Mortgage

Money Market

Mortgagee

Mortgage Market

Mortgage Priority

Mortgagor

Web Links

Web links are included for general interest regarding selected chapter topics.

Bank Act	For a current listing of bank schedules, go to ***www.canada.justice.gc.ca*** and search *Bank Act* under *Laws* (located in upper portion of the web site banner).
Bank of Canada	Mortgage statistics published for various mortgage sources are available in the Weekly Financial Statistics report published by the Bank of Canada. For more information concerning credit measures, go to ***www.bankofcanada.ca***.
Credit Unions	Many credit unions in Ontario are members of the Credit Union Central of Ontario (CUCO). CUCO provides operational and financial services to member credit unions. For additional information about credit unions, go to ***www.cucentral.on***.
Financial Services Commission of Ontario	For more information concerning regulation of mortgage brokers, go to the Financial Services Commission of Ontario web site at ***www.fsco.gov.on.ca***.
Genworth Financial Canada	For additional details regarding programs offered by Genworth Financial Canada, go to ***www.genworth.ca***.
Canada Mortgage and Housing Corporation	Go to the CMHC web site (***www.cmhc.ca***) for detailed information regarding the mortgage loan insurance program and other programs offered by this government agency.

Strategic Thinking For Your Career

Questions are included to assist in developing your new career. No answers are provided.

1. I need to gain more familiarity with mortgage documents. Do I have a personal source (e.g., my own mortgage) or should I go to the local land registry office to expand my knowledge of such documents?

2. What common mortgage privileges are commonly found in today's marketplace?

3. Which lenders in my area offer mortgage products to prime and/or sub-prime borrowers?

4. Are there lenders (or departments within local lenders) that specialize in commercial mortgage products?

5. What detailed online information is available regarding mortgage default insurance providers discussed in this chapter?

6. What legal and non-legal default remedies are most commonly used by local lenders?

Chapter Mini-Review

Solutions are located in the Appendix.

1. The mortgagor gives or lends the money and registers the mortgage against the property in the land registry office.

   ○ True   ○ False

2. A chattel mortgage is given on movable objects or personal property.

   ○ True   ○ False

3. Subsequent mortgagees, over and above the first mortgagee, have the right to be notified regarding default action being taken by the first mortgagee, but cannot make payments on behalf of the mortgagor to stave off such action.

   ○ True   ○ False

4. A lease that is entered into prior to the registration of a mortgage generally has priority over that mortgage.

   ○ True   ○ False

5. The requirement that a mortgagor will provide insurance on the buildings is one of the implied covenants under the *Land Registration Reform Act*.

   ○ True   ○ False

6. The mortgagee can only assign a mortgage with the express written consent of the mortgagor.

   ○ True   ○ False

7. A mortgagee can only pursue legal remedies for mortgage default once he or she has exhausted all non-legal remedies.

   ○ True   ○ False

8. A legal remedy in which the mortgagor forfeits his or her equity of redemption along with any equity that he or she may have in the property is referred to as a judicial sale.

   ○ True   ○ False

9. Under a power of sale, the mortgagee can force the sale of the mortgaged property when default occurs.

   ○ True   ○ False

10. Money markets are typically associated with short term borrowing with capital markets focused on longer term borrowing.

    ○ True   ○ False

11. The secondary market is focused on sub-prime lending involving higher risk levels with borrowers having B and C level credit.

    ○ True   ○ False

12. Mortgage brokers in Ontario are regulated by the Financial Services Commission of Ontario.

    ○ True   ○ False

13. High ratio mortgages can only be insured by Canada Mortgage and Housing Corporation.

    ○ True   ○ False

14. Creditor life insurance is another name for mortgage default insurance.

    ○ True   ○ False

Active Learning Exercises

Solutions are located in the Appendix.

■ **Exercise 1   Multiple Choice**

1.1   A chattel mortgage:

    a.   May be registered pursuant to procedures set out in the *Personal Property Security Act*.

    b.   May be registered pursuant to procedures set out in the *Mortgages Act*.

    c.   May be registered pursuant to procedures set out in the *Mortgage Brokerages, Lenders and Administrators Act, 2006*.

    d.   Is not normally registered in the Province of Ontario.

1.2   Under a judicial sale:

    a.   The mortgagor must release all interests that he or she may have in the land at the point of electing to involve the Court in the sale.

    b.   Any surplus, after obligations to encumbrancers are satisfied, would be paid to the mortgagor (subject to court and related costs).

    c.   The Court evicts the mortgagor and takes possession of the property.

    d.   The mortgagor does not receive any surplus after obligations to encumbrancers and court costs are paid.

1.3   Mortgagor Jones has an existing first mortgage with Lender Inc. that is coming due and she wants to renew. However, Jones also has an existing second mortgage and wants that second mortgage to remain as such, while replacing the existing first. Which of the following privileges is needed relating to the second mortgage to accommodate this?

    a.   Prepayment.

    b.   Transfer.

    c.   Renewal.

    d.   Postponement.

1.4   Mortgagor Smith has encountered significant financial problems and wants to be released from all interests in a mortgaged property. The mortgagee agrees to take over the property with no further action against Smith for monies owed. This arrangement is best described as a:

    a.   Foreclosure.

    b.   Quit Claim Deed.

    c.   Power of Sale.

    d.   Judicial Sale.

1.5   When a mortgagee takes possession of a property due to the mortgagor's default, he or she:

     a.   Must respect the legal rights of a tenant, if any, now occupying the property.

     b.   Is not permitted to take any other legal action against the mortgagor.

     c.   Must not hire agents for upkeep or repair of the property.

     d.   Is not governed by provisions of the *Mortgages Act*.

1.6   A mortgage broker:

     a.   Is regulated under the *Real Estate and Business Brokers Act*.

     b.   Can represent either the lender or the borrower.

     c.   Can only represent the lender.

     d.   Cannot receive any payment from borrowers for services performed in securing financing.

1.7   Which of the following is a correct statement regarding provisions set out in the *Mortgages Act*?

     a.   A mortgagee is free to use insurance money received relating to damage to the mortgaged property in whatever way he or she sees fit.

     b.   A mortgagee can pursue both the original mortgagor and a new buyer of a home who assumes the mortgage for any default of that mortgage.

     c.   When funds are received under a power of sale, payment of rent deposits to tenants must be made prior to paying costs relating to the power of sale action.

     d.   A copy of the mortgage must be received by the mortgagor (or his/her agent) within 30 days of signing.

1.8   The secondary mortgage market:

     a.   Focuses on higher risk borrowers with B and C level credit.

     b.   Involves the trading of existing mortgages.

     c.   Is not involved with securitization of mortgages.

     d.   Focuses on new loans for property financing and rehabilitation of existing structures.

SECTION V   PROPERTY FINANCING

■ Exercise 2   Matching

Match the words in the left column with the appropriate descriptions in the right column (not all descriptions are used).

____	*Subsequent Encumbrancers*
____	*Equity of Redemption*
____	*Common Expenses*
____	*Holdback*
____	*Quit Claim Deed*
____	*Prepayment*

a. *Type of Lien Registered by a Condominium Corporation*

b. *Privilege Granted by a Mortgagee to a Mortgagor*

c. *Construction Lien Act*

d. *Right to Prevent Default and Right to be Notified*

e. *Right to Redeem the Property*

f. *Release any Rights in a Parcel of Land*

g. *Legal Occupancy of the Mortgaged Property by the Mortgagee*

■ Exercise 3   Power of Sale

Funds received by a mortgagee under power of sale must be disbursed in a precise order according to the *Mortgages Act*. Place the following in the correct order (i.e., **1**, **2**, **3**, **4** and **5**).

Discharge of all principal money due relating to the mortgage.	
Payment to the tenants of rent deposits made pursuant to the *Residential Tenancies Act* where the rent deposit was not applied in payment for the last rent period and the residue shall be paid to the mortgagor.	
Discharge of all interest and costs relating to the mortgage.	
Payment of all expenses incurred in any sale or attempted sale.	
Payment of amounts to subsequent encumbrances based on their priority.	

CHAPTER 14

Mortgage Lending Practices

Introduction

Real Estate as a Professional Career detailed fundamentals of how the mortgage financing process works, including mortgage qualification steps using gross debt service and total debt service ratios, along with basic mortgage calculations involving simple interest, blended mortgage payments, amortization and mortgage averaging. Chapter 14 builds on this foundation through a more detailed discussion of residential mortgage application/processing procedures, common mortgage products and financing techniques to assist buyers and sellers.

The chapter is divided into two primary sections addressing residential and commercial mortgage underwriting practices. With residential mortgages, the emphasis is placed on the borrower and the property. Borrower documentation is discussed along with details of how credit bureaus operate followed by mortgage processing procedures and costs including mortgage commitments and the range of mortgage products available in the Ontario marketplace. Advanced calculator skills are also introduced.

Commercial underwriting is broadly discussed in terms of both large and small business loans including typical documentation, alternative lending sources and prevalent lending practices used by lenders when addressing lending risk. The chapter concludes with specialized terminology and practices that are commonly encountered in commercial mortgage financing.

Chapter 14 advances concepts and techniques that form a foundation for advanced mortgage discussions in *The Commercial Real Estate Transaction* and *Principles of Mortgage Financing.*

Learning Outcomes

At the conclusion of this chapter, students will be able to:

- Outline methods used for borrower pre-approvals and typical borrower documentation required for residential mortgage applications.
- Describe how a credit bureau operates with particular emphasis on credit reports and credit scores, including what factors impact an individual's credit score.
- Discuss selected adverse property conditions that may impact the approval of a residential mortgage.
- Explain the fundamentals underlying residential mortgage processing with particular reference to origination software, preparation of a mortgage commitment, underwriting costs and other fees.
- Discuss mortgage products with reference to fixed vs. variable, open vs. closed, payment flexibility options, incentives and custom packages.
- Describe seven techniques that may assist in mortgage negotiations and utilize selected advanced calculator skills involving unknown terms, amortizations and payment frequencies.
- Outline commercial underwriting procedures with particular emphasis on mortgage documentation packages and special considerations for small business financing.
- Detail alternative sources of funds including private investors, seller take backs and sale/leasebacks.
- List and discuss examples of selected commercial lending practices that better assure investment security when advancing mortgage funds to commercial enterprises.
- Define and describe thirteen specialized products used in commercial (and in selected residential) situations.

RESIDENTIAL UNDERWRITING

Mortgage underwriting is a process (also commonly referred to as mortgage qualification) undertaken by a lender to evaluate the credit worthiness of the applicant and assess the property being offered as security for the mortgage. Underwriting involves applying specific lender credit policies leading to the acceptance (including applicable conditions) or rejection of the application.

Residential mortgage applications focus on both the property and the applicants. Underwriting for commercial loans is addressed later in this chapter. A pre-approval (i.e., **pre-approved buyer**) involves lender preliminary approval of the applicant, with any final financing commitment subject to inspection of the chosen property and other conditions as stated in the pre-approval letter. Residential mortgages follow a more or less standardized processing procedure involving seven steps from initial contact with the lender to final closing of the mortgage (coincident with the sale closing).

Pre-Approved Buyer

Approval of a buyer for a mortgage by a lender, subject to various conditions and limitations.

Seven Typical Processing Steps

STEP 1	Pre-Approval *(Optional)*
STEP 2	Mortgage Application Prepared
STEP 3	Lender Review of Application
STEP 4	Commitment Letter Prepared and Forwarded
STEP 5	Commitment Letter Signed/Condition(s) Waived
STEP 6	Mortgage Documents Prepared
STEP 7	Mortgage Transaction Completed Coincident With Closing

THE BORROWER

Pre-Approval

Pre-approved mortgage financing has become increasingly popular as it adds negotiating strength in the marketplace. The buyer becomes virtually a cash buyer, *subject to the conditions of the pre-approval.* Although no standard pre-approval form exists, most consist of a confirmation document setting out the maximum amount that can be borrowed, the interest rate to be charged (guaranteed for a fixed period) and the monthly payments. The confirmation is subject to an appraisal of the property being mortgaged. *Always read pre-approval documents with extreme care.*

EXAMPLE   *Pre-Approved Buyer*

James and Judy Jones are contemplating a home purchase and have gone to the Canadian National Bank for a pre-approved mortgage. They received a pre-approved mortgage certificate concerning the maximum approved mortgage. Now the Joneses can negotiate with confidence, knowing just how much Canadian National Bank will lend them and how much they are able to spend for their home subject to specified conditions; e.g., an appraisal.

THE CANADIAN NATIONAL BANK	**Date:** January 15, 20xx
Pre-Approved Mortgage Certificate	**Name:** James and Judy Jones
	Address: 123 Main Street, Anycity, Ontario

This is to certify that the above person(s) named has/have qualified for the following mortgage, subject to a satisfactory appraisal of the property and a credit review by the Bank at the time of actual mortgage application.

Amount:	$230,000
Interest Rate:	6.5%
Monthly Payment:	$1493.37

The mortgage amount is based on details supplied at the time of application for a certificate. The interest rate is guaranteed for 60 days from the date stated above provided that the mortgage is fully advanced within a 60-day period. The pre-approval is for a five-year term mortgage, but a shorter term may be selected, the interest rate will either be the rate in effect as of the date of this certificate, or at the time at which the selection is made, whichever is less.

The monthly payment of $1,493.37 includes principal and interest repayment only. Based on our estimate, the taxes would be approximately $3,800 per annum and the heating costs would be approximately $1,240.00 per annum. Based on the mortgage amount on this Pre-approved Mortgage Certificate and the downpayment stated in your application, you should consider purchasing a home in the range of $260,000 to $300,000.

Branch Manager/Lending Officer
Tel: (800) 555-1212

Mortgage Application

Once an offer is accepted regarding a property and financing is required, the application is forwarded to the lender for review (assuming that no pre-approval was granted). The lender scrutinizes applications based on the 5 C's of credit, applies GDS and TDS ratios (as discussed in *Real Estate as a Professional Career*; see Chapter 8) and completes a **credit report** through a **credit bureau**.

The Five C's of Credit

CHARACTER   Employment reliability and overall risk

CAPITAL   Available financial resources; assets/liabilities

CAPACITY   Ability to pay; GDS/TDS

COLLATERAL   Condition of property to be mortgaged

CREDIT   Credit record

Credit Report

A report on the credit position of a borrower, typically including a three-digit credit score to assess credit standing.

Typically, income-related supporting documents are required for initial qualifying with additional items set out in the mortgage commitment. Commercial mortgages, discussed later in this chapter, require more extensive documentation including feasibility reports, construction/site analysis, income/expense statements and detailed borrower information.

Lenders employ staff or contract qualified appraisers and real estate brokers/salespersons to complete an appraisal. Currently, some lenders are limiting the physical inspection to exterior only (if the homeowner has significant equity). Lender criteria vary concerning acceptable properties. Location, size and condition are primary considerations, with older and unique homes falling under the closest scrutiny. Lenders may require holdbacks from mortgage funds to repair identified items; e.g., outdated wiring.

Borrower Documentation

Lender requirements vary, but minimum documentation in support of income typically includes:

- employment and income verification (income verification must normally be supported by a Notice of Assessment (NOA), T4s or T4As, income tax return and/or employer letter/pay stubs);
- down payment source and amount;
- credit report;
- completed loan application;
- copy of agreement of purchase and sale; and
- copy of property valuation.

Lenders may wish to gain a more complete picture about a salaried applicant by seeking past years' income documents, assurances of future income stability given present income fluctuations and additional information about other income sources.

Self-employed persons should demonstrate at least three years' successful operation. Income tax receipts alone are not normally sufficient. Documents must show profit generated as well as income earned in order to confirm that debt obligations can be handled.

Additional Qualifying Income	CURIOSITY

Lender policies will vary, but generally financial institutions considering additional income of an applicant will consider the following:

- Overtime/secondary income/bonuses if reasonable and consistently earned.
- Net income (gross rent less operating expenses) from rental properties.
- Investment income if reasonable and consistent.
- Alimony/child support if fully and regularly received. Conversely, such amounts are typically deducted from the person making such payments.
- Employment insurance (in the case of cyclical income patterns), if likely to continue in future.

Important: *Various income sources are generally unacceptable as additional qualifying income.* These would include a one-time capital gain, income that cannot be verified, social assistance payments, retained earnings for a corporation, education benefits, income tax refunds or credits, and projected future income.

Credit Bureau

A credit bureau is a central clearing house, also referred to as a *credit investigating agency*, for all types of credit related information. Essentially, companies involved in lending money provide the bureau with customer information and, in return, have access to the files established for each consumer. The credit bureau receives information not only from lenders (credit grantors) but also from public record sources (judgments, bankruptcies). Most companies using credit cards within Canada, such as financial institutions, oil companies and department stores, use the service. Selected banks input information and the major Canadian-based automobile financing companies are also part of the system.

CREDIT INFORMATION

The credit bureau provides consumer credit information that is usually updated on a 60-day basis. This varies depending on how information is transmitted between individual lenders and the bureau. Often, information is sent electronically which has improved both the accuracy and timeliness. Of course, the consumer has the ability not only to verify information being held on file but also to dispute or alter incorrect data.

Credit bureaus only compile information relating to credit. No data is collected relating to personal habits, affiliations, political or social connections. Further, not all credit information about an individual will be found in the records. The completeness of data is limited by the number of lenders that participate as members with the bureau in any particular locale. The report on an individual may be limited but still a useful indicator of the positive and negative aspects of a personal credit history.

CREDIT REPORT

Credit bureaus in Canada produce reports using a common or standardized language to ensure that reporting is consistent and that all credit grantors use the same terms to describe specific types of pay habits. Currently, there are two major credit bureaus operating in Canada that provide credit reports: Equifax Canada and TransUnion. Examples are provided on their respective web sites.

The credit report provides personal information about the individual (address and employment), bank account information, credit history, status of revolving accounts (accounts with an open-ended term; e.g., credit cards), bankruptcies and/or proposals, judgments and garnishments.

WEB LINKS

Credit Reports   For examples of credit reports and various credit-related products (including online services) offered by credit bureaus in Canada, go to the Equifax Canada web site at *www.equifax.ca* and the TransUnion web site at *www.transunion.ca*.

CREDIT SCORE

The FICO® score, developed by Fair, Isaac and Company, Inc. is a number between 300 and 900 that lenders use in assessing an applicant's credit standing and his or her probability of becoming delinquent regarding a particular loan. Both Equifax Canada and TransUnion provide credit scores (sometimes referred to as bureau scores) based on FICO. As a statistical measure, the credit score is determined by selecting variables within the credit reporting structure (e.g., payment history, delinquencies and requests for credit) placing numerical weights on these components and calculating a final score.

As a general guideline, the higher the credit score, the higher the likelihood of being approved for loans. However, it is important to emphasize that the credit score is only one of several factors taken into consideration when making decisions about mortgage applications.

For real estate practitioners, credit reports are a key ingredient in the mortgage approval process. Many different scoring arrangements are possible based on variables used and weightings applied. Credit reporting bureaus offer both standardized scoring based on credit report data, as well as custom models to address specific lender and other client needs.

Becoming Credit Score Savvy   MARKET PERSPECTIVE

Score Factors

Various factors impact an individual's credit score. Here are some general guidelines and tips:

- Timeliness of payments is very important.
- Consumers should avoid late payments (i.e., 30 days or more).
- Credit reporting agencies closely track amount of credit card debt and loans outstanding. High remaining balances can impact the rating despite prompt installment payments.

- Any collection procedures or judgments will also directly affect the score.
- Opening of several credit accounts and requests for credit reports by creditors over a short period of time can also prove detrimental.
- The number of credit inquiries made can impact the credit score.

Formulae underlying scoring models are very complex. Following is a general estimate of factors that impact credit score:

Payment History 35%	Credit Owed 30%	Credit History 15%	Type of Credit 10%	New Credit 10%

(including inquiries)

Score Range

According to Equifax Canada's Score Power information, approximately 1 in 4 Canadians have a score between 750 and 799 with only 5% above 850. (Reminder: The minimum score is 300 and the maximum is 900.) An acceptable score will vary based on the lender's credit policies.

Borrowers may improve personal scores through a number of credit practices. First, review your personal credit report to ensure accuracy and dispute any inaccurate items. Corrections to incorrect information can positively affect the score. Of course, the best strategies are implementing prudent credit practices, promptly paying bills and avoiding excessive debt.

No Credit Score

Not all borrowers will have a credit score. Reporting agencies are unable to calculate a score unless sufficient credit information is available; e.g., at least one updated account and one account trade that has been opened for a few months. Minimum requirements will vary by agency.

Scores and Lending Decisions

The credit score is a very important consideration in a lender's decision, but many other factors come into play. For example, in the case of a mortgage, the lender will take into consideration the range of services currently provided to that customer, the borrower's equity and the property being mortgaged. As well, information supplied by the customer may clarify or otherwise address matters that are contained in the credit report that negatively impacted scoring.

THE PROPERTY

Financial institutions establish lending criteria for various types of properties, conditions of those properties and whether a first mortgage or subsequent (e.g., second, third and so on) is being arranged. The lender may refuse to finance specific properties or seek an increased equity position (larger downpayment) by restricting the mortgage amount, demanding a higher interest rate, requiring certain repairs including a holdback on funds until the repairs are completed, or any combination thereof. The decision made varies based on the specific lender's mortgage underwriting policies and procedures.

Adverse Property Conditions

Various conditions can adversely impact the approval of a mortgage, the interest rate charged and whether specific holdbacks are required. A list of situations or conditions that might affect approval are included. However, specific lending policies on such matters can vary in the marketplace. Contact local lenders to better assess what are acceptable and not acceptable conditions from an underwriting perspective.

Physical Detractions

- Certain types of siding (e.g., insulbrick).
- Lack of a central heating system and reliance on space heaters.
- Outdated wiring system, such as a 60-amp service.
- Low water gallonage per minute test, usually under two gallons per minute.
- Dug well.
- Partial basement and/or dirt floor.
- Major amenities in structural state of disrepair (e.g., a pool).

Legislative Inadequacies

- Failure to comply with local building codes.
- Non-compliance with local zoning by-laws.

Other Limiting Factors

- Non-conformance (other than zoning) with prevailing property types in the area.
- Interior and exterior design weaknesses.
- Deteriorating neighbourhood.

Lender Holdback

A lender holdback refers to funds not advanced by the lender until specific requirements and/or conditions are met by the borrower. A lender typically requires a holdback of funds involving resale properties until certain work is completed or repairs are made to a property being considered for mortgage financing. This could apply when electrical service must be brought up to standard, the furnace replaced, siding installed or structural changes made.

Normally when a holdback is required, a specified time limit is set for completion of work along with a re-inspection of the property. Frequently such holdbacks pertain to household improvements of a relatively minor structural or cosmetic nature. If substantial alterations are undertaken (e.g., an addition) mortgage funds are normally advanced in progressive stages as construction proceeds.

> **EXAMPLE** *Jones Seeks Financing*
>
> ABC Lending Inc. is offering conventional mortgages in isolated areas of the province but emphasizes that amounts advanced and ultimate approval can be affected by certain factors set out in lending criteria policies.
>
> Buyer Jones requires financing on his recent purchase of an older two-storey house located 15 miles north of the village of Smallville in rural Ontario. The home cost $195,000 and Jones is seeking a mortgage of $150,000 at the prevailing interest rate (6.5%) with a 25-year amortization. Upon inspecting the property, the appraiser estimates the market value at $193,500, but identifies the following limiting factors:
>
> - No central heating system–reliance on space heaters;
> - Dug well; and
> - Partial basement with dirt floor.
>
> The lender, considering these factors, is prepared to lend $140,000, but requires an interest rate of 7.75% and a 20-year amortization. More importantly, the lender will not advance any funds without proof that a central heating system has been installed. Further, the lender will advance $120,000 following the heating system installation. The balance of $20,000 will be advanced once the well is drilled by an approved well driller and the concrete floor is poured in the partial basement, which must meet building code specifications.

MORTGAGE PROCESSING

Historically, mortgage processing was established by means of paper-based procedures involving cumbersome and often time consuming practices that impacted both borrower and lender. Paperwork could be extensive and approvals could take weeks. In recent years, origination software has changed all that.

Origination Software

While lenders have had internal, electronic communication systems for some time, origination (point-of-sale) software has expanded this capability to encompass mortgage brokers and consumers in an online delivery system that includes electronic access to lenders, credit bureaus, online valuations, title insurers, land registry offices and specialized service providers (e.g., mortgage fraud online detection systems).

Mortgage brokers and lenders can prepare online applications, attach electronic credit reports, perform various mortgage calculations, submit applications and receive approvals, validate information and prepare documents to coincide with the real estate closing. The latest versions of origination software also permit potential borrowers to compare lender offers and input data ready for review by mortgage brokers and lenders. Processes that once took weeks to complete can now be accomplished in hours and minutes.

Mortgage Commitment

The lender, once the underwriting process is complete, prepares a **mortgage commitment** setting out terms and conditions for acceptance by the borrower. At present, most mortgage commitments are prepared and electronically transmitted. From the borrower's perspective, careful review is essential to ensure alignment with the financing condition in the agreement of purchase and sale.

Upon signing the commitment, the buyer removes the condition in the agreement of purchase and sale. The lender then prepares mortgage documents and arranges the closing funds ready for disbursement. In most instances, the lawyer acting for the buyer handles the mortgage being registered coincident with the closing of the real estate transaction.

Mortgage Commitment

A written confirmation to a prospective borrower regarding terms and conditions under which a mortgage will be granted and funds advanced to that borrower.

FORM CONTENT

Information contained in the commitment will vary, but typically includes the mortgagor(s) name, property address, legal description, loan amount, payment arrangements (including property tax installment, if applicable), mortgage advance date (typically coincides with the closing date), interest adjustment date, first payment date, term and maturity date.

Commitments usually fix a mortgage rate for a specified time period; e.g., 60 days. If the rate drops during the period, the lower rate usually applies. A typical mortgage commitment is illustrated. Terms and conditions will vary based on the lender used and circumstances relating to a particular borrower and property.

MORTGAGE LOAN COMMITMENT   Loan No. A10461

To

    Mr. Anthony Smith
    R.R. #1, Anycity

Loan Amount

Basic Loan	$152,000
Mortgage Insurance Premium	0
Total Loan	$152,000

Property

Civic Address	42 Leafy Drive, Anycity
Legal Description	Lot 23, Plan 99M–1631

Terms

Interest Rate	8.25%
Term	5 Years
Amortization	25 Years
I.A.D.	September 1, 20xx
First Payment Date	October 1, 20xx

Type of Mortgage

    Conventional

Repayment   Repayable in blended monthly installments of $1,184.43 plus an amount which in our opinion is sufficient to enable us to pay the property taxes on your behalf by the first due date of the tax bill each year, currently estimated at $196.64. It is understood that repayment will be by preauthorized cheque drawn on your bank.

Taxes   In order to satisfy the foregoing tax requirement, we shall withhold funds from our mortgage advance to accumulate sufficient credit in your tax account. The amount of $1,245.00 will be deducted for this purpose.

Fire Insurance   We shall require evidence of fire insurance coverage in the amount of not less than $140,000 taken with an insurer acceptable to us. Such policy must contain the standard Insurance Bureau of Canada mortgage clause and must indicate our interest as first mortgagee.

Survey Requirement   An acceptable survey prepared by a duly certified Land Surveyor is to be furnished to our Solicitor prior to the disbursement of funds.

Solicitor   B. Watson be appointed to act on our behalf in this transaction. All documentation including but not limited to survey, title and insurance must be acceptable to us prior to the advance of funds.

Costs   A processing fee amounting to $50.00 will be deducted from our advance of funds. Should the loan not be proceeded with, this fee will still be payable in any event. You are to pay all legal and survey costs incurred in this transaction.

General Conditions

    (i)   This approval is based upon and subject to the accuracy of information furnished in connection with your application.

    (ii) In cases where there is a construction loan, advances will be made at the discretion of the lender, who will always retain sufficient funds to complete construction.

    (iii) Funds are available under this mortgage until October 1, 20xx at which time, this commitment may be amended or withdrawn at our option.

Privileges   There is a 10% prepayment privilege. See Attached. This mortgage is open for full discharge with 3 months bonus. See attached. Mortgagor is responsible for total 20xx taxes.

Special Conditions   If this mortgage loan covers a newly constructed house or house being constructed for sale, our Solicitor will be required to obtain a certified copy of the New Home Enrollment form, endorsed by ONHWP before making any mortgages advances.

Acceptance of Offer   This offer of mortgage loan is open for acceptance by you until the close of business on August 7, 20xx by which time, the enclosed copy of this letter, duly executed, plus a deposit of $NIL being a Standby Fee shall be in our hands. The aforementioned deposit without interest will be refunded to you upon the disbursement of mortgage funds, but will be retained by us if this commitment is cancelled by you after acceptance as liquidated damages and not as a penalty.

This commitment is not transferable and the benefit may not be assigned. If the above conditions are satisfactory to you, please indicate your acceptance by signing and returning the enclosed copy to us, at the above address.

Accepted as above, this _____ day of _____ , 20xx

_____
Applicant's Signature

Fire Insurance

Fire insurance coverage is normally cancelled by the seller and rewritten by the buyer, prior to the closing date. The mortgage document (and often the mortgage commitment) outlines the precise coverages required. Full replacement value coverage ensures the mortgagee that the total risk is insured against loss. Limited insurance to cover only the mortgage amount would unnecessarily expose the mortgagee in case of a partial loss. Sufficient funds may not be available to fully correct the damage.

Taxes

The lender normally specifies a method by which taxes are paid. The commitment may contain a provision whereby an amount (usually between ¼ and ½ of the estimated annual taxes) is withheld for payment of taxes so that such payments are always current. Lenders usually adjust the monthly amount to gradually build a tax reserve.

Limiting Conditions

Limiting conditions will vary but can include stipulations such as written verification that the taxes are not in arrears, proof of fire insurance, satisfactory evidence of title and the provision of a survey acceptable to the mortgage (or title insurance that eliminates the lender's need for a survey). The application fee paid for underwriting the mortgage may not be refunded if any or all of these limiting conditions are not fulfilled and/or the loan is not advanced.

Underwriting and Other Costs

Most lenders assess a fee for underwriting expense when arranging a mortgage.

- A conventional mortgage typically involves an application fee plus the cost of an appraisal. Mortgage default insurance fees are normally not applicable, but can be imposed based on lender requirements.
- High ratio mortgages through CMHC or private insurance providers (e.g., Genworth Financial Capital and AIG United Guaranty) are subject to an application fee and an insurance premium, with graduated upward rates as the loan-to-value ratio rises. Mortgage insurance fees are subject to provincial sales tax, which must be paid on closing.
- High ratio mortgages under the *National Housing Act*, administered by CMHC, are similarly graduated and subject to an application fee and insurance premium. Mortgage default insurance premiums can be paid up front or added to the mortgage amount (the latter being by far the most common practice).

An example is provided outlining fictitious rates and premiums for mortgage default insurance. As a reminder, all mortgages with a loan-to-value ratio of 80% or more must be insured. The lender may require mortgage default insurance for lower loan-to-value ratios based on internal policies. Practitioners should access web sites for CMHC and private providers to obtain current premiums and requirements.

CALCULATING MORTGAGE DEFAULT INSURANCE PREMIUMS

Based on fictitious ratios and premiums. Contact CMHC or a private provider (e.g., Genworth Financial Canada or AIG United Guaranty).

LOAN-TO-VALUE RATIO	PREMIUM BASED ON LOAN AMOUNT*
Up to and including 65%	0.50%
Up to and including 75%	0.65
Up to and including 80%	1.00
Up to and including 85%	1.75

LOAN-TO-VALUE RATIO	PREMIUM BASED ON LOAN AMOUNT*
Up to and including 90%	2.00
Up to and including 95%	2.75
Up to and including 100%	3.10

EXAMPLES

PURCHASE PRICE**	DOWN PAYMENT	MORTGAGE AMOUNT	LTV (%)	PREMIUM (%)	PREMIUM ($)
299,000	54,000	245,000	82	1.75	4,287.50
249,000	15,000	234,000	94	2.75	6,435.00
210,000	45,000	165,000	79	1.00	1,650.00

* Additional premium surcharges may apply; e.g., with selected types of variable rate mortgages and progress advances (new construction). Harmonized sales tax applies to insurance premium.

** Insured loans are subject to maximum house price.

MORTGAGE BROKER FEES

Mortgage brokers can receive fees for services provided to the borrower and/or the lender. Borrower fees are typically associated with commercial mortgages or residential mortgages requiring additional services by the broker. For most residential mortgages, the lender pays the fee. This fee is determined according to the mortgage amount.

Brokers and lenders use basis points when calculating fees; i.e., 100 basis points equals one percent. For example, if a mortgage broker is paid 75 basis points on a $200,000 mortgage, he or she would receive $1,500 ($200,000 x .0075). Mortgage brokers are required to make disclosures regarding fees in accordance with the *Mortgage Brokers, Lenders and Administrators Act, 2006*.

LEGAL FEES

Lawyers typically charge a fee for preparing and registering the mortgage. Often, the fee for the transfer of title and arranging the mortgage are combined. Additional legal costs include specific fees/disbursements relating to the title search, arranging title insurance, conducting a title search (including an access fee to Teranet) and mortgage registration fees.

MORTGAGE PRODUCTS

Most mortgage products flow from four basic payment arrangements: **interest only**, **interest accruing**, **interest plus specified principal** and **blended (amortized)**. The final option can be either a fixed or variable rate.

Interest Only	The borrower does not repay any principal, but remits interest payments at regular, specified intervals. The principal amount is due at the end of the mortgage term. Interest only mortgages are sometimes used in short-term seller take backs or interim financing to avoid complex interest calculations. A promissory note is typically based on an interest only arrangement.
Interest Accruing	The lender receives no payment of interest or principal during the mortgage term. Interest due and payable is accrued. Consequently, the lender's risk actually grows during the term. Interest accruing mortgages are rarely found in today's marketplace and, if used at all, would undoubtedly be for a very short time period. Interest accruing arrangements are often found in student loan programs, where interest owed is added to the amount outstanding (referred to as interest capitalization). The individual does not have to make payments while enrolled in full-time studies, but the loan amount increases by the amount of unpaid interest. Such plans may also include subsidized rates and interest-free periods.
Interest Plus Specified Principal	This plan, sometimes referred to as a straight principal reduction plan, requires the borrower to repay a fixed principal amount at specified times during the term. At regular intervals, the borrower is also asked to pay interest on the outstanding balance. For example, a loan of $60,000 might require quarterly principal payments of $2,000 together with interest on the unpaid balance for each quarter.
Blended (Amortized)	This plan provides for equal payments made at regular specified intervals during the mortgage term. Each payment is a blend of principal and interest based on the amortized schedule for the mortgage. Blended mortgages can be either fixed or variable. The fixed mortgage has a set interest rate for the blended mortgage during the mortgage term. The variable rate mortgage has an interest rate that varies based on the lender's prime rate or some other identified index. As rates rise or fall, payments or the amortization period are adjusted accordingly. The blended plan dominates the residential market.

Fixed vs. Variable

The standard blended mortgage is generally referred to as a fixed mortgage; i.e., a blended principal/interest payment is fixed throughout the term. However, increasing lender competition has produced a myriad of prepayment or open privileges (see next topic titled *Open vs. Closed*).

Longer-term fixed mortgages are popular when rates are expected to trend upwards. Short term fixed may offer attractive rates, but renewal timing can be problematic in volatile mortgage markets; e.g., a six-month mortgage which renews just as interest rates spike.

Variable rate mortgages fluctuate with the applicable bank prime rate. Corresponding adjustments are made to payments or amortization. Typically, payment adjustments are made quarterly, half-yearly or yearly…but many variations exist.

Capped variable rate mortgages set limits on rate increases/decreases and a lock-in (sometimes referred to as convertible option) provides for conversion to fixed. Read the fine print on the lock-in, particularly what administrative costs and interest rate apply.

Open vs. Closed

Closed and open mortgages are commonly misunderstood. Terminology found in the marketplace can be confusing. A closed mortgage may become open and an open mortgage may be partially closed.

A fully-closed mortgage does not permit principal repayment before maturity (other than regularly scheduled payments). However, market circumstances can alter the lender's perspective. For example, a mortgage written at 4% is a poor investment if current rates are hovering at 8%. The lender, in allowing prepayment, could free up funds for potentially higher returns. Further, legislation also has a bearing. The *Interest Act* (federal) provides that a mortgagor (other than a corporation) may, after five years, pay off the mortgage subject to a three months' interest penalty.

Conversely, an open mortgage may not actually be fully open. The lender may require a penalty or, at minimum, notice. Creative mortgage products now contain both open and closed provisions. In other words, only part of the principal may be open without notice or penalty; e.g., a one-time 10% principal reduction (remember, 90% remains closed) or the mortgage may be periodically open subject to notice but no penalty; e.g., an option for 10% principal reduction on each anniversary date.

Inventive combinations have also appeared; e.g., the 20 plus 20 mortgage (or variation thereof). Twenty percent of the outstanding principal can be paid on each anniversary, as well as increasing periodic payments by 20% on that same date.

Read the Fine Print	CAUTION

Carefully analyze every mortgage product. Privileges, stipulations and conditions often lie buried deep in the preprinted wording. Pay particular attention to prepayment privileges. Get specifics. Remember…the best way to reduce borrowing costs is to pay off the mortgage earlier.

EXPANDED PAYMENT FLEXIBILITY

Today's mortgage market is highly competitive. Lenders have added more flexibility to attract consumers by including doubling up features (the doubling of any scheduled principal interest payment), offering of monthly, semi-monthly, bi-weekly and weekly payment options, and the ability to skip payments (e.g., borrower may skip a payment for every doubling payment that is made). In that way, borrowers have more flexibility to handle variations in cash flow or more effectively deal with unexpected expenses.

INCENTIVES

Creative incentives are commonplace in today's market. Cash backs have been popular, as buyers receive dollars to assist with closing costs. Typically, the cash back is 2% or 3% for longer term, fixed mortgages. However, such benefits are built in the rate structure. Borrowers typically pay back that amount and more in higher fixed rates. Reward miles have struck a note with consumers. Mortgage payments translate into travel miles.

These and similar offerings are worth investigation, but carefully shop the market. As a general guideline, arranging the best package is a matter of risk and cost. Some want to gamble, some don't. Some need extra cash today, others seek long-term assurances… and some just love reward miles. The bottom line—it's easy to customize the financing package to suit circumstances.

SECTION V   PROPERTY FINANCING

CUSTOM PACKAGES

Lenders are also customizing packages to suit specific market niches. For example, family plans have attracted consumers. Under this mortgage arrangement, a borrower can obtain financing against the principal residence to assist his or her adult child in purchasing accommodation when in post-secondary education or assisting a fixed-income parent in securing a home. Other packages are designed for new immigrants, owner-occupied rental properties (including upgrades to these rental units) and secondary homes (e.g., cottages).

NEGOTIATIONS

While residential financing is fairly straightforward, challenges can arise with qualifying and related issues. Seven creative approaches are presented that can assist new practitioners when working with buyers and sellers, should difficulties arise in the financing process.

Increase Amortization

Lenders may consider a longer amortization given strong borrower covenant, thereby reducing mortgage payments and, in turn, permitting lower income qualification levels for GDS/TDS purposes.

> **EXAMPLE**   *The Older Cottage*
>
> Buyer Ramos wants to purchase and renovate an aging cottage. Fifteen-year amortizations are typical for this property type. The monthly payment is $1,360.25 ($150,000 @ 7.25%, 15-year am.). Ramos' income of $45,500 falls short of the lender's 32% GDS requirement of $51,009.42.
>
> The lender extends the amortization to 25 years, given the applicant's 18-year employment record. Ramos now exceeds the minimum GDS income requirement of $40,270.42 based on the lowered $1,073.88 monthly payment.

Refinance/Debt Consolidation

Consolidating short-term debts into a longer-term amortized loan can reduce monthly financial commitments and free up borrower credit for qualifying purposes.

> **EXAMPLE**   *TDS Ratio*
>
> Buyer Burgess currently owes $13,000 in various small loans with differing, short amortizations. The total monthly payment of $287.50 places Burgess' TDS at 44%. By securing a debt consolidation loan at 9.5% with a 15-year amortization, the monthly payments are reduced from $287.50 to $134.32 and TDS is reduced to an acceptable level from the lender's perspective.

Use Leverage

Effective use of borrowed funds can result in wealth building, assuming rising real estate values. As a cautionary note, practitioners are reminded that while positive leverage is desirable, negative leverage can have serious adverse consequences during market downturns.

> **EXAMPLE** *Leverage*
>
> Buyer Leonardo has a $100,000 down payment and can obtain a 6.5% mortgage for construction of his $300,000 new home. The LTV is 66 2/3%. Leonardo also has access to an attractive, low risk investment returning 10% annually over five years.
>
> By increasing the LTV to 90% with $30,000 down, the buyer has freed up $70,000 for the alternative investment. In effect, Leonardo is using other people's money to increase (leverage) the yield on available funds.

Caution is advised in such matters. While positive leverage increases yield, negative leverage has the reverse effect. Many investors have experienced the financial hardships of negative leverage, particularly in a declining real estate market. Leverage is most commonly associated with income-producing properties and is discussed in relation to commercial properties in *The Commercial Real Estate Transaction.*

Include a Guarantor

A person may co-sign as a guarantor, thereby reducing risk from the lender's perspective and resulting in the applicant's approval. The guarantor is providing a separate personal covenant over and above a named party in a contract regarding some obligation, such as a mortgage, personal loan or lease.

> **EXAMPLE** *Father as Guarantor*
>
> Buyer Morton's GDS ratio is 34% with the TDS at 42%, both slightly above the lender's requirements. The application is refused. The buyer's father agrees to be a guarantor on the mortgage and signs a guarantor clause which states that he will jointly and severally be responsible for the mortgage.

In a mortgage, the guarantor normally agrees to do the following:

- Perform and carry out the covenants as outlined in the mortgage document; and
- Make such payments on dates set out in the mortgage document.

The guarantor does not normally receive a release until all covenants outlined in the mortgage document are satisfied. Further, the mortgagee does not have to exhaust all avenues against the original mortgagor before turning to the guarantor. The guarantor will not usually be notified that a default has occurred and remedies that might be taken need not be the same as exercised against the mortgagor nor with the same degree of leniency.

A variety of clauses can be used for the purposes of adding a guarantor either within the mortgage document or as an attachment. Typically, this clause creates a separate personal covenant that can be acted upon by the mortgagee. The lender's position is further secured and risk reduced. Applicants who would otherwise not be able to qualify may find this an acceptable avenue, given the agreement of a third party to become involved in the mortgage transaction.

Improve the Borrower's Qualifying Profile

Many borrowers overlook funds that can increase down payment, while improving their overall covenant. Don't forget about often overlooked sources: cash value life insurance, negotiable stocks/bonds, gifts, future bonuses (confirmed by employer), income tax refunds and pledging of future dividends.

Use the Right Lender

The buyer has limited resources, a few financial problems in the past and doesn't fit the ideal borrower profile. Get expert mortgage advice and seek lenders specializing in non-confirming (sub prime) loans. Underwriting fees and mortgage rates will probably be higher, but the borrower can secure credit and start building equity (and a better future credit rating).

Shop for the Total Package, Not Just Rates

Don't let clients immediately leap at the lowest rate. Other costs (e.g., underwriting fees, appraisal costs, application/processing charges, discharge penalties) add up quickly. Further, attractive introductory rates for variable mortgages may be prelude to higher lock-in rates. The client should carefully compare and seek out the best, tailor-made package.

CALCULATOR SKILLS

A working knowledge of financing options is key to effective negotiations. Routinely, practitioners are involved in discussions about mortgages and financing options. Calculator techniques can help in quickly addressing many questions posed by buyers and sellers.

In *Real Estate as a Professional Career*, interest rate and blended mortgage basics were covered. However, the HP 10BII has many features that can assist when working with clients and narrow financing options to suit a particular transaction. A case study is provided to illustrate selected techniques and improve your skills.

Case Study	ADVANCED CALCULATIONS: UNKNOWN TERMS, AMORTIZATIONS AND PAYMENT FREQUENCIES

The HP 10BII's built-in options are handy when discussing mortgage market options with clients. Becoming adept with keystrokes can help narrow financing options, assist clients shopping the market, provide meaningful comparisons, and help buyers and sellers make informed decisions.

SCENARIO 1: ANALYZING MORTGAGE TERMS

Mortgage calculations would be easy if the buyer simply wanted to know the payment, but what about the tougher questions: *If my mortgage payments were $200 higher, how much larger mortgage could I afford? What if I reduce the amortization, how does that affect my payment? What happens to the payment if the commitment comes back at 5.5% instead of 5.0%?*

Think in terms of unknowns. In the simplest case, the mortgage amount, interest rate and amortization are known, but the payment is not. The buyer client is only changing the unknowns. Fortunately, the HP 10BII stores the knowns. Just insert new variables and recalculate. A series of examples illustrate the point.

MORTGAGE VARIABLE	KEYSTROKE	MORTGAGE VARIABLE	KEYSTROKE
Number of Payments Per Year	P/YR	Current Amount of Mortgage/Present Value	PV
Number of Payments (Mortgage Amortization x # Payments per Year)	N	Future Amount of Mortgage/Future Value (if not zero)	FV
Interest Rate Per Year	I/YR	Amount of Each Payment	PMT

Case Study   ADVANCED CALCULATIONS: UNKNOWN TERMS, AMORTIZATIONS AND PAYMENT FREQUENCIES

Calculating an Unknown Payment

Enter values for N, I/YR, and PV. The payment amount is calculated by pressing PMT (assuming FV is zero). The monthly payment required to fully amortize a $150,000 mortgage, 25-year term and 6.5% interest rate (compounded semi-annually, not in advance) is calculated by:

Compile Mortgage Details

N = 300 (12 x 25)   I/YR = 6.5%   PV = $150,000   FV = $0   PMT = Unknown

CALCULATE MONTHLY PAYMENT	KEYSTROKES	DISPLAY
Clear all variables	C ALL	0.00
Store # of payment periods	300 N	300.00
Store adjusted interest rate**	(see Canadian Mortgage Keystrokes)	6.41
Store present value	150000 PV	150,000.00
Calculate the monthly payment	PMT	1,004.74

The monthly payment is $1,004.74.

** The interest rate must be adjusted, as interest is compounded semi-annually but payments are made monthly. Follow the instructions for Canadian mortgages and store the value for I/YR. See *Reminders* on the following page.

Calculate a Revised Mortgage Amount

The buyer realizes that selected income was mistakenly omitted in the GDS calculation. A higher monthly payment of $1,100 results. What impact does this have on the mortgage amount, if all remaining terms stay the same? If PMT, N and I/YR are stored, pressing PV will calculate the mortgage present value (the amount to be loaned).

	KEYSTROKES	DISPLAY
Store the new payment	1100 +/- PMT	−1,100.00
Recalculate the present value (mortgage amount)	PV	164,222.30

The new mortgage amount based on a $1,100 monthly payment is $164,222.

Calculate Payment With a Different Amortization

The broker advises you that two lenders will consider the buyer's application based on a 30-year amortization (360 payments). Store the new amount in N and recalculate the monthly payment.

	KEYSTROKES	DISPLAY
Store the new number of payments	360 N	360.00
Recalculate the payment	PMT	−1,028.69

The new 30-year amortized mortgage payment is $1028.69. (A negative appears before the number—See Reminders).

Calculate Payment With a Different Interest Rate

As a final step in negotiations, you discover that the buyer may qualify for a 6.0% interest rate. Complete the keystrokes for Canadian mortgages. The interest rate is automatically stored in I/YR.

	KEYSTROKES	DISPLAY
Store adjusted interest rate**	(see Canadian Mortgage Keystrokes)	5.93
Recalculate the payment	PMT	−976.83

The new mortgage payment is $976.83 (based on a 30-year amortized mortgage of $164,222).

Case Study **ADVANCED CALCULATIONS: UNKNOWN TERMS, AMORTIZATIONS AND PAYMENT FREQUENCIES**

REMINDERS

1. Canadian Mortgage Keystrokes

- Enter the nominal rate and press [ ] [NOM%] .

- Enter the number of compounding periods in a year (2) and press [ ] [P/YR] .

- Solve for the effective rate by pressing [ ] [EFF%] .

- Enter the number of payment periods in a year and press [ ] [P/YR] .

- Solve for the adjusted nominal rate by pressing [ ] [NOM%] .

The last step automatically stores the adjusted nominal rate as [I/YR] . Mortgages require an end of period calculation: Pressing [ ] [BEG/END] toggles between begin and end mode. Ensure the calculator display does not show BEGIN.

2. Negative/Positive Signs

Negative or positive cash flow depends on one's perspective. The lender views mortgage funds advanced (outgoing) as a negative, and incoming mortgage payments, as a positive. The borrower views mortgage funds received (incoming) as a positive, and outgoing mortgage payments, as a negative. The HP 10BII defaults to the borrower's perspective.

SCENARIO 2: USING THE AMORTIZATION FUNCTION

Demonstrate your skills with more indepth analysis of mortgage options. Once all mortgage details are stored, the amortization function provides principal, interest and balance details. Results could be used to develop a detailed amortization schedule.

The amortization function is accessed by pressing [ ] [AMORT] . By default, this keystroke will provide amortization details for the end of the first year of payments (after the 12 th month). The calculator display will show the period being amortized. Pressing the [=] button scrolls through the details in the following order:

- The amount applied to principal in the range of payments.

- The amount applied to interest in the range of payments.

- The outstanding balance as of the end of the range of payments. The remaining balance equals the initial mortgage less the amount applied toward the principal.

Once an initial amortization has been calculated, pressing [ ] [AMORT] calculates the amortization for the next range of payments using the same increment as the first calculation (one year by default).

- To amortize a single payment, enter the payment number (i.e., 6 for an amortization after 6 months) followed by [INPUT] [ ] [AMORT] .

- To amortize a specific range of payments (i.e., from 6 to 18 months) enter **6** [INPUT] **18** [ ] [AMORT] .

Example—Mortgage Amortization

Buyer McKay obtained a $185,000 mortgage amortized over 20 years, at 6.25% compounded semi-annually.

- a. Calculate the principal and interest paid in the first 5 years of the mortgage.

- b. Calculate the lump sump payment that would completely repay the mortgage at the end of Year 15.

TASK 1 CLEAR ALL VARIABLES & CHECK MODE	KEYSTROKES	DISPLAY
Clear all previously stored variables	[ ] [C ALL]	**0.00**
If display shows BEGIN, press [ ] [BEG/END] to switch to END mode.		

Case Study | ADVANCED CALCULATIONS: UNKNOWN TERMS, AMORTIZATIONS AND PAYMENT FREQUENCIES

TASK 2 ADJUST THE INTEREST RATE FOR SEMI-ANNUAL COMPOUNDING	KEYSTROKES	DISPLAY
Enter the nominal rate and press [ ] [NOM%]	6.25 [ ] [NOM%]	**6.25**
Enter the number of compounding periods in a year and press [ ] [P/YR]	2 [ ] [P/YR]	**2.00**
Solve for the effective rate by pressing [ ] [EFF%]	[ ] [EFF%]	**6.35**
Enter the number of payment periods in a year and press [ ] [P/YR]	12 [ ] [P/YR]	**12.00**
Solve for the adjusted nominal rate by pressing [ ] [NOM%]	[ ] [NOM%]	**6.17**

This last step automatically stores the adjusted nominal rate (6.17) as [I/YR]

TASK 3 STORE VALUES & CALCULATE PAYMENT	KEYSTROKES	DISPLAY
Store the amortization period of the mortgage	240 [N]	**240.00**
Store the present value of the mortgage	185000 [PV]	**185,000.00**
Calculate the monthly payment	[PMT]	**–1,343.62**

TASK 4 CALCULATE PRINCIPAL & INTEREST PAID BY END OF YEAR 5	KEYSTROKES	DISPLAY
Enter the range of payments to amortize (from Month 1–60)	1 [INPUT] 60	**60**
Calculate amortization	[ ] [AMORT]	**1–60**
View principal paid	[=]	**–27,497.10**
View interest paid	[=]	**–53,120.10**

TASK 5 CALCULATE OUTSTANDING BALANCE AT END OF YEAR 15	KEYSTROKES	DISPLAY
Enter the range of payments to amortize (from Month 1–180)	1 [INPUT] 180	**180**
Calculate amortization	[ ] [AMORT]	**1–180**
Scroll to outstanding balance	[=][=][=]	**69,215.90**

At the end of Year 5, $27,497.10 has been applied towards the mortgage principal, $53,120.10 has been applied towards interest. At the end of Year 15, Buyer McKay could completely repay the mortgage for $69,215.90.

NOTES • The value for N could have been entered by pressing **20** [ ] [x P/YR].

     • At this point any variable could be changed and the terms recalculated and a new amortization schedule produced.

● SCENARIO 3: USING DIFFERENT PAYMENT FREQUENCIES

Buyers may want to analyze payment options, e.g., weekly, bi-weekly, semi-monthly and monthly. Assume the client in Scenario 2 wants bi-weekly payments rather than monthly. The procedure for calculating payments and amortization is identical to Scenario 2, except where the number of payments per year (26 bi-weekly payments per year), amortization period (20 years x 26 payments/year), and range of payments to amortize (5 years x 26 payments/year) are entered. A "●" has been placed beside each entry in Scenario 2 that would require altered entries. The bi-weekly payment would be $619.28. Over the 20-year amortization the client would pay $447.27 less interest than if monthly payments were chosen ($137,021.52 total interest for bi-weekly payments versus $137,468.79 total interest for monthly payments).

NOTE To reset from 26 payments per year, enter 12 [ ] [P/YR]. To confirm the change, press [ ] [C ALL].

COMMERCIAL UNDERWRITING

Business financing differs from residential given inherent complexities, as well as a somewhat different perspective for underwriting, particularly with large commercial transactions. Underwriters looking at small business operations typically focus their attention on *business specifics*, *property details* and *borrower covenant*. As mortgage amount increases, business performance is emphasized with far less concern regarding personal covenant.

Commercial lenders consider risk and return in the decision-making process. Debt financing is actually little more than shifting equity from mortgagor to mortgagee as a trade off against long term goals. Lenders have inundated the market with clever methods to meet most borrowers' needs while seeking safeguards. Institutional lenders have refined criteria and rules of thumb to more rigidly structure the underwriting process.

Practitioners should clearly understand the most typical approaches and usual documentation required. Commercial salespersons also require a knowledge of unique forms of financing such as development loans, letters of guarantee, lines of credit, and gap, bridge and standby loans to discuss financing options with clients and customers.

Mortgage Documentation Package

Commercial mortgage applications require significantly more documentation than their residential counterparts. The typical mortgage documentation package contains information relevant to a lender in making a mortgage financing decision regarding a specific project or property. The package (sometimes referred to as a *mortgage request package*) can be used for both residential and commercial mortgaging, but is most commonly associated with industrial, office/retail and investment properties.

The range of materials varies significantly by property type, project scope, lender requirements and the specific investor.

- Site and property information along with relevant statistics, sketches, valuation estimates and associated supporting documentation.
- Fully completed mortgage application, appraisal, verification of income/salaries, credit check, verification of resources and other financial commitments, and the agreement of purchase and sale.
- In the case of resale properties, the lender will usually insist on financial statements for at least the past three to five years, along with a review of existing leases on the property.

- For new construction, pro forma income statements, letters of commitment from prospective tenants (or suitable analysis identifying potential for lessees), details concerning principals involved in the project, feasibility studies and applicable construction information (if relevant) are normally requested.

The overall structure of a typical documentation package is illustrated, but scope and format varies significantly in the marketplace.

TYPICAL DOCUMENTATION PACKAGE

PART 1 Summary Statement of Objectives

PART 2 Site Description
(general description, site data and relevant statistics)

PART 3 Improvements
(detailed description of existing or planned improvements)

PART 4 Financial Profile
(personal and/or corporate)

PART 5 Mortgage Financing Request
(amount, terms and special requirements)

APPENDIX Support Documentation
(fully completed mortgage application, credit references and financial information)

Practitioners are advised to seek information from lending institutions regarding local practices and procedures. As a general rule, more information is better than less. The lender must be comfortable with both borrower and project, as large commercial loans represent a significant commitment by the lender.

Small Business Financing

Small business financing is typically offered through a separate department or distinct division within a commercial banking division. Given the wide range of businesses (e.g., garages, retail shops, restaurants and repair facilities) lenders rarely use a standardized approach as information required will vary. Also, practitioners will find lenders that focus on specific business classifications; e.g., warehouses, golf courses and bars. Lenders are able to lend confidently for such classifications, as they fully understand the risks associated with these enterprises.

In addition, practitioners will encounter lenders who specialize in difficult to finance businesses that could include rural business operations, small non-owner occupied commercial businesses, start-ups and home office configurations. As with other specialty areas, lenders normally seek added return to offset risk.

CANADA SMALL BUSINESS FINANCING PROGRAM

In addition to in-house mortgage, lenders may avail themselves of the **Canada Small Business Financing (CSBF) Program**. This federal financing program was created to assist entrepreneurs by way of loans, including capital leases, when establishing and improving small businesses. The federal government guarantees 85% of lenders' losses due to default. The CSBF program is not available for farming, charitable or religious enterprises.

Loans are available for buying and improving real property, along with the acquisition of new or used equipment. CSBF loans have proven particularly effective with startup businesses requiring significant leasehold improvements; e.g., restaurant equipment and computer hardware/software. Local lenders will have current information regarding maximum term and loan amount under this program. A personal guarantee may be required and registration, as well as administration, fees apply.

WEB LINKS
Canada Small Business Financing Program   For more information concerning this federal financing program, go to *www. ic.gc.ca/csbfa*.

ALTERNATIVE SOURCES

While most emphasis is placed on institutional lenders and their role in commercial financing, alternative sources of debt financing are also available to the commercial marketplace including private investors, seller take back arrangements and sale/leasebacks.

Private Investors

Private investors may offer greater scope given more relaxed lending criteria, safety margins or other approval considerations. In addition, application forms, underwriting requirements and the mortgage approval process may be simplified. On the converse, buyers need to be aware of limited legislation imposed on such investors. Ensure that the buyer's lawyer is involved in all aspects of the mortgage transaction. Be very specific in detailing mortgage particulars within the agreement of purchase and sale.

Reliable sources of private money often include: seller take back mortgages, local developers/investors and lawyers acting for clients (e.g., private investors, trusts and estates). Specialized investors frequently advertise availability of funds in appropriate trade magazines or local/regional/national newspapers.

Seller Take Back

The seller take back mortgage is a popular negotiating tool in both residential and commercial markets, particularly when financing proves difficult through conventional lenders and/or seller participation provides a better overall package in negotiations. The buyer may be attracted to this type of financing as it can avoid certain costs, paper work and regulations of conventional lenders. The seller may be drawn to the STB if his/her property remains unsold. Further, a mortgage might be a worthwhile investment for the seller.

From a real estate practitioner's perspective, the STB is an excellent vehicle provided that the client is given a full explanation before any commitment. Every seller should be given the opportunity to take back a mortgage and, at the same time, be provided with sufficient information to make a well-informed decision on the matter. An example is provided in which the seller is seeking further information when considering a STB. STBs may be seriously considered in the following situations:

Seller Motivation	The seller is anxious to sell and has no real concerns about taking back a mortgage to hasten the sale of his/her property.
Underwriting Fundamentals	The market is strong, the equity position of the buyer is adequate (i.e., downpayment) and the buyer can qualify to make the required mortgage payments.
Limited Appeal	The property has limited buyer appeal due to age, condition or location and financing would improve overall marketing impact.
Increased Competition	The number of competing houses is increasing and a competitive advantage from a financing perspective is required to increase saleability.
Sale Potential	Buyers for the mortgage are available should the seller wish to sell the STB.

Sale/Leaseback

Sale/Leaseback

The sale of a property with the leaseback of that property to the original owner.

A **sale/leaseback** involves the sale of a property by an owner with the lease back of the property to that original owner. The sale/leaseback arrangement can prove beneficial to both the seller and buyer of property. The seller liquidates his/her equity in the land and building to use for other purposes, while retaining the location under a long-term lease arrangement. The buyer, as an investor, is assured of a long-term cash flow and the seller may have an option to repurchase the property following the lease.

Obviously, certain risks are associated with the sale/leaseback. The investor is relying on the tenant to make regular lease payments, thereby ensuring the anticipated rate of return. Any default can adversely affect investor cash flow. On the converse, the land may appreciate substantially during the lease period with the investor enjoying capital appreciation even though the building may have depreciated significantly during the extended lease period.

COMMERCIAL LENDING PRACTICES

Debt is intrinsically tied to most commercial transactions and the success of ventures often rests in the availability and suitability of financing. Mortgaging directly affects cash flows and yields and most acquisitions hinge on favourable debt financing. The optimum arrangement is twofold:

- the lender is provided reasonable security; and
- the investor is afforded the opportunity to enhance yield.

Criteria vary by commercial lender, market conditions and type of project and are essentially designed to give the lender reasonable assurances of investment security when advancing funds. Typical criteria are highlighted for illustration purposes only and are not exhaustive in nature.

Loan-to-Value Ratio

Most lenders use a conservative loan-to-value ratio (also referenced as the loan ratio) as their first line of risk defense. Additional security or collateral is usually sought in instances when the loan-to-value ratio meets or slightly exceeds a predetermined comfort level for the lender. Loan-to-value ratios vary by lender and type of property. Institutional lenders are restricted by law to a maximum 75%.

> **EXAMPLE**   *Risk and Loan-to-Value Ratio*
>
> Lender Inc. will advance 75% of value on most commercial projects. However, this ratio is reduced to 65% for older structures and situations identified as higher risk by the institution. McKay approaches Lender Inc. for debt financing on a property valued at $750,000. The risk assessment by Lender Inc. can significantly influence approved amounts.
>
> - Lender Inc. initially considers a mortgage based on 75% of value:
>
> $750,000 x .75 = **$562,500** (loan amount).
>
> - Lender Inc. perceives addition risk and revises loan-to-value ratio. New amount based on 65% of value:
>
> $750,000 x .65 = **$487,500** (loan amount).
>
> Perception of risk on the lender's part has lowered mortgage advance funds by $75,000.

Debt Coverage Ratio

This ratio, comparing net operating income to total debt service, is also referred to as the debt service coverage ratio. The **debt coverage ratio** is frequently used by loan and mortgage underwriters to establish whether or not a business or rental property is capable of handling a specific debt payment level.

Debt Coverage Ratio

A ratio used by commercial mortgage underwriters to assess lending risk by comparing net operating income to total debt service.

The debt coverage ratio is calculated by dividing net operating income (NOI) by total debt service (principal and interest payments). The ratio should be in a positive range (i.e., above 1) in order for income to properly address total debt service. Lenders often require a debt coverage ratio of 1.2 or higher when considering loan applications for rental property and other commercial ventures. In other words, for $1.00 of debt, a net operating income of $1.20 is available to service that debt.

Simply put, as the ratio moves above one, lender risk is reduced; when it moves below one, risk increases.

> **EXAMPLE**   *Lender DCR Met*
>
> A buyer is seeking financing for an existing rental property. The lender requires a DCR of 1.2. A reconstructed operating statement has been prepared based on the previous year's income and expenses. The net operating income is $28,373. The borrower is seeking a loan with monthly payments of $1,670 per month.
>
> The DCR is:
>
> $$\frac{\text{NOI}}{\text{Debt Service}} = \frac{\$28{,}373}{12 \times \$1{,}670} = \frac{\$28{,}373}{\$20{,}040} = \mathbf{1.42}$$
>
> The rental property meets the lender's criteria.

EXAMPLE   *Lender DCR Not Met*

Lender Inc. will advance mortgage funds based on a DCR of 1.20. An investor approaches Lender Inc. seeking a mortgage of $375,000, amortized over 20 years, at 8.00%. The investor reports a net operating income of $39,316.

Annual Debt Service:	3,106.34 x 12 = 37,276.09
Debt Coverage Ratio:	39,316 ÷ 37,276 = 1.05

The DCR does not meet or exceed 1.20 and therefore does not meet Lender Inc.'s criteria for advancing mortgage funds.

Safety Margin

Some lenders apply a safety margin when lending based on net operating income. In effect, the margin accomplishes the same net result as the debt coverage ratio in that the mortgage amount is directly linked to net operating income.

The safety margin represents either a dollar or percentage factor that serves as a financial cushion for the lender between the obligation of an owner to pay annual debt service and the forecasted net operating income from the property under consideration. In other words, the lender seeks additional security to ensure that not every dollar of net operating income is dedicated to addressing mortgage payments. A safety margin is typically required by a lender when considering income property in commercial mortgage qualification.

EXAMPLE   *The Multi-Residential Building*

The Canadian National Bank is concerned about Seller Smith's income stream derived from a multi-residential building located in Anycity. According to the reconstructed worksheet prepared by Salesperson Lane of ABC Realty Inc., the net operating income is $105,256. In theory, this amount could be devoted totally to debt service payments. However, a safety margin of 20% is required by the lender.

Safety Margin/Mortgage Qualification for 1937 Lakefront Drive, Anycity	
Net Operating Income *(Forecasted for Upcoming Year)*	$105,256
Lender Safety Margin *(20% of Net Operating Income)*	21,051
Amount Available for Annual Debt Service *(105,256 – 21,051)*	84,205
Amount Available for Monthly Debt Service *(84,205 ÷ 12)*	7,017

Assuming that a 7% mortgage can be obtained from the Canadian National Bank with a 25-year amortization, Seller Smith would qualify for a mortgage of approximately $1,001,845. This amount is calculated by referring to the Mortgage Payment Factors. The payment factor per $1,000 is 7.004158 for a 7% mortgage with a 25-year amortization. Therefore, the amount of the mortgage can be determined by dividing Smith's amount available for monthly debt service by the factor to arrive at the number of 000s (thousands) in mortgage principal. In this instance, Smith can qualify for 7,017 ÷ 7.004158 = 1001.833 (000s) in mortgage amount which equals $1,001,833 (answer is arrived at by moving the decimal three places to the right).

EXAMPLE   *Retail Complex: Reduced Mortgage Amount*

Potential Gross (Rental) Income	**$234,500**
Less: Vacancy and Credit Losses	−12,440
Effective Rental Income	**222,060**
Add: Other Income	+14,300
Gross Operating Income	**236,360**
Less: Operating Expenses	−202,500
Net Operating Income	**33,860**

Analysis

Annual Debt Service $33,860 ($2,821.67 per month)
(if based on 100% of NOI)

Annual Debt Service $25,395 ($2,116.25 per month)
(based on 75% of NOI, 25% safety margin)

The increased safety margin effectively lowers the approved mortgage payment by $705.42. This payment translates into a reduced mortgage amount of:

$705.42 ÷ 7.473210   *(monthly payment factor per $1,000 for 7.75% mortgage)*

= 94.3931724 (expressed per 000's) or **$94,393.17**.

Risk and Capitalization Rate

Lenders may elect to reduce risk and augment investment security by increasing the capitalization rate. A cap rate increase lowers value for lending purposes.

EXAMPLE   *Higher Cap Rate Due to Risk*

Market research indicates that a capitalization rate for a 30-suite residential apartment building is 9.27. The lender, however, feels that this market-extracted rate is too low in relation to risk. Added risk might be justified given property location and age of the structure. The lender is concerned that long term rents may stabilize while operating expenses and maintenance will undoubtedly increase. The lender, lacking adequate comparables, establishes a cap rate based on a low-risk investment rate (bonds, mortgages) plus a risk factor. This factor represents a perception of risk and is largely a subjective interpretation based on many factors relating to the property and the marketplace.

Thirty-year bond rate:	7.20
Risk Factor (3.5% above bond rate)	3.50
Capitalization Rate	**10.70**

Assuming a net operating income of $443,292, the value can be significantly affected:

Capitalized Value Based on Market Rate: 443,292 ÷ 9.27   = $4,782,006

Capitalized Value Based on Lender Rate: 443,292 ÷ 10.70   = $4,142,916

If the lender will advance 75% of appraised value, the lending value is reduced by $639,090 and the resulting maximum mortgage would be:

$4,142,916 x .75 = **$3,107,187**

Operating Statement Adjustments

Lenders may require certain adjustments to reconstructed worksheets based on a review of the owner's operating statements and past experience with similar structures. For example, market data may suggest vacancy and credit losses other than stated on the reconstructed operating statement. Also, the lender may wish to include a reserve for replacement of specific items not included in the statement.

EXAMPLE   *The Retail Property*

The owner of an older, four-unit retail structure approaches a lender with the following reconstructed operating statement (all figures are rounded to the nearest dollar). For this exercise, assume a cap rate for lending purposes of 9.50 and the loan-to-value ratio of 0.75.

Potential Gross (Rental) Income	**$334,500**
Less: Vacancy and Credit Losses *(3.5% of Potential Rental Income)*	−11,707
Effective Rental Income	322,793
Add: Other Income	+14,300
Gross Operating Income	337,093
Less: Operating Expenses	−302,500
Net Operating Income	34,593

Lending Value:	$34,593 ÷ .095	= $364,137
Mortgage:	$364,137 x .75	= **$273,103**

Lender Inc., after reviewing the documentation, modifies the worksheet based on vacancy and credit losses of 5% and a reserve of $4,400 relating to electrical upgrades. The altered calculations are as follows:

Potential Gross (Rental) Income	**$334,500**
Less: Vacancy and Credit Losses *(5% of Potential Rental Income)*	−16,725
Effective Rental Income	317,775
Add: Other Income	+14,300
Gross Operating Income	332,075
Less: Operating Expenses	−302,500
Less: Reserve	−4,400
Net Operating Income	25,175

Lending Value:	$25,175 ÷ .095	= $265,000
Mortgage:	$265,000 x .75	= **$198,750**

Slight modifications can have significant impact. In this instance, the approved mortgage is $74,353 less than originally anticipated.

SPECIALIZED PRODUCTS

Certain unique products are used in commercial lending given specialized needs when arranging financing for new projects and existing properties. Thirteen products are highlighted in alphabetical order for illustration purposes, some of which also apply to residential financing.

Bridge Loan

A **bridge loan**, as an interim form of financing, is used in a variety of residential and commercial transactions. Bridging may occur when a buyer is committed to completing the purchase of a property on a specific date, but will not have sufficient funds until a later time. This frequently arises when the buyer's property has sold with a late closing date, or the property remains unsold. Lending institutions may be prepared to advance funds under a bridge loan based on the borrower's personal covenant, verification of relevant documentation and a direction for the payment of funds on completion of a sale, or when a mortgage is placed on the unsold property.

The bridge loan is also found in new construction. Bridge loans can assist a developer between scheduled advances (normally received through either an interim or permanent lender). The bridge loan is intended to provide cash to pay immediate expenses while awaiting the next formal advance and is said to bridge the distance between advances.

> **Bridge Loan**
>
> An interim form of financing typically used when a buyer has to close one sale prior to receiving funds from another sale.

> **EXAMPLE**   **The Expansion**
>
> Seller Smith outgrew his current commercial building and sold the property with a scheduled closing date of May 31, 20xx, which cannot be changed. He can remain in the property as a tenant until his new premises are available. Smith will net approximately $350,000 from the sale. However, his new building purchased with a negotiated selling price of $950,000 closes on April 30th. Smith requires a $300,000 downpayment in addition to the new first mortgage of $650,000. The downpayment will come from equity in his current property. The bank arranging the first mortgage agrees to advance the additional funds by way of a bridge loan until the prior property closes.

Development Loan

A **development loan** (sometimes referred to as *construction loan*) is advanced by a lender to a company for the specific purpose of servicing and improving land to the point of building construction. The term of the loan is normally one to three years. The payout of the loan occurs when the serviced land is sold to builders or to a general developer for the construction of new homes, a plaza or a rental project. Normally this type of loan is not amortized over a specific period of time, but takes the form of a collateral loan with specific guarantees and interest only payments throughout the term.

> **Development Loan**
>
> A loan advanced for servicing and improving land prior to building construction.

> **EXAMPLE**   *Residential Development Loan*
>
> Developer Reed is considering the purchase of a five-acre tract of land for residential development. The asking price is $1,499,000. Reed estimates that servicing of the property, associated costs for rezoning of the lands and other development costs will amount to $1,085,000 excluding Reed's own time and interest on monies invested. The final development will contain 30 residential lots with an estimated value of $4,250,000.
>
> A lender is interested in a development loan for $2,300,000 to be paid in successive stages starting at the point of purchase and being fully advanced on completion of servicing. No principal payments are required, the term is for two years and interest must be paid monthly based on amounts advanced. Reed is also required to make partial discharges ($140,000 per lot) for lots sold during the two-year period.

Gap Loan

A gap loan is an interim financing vehicle that provides funding between construction advances and the placement of permanent financing. While no standard scenario exists, a **gap loan** is normally associated with the following circumstance.

A large construction project has an interim lender that advances funds based on projected costs. A permanent lender advances funds at project completion and the assurance of an income stream on the property. In some cases, the project is completed and final draws have been taken under interim financing, but the permanent lender has only advanced part of the take-out funds, due to the borrowers failure to secure full rental of all space as required in the mortgage commitment; e.g., the permanent lender advances 75% of the total commitment because 25% of the floor space remains unrented. The gap loan is used to augment permanent financing advanced until full rental is achieved.

> **EXAMPLE**   *Office Building*
>
> Developer Reed is constructing an office building for $10,000,000 with an agreed take-out loan from a permanent lender for $7,500,000 based on 90% occupancy of the completed structure. The interim lender has agreed to provide three consecutive draws of $2,000,000 based on pre-determined stages of construction completion. The interim lender provides all draws as agreed totalling $6,000,000. The permanent lender subsequently advances $6,000,000 to repay the interim lender, but withholds $1,500,000 awaiting required occupancy levels. The developer, lacking sufficient funds to complete final construction secures a gap loan from a different lender for $1,500,000 until all funds from the permanent lender are advanced.

Interim Financing

Short-term or temporary financing is used to address immediate needs as distinguished from long-term debt structure. For real estate purposes, interim financing can involve any type of temporary arrangement until a permanent mortgage is put in place. Often, interim financing for new commercial projects involves temporary or gap funds to be used until scheduled advances are received in relation to the project.

EXAMPLE 1   *Interim Financing: Residential*

Seller Smith requires minimal funding to construct a new home as the majority of funds are coming from personal savings. Smith anticipates that, although some interim money may be required, he will be able to pay off this debt in a few months.

In total, Smith requires about $60,000 for a period not to exceed six months. If a mortgage was taken out on the new property, he would undoubtedly incur various legal, appraisal and incidental disbursement expenses. Instead, he secures a personal loan from his bank as a form of interim financing and largely avoids various processing costs.

EXAMPLE 2   *Interim Financing: Commercial*

Investor McKay is constructing a retail mall valued at $2,700,000. He has arranged a mortgage of $2,000,000 that is to be advanced in three stages during the development. Construction delays have affected the draw schedule by several weeks and McKay requires interim funds to pay several large invoices and take advantage of early payment discounts offered by several sub-contractors. McKay arranges interim financing (gap loan) amounting to $325,000 that will be repaid on receipt of the next construction draw.

Letter of Commitment

A letter of commitment is a written commitment by a lender setting out terms under which a loan or mortgage will be granted to a borrower. The terms typically include a specific interest rate together with a time period that the lender is bound by the commitment.

Often referred to as a mortgage commitment, this document also details any special privileges (e.g., repayment privileges), fire insurance requirements, survey requirements, processing costs and special conditions. Practitioners should note that a mortgage commitment is a *conditional lender approval* subject to terms and conditions set out in that commitment.

Letter of Credit

This letter or document is issued by a lending institution on behalf of a customer authorizing the person named to withdraw a specified amount of money based on certain prearranged terms and conditions. Letters of credit are most commonly associated with commercial ventures.

Letter of Guarantee

The letter of guarantee is often used in development projects involving a municipal body. The letter of guarantee assures the existence of funds and provides a form of promise on the part of the lending institution to step in and complete the development using its own resources, if such is necessary. The lending institution provides this guarantee to assure municipal authorities of the developer's solvency, given that a lender is prepared to back the company and the project.

Letter of Intent

A letter of intent is a written, general understanding of the parties setting out various provisions, covenants, terms and other matters that may ultimately lead to a detailed agreement between those parties. A letter of intent is viewed as a preliminary agreement between the parties and is not a formal contract.

> **EXAMPLE** *Complicated Negotiations*
>
> Owner Smith and Buyer Jones are attempting to negotiate a complex sale involving an industrial property, a wide range of fixtures and chattels, business contracts and other assets of Smith's corporation. As a further complication, the sale will require certain zoning amendments, approvals by the applicable ministry/department and a detailed accounting analysis to determine tax implications for both buyer and seller.
>
> The parties have agreed to enter into a brief letter of intent (agreement) setting out the purchase price subject to modifications, anticipated closing date and general conditions to be fulfilled. Most importantly, the entire agreement is subject to a more detailed contract being signed within a 60-day period. Essentially, the 60 days will afford both parties sufficient time to clear a number of potential hurdles prior to a formal agreement.

The letter of intent can, for example, be used in real estate transactions to provide an overall framework between a developer and owner of the lands, or a commercial landlord and a potential tenant. Generally, a letter of intent is simply a statement of general understanding and does not constitute a formal contract, nor does it create any obligation or liability unless such terms are specifically detailed.

Line of Credit

A line of credit is a highly flexible form of interim financing based on past performance and strength of personal or corporate covenants. In real estate development, a line of credit is used either in lieu of mortgages and associated advances or in addition to them. Monies advanced are secured by demand notes up to a limit specified by the applicable lender.

The line of credit, in effect, can provide interim financing or complement existing arrangements. The interest charged is normally higher than conventional mortgage rates. While it is common to see a line of credit rate one or two points above conventional mortgage rates, the rate charged depends on a host of circumstances surrounding the project, the borrower and the lender.

The demand notes underlying a line of credit can be for a specified period. More commonly, a stated amount of credit is established and all notes are processed in line with that maximum. Typically, all such notes are on a demand basis, that is, the loan may be called at the lender's option. Normally, the financial status of the borrower is reviewed on an annual or semi-annual basis.

Standby Loan

Standby Loan

A loan commitment for preliminary financing with the expectation of more favourable, permanent financing.

A **standby loan** refers to a pre-construction loan commitment arranged between a developer and a lender for preliminary financing as opposed to more permanent, long-term mortgaging. Practitioners will encounter standby loans most frequently in development projects.

The lender is attracted to this arrangement, as the rate charged is normally two to four points higher and an upfront fee (often referred to as a standby fee) is normally required. The developer, with a standby commitment, can pursue construction financing and gain additional time to secure a more favourable permanent mortgage arrangement for a particular project.

The standby loan is really a form of guarantee of credit for the project. It is rarely used except when interest rates are high but expected to lower before completion of the project. The standby loan is exercised and then discharged in favour of more attractive rates offered by a permanent lender at some point in the future.

SECTION V PROPERTY FINANCING

Wraparounds (WRAPs)

Wraparound Mortgage

A new mortgage that wraps around existing financing.

A **wraparound mortgage** is a new mortgage that wraps around existing financing in which the WRAP mortgage collects payments from the mortgagor, makes payments on the original mortgage(s) and retains the balance. The WRAP is not a first mortgage, but rather sits in subsequent priority as a second, third or higher, based on the number of mortgages being wrapped. The wraparound is most commonly used to retain the benefits of a low-interest, long-term mortgage(s) while seeking additional capital or extending an existing debt for a longer term.

The use of WRAPs is often highest in tight money markets and/or in instances where refinancing costs are prohibitive. This financing arrangement has traditionally enjoyed popularity by providing attractive yields to investors while affording lower payments to borrowers that would otherwise be unavailable or economically unfeasible. The wraparound is most effective with longer term mortgages.

In Canada, the roll-over mortgage (short term/long amortization) has largely negated its role, but this may change should debt markets move to longer mortgage terms.

Blanket Mortgage

A blanket mortgage is a single mortgage on two or more properties forming security for a loan. A blanket mortgage allows the lender to gain recourse against all properties upon default and further protect his/her interest by not allowing the sale of any of the properties without specific permission. Blanket mortgages are used in situations involving both residential and commercial properties.

> **EXAMPLE**   *The Warehouse Renovation*
>
> Owner Smith wants to renovate an older building and wants to use the property for warehousing. The property is valued at $590,000 but is having difficulty securing a mortgage for $300,000 given the current condition of the property. His bank will, however, increase the existing first mortgage on his main manufacturing facility, valued at $1,850,000 from the current amount of $600,000 to $935,000, provided that the mortgage is registered against both properties.
>
> Both parties achieve their objectives—Smith is able to secure the required funds and will probably receive a more favourable interest rate than would be available for the older building —the bank increased business with a client, maintained a conservative loan to value ratio ($935,000 ÷ 1,850,000 or .51) on the primary property and obtained additional security (the warehouse now valued at $590,000).

A variation on blanket financing is found in large construction projects, particularly new home developments and condominium projects. A lender supplies a blanket mortgage over the entire condominium project for construction purposes and is fully secured by the developer's covenant during the construction stages. Upon completion, the condominium units are marketed and the lender is correctly positioned to provide financing for individual buyers. This is accomplished by fracturing the blanket mortgage. Once sold, the buyer must qualify for the unit and upon approval, a mortgage is created for that property to be registered at closing.

Participation Financing

For real estate purposes, participation financing typically refers to special purpose financing involving the lender in direct participation with the borrower in some profit or owner-ship position for a particular venture. (Note: This term is also found in banking circles when referring to a large loan or mortgage shared by a group of financial institutions, typically to distribute risk over a broader financial base.)

A variety of participation financing arrangements are possible. However, most can be grouped under two major categories.

- **Income Participation**   The lender's involvement in the cash flow, net income and/or potential income of the enterprise.
- **Equity Participation**   The lender's participation in proceeds of the disposition of the property and/or business enterprise.

Participation mortgages often appear in tight money situations and times of high interest rates. The lender may grant a participation mortgage in order to reduce the effective interest rate charged, increase the mortgage amount to the borrower and/or extend the term. The lender, in return, receives a percentage of equity or a share of income received. Alternatively, the lender may seek a percentage participation in gross sales activity.

EXAMPLE   *The Shopping Complex*

Developer Reed is attempting to secure $5,500,000 in financing for a neighbourhood shopping complex. A lender will provide the funds provided that a 3% of gross income participation factor is included in the package. In return, the lender will advance funds at 1% less than comparable lenders for five years. To facilitate this arrangement, the lender has certain requirements.

- Reed must report gross sales activity from all tenants within the project during the term of the mortgage.

- All tenants must be on a percentage lease arrangement, with the participation portion being no less than 3% of the amount exceeding base sales for the minimum rents as established and agreed between the lender and Reed.

- Reed will report all gross sales activity within 30 days of receiving reports of gross sales from tenants. The tenants must provide such reports no later than the tenth day after the last day of each calendar month of the term, including the calendar month in which the first day of the term occurs. The lender will require an original written statement from each tenant or by an authorized officer or independent auditor of the tenant, showing the gross sales for the preceding calendar month.

- Reed will remit payments directly to the lender in accordance with statements provided by the tenants.

- If Reed fails to deliver the statements within the stipulated time, the lender, in addition to any rights in the mortgage document, may employ an independent chartered accountant qualified to practice in the provincial jurisdiction in which the property is situated, to examine the books and records of Reed and report upon and certify the amount of gross sales due to the lender.

Commercial vs. Residential Mortgages

PERSPECTIVE

While underwriting procedures may vary, no significant differences are found in legal documents registered in the land registry office. For example, most *basic* provisions in standard sets of charge terms vary only slightly from residential versions. However, noteworthy differences can arise by way of additional clauses to address complexities in commercial ventures. Five are highlighted for illustration purposes only.

Annual Provision of Rental Information	Lender Inc. requires a detailed report of tenancy payments each year for multi-unit residential, commercial and industrial properties. The particulars required are set out on a standard form providing details of total rents collected, vacancies, rental, absorption within the year for vacant space, rent increases and other related information.
Annual Provision of Financial Statements	Audited statements are required for the full fiscal year (Balance Sheet, Profit and Loss Statement).
Assignment of Lease	Upon occasion, we require that all present and future leases be assigned to us. Sometimes, this provision is included within the mortgage document. In others, it may appear as a separate schedule titled Assignment of Leases with details of all existing leases attached to the assignment document.
Assignment of Profits	In selected instances, Lender Inc. will require that all profits from the business operation be assigned. In case of default, profits can be applied against mortgage arrears.
Lessee Responsibilities	Specific covenants may be included reflecting unique agreements between the mortgagor and individual lessees. For example, arrangements regarding fixtures may be required based on the extent of tenant improvements within the complex and the exclusion of these items if there was a foreclosure.

KNOWLEDGE INTEGRATION

Notables

- Mortgage underwriting is a process undertaken by a lender to evaluate the credit worthiness of an applicant and assess the property being offered as security.

- Pre-approvals are typically subject to conditions. Always read with extreme care.

- Required borrower documentation can vary by lender. Typical minimum documentation includes employment and income verification.

- Two credit bureaus operate in Ontario: Equifax Canada and TransUnion.

- Adverse property conditions can impact the approval of a mortgage and a lender may require a holdback until specific requirements and/or conditions are met.

- The mortgage commitment sets out terms and conditions of a proposed mortgage for acceptance by the borrower.

- Underwriting and related costs can vary based on whether a conventional or high ratio mortgage is being arranged.

- The current mortgage market offers a wide variety of fixed, variable, open and closed mortgages. Read the fine print carefully relating to all privileges, stipulations and conditions.

- Commercial underwriting can vary somewhat depending on whether a large commercial mortgage or small business financing is being arranged.

- As a general guideline: the larger the commercial mortgage, the greater the emphasis that is placed on business and property with less focused on the personal covenant.

- Commercial mortgage documentation packages can be complex; the range of materials varies by property type and size.

- Alternative lending sources offer greater scope to commercial practitioners seeking creative financing solutions.

- Commercial lending practices are designed to provide reasonable lender security combined with investor opportunity to enhance yield.

Glossary

Blended (Amortized) Payment Plan	Interest Accruing Payment Plan
Bridge Loan	Interest Only Payment Plan
Canada Small Business Financing Program	Interest Plus Specified Principal Payment Plan
Credit Bureau	Mortgage Commitment
Credit Report	Pre-Approved Buyer
Debt Coverage Ratio	Sale/Leaseback
Development Loan	Standby Loan
Gap Loan	Wraparound Mortgage

SECTION V   PROPERTY FINANCING

Web Links

Web links are included for general interest regarding selected chapter topics.

Credit Reports For examples of credit reports and various credit-related products (including online services) offered by credit bureaus in Canada, go to the Equifax Canada web site at ***www.equifax.ca*** and the TransUnion site at ***www.transunion.ca***.

Canada Small Business Financing Program For more information concerning this federal financing program, go to ***www.ic.gc.ca/csbfa***.

Strategic Thinking For Your Career

Questions are included to assist in developing your new career. No answers are provided.

1. What local information can I obtain from local lenders regarding conditions typically included in a pre-approval form for a buyer?

2. What information is contained in my personal credit report?

3. Can my intended employing broker give me more information about typical adverse conditions in property that cause problems in obtaining a mortgage?

4. Which lenders in the local marketplace offer small business financing or other specialty services?

5. What financing problems or obstacles do salespeople most commonly encounter in the local marketplace?

Chapter Mini-Review

Solutions are located in the Appendix.

1. Credit reports typically provide a credit score that can range from 600 to 1000.

   ◯ True   ◯ False

2. Lenders may require a Notice of Assessment issued by the Canada Revenue Agency to verify income of prospective borrowers.

   ◯ True   ◯ False

3. A mortgage commitment typically sets out terms and conditions for acceptance by the borrower that is valid for a specified time period.

   ◯ True   ◯ False

4. If a high ratio mortgage is obtained for $227,500 and the mortgage default premium is 2.75% of the mortgage, the amount due for this insurance would be $625.63.

   ◯ True   ◯ False

5. With a variable rate mortgage, the payment may be adjusted on a periodic basis to reflect changes in interest rates.

   ◯ True   ◯ False

6. Opening of several credit accounts within a short period of time can adversely impact a credit score.

   ◯ True   ◯ False

7. A guarantor on a mortgage agrees to perform and carry out covenants outlined in the mortgage document.

  ◯ True   ◯ False

8. The Canada Small Business Financing Program is a provincial program designed to assist entrepreneurs by way of loans.

  ◯ True   ◯ False

9. A seller take back can be an effective alternate source of mortgage funds when a property has limited appeal and the number of competing properties is increasing.

  ◯ True   ◯ False

10. An increase in the capitalization rate by a lender has the net effect of increasing a property's value for lending purposes.

  ◯ True   ◯ False

11. A bridge loan is an interim form of financing used for commercial properties, but not for residential properties.

  ◯ True   ◯ False

12. A gap loan could involve a lender providing funds to assist a developer who is facing construction delays and, consequently, is unable to receive construction advances to address immediate costs.

  ◯ True   ◯ False

13. A line of credit is normally granted by a lender based on past performance of the borrower client and that borrower's strength of covenant (personal or corporate).

  ◯ True   ◯ False

Active Learning Exercises

Solutions are located in the Appendix.

▣ Exercise 1   Mortgage Default Insurance Calculations

Calculate the mortgage default insurance premiums (excluding any applicable taxes) for the four mortgages listed below, based on the following fictitious scale.

LOAN-TO-VALUE RATIO	PREMIUM BASED ON LOAN AMOUNT
Up to and including 65%	0.50%
Up to and including 75%	0.65
Up to and including 80%	1.00
Up to and including 85%	1.75
Up to and including 90%	2.00
Up to and including 95%	3.25
Up to and including 100%	3.40

PURCHASE PRICE	DOWN PAYMENT	MORTGAGE AMOUNT	LTV (%)	PREMIUM (%)	PREMIUM ($)
$343,250	$53,250				
$243,700	$21,000				
$210,000	$47,000				
$167,000	$9,000				

▇ Exercise 2   Mortgage Balance and Recalculation

Mr. and Mrs. Hutchings are arranging a mortgage for $184,500 at 6.75% calculated semi-annually, not in advance, amortized over 25 years and due in five years.

2.1   Calculate the monthly payment that must be paid by the owners.

2.2   Calculate the outstanding balance at the end of the 5-year term.

2.3   How much would the monthly payment have to be increased if a $190,000 mortgage was arranged with the same terms?

■ Exercise 3   Interest Paid

Buyer Thompson is concerned about interest paid on financing provided by three lenders. Which of the following has the least amount of interest paid over the full amortization period?

Alternative A   A $225,000 mortgage, at 6.5% amortized over 20 years.

Alternative B   A $225,000 mortgage, at 5.75% amortized over 25 years.

Alternative C   A $230,000 mortgage, at 5.65% amortized over 25 years.

■ Exercise 4   Principal and Interest

Robert and Cynthia Baird are contemplating the purchase of a $255,000 home with a $35,000 down payment, an interest rate of 5.75% (compounded semi-annually, not in advance) and a 25-year mortgage amortization. They will be paying a high ratio insurance fee in cash on closing. Calculate the following:

4.1   The bi-weekly mortgage payment.

4.2   The amount of interest and principal paid in the first payment of this mortgage.

■ Exercise 5   Unknown Principal Amount

A property owner states today that his mortgage is fully amortized in eight years, has a 6.0% rate and has blended monthly payments of $1,544.00 monthly. What is the outstanding balance today?

■ Exercise 6   The Reconstructed Operating Statement

Investor McKay is developing a reconstructed worksheet in readiness for Lender Inc. and has asked for your assistance.

6.1   Complete the worksheet and estimate of value based on the following assumptions: Other income represents 5% of potential rental income; the vacancy factor is 4% and the cap rate is 9.25 with a loan-to-value ratio of .75. Based on the estimated value, calculate the loan that could be arranged based on McKay's reconstructed worksheet.

Potential Gross (Rental) Income		$443,800
Less: Vacancy and Credit Losses	–	
Effective Rental Income	=	
Add: Other Income	+	
Gross Operating Income	=	
Less: Operating Expenses	–	379,500
Net Operating Income	=	
Estimate of Value		
Amount of Mortgage		

6.2   Lender Inc. is considering the mortgage documentation package, but will apply various rules and assumptions in reviewing the application. The vacancy factor must be 5%, a minimum cap rate of 9.50 is required and given the age of the structure, the loan-to-value ratio is .70.

Based on this information, and assuming other income is 5% of potential rental income, determine the maximum mortgage that Lender Inc. will approve.

Potential Gross (Rental) Income	$443,800
Less: Vacancy and Credit Losses	−
Effective Rental Income	=
Add: Other Income	+
Gross Operating Income	=
Less: Operating Expenses	− 379,500
Net Operating Income	=
Estimate of Value	
Amount of Mortgage	

▣ Exercise 7   Debt Coverage Ratio

National Lending Inc. recently arrived in Southgate and is attempting to gain a foothold in the commercial marketplace. The debt coverage ratio is used primarily when assessing risk. Savard submits a reconstructed worksheet showing a NOI of $37,393. National Lending Inc. requires a minimum cap rate of 9.5, a DCR of 1.20 and a loan-to-value ratio of 75%.

7.1   What is the maximum loan permitted based on the cap rate and loan-to-value ratio? Show all calculations.

7.2   If National Lending Inc. is prepared to mortgage the property at 8.25%, amortized over 20 years, does this mortgage fall within the DCR guidelines of 1.20? Show all calculations.

■ Exercise 8   Risk and Cap Rates

Investor McKay is shopping the market for the most suitable mortgage financing for his multi-residential building that produces a net operating income of $37,500. Following are lending criteria from three lenders. Market research indicates that the capitalization rate for such property is 9.55. Which of the following lenders will advance the largest mortgage?

	LENDER A	LENDER B	LENDER C
CAP RATE	10.25 *Established by risk analysis*	9.55 *Market cap rate*	9.75 *Established by risk analysis*
LOAN-TO-VALUE RATIO	60%	75%	70%
VALUE ESTIMATE			
MORTGAGE			

◼ **Exercise 9 Specialized Financing Products**

Chapter 14 introduced or reviewed important terminology regarding alternative financing products. Upon occasion, commercial practitioners may be asked to explain, or more precisely, compare various terms when completing a listing proposal or assisting a buyer/tenant. Compare the following, remembering that the word *compare* includes both similarities and differences.

9.1   Gap Loan vs. Bridge Financing

9.2   Standby Loan vs. Letter of Guarantee

SECTION VI

INTRODUCTION TO REAL ESTATE TRADING

A housing boom is underway with over 3,700 acres of land under residential development. New subdivision names are sprouting up weekly: Grenadier Heights, Baby Point, Leaside, Scarborough Beach Park and Kingsway Park.

New commercial buildings on Bay and Front are in demand, as are harbour front locations for the newly announced waterfront development. Investment in Toronto's downtown shoreline is skyrocketing. Real estate talk is everywhere and real estate trading requirements are on people's minds.

The Telegram's weekly real estate and building page is focused on the new Code of Ethics and the need for real estate brokers to fully understand the new legislation and public policies which affect real estate trading. **The Year: 1927.**

Three years later, the Legislative Committee would assent to the *Act for the Prevention of Frauds in Connection with Real Estate Brokers and Salesmen*—the original legislation from which today's *Real Estate and Business Brokers Act, 2002* ultimately evolved. How we trade real estate, how we represent others and what trading practices must be followed have been evolving for over 80 years.

Source: Selected historical facts have been excerpted from *No Mean Business* (Toronto Real Estate Board, 1989).

CHAPTER 15

Trading and Agency Relationships

Introduction

The *Real Estate and Business Brokers Act, 2002* and Regulations became law on March 31, 2006, replacing the previous *Real Estate and Business Brokers Act* and creating a new legislative framework for the registration and regulation of real estate brokerages, brokers and salespeople in the trading of real estate.

The Act also expanded requirements regarding how brokerages and their representatives represent others in the listing and selling process. Representation is central to the trading of real estate. Under common law, real estate brokerages are agents and must adhere to principles and procedures established over many years by the Courts. These brokerages and their duly authorized representatives must also ensure full compliance with regulatory requirements set out in REBBA 2002.

Real estate trading services historically provided by brokerages are based on agency: a relationship involving one party (the agent) who accepts responsibility for representing the other party (the principal). Establishing an agency relationship and the granting of agency authority results in various obligations that are owed to clients, along with a select few that are owed to customers.

This chapter, along with discussing the Act, explains general, fiduciary and regulatory obligations together with detailed examples. This is followed by an analysis of duty of care requirements that apply to everything that is done for clients and limited obligations that extend to customers. It further discusses duties owed by the principal to the agent and is concluded with a discussion of agency termination.

Learning Outcomes

At the conclusion of this chapter, students will be able to:

- Outline the REBBA 2002 regulatory structure involving the Act and six Regulations, with particular emphasis on how real estate is traded in Ontario.

- Define a trade, identify key trading exemptions and discuss how common law and regulatory terminology differs in regard to representation when brokerages, through their representatives, are providing services relating to a trade in real estate.

- Discuss the role of a brokerage as an agent in the trading process including how agency relationships are established.

- Differentiate between actual and implied authorities when a principal grants agency authority to a real estate brokerage, including typical limitations on that brokerage authority.

- Detail which duties are owed to principals (clients) and customers.

- Identify and explain eight general obligations owed by an agent to a principal.

- Discuss what is meant by the term *fiduciary*, and identify and explain five fiduciary obligations owed by an agent to a principal.

- Identify and explain six regulatory obligations owed by an agent to a principal.

- Explain how the extent of duty of care varies with clients and customers, and outline how duty of care standards are established.

- Outline three general obligations owed by the principal to the agent in an agency relationship.

- Discuss how an agency relationship is terminated by either an act of the parties or by operation of law.

REAL ESTATE TRADING

Knowledge of REBBA 2002 is essential to anyone involved in real estate trading, whether registered under the Act or exempted from it. For those registered under the Act, their livelihood depends on strict adherence to its requirements. There is no excuse for ignorance of the law.

Certain REBBA 2002 regulatory requirements were introduced in *Real Estate as a Professional Career* when discussing salesperson registration and the relationship involving brokerages, brokers and salespersons. However, a much broader awareness of its provisions is necessary, as trading-related requirements are the foundation of this discussion regarding representation and subsequent detail analysis in *The Residential Real Estate Transaction* and *The Commercial Real Estate Transaction*.

Regulatory Structure

REBBA 2002 consists of the statute and six regulations, three of which have direct bearing on real estate trading including day-to-day listing/selling activities and brokerage administration. The remaining three focus on regulation-making powers associated with the Ministry of Small Business and Government Services (the Ministry) and the Real Estate Council of Ontario (the Administrative Authority), and Code of Ethics issues involved in the transition from the old to the new Act.

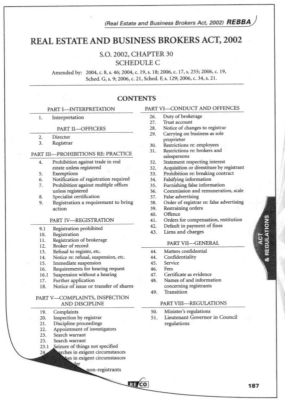

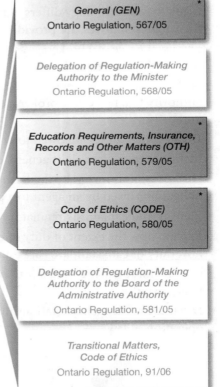

For ease of reference, the following key words are used in this text to identify either the Act or the three relevant regulations.

REBBA　Real Estate and Business Brokers Act, 2002

GEN　General, Ontario Regulation, 567/05

OTH　Education Requirements, Insurance, Records and Other Matters, Ontario Regulation, 579/05

CODE　Code of Ethics, Ontario Regulation, 580/05

WEB LINKS

REBBA 2002　For direct references to the Act/Regulations, go to *www.e-laws.gov.on.ca*. The RECO web site also provides a link to the legislation. Go to *www.reco.on.ca*.

Guide to REBBA 2002　The online guide is available at *www.reco.on.ca/onlineguide*. This handy guide provides key information about the Act and Regulations and is an excellent study resource throughout the pre-registration courses.

Understanding the Legislation

REBBA 2002 is a complex document and requires detailed study in order to fully grasp all aspects of the legislation when discussing trading-related activities.

TERMINOLOGIES

REBBA 2002 introduces various terms that, while straightforward, require more close scrutiny as they may differ somewhat from terms used in the marketplace. Following are a few examples:

LEGISLATIVE TERM	COMMONLY USED MARKETPLACE TERM
Representation	Agency
Representation Agreement	Listing (Seller Agency) Agreement / Buyer Agency Agreement
Agreement (Conveyance of Interest in Real Estate)	Agreement of Purchase and Sale
Multiple Representation	Dual Agency
Convey Offer	Present Offer
Acquisition/Divestiture by Registrant	Purchase/Sale by Registrant

Interrelated Topics

Many regulatory requirements include references from both within the Act and one or more Regulations. For example, when searching topics relating to commissions, provisions are located not only in REBBA (the Act) but also in the General Regulation (GEN) and the Code of Ethics (CODE). Registrants cannot simply look at one provision, as others may further define or expand the provision.

As an example, when searching for branch office responsibilities and trust accounts, branch office provisions are set out in the Act (REBBA), the General Regulation (GEN) and the Code of Ethics (CODE), with trust account procedures found under the Act (REBBA) and two regulations (GEN and OTH).

Market Complexities

This legislation is unavoidably more complex in order to properly address an increasingly sophisticated marketplace. For example, where once a single provision under the previous Act addressed brokerage compliance with the Code of Ethics, the new legislation has three interrelated requirements:

- Brokerages must ensure that salespersons and brokers within their employ comply with the Act (REBBA, Sec. 26);
- Salespersons and brokers must agree not to do anything that would cause the brokerage to be in violation of the Act (CODE, Sec. 2);
- The broker of record must ensure that the brokerage complies with the Act (REBBA Subsec. 12(2)) and that adequate supervision is provided both within the brokerage and any branch offices (GEN, Sec. 30 and 31).

In addition, many trading requirements necessitate detailed treatment given their importance in consumer protection. As an example, disclosure requirements set out in the Act and Regulations outline more than 15 disclosure obligations concerning such matters as competing offers, informing buyers and sellers of compliance with insurance requirements and detailing how multiple representation will impact clients and customers in terms of information and services provided.

 # HOW PROPERTY IS TRADED

Real estate trading is regulated by REBBA 2002, unless specifically exempted under that Act. The majority of real estate in Ontario is traded through persons registered under the Act. Prior to the 1940's, real estate brokers did not play a significant role. Property transactions were typically more simple and straightforward. Often, particularly in rural areas, properties were held by family members over several generations and transactions were few. When sales were made, normally the buyer had a detailed knowledge of the property being acquired and the parties usually knew each other before the transaction occurred.

As the market became more complex, and relocation of buyers/sellers more commonplace, real estate transactions became increasingly formalized. To compound matters, a host of regulations regarding property began impacting how properties were marketed and sold; e.g., planning and land use regulations, environmental controls, matrimonial status considerations and taxation. The mid-1900's witnessed a tremendous growth in real estate transactions (particularly following the Second World War). These expanding markets necessitated new approaches to real estate trading. Consumers began discovering the many advantages of having an agent working on their behalf in order to market property. Initially, sellers availed themselves of such services, but in the 1970's to 1990's, buyers also sought out registrants to represent their interests when locating suitable properties. Prior to that time, buyers were not represented, but rather treated as customers— an important point warranting detailed discussion later in this chapter.

The involvement of specialists has not abated, but in fact expanded. Persons offering services to both residential and commercial buyers and sellers now include property inspectors, building inspectors, environmental auditors, surveyors, and title insurers.

Definition of Trade

The definition of trade under REBBA 2002 encompasses activities not only directly related to the sale, exchange, option, lease, rental, or other acquisition or transaction, but also any act, conduct or negotiation in the furtherance of such matters.

INTERPRETATION

1. (1) "trade" includes a disposition or acquisition of or transaction in real estate by sale, purchase, agreement for purchase and sale, exchange, option, lease, rental or otherwise and any offer or attempt to list real estate for the purpose of such a disposition, acquisition or transaction, and any act, advertisement, conduct or negotiation, directly or indirectly, in furtherance of any disposition, acquisition, transaction, offer or attempt, and the verb "trade" has a corresponding meaning; ("opération", "mener des opérations").

Trading Exemptions

While all persons trading in real estate must be registered, exemptions for certain persons are set out under the Act (See REBBA, Sec. 4). The Act details eleven exemptions, the most notable of which are detailed below.

- **Auctioneer**   If the trade is made in the course of and as part of the auctioneer's business.

- **Full-Time Salaried Employee of a Party to a Trade**   If the employee involved in the trade is acting for and on behalf of his or her employer in respect of land situated in Ontario; e.g., a full-time employee of a builder.

- **Solicitor**   A solicitor of the Superior Court of Justice who is providing legal services if the trade in real estate is itself a legal service or is incidental to and directly arising out of the legal services.

- **Residential Tenancies**   A person who trades in real estate solely for the purpose of arranging leases to which the *Residential Tenancies Act* applies.

Trading and Representation

A real estate brokerage, when involved with trading as set out in REBBA 2002, is legally viewed as an agent under common law. Salespersons and brokers, as individual registrants, are representatives of the agent and act on the agent's behalf. Common law represents principles, customs and procedures recognized over many years by the courts. Many types of agents (e.g., insurance and investment) operate under common law.

REBBA 2002 does not refer to the common law term *agency* and related words (e.g., *agent*, *agency relationship* and *agency duties*). The legislation instead refers to *representation*, which is viewed as generally analogous to agency in terms of roles performed and duties/responsibilities carried out. The Act also sets out various duties that must be followed, along with requirements concerning representation agreements (i.e., agreements under which the brokerage owes certain duties to the **client** when representing that individual), as opposed to agreements other than representation agreements (i.e., service agreements in which the person to whom the service is being provided is not being represented).

However, to properly understand requirements set out in the Act, a solid understanding of agency law is essential including what duties are owed to clients and **customers**.

AGENCY RELATIONSHIPS

The following discussion includes agency text that has been adapted with permission from *Agency Fundamentals: The National Perspective* published by the Alliance for Canadian Real Estate Education. In doing so, the Real Estate Council of Ontario wishes to promote consistency in agency training and generally advance greater uniformity in real estate education across Canada.

    The terms *agency* and *representation* are judged to be analogous and used interchangeably given terminology differences between agency law and statutory law (as detailed in REBBA 2002).

Agency is a relationship between two parties in which one party (the **agent**) accepts responsibility for representing the other party (the **principal**) in dealing with a **third party**. Agency may be broadly defined as *a consensual relationship between two persons created by law by which one person, the principal, has the right to control the conduct of the agent and the agent has the power to affect the legal relations of the principal with third parties.* The real estate brokerage, as the agent, is employed by a buyer or seller to perform professional services. The **agency relationship** is typically documented using a representation agreement.

Principal

A **principal** (client) is an individual who authorizes an agent to act on his/her behalf in an agency relationship. This relationship between principal and agent can be created by express or implied agreement. The principal has two primary duties to the agent, as well as obligations set out in a representation agreement (see additional discussion later in this chapter).

INDEMNIFICATION

The principal is obligated to compensate or indemnify the agent for liabilities incurred while carrying out responsibilities under the relationship. If the agent is not acting within the authority given (actual or implied authority), or is acting unlawfully, the principal would not be responsible. In real estate, the duty to reimburse for expenses under the general responsibility of indemnification does not normally apply. For example, expenses involving property promotion are waived in return for anticipated commission pursuant to a representation agreement. However, indemnification does apply in specific fields relating to real estate brokerage; i.e., property management.

REMUNERATION

Under common law, an agent is entitled to payment for services rendered as agreed between the agent and the principal. Remuneration provisions are typically set out by

---

Third Party

An individual who is not directly connected with a legal transaction, but may be affected by it. The terms 'third party' and 'customer' are generally analogous when discussing real estate agency relationships in Ontario.

Principal

An individual who authorizes an agent to act on his or her behalf in an agency relationship.

Agency Relationship

A relationship between an agent and a principal in which the agent represents that principal when dealing with a third party. Agency relationships are typically established in real estate by the signing of a representation agreement. See also Agency.

way of a **seller representation agreement** or **buyer representation agreement**. The REBBA 2002 Code of Ethics contains specific requirements concerning representation agreements (CODE, Sec. 11, 13 and 14).

Third Party

This legal term generally refers to any individual who is not directly connected with a legal transaction, but may be affected by it. As an example, a seller signs a representation agreement with a brokerage. In doing so, an agency relationship is established between the seller and the brokerage, with any potential buyer being viewed as a third party. Registrants should note that the terms *third party* and *customer* are generally analogous for purposes of discussions involving agency in Ontario.

Terminology Challenges | MARKET PERSPECTIVE

Differing perspectives by the courts, regulators, real estate brokerages and consumers have so far thwarted universal agency terminology. While real estate brokerages are agents governed by the law of agency, rarely is traditional agency terminology (e.g., agent, principal and third party) found in the legislation, rules, by-laws and codes of ethics. REBBA 2002, for example, focuses on registration, registrants and specific registrant categories including brokerage, broker and salesperson. More importantly, REBBA 2002 does not refer to agency, but rather representations. Fortunately, the terms are generally viewed as analogous.

To compound matters, brokers and salespeople use terms most familiar to them (buyer, seller, client, customer, seller brokerage, buyer (co-operating) brokerage and the like). Lastly, the Courts gravitate to purchaser, vendor, principal and third party. Misunderstandings understandably arise, but fortunately regulators across Canada are moving towards a uniform set of terms to better facilitate communication between registrants and regulatory bodies.

However, full alignment with legal terminology will be a much greater challenge. Such initiatives usually take considerable time, as the law pertaining to the real estate brokerage industry is viewed as but a segment of the much broader field of law governing real estate transactions; i.e., the law of vendor and purchaser. Attempts to remedy the situation are further compounded by the well-known legal fondness for tradition.

Following are several guidelines that apply to this text:

- Buyer and seller can be *client* or *customer*.

- The *client (principal)* has an agency relationship with the *agent (brokerage)*.

- The *customer (third party)* does not have an agency relationship with the *agent (brokerage)*, but is entitled to fairness and honesty.

- The *customer* (buyer or seller) of one brokerage may be the *client* of another.

- A *brokerage* (sole proprietorship, partnership or corporation) is the *agent* in an agent/principal relationship.

- Brokerages employ *brokers* and *salespersons*. One of the brokers is designated as the broker of record and responsible for the brokerage.

- For agency discussion purposes, the terms *broker* and *salesperson* are used interchangeably, as responsibilities owed to clients and customers and duties performed are essentially the same.

- All brokerages, brokers and salespersons are registrants for regulatory purposes.

THE AGENT

For real estate purposes, an agent refers to a brokerage which is expressly or implicitly authorized to act for or represent another person in a trade in real estate. A real estate brokerage, as an agent, is typically employed by a buyer or seller to perform professional

services. The brokerage and its representatives must obey the principal's lawful instructions, although not necessarily be subject to detailed, direct control or supervision as to how work is to be done. The brokerage does not have direct authority to bind the principal; i.e., sign an agreement on behalf of that principal.

Brokers: Middlemen or Agents?

The term *broker*, strictly speaking, refers to a middleman who acts for others in negotiating contracts; e.g., brokering a deal between opposing parties for a fee. An agency relationship does not automatically attach, as the true middleman is but an intermediary or go-between, and provides an objective, impartial role in the negotiating process.

The terms *broker* and *agent* have become virtually synonymous given that skills used in performing the function are essentially the same. Once linked, the two have become indistinguishable. Therefore, in modern real estate, all duties and obligations inherent in agency attach to brokerages (as REBBA 2002 recognizes the brokerage as the actual agent).

Can a Broker be a Middleman?   CURIOSITY

Yes, but caution is advised. Some registrants argue that they are simply middlemen who bring the parties together. Those parties then make their own contract without any further intervention by the middleman. However, to have this intermediary or go-between role, the registrant must neither profess to act as an agent, nor exercise judgement in carrying out any function related to the listing or sale. This definitely is not the role normally played by real estate **brokerages** and their authorized **salespersons** and **brokers**. Further, the courts also regard registrants as more than middlemen because they possess specialized skills and knowledge and openly promote such specialized skills and knowledge to those who consider employing their services.

However, it is legally possible for a brokerage to act as a middleman or go-between if such is fully disclosed to the customer, and the customer is fully informed in that regard and provides his or her written **informed consent**.

Brokerage vs. Broker

The Real Estate Council of Ontario, with the proclamation of REBBA 2002, moved away from *broker* in favour of *brokerage* to identify the person or legal entity (i.e., sole proprietorship, partnership or corporation) authorized to trade in real estate. The brokerage, for regulatory purposes, is the agent with others employed or appointed to act on behalf of the brokerage being identified as brokers and/or salespersons. Skills required in performing the broker or salesperson functions are essentially the same.

REBBA 2002 also introduced a new level of compliance control within brokerages referred to as the broker of record. Every real estate brokerage must designate a broker of record to ensure brokerage compliance with the Act and Regulations and effective administrative control within the brokerage.

Brokers and Salespersons

Brokers and salespersons are employed by a brokerage and authorized to trade on behalf of their respective brokerages. As such, they lack the legal capacity to trade on their own account and are viewed as having an employee/employer relationship with the brokerage. In recent years, brokerages have been employing brokers and salespersons as independent contractors, but such strategies are for taxation purposes only and do not disrupt, or in any way minimize, the fundamental employee/employer relationship.

The Real Estate Council of Ontario has been steadfast in reinforcing the employee/employer relationship. Brokers and salespersons, as independent contractors, are not independent from the regulatory framework, nor are they relieved of agency obligations. Brokers and salespersons are legally an extension of the brokerage and have the same responsibilities and duties. For purposes of this text, the term *brokerage* is deemed to include employed brokers and salespersons.

Who is the Agent?   MARKET MEMO

The term agent is a classic example of the terminology challenge.

- It's common practice for consumers to refer to salespeople and brokers as agents even though they're not technically agents (as the brokerage is the agent).

- Salespeople and brokers often, inadvertently or otherwise, contribute to this mistaken identity and commonly refer to each other as agents.

- Lawyers and courts refer to an agent within the context of an agent/principal relationship.

- Most, but not all, regulatory jurisdictions refer to the brokerage as the agent. In some instances, the term 'broker' is still used.

- Until recently, salespeople in Alberta were officially agents but are now referred to as associates.

Varying Roles/Responsibilities

The *concept* of agency applies to all agents where common law exists; i.e., all Canadian provinces except Quebec. However, the *practice* of agency varies according to the profession or trade and related legislation. Similarly, the *extent* of authority can also vary by profession. Agency relationships are not unique to real estate, but are common to many professions. Regardless, a person is appointed or employed as an agent to act in some capacity on behalf of a principal. Differences involve the authorities granted and services provided. Examples include:

- A lawyer representing a client in negotiating a contract.
- A travel agent making travel arrangements for a client.
- A stockbroker making stock and mutual fund investments for a client.
- A property manager overseeing an investment property.
- An insurance agent obtaining insurance for a client from an insurance company.
- A real estate brokerage representing a client in a real estate transaction.

EXAMPLE   *Extent of Authority*

- A lawyer can have broad authority to stand in for another; e.g., a general power of attorney (sometimes referred to as general agency).

- A sports agent may be more limited given defined negotiating parameters to bind his or her principal, but still have reasonably extensive authority to act on behalf of that principal.

- A real estate agent is usually further limited to specific duties (sometimes referred to as specific or special agency) and does not have direct authority to bind the principal; i.e., sign on his or her behalf.

Key Elements

Five key elements are contained within an agency relationship:

The relationship is the creation of law.	The law, not the intention of the parties, determines whether an agency relationship has been established; if a contract does exist between agent and principal; if obligations have been fulfilled by these parties; and if the agent has fulfilled duties imposed by statute and the law of agency.
The relationship is consensual in nature and may be gratuitous.	The relationship has its basis in the parties' consent, not necessarily in a contractual relationship. This consent can be written, verbal or implied by conduct (i.e., **implied agency**).
The control of conduct rests with the principal.	The agent must at all times obey the lawful instructions of his/her principal. The principal may or may not exercise such control, but the right exists and ends with termination of the agency relationship.
The relationship is fiduciary in nature.	An agent becomes a **fiduciary** in the eyes of the law and must act at all times in the principal's best interests. Note: Court cases have identified some instances where this does not apply, but none relate to real estate brokerages.
The agent may affect his/her principal's legal position.	The extent can vary, as some agents have more direct impact on the principal's legal position than others. For example, an agent for an entertainer may negotiate and finalize agreements, while a real estate brokerage is more restricted to showing property and presenting offers. Regardless, the ability to somehow affect relations between a principal and a third party remains.

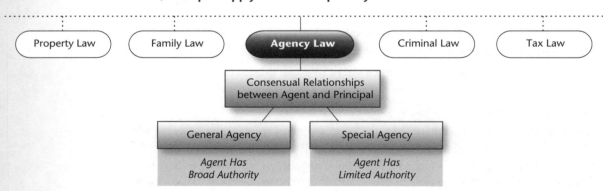

THE LEGAL SYSTEM

Rules/Principles Apply to Various Specialty Areas of the Law

Property Law — Family Law — **Agency Law** — Criminal Law — Tax Law

Consensual Relationships between Agent and Principal

General Agency — Special Agency

Agent Has Broad Authority — *Agent Has Limited Authority*

Source: © Alliance for Canadian Real Estate Education, 2006. *Agency Fundamentals: The National Perspective.*

ESTABLISHING AN AGENCY RELATIONSHIP

An agency relationship can be created in a number of ways including by agreement, by ratification, by estoppel or by operation of law. Typically the most common method associated with real estate brokerages is agency based on a written agreement between the client and the brokerage (e.g., seller representation agreement or buyer representation agreement).

While a written agreement is not essential to an agency relationship (as agency relationships can be oral or implied given the conduct of the parties), it is always the preferred method. Registrants must at all times avoid putting themselves in a position where the Court determines whether or not an agency relationship has been established under a particular set of circumstances. The importance of a written agreement cannot be overemphasized.

BY AGREEMENT

- A definite understanding which may be an express agreement (written or verbal). Alternatively, the agreement can be implied given circumstances and the relationship of the parties.
- Common law does not require a written agreement nor a particular form, but such is strongly encouraged.
- To receive commission, the brokerage must prove that a contract existed. The best solution: a written, signed agreement. Provincial legislation may require written agreements to enforce commission arrangements.

EXAMPLE
Written, Oral and Implied Agreements

Written: A buyer representation agreement is signed by the buyer.

Oral: The seller permits the salesperson to show the property and agrees upon a commission, but with no signed listing.

Implied: The seller and the brokerage act in a manner which suggests that an express agreement exists, but no formal understanding is reached between them.

BY RATIFICATION

- An agent's authority can be granted retroactively. Ratification applies if the agent has acted either without authority or in excess of granted authority. In such instances, the principal subsequently agrees to be bound by such unauthorized acts.

EXAMPLE
Seller and Buyer Ratification

Seller Representation:
The salesperson shows a property with no authority and drafts an offer. The seller, while not originally planning on selling, signs the agreement thereby ratifying the agency relationship.

Buyer Representation:
The salesperson locates a property with no authority from the buyer and drafts an offer. The buyer, while originally planning on buying, signs the agreement thereby ratifying the agency relationship.

The remaining two methods are uncommon, but legally possible in real estate agency relationships.

BY ESTOPPEL

- Occurs where one person (the principal) acts in such a way as to lead a third party to believe that another person (the agent) has authority to act on behalf of the principal.

- Must be clear evidence that the principal has by words or conduct held out that another person has the authority to act on his/her behalf.

- Estoppel does not protect the brokerage, but provides recourse by the third party against the principal and/or the brokerage.

EXAMPLE

Buyer Takes Action

The seller clearly indicates to a prospective buyer that the brokerage is acting on his behalf and has the authority to negotiate and sign an agreement with the buyer. The buyer enters into an agreement based on that instruction, but the seller subsequently refuses to close the sale, arguing that the brokerage had no such authority. The buyer takes legal action against the seller given this misrepresentation.

BY OPERATION OF LAW

- A right or liability that is created for a party (regardless of that party's original intention) based on established legal principles.

- Circumstances can arise where a duty is imposed on one party to act on behalf of another, despite the fact that no agency relationship existed; e.g., agent of necessity when immediate action must be taken to save the principal's property.

EXAMPLE

Imminent Danger

A carrier of perishable goods might be viewed as an agent of necessity, as might a property manager in control of a structure facing imminent danger. In both instances, certain actions might need to be taken, but nevertheless were never spelled out in the agreement between the parties.

GRANTING AGENCY AUTHORITY

An **authority** is legally defined as a right or permission granted by one person to another to act. From a real estate brokerage perspective, the seller client typically gives an express, written authority to the brokerage to offer his or her property for sale or the buyer client authorizes the brokerage to locate suitable property for him or her.

Such authority is set out by specific instructions within the seller representation agreement or buyer representation agreement regarding what may be done by the brokerage on behalf of the respective client.

These are *actual authorities* intentionally conferred on the brokerage, as distinct from *implied authorities* that are assumed given the nature of the relationship. For example, the seller may give an actual authority to advertise the property, but the relationship implies that additional assumed authorities are granted to the brokerage regarding advertising specifics (i.e., the preparation of advertising materials and the selection of appropriate media).

Similarly, a buyer can provide an express, written authority to the brokerage to locate suitable property. The actual authority will set out this instruction, as well as typically identify the general geographic area of interest to that client. However, the implied authority assumes that the brokerage will select those methods most appropriate to locate the property.

In summary, the actual authority is given by the principal to the agent created by the terms of the agreement. The implied authorities allow the agent to get the job done properly. The agent may:

- Undertake incidental activities consistent with express provisions in the agency document.
- Perform such other acts usual to real estate brokerages and carry out the tasks at hand (i.e., marketing a property or seeking a suitable property), which are not specifically detailed in the agreement.

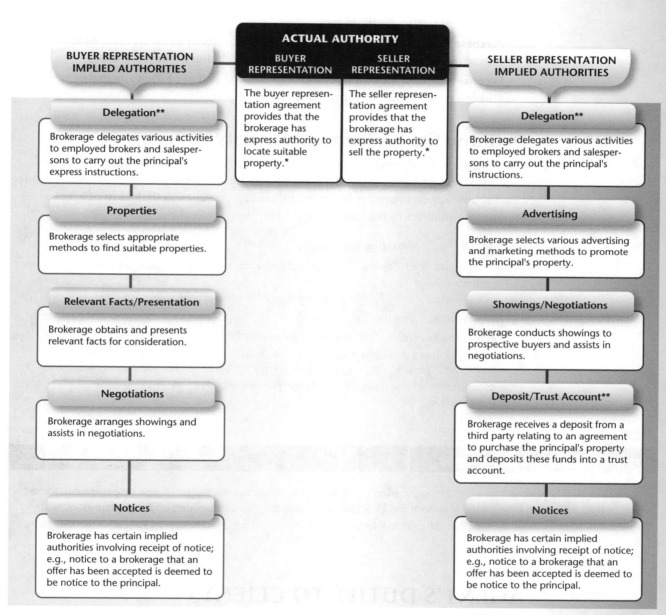

* Actual authorities within agency agreements have expanded significantly as brokerages seek more explicit arrangements from clients. See also the sub-topic *Defining the Brokerage Authority* on the following page.

** Certain implied authorities are further supported by provincial legislation; e.g., the authority to delegate to employed, appointed or authorized brokers and salespersons, and the authority upon receipt of a deposit for the placement of same into a (real estate) trust account.

Source: © Alliance for Canadian Real Estate Education, 2006. *Agency Fundamentals: The National Perspective.*

Limits on Brokerage Authority

While brokerages can pursue reasonable activities flowing from express authority in a representation agreement, certain noteworthy limitations arise from legal precedents and common practices:

- **Contract**   While an authority is given (e.g., to market the property or seek out appropriate property), the authority is limited. Brokerages and their representatives do not have the authority to sign a contract on behalf of a principal, unless so instructed.
- **Delegation**   Delegation by the brokerage to use other brokerages in the marketing/selling process is not presumed under agency law, as the agency obligation is a personal one to that particular brokerage.
- **Purchase Price**   Brokerages have no implied authority to receive all or part of the purchase price, but can only receive a deposit relating to the purchase.
- **Expense**   Brokerages cannot incur expenses on behalf of the principal or seek reimbursement without express authority.

Defining the Brokerage Authority

Seller representation agreements are expanding as brokerages seek clearly delineated responsibilities and authorities, rather than leaving such issues to open debate. A similar trend is now appearing in buyer representation agreements, as that form of agency relationship matures in the Canadian marketplace.

EXAMPLE   *Marketing the Property*

A few years ago, the following statement sufficed as an express authority in a seller representation agreement:

I agree to allow you to market my property . . .

A typical current instruction now reads:

I agree to allow you to show and permit prospective buyers to fully inspect the Property during reasonable hours and I give you the sole and exclusive right to place "For Sale"/"For Lease" and "Sold"/"Leased" sign(s) upon the Property. I further agree that you shall have sole and exclusive authority to make all advertising decisions relating to the Property during the Listing Period.

The Principal's Instructions   CAUTION

Registrants should exercise caution regarding implied authorities, as such issues are a matter of legal interpretation. Make certain that sellers and buyers clearly understand all actual and implied authorities granted under the representation agreement. Keep in mind, as well, that the principal can withhold consent to any specific authority at his or her discretion.

AGENT'S DUTIES TO CLIENTS AND CUSTOMERS

An agreement to become an agent for another person and represent his or her interests carries with it significant duties and obligations. Most are shared by all agents who act in an advisory capacity, while some relate specifically to agents in real estate.

Levels of Obligation (Plus Duty of Care)

A real estate brokerage acting in an agency capacity with a *client* is responsible for duties outlined in the representation agreement, as well as general (set out in agency law), fiduciary and regulatory obligations (set out in REBBA 2002). A brokerage also owes selected general obligations (specifically, exercising care/skill and ensuring honesty) and regulatory obligations to *customers*.

A **duty of care** is owed to clients for everything that is done or ought to be done for those clients. The duty of care owed to customers is more limited.

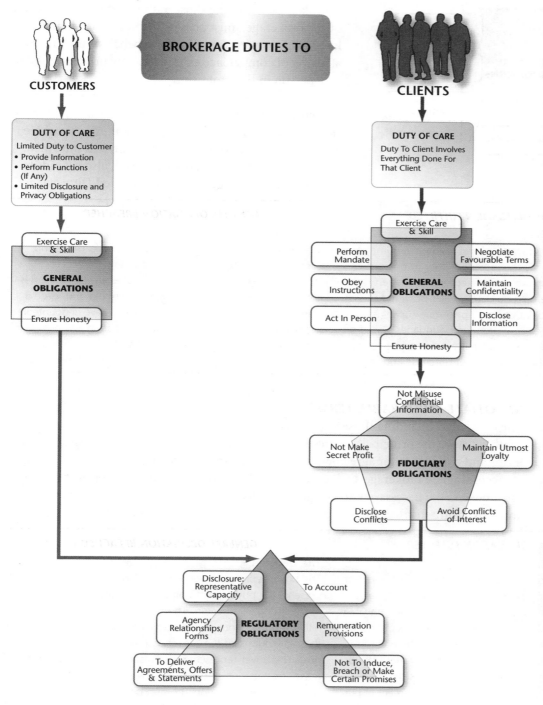

Source: © Alliance for Canadian Real Estate Education, 2006. *Agency Fundamentals: The National Perspective* (with modifications).

General Obligations

Eight **general obligations** apply to real estate brokerages (and to those authorized to act on behalf of those brokerages) when representing a client. Two of these obligations (*Exercise Care & Skill* and *Ensure Honesty*) apply to customers. See the subsequent topic titled *Duty of Care*. Two examples are provided below for each obligation: one in which the brokerage and/or its representative acts properly, and the other where the duty is breached.

EXERCISE CARE AND SKILL

A brokerage, including those authorized to act on behalf of the brokerage, must possess the necessary skills and knowledge to perform services on behalf of the principal at a level of competence expected of any prudent, reasonable person in the profession.

A brokerage and its authorized representatives must also ensure the completeness and accuracy of all information provided and recommend relevant experts, where applicable, to ensure that principals are well informed. The obligation to exercise care and skill also extends to customers. See the subsequent topic titled *Duty of Care*.

GENERAL OBLIGATION FULFILLED	GENERAL OBLIGATION BREACHED
The Up-To-Date Survey	**The Water Stain**
A salesperson, when showing a rural residential home to a buyer client, is asked by the buyer whether or not certain trees and part of a stream are located on the property. The salesperson gives the buyer a dated, seller-provided survey. He also informs his client that an up-to-date survey is necessary to precisely locate property boundaries. Based on this information, the buyer asks that an appropriate condition be included in the agreement of purchase and sale.	A buyer client, when viewing a property, asks the listing salesperson if water staining on the basement wall is cause for concern. The salesperson assures the buyer that such is not the case, as the stain is probably very old and, even if there had been a problem, the seller would have undoubtedly resolved it. The buyer relies on this information and buys the home, but later discovers significant water leakage and takes legal action against the brokerage and the salesperson.

NEGOTIATE FAVOURABLE TERMS

The brokerage, including those authorized to act on behalf of the brokerage, must diligently advance the principal's interests by assisting in negotiations and drafting favourable terms and conditions for agreements arising from such negotiations.

Accordingly, a brokerage, including those authorized to act on behalf of the brokerage, must possess the necessary knowledge and skills to successfully negotiate agreements and also ensure that legally binding agreements are drafted on behalf of its principals.

GENERAL OBLIGATION FULFILLED	GENERAL OBLIGATION BREACHED
Amending the Offer	**The Decision**
The seller wants to accept an offer presented by a salesperson employed by a co-operating brokerage. The listing salesperson suggests that she and the seller client meet privately to discuss the matter. The salesperson then points out certain concerns about selected clause wordings in the offer and recommends two changes that could result in more favourable terms from the seller's perspective. The seller readily agrees, a counter-offer is prepared and the agreement of purchase and sale is successfully negotiated between the parties.	The buyer representative from a co-operating brokerage presents the buyer client's offer to the seller in the presence of the listing salesperson. The seller signs back the offer at full listing price, but readily admits to both salespeople that he would *split the difference*, if necessary, to make the deal. The buyer representative presents the sign back but makes no mention of the seller's comment to his buyer client. The buyer accepts the sign back unaware of the possibility of more favourable terms.

MAINTAIN CONFIDENTIALITY

Trust is focal to the agency relationship. Accordingly, the brokerage, including those authorized to act on behalf of the brokerage, must maintain confidentiality regarding all matters that could adversely impact the principal or in any way undermine that principal's position during negotiations.

All information received from the client or obtained as a result of representing the client must be kept confidential. Common examples include the client's personal information, motivation for buying/selling, and amount to be paid or accepted during negotiations. This duty of confidentiality survives termination of the representation agreement and the closing of the transaction.

GENERAL OBLIGATION FULFILLED	GENERAL OBLIGATION BREACHED
Financial Difficulties	**The Real Reason**
The listing salesperson is aware that the seller has financial difficulties. The seller client wants this kept confidential, as it could affect his negotiations with potential buyers. The salesperson does not mention this information to a prospective buyer and a sale is successfully negotiated between the parties.	The seller is anxious to sell his home, given a job loss and an immediate need to relocate. The salesperson from the listing brokerage also represents an interested buyer client. The buyer, uncertain as to offering price, asks the salesperson's advice. The salesperson suggests $290,000, which is significantly less than the $340,000 asking price. When the buyer expresses concern that this low offer may not be accepted, the salesperson assures her not to worry, because *time is on their side and the seller has to make a quick decision.*

DISCLOSE INFORMATION

A brokerage acting as an agent, including those authorized to act on behalf of the brokerage, has a duty to disclose information broadly grouped under two categories:

- Information pertinent to the principal/agent relationship (i.e., actual or potential conflicts); and
- Matters relating to the transaction (i.e., situations or events involving the property, the offer or third parties) which impact the principal.

The first category relates to fiduciary obligations (more fully discussed later in this chapter), while the second is viewed legally as a general obligation applying to all agent/principal relationships. Both duties assume forthright disclosure before the principal makes a decision or takes an action affecting his or her interest.

GENERAL OBLIGATION FULFILLED	GENERAL OBLIGATION BREACHED
Personal Circumstances	**Wiring Deficiencies**
The seller is seriously considering an offer presented by a salesperson from a co-operating brokerage. However, the listing salesperson is aware of certain personal circumstances about the buyer that would affect his client's decision. In private, he discloses this information to his seller client. The seller, taking these facts into consideration, rejects the offer.	The buyer representative is aware that an older commercial property, being considered by his buyer client, has wiring deficiencies that would prove costly to repair. Further, given this and other general deterioration, insurance would be difficult to obtain or very expensive, if available at all. The salesperson does not disclose this important information, as he is anxious to make the deal and further his own interests.

ENSURE HONESTY

A brokerage as an agent, including those authorized to act on behalf of the brokerage, must demonstrate honesty of intent and ensure adherence to facts. Honesty extends to all dealings and brokerages must ensure that the client is not in any way misled and that all known facts are disclosed, including the role of the agent in performing services. This general obligation of honesty also extends to customers.

A brokerage acting fraudulently may not only incur liability to a client, but also to a third party (customer) induced to enter into a transaction with the client. For example, liability can arise if a buyer customer is not informed about material latent defects, which are known by the brokerage.

GENERAL OBLIGATION FULFILLED	GENERAL OBLIGATION BREACHED
The Nearby School	**The Anxious Buyer**
A buyer client with two children, ages six and eight, asks the seller when viewing his property about the nearest school. The seller indicates a nearby location, knowing that the identified school is limited to grades seven and eight. The buyer representative, overhearing this comment, informs his client that the correct school (given her children's ages) is approximately five miles distant. The buyer decides to look at other property.	A prospective buyer attends an open house conducted by the listing salesperson for her seller client. The prospective buyer immediately begins discussing personal information, such as available cash to buy a house and the fact that she must find a suitable property within the next two weeks. The listing salesperson knowingly encourages the buyer to provide additional information, without explaining that she represents the seller and promotes the seller's interests.

ACT IN PERSON

A brokerage as an agent, including those authorized to act on behalf of the brokerage, must perform duties personally, unless instructed otherwise. Seller representation agreements commonly extend authority to brokers and salespersons authorized to trade for that brokerage. Such authority can be implied.

Further, the principal frequently extends such authority through a multiple listing service (MLS®) agreement to other real estate board members, but could also extend it to non-affiliated brokerages. Such authority is limited by regulators to those registered to trade in real estate, or exempted under REBBA 2002.

GENERAL OBLIGATION FULFILLED	GENERAL OBLIGATION BREACHED
The Exclusive Agreement	**The Missed Open House**
A salesperson, when listing the seller's property on behalf his employing brokerage, provides detailed information about agency relationships and fully discloses the brokerage's role as the agent. The seller clearly understands that he is authorizing the brokerage and all registrants employed by that brokerage to act on his behalf, when signing an exclusive seller representation agreement.	A listing salesperson is unable to attend the Saturday afternoon open house scheduled for his seller client, because a valued buyer client arrived in town and wants to see several properties. The salesperson arranges for his unregistered assistant to take over for a couple of hours until he can get to the open house. The seller is unaware that an unauthorized, unregistered person is conducting the open house, which is in violation of REBBA 2002.

OBEY INSTRUCTIONS

A brokerage, including those authorized to act on behalf of the brokerage, is obligated to obey the instructions of the principal. However, this obligation only extends to lawful instructions.

As an example, the brokerage would not have to follow an instruction to create a false document for a buyer client seeking mortgage financing, nor obey a seller client demanding misleading advertising content relating to his property, or a client instructing the brokerage to breach human rights legislation.

GENERAL OBLIGATION FULFILLED	GENERAL OBLIGATION BREACHED
The Condominium Listing A seller, when listing her $1,500,000 penthouse condominium, wants all buyers to show appropriate identification before viewing the property. She also requires the listing salesperson to be present for all showings and report back any comments made by prospective buyers during such showings. The listing salesperson agrees to these client instructions.	**The Underground Tank** The seller client is aware that his property has an old, buried oil tank, but its location is not readily discernible to the casual observer. He informs the listing salesperson not to mention this fact to anyone. Both the seller and the salesperson know that legislative requirements require the removal of unused, underground tanks. The salesperson does not disclose this material fact to the buyer. The buyer subsequently discovers the rusted tank and associated ground contamination after closing. Legal action is taken against the seller, the brokerage and the salesperson.

PERFORM MANDATE

An agent and its representative(s) must perform the mandate as set out in the representation agreement between the parties and act within specific authorities granted. The agent and/or its representatives should seek clarification when doubt exists regarding such authorities.

A brokerage, including those authorized to act on behalf of the brokerage, is not legally obliged to act, unless specific terms are set out in the agreement. However, a brokerage's non-performance of obligations usual to the industry may give rise to successful legal action for negligence.

GENERAL OBLIGATION FULFILLED	GENERAL OBLIGATION BREACHED
The Advertising Strategy The seller representation agreement provides authorization for the listing brokerage to undertake such marketing activities as it deems effective to sell the property. In accordance with this instruction, the brokerage places a for sale sign on the property, advertises the property through the local newspaper, markets the home using exclusive Internet-based promotion and shows the property to prospective buyers during reasonable hours.	**Multiple Representation** The seller representation agreement clearly states that the brokerage and its representatives must fully discuss agency relationships, including the possibility of multiple representation. The salesperson employed by the brokerage, while working with the seller client, fails to disclose the fact that the brokerage is also representing the buyer who submits an offer. As such, the brokerage and its representative have not carried out obligations outlined in the seller representation agreement and are in violation of REBBA 2002 disclosure requirements.

Fiduciary Obligations

A fiduciary must maintain utmost loyalty and protect the interests of the principal (client), avoid conflicts of interest, disclose conflicts, not make secret profits and not misuse confidential information. Fiduciary relationships arise in many different situations including a lawyer working on behalf of a client, a trustee on behalf of an estate and a real estate brokerage on behalf of a seller or buyer.

WRITTEN AGREEMENT NOT REQUIRED

While the relationship is typically established by an express written agreement (at the point of signing an appropriate seller representation agreement or buyer representation agreement), it would appear that a fiduciary relationship can arise if a representative of a brokerage receives confidential information from a seller or buyer and that representative in some way (by words and/or conduct) leads the seller or buyer to believe that he or she will act in the seller's or buyer's best interests (or takes no action to correct the seller's/buyer's mistaken belief that his or her interests will be protected).

Therefore, a fiduciary relationship can exist even when brokerages:

- Have not entered into written representation agreements with sellers or buyers.
- Are acting gratuitously for their clients.
- Are engaged in joint ventures with their clients.

However, the Code of Ethics requires that a registrant must reduce a verbal representation agreement with a buyer or seller to writing before an offer is made, have it signed on behalf of the brokerage and submit it to that buyer or seller for signature (CODE, Sec. 13 and 14).

PREMISES UNDERLYING A FIDUCIARY RELATIONSHIP

A fiduciary relationship is based on three fundamental premises that, in turn, flow to five **fiduciary obligations**.

Trust & Confidence   Case law has established that various elements must be present to create a fiduciary relationship. The key factor for real estate brokerages is whether the client places trust and confidence in the brokerage and relies on advice given.

As such, a client becomes dependent on and vulnerable to the brokerage. Fiduciary obligations typically attach to the relationship at point of signing a representation agreement, but the relationship might also be formed by way of a verbal agreement or upon sharing confidential information depending on the actions of the parties at the time the confidential information was shared. Remember, a fiduciary relationship can be created even when no agreement is reached, but is warranted by the facts.

Best Interests   In a fiduciary relationship, the brokerage must at all times act in the client's best interests. Fiduciaries must never permit their own interests, or those of third parties, to override this fundamental duty. The client's informed consent must be obtained if such interests come into conflict, either directly or indirectly, with the client's interests.

Loyalty Loyalty is focal to any fiduciary relationship and, in fact, encompasses all other obligations within its scope. The agent must ensure that the client's best interests are served and that such interests always take priority over personal and third party interests.

Implied Representation | CAUTION

Caution is always advised as a fiduciary relationship can arise when brokerages and/or their representatives have, in some way, implied that a relationship exists (due either to some action or inaction, particularly in regards to confidential information), are working gratuitously for clients or are engaged in joint ventures with clients.

> **Example:** *Buyer Divulges Confidential Information*
>
> The salesperson is showing his seller client's home to a prospective buyer customer. When viewing the property, the buyer casually mentions that the property may be beyond her financial abilities given a limited downpayment of approximately $25,000. The salesperson does nothing to dissuade the buyer from providing further details. In fact, the salesperson encourages the buyer to provide more details so that he can assist in advancing her interests. The buyer, now believing that she can rely on the salesperson to protect her interests, offers additional personal and confidential information. Once again, the salesperson does nothing to make the customer believe otherwise and encourages further dialogue. As such, the conduct of the parties would suggest that a relationship has been created and fiduciary obligations are owed.

Specific Fiduciary Obligations

Fiduciary obligations are difficult to quantify, but can be generally grouped under five categories. As with general obligations, two examples are provided for each: one in which the brokerage and/or its representative acts properly, and the other where the duty is breached.

MAINTAIN UTMOST LOYALTY

This obligation effectively encompasses all other fiduciary duties. The client's interests take precedence over the brokerage's and its representatives, and that of any other party. Maintaining loyalty is best achieved only by representing the interests of one party to a transaction; i.e., single representation. Difficulties can arise, for example, when a brokerage attempts to act for both buyer and seller (i.e., multiple representation) or two buyers who are competing for the same property, as the clients have divergent interests. Issues regarding multiple representation are discussed in the next chapter.

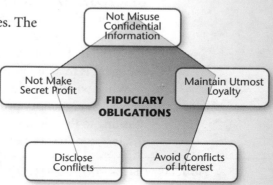

In a sense, any breach of an obligation could be said to constitute a breach of loyalty, as the brokerage is not acting in the client's best interests. However, strictly and narrowly speaking, a breach of loyalty occurs when another's interests (be it the brokerage's or the client's) are in play.

FIDUCIARY OBLIGATION FULFILLED	FIDUCIARY OBLIGATION BREACHED
Property in Demand	**The Competing Offer**
The salesperson locates a property that meets his client's needs. The salesperson, however, is also impressed with the property and might consider acquiring it himself. Putting aside his own interests, he introduces the property to his client who subsequently buys it.	The seller's salesperson has an offer, but is informed that another salesperson will be getting a competing offer later in the day. He does not inform the seller and presents his brokerage's offer immediately without regard to the client's best interests.

AVOID CONFLICTS OF INTEREST

Many forms of conflict can arise in real estate brokerages. A conflict of interest can involve the brokerage acting for two clients at the same time (i.e., multiple representation), the brokerage (or its authorized representative) acquiring the client's property, selling owned property to the client, being in some way either directly or indirectly involved with the transaction or having some other association that creates a potential or actual conflict of interest. A brokerage or its authorized representative might also divulge confidential information to a third party that could in turn be used to the disadvantage of the client's interests, such as making a secret profit in the absence of fully informed consent by the client.

FIDUCIARY OBLIGATION FULFILLED	FIDUCIARY OBLIGATION BREACHED
The Second Client	**The Relative's Home**
The salesperson, originally working with a seller client, is approached by a buyer who also wants to be represented. The salesperson explains dual agency and the conflict of interest that arises. Based on the discussion, the buyer elects to receive services as a customer.	The buyer client is unaware that the listed property is owned by a close relative of the salesperson. The salesperson does not disclose this fact and negotiates the deal despite an apparent conflict of interest.

DISCLOSE CONFLICTS

This fiduciary duty requires that the agent or its representatives disclose any personal or third party interests which either do or might conflict with the interests of the principal. The principal must have full knowledge of the exact nature and extent of the conflicts, if the agent is to avoid potential liability for breach of his or her fiduciary obligations.

While written disclosure is not mandated by common law, practical considerations (as well as regulatory provisions set out in REBBA 2002) require a signed document attesting to the client's awareness of, and consent to, the certain conflicts. Failure to openly disclose conflicts can give rise to registrant liability.

FIDUCIARY OBLIGATION FULFILLED	FIDUCIARY OBLIGATION BREACHED
The Written Disclosure	**The Altered Circumstance**
The salesperson wants to buy the listed property. When drafting the offer, she also prepares a written disclosure confirming that she is registered under the applicable provincial real estate statute, is employed by the brokerage with whom the property is listed and also discloses all other facts that are relevant under the circumstance.	The salesperson, originally not interested in his client's property, realizes its true value when two offers are immediately forth coming. He hurriedly decides to submit a competing offer through a numbered company, but makes no disclosure. The seller remains unaware of this fact during negotiations and accepts the numbered company's offer.

NOT MAKE SECRET PROFIT

This obligation prohibits an agent from profiting unlawfully at the expense of the principal. This obligation can involve profits from various activities. Three examples are highlighted.

- **Improper Advice/Breach of Loyalty**   An agent might attempt to profit from the principal's trust and reliance on advice given. In doing so, the brokerage or its representatives could further personal interests to the detriment of the client.

- **Payment from Other Party**   Real estate brokerages are not permitted to accept commissions or other remuneration from both parties to a transaction unless full disclosure is made to the client, including the amount being received, and the client consents to the payment. Simple disclosure is not sufficient. If such payment is received without the client's consent, the payment goes to the client and is not simply returned to the payor.

- **Payment by Third Party**   A brokerage or its representatives must not receive a secret profit from someone who is providing services relating to the transaction (e.g., a home inspector, appraiser or mortgage broker/agent) or is providing services that are incidental to the transaction (e.g., a moving company, renovation contractor or decorator). Such profit must be openly disclosed to the client.

FIDUCIARY OBLIGATION FULFILLED	FIDUCIARY OBLIGATION BREACHED
The Bonus	**The Flat Fee**
A salesperson is representing a buyer client and will receive remuneration from that client upon locating, and upon her purchase of, a suitable property. The salesperson approaches a *for sale by owner* (FSBO) who offers a bonus should the buyer client purchase his property. The salesperson makes full disclosure of this bonus to the buyer client.	The listing salesperson, in addition to receiving a commission from his seller client, receives a flat fee from the buyer customer for services performed in bringing about the negotiated sale. This amount received from the buyer customer is not disclosed to the seller client and, therefore, constitutes a secret profit.

NOT MISUSE CONFIDENTIAL INFORMATION

A brokerage or its representatives acquire confidential information by the very nature of the client relationship, which is established based on trust and loyalty. The brokerage or its representatives must never use confidential information obtained from that relationship to its own advantage, nor to harm the principal or interfere with his/her endeavours.

Information gained from a client can be far reaching; i.e., confidential details about the client, the property and/or the transaction. While disclosure to anyone can be harmful to the principal, providing confidential information to another party to the transaction can have significant detrimental impact on the client. This requirement obviously excludes any information about the client, the property or the transaction that, by law, the brokerage is required to disclose. For example, suspicious transactions, money laundering and terrorist financing involving a client (or customer) must be disclosed to the Financial Transactions and Reports Analysis Centre of Canada (FINTRAC). This and related topics are discussed in *The Residential Real Estate Transaction*.

FIDUCIARY OBLIGATION FULFILLED	FIDUCIARY OBLIGATION BREACHED
Seller's Confidentiality	**Breach of Buyer's Confidentiality**
The seller client informs the salesperson in confidence that a divorce is pending and financial commitments demand a quick sale. The listing salesperson keeps this information confidential, as disclosure to another party (e.g., the potential buyer) would impair the principal's negotiating position.	The buyer client informs his salesperson in confidence that while the initial offer is $247,000, he is willing to go to $265,000 if necessary. The salesperson discloses this fact to the seller's agent during negotiations and breaches his fiduciary responsibility to the buyer client.

Regulatory Obligations

Agents owe their principals various **regulatory obligations** beyond those imposed by common law (i.e., general and fiduciary obligations). Five common obligations are highlighted. Two examples are provided for each obligation: one in which the brokerage or its representative acts in accordance with the regulatory obligation, and the the brokerage or its representative does not.

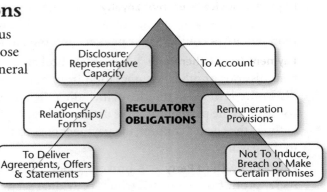

other in which

TO ACCOUNT

This obligation focuses on the agent's regulatory responsibility to account for and safeguard money, documents and property entrusted to that agent. These provisions are set out in trust account provisions in the *Real Estate and Business Brokers Act, 2002* and the Regulations. Further, brokerages must adhere to strict procedures regarding proper record keeping. Handling of trust account funds by registrants is discussed in *The Real Estate Transaction – General.*

REGULATORY OBLIGATION FULFILLED	REGULATORY OBLIGATION BREACHED
Deposit	**Lost Document**
A salesperson receives a deposit and returns immediately to the brokerage, which in turn places the funds in the real estate trust account within the specified regulatory time limit.	The salesperson successfully negotiates an agreement, but misplaces a schedule (addendum) that should have been attached to the contract. The principal suffers loss and the brokerage faces litigation, as well as regulatory action, due to faulty record-keeping practices.

REMUNERATION PROVISIONS

Common law merely requires that brokerages establish the existence of an agreement and confirmation that the applicable event occurred relating to the payment of commission or other remuneration. Common law places no restraint on how the commission is calculated. However, regulatory frameworks impose limitations, particularly regarding how remuneration is established (i.e., calculated) and rights to recover commission, including the requirement to be registered/licensed in that jurisdiction.

Sec. 36 of REBBA 2002 requires that the commission or other remuneration must be an agreed amount or percentage of sale price/rental price, but not both. Further, Section 9 of the Act provides that no legal action can be taken for the collecting of a commission, unless the person who brings such action is either registered or exempt from registration.

REGULATORY OBLIGATION FULFILLED	REGULATORY OBLIGATION BREACHED
Percentage of Sale Price	**Rate and Percentage of Sale Price**
The commission rate in the seller representation agreement was agreed upon as 4.5% on the first $250,000 of the selling price and 2.5% on the balance. The property was listed at $459,000 and subsequently sold for $450,000. In accordance with the agreement, a commission was paid by the seller to the brokerage in the amount of $16,250 ($11,250 + 5,000).	The brokerage completed a seller representation agreement in which the commission was to be calculated based on 3.5% of the sale price, plus a flat fee of $4,000. This arrangement violates Sec. 36 of the Act. The computation of remuneration must be a percentage of sale price or an agreed upon amount, but not both.

NOT TO INDUCE, BREACH OR MAKE CERTAIN PROMISES

Provincial jurisdictions generally prohibit brokerages from inducing a party to break a contract for the purpose of entering into another agreement. This requirement is set out in Sec. 33(1) of the Act. Further, brokerages and their authorized representatives cannot make certain promises (e.g., to resell the property) unless these are put in writing, signed by the brokerage and delivered to the party to whom the promise is made. REBBA 2002 addresses these requirements in the General Regulation (GEN), Sec. 25.

REGULATORY OBLIGATION FULFILLED	REGULATORY OBLIGATION BREACHED
Multiple Representation and the Signed Deal	**The Promise**
The listing salesperson, ten days following acceptance of an offer by his buyer client, is asked by the buyer how to get out of the deal in order to purchase a better property, which has subsequently appeared on the market. The salesperson informs the client that he cannot advise on such matters.	The salesperson, anxious for a sale on the listed property, promises the buyer (in the presence of others) that he will guarantee the sale of the buyer's current home. Nothing is put in writing, but the buyer relies on this representation to his detriment, lodges a complaint with the regulatory body and also commences litigation.

TO DELIVER AGREEMENTS, OFFERS AND STATEMENTS

Most Canadian jurisdictions include regulatory requirements concerning delivery of agreements, offers and other related statements. In Ontario, REBBA 2002 requires the prompt delivery of written agreements in connection with a trade in real estate. This provision found in the Code of Ethics (Sec. 12, 28 and 29) includes buyer and seller representation agreements, service agreements, agreements of purchase and sale, and deposits, as well as notices, amendments and other documents relating thereto.

REGULATORY OBLIGATION FULFILLED	REGULATORY OBLIGATION BREACHED
The Seller Representation Agreement	**The Offer**
The sellers sign an exclusive seller representation agreement and immediately after execution receive a copy of the agreement.	The buyer signs an offer which is subsequently accepted by the seller. However, following acceptance, the buyer returns to her distant home. The salesperson informs the buyer that he will send a copy, but none is ever received. The buyer assumes that the deal was cancelled and ultimately does not close the sale. The salesperson has not only failed to meet the delivery requirement as set out in that particular provincial jurisdiction, but may also face litigation concerning the cancelled sale.

AGENCY RELATIONSHIPS/FORMS

Traditionally, jurisdictions have not regulated agency relationships, nor addressed content of representation agreements. However, such initiatives are now underway in various provinces. In Ontario, REBBA 2002 has certain requirements regarding such agreements. For example, the Code of Ethics (Sec. 11) requires that a date must be specified as to when the agreement takes effect and the date on which it expires. Representation agreements are analyzed in *The Real Estate Transaction – General*.

REGULATORY OBLIGATION FULFILLED	REGULATORY OBLIGATION BREACHED
The Seller Representation Agreement The brokerage completes an agreement with the seller and fully complies with regulatory requirements by ensuring that the agreement has a specific date on which the agreement takes effect and the date on which it expires. The agreement also sets out the method for calculating remuneration and details the services that will be provided under this agreement.	**The Buyer Representation Agreement** The salesperson prepares a buyer representation agreement, but neglects to include an expiry date. Also, the buyer does not sign the agreement, but insists that the arrangement be verbal only. The agreement does not meet REBBA 2002 requirements regarding the date. Interestingly, the Act and Regulations do not require a signature (as a representation agreement can be written, oral or implied), but problems may arise, particularly when proving entitlement to commission.

DISCLOSURE: REPRESENTATIVE CAPACITY

Timely disclosure of representative capacity and guidelines regarding what triggers this type of disclosure have become focal regulatory issues. The *Real Estate and Business Brokers Act, 2002* requires that a brokerage and its representatives must provide certain information as early as is practically possible and before entering an agreement in respect of a trade in real estate (Code of Ethics, Sec. 10). Such disclosure ensures that consumers are informed regarding what roles registrants perform in real estate transactions, including the range of available services. The disclosure requirement also addresses the possibility of multiple representation and the consequent implications for buyer and/or seller clients. Further, the brokerage and its representatives must use their best efforts to obtain a written acknowledgement from the consumer that such information has been received and understood.

REGULATORY OBLIGATION FULFILLED	REGULATORY OBLIGATION BREACHED
Timely Disclosure The listing salesperson, on behalf of her brokerage, meets with the seller regarding the sale of his property. The salesperson, as part of the presentation, clearly outlines her representative capacity, available services and the possibility of multiple representation. She provides the seller with an informative brochure and has the seller provide his written acknowledgement that this disclosure was made.	**The Uninformed Buyer** A salesperson, on behalf of his brokerage, lists the seller's home and subsequently schedules an open house. A prospective buyer arrives at the open house and immediately wants an offer drafted. The salesperson prepares the offer, has the buyer sign and then presents the offer to his client for acceptance. The salesperson does not, at any point, discuss his role or any associated disclosures as required by REBBA 2002.

Duty of Care

Brokerages and their representatives owe both clients and customers a duty of care, *but the extent of that duty differs considerably*. With clients, the duty applies to everything that is done or ought to be done for a client. With customers, the duty is limited to the giving of information, responding to questions and doing anything that the salesperson has agreed to do for the customer. Accordingly, duty of care owed to customers involves:

- honesty;
- reasonable care and skill in ensuring accurate information; and
- reasonable care and skill in performing functions to which the brokerage has agreed.

DUTY OF CARE	DUTY OF CARE
Limited Duty to Customer	Duty To Client Involves Everything Done for That Client
• Provide Information	
• Perform Functions (If Any)	
• Limited Disclosure and Privacy Obligations	

Brokers and salespersons must conduct themselves in accordance with a standard of care expected of knowledgeable registrants. Failure to do so exposes brokerages and their representatives to liability for professional negligence.

As a cautionary note, registrants must always exercise reasonable care and skill with customers to ensure that accurate information is provided and that functions agreed to are properly performed. However, such information and functions should be limited, otherwise a client relationship may be established and multiple representation may result (see Chapter 16 for detailed discussion of multiple representations).

> **EXAMPLE**   *Client Duty of Care—Advice Regarding Offer*
>
> The seller asks for advice on whether or not to accept an offer. The salesperson meets an acceptable duty of care by providing input based on knowledge of existing sales, reviewing the benefits/drawbacks of the offer, pointing out any particular difficulties that might be encountered (i.e., the removal of any conditions) and answering seller questions as the need arises when reviewing the agreement.

> **EXAMPLE**   *Customer Duty of Care—Regarding Home Inspection*
>
> The buyer, as a customer, asks for advice regarding the condition of the seller's home. The salesperson states that the seller is his client, but that in all honesty many buyers seek out a home inspector, as the responsibility rests with the buyer to satisfy himself or herself regarding the condition of the property.

STANDARDS IMPOSED UNDER DUTY OF CARE

The standard of care is based on how ordinary and prudent members of the real estate industry would conduct themselves under similar circumstances. The standard expected is not of perfection, but of reasonableness according to how knowledgeable, well-trained registrants would act.

The standard is objective (i.e., based on facts and criteria), without regard for personal interpretations or intervening circumstances. What a registrant can't argue in court include:

- *I just got my registration to sell real estate.*
- *I wasn't familiar with this type of property.*
- *I don't have any experience with that type of property; e.g., commercial.*
- *I didn't charge for my services (i.e., acted gratuitously).*
- *I did the best that I could under the circumstances.*
- *I didn't realize that I had to do that; i.e., conduct deviates from normal brokerage practices.*

ESTABLISHING THE STANDARD

The objective standard is typically established in court by determining from industry experts, applicable laws, regulatory rules and codes of ethics, how reasonable and prudent registrants would have acted under similar circumstances. An important exception involves a registrant who claims to possess special expertise or experience. He or she will be judged according to that higher standard.

EVOLUTION OF CUSTOMER DUTY OF CARE

The Hedley Byrne case (Hedley Byrne & Co. Ltd. v. Heller & Partners Ltd. [1964] AC 465) was an important legal milestone. This British case, ultimately settled in the House of Lords, has always been reaffirmed in Canadian courts. Essentially, the case established that a representation (whether written or spoken) can give rise to action for damages, apart from any agency relationship; i.e., representations made to a customer. A duty of care is implied when:

- One party seeks information from another who has special skills (such as a salesperson or broker);
- That party trusts the person to exercise due care; and
- The party giving the advice knows or ought to know that reliance is being placed on such advice.

If the person receiving this information suffers economic loss, damages can result due to negligent misrepresentation.

WHAT THIS MEANS TO REGISTRANTS

Duty of care focuses on reasonableness, not perfection. However, registrants can avoid many pitfalls and problems if certain simple duty of care rules are followed.

Seek Advice When Appropriate	Be aware of the limits of individual expertise. Personally seek assistance and/or recommend that the client or customer obtain legal or other appropriate advice.
Diligently Prepare Contracts and Other Documents	Make certain that contracts are properly worded, documents are delivered appropriately and persons signing are aware of associated implications.
Keep in Step with Relevant Issues	Be well informed about issues impacting property; e.g., zoning, local improvement charges and HST.
Make Reasonable Inquiry	Don't simply rely on information supplied by others (even a client) regarding material matters affecting the property. If something is questionable, check it out.
Verify the Accuracy of Information	Be particularly careful with listing details and double check information.

Documenting Non-Agency Relationships   MARKET MEMO

Brokerages commonly enter into agency relationships with buyers and sellers. However, circumstances can arise where a buyer or seller is given only selected services as a customer and the parties wish to document this by way of a service agreement; i.e., a non-agency relationship.

EXAMPLE

The seller as a for sale by owner does not want to be represented, but agrees to pay a commission if a sale is effected with the brokerage's buyer client. A *Seller Customer Service Agreement (Commission Agreement for Property Not Listed)*, OREA Form 201 might be used.

Alternatively, a sophisticated buyer may seek customer status rather than being represented by the brokerage. A *Buyer Customer Service Agreement (For Use When the Buyer is Not Represented By the Brokerage)*, OREA Form 310 might be used.

Canadian jurisdictions, including Ontario, have traditionally shied away from specific forms designed for non-agency arrangements, but increased regulatory requirements involving customers have necessitated the introduction of customer service agreements or customer acknowledgements. Services provided under such agreements do not require the exercising of discretion or judgement, as is the case with representation agreements. Detailed discussion is included in *The Real Estate Transaction – General*.

PRINCIPAL'S DUTIES TO AGENT

Three obligations are owed by the principal when entering an agency relationship: indemnification, remuneration and obligations set out in the representation agreement. The principal does not owe any fiduciary or regulatory obligations to the agent.

General Obligations

INDEMNIFY

As a general rule of agency, the principal must compensate an agent for loss or damage incurred in carrying out lawful acts. Indemnity also extends to reimbursement for expenses incurred. However, by the terms of most real estate representation agreements the right to reimbursement does not generally apply when, for example, real estate brokerages receive a commission (unless specifically stated in the agreement).

EXAMPLE   *The Appliances*

A buyer sued both the seller and the seller's real estate brokerage due to the fact that five expensive appliances that were stated to be included in the purchase price on the *Agreement of Purchase and Sale* were removed from the property by the seller on completion of the transaction.

The court held that the seller must indemnify the brokerage and assume the full liability for the loss suffered by the buyer.

REMUNERATE

The principal is obligated to remunerate the agent (typically by way of commission) assuming that the agent is duly authorized by provincial legislation to trade in real estate and that the terms of a representation agreement are performed.

EXAMPLE   *The Exclusive Representation Agreement*

ABC Realty Inc. has listed the seller's property which provides for the following:

> **COMMISSION:** *In consideration of you listing the property, I agree to pay the listing brokerage a commission of 5.25% of the sale price of the Property or for any valid offer to purchase or lease the Property from any source whatsoever obtained during the Listing Period and on the terms and conditions set out in this Agreement OR such other terms and conditions as I may accept.*

The commission is due and payable if the terms as set out are fulfilled.

OBLIGATIONS IN THE AGREEMENT

The principal must also perform other obligations as agreed and set out in the representation agreement. The following illustration details typical remuneration-related provisions involving a seller representation agreement. See subsequent Curiosity titled *Principal's Obligations: Buyer Representation Agreement* for typical provisions found in a buyer representation agreement.

LEASE	HOLDOVER PROVISION	DEPOSIT	TAXES	REFERRAL OF ENQUIRIES	OTHER
Obligation to pay commission may extend to any lease.	Obligation to pay extends for a specified period beyond the agreement term for persons introduced to the property or to the seller during the currency of the representation agreement.	The brokerage has the right to apply any deposit against commission.	The principal agrees to remit commission, plus applicable harmonized sales tax (HST).	The principal shall advise the brokerage immediately of enquiries from any source whatsoever during the currency of the listing.	Other obligations that may be contracted between the parties.

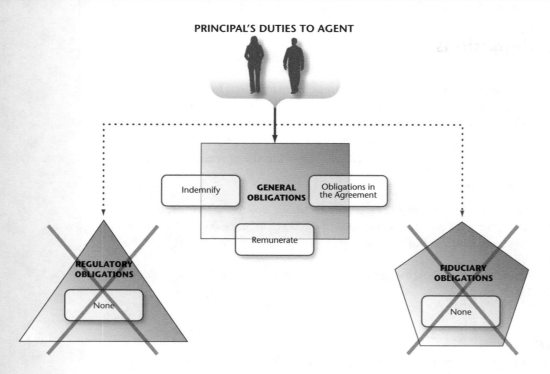

Source: © Alliance for Canadian Real Estate Education, 2006. *Agency Fundamentals: The National Perspective.*

SECTION VI   INTRODUCTION TO REAL ESTATE TRADING

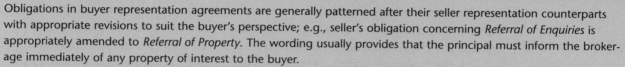

Principal's Obligations: Buyer Representation Agreement | CURIOSITY

Obligations in buyer representation agreements are generally patterned after their seller representation counterparts with appropriate revisions to suit the buyer's perspective; e.g., seller's obligation concerning *Referral of Enquiries* is appropriately amended to *Referral of Property*. The wording usually provides that the principal must inform the brokerage immediately of any property of interest to the buyer.

However, an additional provision may be included relating to receiving remuneration from the seller brokerage:

- The buyer brokerage is entitled to receive/retain remuneration from the seller brokerage or seller.

- Buyer will be informed of amount payable.

- No remuneration is due from the buyer if such amount received from the seller brokerage is more. If less, the buyer may be responsible for the shortfall.

- Such payment does not make the buyer brokerage either the agent or sub-agent of the seller brokerage or the seller.

AGENCY TERMINATION

An agency relationship can be terminated by acts of the parties or operation of law. Such termination does not disturb legal rights and obligations associated with the relationship, unless otherwise agreed to by the parties.

BY AGREEMENT

Mutual Consent
The principal and agent mutually agree to terminate the agency (e.g., signing of a mutual consent form).

Revocation
The principal has the power to revoke the authority of the brokerage, however, such revocation may be either lawful or unlawful. If unlawful, the principal can be liable for damages (i.e., breach of duties under the agreement).

Expiry
The agency relationship terminates on the date agreed to by the parties, subject to remuneration obligations (i.e., holdover period) and any representation renewal agreement. However, all fiduciary responsibilities do not terminate. Some carry on, such as confidentiality of information.

Completion/Performance
The relationship terminates when the ultimate purpose of the agreement is achieved (i.e., the property is sold and title is transferred).

OPERATION OF LAW

Impossibility
The relationship ends if the subject matter of the agency ceases to exist (e.g., the building is destroyed by fire).

Illegality
The relationship ends if the agency purpose or the agency relationship is unlawful (e.g., the brokerage's registration is revoked).

Death, Mental Incapacity or Bankruptcy
The relationship generally terminates with the death, bankruptcy or mental incapacity of either the agent or the principal. (Note: An exception can involve the principal's death assuming a representation agreement provision extends obligations to the person's estate.)

Continuance of Rights/Obligations

Termination by either principal or agent does not affect the rights of either party nor any associated obligations owed by one to the other, unless the parties agree otherwise. Termination of the brokerage as agent does not generally impact the relationship between the client and a third party (e.g., a buyer). However, subsequent negotiations between the brokerage and the third party could affect the client's legal position in relation to that third party. Two examples are provided that result in legal action. The outcome of any such action depends on circumstances concerning the particular situation.

EXAMPLE *Seller Refuses to Co-operate*

A seller listed his property with a brokerage for a 90-day period. During the initial two weeks, the brokerage showed the property to four buyers. One buyer expressed interest and wanted to re-inspect the home, however, the seller refused stating that he had decided not to sell the property. The seller also would not sign a mutual release, but effectively terminated the agency relationship by ceasing all communication with the brokerage. Several weeks later, the brokerage discovered that the seller sold the property privately to the interested buyer previously introduced and took legal action for commission based on rights set out in the seller representation agreement.

EXAMPLE *Brokerage Misrepresentation*

Salesperson A, on behalf of the brokerage, entered into a 90-day listing with the seller for a commercial property. A buyer client was introduced to the property by Salesperson B, another salespserson employed by the brokerage. The sale closed one month following expiration of the representation agreement. After closing, the new owner discovered that the property could not be used for car repairs, despite assurances to the contrary by Salesperson B. The seller had provided a list of relevant usage limitations to Salesperson A, but this information was apparently not conveyed to the buyer. The new owner took legal action against the brokerage for breach of duties under the buyer representation agreement.

KNOWLEDGE INTEGRATION

Notables

- REBBA 2002 consists of the statute and six regulations, three of which have a direct bearing on real estate trading.

- A real estate brokerage, when involved in trading, is legally viewed as an agent under common law, but must also adhere to regulatory requirements regarding representation.

- An agency relationship between agent and principal can be express (written or oral) or implied. Written agreements are essential from a registrant's perspective.

- Agency is created by four methods; the most relevant to real estate is *by agreement*.

- Agency terms can be confusing given differing perspectives of the courts, legislators, real estate brokers and consumers.

- Agency applies to all types of agents wherever common law exists. However, the practice and extent of agency authority varies by profession.

- For real estate agency purposes, the terms *brokerage* and *agent* have become legally synonymous.

- Agent authority is best described in terms of actual and implied authorities.

- Obligations of an agent (i.e., brokerage) and its representatives are grouped under three categories: general, fiduciary and regulatory.

- Fiduciaries must at all times act in the client's best interests and never permit their own interests or that of a third party to override this duty.

- Real estate brokerages owe clients and customers a duty of care, but the extent of such duties varies depending on whether a client or customer relationship exists.

- The standard of care is not one of perfection, but rather of reasonableness; that is, how prudent members of the real estate industry would conduct themselves under the circumstances.

Glossary

Agency

Agency Relationship

Agent

Authority

Brokerage

Broker

Buyer Representation Agreement

Client

Customer

Duty of Care

Fiduciary

Fiduciary Obligations

General Obligations

Implied Agency

Informed Consent

Principal

Regulatory Obligations

Salesperson

Seller Representation Agreement

Third Party

Web Links

Web links are included for general interest regarding selected chapter topics.

REBBA 2002   For direct references to the Act/Regulations, go to *www.e-laws.gov.on.ca*. The RECO website also provides a link to the legislation. Go to *www.reco.on.ca*.

Guide To REBBA 2002   The online guide is available at *www.reco.on.ca/onlineguide*. This handy guide provides key information about the Act and Regulations and is an excellent study resource throughout the pre-registration courses.

Strategic Thinking For Your Career

Questions are included to assist in developing your new career. No answers are provided.

1. What specific authorities are included in representation agreements used in the local marketplace?

2. Can I fully explain general, fiduciary and regulatory obligations to clients and customers and can I differentiate between the duty of care owed to clients and customers?

3. What is the best way for me to avoid conflicts of interest when faced with the possibility of representing two clients in the same transaction?

4. What type of conduct with a buyer customer might lead that buyer to mistakenly assume that he or she is a client?

Chapter Mini-Review

Solutions are located in the Appendix.

1. A seller representation agreement is often referred to in the marketplace as a listing agreement.
   ○ True   ○ False

2. Agency describes a relationship in which one party (the agent) accepts responsibility for representing another (a third party).
   ○ True   ○ False

3. The term *agent* refers to a salesperson registered pursuant to REBBA 2002.
   ○ True   ○ False

4. An agency relationship created by agreement can either be express or implied.
   ○ True   ○ False

5. An agent's authority can be granted retroactively.
   ○ True   ○ False

6. While agency relationships are commonplace, situations can arise in which a buyer or seller is provided only selected services as a customer.
   ○ True   ○ False

7. The terms *agency* and *representation* are generally analogous for purposes of discussing agency relationships as they impact real estate brokerage.
   ○ True   ○ False

8. A real estate brokerage's actual agency authorities are typically set out in writing in a representation agreement.
   ○ True   ○ False

9. A real estate brokerage's agency authority is subject to only three limitations.

   ◯ True   ◯ False

10. Real estate agency relationships are generally assumed to give rise to fiduciary obligations.

    ◯ True   ◯ False

11. A fiduciary relationship, which is enforceable by the courts, can only be created by written agreement.

    ◯ True   ◯ False

12. A major element in determining if a fiduciary relationship has been established is whether or not the client has agreed to pay remuneration.

    ◯ True   ◯ False

13. Real estate brokerages are not permitted to accept commissions from anyone other than the principal in a transaction, unless full disclosure is made to that client.

    ◯ True   ◯ False

14. A salesperson who claims to have special expertise will be judged in court according to that higher standard.

    ◯ True   ◯ False

15. A salesperson employed by a brokerage owes a customer both honesty and confidentiality when fulfilling his/her duty of care.

    ◯ True   ◯ False

16. An agency relationship can only be terminated by operation of law.

    ◯ True   ◯ False

Active Learning Exercises

Solutions are located in the Appendix.

■ Exercise 1: Agency (Matching)

Match the description in the left column with the appropriate phrase/word in the right column (not all phrases/words are used).

____ Fiduciary Relationship	a. Customer
____ Adopts Agent's Actions	b. Client
____ Representation Agreement	c. Excludes Quebec
____ Third Party	d. Express Agreement
____ Common Law	e. Estoppel
	f. Ratification

■ Exercise 2: Authorities and Obligations (Fill-in-the-Blanks)

2.1 Actual authorities are typically set out by way of a (an)

.... agreement.

2.2 A brokerage selecting various advertising and promotion methods relating to a seller representation agreement is usually operating under a (an)

.... authority.

2.3 Certain .... obligations are

established under REBBA 2002, as distinct from common law.

2.4 Two elements essential in a fiduciary relationship are *trust* and

....

2.5 A general obligation that requires a brokerage to possess the necessary abilities

to perform agency duties is best described by the phrase

....

2.6 A brokerage that avoids conflicts of interest is adhering to agent obligations

commonly grouped under the category of

....

■ Exercise 3: Duty of Care/Standard of Care

Identify which of the following circumstances are examples of duty of care in the marketplace:

☐ The salesperson informs the buyer customer that many buyers seek out the services of a home inspector.

☐ The salesperson takes accurate room measurements and includes these on the seller representation agreement.

☐ The customer asks about arranging a new mortgage and the salesperson provides the buyer with a list of lenders that typically lend on that type of property.

☐ The seller client asks the salesperson not to divulge that a marital dispute is the primary reason for listing the home.

☐ The salesperson, when asked by the buyer about legal matters involving the house purchase, advises the client to seek appropriate expert advice.

▣ Exercise 4: Multiple Choice

4.1 Which of the following terms best describes duties performed by a real estate brokerage in seller representation?

   a. Middleman Role.

   b. General Agency.

   c. Special Agency.

   d. Third Party Agency.

4.2 Which of the following best describes the key difference between clients and customers?

   a. The duty of care owed to customers exceeds that owed to clients.

   b. The term *client* relates to an agency relationship, while *customer* refers to a non-agency relationship.

   c. Clients are owed greater fiduciary obligations than those owed to customers.

   d. No significant differences exist between fiduciary duties owed to clients and customers.

4.3 A seller permits a salesperson employed by a brokerage to show his property, agrees that the brokerage will represent his interests and discusses remuneration to be paid. However, the seller does not sign the seller representation agreement provided to him. The property is subsequently sold to a buyer by that brokerage. This situation is best described as:

   a. Creating agency by oral agreement.

   b. Establishing an agency relationship by operation of law.

   c. A good example of a salesperson performing his/her general obligation of confidentiality.

   d. A good example of duty of care as it applies in the marketplace.

4.4 A salesperson, when listing a property, elects to focus most of her advertising efforts on the Internet rather than print media, given the particular features of the home. The seller is not aware of this specific advertising decision. This action is best described as:

   a. An actual authority.

   b. An express agreement.

   c. An implied authority.

   d. A legislated authority.

4.5   A buyer's representative is unaware of potential water problems within a particular neighbourhood, but accidentally overhears the seller customer discussing his problems with water quality and adequate supply. The listing brokerage has made no mention of this matter. The prospective buyer client is keenly interested in the property. After leaving the property, the salesperson informs the buyer regarding what was overheard. This scenario is best described by which of the following general obligations?

    a.   Obedience.

    b.   Negotiate Favourable Terms.

    c.   Confidentiality.

    d.   Disclosure.

4.6   A salesperson is instructed by the seller client not to divulge mould problems associated with the listed property. The salesperson agrees once the seller assures him that the problem has gone away. Further, evidence of any problem is not readily visible from a cursory inspection. The buyer, as a customer, discovers the problem subsequent to completion of the sale and takes legal action. Regardless of the outcome, which of the following general or fiduciary obligations will be most closely scrutinized by the Courts?

    a.   Obedience.

    b.   Loyalty.

    c.   Conflict.

    d.   Confidentiality.

4.7   A buyer client is pursuing legal recourse, because the salesperson failed to inform her that the basement apartment in the purchased home was not legal. The salesperson, in his defense, argues that he only recently obtained his salesperson's registration and can't be expected to know about such matters. Which of the following statements best describes the merits of the salesperson's argument?

    a.   The argument has legal merit, as recently registered salespersons are not expected to have such knowledge.

    b.   The argument has little legal merit, as a duty of care is owed regardless of experience level.

    c.   The argument has legal merit, as the standard of care is subjectively interpreted by the Courts.

    d.   The argument has little legal merit, as a salesperson cannot be held liable for inaccurate statements.

CHAPTER 16

Representation

Introduction

The *Real Estate and Business Brokers Act, 2002* and the Regulations contain various provisions relating to representation and related disclosures that must be made to buyers and sellers in real estate transactions. Registrants must be clear in describing the nature of representation that they are providing to clients, as well as services offered to customers.

This chapter analyzes representation from several different perspectives; namely, single representation (seller or buyer) including obligations owed, multiple representation and the challenges facing registrants in regard to competing interests and imputed knowledge, other conflicts of interest that can arise with competing sellers and buyers, sub-agency possibilities in the marketplace and requirements regarding service agreements involving customers.

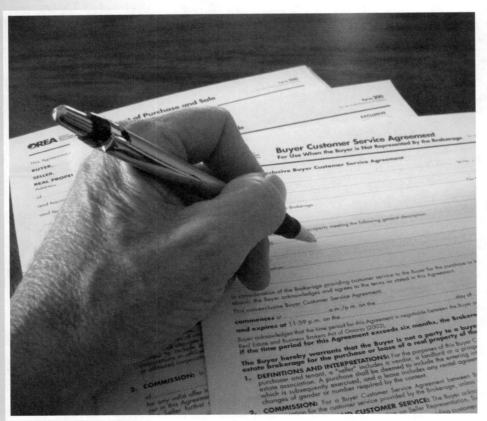

Various learning aids are included to expand awareness including scenarios detailing general, fiduciary and regulatory obligations, examples including typical wordings used in representation and customer service forms, and direct reference to regulatory compliance set out in REBBA 2002.

Key disclosure provisions concerning representation and service agreements are found in the Code of Ethics. While such agreements can be written, oral or implied, registrants are required to reduce these agreements to writing and submit them to buyers and sellers for signature.

Learning Outcomes

At the conclusion of this chapter, students will be able to:

- Define and describe single representation including regulatory requirements contained in the Code of Ethics concerning duties owed to clients vs. customers.
- Detail basic obligations owed to a client under single representation as set out in common law.
- Explain REBBA 2002 compliance requirements for single representation including the need for agreements to be in writing and required disclosures.
- Identify key challenges facing registrants in regard to multiple representation, with particular reference to competing interests and imputed knowledge.
- Explain REBBA 2002 compliance for multiple representation including the need for informed, written consent and required disclosures.
- Discuss other conflicts of interest involving competing buyers and competing sellers.
- Explain the importance and the procedure used in the disclosure of interest by registrants.
- Briefly outline how sub-agency could be used in selected representation situations.

REPRESENTATION: OVERVIEW

Selected materials from *Agency Fundamentals: The National Perspective* (Alliance for Canadian Real Estate Education, 2006) are included with permission. In doing so, the Real Estate Council of Ontario wishes to advance consistency in agency training and promote greater uniformity in real estate education across Canada.

Agency relationships between principal and agent can be grouped under two categories:

Single Representation   Brokerage represents buyer or seller with the other party (i.e., the seller or buyer respectively) being a third party (customer).

Multiple Representation   Brokerage represents more than one party, typically the buyer and the seller.

A registrant's perspective in any transaction is relative to his or role. For example, if a brokerage and its representatives are representing the seller as a client, the third party will normally be the buyer who is viewed as a customer. Conversely, if the brokerage and its representatives are representing the buyer client, then the seller becomes the third party. Of course, in some instances, the brokerage and its representatives are representing both buyer and seller (multiple representation trading).

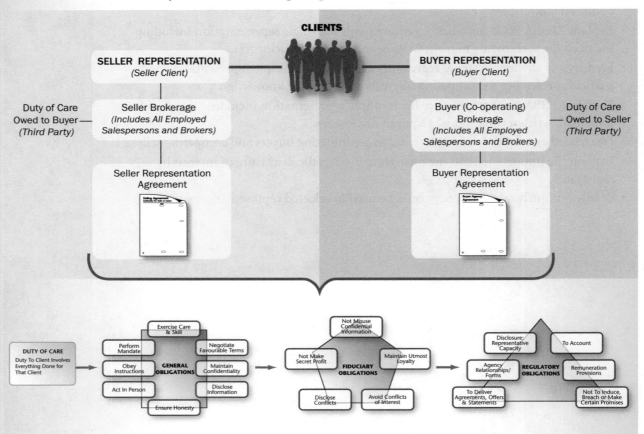

Source: © Alliance for Canadian Real Estate Education, 2006. *Agency Fundamentals: The National Perspective.*

SINGLE REPRESENTATION

Single representation is a relationship between a seller or buyer and an agent wherein the agent is considered in law to represent only the principal. In single representation involving the seller, the buyer is often represented by another brokerage (the **co-operating brokerage**). Further, the brokerage representing the seller typically assumes that the co-operating brokerage is representing the buyer. The seller's representative owes that third party buyer a limited duty of care. In buyer representation, the reverse applies in which the buyer is represented by one brokerage, with the seller typically represented by another brokerage.

> **Co-operating Brokerage**
>
> A brokerage (typically representing the buyer) who is co-operating with a listing brokerage in a real estate trade.

With the rise of buyer representation in the 1990's, the term *single representation (or single agency)* is sometimes used to refer to brokerages that only work with either buyers or sellers. For example, a brokerage dealing only with buyers would not offer representation services to sellers or, conversely, a brokerage representing only sellers would not offer client services to buyers. While this approach has been used in the United States, the concept has not gained any prominence in the Canadian marketplace.

Seller Representation

In **seller representation**, the brokerage represents the seller as a client. The seller brokerage and all salespeople employed by that brokerage promote the listed property, seek out qualified buyers and use their professional negotiation skills to advance the seller's interests. General and fiduciary duties are owed to the seller/client, along with a limited duty of care to the customer. Regulatory obligations also apply as set out in REBBA 2002.

> **Seller Representation**
>
> A form of single representation in which the brokerage represents the seller as a client.

The Code of Ethics (Ontario Regulation 580/05) provides that a registrant's loyalty rests with the client by protecting and promoting his/her best interests. The Code also requires that, in doing so, the registrant must also deal honestly and with integrity with every person with which he or she is involved in the course of a trade and provide conscientious service to both clients and customers.

FAIRNESS, HONESTY, ETC.   CODE

3.   A registrant shall treat every person the registrant deals with in the course of a trade in real estate fairly, honestly and with integrity. O. Reg. 580/05, s. 3.

BEST INTERESTS

4.   A registrant shall promote and protect the best interests of the registrant's clients. O. Reg. 580/05, s. 4.

CONSCIENTIOUS AND COMPETENT SERVICE, ETC.

5.   A registrant shall provide conscientious service to the registrant's clients and customers and shall demonstrate reasonable knowledge, skill, judgment and competence in providing those services. O. Reg. 580/05, s. 5.

EXAMPLES   *Seller Representation*

SEC. 3.   FAIRNESS, HONESTY, ETC.

A salesperson representing the seller is showing the property to a prospective buyer customer. The customer, unfamiliar with rural properties, enquires as to the condition of the well and septic system. While not representing the buyer, the salesperson honestly informs the buyer that most buyers would seek the assistance of a home inspector or other qualified individual regarding such matters. The salesperson also tells the buyer that he can obtain additional information about well and septic requirements from the local municipality.

SEC. 4.   BEST INTERESTS

A salesperson is presenting a $386,000 offer to the seller client for her property listed at $399,500. The seller wants to know if this offer is reasonable or should it be signed back for a higher amount. The salesperson provides any information known about the buyer that will assist in this decision, updates the seller on recent sales in the area and advises her regarding general market conditions. At the same time, the salesperson clearly indicates to the seller that the ultimate decision of whether to accept or reject the offer rests solely with her. The seller, upon considering information provided by the salesperson, decides to accept the offer.

SEC. 5.   CONSCIENTIOUS AND COMPETENT SERVICE, ETC.

A salesperson is asked by the seller client to review an offer received on his commercial property located at 11233 Main Street. The salesperson fully discusses all conditions and other wordings within the offer, pointing out relevant items that are beneficial to the seller or, conversely, could pose problems for the client. A counter offer is prepared and promptly returned to the buyer by the seller's salesperson for further consideration. The salesperson representing the seller also answers various questions about the counter offer in a conscientious manner to further the negotiations, while at the same time representing the best interests of her client.

Buyer Representation

| *Buyer Representation*
| A form of single representation in which the brokerage represents the buyer as a client.

In **buyer representation**, the brokerage represents the buyer as a client. The buyer brokerage (often referred to as the co-operating brokerage) and all salespersons employed by that brokerage must promote the buyer's interests, locate a suitable property and use their professional negotiation skills to advance the buyer's interests. General and fiduciary obligations are owed to the buyer/client, along with a limited duty of care to the customer, who in this instance would be the seller. Regulatory obligations also apply and include the three key provisions already highlighted; i.e., Code of Ethics, Sec. 3, 4 and 5.

COMMISSION

In Canadian jurisdictions, the seller typically pays commission or other remuneration to the seller's brokerage who, in turn, disburses the agreed portion to the buyer's (co-operating) brokerage. The buyer must be informed of this arrangement and of the amount of the remuneration to be received by the buyer's brokerage from the seller's brokerage. Alternatively, the buyer's brokerage can be paid directly by the buyer in which case such amount does not form part of the sale proceeds.

As an important qualification, a buyer's brokerage could be paid by the seller or could potentially seek remuneration from both. The real estate brokerage, as with all agents in a fiduciary relationship, must disclose such arrangements to the client (or clients) and receive their fully informed consent. This obligation also extends to receipt of money from third parties, such as referral fees paid by persons involved in the transaction (e.g., mortgage brokers, lenders and lawyers) or those providing incidental services (e.g., moving companies and interior decorators).

EXAMPLES   *Buyer Representation*

SEC. 3.   FAIRNESS, HONESTY, ETC.

A salesperson representing the buyer has shown his client the seller's property. The seller is not represented and is offering his home as a 'For Sale by Owner.' The salesperson presents the offer to the seller on behalf of his client. The seller, upon delivery, wants to discuss his negotiating position with the salesperson. The salesperson immediately advises the seller that he represents the buyer and honestly informs the seller that he should seek out the services of another real estate brokerage or a lawyer regarding such matters.

. . . .

SEC. 4.   BEST INTERESTS

Salesperson A is presenting a counter offer from his seller client for $489,000. The counter offer was made based on an initial offer by the buyer of $473,000 on the property listed at $499,900. The buyer, in considering the counter offer, wants to know if the amount countered is realistic. Salesperson B provides his buyer client details about comparable properties that are for sale, have been sold or have expired (unsold) over the past two months in that particular area. Salesperson B also updates the buyer on recent market trends and generally ensures that his buyer client is well informed prior to making a decision about the seller's counter offer.

. . . .

SEC. 5.   CONSCIENTIOUS AND COMPETENT SERVICE, ETC.

A salesperson is asked by his buyer client and seller customer about a problem regarding a tax matter that has cropped up during negotiations. The salesperson explains to both parties that he is obligated to provide conscientious and competent service to both of them, but that such matters go well beyond his area of knowledge and expertise. As such, he strongly advises both client and customer to seek expert advice from their respective accountants.

Basic Obligations: Single Representation

As previously discussed, various general and fiduciary obligations are owed to a client under single representation. The Agency Task Force of the Canadian Regulators Group (of which RECO is a member) developed a list of all obligations imposed by common law and inherent in the single representation relationship. The following chart provides a handy reference to specific duties that must be carried out when registrants are involved in seller client and buyer client relationships.

The Agency Task Force recommended that these obligations be expressly spelled out in representation agreements so that registrants and clients are fully aware of them. These obligations are fundamental to any discussion of representation, and must be fully understood and practised by all registrants.

BASIC OBLIGATIONS—SINGLE REPRESENTATION

Basic obligations are owed to a client in a single representation relationship. All obligations illustrated are imposed by common (case) law and inherent in the relationship.

Buyer Single Representation

Locate Property—Promote Buyer's Best Interests

(a) to use best efforts in locating a property in the specified market area(s) that meets the material requirements identified by the buyer and to promote the interests of the buyer;

Advise Seller—Brokerage is Representative of Buyer

(b) at the earliest reasonable opportunity, to advise any seller in whose property the buyer is interested that the brokerage is the representative of the buyer;

Act as the Buyer's Representative

(c) subject to the provisions of the agreement related to a change in representative capacity, to act as only the buyer's representative;

Obey Lawful Instructions

(d) to obey all lawful instructions of the buyer;

Fulfill Fiduciary Obligations

(e) to fulfill its fiduciary obligations of loyalty, confidentiality and of full disclosure of all conflicts of interest that may arise between the buyer's interests and those of the brokerage and its representatives, sellers or competing buyers;

No Sub-Agency Without Consent

(f) not to appoint another brokerage to act on behalf of the buyer as sub-agent without the prior written consent of the buyer;

Exercise Reasonable Care and Skill

(g) to exercise reasonable care and skill in the performance of the agreement;

Seek Out Available Properties

(h) to seek out and advise the buyer in a timely manner of available properties in the market area which may meet the buyer's requirements, including those listed with other brokerages, those "for sale by owner" and other available properties known to the brokerage or its representatives;

Discover Relevant Facts

(i) to use best efforts to discover relevant facts pertaining to any property for which the buyer is considering making an offer;

Disclose Relevant Facts

(j) to disclose, in a timely manner, to the buyer all relevant facts known to the brokerage or its representatives affecting a property or transaction;

Obtain Expert Advice

(k) to advise the buyer to obtain expert advice on matters of importance to the buyer;

Timely Presentation of Offers and Counter-Offers

(l) to present, in a timely manner, all offers and counter-offers to and from the buyer even when a property is already the subject of an agreement of purchase and sale;

Keep Buyer Informed

(m) to keep the buyer fully informed regarding the progress of the transaction;

Disclose Competing Offers

(n) to disclose to the buyer the existence and terms of any competing offers known to the brokerage or its representatives for a property in which the buyer is interested;

Negotiate Favourable Terms

(o) to assist the buyer in negotiating favourable substance and conditions, and in preparing a legally binding agreement of purchase and sale;

Comply with Regulatory Requirements

(p) to comply with all relevant provisions of the [name of Act] and its regulations, and the rules and by-laws of the [name of governing body].

Seller Single Representation

Market Property—Promote Seller's Best Interests

(a) to use best efforts to market the property and to promote the interests of the seller;

Advise Buyer—Brokerage is Representative of Seller

(b) at the earliest reasonable opportunity, to advise any buyer interested in the property that the brokerage is the seller's representative;

Act as the Seller's Representative

(c) subject to the provisions of the agreement related to a change in representative capacity, to act as only the seller's representative;

Obey Lawful Instructions

(d) to obey all lawful instructions of the seller;

Fulfill Fiduciary Obligations

(e) to fulfill its fiduciary obligations of loyalty, confidentiality and of full disclosure of all conflicts of interest that may arise between the seller's interests and those of the brokerage, including its representatives, or buyers;

No Sub-Agency Without Consent

(f) not to appoint another brokerage to act on behalf of the seller as sub-agent without the seller's prior written consent;

Exercise Reasonable Care and Skill

(g) to exercise reasonable care and skill in the performance of the agreement;

Negotiate Favourable Terms

(h) to assist the seller in negotiating favourable terms and conditions with a buyer and in preparing and complying with a legally binding agreement of purchase and sale for the property;

Disclose Material Latent Defects to Buyers

(i) to disclose to buyers all material latent defects affecting the property known to the brokerage or its representatives;

Timely Presentation of Offers and Counter-Offers

(j) to present, in a timely manner, all offers and counter-offers to and from the seller even when the property is already the subject of an agreement of purchase and sale;

Disclose Relevant Facts to Seller

(k) to disclose, in a timely manner, to the seller, all relevant facts affecting the transaction known to the brokerage or its representatives;

Keep Seller Fully Informed

(l) to keep the seller fully informed regarding the progress of the transaction;

Obtain Expert Advice

(m) to advise the seller to obtain expert advice on matters of importance to the seller;

Comply with Regulatory Requirements

(n) to comply with all provisions of the [name of Act] and its regulations, and the rules and by-laws of the [name of governing body].

Source: © Alliance for Canadian Real Estate Education, 2006. *Agency Fundamentals: The National Perspective.*

Scenarios: Single Representation

SELLER REPRESENTATION

Seller Smith authorizes ABC Realty Inc. to represent him by signing an MLS® listing agreement. Buyer Jones, not represented by a brokerage, purchases the property as a customer.

ANALYSIS	Seller Smith		Buyer Jones	
	Obligations*	Duty of Care**	Obligations*	Duty of Care**
ABC Realty Inc.	■	■		■
Salesperson Lee	■	■		■
Other Salespeople at ABC Realty Inc.	■	■		■

BUYER REPRESENTATION

Buyer Jones authorizes XYZ Real Estate Ltd. to find a suitable home and signs a buyer representation agreement. Seller Smith wants to sell his home, but is not interested in being represented during negotiations but is willing to pay remuneration. XYZ Real Estate Ltd. sells the property to Buyer Jones with Seller Smith as a customer.

ANALYSIS	Seller Smith		Buyer Jones	
	Obligations*	Duty of Care**	Obligations*	Duty of Care**
XYZ Real Estate Ltd.		■	■	■
Salesperson Martin		■	■	■
Other Salespeople at XYZ Real Estate Ltd.		■	■	■

SELLER REPRESENTATION AND BUYER REPRESENTATION

Seller Smith authorizes ABC Realty Inc. to represent him by signing a seller representation agreement. The listing salesperson is Salesperson Lee. Salesperson Martin of XYZ Real Estate Ltd., the buyer brokerage, arranges an appointment to show the property to his client Buyer Wilson.

ANALYSIS	Seller Smith		Buyer Wilson	
	Obligations*	Duty of Care**	Obligations*	Duty of Care**
ABC Realty Inc.	■	■		■
Salesperson Lee	■	■		■
Other Salespeople at ABC Realty Inc.	■	■		■
XYZ Real Estate Ltd.		■	■	■
Salesperson Martin		■	■	■
Other Salespeople at XYZ Real Estate Ltd.		■	■	■

* Includes general, fiduciary and regulatory obligations.

** *Reminder:* Duty of care to the client applies to everything that is done and that ought to be done for the client. Duty of care to the customer is limited to providing information and performing functions (if any), along with limited disclosure and privacy obligations.

REBBA 2002 Compliance

INFORMATION BEFORE AGREEMENT

The Code of Ethics (Sec. 10) requires that buyers and sellers be provided certain information as early as practically possible and before entering an agreement in respect of trading in real estate. Further, the brokerage must use its best efforts to obtain a written acknowledgement that such information has been received.

INFORMATION BEFORE AGREEMENTS `CODE`

10. (1) Before entering into an agreement with a buyer or seller in respect of trading in real estate, a brokerage shall, at the earliest practicable opportunity, inform the buyer or seller of the following:

1. The types of service alternatives that are available in the circumstances, including a representation agreement or another type of agreement.

2. The services that the brokerage would provide under the agreement.

3. The fact that circumstances could arise in which the brokerage could represent more than one client in respect of the same trade in real estate, but that the brokerage could not do this unless all of the clients represented by the brokerage in respect of that trade consented in writing.

4. The nature of the services that the brokerage would provide to each client if the brokerage represents more than one client in respect of the same trade in real estate.

5. The fact that circumstances could arise in which the brokerage could provide services to more than one customer in respect of the same trade in real estate.

6. The fact that circumstances could arise in which the brokerage could, in respect of the same trade in real estate, both represent clients and provide services to customers.

7. The restricted nature of the services that the brokerage would provide to a customer in respect of a trade in real estate if the brokerage also represents a client in respect of that trade. O. Reg. 580/05, s. 10 (1).

(2) The brokerage shall, at the earliest practicable opportunity and before an offer is made, use the brokerage's best efforts to obtain from the buyer or seller a written acknowledgement that the buyer or seller received all the information referred to in subsection (1). O. Reg. 580/05, s. 10 (2).

EXAMPLE   *Seller Representation*

Salesperson Ward is preparing a seller representation agreement for Owner Jones. Ward discusses various matters regarding representation, including the possibility of multiple representation (discussed later in the chapter) in accordance with the Code of Ethics (Sec. 10). The seller acknowledges that information about agency relationships has been received, and that the listing brokerage may enter into representation agreements with buyers and also provide customer services to both buyers and sellers.

Ward then has the seller carefully review the representation agreement and answers any questions to ensure the owner's informed consent. The seller's signature on the representation agreement provides written acknowledgement, as required by Sec. 10(2), for the registrant and the brokerage.

The applicable provisions of the brokerage's seller representation agreement are reprinted on the following page, with seller acknowledgements highlighted.

EXAMPLE   *Seller Representation (continued)*

4. **REPRESENTATION:** The Seller acknowledges that the Listing Brokerage has provided the Seller with information explaining agency relationships, including information on Seller Representation, Sub-agency, Buyer Representation, Multiple Representation and Customer Service.

The Seller authorizes the Listing Brokerage to co-operate with any other registered real estate brokerage (co-operating brokerage), and to offer to pay

the co-operating brokerage a commission of....................% of the sale price of the Property or..

.... out of the commission the Seller pays the Listing Brokerage.

The Seller understands that unless the Seller is otherwise informed, the co-operating brokerage is representing the interests of the buyer in the transaction. The Seller further acknowledges that the Listing Brokerage may be listing other properties that may be similar to the Seller's Property and the Seller hereby consents to the Listing Brokerage listing other properties that may be similar to the Seller's Property without any claim by the Seller of conflict of interest. The Seller hereby appoints the Listing Brokerage as the Seller's agent for the purpose of giving and receiving notices pursuant to any offer or agreement to purchase the property. Unless otherwise agreed in writing between Seller and Listing Brokerage, any commission payable to any other brokerage shall be paid out of the commission the Seller pays the Listing Brokerage, said commission to be disbursed in accordance with the Commission Trust Agreement.

MULTIPLE REPRESENTATION: The Seller hereby acknowledges that the Listing Brokerage may be entering into buyer representation agreements with buyers who may be interested in purchasing the Seller's Property. In the event that the Listing Brokerage has entered into or enters into a buyer representation agreement with a prospective buyer for the Seller's Property, the Listing Brokerage will obtain the Seller's written consent to represent both the Seller and the buyer for the transaction at the earliest practicable opportunity and in all cases prior to any offer to purchase being submitted or presented.

The Seller understands and acknowledges that the Listing Brokerage must be impartial when representing both the Seller and the buyer and equally protect the interests of the Seller and buyer. The Seller understands and acknowledges that when representing both the Seller and the buyer, the Listing Brokerage shall have a duty of full disclosure to both the Seller and the buyer, including a requirement to disclose all factual information about the Property known to the Listing Brokerage.

However, the Seller further understands and acknowledges that the Listing Brokerage shall not disclose:
- that the Seller may or will accept less than the listed price, unless otherwise instructed in writing by the Seller;
- that the buyer may or will pay more than the offered price, unless otherwise instructed in writing by the buyer;
- the motivation of or personal information about the Seller or buyer, unless otherwise instructed in writing by the party to which the information applies or unless failure to disclose would constitute fraudulent, unlawful or unethical practice;
- the price the buyer should offer or the price the Seller should accept; and
- the Listing Brokerage shall not disclose to the buyer the terms of any other offer.

However, it is understood that factual market information about comparable properties and information known to the Listing Brokerage concerning potential uses for the Property will be disclosed to both Seller and buyer to assist them to come to their own conclusions.

Where a Brokerage represents both the Seller and the Buyer (multiple representation), the Brokerage shall not be entitled or authorized to be agent for either the Buyer or the Seller for the purpose of giving and receiving notices.

Multiple Representation And Customer Service: The Seller understands and agrees that the Listing Brokerage also provides representation and customer service to other sellers and buyers. If the Listing Brokerage represents or provides customer service to more than one seller or buyer for the same trade, the Listing Brokerage shall, in writing, at the earliest practicable opportunity and before any offer is made, inform all sellers and buyers of the nature of the Listing Brokerage's relationship to each seller and buyer.

MINIMUM CONTENT

The Code of Ethics (Sec. 11) sets out minimum information that must be contained in single representation agreements between registrants and buyers/sellers. These include:

- Effective date of the agreement.
- Amount of commission/other remuneration.
- Amount payable to a co-operating brokerage.
- How commission will be paid.
- Services being provided under the agreement.
- Provision for agreement exceeding six months (i.e., date to be prominently displayed on first page with space for required buyer or seller initials).
- Agreement contains only one expiry date.

CONTENTS OF WRITTEN AGREEMENTS   `CODE`

11. (1) A brokerage shall not enter into a written agreement with a buyer or seller for the purpose of trading in real estate unless the agreement clearly, comprehensibly and prominently,

   (a) specifies the date on which the agreement takes effect and the date on which it expires;

   (b) specifies or describes the method for determining,

      (i) the amount of any commission or other remuneration payable to the brokerage, and

      (ii) in the case of an agreement with a seller, the amount of any commission or other remuneration payable to any other brokerage;

   (c) describes how any commission or other remuneration payable to the brokerage will be paid; and

   (d) sets out the services that the brokerage will provide under the agreement. O. Reg. 580/05, s. 11 (1).

(2) A brokerage shall not, for the purpose of trading in real estate, enter into a written agreement with a buyer or seller that provides that the date on which the agreement expires is more than six months after the date on which the agreement takes effect unless,

   (a) the date on which the agreement expires is prominently displayed on the first page of the agreement; and

   (b) the buyer or seller has initialled the agreement next to the date referred to in clause (a). O. Reg. 580/05, s. 11 (2).

(3) A brokerage shall ensure that a written agreement that is entered into between the brokerage and a buyer or seller for the purpose of trading in real estate contains only one date on which the agreement expires. O. Reg. 580/05, s. 11 (3).

COPIES OF AGREEMENTS

The Code of Ethics requires that each person entering into a written representation agreement must immediately receive a copy of that agreement.

COPIES OF WRITTEN AGREEMENTS   `CODE`

12. If a brokerage and one or more other persons enter into a written agreement in connection with a trade in real estate, the brokerage shall ensure that each of the other persons is immediately given a copy of the agreement. O. Reg. 580/05, s. 12.

AGREEMENT IN WRITING

For purposes of common law, an agreement involving single representation can be written, oral or implied. From a statutory perspective, the Code of Ethics (Sec. 13 and 14) states that representation agreements with buyers and sellers must be reduced to writing, signed by the brokerage and submitted to the buyer or seller client. The Code does not require a signature, but registrants need to be aware of practical issues and risks associated with an unsigned representation agreement. In particular, proving entitlement to commission may become a problem.

SELLER REPRESENTATION AGREEMENTS   `CODE`

13. If a brokerage enters into a seller representation agreement with a seller and the agreement is not in writing, the brokerage shall, at the earliest practicable opportunity and before any buyer makes an offer, reduce the agreement to writing, have it signed on behalf of the brokerage and submit it to the seller for signature. O. Reg. 580/05, s. 13.

BUYER REPRESENTATION AGREEMENTS

14. If a brokerage enters into a buyer representation agreement with a buyer and the agreement is not in writing, the brokerage shall, before the buyer makes an offer, reduce the agreement to writing, have it signed on behalf of the brokerage and submit it to the buyer for signature. O. Reg. 580/05, s. 14.

NOTE: This discussion focuses on key regulatory compliance issues relating to representation. Detailed analysis of forms and procedures are addressed in *The Real Estate Transaction – General* when analyzing representation agreements and related trading practices.

Single Representation: Forms

Two residential representation forms published by the Ontario Real Estate Association are provided at the end of this chapter for illustrative purposes. Topics involving representation are highlighted. Detailed analysis of these forms and associated procedures are covered in *The Real Estate Transaction – General.*

- OREA Form 200: *Listing Agreement, Authority to Offer for Sale*
- OREA Form 300: *Buyer Representation Agreement, Authority for Purchase or Lease*

MULTIPLE REPRESENTATION

Multiple representation is a relationship in which a brokerage represents two or more parties at the same time in the same transaction, most commonly buyer and seller. The underlying legal assumption is that all representatives in a brokerage share each other's confidences; i.e., knowledge of confidential matters is imputed to all other representatives. Consequently, multiple representation can arise in various circumstances. Most commonly, this situation arises when the same salesperson or broker in a brokerage represents both buyer and seller or two different salespeople within that brokerage (located in the same office or different branch offices) represent the buyer and the seller respectively.

Multiple representation is not prohibited by law but, given that an inherent conflict of interest exists between the interests of the seller and the buyer, this practice must be strictly regulated.

Brokerage Options

Multiple representation raises significant problems and inherent risks for brokerages given the issue of conflicting interests. In effect, the brokerage must either avoid multiple representation or ensure that such is practised with the full and informed consent of both clients (including the clients' understanding of the implications of that consent). Alternatively, when practising multiple representation, brokerages and their representatives must fully comply with regulatory requirements as set out in REBBA 2002. While multiple representation is legally permissible and regulatory procedures are in place to handle such matters, The Canadian Real Estate Association and the Canadian Regulators Group have discouraged its practice.

An effective way to avoid multiple representation is to represent one party, while giving the other party customer status, thereby avoiding the legal pitfalls associated with multiple representation. This approach is particularly effective in situations involving the same salesperson or broker. As a final note, if multiple representation is practised and a dispute develops and remains unresolved, the brokerage and its representatives cannot continue to act for both parties.

Scenario: Multiple Representation

Seller Smith authorizes ABC Realty Inc. to represent him by signing an MLS® listing agreement. The seller acknowledges that a buyer, also represented by the brokerage, is purchasing the property as a client. Salesperson Lee is providing client services to both Seller Smith and Buyer Jones.

ANALYSIS	Seller Smith		Buyer Jones	
	Obligations*	Duty of Care**	Obligations*	Duty of Care**
ABC Realty Inc.	☐	☐	☐	☐
Salesperson Lee	☐	☐	☐	☐
Other Salespeople at ABC Realty Inc.	☐	☐	☐	☐

*   Includes general, fiduciary and regulatory obligations.

** *Reminder:* Duty of care to the client applies to everything that is done and that ought to be done for the client. Duty of care to the customer is limited to providing information and performing functions (if any), along with limited disclosure and privacy obligations.

REBBA 2002 Compliance

Provisions in REBBA 2002 are intended to minimize potential problems by ensuring that registrants and clients are both clear about the nature of services being provided under multiple representation. Recall that the Code of Ethics (Sec 10: Information Before Agreements) requires that the registrant discuss with the seller or buyer that circumstances could arise in which the brokerage and its representatives could represent more than one client.

In addition, the Code of Ethics has specific requirements that must be met before the occurrence of multiple representation. Such requirements focus on informed, written consent by the clients and detailing specific differences between obligations owed under single representation vs. multiple representation.

INFORMED, WRITTEN CONSENT

Registrants must not represent more than one client in respect of a real estate trade unless all of the clients represented give informed, written consent.

MULTIPLE REPRESENTATION   `GEN`

22. A registrant shall not represent more than one client in respect of the same trade in real estate unless all of the clients represented by the registrant in respect of that trade consent in writing. O. Reg. 567/05, s. 22.

The obtaining of informed consent is crucial to proper disclosure. Informed consent is consent given by a person assuming a clear understanding by that individual of relevant facts and reasonable implications concerning a proposed action that would be prohibited in the absence of informed consent of the person affected. Informed consent also assumes that the individual has legal capacity (i.e., the ability to understand the nature of the consent) and that he or she is not limited in that capacity due to circumstances such as mental incompetence, intoxication or illiteracy. Reasonable care should always be taken to ensure that the person understands the disclosure prior to giving consent.

Proving informed consent can be difficult, as evidenced by numerous court cases (particularly litigation involving the medical profession). Individuals may confirm understanding, but honestly lack a full appreciation of relevant facts, or they may agree to a particular course of action while not completely comprehending the ramifications. Alternatively, individuals may initially provide consent, but then attempt to deny or withdraw this consent for legal advantage.

As a general guideline, common law presumes that an adult is competent to give informed consent for most day-to-day business dealings. That said, real estate registrants must take reasonable steps to ensure that an individual understands relevant facts and implications, and confirm that understanding in writing accompanied with a signature. If doubt exists, discuss the matter further and seek added confirmation from the individual; e.g., ask the customer or client to reiterate the main points discussed prior to obtaining his or her signature. In cases where a person's capacity remains in doubt, the registrant should recommend that the party seek independent legal advice.

DISCLOSURE BEFORE MULTIPLE REPRESENTATION

The Code of Ethics (Sec. 16) requires that certain information must be disclosed prior to multiple representation. Specifically, brokerages must inform the clients that the brokerage proposes to represent more than one client in the same trade and also outline differences in obligations had the client received single representation, as compared with multiple representation.

DISCLOSURE BEFORE MULTIPLE REPRESENTATION   CODE

16. A brokerage shall not represent more than one client in respect of the same trade in real estate unless it has disclosed the following matters to the clients or prospective clients at the earliest practicable opportunity:

   1. The fact that the brokerage proposes to represent more than one client in respect of the same trade.

   2. The differences between the obligations the brokerage would have if it represented only one client in respect of the trade and the obligations the brokerage would have if it represented more than one client in respect of the trade, including any differences relating to the disclosure of information or the services that the brokerage would provide. O. Reg. 580/05, s. 16.

EXAMPLE   *Multiple Representation*

A salesperson is listing a commercial property for sale on behalf of his brokerage. He explains to the seller, in accordance with the Code of Ethics (Sec. 10: Information Before Agreements), the various services available through the brokerage, the services provided when offering single representation, the possibility that multiple representation could occur, the fact that the respective clients would have to provide their informed written consent and that restricted services would result if multiple representation did occur.

Subsequent to listing the property, the brokerage through its salesperson, has a buyer client interested in the property. The salesperson seeks and obtains written consent from both clients in accordance with the General Regulation (Sec. 22) and details the differences regarding what services are provided under this multiple representation arrangement (Code of Ethics, Sec. 16: *Disclosure Before Multiple Representation*).

NOTE: Code requirements involving multiple representation as set out in *Sec. 10: Information Before Agreements* were addressed earlier under *Single Representation* and have not been repeated here.

Implied Multiple Representation   CAUTION

A real danger with multiple representation lies not so much in representing more than one party, which can be largely addressed through proper disclosure procedures, but rather with implied relationships. Salespeople can inadvertently give the impression through words and actions that a client relationship does exist. No formal document need exist for unintended multiple representation.

This situation is most likely to occur in a traditional relationship when the seller has listed his or her property with a brokerage and is represented by that brokerage. The brokerage and all employed representatives owe general and fiduciary duties to the seller, as set out in the seller representation agreement. However, one of the salespeople could inadvertently assist the buyer through some form of counselling and advice.

The seller is under the impression that the brokerage works solely in his/her best interest. The buyer, upon receiving counselling, is incorrectly led to believe that an implied relationship exists, given that the salesperson is working in his/her best interest. The result is implied (or unintended) multiple representation.

The Courts will recognize a multiple representation relationship when such is warranted by the facts. In other words, while the documents may state that no relationship exists, the actions of salespeople may establish otherwise. Further, registrants should be aware that the existence of a multiple relationship is *not* contingent on:

- the intention of brokerages or their clients to establish such a relationship;
- knowledge of brokerages or their clients of the existence of such a relationship; nor
- brokerages being remunerated by both parties to transactions.

Caution is strongly advised in all such matters, as litigation can ensue and the injured party may seek and receive damages incurred.

> **EXAMPLE**   *The Open House*
>
> Salesperson Lee completed a representation agreement with Seller Smith. During the conversation, Lee was very explicit regarding his duties to Smith as a client and stated that all buyers would be treated as customers. Buyer Jones got an entirely different impression from Lee at an open house. Lee was forthright in providing information about Smith's circumstances concerning the sale and assured Jones that he could get the property for a low price. Given Lee's actions, the brokerage is now involved in multiple representation by creating an implied client relationship with the buyer.

COMPETING BUYERS/SELLERS

Multiple representation normally focuses on situations in which buyers and sellers are involved in the same trade. However, other conflicts of interest can arise in which the brokerage is representing individuals with competing interests, but not within the same trade; e.g., a brokerage may have two or more buyer clients who are competing for the same property, but not involved in the same trade. Both multiple representation involving the same trade and other conflicts not involving the same trade can be broadly grouped under the heading of **concurrent representation**.

Concurrent Representation

A legal term generally referring to a brokerage representing two clients at the same time. Multiple representation is a form of concurrent representation that not only involves representing two clients at the same time, but also in the same trade.

Competing Buyers

Assume that a brokerage has two or more buyers as clients who are concurrently competing for the same property. Given the fiduciary relationship with both, the brokerage and its representatives cannot allow a conflict of interest to exist without the informed consent of the clients. While not a typical multiple representation situation, the buyers are in direct competition. Clearly, the brokerage and its representatives from a common law perspective must:

- Disclose the nature of the conflict and seek the informed consents of both buyer clients.
- Discuss how the brokerage intends to proceed under the circumstances with both buyer clients.
- Outline implications for the buyer clients when giving consent to this conflict of interest.

STATUTORY DISCLOSURE

The issue of competing buyers has caused considerable discussion over the years. Such activities have not traditionally fallen under the definition of *multiple representation* (as the buyers are not involved in the same trade, but rather different trades involving the same property). The Registrar has stated that, for purposes of REBBA 2002, competing buyers are viewed statutorily as falling under multiple representation and regulatory disclosure requirements apply.

As a qualifier regarding the timing of such disclosure, registrants might not be initially aware of competing buyers given that different registrants within the brokerage could be working with separate buyers looking at the same property. However, disclosure requirements must be fulfilled when such a circumstance becomes known during negotiations.

EXAMPLE   *Disclosure: Competing Buyers*

Salesperson Williams is reviewing various provisions in a buyer representation agreement. He wants to ensure that the buyer fully understands that conflicts can arise beyond representing both buyer and seller in the same trade. He carefully reviews the following clause wording:

> *The Buyer further acknowledges that the Brokerage may be entering into buyer representation agreements with other buyers who may be interested in the same or similar properties that the Buyer may be interested in buying or leasing and the Buyer hereby consents to the Brokerage entering into buyer representation agreements with other buyers who may be interested in the same or similar properties without any claim by the Buyer of conflict of interest.*

> *Source: ©OREA 2008, Form 300, Buyer Representation Agreement, Authority for Purchase or Lease.*

Competing Sellers

Unlike competing buyers where conflicting interests are evident, the circumstance of representing two or more sellers does not typically invoke such conflict, because the brokerage can loyally serve the interests of each seller as remuneration is due upon effecting a sale and, consequently, the interests of the brokerage and those of the sellers generally align. Regardless, representation agreements now typically include reference to such conflicts of interest and seek the buyer's or seller's consent, as the following examples illustrate. At time of printing, no statutory directive has been issued in regard to competing sellers.

EXAMPLE   *Disclosure: Competing Sellers*

Salesperson James is reviewing various provisions in a seller representation agreement. She wants to ensure that the seller understands that conflicts can arise beyond representing both buyer and seller in the same trade. She carefully reviews the following clause wording,

> *The Seller further acknowledges that the Listing Brokerage may be listing other properties that may be similar to the Seller's Property and the Seller hereby consents to the Listing Brokerage listing other properties that may be similar to the Seller's Property without any claim by the Seller of conflict of interest.*

> *Source: ©OREA 2008, Form 200: Listing Agreement, Authority to Offer for Sale.*

Sequential Representation   CURIOSITY

Sequential representation involves a situation in which a brokerage is potentially placed in a multiple representation in a subsequent transaction owing to a client relationship established by a previous agreement. For example, a salesperson acts for the seller client by listing and selling his property. Subsequently, the same salesperson working with the seller, who is now looking to buy, locates a property listed with his or her employing brokerage.

Given the prior relationship, the salesperson would be aware of certain confidences shared by the seller when previously marketing his client's property. Accordingly, he is well advised to maintain his client relationship with the seller (now seeking property) in order to protect confidential information, even though maintaining this relationship will create a multiple representation calling for the appropriate disclosures. If the salesperson elected to offer the seller (now buyer) customer status only, he or she would have to disclose such confidences to the second client given the fiduciary obligation to maintain utmost loyalty to that subsequent seller client.

EXAMPLE   *Seller Smith/Buyer Smith*

Salesperson Lee of ABC Realty Inc. completes a seller representation agreement with Seller Smith and sells his home. Lee then subsequently represents Seller Jones whose home Smith (now Buyer Smith) is seeking to acquire. Lee and ABC Realty Inc. have an inherent conflict of interest given the previous representation relationship and confidential information acquired during that relationship. As a result, Lee and his brokerage face multiple representation, along with its inherent risks given the nature of the preceding relationship.

The Registrar has prepared an informative *Registrar's Bulletin* regarding representation responsibilities and related disclosure requirements (see subsequent pages). Detailed discussion of multiple representation and the use of applicable forms in the marketplace is addressed in *The Real Estate Transaction – General.*

Effective March 31, 2006

Representation

The *Real Estate and Business Brokers Act, 2002* (the "Act") contains a number of provisions related to disclosures registrants must make to the buyers and sellers they represent in real estate transactions. In general, registrants are required to be clear about the nature of services they are providing when they enter into agreements to represent or provide services to others in real estate transactions.

Three definitions that registrants need to fully understand to meet their obligations toward buyers and sellers are the definitions of *"client"*, *"customer"* and *"representation agreement"*. Under the Act a client is someone who is represented under a representation agreement with a brokerage. With respect to brokers and salespersons, persons are clients if the person has a representation agreement with the brokerage that employs the broker or salesperson and they are providing services to the person or representing the person on behalf of the brokerage in the transaction.

Representation agreements can be written, oral or implied. The key determinant is that the brokerage and the person have agreed that the brokerage will represent the person in respect of the trade. Although, the Act and its regulations do not define the term *"represent"* explicitly, it is meant to apply to situations when the registrant is acting as a fiduciary *"agent"* of the person from the perspective of the common law. In other words, the registrant has fiduciary obligations toward the person and is acting in their best interests in the transaction in terms of the advice and services that are provided. A customer is a person who has entered into a service agreement with a brokerage related to a real estate transaction, but who is not being represented by that brokerage as a client. This might apply to a situation in which a brokerage has entered into an agreement with a person to facilitate a real estate transaction, but the brokerage or its representatives are not providing any financial or fiduciary advice to the person as part of that agreement.

Although agreements with buyers and sellers can be written, oral or implied, registrants are required under the Act's regulations to reduce these agreements to writing and submit them to buyers and sellers for signature.

Sec. 10 of the Code of Ethics (Ont. Reg. 580/05) establishes minimum disclosures that must be made to buyers and sellers prior to entering into agreements with them. Registrants are required to describe the services that will be provided and the alternatives available to the potential client or customer. With respect to multiple representation, registrants are required to inform prospective buyers and sellers about the possibility of multiple representation, including a description of the services the brokerage would provide in those situations. Registrants also have to make it clear to buyers and sellers that they cannot represent multiple clients in a transaction unless all of the potential clients consent in writing to that representation.

Sec. 16 of the Code, requires further disclosures regarding multiple representation at the point in time where a registrant might enter into a multiple representation situation. Registrants are

Representation

obligated to describe how the services provided to the client will differ from a single representation situation including any differences in the disclosure of information made to the client. Sec. 17 of the Code requires the registrant to make these disclosures at the earliest practical opportunity and in all cases before an offer to purchase in made.

Sec. 10, 16 and 17 of the Code operate in conjunction with Sec. 22 of Ont. Reg. 567/05 (GEN) which states:

MULTIPLE REPRESENTATION

22. A registrant shall not represent more than one client in respect of the same trade in real estate unless all of the clients represented by the registrant in respect of that trade consent in writing.

At the point that a registrant wishes to represent more than one client with respect to a real estate transaction, it must obtain the written consent of all of the parties it is representing. This written consent is required in situations where a single brokerage represents two parties to a trade even if different salespersons or brokers are representing the two parties to the trade. Given that the brokerage has a fiduciary relationship with more than one party to a trade, it must be clear to those parties about how information will be exchanged related to the transaction and how services will be provided in such a situation.

Consent to multiple representation is required not only when a brokerage is representing both the buyer and seller in a transaction, but in situations where the brokerage is representing multiple buyers in a single transaction. In the case of multiple buyers, it may not be clear that a single brokerage is representing multiple buyers until one or more buyers have expressed interest in the same property.

In such situations, consent to the multiple representation would be required when the brokerage becomes aware that it is operating in a multiple representation situation.

In situations where a client or clients refuse to consent to a multiple representation, the brokerage must release one or more of its clients to seek alternate representation with respect to the transaction. The registrant cannot represent more than one party to a trade without the written consent of all parties it is representing.

With respect to services provided to customers, Sec. 10 of the Code requires registrants to disclose to buyers and sellers that they may represent more than one customer in a transaction. A brokerage does not require a customer's or client's written consent to provide services to an additional customer in a transaction. However, both Sec. 10 and 17 of the Code require registrants to clarify for all parties the nature of services they are providing to each party in situations where: a brokerage is providing services to more than one party in a transaction; or representing a client and providing services to a customer in the same transaction.

Sec. 11 of the Code also identifies minimum information that must be contained in agreements between registrants and buyers and sellers. Required information includes effective dates, amounts of remuneration or commission and a description of the services the brokerage is providing under the agreement. Sec. 12 of the Code requires brokerages to given copies of these agreements to buyers and sellers. Sec. 13, 14 and 15 of the Code require brokerages to reduce representation and service agreements to writing and submit them to buyers and sellers for signature.

CONTACT RECO:

Address
3250 Bloor Street West,
East Tower, Suite 600
Toronto, Ontario
M8X 2X9

By E-mail
Registration:
registration@reco.on.ca

Office of the Registrar:
AsktheRegistrar@reco.on.ca

General information:
information@reco.on.ca

For more information about the services provided by RECO, visit: www.reco.on.ca

DISCLOSURE OF INTEREST

Registrants must also disclose any existing or contemplated interest that they have in real estate which they are either divesting or acquiring. The registrant must deliver a notice to all other parties to the agreement and receive acknowledgement in writing of receipt of this notice from those parties. The notice must contain a statement concerning the registrant's status (i.e., brokerage, broker or salesperson), full disclosure of known facts that affect or will affect value and particulars of any subsequent negotiations (if an acquisition is involved).

ACQUISITION OR DIVESTITURE BY REGISTRANT   `REBBA`

32. (1) Unless the registrant first delivers to all other parties to the agreement the notice described in subsection (2) and the other parties have acknowledged in writing receipt of the notice, no registrant shall, directly or indirectly,

  (a) purchase, lease, exchange or otherwise acquire for himself, herself, or itself, any interest in real estate, or make an offer to do so; or

  (b) divest himself, herself, or itself of any interest in real estate, or make an offer to do so. 2004, c. 19, s. 18 (21).

Contents of notice

(2) The notice referred to in subsection (1) shall be in writing and shall include,

  (a) a statement that the registrant is a brokerage, broker or salesperson, as the case may be;

  (b) full disclosure of all facts within the registrant's knowledge that affect or will affect the value of the real estate; and

  (c) in the case of a transaction described in clause (1) (a), the particulars of any negotiation, offer or agreement by or on behalf of the registrant for the subsequent sale, lease, exchange or other disposition of an interest in the real estate to any other person. 2004, c. 19, s. 18 (21).

The Code of Ethics complements this disclosure provision by requiring that a registrant must disclose any interest that the registrant has in the real estate (or any person related to the registrant), to both clients and customers, at the earliest practicable opportunity and before an offer is made.

DISCLOSURE OF INTEREST   `CODE`

18. (1) A registrant shall, at the earliest practicable opportunity and before any offer is made in respect of the acquisition or disposition of an interest in real estate, disclose in writing the following matters to every client represented by the registrant in respect of the acquisition or disposition:

  1. Any property interest that the registrant has in the real estate.

  2. Any property interest that a person related to the registrant has in the real estate, if the registrant knows or ought to know of the interest. O. Reg. 580/05, s. 18 (1).

(2) A brokerage shall, at the earliest practicable opportunity and before any offer is made in respect of the acquisition or disposition of an interest in real estate, disclose in writing the matters referred to in paragraphs 1 and 2 of subsection (1) to every customer with whom the brokerage has entered into an agreement in respect of the acquisition or disposition. O. Reg. 580/05, s. 18 (2).

(3) A broker or salesperson shall, at the earliest practicable opportunity and before any offer is made in respect of the acquisition or disposition of an interest in real estate, disclose in writing the matters referred to in paragraphs 1 and 2 of subsection (1) to every customer of the broker or salesperson with whom the brokerage that employs the broker or salesperson has entered into an agreement in respect of the acquisition or disposition. O. Reg. 580/05, s. 18 (3).

SUB-AGENCY

Sub-agency involves the authorization by one brokerage to another brokerage to assist in advancing the interests of the principal, with the express consent of that principal. The sub-agent owes all of the same general, fiduciary and regulatory obligations to the principal, as does the agent. *(Note: REBBA 2002 does not address sub-agency (i.e., sub-representation) and, consequently, traditional agency terminology is used when discussing this topic.)*

Sub-Agency: Is it Still Viable? CURIOSITY

Sub-agency once dominated residential markets, due largely to the MLS® system with all co-operating brokerages acting as sub-agents of the seller brokerage. While this approach has faded as the industry has searched for ways to avoid dual agency, does it still have a role in the marketplace? The answer: a qualified 'yes,' as certain circumstances may warrant this approach.

Assume, for example, that a large commercial client is seeking specific locales across a particular province for an expanding franchise. The client might retain a primary brokerage as the agent who, in turn, would seek the assistance of sub-agents in locating suitable properties for presentation to the client.

Alternatively, a land developer/builder with several residential subdivisions in various communities might seek out a primary brokerage to co-ordinate all marketing efforts, with the brokerage then seeking sub-agency relationships with local brokerages to sell the new houses at individual sites.

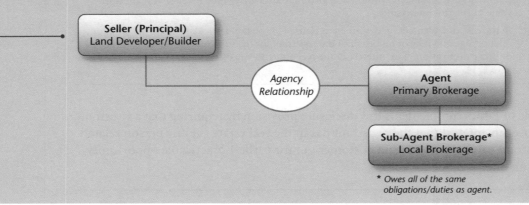

* Owes all of the same
obligations/duties as agent.

Sub-Agency: Scenario

Seller Smith selects ABC Realty Inc., through Salesperson Lee, to represent him in the sale of his specialized commercial retail property. Lee has expertise regarding such retail space, as does a representative of XYZ Real Estate Ltd. (located in a distant community). Smith signs an exclusive seller representation agreement with ABC Realty Inc. and agrees that Lee can seek out Salesperson Martin from XYZ Real Estate Ltd. to assist in marketing the property. Martin locates Buyer Jones who, as a customer, purchases the Smith property.

ANALYSIS	Seller Smith		Buyer Jones	
	Obligations*	Duty of Care**	Obligations*	Duty of Care**
ABC Realty Inc.	☐	☐		☐
Salesperson Lee	☐	☐		☐
Other Salespeople at ABC Realty Inc.	☐	☐		☐
XYZ Real Estate Ltd.	☐	☐		☐
Salesperson Martin	☐	☐		☐
Other Salespeople at XYZ Real Estate Ltd.	☐	☐		☐

* Includes general, fiduciary and regulatory obligations.

** *Reminder:* Duty of care to the client applies to everything that is done and that ought to be done for the client. Duty of care to the customer is limited to providing information and performing functions (if any), along with limited disclosure and privacy obligations.

Servicing the Customer

PERSPECTIVE

Chapter 16 focuses on representation, but **service agreements** involving customer status are gaining prominence, as registrants seek ways to offer non-representation services to consumers. Such agreements can also be effective in avoiding multiple representation and associated conflicts of interest; i.e., treating one party as the client by way of a representation agreement and the other as the customer with written confirmation by way of a service agreement. Such agreements are proving effective in minimizing confusion leading to implied representation while, at the same time, more clearly delineating responsibilities owed to customers, as distinct from those owed to clients. Regulatory requirements and form completion are detailed in *The Real Estate Transaction – General*.

Listing Agreement
Authority to Offer for Sale

OREA Ontario Real Estate Association

Form 200
for use in the Province of Ontario

This is a Multiple Listing Service® Agreement   **MLS®** (Seller's Initials)   **OR**   Exclusive Listing Agreement   **EXCLUSIVE** (Seller's Initials)

BETWEEN:

Brokerage:...

....(the "Listing Brokerage") Tel.No. (..........)..

Seller(S):..(the "Seller")

In consideration of the Listing Brokerage listing the real property **for sale** known as...

....(the "Property")

the Seller hereby gives the Listing Brokerage the **exclusive and irrevocable** right to act as the Seller's agent,

commencing at 12:01 a.m. on the..day of.., 20............,

until 11:59 p.m. on the..day of..., 20............ (the "Listing Period"),

{ Seller acknowledges that the length of the Listing Period is negotiable between the Seller and the Listing Brokerage and, if a MLS® listing, may be subject to minimum requirements of the real estate board, however, in accordance with the Real Estate and Business Brokers Act (2002), **if the Listing Period exceeds six months, the Listing Brokerage must obtain the Seller's initials.** }   (Seller's Initials)

to offer the property **for sale** at a price of: Dollars (CDN$)..

....Dollars

and upon the terms particularly set out herein, or at such other price and/or terms acceptable to the Seller. It is understood that the price and/or terms set out herein are at the Seller's personal request, after full discussion with the Listing Brokerage's representative regarding potential market value of the Property.

The Seller hereby represents and warrants that the Seller is not a party to any other listing agreement for the Property or agreement to pay commission to any other real estate brokerage for the sale of the property.

1. **DEFINITIONS AND INTERPRETATIONS:** For the purposes of this Listing Agreement ("Authority" or "Agreement"), "Seller" includes vendor, a "buyer" includes a purchaser, or a prospective purchaser and a "real estate board" includes a real estate association. A purchase shall be deemed to include the entering into of any agreement to exchange, or the obtaining of an option to purchase which is subsequently exercised. This Agreement shall be read with all changes of gender or number required by the context. For purposes of this Agreement, anyone introduced to or shown the Property shall be deemed to include any spouse, heirs, executors, administrators, successors, assigns, related corporations and affiliated corporations. Related corporations or affiliated corporations shall include any corporation where one half or a majority of the shareholders, directors or officers of the related or affiliated corporation are the same person(s) as the shareholders, directors, or officers of the corporation introduced to or shown the Property.

2. **COMMISSION:** In consideration of the Listing Brokerage listing the Property, the Seller agrees to pay the Listing Brokerage a commission

   of............................% of the sale price of the Property or...
   for any valid offer to purchase the Property from any source whatsoever obtained during the Listing Period and on the terms and conditions set out in this Agreement **OR** such other terms and conditions as the Seller may accept.
   The Seller further agrees to pay such commission as calculated above if an agreement to purchase is agreed to or accepted by the Seller or

   anyone on the Seller's behalf within............................ days after the expiration of the Listing Period **(Holdover Period)**, so long as such agreement is with anyone who was introduced to the Property from any source whatsoever during the Listing Period or shown the Property during the Listing Period.
   If, however, the offer for the purchase of the Property is pursuant to a new agreement in writing to pay commission to another registered real estate brokerage, the Seller's liability for commission shall be reduced by the amount paid by the Seller under the new agreement.
   The Seller further agrees to pay such commission as calculated above even if the transaction contemplated by an agreement to purchase agreed to or accepted by the Seller or anyone on the Seller's behalf is not completed, if such non-completion is owing or attributable to the Seller's default or neglect, said commission to be payable on the date set for completion of the purchase of the Property.
   Any deposit in respect of any agreement where the transaction has been completed shall first be applied to reduce the commission payable. Should such amounts paid to the Listing Brokerage from the deposit or by the Seller's solicitor not be sufficient, the Seller shall be liable to pay to the Listing Brokerage on demand, any deficiency in commission and taxes owing on such commission.
   All amounts set out as commission are to be paid plus applicable taxes on such commission.

3. **FINDERS FEES:** The Seller acknowledges that the Brokerage may be receiving a finder's fee, reward and/or referral incentive, and the Seller consents to any such benefit being received and retained by the Brokerage in addition to the commission as described above.

INITIALS OF LISTING BROKERAGE: ( )   **INITIALS OF SELLER(S):** ( )

Form 200 Listing Agreement—Authority to Offer for Sale, Page 2 of 3

4. REPRESENTATION: The Seller acknowledges that the Listing Brokerage has provided the Seller with information explaining agency relationships, including information on Seller Representation, Sub-agency, Buyer Representation, Multiple Representation and Customer Service. The Seller authorizes the Listing Brokerage to co-operate with any other registered real estate brokerage (co-operating brokerage), and to offer to pay

the co-operating brokerage a commission of.....................% of the sale price of the Property or...

.... out of the commission the Seller pays the Listing Brokerage.

The Seller understands that unless the Seller is otherwise informed, the co-operating brokerage is representing the interests of the buyer in the transaction. The Seller further acknowledges that the Listing Brokerage may be listing other properties that may be similar to the Seller's Property and the Seller hereby consents to the Listing Brokerage listing other properties that may be similar to the Seller's Property without any claim by the Seller of conflict of interest. The Seller hereby appoints the Listing Brokerage as the Seller's agent for the purpose of giving and receiving notices pursuant to any offer or agreement to purchase the property. Unless otherwise agreed in writing between Seller and Listing Brokerage, any commission payable to any other brokerage shall be paid out of the commission the Seller pays the Listing Brokerage, said commission to be disbursed in accordance with the Commission Trust Agreement.

MULTIPLE REPRESENTATION: The Seller hereby acknowledges that the Listing Brokerage may be entering into buyer representation agreements with buyers who may be interested in purchasing the Seller's Property. In the event that the Listing Brokerage has entered into or enters into a buyer representation agreement with a prospective buyer for the Seller's Property, the Listing Brokerage will obtain the Seller's written consent to represent both the Seller and the buyer for the transaction at the earliest practicable opportunity and in all cases prior to any offer to purchase being submitted or presented.

The Seller understands and acknowledges that the Listing Brokerage must be impartial when representing both the Seller and the buyer and equally protect the interests of the Seller and buyer. The Seller understands and acknowledges that when representing both the Seller and the buyer, the Listing Brokerage shall have a duty of full disclosure to both the Seller and the buyer, including a requirement to disclose all factual information about the Property known to the Listing Brokerage.

However, the Seller further understands and acknowledges that the Listing Brokerage shall not disclose:
- that the Seller may or will accept less than the listed price, unless otherwise instructed in writing by the Seller;
- that the buyer may or will pay more than the offered price, unless otherwise instructed in writing by the buyer;
- the motivation of or personal information about the Seller or buyer, unless otherwise instructed in writing by the party to which the information applies or unless failure to disclose would constitute fraudulent, unlawful or unethical practice;
- the price the buyer should offer or the price the Seller should accept; and
- the Listing Brokerage shall not disclose to the buyer the terms of any other offer.

However, it is understood that factual market information about comparable properties and information known to the Listing Brokerage concerning potential uses for the Property will be disclosed to both Seller and buyer to assist them to come to their own conclusions.

Where a Brokerage represents both the Seller and the Buyer (multiple representation), the Brokerage shall not be entitled or authorized to be agent for either the Buyer or the Seller for the purpose of giving and receiving notices.

Multiple Representation And Customer Service: The Seller understands and agrees that the Listing Brokerage also provides representation and customer service to other sellers and buyers. If the Listing Brokerage represents or provides customer service to more than one seller or buyer for the same trade, the Listing Brokerage shall, in writing, at the earliest practicable opportunity and before any offer is made, inform all sellers and buyers of the nature of the Listing Brokerage's relationship to each seller and buyer.

5. REFERRAL OF ENQUIRIES: The Seller agrees that during the Listing Period, the Seller shall advise the Listing Brokerage immediately of all enquiries from any source whatsoever, and all offers to purchase submitted to the Seller shall be immediately submitted to the Listing Brokerage before the Seller accepts or rejects the same. If any enquiry during the Listing Period results in the Seller accepting a valid offer to purchase during the Listing Period or within the Holdover Period after the expiration of the Listing Period, the Seller agrees to pay the Listing Brokerage the amount of commission set out above, payable within five (5) days following the Listing Brokerage's written demand therefor.

6. MARKETING: The Seller agrees to allow the Listing Brokerage to show and permit prospective buyers to fully inspect the Property during reasonable hours and the Seller gives the Listing Brokerage the sole and exclusive right to place "For Sale" and "Sold" sign(s) upon the Property. The Seller consents to the Listing Brokerage including information in advertising that may identify the Property. The Seller further agrees that the Listing Brokerage shall have sole and exclusive authority to make all advertising decisions relating to the marketing of the Property for sale during the Listing Period. The Seller agrees that the Listing Brokerage will not be held liable in any manner whatsoever for any acts or omissions with respect to advertising by the Listing Brokerage or any other party, other than by the Listing Brokerage's gross negligence or wilful act.

7. WARRANTY: The Seller represents and warrants that the Seller has the exclusive authority and power to execute this Authority to offer the Property for sale and that the Seller has informed the Listing Brokerage of any third party interests or claims on the Property such as rights of first refusal, options, easements, mortgages, encumbrances or otherwise concerning the Property, which may affect the sale of the Property.

8. INDEMNIFICATION AND INSURANCE: The Seller will not hold the Listing Brokerage responsible for any loss or damage to the Property or contents occurring during the term of this Agreement caused by the Listing Brokerage or anyone else by any means, including theft, fire or vandalism, other than by the Listing Brokerage's gross negligence or wilful act. The Seller agrees to indemnify and save harmless the Listing Brokerage and any co-operating brokerage from any liability, claim, loss, cost, damage or injury, including but not limited to loss of the commission payable under this Agreement, caused or contributed to by the breach of any warranty or representation made by the Seller in this Agreement or the accompanying data form. The Seller warrants the Property is insured, including personal liability insurance against any claims or lawsuits resulting from bodily injury or property damage to others caused in any way on or at the Property and the Seller indemnifies the Brokerage and all of its employees, representatives, salespersons and brokers (Listing Brokerage) and any co-operating brokerage and all of its employees, representatives, salespersons and brokers (co-operating brokerage) for and against any claims against the Listing Brokerage or co-operating brokerage made by anyone who attends or visits the Property.

9. FAMILY LAW ACT: The Seller hereby warrants that spousal consent is not necessary under the provisions of the Family Law Act, R.S.O. 1990, unless the Seller's spouse has executed the consent hereinafter provided.

10. VERIFICATION OF INFORMATION: The Seller authorizes the Listing Brokerage to obtain any information affecting the Property from any regulatory authorities, governments, mortgagees or others and the Seller agrees to execute and deliver such further authorizations in this regard as may be reasonably required. The Seller hereby appoints the Listing Brokerage or the Listing Brokerage's authorized representative as the Seller's attorney to execute such documentation as may be necessary to effect obtaining any information as aforesaid. The Seller hereby authorizes, instructs and directs the above noted regulatory authorities, governments, mortgagees or others to release any and all information to the Listing Brokerage.

INITIALS OF LISTING BROKERAGE ⬭   **INITIALS OF SELLER(S):** ⬭

Form 200 Revised 2012 **Page 2 of 3**

11. **USE AND DISTRIBUTION OF INFORMATION:** The Seller consents to the collection, use and disclosure of personal information by the Brokerage for the purpose of listing and marketing the Property including, but not limited to: listing and advertising the Property using any medium including the Internet; disclosing Property information to prospective buyers, brokerages, salespersons and others who may assist in the sale of the Property; such other use of the Seller's personal information as is consistent with listing and marketing of the Property. The Seller consents, if this is an MLS® Listing, to placement of the listing information and sales information into the database(s) of the appropriate MLS® system(s), and to the posting of any documents and other information (including, without limitation, photographs, images, graphics, audio and video recordings, virtual tours, drawings, floor plans, architectural designs, artistic renderings, surveys and listing descriptions) provided by or on behalf of the Seller into the database(s) of the appropriate MLS® system(s). The Seller hereby indemnifies and saves harmless the Brokerage and/or any of its employees, servants, brokers or sales representatives from any and all claims, liabilities, suits, actions, losses, costs and legal fees caused by, or arising out of, or resulting from the posting of any documents or other information (including, without limitation, photographs, images, graphics, audio and video recordings, virtual tours, drawings, floor plans, architectural designs, artistic renderings, surveys and listing descriptions) as aforesaid. The Seller acknowledges that the MLS® database is the property of the real estate board(s) and can be licensed, resold, or otherwise dealt with by the board(s). The Seller further acknowledges that the real estate board(s) may: during the term of the listing and thereafter, distribute the information in the MLS® database to any persons authorized to use such service which may include other brokerages, government departments, appraisers, municipal organizations and others; market the Property, at its option, in any medium, including electronic media; during the term of the listing and thereafter, compile, retain and publish any statistics including historical MLS® data and retain, reproduce and display photographs, images, graphics, audio and video recordings, virtual tours, drawings, floor plans, architectural designs, artistic renderings, surveys and listing descriptions which may be used by board members to conduct comparative analyses; and make such other use of the information as the Brokerage and/or real estate board(s) deem appropriate, in connection with the listing, marketing and selling of real estate during the term of the listing and thereafter.

> In the event that this Agreement expires or is cancelled or otherwise terminated and the Property is not sold, the Seller, by initialling:
>
>   (   )   (   )
>
>   **Does**   **Does Not**
>
> consent to allow other real estate board members to contact the Seller after expiration or other termination of this Agreement to discuss listing or otherwise marketing the Property.

12. **SUCCESSORS AND ASSIGNS:** The heirs, executors, administrators, successors and assigns of the undersigned are bound by the terms of this Agreement.

13. **CONFLICT OR DISCREPANCY:** If there is any conflict or discrepancy between any provision added to this Agreement (including any Schedule attached hereto) and any provision in the standard pre-set portion hereof, the added provision shall supersede the standard pre-set provision to the extent of such conflict or discrepancy. This Agreement, including any Schedule attached hereto, shall constitute the entire Agreement between the Seller and the Listing Brokerage. There is no representation, warranty, collateral agreement or condition which affects this Agreement other than as expressed herein.

14. **ELECTRONIC COMMUNICATION:** This Listing Agreement and any agreements, notices or other communications contemplated thereby may be transmitted by means of electronic systems, in which case signatures shall be deemed to be original. The transmission of this Agreement by the Seller by electronic means shall be deemed to confirm the Seller has retained a true copy of the Agreement.

15. **SCHEDULE(S):**...and data form attached hereto form(s) part of this Agreement.

THE LISTING BROKERAGE AGREES TO MARKET THE PROPERTY ON BEHALF OF THE SELLER AND REPRESENT THE SELLER IN AN ENDEAVOUR TO OBTAIN A VALID OFFER TO PURCHASE THE PROPERTY ON THE TERMS SET OUT IN THIS AGREEMENT OR ON SUCH OTHER TERMS SATISFACTORY TO THE SELLER.

.... DATE..................................... ....
(Authorized to bind the Listing Brokerage)   (Name of Person Signing)

THIS AGREEMENT HAS BEEN READ AND FULLY UNDERSTOOD BY ME AND I ACKNOWLEDGE THIS DATE I HAVE SIGNED UNDER SEAL AND HAVE RECEIVED A TRUE COPY OF THIS AGREEMENT. Any representations contained herein or as shown on the accompanying data form respecting the Property are true to the best of my knowledge, information and belief.

SIGNED, SEALED AND DELIVERED I have hereunto set my hand and seal:

.... ● DATE..................................... ....
(Signature of Seller)   (Seal)   (Tel. No.)

.... ● DATE..................................... ....
(Signature of Seller)   (Seal)

SPOUSAL CONSENT: The undersigned spouse of the Seller hereby consents to the listing of the Property herein pursuant to the provisions of the Family Law Act, R.S.O. 1990 and hereby agrees that he/she will execute all necessary or incidental documents to further any transaction provided for herein.

.... ● DATE..................................... ....
(Spouse)   (Seal)

DECLARATION OF INSURANCE

The broker/salesperson..
                                         (Name of Broker/Salesperson)

hereby declares that he/she is insured as required by the Real Estate and Business Brokers Act (REBBA) and Regulations.

....
(Signature(s) of Broker/Salesperson)

Form 300   Buyer Representation Agreement—Authority for Purchase or Lease, Page 1 of 3

OREA Ontario Real Estate Association

Buyer Representation Agreement
Authority for Purchase or Lease

Form 300
for use in the Province of Ontario

This is an Exclusive Buyer Representation Agreement

BETWEEN:

BROKERAGE:.., Tel.No. (..........)...............................

ADDRESS:..

.... Fax.No. (..........).................................
hereinafter referred to as the Brokerage.

AND:

BUYER(S):..., hereinafter referred to as the Buyer,

ADDRESS:..

The Buyer hereby gives the Brokerage the **exclusive and irrevocable authority** to act as the Buyer's agent

commencing at.......................a.m./p.m. on the...day of..................................., 20............,

and expiring at 11:59 p.m. on the...day of................................., 20.............(Expiry Date).

{ Buyer acknowledges that the time period for this Agreement is negotiable between the Buyer and the Brokerage, however, in accordance with the Real Estate and Business Brokers Act of Ontario (2002), **if the time period for this Agreement exceeds six months, the Brokerage must obtain the Buyer's initials.** }   ⬭ (Buyer's Initials)

for the purpose of locating a real property meeting the following general description:

Property Type (Use):..

....

Geographic Location:...

....

The Buyer hereby warrants that the Buyer is not a party to a buyer representation agreement with any other registered real estate brokerage for the purchase or lease of a real property of the general description indicated above.

1. **DEFINITIONS AND INTERPRETATIONS:** For the purposes of this Buyer Representation Agreement ("Authority" or "Agreement"), "Buyer" includes purchaser and tenant, a "seller" includes a vendor, a landlord or a prospective seller, vendor or landlord and a "real estate board" includes a real estate association. A purchase shall be deemed to include the entering into of any agreement to exchange, or the obtaining of an option to purchase which is subsequently exercised, and a lease includes any rental agreement, sub-lease or renewal of a lease. This Agreement shall be read with all changes of gender or number required by the context. For purposes of this Agreement, Buyer shall be deemed to include any spouse, heirs, executors, administrators, successors, assigns, related corporations and affiliated corporations. Related corporations or affiliated corporations shall include any corporation where one half or a majority of the shareholders, directors or officers of the related or affiliated corporation are the same person(s) as the shareholders, directors, or officers of the corporation introduced to or shown the property.

2. **COMMISSION:** In consideration of the Brokerage undertaking to assist the Buyer, the Buyer agrees to pay commission to the Brokerage as follows: If, during the currency of this Agreement, the Buyer enters into an agreement to purchase or lease a real property of the general description indicated above, the Buyer agrees the Brokerage is entitled to receive and retain any commission offered by a listing brokerage or by the seller. The Buyer understands that the amount of commission offered by a listing brokerage or by the seller may be greater or less than the commission stated below. The Buyer understands that the Brokerage will inform the Buyer of the amount of commission to be paid to the Brokerage by the listing brokerage or the seller at the earliest practical opportunity. The Buyer acknowledges that the payment of any commission by the listing brokerage or the seller will not make the Brokerage either the agent or sub-agent of the listing brokerage or the seller.

INITIALS OF BROKERAGE: ⬭   **INITIALS OF BUYER(S):** ⬭

Form 300   Buyer Representation Agreement—Authority for Purchase or Lease, Page 2 of 3

If, during the currency of this Agreement, the Buyer enters into an agreement to purchase or lease any property of the general description indicated

above, the Buyer agrees that the Brokerage is entitled to be paid a commission of.......................% of the sale price of the property or

....

The Buyer agrees to pay directly to the Brokerage any deficiency between this amount and the amount, if any, to be paid to the Brokerage by a listing brokerage or by the seller. The Buyer understands that if the Brokerage is not to be paid any commission by a listing brokerage or by the seller, the Buyer will pay the Brokerage the full amount of commission indicated above.

The Buyer agrees to pay the Brokerage such commission if the Buyer enters into an agreement within ....days after the expiration of this Agreement **(Holdover Period)** to purchase or lease any real property shown or introduced to the Buyer from any source whatsoever during the term of this Agreement, provided, however, that if the Buyer enters into a new buyer representation agreement with another registered real estate brokerage after the expiration of this Agreement, the Buyer's liability to pay commission to the Brokerage shall be reduced by the amount paid to the other brokerage under the new agreement.

The Buyer agrees to pay such commission as described above even if a transaction contemplated by an agreement to purchase or lease agreed to or accepted by the Buyer or anyone on the Buyer's behalf is not completed, if such non-completion is owing or attributable to the Buyers default or neglect. Said commission, plus any applicable taxes, shall be payable on the date set for completion of the purchase of the property or, in the case of a lease or tenancy, the earlier of the date of occupancy by the tenant or the date set for commencement of the lease or tenancy. All amounts set out as commission are to be paid plus applicable taxes on such commission.

3. **REPRESENTATION:** The Buyer acknowledges that the Brokerage has provided the Buyer with written information explaining agency relationships, including information on Seller Representation, Sub-Agency, Buyer Representation, Multiple Representation and Customer Service. The Brokerage shall assist the Buyer in locating a real property of the general description indicated above and shall represent the Buyer in an endeavour to procure the acceptance of an agreement to purchase or lease such a property.

The Buyer acknowledges that the Buyer may not be shown or offered all properties that may be of interest to the Buyer. The Buyer hereby agrees that the terms of any buyer's offer or agreement to purchase or lease the property will not be disclosed to any other buyer. The Buyer further acknowledges that the Brokerage may be entering into buyer representation agreements with other buyers who may be interested in the same or similar properties that the Buyer may be interested in buying or leasing and the Buyer hereby consents to the Brokerage entering into buyer representation agreements with other buyers who may be interested in the same or similar properties without any claim by the Buyer of conflict of interest. The Buyer hereby appoints the Brokerage as agent for the purpose of giving and receiving notices pursuant to any offer or agreement to purchase or lease a property negotiated by the Brokerage.

MULTIPLE Representation: The Buyer hereby acknowledges that the Brokerage may be entering into listing agreements with sellers of properties the Buyer may be interested in buying or leasing. In the event that the Brokerage has entered into or enters into a listing agreement with the seller of a property the Buyer may be interested in buying or leasing, the Brokerage will obtain the Buyer's written consent to represent both the Buyer and the seller for the transaction at the earliest practicable opportunity and in all cases prior to any offer to purchase or lease being submitted or presented.

The Buyer understands and acknowledges that the Brokerage must be impartial when representing both the Buyer and the seller and equally protect the interests of the Buyer and the seller in the transaction. The Buyer understands and acknowledges that when representing both the Buyer and the seller, the Brokerage shall have a duty of full disclosure to both the Buyer and the seller, including a requirement to disclose all factual information about the property known to the Brokerage.

However, The Buyer further understands and acknowledges that the Brokerage shall not disclose:
- that the seller may or will accept less than the listed price, unless otherwise instructed in writing by the seller;
- that the Buyer may or will pay more than the offered price, unless otherwise instructed in writing by the Buyer;
- the motivation of or personal information about the Buyer or seller, unless otherwise instructed in writing by the party to which the information applies or unless failure to disclose would constitute fraudulent, unlawful or unethical practice;
- the price the Buyer should offer or the price the seller should accept; and
- the Brokerage shall not disclose to the Buyer the terms of any other offer.

However, it is understood that factual market information about comparable properties and information known to the Brokerage concerning potential uses for the property will be disclosed to both Buyer and seller to assist them to come to their own conclusions.

Where a Brokerage represents both the Seller and the Buyer (multiple representation), the Brokerage shall not be entitled or authorized to be agent for either the Buyer or the Seller for the purpose of giving and receiving notices.

Multiple Representation And Customer Service: The Buyer understands and agrees that the Brokerage also provides representation and customer service to other buyers and sellers. If the Brokerage represents or provides customer service to more than one seller or buyer for the same trade, the Brokerage shall, in writing, at the earliest practicable opportunity and before any offer is made, inform all sellers and buyers of the nature of the Brokerage's relationship to each seller and buyer.

4. **REFERRAL OF PROPERTIES:** The Buyer agrees that during the currency of this Buyer Representation Agreement the Buyer will act in good faith and work exclusively with the Brokerage for the purchase or lease of a real property of the general description indicated above. The Buyer agrees that, during the currency of this Agreement, the Buyer shall advise the Brokerage immediately of any property of interest to the Buyer that came to the Buyer's attention from any source whatsoever, and all offers to purchase or lease submitted by the Buyer shall be submitted through the Brokerage to the seller. If the Buyer arranges a valid agreement to purchase or lease any property of the general description indicated above that came to the attention of the Buyer during the currency of this Agreement and the Buyer arranges said agreement during the currency of this Agreement or within the Holdover Period after expiration of this Agreement, the Buyer agrees to pay the Brokerage the amount of commission set out above in Paragraph 2 of this Agreement, payable within (5) days following the Brokerage's written demand therefor.

5. **INDEMNIFICATION:** The Brokerage and representatives of the Brokerage are trained in dealing in real estate but are not qualified in determining the physical condition of the land or any improvements thereon. The Buyer agrees that the Brokerage will not be liable for any defects, whether latent or patent, to the land or improvements thereon. All information supplied by the seller or landlord or the listing brokerage may not have been verified and is not warranted by the Brokerage as being accurate and will be relied on by the Buyer at the Buyer's own risk. The Buyer acknowledges having been advised to make their own enquiries to confirm the condition of the property.

6. **FINDERS FEE:** The Buyer acknowledges that the Brokerage may be receiving a finder's fee, reward and/or referral incentive, and the Buyer consents to any such benefit being received and retained by the Brokerage in addition to the commission as described above.

INITIALS OF BROKERAGE: ⬭   INITIALS OF BUYER(S): ⬭

Form 300   Revised 2011   Page 2 of 3

Form 300   Buyer Representation Agreement—Authority for Purchase or Lease, Page 3 of 3

7. **CONSUMER REPORTS: The Buyer is hereby notified that a Consumer Report containing credit and/or personal information may be referred to in connection with this Agreement and any subsequent transaction.**

8. **USE AND DISTRIBUTION OF INFORMATION:** The Buyer consents to the collection, use and disclosure of personal information by the Brokerage for such purposes that relate to the real estate services provided by the Brokerage to the Buyer including, but not limited to: locating, assessing and qualifying properties for the Buyer; advertising on behalf of the Buyer; providing information as needed to third parties retained by the Buyer to assist in a transaction (e.g. financial institutions, building inspectors, etc...); and such other use of the Buyer's information as is consistent with the services provided by the Brokerage in connection with the purchase or prospective purchase of the property.

    The Buyer agrees that the sale and related information regarding any property purchased by the Buyer through the Brokerage may be retained and disclosed by the Brokerage and/or real estate board(s) (if the property is an MLS® Listing) for reporting, appraisal and statistical purposes and for such other use of the information as the Brokerage and/or board deems appropriate in connection with the listing, marketing and selling of real estate, including conducting comparative market analyses.

9. **CONFLICT OR DISCREPANCY:** If there is any conflict or discrepancy between any provision added to this Agreement and any provision in the standard pre-set portion hereof, the added provision shall supersede the standard pre-set provision to the extent of such conflict or discrepancy. This Agreement, including any provisions added to this Agreement, shall constitute the entire Agreement between the Buyer and the Brokerage. There is no representation, warranty, collateral agreement or condition, which affects this Agreement other than as expressed herein.

10. **ELECTRONIC COMMUNICATION:** This Buyer Representation Agreement and any agreements, notices or other communications contemplated thereby may be transmitted by means of electronic systems, in which case signatures shall be deemed to be original. The transmission of this Agreement by the Buyer by electronic means shall be deemed to confirm the Buyer has retained a true copy of the Agreement.

11. **SCHEDULE(S):**.. attached hereto form(s) part of this Agreement.

THE BROKERAGE AGREES TO REPRESENT THE BUYER IN LOCATING A REAL PROPERTY OF THE GENERAL DESCRIPTION INDICATED ABOVE IN AN ENDEAVOUR TO OBTAIN THE ACCEPTANCE OF AN AGREEMENT TO PURCHASE OR LEASE A PROPERTY ON TERMS SATISFACTORY TO THE BUYER.

....   DATE.................................   ....
(Authorized to bind the Brokerage)   (Name of Person Signing)

THIS AGREEMENT HAS BEEN READ AND FULLY UNDERSTOOD BY ME AND I ACKNOWLEDGE THIS DATE I HAVE SIGNED UNDER SEAL AND HAVE RECEIVED A TRUE COPY OF THIS AGREEMENT. Any representations contained herein are true to the best of my knowledge, information and belief.

SIGNED, SEALED AND DELIVERED I have hereunto set my hand and seal:

....   ● DATE.................................   ....
(Signature of Buyer)   (Seal)   (Tel. No.)

....   ● DATE.................................   ....
(Signature of Buyer)   (Seal)

DECLARATION OF INSURANCE

The broker/salesperson...
                                                    (Name of Broker/Salesperson)

hereby declares that he/she is insured as required by the Real Estate and Business Brokers Act (REBBA) and Regulations.

....
                                                    (Signature(s) of Broker/Salesperson)

KNOWLEDGE INTEGRATION

Notables

- Single representation involves an agent representing either buyer or seller with the other party being a third party (i.e., a customer).

- The Code of Ethics sets out specific requirements regarding protecting and promoting the client's interests, as well as duties to others involved in the transaction.

- The Agency Task Force has developed a list of obligations imposed by common law regarding single representation.

- The Code of Ethics sets out specific requirements regarding information provided before agreements, contents of such agreements and prompt delivery of signed agreements.

- Multiple representation has certain inherent risks given issues concerning competing interests and imputed knowledge.

- Brokerages and their representatives must fully comply with REBBA 2002 disclosure and related requirements.

- Other conflicts of interest must be fully disclosed, as with multiple representation, and registrants must ensure that informed consent is obtained.

- Representation agreements now typically contain reference to conflicts involving competing buyers and sellers and the need to seek the client's informed consent.

- Registrants must meet strict disclosure requirements when acquiring or disposing of real estate.

- Sub-agency once dominated residential markets, but now has faded in popularity. However, this variation can be effective in selected circumstances.

- Service agreements can be effective both in avoiding multiple representation and offering alternatives to representation.

Glossary

Buyer Representation

Concurrent Representation

Co-operating Brokerage

Multiple Representation

Seller Representation

Sequential Representation

Service Agreement

Single Representation

Sub-Agency

Strategic Thinking For Your Career

Questions are included to assist in developing your new career. No answers are provided.

1. What procedures are followed in my intended employing brokerage regarding single and multiple representation?

2. When representing a client, what type of confidential information could be particularly damaging to the client, if overheard by others in the brokerage?

3. If a dispute arises between two clients in a multiple representation situation, what procedure does my intended employing brokerage follow to resolve the matter?

4. Can I readily outline to potential clients the various compliance requirements for representation agreements?

5. What potential conflicts arise when a brokerage and its representatives attempt to represent competing buyers negotiating over the same property?

Chapter Mini-Review

Solutions are located in the Appendix.

1. Agency relationships can be grouped under two main categories: single representation and multiple representation.

   ◯ True   ◯ False

2. In single representation, the brokerage and its representatives owe the client both general and fiduciary obligations.

   ◯ True   ◯ False

3. Typically, the brokerage representing the seller assumes that the co-operating brokerage is NOT representing the buyer, but instead is treating that buyer as a customer.

   ◯ True   ◯ False

4. According to REBBA 2002, a brokerage and its representatives must be fair and honest to the buyer as a customer, but duties do not extend to offering conscientious service.

   ◯ True   ◯ False

5. In single buyer representation, one of the common law obligations to the client is to disclose, in a timely manner, all relevant facts known to the brokerage and its representatives about the property or transaction.

   ◯ True   ◯ False

6. When offering single representation, a brokerage and its representatives must represent the interests of the client, but do not owe a duty of care to that client.

   ◯ True   ◯ False

7. One of the challenges for brokerages involved with multiple representation is to handle conflicting instructions from two principals.

   ◯ True   ◯ False

8. A salesperson representing a client, who suggests in confidence to the customer that he or she could work in his or her best interests at the same time, faces the legal perils of implied representation.

    ◯ True   ◯ False

9. If two salespeople within a brokerage are representing competing buyers, they must follow disclosure procedures as set out for all multiple representation situations.

    ◯ True   ◯ False

10. If ABC Realty Inc. represents the seller and XYZ Real Estate Ltd. is appointed as a sub-agent, then XYZ Real Estate Ltd. owes the same general, fiduciary and regulatory obligations to the seller as does ABC Realty Inc.

    ◯ True   ◯ False

Active Learning Exercises

Solutions are located in the Appendix.

▣ Exercise 1   Multiple Choice

1.1 Provisions in REBBA 2002 (General Regulation and the Code of Ethics) regarding multiple representation:

    a. Require that only single representation can be offered by brokerages in Ontario.

    b. Do not require a written agreement between the brokerage and the client.

    c. Require that clients provide consent in writing to multiple representation.

    d. Require that customers provide consent in writing to multiple representation.

1.2 Which of the following is most correct in the case of single representation?

    a. General and fiduciary duties are owed to the seller client, but not a duty of care.

    b. Regulatory obligations can apply to both customers and clients.

    c. Fiduciary duties are owed to both buyer and seller.

    d. The brokerage representing a seller client must have a signed seller representation agreement.

1.3 Salesperson Lee, on behalf of ABC Realty Inc., lists the seller's property and then locates a suitable new home for his client. The new home is listed by another salesperson in the same brokerage. If Lee represents the seller (now a buyer) in purchasing this listed property, he is facing a situation legally referred to as:

    a. Sequential Representation.

    b. Concurrent Representation.

    c. Limited Representation.

    d. Customer Representation.

1.4 Which of the following is NOT a true statement regarding multiple representation?

a. The brokerage and its representatives must act impartially to protect the interests of both clients.

b. Implied multiple representation may be recognized by the Court based on the facts, and not simply based on what documents have been signed by the buyer or seller.

c. One of the limitations regarding disclosure is that the seller's brokerage and its representatives will not disclose the seller's motivation or any personal information, unless so instructed by the seller.

d. Imputed knowledge, from a legal perspective, refers to the fact that all registrants within a brokerage share each other's confidences.

1.5 A salesperson, on behalf of the brokerage, agrees to represent the seller when listing his home and then also agrees to represent a buyer in the purchase of that home. The most appropriate term describing this circumstance is:

a. Multiple Representation.

b. Duty of Care.

c. Sequential Representation.

d. Single Representation.

1.6 The salesperson, as a representative of a brokerage, has been working first with the seller as a client and then with a buyer client under a multiple representation relationship for more than a week, attempting to put a deal together. The problem revolves around the offered price and the closing date. To move things along, the salesperson casually mentions to the buyer that the seller is getting anxious and will probably accept a lower price, if the seller's closing date is met. The seller has not given the salesperson authority to make that statement. Which of the following best describes this situation?

a. Even a minor advantage given to one client over the other can dramatically tip the negotiating scale.

b. Conflicting instructions from buyer and seller clients involved in the same trade rarely result in a conflict for the salesperson and the brokerage.

c. The first client can have a disadvantage in a multiple representation, as more confidential information is normally provided by that client than by the second client.

d. The salesperson does not need the client's authority to divulge this information.

1.7 Which of the following statements is correct?

a. A seller brokerage involved in multiple representation with seller and buyer clients owes its ultimate allegiance and loyalty to the seller, as the seller will typically be paying the commission.

b. A service agreement can be effective in avoiding multiple representation when a salesperson in a brokerage is working with a seller client and is approached by a buyer to purchase the seller's property.

c. Representing competing buyers is described as a form of sequential representation.

d. Offers, but not counter-offers, are to be communicated promptly to the buyer or seller under single representation.

■ Exercise 2   Multiple Representation

Identify which of the following circumstances are examples of multiple representation.

- [ ] Two salespersons in the same brokerage representing different clients in the same transaction.
- [ ] Two salespersons from different brokerages representing buyer and seller clients in the same transaction.
- [ ] Two salespersons from different branches of the same brokerage representing different clients in the same transaction.
- [ ] Two salespersons from the same brokerage; one representing the seller as a client and the other providing services to a customer in the same transaction.
- [ ] A salesperson from a brokerage representing a seller client and an appraiser from the same brokerage providing an evaluation of the seller client's home to a buyer who wishes to purchase the seller's home.

■ Exercise 3   Obligations to Seller and Buyer (Fill-in-the-Blanks)

ABC Realty Inc. has listed a unique, six-outlet bistro operation called Bistro Best. Salesperson Lee of ABC Realty Inc. obtains the seller's consent to involve another brokerage as a sub-agent to market the enterprise. Salesperson Martin, employed by XYZ Real Estate Ltd. (the sub-agent) interests ACME Holdings Inc. as a customer in looking at the property and has an appropriate agreement signed with ACME. Based on this scenario, check off which obligations (general, fiduciary and regulatory), as well as duty of care, apply to the respective brokerages.

ANALYSIS	Seller Bistro Best		Buyer ACME Holdings Inc.	
	Obligations*	Duty of Care**	Obligations*	Duty of Care**
ABC Realty Inc.				
Salesperson Lee				
Other Salespeople at ABC Realty Inc.				
XYZ Real Estate Ltd.				
Salesperson Martin				
Other Salespeople at XYZ Real Estate Ltd.				

*   Includes general, fiduciary and regulatory obligations.

** *Reminder:* Duty of care to the client applies to everything that is done and that ought to be done for the client. Duty of care to the customer is limited to providing information and performing functions (if any), along with limited disclosure and privacy obligations.

APPENDIX

GLOSSARY

KEYWORD	DESCRIPTION
Abstract	A written history of the title to a parcel of real estate as recorded in a Land Registry Office.
Accessory Apartment	A self-contained unit within a house.
Adjusted Sale Price	Sale price of a comparable property under the direct comparison approach following all adjustments in comparison with the subject property being appraised.
Advertising	Activities intended to inform and otherwise favourably influence individuals through the use of various media. A broader definition of advertising has been developed by the Real Estate Council of Ontario, which is used for regulatory compliance.
Agency	A relationship between two parties in which one party (the agent) accepts responsibility for representing the other party (the principal) in dealing with a third party.
Agency Relationship	A relationship between an agent and a principal in which the agent represents that principal when dealing with a third party. Agency relationships are typically established in real estate by the signing of a representation agreement. See also **Agency**.
Agent	For real estate purposes, an agent is a brokerage which is expressly or implicitly authorized to act for a principal.
Air Rights	Rights above the physical surface of the land.
Appraiser	An individual having the necessary training, experience and/or qualifications to estimate the value of real property.
Areas of Natural and Scientific Interest	Natural heritage areas identified by the Ministry of Natural Resources.
Authority	The legal power or right given by a principal and accepted by the agent to act on the principal's behalf in business transactions with a third party. Authority relating to a representation agreement is typically analyzed in terms of actual and implied authorities.
Automated Valuation Model	A computer-based program that relies on statistical methods to arrive at property values.

KEYWORD	DESCRIPTION
Bacteriological Testing	Testing of water to assess water quality and existence of contamination.
Balloon Framing	One of two framing methods commonly used in residential construction.
Blended (Amortized) Payment Plan	One of four traditional payment plans in which principal and interest payments are combined in accordance with an amortization schedule.
Boiler	Central heating system typically with pipe distribution system throughout the structure.
Brick Veneer	A wood frame wall with an exterior layer of brick.
Bridge Loan	An interim form of financing typically used when a buyer has to close one sale prior to receiving funds from another sale.
Bridging/Bracing	Cross members between joists facilitating weight transfer and minimizing joist twisting.
Broker	An individual who has prescribed qualifications to be registered as a broker under REBBA 2002 and is employed by a brokerage to trade in real estate.
Brokerage	A corporation, partnership or sole proprietorship that trades in real estate on behalf of others.
Building Inspector	An individual appointed by the local municipality to enforce Ontario Building Code provisions.
Building Permit	A document issued by the municipal authority certifying the blueprints for construction and allowing work to commence.
Bundle Of Rights	Rights of ownership associated with the possession, use, enjoyment and disposition of real estate.
Buyer Agency	An agency relationship in which the broker owes fiduciary duties to the buyer.
Buyer Representation	A form of single representation in which the brokerage represents the buyer as a client.
Buyer Representation Agreement	An agreement setting out the agency relationship between a brokerage and a buyer in which the brokerage is acting as an agent for the buyer, who is the principal (client).

APPENDIX

KEYWORD	DESCRIPTION
Canada Small Business Financing Program	A federal financing program offered through various institutional lenders to entrepreneurs for buying startup and existing business operations.
Canadian Environmental Protection Act	Federal legislation viewed as an enabling statute to establish a statutory framework for provincial activities.
Capital Market	An international financial market where borrowers seek funding from savers (investors) to meet financial obligations and achieve economic goals.
Chain of Title	A series of conveyances and other documents linking current ownership back to an historical point.
Charge	The name given to a mortgage document when title is registered under the *Land Titles Act*.
Charge/ Mortgage of Land	Standard form (Form 2) for registering a charge/mortgage.
Chattel	Personal property which is tangible and moveable.
Chattel Mortgage	A lien or interest on assets (moveable or personal property) that is taken to secure a loan.
Client	A person who is represented by a brokerage pursuant to a representation agreement.
Committee of Adjustment	A committee charged with the responsibility for granting minor variances under the *Planning Act*.
Comparative Sales Method	A procedure used by appraisers to establish site values under the cost approach.
Comparative Square Metre/ Foot Method	A procedure used by appraisers to establish building costs under the cost approach.
Concession	Strips of land making up a township, each separated by a road allowance.
Concurrent Ownership	Two or more persons having ownership at the same time.

APPENDIX

KEYWORD	DESCRIPTION
Concurrent Representation	A legal term generally referring to a brokerage representing two clients at the same time. Multiple representation is a form of concurrent representation that not only involves representing two clients at the same time, but also in the same trade.
Condominium	The fee simple ownership of a specified amount of space (the unit) in a multiple dwelling or other multi-occupancy building with tenancy in common ownership of portions used jointly with other owners (the common elements).
Consent	An approval granted by a consenting authority pursuant to the *Planning Act.*
Conservation Authority	An agency authorized under conservation legislation to oversee regulated areas.
Conservation Land Tax Incentive Program	A provincial program providing tax exemption for conservation lands.
Co-operating Brokerage	A brokerage (typically representing the buyer) who is co-operating with a listing brokerage in a real estate trade.
Co-operative (Housing)	A joint ownership alternative in which a property is owned by a corporation and members have a lease for a specific unit. A co-operative can be either with share capital (equity co-operative) or without share capital (non-profit co-operative).
County	One of the larger divisions of land in Ontario for administrative purposes.
Credit Bureau	A clearing house for credit-related information.
Credit Report	A report on the credit position of a borrower, typically including a three-digit credit score to assess credit standing.
Crown Patent	Original deed issued from the Crown (government) representing the root of title for a particular property.
Curtain Principle	A principle under land titles which states that the register is the sole, current source of information and individuals need not be concerned with prior recorded information.
Customer	A person who has entered into some form of service agreement with a brokerage, but is not represented by that brokerage by way of a representation agreement.

APPENDIX

KEYWORD	DESCRIPTION
Debt Coverage Ratio	A ratio used by commercial mortgage underwriters to assess lending risk by comparing net operating income to total debt service.
Declaration	A condominium document required for registration that sets out the responsibilities of the owners and condominium corporation.
Deed	An instrument in writing, duly executed and delivered, that conveys title or an interest in real property.
Description	A diagrammatic presentation of the condominium property and structures on that property.
Development Loan	A loan advanced for servicing and improving land prior to building construction.
Direct Capitalization	The process of converting the income generated by a property into capital value by means of a capitalization rate, as opposed to discounting future cash flows through yield capitalization.
Discharge of Charge/ Mortgage	Standard form (Form 3) relating to discharge of a charge/ mortgage.
Distribution Panel	An electrical panel between the service entrance wires and power distribution within a structure.
Document General	Standard form (Form 4) relating to land registration process.
Dominant Tenement	The estate that derives benefit from a servient tenement, as in a right-of-way.
Double Front Township	A township originally consisting of 100-acre half-lots.
Draft Plan Approval	Initial step in the subdivision approval process under the *Planning Act*.
Drywall	Pre-manufactured wallboard typically built using gypsum.
Duty of Care	Duty owed to clients and customers established by objective standard. The duty of care to a client involves everything done by the agent for that client, but the duty is more limited in the case of customers.

APPENDIX

KEYWORD	DESCRIPTION
E-Registration	See Electronic Registration (below).
Easement	A right enjoyed by one landowner over the land of another.
Economic Life	The span of time in which a structure adds value to a property, as distinct from the number of years that the structure exists.
Economic Age-Life Depreciation Method	A measure of depreciation of a property based on the anticipated life of the structure.
Effective Age	The age of a structure based on its condition and utility, as opposed to its chronological age.
Effective Gross Income	Potential gross (rental) income plus other income and less vacancy and credit losses. Terminology may vary in the marketplace.
Electrical Inspection	An analysis of a structure's electrical components, normally conducted by a local utility or an electrical expert.
Electrical Service Size	The number of amps provided to a structure(s) through a primary service wire.
Electronic Registration (E-Registration)	An online procedure for property registration in the Province of Ontario.
Energy Audit	An analysis of energy loss in a structure, typically including recommendations.
Environmental Protection Act	Provincial legislation impacting the ownership and use of property within Ontario.
Equitable Mortgage	An historical term differentiating a mortgage against equity from a legal mortgage against title.
Equity of Redemption	The right of the mortgagor to reclaim clear title to the property upon full repayment of the debt.
Escheat	The reversion of property to the state in the event the owner thereof dies leaving no will.
Estate	An interest in land; i.e., the status or extent of rights associated with tenure.

APPENDIX

KEYWORD	DESCRIPTION
Expropriation	Taking of private property by the state for public use, with fair compensation to the owner, through the exercise of the right of eminent domain.
External Obsolescence	Depreciation resulting from loss of utility or marketability due to locational or general economic factors.
Fee Appraiser	Professional appraisers who market services on the basis of time, cost and effort required to arrive at a value estimate.
Fee Simple	The highest estate or absolute right in real property.
Fiduciary	A term generally referring to a position of trust. An agent (i.e., a real estate brokerage) as a fiduciary must maintain utmost loyalty and protect the interests of the principal (client).
Fiduciary Obligations	Obligations owed by an agent in a fiduciary relationship with a principal. REBBA 2002 does not specifically discuss agency duties and responsibilities including fiduciary and general obligations as set out in common law. However, the Act addresses such legal principles through use of the term *representation* and associated words; e.g., *multiple representation* and *representation agreement*.
Final Estimate of Value	Value estimate determined in the appraisal process by reconciling alternate value estimates arrived through the cost, direct comparison and income approaches.
Final Plan Approval	Final step in the subdivision approval process under the *Planning Act*.
Fireplace	A heating device typically providing warmth through radiant and convection methods.
Fixture	Permanent improvements to a property that may not be removed at the expiration of the term of lease or tenure.
Flashing	Tin, aluminum, copper or galvanized steel sheets used as part of a roofing system.
Flat Depreciation Method	A specific depreciation rate applied by appraisers in determining depreciation for improvements under the cost approach.
Flood Plain	Area along a stream or watercourse that is subject to flood hazard.

KEYWORD	DESCRIPTION
Flood Proofing	Structural or related methods that minimize flooding for a flood-prone property.
Footing	The widened section, usually concrete, at the base or bottom of a foundation wall, pier or column.
Form Report	A standardized appraisal report format typically associated with property valuations for residential property; e.g., mortgage applications.
Foundation	The base, typically concrete but other materials are used, upon which a structure is built.
Fractional Interest	A single right, within the bundle of rights, in fee simple ownership.
Framing	The rough timber work of a house, including the flooring, roofing, partitioning, ceiling and beams.
Functional Obsolescence	Depreciation resulting from the loss of utility and hence value; e.g., poor design or unacceptable style.
Furnace	A central heating device typically with a distribution system throughout the structure.
Future Estate	An interest in land that arises at the end of a life estate.
Gap Loan	Interim financing that provides funding between construction advances and the placement of permanent financing.
General Obligations	Obligations owed by an agent to a principal as set out in common law. Other obligations are grouped under fiduciary and regulatory.
Geographic Information System (GIS)	A property information database, often with web-enabled data browser, providing access to data layers; e.g., property boundaries, municipal requirements/stipulations, structural features and environmental details concerning specific properties.
Green Roof	A roof constructed of various landscaping materials.
Heating System	A system used to warm structures including, but not limited to, warm air, steam, hot water, radiant and electrical.
Hot Water Heater	A device used for heating water that typically, but not always, has a tank or reservoir.

APPENDIX

KEYWORD	DESCRIPTION
HVAC System	An acronym for heating, ventilation and air-conditioning.
Implied Agency	An agency relationship that is suggested to exist based on the facts and circumstances, as distinct from an express agreement which is explicitly written or stated.
Implied Covenants	Obligations of a mortgagor as set out in the *Land Registration Reform Act*, which apply to a Charge/Mortgage of Land registered in land titles or registry.
Income Approach	An approach to estimating value based on the theory that the value of an investment property is the present worth of the future benefits (i.e., income) which the property is capable of producing.
Inert Gas Fill	Gas, such as argon or krypton, inserted between glass panes in windows.
Informed Consent	A consent given by a person who has legal capacity, based on that individual's clear understanding of relevant facts and implications concerning a particular course of action.
Insurance Principle	A principle under land titles which states that the current information in the register is insured pursuant to the Land Titles Assurance Fund.
Interest Accruing Payment Plan	One of four traditional payment plans in which interest accrues with no payments required. The interest and principal are due at the end of the mortgage term.
Interest Only Payment Plan	One of four traditional payment plans in which interest is repaid on an unamortized loan with the full principal coming due at the end of the mortgage term.
Interest Plus Specified Principal Payment Plan	One of four traditional payment plans in which principal is reduced through scheduled payments with interest due and payable on the outstanding balance at times set out in the mortgage.
Joint Tenancy	Ownership of land by two or more persons whereby, on the death of one, the survivor or survivors take the whole estate.
Joist	One of a series of horizontal wood members, usually 2-inch nominal thickness, used to support a floor, ceiling or roof.

APPENDIX

KEYWORD	DESCRIPTION
Land Severance	The division of land by means of a consent under the *Planning Act*.
Land Titles	One of two land registration systems found in Ontario.
Land Transfer Tax Affidavit	Standard form relating to land transfer tax for the conveyance of a real estate interest.
Leasehold Estate	An interest in land for a specified period of time.
Legal Mortgage	A mortgage involving the transferral of an interest in land as security for debt repayment, as distinct from an equitable mortgage–now largely viewed as an historical distinction given present registration practices for charges.
Letter of Opinion	A brief letter setting out an estimate of value, typically with only limited details concerning the property.
Life Estate	An ownership right to an individual for a lifetime period.
Limiting Conditions	A range of stipulations and assumptions underlying an appraisal report.
Locational Obsolescence	Depreciation resulting from loss of value due to negative influences from external factors; e.g., railway tracks and commercial uses directly adjacent to residential property.
Lot	A parcel of land. Lots formed part of the basic land description system in Ontario.
Low-E	Low emissivity refers to the ability of a surface to reflect long-wave radiation and typically is used in reference to windows.
Lower Tier Municipality	A municipality involved in planning-related activities.
Matrimonial Home	Special status given to selected properties pursuant to the *Family Law Act*.
Metal Siding	Structural siding typically made of aluminum or steel.
Metes and Bounds	A system of land description whereby all boundary lines are set forth by use of terminal points and angles—metes referring to limits or limiting marks, and bounds referring to boundary lines.
Mineral Right	Rights regarding minerals on or below the land.

APPENDIX

KEYWORD	DESCRIPTION
Minor Variance	Small variations from the zoning by-laws.
Mirror Principle	A principle under land titles which states that the register of title is a mirror of (i.e., reflects) the current facts about any specific property on that register.
Money Market	A sector of the financial market dealing with short-term investments (usually one year or less), as distinct from longer term investments in the capital market.
More or Less	Term often found in a property description intended to cover slight, unimportant or unsubstantial inaccuracies of which both parties are willing to assume the risk.
Mortgage Commitment	A written confirmation to a prospective borrower regarding terms and conditions under which a mortgage will be granted and funds advanced to that borrower.
Mortgage Market	A segment of the financial market representing one investment option within the broader capital market. Other options include, but are not limited to, commodities, stocks, bonds, securities, business ventures and foreign currencies.
Mortgage Priority	The legal priority of mortgages determined by time of registration, subject to various exceptions.
Mortgagee	The one to whom property is given as security for the payment of a mortgage debt; i.e., the lender or creditor.
Mortgagor	The one who gives the mortgage; i.e., the borrower or debtor.
Multiple Representation	Two or more clients in a real estate transaction are represented by a real estate brokerage.
Narrative Report	A detailed appraisal report typically prepared by a fee appraiser.
Net Operating Income	Net income following deduction of all expenses from effective gross income.
Non-Conforming Structure	A structure that lawfully existed prior to the current zoning by-law.
Non-Conforming Use	A use that existed prior to the current zoning by-laws.
Occupancy Permit	A municipal permit issued following final inspection permitting occupancy of a structure.

APPENDIX

KEYWORD	DESCRIPTION
Official Plan	A formal projection of development of a planning area for a specified future period of time.
One Zone Flood Plain	A regulated area in which the entire area is considered to be a floodway.
Ontario Building Code	A provincial code establishing minimum standards for building design.
Ontario Fire Code	A provincial code setting out compliance criteria for fire safety.
Order	An enforcement method used by the Ministry of the Environment to ensure compliance with the *Environmental Protection Act*.
Paired Sales	Sales of two or more identical properties in different locations to arrive at a value for local adjustments under the direct comparison approach.
Partnership	A contractual relationship between two or more parties, typically evidenced by a partnership agreement. A partnership is one of three entities that may be permitted to act as a real estate brokerage and trade in real estate on behalf of others.
Payback	A term frequently associated with investment return; i.e., payback period. For example, a payback period typically represents the time required for net cash flows to equal initial cash outlay. Other payback measures exist in the marketplace. The term payback is sometimes referenced in appraisal, the value of an improvement for adjustment purposes under the direct comparison approach.
Personal Property	All property, except land and the improvements thereon.
Physical Deterioration	Depreciation resulting from physical condition of an improvement due to wear and tear, decay and structural defects.
Pitch	The roof slope defined as a ratio of rise over run.
Plan of Subdivision	A detailed survey indicating lots, blocks of land, road allowances, etc.
Plan of Survey	A survey that is not registered in a Land Registry Office, but is commonly attached to another document; e.g. a deed/transfer of land.

APPENDIX

KEYWORD	DESCRIPTION
Planning	The orderly development of land through a structured planning process.
Planning Act	Legislation that establishes the statutory framework for orderly planning in the province.
Platform Framing	One of two framing methods commonly used in residential construction.
Plumbing System	Piping and associated fittings for water supply and waste disposal.
POLARIS	An acronym for Province of Ontario Land Information System which is integral to the automation of land records in Ontario.
Pre-Approved Buyer	Approval of a buyer for a mortgage by a lender, subject to various conditions and limitations.
Profit a Prendre	The right to enter and take something from the land.
Potential Gross (Rental) Income	Income that a property will produce with 100% occupancy at market rent, assuming competent, prudent management. Terminology may vary in the marketplace.
Principal	An individual who authorizes an agent to act on his or her behalf in an agency relationship.
Provincial Interests	Specific premises and objectives set out under the *Planning Act* to guide various authorities in carrying out the planning process.
Provincial Policy Statement	A general statement or principle issued by the Ministry of Municipal Affairs and Housing relating to long-term planning directions.
R-2000	An energy efficiency program relating to new residential construction.
R-Value	A measure of thermal resistance.
Rafter	Building component used to support the roof sheathing.
Real Property	Tangible and intangible attributes of land and improvements.

KEYWORD	DESCRIPTION
Reconciliation	One of several steps in the appraisal process by which the appraiser arrives at a final value estimate. See also **Monthly Reconciliation** regarding REBBA 2002 requirements concerning reconciliation of a real estate trust account.
Reconstructed Operating Statement	A statement used in the income approach to value, typically representing a one-year analysis of income expenses, derived from an owner's statement with adjustment to reflect typical income and expenses.
Reference Plan (R-Plan)	A survey that normally describes more than one interest in land (each interest identified as a Part), which is deposited in a Land Registry Office.
Registry	One of two land registration systems found in Ontario. Registry is currently being phased out in the province.
Regulatory Obligations	Obligations imposed by regulatory authorities which are owed by the agent to the principal over and above those imposed by common law and fiduciary obligations.
Replacement Cost	The cost of construction, at current prices, of a structure having equal utility.
Representation Agreement	An agreement by which a person and the real estate brokerage have agreed that the brokerage will represent that person as a client.
Reproduction Cost	The cost of construction, at current prices, of an exact duplicate using the same materials, standards, design, etc.
Restrictive Covenant	A limitation placed upon the use of property, contained in the deed.
Right	An interest in property.
Right Of Survivorship	The distinguishing feature of joint tenancies which provides that, where land is held in undivided portions by co-owners, upon the death of any joint owner, his interest in the land will pass to the surviving co-owner, rather than to his estate.
Right-of-Way	The right to pass over another's land, more or less frequently, according to the nature of the easement.

APPENDIX

KEYWORD	DESCRIPTION
Riparian Rights	The rights of the owner of lands on the banks of watercourses, to take advantageous use of the water on, under or adjacent to this land, including the right to acquire accretions, wharf slips and fish therefrom.
Sale/Leaseback	The sale of a property with the leaseback of that property to the original owner.
Salesperson	An individual meeting prescribed qualifications to be registered as such under REBBA 2002 and who is employed by a brokerage to trade in real estate.
Schedule	Form 5 is used as a standard attachment to other prescribed land registration forms.
Sectional Township	A township originally consisting of 1000-acre sections with subsequent divisions into lots.
Seller Representation	A form of single representation in which the brokerage represents the seller as a client.
Seller Representation Agreement	An agreement setting out the agency relationship between a brokerage and a seller in which the brokerage is acting as an agent for the seller, who is the principal (client). Also, referred to as a listing agreement.
Sequential Representation	A situation in which a brokerage finds itself in a multiple representation situation with two clients, due to a previous client relationship that existed with one of the parties.
Service Agreement	An agreement in which the brokerage provides services to the customer, as distinct from a representation agreement with a client.
Servient Tenement	Land over which an easement exists in favour of the dominant tenement.
Sewage System (OnSite)	A private system, identified by various classes, for the disposal of waste.
Sheathing	Roofing panels that support the roof covering (i.e., shingles) and other loads (e.g., snow).
Shingle	A relatively thin and small unit of roofing, laid in overlapping layers as a roof covering or as cladding on the sides of buildings.

KEYWORD	DESCRIPTION
Sick Building Syndrome	Illness associated with poor air quality in structures.
Single Front Township	A township originally consisting of 200-acre lots.
Single Representation	A relationship between a seller or buyer and a brokerage in which the brokerage represents the seller or buyer as a client.
Site Plan Control Agreement	An agreement setting out terms for property development within a site plan control area.
Site Plan Control Area	An area designated for site plan control within a municipality.
Site-Specific Exemptions	Properties that are specifically exempted under a zoning by-law.
Standard Charge Terms	A document containing mortgage terms and conditions registered by a mortgagee in land registry which can be referenced in a Charge/Mortgage of Land.
Standby Loan	A loan commitment for preliminary financing with the expectation of more favourable, permanent financing.
Sub-Agency	An agency relationship in which a brokerage representing a seller or buyer seeks the assistance of another brokerage in transacting the affairs of that principal (with express or implied consent of the principal).
Subdivision	From a planning perspective, the process of taking an individual piece of land and separating it into parts.
Subdivision Plan	A plan prepared in compliance with the *Planning Act*.
Surface Rights	Rights associated with ground level as opposed to mineral or air rights.
Survey	The accurate mathematical measurement of land and buildings thereon, made with the aid of instruments.
Surveyor's Real Property Report	A plan of survey consisting of two parts: Plan of Survey and The Written Report.
Tenants In Common	Ownership of land by two or more persons; unlike joint tenancy in that interest of deceased does not pass to the survivor, but is treated as an asset of the deceased's estate.

APPENDIX

KEYWORD	DESCRIPTION
Tenure	A method of land holding for a temporary time period, but does not involve ownership of the land.
Teranet	A company responsible for the automation of property records in Ontario.
Teraview	A software package providing an electronic gateway to automated property records in Ontario.
Third Party	An individual who is not directly connected with a legal transaction, but may be affected by it. The terms 'third party' and 'customer' are generally analogous when discussing real estate agency relationships in Ontario.
Time Resale Method	A technique used in appraisals to make time adjustments based on research into comparable properties that have sold and resold within a short period of time. Such comparables are then applied in the direct comparison approach. Practitioners may encounter differing terminology for this technique in the marketplace.
Title	The means of evidence by which the owner of land has lawful ownership thereof.
Title Insurance	Insurance for owners and lenders regarding various risks and undisclosed interests affecting title.
Township	Division of a county into several distinct areas for administrative purposes.
Transfer/Deed of Land	Standard form (Form 1) for conveyance of a real estate interest.
Truss	A roof component performing a similar function to a rafter, typically pre-engineered and delivered to the construction site.
Two Zone Flood Plain	A regulated area in which the flood plain is divided into a floodway and flood fringe.
Upper Tier Municipality	A regional, county or district involved in planning-related activities.
Vinyl Siding	Structural siding made of polyvinyl chloride, most noted for its dent-resistant qualities.

APPENDIX

KEYWORD	DESCRIPTION
Volatile Organic Compounds	Products that have gas emissions which can impact indoor air quality.
Water Well	Drilled, bored or dug wells for accessing water.
Water Well Record	A record maintained regarding the initial installation of a water well.
Wetlands	Lands covered by shallow water, as well as areas where the water table is close to or at the surface.
Wraparound Mortgage	A new mortgage that wraps around existing financing.
Yield Capitalization	The conversion of a projected income stream into an estimate of value by analyzing forecasted operations and sale proceeds over a specified holding period.
Zoning By-law	A by-law that defines zones for various types of uses and sets selected standards for erecting buildings.
Zoning Classifications	Specific property divisions within a zoning by-law (e.g., residential and commercial), along with further sub-classifications (e.g., single-family and duplex).

APPENDIX

SOLUTIONS

CHAPTER 1
THE EVOLUTION OF OWNERSHIP

Chapter Mini-Review

1. The major distinction between real property and personal property is the feature of mobility.

    True   ◯ False

   Real property is immovable, whereas personal property is movable.

2. Fee simple ownership is the highest estate in real property and includes the most rights and fewest limitations.

    True   ◯ False

   Fee simple ownership is the highest form of ownership, compared with lesser estates such as leasehold estate and life estate.

3. An estate to uses involves granting an interest in real estate to someone for a lifetime period.

   ◯ True   **False**

   Estate to uses has fallen into disuse, but essentially was used to avoid a dower right. Life estate represents a lifetime interest.

4. A matrimonial home represents a distinct status afforded to a property pursuant to the *Family Law Act* in recognition of the equal partnership-marriage relationship.

    True   ◯ False

   The *Family Law Act* recognizes the concept of an equal partnership-marriage relationship and provides a code for the orderly and equitable settlement of the spouses' affairs including the matrimonial home.

5. In the case of an easement, the land receiving the benefit is known as the dominant tenement.

    True   ◯ False

   Conversely, the land over which an easement exists is known as the servient tenement.

6. Property inherited or received as a gift is included when applying the net family concept for the equal division of property on marriage breakdown.

   ◯ True   **False**

   Property inherited or received as a gift by one spouse is excluded under the net family concept for the equal division of property on marriage breakdown or death.

7. Expropriation is the taking of land without consent of the owner and may be done without compensation to the owner.

   ◯ True   **False**

   Expropriation is the taking of private property, but with fair compensation to the owner.

8. According to the doctrine of escheat, an individual's property will automatically revert to the Crown if he dies intestate.

   ◯ True   **False**

   The property would revert to the Crown if the individual dies intestate *and* has no legally qualified heir.

APPENDIX

9. If two individuals own a parcel of vacant land as joint tenants and one dies with or without a will, the interest in the property will revert to the remaining joint tenant.

✔ **True**   ◯ False

Joint tenancy includes the right of survivorship and on the death of one joint tenant, the surviving tenant or tenants acquire the whole interest in the property.

10. The power to regulate includes the government's right to regulate privately owned property.

✔ **True**   ◯ False

Privately owned property is impacted by many Acts and Regulations, particularly regarding land planning and land use.

11. A condominium is created through the registration of a declaration and description.

✔ **True**   ◯ False

A condominium is created in law when both the declaration and the description are registered.

12. Housing co-operatives in Ontario can be either equity co-operatives or private corporation co-operatives.

◯ True   ✔ **False**

Housing co-operatives can be either equity co-operatives (with share capital) or non-profit co-operatives (without share capital).

13. The act of severance can change a joint tenancy into a tenancy in common.

✔ **True**   ◯ False

If joint tenants sever their joint tenancy, they automatically become tenants in common.

14. Air rights could be alternatively described as a fractional interest of fee simple ownership.

✔ **True**   ◯ False

Air rights represent a fractional interest within a fee simple estate relating to the rights to use space above the physical surface of the land.

15. Personal property of a seller may be included as chattels in a transaction.

✔ **True**   ◯ False

The seller may elect to include various personal property items as part of the purchase price when marketing a property.

16. A limited partnership need not have a general partner, but must have one or more limited partners.

◯ True   ✔ **False**

Limited partnerships must be registered and must have at least one general partner.

APPENDIX

Active Learning Exercises

■ Exercise 1 Real Estate Ownership (What was the Question?)

Complete the correct question for each of the following answers.

1.1 A grant of an interest in land for the lifetime of that individual.

What is a (an)   *life estate*   ?

1.2 A form of ownership in which two or more persons have the same interest, the interest begins at the same time, possession is undivided and title is granted from the same instrument.

What is   *joint tenancy*   ?

1.3 Rights associated with owners of land on the banks of watercourses to take advantageous use of water on, under or adjacent to their land.

What are   *riparian rights*   ?

1.4 A TV satellite dish that is not permanently affixed to the property and is not deemed to be a fixture.

What is a (an)   *chattel*   ?

1.5 An interest in land, referred to as a type of tenement, that includes the owner's right to cross another person's land.

What is a (an)   *dominant tenement*   ?

1.6 Restrictions in a subdivision that control the type of construction and style of homes within that development.

What are   *restrictive covenants*   ?

1.7 A government right to regulate property ownership.

What is   *police power*   ?

APPENDIX

1.8   The Crown or any person authorized by statute to expropriate land.

What is a (an) | **expropriating authority** | ?

1.9   A legal authority to create an easement that is typically used when granting such rights to a public utility or telephone companies.

What is a (an) | **statute** | ?

▣ Exercise 2   Multiple Choice

CH1 **EX2**

2.1   Real property is the freehold ownership of land and improvements, consisting of tangible and intangible elements. Which of the following would NOT be considered real property? **This question requires that the *incorrect* option be identified.**

a.   An exotic flowering tree planted on the land, but protected by a movable greenhouse.

This option is correct. Trees and other vegetation planted on the land are deemed to be fixtures.

b.   An owned underground sprinkler system.

This option is correct. An underground sprinkler system is permanently affixed and deemed to be a fixture.

c.   **A boat firmly secured by ropes inside a boathouse that is an improvement (outbuilding) on the land.**

✅ *THIS IS THE INCORRECT OPTION.* A boat is a chattel, which is temporarily secured by ropes to a structure.

d.   The fruit ripening on a pear tree.

This option is correct. Trees and other vegetation (including fruit) planted on the land are deemed to be fixtures.

2.2   Which of the following statements is NOT true with respect to a fee simple estate? **This question requires that the *incorrect* option be identified.**

a.   An estate in fee simple can be held by several persons.

This option is correct. An estate in fee simple can be held by several persons; e.g., joint tenancy or tenants in common.

b.   An estate in fee simple is the most extensive estate or quantity of ownership of land.

This option is correct. Fee simple has the greatest number of rights in combination with the least limitations.

c.   **An estate in fee simple cannot be held by more than one person.**

✅ *THIS IS THE INCORRECT OPTION.* An estate in fee simple can be held by several persons; e.g., joint tenancy or tenants in common.

d.   In a fee simple estate, the rights of ownership are the most extensive and the limitations the smallest of any estate in land.

This option is correct. Fee simple ownership has the most extensive rights combined with the smallest number of limitations.

APPENDIX

CH1 EX2

2.3 The distinguishing feature of joint tenancy is the right of survivorship. Which of the following best reflects that statement?

a. Upon the death of one of the joint tenants, his or her interest in a property automatically passes to the spouse named in the deceased's will.

Incorrect. The interest of the deceased joint tenant does not pass to a spouse named in his/her will.

b. The interest in a property held in joint tenancy is not an interest in the land; it is merely a right to use the land for a certain time period.

Incorrect. Joint tenancy involves an interest in land, not a right relating to land.

c. **Upon the death of one of the joint tenants, his or her interest in the property will automatically pass to the other joint tenants and not to the heirs of the deceased.**

✔ *CORRECT.* The interest of the joint tenant automatically passes to the surviving joint tenant or tenants.

d. The joint owners hold different interests in the property and have the right to pass their respective interests to surviving spouses upon death.

Incorrect. Joint tenants have the identical interest in nature, extent and duration. Further, such interest is passed to the surviving joint tenant(s) and not to a surviving spouse (unless that spouse is the joint tenant).

2.4 Which of the following is a characteristic of joint tenancy?

a. Owners must obtain title at different times.

Incorrect. Title must be obtained at the same time.

b. **Owners are all entitled to simultaneous possession of the property.**

✔ *CORRECT.* Owners are entitled to simultaneous possession unless otherwise agreed.

c. Owners must obtain title from different people.

Incorrect. Title must be obtained from the same person or persons.

d. Owners must each have different quantities of interest.

Incorrect. Ownership interest must be identical in nature, extent and duration.

2.5 Which of the following does NOT apply to the *Family Law Act*? **This question requires that the *incorrect* option be identified.**

a. Sets out the orderly and equitable settlement of spouses' affairs in a marriage breakdown.

This option is correct. The *Family Law Act* provides for the equitable settlement of all assets including property.

b. Provides for the orderly division of property in a marriage breakdown.

This option is correct. The *Family Law Act* sets out procedures for the equal division of property on marriage breakdown or death.

c. **States that spouses cannot contract out of the equalizing system to establish and distribute value.**

✔ *THIS IS THE INCORRECT OPTION.* Spouses may contract out of this system with a valid domestic contract.

d. Establishes certain non-owner spousal rights regarding possession of the matrimonial home.

This option is correct. Such a right is a personal one and is not an interest in land.

APPENDIX

2.6 Which of the following is NOT a characteristic of a restrictive covenant? **This question requires that the *incorrect* option be identified.**

CH1 EX2

a. The parcels of land affected by the benefit and burden must be owned by the same person.	✔ *THIS IS THE INCORRECT OPTION.* A restrictive covenant is a contract between two different landowners.
b. The covenant must be negative in nature.	*This option is correct.* The covenant must be negative in nature and represent a burden on the land.
c. The covenant, in order to run with the land, cannot be contrary to public interest.	*This option is correct.* The covenant must be reasonable in nature, not arbitrary and not contrary to the public interest.
d. There must be dominant and servient tenements.	*This option is correct.* Both a dominant and a servient tenement are necessary in order to create a restrictive covenant.

2.7 Which of the following is a characteristic of an easement?

a. An easement does not run with the land.	*Incorrect.* An easement is attached to that land and binds successive owners.
b. An easement remains if both dominant and servient tenements are purchased by the same person.	*Incorrect.* An easement ceases to exist if the dominant and servient tenements merge.
c. The dominant tenement need not directly adjoin the servient tenement but must be reasonably close.	✔ *CORRECT.* The dominant and servient tenements need not adjoin.
d. An easement must confer a burden on the dominant tenement and be reasonably necessary for its use and enjoyment.	*Incorrect.* An easement confers a burden on the servient tenement, not the dominant tenement.

2.8 Which of the following is NOT generally viewed as an interest in land that is less than an estate? **This question requires that the *incorrect* option be identified.**

a. Right-of-way.	*This option is correct.* A right-of-way is a lesser (fractional) interest.
b. Life tenancy.	✔ *THIS IS THE INCORRECT OPTION.* A life tenancy is a type of estate, not a lesser interest.
c. Profit a prendre.	*This option is correct.* Profit a prendre involves a lesser right; i.e., the right to enter land and take something from it.
d. Easement.	*This option is correct.* An easement involves a lesser right enjoyed by one tenement over another.

APPENDIX

2.9 Which of the following statements is correct?

a. **A partnership is a contractual relationship that may involve the ownership of property.**

✓ *CORRECT.* A partnership is a contractual relationship that may own property. However, the mere co-ownership of property does not in itself create a partnership.

b. An equity co-operative involves a non-profit corporation without share capital that owns the land and buildings.

Incorrect. An equity co-operative involves a corporation with share capital with members of the co-operative being shareholders in that corporation.

c. In a condominium, unit owners are not liable for the debts and obligations of the condominium corporation.

Incorrect. Unit owners are liable for the debts and obligations of the condominium corporation.

d. A limited partnership need not be registered.

Incorrect. A limited partnership must be registered.

CH1 EX3

■ Exercise 3   Selling the Matrimonial Home

• Bill's signing of a listing is not, in itself, illegal. However, any agreement that flows from this listing will probably not have legal effect, as due regard was not given to his wife's concern and legal rights (assuming that Bill's spouse refuses to sign the agreement of purchase and sale). The name on the title to the property is not the key issue in terms of the matrimonial home and spousal consent. The *Family Law Act* sets out spousal requirements regarding a matrimonial home. The spouse has rights even though his or her name does not appear on title.

• As a counterbalancing argument, Bill might point out that such consent cannot be unreasonably withheld. However, the Court would undoubtedly give significant weight to his wife's argument that moving could impact the well-being of the children.

• Salespersons should exercise caution when listing property where a marital dispute is involved. Make certain that all parties are in agreement concerning the disposition of the property and seek legal counsel as appropriate. Salespersons should also obtain signatures of both spouses on any listing agreement involving matrimonial property.

CH1 EX4

■ Exercise 4   The Easement

4.1 An easement must have both dominant and servient tenements. Smith will have the dominant tenement (seeking to cross Jones' land from his own) and Jones will have the servient tenement. Other characteristics of an easement include: the easement attaches to the land; separate ownership of the dominant and servient tenements must exist; and the right (in this instance the right of access) must confer a benefit on the dominant tenement. Lastly, while Smith and Jones own abutting lots, the two tenements do not need to be adjoining for a valid easement to exist.

4.2 An easement is extinguished if the ownership of the dominant and servient tenements merge.

4.3 The three other approaches include easement by prescription in which an individual obtains a right-of-way or easement by adverse possession. Second, an easement might be created by implication (e.g., when a piece of land is landlocked, the law implies that an easement exists). Lastly, easements are created by statute (e.g., easement for a public utility across rear yards in a residential subdivision).

4.4 While an exact answer is not provided in this chapter, some readily apparent problems would undoubtedly arise. First, numerous disputes have arisen between neighbours over verbal or poorly

APPENDIX

written documents. Second, suppose that one of the owners sells his property. Would the new owner understand and appreciate the arrangement or could litigation ensue? Also, the easement would probably cause difficulties when closing the sale. Lastly, with no written document, the dominant tenement would not have an effective way to protect his or her interest. Verbal or poorly written documents concerning easements cause all sorts of difficulties. Legal advice is required.

■ Exercise 5   An Ownership Decision

Joint tenancy must have four unities. These unities are:

- Obtain title from the same document.
- Ownership must begin at the same time.
- Each owner has undivided possession of the property.
- The interest of each joint tenant must be identical in nature, extent and duration.

- In the case of tenants in common, only unity of possession is required. Further, tenants in common do not require equal ownership. Right of survivorship only attaches to joint tenancy. For additional discussion of similarities and differences, see the applicable chapter topic.

- In regard to termination of joint tenancy, the joint tenants may voluntarily elect to sever the relationship. The severance can also occur as a consequence of the marriage dissolution. If joint tenants cannot agree on the termination of their joint tenancy, the court can order that the property be sold and the equity distributed between the parties.

■ Exercise 6   Restrictive Covenants

Various restrictive covenants can be encountered in the marketplace. Five possibilities are included:

- May be registered against titles for specific issues; e.g., no storage of fuel in external tanks, television antennae and/or outside clotheslines.
- May apply to properties bordering an environmentally sensitive area, thereby prohibiting any changes to residential rear yards that would impact water runoff.
- May be encountered relating to house construction; e.g., house size and/or exterior appearance.
- May limit the use of the land for a specific purpose; e.g., property can only be used for farming purposes and not developed.
- May restrict the removal of items from the land; e.g., trees or other significant vegetation.

APPENDIX

CHAPTER 2
LEGAL LAND DESCRIPTION

Chapter Mini-Review

1. The single front township is the oldest of the township systems used in Ontario.

   ☑ **True**   ◯ False

   The single front township was laid out in Southern Ontario between 1783 and 1818.

2. A concession is a township roadway.

   ◯ True   ☑ **False**

   A concession is a strip of land that was subsequently divided into lots. Township road allowances are placed between concessions.

3. The sectional township system in Ontario was based on 1,000 acres per section.

   ☑ **True**   ◯ False

   The 1,000 acre sectional township was introduced in 1835.

4. In a double front township, farms were usually patented in half-lots of 100 acres.

   ☑ **True**   ◯ False

   The double front township should be differentiated from the single front township system.

5. The number for a reference plan is always preceded by the number 99.

   ◯ True   ☑ **False**

   The number 99 is a fictitious number. The number used would be the applicable number for the specific land registry office. Note: There are less than 99 land registry offices in Ontario.

6. Plans of subdivision are assigned numbers at the time when the developer acquires the property.

   ◯ True   ☑ **False**

   Plans of subdivision are assigned numbers at the land registry office at the time of registration.

7. A registered plan of subdivision must be prepared by an Ontario Land Surveyor.

   ☑ **True**   ◯ False

   A registered plan of subdivision must be prepared by an Ontario Land Surveyor in order to be registered in the land registry office.

8. A condominium declaration includes a plan of survey, architectural building plans and structural plans (if there are any).

   ◯ True   ☑ **False**

   A condominium description includes these items, not a condominium declaration.

9. Field survey standards for Ontario Land Surveyors are set out in the *Surveyors Act*.

   ☑ **True**   ◯ False

   The *Surveyors Act* details standards of practice while allowing some professional discretion by individual surveyors.

APPENDIX

10. A Surveyor's Real Property Report typically includes the location of pertinent improvements on the property, but not easements on the property.

 True   False

A Surveyor's Real Property Report would normally include any easements or rights-of-way that affect the property being surveyed.

11. A survey, according to the Association of Land Surveyors, includes four components two of which are research and measurement.

 True   False

The remaining components are monumentation, and plan and/or report.

12. A Surveyor's Real Property Report and a reference plan are essentially the same and used for the same purposes.

 True   False

A Surveyor's Real Property Report represents a full survey of the property, including anything that might affect title to the property. A reference plan is a graphic illustration of more than one area (identified as Part 1, Part 2, etc.) pursuant to the *Registry Act* or *Land Titles Act*.

13. A registered plan of subdivision creates a new geographic identity for the land.

 True   False

At point of registration, the land is no longer referred to by its previous legal description, but instead has a new identity with individual lots being identified by plan number and lot number.

14. Direct access by adjacent property owners to 400-series highways in Ontario is permitted provided that the applicable permits are obtained.

 True   False

The 400-series highways are referred to as limited access highways. As such, these highways do not provide direct access by adjacent property owners.

15. A permit issued by the Minister is required for various activities near a highway designated as the King's Highway; e.g., placing, erecting or altering buildings.

 True   False

Such permits are required for other activities as well including the placement of fences, gasoline pumps or other structures, the placing of trees, shrubs or hedges, and the displaying of signs, notices or advertising devices.

16. A geographic information system is typically used instead of a survey to precisely locate property boundaries.

 True   False

A geographic information system presently is descriptive in nature typically with various layers of information. While a GIS does not replace a survey, the two technologies are gradually merging.

17. Compiled plans are largely replacing reference plans within the land registry system.

True   False

Compiled plans were phased out in 1985.

APPENDIX

Active Learning Exercises

▣ Exercise 1   Multiple Choice

1.1   For purposes of land description, most of Southern Ontario was originally divided into counties. Counties were then divided into rectangles called townships. Townships were in turn divided into strips of land running the entire length of the township. The areas between these strips of land were called:

a.	Road allowances.	✅ *CORRECT.* Each concession was separated by a road allowance. These road allowances might not have been opened, but did remain as public property.
b.	Lot lines.	*Incorrect.* Lot lines refer to the boundaries of a specific lot.
c.	Concessions.	*Incorrect.* Concessions refer to the strips of land running the entire length of a township.
d.	Lots.	*Incorrect.* Lots were created within concessions.

1.2   Which of the following statements are correct?
  i.   Land is described in a precise manner so that one piece of land cannot be mistaken for another.
  ii. A description such as the lot with two mature maples or 43 Main Street is not sufficient as a land description in a current legal document.
  iii. When originally laid out, county boundaries might follow natural boundaries (e.g., a river or lake) but most often were straight lines through the bush.
  iv. A concession is normally 66 feet in width.

a.	i., ii. and iv.	*Incorrect.* Statement **iv.** is not correct. A concession is not 66 feet in width. This measurement usually applies to a road allowance.
b.	i., ii. and iii.	✅ *CORRECT.* All three statements are correct.
c.	ii. and iii.	*Incorrect.* Another statement is also correct.
d.	i. and ii.	*Incorrect.* Another statement is also correct.

1.3   In a metes and bounds description, which of the following are correct?
  i.   Some measurements are said to be more or less to compensate for minor errors.
  ii. The description must completely enclose the parcel of land.
  iii. On a survey, straight lines are described in relationship to North.
  iv. The directions are given in bearings within quadrants.

a.	i. and ii.	*Incorrect.* Other statements within the question are also correct.
b.	i., ii. and iii.	*Incorrect.* Statement **iv.** is also correct. Directions are provided using quadrants within the full circle.
c.	i., ii., iii. and iv.	✅ *CORRECT.* All statements provided are correct.
d.	i. and iv. only.	*Incorrect.* Other statements within the question are also correct.

APPENDIX

1.4 Metes and bounds is a system of written land descriptions. Which of the following is correct?   CH2 EX1

a. All boundary lines are described by the use of lot numbers.

Incorrect. Lot numbers are used in plans of subdivision.

b. **All boundary lines are described by the use of terminal points and angles.**

✔ CORRECT. Metes and bounds descriptions essentially describe property through the use of terminal points and angles.

c. All boundary lines are described as whole lots or fractional parts of lots.

Incorrect. Originally, boundary lines were described as whole lots or fractional parts of lots, but as real estate ownership became more complex, other devices were required such as plans of subdivision and condominiums.

d. None of the above.

Incorrect. A correct answer is provided in one of the other options.

1.5 Which of the following is NOT true with respect to a reference plan? **This question requires that the *incorrect* option be identified.**

a. A reference plan is used for ease of description.

This option is correct. Reference plans greatly simplify legal descriptions.

b. Reference plan numbers are always preceded by the letter R.

This option is correct. Reference plans are always identified by the letter R; e.g., 99R–1033.

c. **A reference plan is a plan of subdivision.**

✔ THIS IS THE INCORRECT OPTION. A reference plan is a graphic illustration only and is not a plan of subdivision.

d. A reference plan describes areas that are identified as parts; e.g., PART 1, PART 2, etc.

This option is correct. Parts are clearly identified on reference plans.

1.6 Which of the following is one of the two Parts of a Surveyor's Real Property Report?

a. Part 1—Plan Sheet.

Incorrect. The term *plan sheet* does not apply to a Surveyor's Real Property Report.

b. Part 2—Certification.

Incorrect. Part 2 is the Written Report. A Certification is included in Part 1, the Plan of Survey.

c. **Part 1—Plan of Survey.**

✔ CORRECT. Part 1 is described as the Plan of Survey.

d. Part 2—Reference Plan.

Incorrect. Part 2 is the Written Report, not a Reference Plan.

APPENDIX

1.7 Which of the following statements are true?

    i.   Surveyors are required to prepare field notes for every survey.

    ii.   The Association of Ontario Land Surveyors is the governing body for surveyors.

    iii. The *Surveys Act* sets out requirements for establishment or re-establishment of lines, boundaries and corners.

    iv. The *Surveys Act* sets out requirements for a valid survey.

a.	**i., ii., iii. and iv.**	✅ *CORRECT.* All four statements are correct.
b.	i., ii. and iii.	*Incorrect.* Statement **iv.** is also correct.
c.	i. and ii.	*Incorrect.* One or more other statements are also correct.
d.	ii., iii. and iv.	*Incorrect.* Statement **i.** is also correct.

■ Exercise 2   Getting Your Bearings

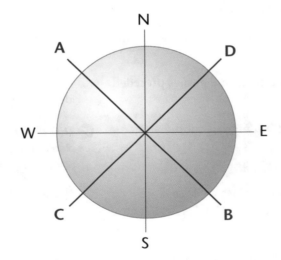

2.1 The line travelling in the direction from C to D has an approximate bearing of

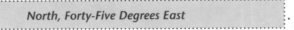

> *North, Forty-Five Degrees East* .

A circle contains 360 degrees and, for purposes of land description, consists of four quadrants each with 90 degrees. The line travelling from C to D proceeds into the northeast quadrant at approximately the midpoint. Therefore the bearing will describe a northerly direction measured from the north-south line (representing 0 degrees) toward the east at 45 degrees.

2.2 What is the reverse (reciprocal) bearing of line C to D?

> *South, Forty-Five Degrees West* .

The reverse bearing merely travels in the opposite direction, namely through the southwest quadrant at the midpoint. In this instance, the bearing will describe a

APPENDIX

southerly direction measured from the north-south line (representing 0 degrees) toward the west at 45 degrees.

2.3   The line travelling in the direction from B to A has an approximate bearing of

> *North, Forty-Five Degrees West*

.

The line travelling from B to A proceeds into the northwest quadrant at the mid point. Therefore the bearing will describe a northerly direction measured from the north-south line (representing 0 degrees) toward the west at 45 degrees.

■ Exercise 3   The Vacant Lot

The first line of the description requires a line moving into the northwest quadrant approximately 20 degrees to the left of the north-south line (representing 0 degrees). Remember, each quadrant contains 90 degrees, so your line should be approximately 2/9ths to the left of the north-south line and run a distance of 294.50 feet.

   The second bearing is 69 degrees southwest and requires a line moving from the first line into the southwest quadrant. The location of the line is 69 degrees to the left of the north-south line. In this instance, you will measure 69/90ths (approximately 7/9ths) of the distance to the left of the north-south line and run a distance of 354.50 feet. When drawing the sketch, a surveyor will indicate the line to be northeast.

   The third bearing will require a new direction into the southeast quadrant. The bearing of the line is 20 degrees to the right of the north-south line. In this instance, you will measure 2/9ths to the right of the north-south line and run a distance of 294.50 feet to the road allowance.

   The final line will require a new direction into the northeast quadrant. The bearing of the line is 69 degrees to the right of the north-south line. In this instance, you will measure 69/90ths (approximately 7/9ths) of the distance to the right of the north-south line and run a distance of 354.50 feet to the point of commencement.

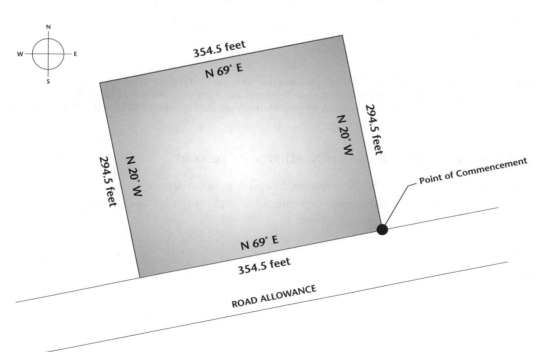

▣ Exercise 4   The Reference Plan

4.1   Part of Lot 2, Concession 1, Township of Anytownship designated as PART 1 on a Reference Plan deposited in the Land Registry Office for the Registry Division of Anycounty as 99R–1033. In practice, practitioners may encounter abbreviated variations; e.g., Pt. Lot 2, Conc. 1, Township of Anytownship, County of Anycounty, more specifically described as PART 1 on 99R–1033.

4.2   February 15, 20xx.

4.3   This reference plan involves property located at the end of a cul-de-sac or dead-end street in a rural area (Part of Lot 2, Concession 1 in the Township of Anytownship). The objective involves extending the road allowance (PART 2 measures 66') and providing additional lots (PARTS 1 and 3). In order to complete the process, PART 2 (along with Parcel A) will ultimately be deeded to the municipality for the road allowance. Reminder: PARTS 1 and 3 are not legally separate lots merely as a consequence of this reference plan, but instead are merely described. Formal severances are required pursuant to the *Planning Act*.

4.4   • A survey cannot be deposited as a separate document with the title to a property, as is the case with a reference plan.
   • A survey lacks certain certificates and related items that are required of a reference plan being deposited under the *Registry Act*.
   • A reference plan normally describes more than one area of land.
   • A reference plan designates the areas of land as PART 1, PART 2, etc.
   • Buildings may or may not be shown on a reference plan.

4.5   The reference plan was introduced to provide a graphic illustration of land only. Reference plans are deposited (not registered) and have no effect on the description of the land until there is a transaction in accordance with the plan. Reference plans were designed to overcome the awkward and often complex wordings of written metes and bounds descriptions. Unfortunately, the use of the phrase reference plan has caused some confusion; perhaps they should have been called reference surveys.

NOTE   As a reminder, the number 99R–1033 indicates that 99 is the land registry office, "R" stands for Reference Plan and 1033 represents the one thousand and thirty-third reference plan registered in that Land Registry Office. The number 99 was arbitrarily selected denoting a fictitious Land Registry Office.

▣ Exercise 5   The House on Northwood Crescent

5.1   The metal shed is located on the hydro and telephone easements and will represent an obstruction should repairs be required. Based on the terms of the easement, the utilities could require its removal.

5.2   August 19, 20xx.

5.3   Two

5.4   Lot 30, Registered Plan 434, Township of Silver, County of Gold.

APPENDIX

CHAPTER 3
LAND REGISTRY AND TITLE REGISTRATION

Chapter Mini-Review

1. An original title issued by the government (Crown) is generally referred to as root of title.

    ✔ **True**   ◯ False

   A root of title can involve several abstract books going back in time to the original farm lot and behind that to the crown patent.

2. The large-scale conversion of registry records into land titles is a process referred to as making first application.

   ◯ True   ✔ **False**

   The large-scale conversion of registry records is referred to as the administrative conversion that is being accomplished pursuant to the land titles conversion project. The first application process involves conversion of individual properties.

3. Chain of title is most commonly associated with land titles.

   ◯ True   ✔ **False**

   Chain of title is associated with registry. The chain of title is typically searched for a 40-year period.

4. Recording of property ownership by its geographic location is known as tract indexing.

    ✔ **True**   ◯ False

   Tract indexing relates to registry and not land titles.

5. A parcel register is used under the registry system.

   ◯ True   ✔ **False**

   Parcel registers are used under the land titles system.

6. Part II of the *Land Registration Reform Act* authorized the automation of property records.

    ✔ **True**   ◯ False

   Part II also provided for the electronic storage and retrieval of these property records. Part I introduced standardized forms and Part III outlined procedures for electronic registration.

7. A combination of block index number and property index number form the PIN (Property Identification Number).

    ✔ **True**   ◯ False

   The PIN number, as described in this question, is assigned when properties are converted to land titles.

8. Teranet is an electronic software operated by Teraview and provides online remote access to automated property records in Ontario land registry offices.

   ◯ True   ✔ **False**

   The reverse is true. Teraview is the electronic gateway operated by Teranet.

APPENDIX

9. A Land Transfer Tax Affidavit normally accompanies every Charge/Mortgage of Land at point of registration in a land registry office.

 ○ True   ✔ False

The Land Transfer Tax Affidavit normally accompanies every Transfer/Deed of Land at point of registration in a land registry office.

10. An implied covenant under a Charge/Mortgage of Land is that the mortgagor will make payments (including interest) and pay taxes.

 ✔ True   ○ False

Various implied covenants are implied pursuant to the *Land Registration Reform Act*.

11. A mortgagor must pay monies owing on a mortgage to a court in order to discharge a mortgage.

 ○ True   ✔ False

A Discharge of Charge/Mortgage is typically registered at the land registry office as a permanent record of the discharge.

12. The Document General is best described as a standard form used to register documents in a land registry office other than a transfer, charge or discharge.

 ✔ True   ○ False

The Document General is essentially a blank form meeting prescribed standards that is used for registration of various miscellaneous documents other than a transfer, charge or discharge.

13. Leasehold interests can only be registered in land titles if the lease does not exceed three years.

 ○ True   ✔ False

On the contrary, leasehold interests must be registered in land titles if the term exceeds three years.

14. A Crown Patent is typically accompanied by certain reservations concerning title to the land.

 ✔ True   ○ False

A typical reservation would involve mineral rights.

15. A national registry of Indian lands is maintained by the Federal government.

 ✔ True   ○ False

The Federal government has been maintaining this registry since 1968. The registry generally parallels provincial registry procedures.

16. A power of attorney cannot be involved in the registration of property.

 ○ True   ✔ False

A power of attorney can be used for land registration purposes and can be registered with the applicable parcel of land in the land registry office.

APPENDIX

Active Learning Exercises

■ Exercise 1   Fill-in-the-Blanks

1.1   Properties in an automated land registry office can be searched using a nine-digit number referred to as the

property identification number (PIN) .

1.2   A sequence of conveyances and encumbrances affecting title over time under the registry system is commonly referred to as a (an)

chain of title .

1.3   The estate of a deceased person is administered by a (an)

estate trustee .

1.4   Public lands under the *Public Lands Act* administered by the government are also

known as *Crown lands* .

1.5   The *mirror* principle under land titles provides that information accurately and completely reflects the present status of land ownership.

1.6   The registration of goods, services and personal property is handled under a

system referred to as *personal property registration system* .

1.7   The Land Transfer Tax Affidavit involves the payment of land transfer tax to the

Ministry of *Finance* .

1.8   Standard charge terms were introduced into the land registration process under

legislation titled *Land Registration Reform Act* .

1.9   A Discharge of Charge/Mortgage is executed by the *mortgagee*

and given to the *mortgagor* verifying that the mortgage has been paid.

1.10 A lessee (tenant) having a lease exceeding 21 years may make application to the registrar in the applicable land registry office to have a (an)

leasehold parcel opened.

APPENDIX

CH3 **EX2**   ■ **Exercise 2   Multiple Choice**

2.1   Teraview gateway software:

a.   Provides for searching of automated records, but does not have e-registration functionality.

Incorrect. Teraview software provides both search and registration functions.

b.   Only permits the user to search property by means of a nine-digit identification number.

Incorrect. Searches can be accomplished using information such as the municipal address and the registered owner's name.

c.   Is designed for use by lawyers and not other individuals.

Incorrect. The software is designed for use by various users; e.g., real estate practitioners, municipal officials and appraisers.

d.   **Accesses various databases within POLARIS.**

✔ *CORRECT.* Teraview accesses the title index, property index and image databases.

2.2   Which of the following is a true statement about the discharge of charge/mortgage?

a.   **When a registered charge/mortgage is paid off, it is necessary to register this document to give evidence of the removal of the claim.**

✔ *CORRECT.* The mere paying off of the debt is not sufficient. Since a document was originally registered on title, a discharge of charge/mortgage must also be registered as evidence of removal of the debt.

b.   The discharge of a charge/mortgage is usually executed by the mortgagor.

Incorrect. The discharge of a charge/mortgage is usually executed by the mortgagee, not the mortgagor confirming that the debt has been paid.

c.   Under land titles, a discharge of a charge/mortgage is typically registered by attaching the discharge to a *Document General*.

Incorrect. The *Document General* is used for purposes other than the registration of a transfer/deed of land, charge/mortgage of land or discharge of charge/mortgage.

d.   The form referred to as the *Discharge of Charge/Mortgage* is also referred to as Form 2.

Incorrect. A *Discharge of Charge/Mortgage* is also referred to as Form 3.

2.3   Which of the following is a true statement about a set of standard charge terms?

a.   The land registrar limits the number of sets of standard charge terms that can be filed in the land registry office.

Incorrect. No limitation is placed on the number of sets of standard charge terms that can be filed in a land registry office.

b.   The concept of standard charge terms was initiated by the *Registry Act*.

Incorrect. The concept of standard charge terms was initiated under the *Land Registration Reform Act*.

c.   **The land registrar assigns a number to each unique set of standard charge terms.**

✔ *CORRECT.* A number is assigned to each unique set of standard charge terms.

d.   A provision stating that the mortgagor will abide by the declaration and all by-laws is required in all sets of standard charge terms.

Incorrect. Terms included in sets of standard charge terms will vary. Note also that a provision requiring that the mortgagor abide with the declaration and by-laws would only apply in the case of condominium.

APPENDIX

2.4 In land titles, the parcel register is deemed to be the sole source of information. Which of the following principles best describes this fact?

a. **Curtain principle.** ✔ *CORRECT.* The curtain principle provides that the register is the sole source of information and persons searching the title need not concern themselves with matters that lie behind the curtain.

b. Insurance principle. *Incorrect.* The insurance principle refers to protection afforded by the Land Titles Assurance Fund.

c. Mirror principle. *Incorrect.* The mirror principle states that information provided reflects the current facts about a specific property.

d. Title principle. *Incorrect.* No such principle exists in relation to land titles.

2.5 The *Land Titles Act* is administered by:

a. The Ministry of Municipal Affairs and Housing. *Incorrect.* The Ministry of Municipal Affairs and Housing is not directly involved with land registry.

b. The Ministry of Financial Institutions. *Incorrect.* The Ministry of Financial Institutions is not involved directly with land registry.

c. **The Ministry of Government Services.** ✔ *CORRECT.* The Ministry of Government Services oversees both registry and land titles and, more specifically, the Real Property Registration Branch of that Ministry.

d. The Ministry of Titles. *Incorrect.* No such government ministry exists in the Province of Ontario.

2.6 The Land Titles Assurance Fund:

a. **Is designed to provide financial compensation for persons wrongfully deprived of land or some interest therein (subject to certain qualifications).** ✔ *CORRECT.* The extent of coverage provided by the fund goes beyond the scope of this course.

b. Refers to a title insurance policy offered by added coverage from a private insurer in Ontario covering property title defects. *Incorrect.* Title insurance policies issued by private insurers should be clearly distinguished from the Land Titles Assurance Fund.

c. Currently applies solely to paper-based and not automated land registry offices. *Incorrect.* The Land Titles Assurance Fund applies to all properties registered under Land Titles.

d. Will not cover situations in which persons are wrongfully deprived of land due to fraud. *Incorrect.* The Land Titles Assurance Fund does cover fraud-related situations, subject to certain qualifications (which go beyond the scope of this course).

APPENDIX

2.7 In a Transfer/Deed of Land, if the purchaser was acquiring the property and the interest/estate being transferred was other than fee simple, in which box on Form 1 would it appear?

a. Box 3.

Incorrect. The property identifier is located in Box 3.

b. Box 5.

Incorrect. The property description is located in Box 5.

c. **Box 7.**

✔ *CORRECT.* The Interest/Estate being transferred is located in Box 7.

d. Box 9.

Incorrect. The spouse of the transferor is located in Box 9.

2.8 In a Charge/Mortgage of Land, the principal amount of the mortgage could appear in two boxes within Form 2. Which are they?

a. Boxes 4 and 10.

Incorrect. Box 10 relates to additional charge/mortgage provisions and not the mortgage amount.

b. **Boxes 4 and 9.**

✔ *CORRECT.* The principle amount is stated in both Box 4 and 9.

c. Boxes 9 and 13.

Incorrect. Box 13 relates to the Chargor(s) address for service.

d. The principal amount does not appear on this form.

Incorrect. The principal amount appears in two boxes on the form.

2.9 Which of the following statements is correct?

a. A power of attorney can only be of a general nature and not for a specific purpose or time period.

Incorrect. A power of attorney can be granted for a specific purpose or a specific time period.

b. **A continuing power of attorney can be used in the conveyance of real property.**

✔ *CORRECT.* A continuing power of attorney can be used in the conveyance of real property.

c. A continuing power of attorney cannot be used if the donor (the person granting the power of attorney) is incapacitated.

Incorrect. A continuing power of attorney continues in force even if the donor is incapacitated.

d. Four different powers of attorney are recognized in Ontario.

Incorrect. Three different powers of attorney are recognized in Ontario.

APPENDIX

◼ Exercise 3   Analyzing the Transfer/Deed of Land and Charge/ Mortgage of Land

3.1   Lot 32, Registered Plan 99 m–165

Buyer	Paul Mark Haines, Susan Gail Haines
Seller	New Home Builders Inc.
Sale Amount	$245,000
Ownership Interest	Fee simple
Other Noteworthy Items	Buyers are taking title as joint tenants.

3.2   Lot 12, Registered Plan 88

Amount	$58,000
Borrower	Paul William Ames, Jane Marie Ames
Lender	Bank of Ontario
Terms	The Set of Standard Charge Terms was filed as #8461.

◼ Exercise 4   Smith's Legal Papers

4.1   • The chargor will make payments including interest and taxes;

   • The chargor has legal right to give charge/mortgage;

   • The chargor will provide insurance on the buildings;

   • The chargor will maintain the building(s) in good repair and will not permit waste to the property;

   • The chargor has no other encumbrances on the property other than those currently registered;

   • Upon default, total monies due shall become payable; and

   • Interest in arrears may be collected.

Various other covenants as provided in the chapter materials.

4.2   A copy of the discharge may in fact have been registered. If not, and if it is not possible to obtain a copy from the lender, Smith may be able to obtain an order from the court to discharge the mortgage.

APPENDIX

CHAPTER 4
MUNICIPAL PLANNING

Chapter Mini-Review

1. Land planning in Ontario is governed by legislation at federal, provincial and local (municipal) levels.

    ✔ **True**   ◯ False

   While all three levels are involved, the federal government only has selected planning-related activities typically focused on airports and oceans/fisheries.

2. A region, county or district would typically be a lower-tier municipality in the two-tier structure found in many parts of Ontario.

   ◯ True   ✔ **False**

   A region, county or district would typically be an upper tier municipality.

3. The provincial policy statement now in effect in Ontario generally discourages urban sprawl.

    ✔ **True**   ◯ False

   The current provincial policy statement promotes intensification as a method to discourage urban sprawl.

4. The Ontario Municipal Board only hears matters concerning land planning and is not involved with other legislation.

   ◯ True   ✔ **False**

   Other disputes and issues are also handled by the Ontario Municipal Board. At present, the OMB is referred to in over 70 public statutes.

5. Committees of adjustment are rarely involved in issues concerning non-conforming uses.

   ◯ True   ✔ **False**

   The three primary functions of a typical committee of adjustment involves minor variances, non-conforming uses and granting of consents.

6. Municipalities use the official plan to assist in forecasting both the size and location of future development.

    ✔ **True**   ◯ False

   The plan also assists in establishing local regulations and standards.

7. The power to grant consents to convey is usually vested either in a committee of adjustment or a land division committee.

    ✔ **True**   ◯ False

   This power is usually vested either in a committee of adjustment or a land division committee, but other possibilities also exist; e.g., the Ministry of Municipal Affairs and Housing may perform this function in certain areas.

8. The *Planning Act* permits the entering into of an Agreement of Purchase and Sale that is conditional upon the procuring of a consent to convey.

    ✔ **True**   ◯ False

   The Act contemplates situations in which a buyer and seller may sign an agreement of purchase and sale conditional upon obtaining the necessary consent.

APPENDIX

9. A plan of subdivision is normally required where more than two or three lots are to be created.

 True   False

If a landowner wishes to divide one parcel of land into several parcels, then a plan of subdivision would be required. The division of land into two or three parcels may be accomplished through severances. Seek guidance from the local planning authority on such matters.

10. An individual seeking a consent to sever would rarely be required to include a sketch of property boundaries along with the application.

 True   **False**

The consent application requires that a sketch be provided outlining boundaries and any abutting lands owned by the applicant.

11. The requirement to publish a notice in a newspaper is one aspect of the overall approval process for a plan of subdivision.

 True   False

Notices must also be sent to land owners within a prescribed distance of the property.

12. A plan of subdivision must be registered in the applicable land registry office, as a final step in the approval process.

 True   False

The plan of subdivision is assigned a number at time of registration, which creates a new legal identity for the land.

Active Learning Exercises

Exercise 1   Multiple Choice

1.1 An owner of a shoe repair store wishes to expand his operation. His store is located in the midst of a residential subdivision zoned for single family use. His commercial operation existed prior to the passage of current planning requirements for the community in question. Under normal circumstances, which of the following will the owner have to appear before in order to gain permission to enlarge his commercial operation?

a. Land Division Committee.   *Incorrect.* The land division committee focuses on consent applications.

b. Municipal Council.   *Incorrect.* The municipal council would normally delegate this authority to a committee of adjustment.

c. Ontario Municipal Board.   *Incorrect.* The Ontario Municipal Board hears appeals to decisions made by selected municipal authorities; e.g., local or regional councils and land division committees.

d. Committee of Adjustment.   *CORRECT.* The committee of adjustment typically addresses matters involving non-conforming uses.

APPENDIX

CH4 **EX1**

1.2 Which of the following is a major function of the Ontario Municipal Board?

a. Administers the *Planning Act*.

Incorrect. The *Planning Act* is administered by the Ministry of Municipal Affairs and Housing.

b. **Hears appeals involving decisions of local committees of adjustment.**

✔ *CORRECT.* The OMB focuses on objections to decisions made by local planning authorities including committees of adjustment.

c. Conducts studies and prepares official plans.

Incorrect. Official plan preparation is accomplished at the municipal level.

d. Conducts research and formulates overall provincial policy statements.

Incorrect. Provincial policy statements are researched and developed at the provincial level.

1.3 Smith owns a Southern Ontario home in an area where the by-law states that minimum side yard clearances are 7 feet, and he wants to build a carport that would extend to within 4 feet of the side yard lot line. Which of the following would Smith *typically* approach to receive approval for this construction?

a. Land Consent Application Committee.

Incorrect. No such committee currently exists within Ontario municipal administrative structures.

b. Municipal Council.

Incorrect. The municipal council would normally delegate this authority.

c. **Committee of Adjustment.**

✔ *CORRECT.* The committee of adjustment would typically address minor variances.

d. Ministry of Municipal Affairs and Housing.

Incorrect. The Ministry of Municipal Affairs and Housing delegates this authority to municipalities. An exception could occur in Northern Ontario, but the question states that this particular property is in Southern Ontario.

1.4 The *Planning Act* addresses the fact that any conveyance of land affecting the right to the land for more than a 21-year period is invalid except for certain circumstances. Which of the following is NOT one of these circumstances? **This question requires that the *incorrect* option be identified.**

a. Where the person granting does not retain the fee or the equity of redemption in or the power or right to grant any land abutting the land that is conveyed.

This option is correct. Section 50 of the *Planning Act* provides for this circumstance.

b. Where the land is being acquired for transmission lines under the *Ontario Energy Board Act*.

This option is correct. Section 50 of the *Planning Act* provides for this circumstance.

c. Where the land is being bought or sold by the Crown, federally, provincially or municipally.

This option is correct. Section 50 of the *Planning Act* provides for this circumstance.

d. **Where the land is being acquired in the hopes of registering a plan of subdivision.**

✔ *THIS IS THE INCORRECT OPTION.* The mere acquisition with intent to subdivide is not sufficient. The land must be within a registered plan of subdivision.

APPENDIX

1.5 According to the *Planning Act*, committees of adjustment are entitled to grant consents. If a committee exceeds stated limitations in this consent authority, the Ministry of Municipal Affairs and Housing may take this power away and transfer it to a:

CH4 EX1

a. Municipal council.

Incorrect. The municipal council would not normally assume this function. See the correct answer below.

b. Provincial arbitrator.

Incorrect. A provincial arbitrator would not be used in such matters.

c. **Land division committee.**

✔ *CORRECT.* The land division committee would usually be granted this authority if the committee of adjustment was not operating within acceptable limits in granting consents.

d. Ontario Municipal Board.

Incorrect. The Ontario Municipal Board hears disputes regarding land planning and is not directly involved in the consent process.

1.6 The municipal government is responsible for various spheres of activities that can directly impact real estate practitioners. Which is NOT one of them? **This question requires that the *incorrect* option be identified.**

a. **Conducting hearings to settle land use disputes.**

✔ *THIS IS THE INCORRECT OPTION.* Hearings are conducted by the Ontario Municipal Board.

b. Flood control provisions that impact flood-prone properties.

This option is correct. Flood control issues fall within the municipal sphere of influence.

c. Sign restrictions (e.g., placement of signs on properties).

This option is correct. Sign restrictions fall within the municipal sphere of influence.

d. Noise, odour, dust and outdoor illumination controls.

This option is correct. Noise, odour, dust and outdoor illumination fall within the municipal sphere of influence.

1.7 Which of the following statements most correctly describes how land could be severed by application for a consent instead of having to obtain approval for a plan of subdivision?

a. A Committee of Adjustment may approve a subdivision plan of no more than 5 lots.

Incorrect. Committees of adjustment are not involved with approvals concerning plans of subdivision.

b. You are limited by statutory law to no more than two lots in an application for a consent.

Incorrect. A specific limitation is not provided in the legislation.

c. You will probably not need a subdivision plan for a project of 50 lots if the services are available to the site.

Incorrect. A plan of subdivision would be required when a proposed development involves 50 lots.

d. **You may possibly obtain a consent to sever if you want to create a small number of lots and your project will not have a major impact on the orderly development of the municipality.**

✔ *CORRECT.* Emphasis should be placed on the word 'possibly.' Many factors are taken into consideration by the approval authority prior to granting a consent.

APPENDIX

▣ Exercise 2   Planning Terminology (Matching)

h.	Airport Facilities	Federal Government
d.	Upper Tier	Regional Government
a.	Form of Judicial Tribunal	Ontario Municipal Board
j.	Grants Spheres of Influence to Municipalities	Municipal Act
f.	Planning Period Usually Spanning 10 to 15 Years	Official Plan
g.	Land Use Controls	Part V, Planning Act
b.	Small or Insignificant Variation	Minor Variance
e.	Clause—Agreement of Purchase and Sale	Planning Act Compliance

No Match: c. One Window Planning Service; i. Provincial Interests.

▣ Exercise 3   The Smith Severance

3.1   Process in obtaining a land severance:

- general consultation with planning staff;
- submit application with fee to appropriate committee granting consents (Application includes a sketch, detailed information on the land being severed and the land being retained, details on services available to the property including roads, etc.);
- surrounding property owners notified and sign posted;
- application is reviewed by various levels of government and related agencies;
- notice of decision is made (with right of appeal);
- various conditions may be attached to the decision as well as a time limit to complete the severance;
- provision of a plan of survey; and
- when conditions are met and survey provided, a certificate is issued.

3.2   The agreement of purchase and sale should include a condition regarding obtaining a severance.

> **NOTE:** The *Planning Act* permits agreements that are conditional on granting a consent. A clause in the OREA Agreement of Purchase and Sale states that the seller must comply with the subdivision control provisions of the *Planning Act* by completion, failing which no interest in land has been created.

Problems that might be encountered:

- Condition may not be fulfilled and sale ultimately cancelled.
- The decision may include various conditions that the seller is unable or unwilling to comply with and the sale would be cancelled.
- Various dates in the agreement might have to be extended if conditions imposed require additional time for compliance.

These problems are not meant to dissuade such agreements. In fact, many properties are transacted pending such consents.

APPENDIX

3.3

Total lot area	21,780
Area to be filled (50% of lot)	21,780 x .50 = 10,890 square feet
Volume of Soil Required	10,890 square feet x 1.5 feet (18 inches) = 16,335 cubic feet
Total Cubic Yards Required	16,335 ÷ 27 (conversion factor: cubic feet to cubic yards) = 605
Total Cost	$4.85 x 605 = $2,934.25 *(Answer may differ slightly due to rounding)*

To be granted the severance, Smith must fulfill the condition (usually within one year from the date of written notice of the decision). Smith must then send a letter to the appropriate agencies confirming that the condition has been satisfied. If not done within the prescribed time limit, the conditional approval is deemed null and void.

APPENDIX

CHAPTER 5
LAND USE RESTRICTIONS

Chapter Mini-Review

1. Minimum setbacks and building coverages are most commonly found in a zoning by-law.

   ☑ **True**   ○ False

   These items are typically found in the zoning by-law. Setbacks involve permissable distances between structures (as defined in the by-law) and lot lines. Building coverages refer to total area occupied by defined structures in relation to total lot size.

2. Requirements concerning non-conforming structures and non-conforming uses are outlined in the Ontario Building Code.

   ○ True   ☑ **False**

   Requirements concerning non-conforming structures and non-conforming uses are typically located in the zoning by-law.

3. An inspector is permitted to enter onto the lands subject to a building permit at reasonable times for inspections.

   ☑ **True**   ○ False

   If corrective action is needed upon entering the lands, the inspector may make an order to that effect.

4. The Ontario Fire Code applies only to new residential construction.

   ○ True   ☑ **False**

   The Ontario Fire Code establishes fire safety levels for existing buildings.

5. A regulated area, for purposes of a conservation authority, can be generally described as lands adjacent to a water-course that require special attention owing to various matters including the potential for flooding.

   ☑ **True**   ○ False

   The regulated area can also include areas involving erosion damage and pollution problems.

6. Flood proofing can be described as either active or passive.

   ☑ **True**   ○ False

   Active flood proofing involves action taken during rising waters; e.g., sand-bagging; passive flood proofing involves construction activity; e.g., floodwalls.

7. A two-zone flood plain is sometimes used when certain parts of the flood plain are considered less hazardous and development is possible subject to conditions.

   ☑ **True**   ○ False

   A two-zone flood plain might be used when the flood plain area has different elevations with varying degrees of risk.

8. Wetlands may be eligible for the Conservation Land Tax Incentive Program.

   ☑ **True**   ○ False

   Certain requirements apply, such as a minimum total size, in order to qualify for the program.

9. The *Environmental Protection Act* (EPA) is a federal statute administered by the Ministry of Fisheries and Oceans.

○ True   ✔ **False**

The *Environmental Protection Act* is a provincial statute administered by the Ministry of the Environment.

10. The *Greenbelt Act* protects environmentally sensitive land in Northern Ontario.

○ True   ✔ **False**

The *Greenbelt Act* protects environmentally sensitive land in Southern Ontario.

11. A permit is usually required to build a house within rural areas that are part of the Niagara Escarpment Development Control Area.

✔ **True**   ○ False

A permit is also typically required to change an existing structure.

12. The Oak Ridges Moraine is a low-lying wetland located near Peterborough.

○ True   ✔ **False**

The Oak Ridges Moraine is a series of sandy hills stretching from the Niagara Escarpment to the Trent River (east of Peterborough).

Active Learning Exercises

▦ **Exercise 1   Land Use Restrictions and Codes (Fill-in-the-Blanks)**

1.1   The ⁞ *Conservation Authority* ⁞ has authority regarding permission to dump fill within a regulated area.

1.2   The continued lawful use of a building that existed prior to an adoption of a local zoning by-law is referred to as a (an) ⁞ *legal non-conforming use* ⁞.

1.3   The ⁞ *Ontario Fire Code* ⁞ addresses, among other things, retrofit standards for occupancy of various building types including accessory apartments.

1.4   A regulated area in which the entire flood plain is considered to be a floodway is called a ⁞ *One Zone Flood Plain* ⁞.

APPENDIX

1.5 Responsibility for inspecting a new residential structure within a municipality falls to inspectors operating under the [*Ontario Building Code*] .

1.6 A fire that involves grease or flammable liquids is classified as a Class [*B*] Fire.

1.7 One of the main objectives underlying a (an) [*zoning by-law*] is to ensure that adjacent lands have compatible uses.

1.8 Owners of eligible conservation land may receive a (an) [*tax incentive*] under a program administered by the Ministry of Natural Resources.

1.9 Land identified for a future use that can be subsequently amended within a zoning by-law is commonly referred to as a (an) [*holding*] provision.

1.10 The conservation authority uses a period of [*100*] years in assessing flooding hazards along waterways.

1.11 The *Greenbelt Act* protects approximately 1.8 million acres of environmentally sensitive land and also prime [*agricultural land/specialty crops*] .

1.12 Protection of fish habitat is primarily the responsibility of the provincial Ministry of [*Natural Resources*] .

APPENDIX

■ Exercise 2   Matching

f.	Temporary Use Provision	Zoning By-Law
c.	Preventative Order	Ministry of the Environment
a.	Part 9: Retrofit	Ontario Fire Code
b.	Grade Requirements and Sight Distances	Entrance Permit
d.	Land Draining into a Stream or River	Watershed
h.	Withstand Passage of Flame	Fire Resistance Rating
g.	Canadian Environmental Protection Act	Federal Legislation

No Match: e. Greenbelt Act; i. Oak Ridges Moraine.

■ Exercise 3   The Smith Property in Northside

3.1 Lot has 2,400 square metres (40m x 60m = 2,400 sq.m.) and meets minimum size standards. Forty metre frontage exceeds minimum Northside requirements.

3.2 Maximum lot coverage: 360 sq. m (15% of 2,400 sq. m.).

3.3 Various rectangular-shaped bungalows could be used. For example, a rectangular bungalow of 245 square metres (2,636 square feet) will fit on the lot with setbacks using a 12m (width) x 20.42m (depth) rectangular design and attached garage of 63 square metres. If this shape is used, the dimensions of the garage must be carefully established.

   The maximum width of the house and garage was determined as follows:

   • Total frontage of 40m less the 20m side yard requirement.

   • Side yard requirement: 10 m x 2 side yards = 20m.

   • Maximum: Total frontage 40m – 20m = 20m

   NOTE The maximum width allowable under the Township of Northside by-laws is 20m (rounded). If 12m applies to the house, then only 8m remains for the garage frontage measurement.

   • Maximum house/garage depth is slightly more complex.

   • The property is located on a county road, therefore the setback must be 23 metres from the centreline of the road. Since the distance from the centreline of the road allowance to the front of the property is 10 metres (representing one-half of the standard 66 foot road allowance), the house must be built a minimum of 13 metres from the lot line.

   • The minimum rear yard is 10 metres.

   • Therefore, the maximum depth of the house and garage is 60m less (13 + 10) = 37 metres.

3.4 The addition of a 48-square metre structure does not exceed total permitted coverage (15% of total lot size.) Various placements are possible given set-backs. Make certain that all structures are located within side and rear yard requirements.

APPENDIX

■ Exercise 4   The Severed Property

Items of possible concern include:

- A second severance in such a short time span may pose problems. The municipality might object under the provisions of the Official Plan for various reasons; e.g., environmental issues, availability of services or overall public interest.
- The proposed 120' x 200' lot does not comply with minimum frontage and lot size requirements. Frontage is 36.58 m (120') and lot size is 2,229.67 sq. m. (24,000 sq. ft.). See zoning by-laws for Township of Northside in Exercise 3.
- Timing issues and steps required to complete the severance process could represent a significant delay for a prospective buyer.
- Fire and building code issues concerning the accessory apartment might be a significant factor. Does the apartment fall within minimum standards acceptable for accessory apartments? What about methods of egress, smoke alarms, etc?
- Is the small motor repair business a non-conforming use? Will the buyer be permitted to continue this use?

■ Exercise 5   The Accessory Apartment

5.1   The Fire Code, Section 9.8 applies to this existing structure; i.e., fire separation for each dwelling unit, escape (egress) from each dwelling unit, smoke alarms and electrical safety. Various options apply to these requirements. Students are not expected to know specific retrofit provisions, but merely demonstrate general awareness.

Compliance with zoning by-laws is required. The salesperson should fully discuss the matter with the seller and municipal representatives, as the need arises. While new accessory apartments may not be permitted, existing units may be allowed as non-conforming uses. The accessory unit will also require an electrical inspection.

5.2   The fire department has stated that the main wall between the units is not adequate. The 30-minute fire resistant rating refers to the length of time that a material will withstand the passage of flame.

Accessory apartments require two acceptable methods of egress. The egress normally must be to an approved open space or to the outside. It must be a continuous path of travel provided by a doorway, hallway, corridor, exterior passageway, balcony, lobby, stair ramp or other acceptable combination thereof. In this particular situation, only one exists.

The second egress must be installed and cannot be shared (i.e., a method of exit that is also used by the other unit). Specified doors must be equipped with approved closures (closing devices) and the solid core door ensures a high fire-resistance rating.

CHAPTER 6
STRUCTURES AND COMPONENTS

Chapter Mini-Review

1. The ranch style bungalow is currently widely used in new urban residential construction projects in Ontario.

   ○ True   ✔ False

   The ranch style bungalow is rarely used in urban areas owing to the large lot size required.

2. The typical split entrance bungalow has bedroom areas on a higher level than the kitchen, dining room and living room.

   ○ True   ✔ False

   The split entrance or bi-level bungalow usually has a split entrance with stairs leading to main level living areas (including kitchen, dining room, living room and bedrooms) and to the lower basement area.

3. Industrial buildings can be broadly grouped under three categories: general purpose, unique purpose and retail purpose.

   ○ True   ✔ False

   The three categories are general purpose, special purpose and single purpose.

4. In wood frame construction, wooden sills are placed on the rim of the foundation walls and are attached by bolts embedded in the foundation wall.

    ✔ True   ○ False

   The sill is a level, continuous pad between the foundation top and the bottom of the framing system.

5. Efflorescence is the result of water carrying dissolved salts to the surface of masonry, then evaporating and leaving salt stains on the surface.

    ✔ True   ○ False

   Efflorescence is a whitish mineral deposit which suggests moisture penetration of the masonry, but does not tell a great deal about the severity of the problem.

6. Bridging is only used in roofing areas and acts to restrain the roof rafters from twisting and also helps to transmit loads from one rafter to another.

   ○ True   ✔ False

   Bridging is used to restrain the joists from twisting and helps to transmit loads from one joist to the next.

7. The subfloor may cause squeaks if not properly secured to joists.

    ✔ True   ○ False

   Subflooring that is not properly secured often will squeak when the weight of someone walking on a floor temporarily pushes the subfloor down onto the joist.

8. Vapour barriers are rarely used in the construction of new home basements.

   ○ True   ✔ False

   Vapour barriers are required under the building code when insulating basement walls in new houses.

APPENDIX

9. Concrete block basement walls are typically covered with parging then damp-proofing.

     True   ◯ False

    Basement walls are covered with coatings and/or membranes to hinder the process of water vapour entering through the walls.

10. A post or column typically carries the load of a beam down to the footings.

     True   ◯ False

    Typical materials for a post or column include concrete block, poured concrete, wood or steel.

11. Collar ties are used to connect joists in order to avoid joist twisting.

    ◯ True   ✔ False

    Collar ties are used with rafters, not joists.

12. Shelter tubes are used for drainage in and around basement areas.

    ◯ True   ✔ False

    Shelter tubes are small tunnels used by termites.

13. Wood rot is caused by a fungus that attacks the wood.

     True   ◯ False

    Fungus attacks the wood cells causing the cells and the wood as a whole to collapse.

14. Drainage tile can either be found in internal or external drainage systems.

     True   ◯ False

    Drainage tile is used in both internal and external drainage systems.

15. Platform framing is differentiated from balloon framing in that trusses are used instead of rafters.

    ◯ True   ✔ False

    Platform framing is differentiated from balloon framing by the fact that platforms are built for each level of the structure.

APPENDIX

Active Learning Exercises

▨ Exercise 1   Matching

e.	Efflorescence	Whitish Mineral Deposit
h.	Floor Support	Joist
f.	Floor Flexibility	Deflection
a.	Continuous Wall Studs	Balloon Framing
g.	Chords/Webs	Roof Trusses
c.	Sloped Roof	Roof Pitch
d.	Small Wall	Knee Wall

No Match: b. Rafter Spread; i. Subfloor.

▨ Exercise 2   Multiple Choice

2.1 In a typical one and one-half storey house, what percentage of the total living area is usually contained on the first floor?

a.	60%	✅ *CORRECT.* The typical first floor coverage is 60%.
b.	90%	*Incorrect.* The 90% figure is too high.
c.	40%	*Incorrect.* The 40% figure is too low.
d.	75%	*Incorrect.* The 75% figure is too high.

2.2 Split level homes:

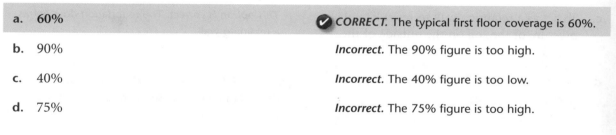

a.	Have few stairways.	*Incorrect.* A common criticism of split levels involves the number of stairways leading to various levels in the home.
b.	Can involve as many as five levels.	✅ *CORRECT.* Split levels typically have three or four levels, but more elaborate models can include five.
c.	Are most commonly classified as either backsplits or front splits.	*Incorrect.* Split level homes are most commonly classified as backsplits or sidesplits.
d.	None of the above.	*Incorrect.* A suitable answer option is provided.

APPENDIX

CH6 **EX2**

2.3   In the construction of a new home, the purpose of installing footings is:

a.   To provide a solid base for installation of roof trusses.

Incorrect. Footings relate to the foundation, not the roof and related components.

b.   To provide extra strength for the overlapping of floor joists.

Incorrect. Footings are not directly related to floor joists. A more suitable answer should be selected.

c.   **To transmit the weight of the house to the soil without allowing the house to sink.**

✔ *CORRECT.* Footings are located at the base or bottom of a foundation wall, pier or column.

d.   To prevent moisture damage when water seeps down exterior finishes and is trapped next to the foundation.

Incorrect. Parging and membranes help prevent water seepage.

2.4   Which of the following is NOT one of the functions of a foundation?
This question requires that the *incorrect* option be identified.

a.   To carry the weight of the house below the frost line to prevent heaving.

This option is correct. The foundation is designed to carry the weight of the house.

b.   To transmit the weight from the above grade walls and floors down to the footings.

This option is correct. The foundation transmits the weight of the structure to the footings.

c.   To act as a retaining wall to resist lateral pressure of the soil on the outside of the foundation.

This option is correct. The foundation does act as a retaining wall.

d.   **To provide a base for installation of roof trusses.**

✔ *THIS IS THE INCORRECT OPTION.* The foundation does not provide a base for installation of roof trusses.

2.5   Which of the following correctly identifies the vertical wall framing members to which wall sheathing and cladding are attached?

a.   Beams.

Incorrect. Beams are designed to carry floor and wall loads.

b.   Joists.

Incorrect. Joists are laid on end and designed to support floor loads.

c.   **Studs.**

✔ *CORRECT.* Studs are vertical wall framing components.

d.   Sills.

Incorrect. Sills are located between the top of the foundation and the bottom of the framing system.

APPENDIX

2.6 What are the horizontal framing members over door and window openings?

a. **Lintels.** ✔ *CORRECT.* Lintels are installed above door and window openings during the framing process.

b. Studs. *Incorrect.* Studs are vertical framing components within the wall system.

c. Sills. *Incorrect.* Sills are located between the foundation and the framing.

d. Knee Walls. *Incorrect.* Knee walls are structural components used in the roof structure.

2.7 Which of the following would NOT be a sign of termite infestation? **This question requires that the *incorrect* option be identified.**

a. The presence of frass inside damaged wood. *This option is correct.* The presence of frass inside damaged wood is an indication of termite infestation.

b. **The presence of shelter tubes.** *This option is correct.* The presence of shelter tubes is an indication of termite infestation.

c. **Signs of wood debris.** ✔ *THIS IS THE INCORRECT OPTION.* Termites consume the wood debris.

d. Indications of damaged wood when probed. *This option is correct.* Typically, the wood must be probed to assess the extent of damage.

2.8 The presence of efflorescence in a concrete basement:

a. **Indicates that moisture was present.** ✔ *CORRECT.* Efflorescence does indicate that moisture was present.

b. Clearly indicates the severity and extent of a moisture problem. *Incorrect.* The presence of efflorescence does not indicate the severity and extent of a moisture problem.

c. Occurs typically in the summer due to humidity. *Incorrect.* Efflorescence can occur at various times of the year.

d. Is found with poured concrete walls, but not concrete block walls. *Incorrect.* Efflorescence can be found in both poured concrete and concrete block walls.

`CH6` `EX2`

2.9 What component of a structure could be most directly affected if a top chord is cut or damaged?

    a. Joist.   *Incorrect.* A chord does not relate to joists.

    b. Roof truss.   ✔ *CORRECT.* The top chord is part of the roof truss.

    c. Roof sheathing.   *Incorrect.* While roof sheathing might be indirectly impacted by the cutting of a top cord, another component is most directly affected.

    d. None of the above.   *Incorrect.* A suitable answer option is provided.

`CH6` `EX3`

▣ Exercise 3   Fill-in-the-Blanks

3.1. Jim, we're having trouble with the gusset plates and web members on that recent shipment. They are separating during installation.

> *roof truss*

3.2 Have you seen that bag of metal "H" clips? We want to install the panels by the end of the day.

> *roof sheathing (plywood)*

3.3 Once Bill's crew has installed the sills and joists, we'll start laying it.

> *subfloor (or flooring system)*

3.4 Jim, do you want both solid blocking and cross bridging?

> *joists*

3.5 We've just finished the expansion joints and are ready to pour.

> *concrete walls/floor (or foundation)*

3.6 We've only got enough studs to complete the first level on Lot 18, then we'll build the floor system for the second level and proceed with the second floor studs tomorrow.

> *platform construction (wall system)*

3.7 What size of lintel do you want to use above the bow in the living room on Lot 21?

> *window*

APPENDIX

3.8 Jim, can you ask one of the other guys to help? I'm having trouble installing the collar ties and lateral braces.

> *roof rafters*

■ Exercise 4 The Riverside Drive Property

Possible causes include:

- Improper lot drainage (lack of minimum slope);
- Poor basement wall damp-proofing;
- Problems with weeping tile around foundation;
- Backfill around house may have settled for some reason;
- High water table due to proximity to river combined with poor drainage;
- Lack of eavestroughs and/or downspouts; and
- Leakage through basement windows.

NOTE: The problem may involve a combination of circumstances; e.g., drainage problems compounded by upper floor and wall system seepage (i.e., leaks running down wall cavities into basement and/or plumbing leaks). Cracks and gaps in the basement walls could also be a contributing factor, particularly if the walls are shifting due to footing problems.

■ Exercise 5 The Renovated House

5.1 Possible answers include discussion of:

- Incorrect spacing/span of joists.
- Lack of bridging/bracing.
- Removal of bearing walls by owner; i.e., removal has effectively made the joists over spanned (undersized). Generally speaking, the alterations made below the master bedroom could have directly affected the structural integrity of the upper floor.
- Squeaking noise could simply involve subflooring and is a reality even in homes that are well constructed. However, given the alterations made by the seller, it could indicate problems with sagging under live weight and deflection problems due to the overall weakening of the supporting structure on the main level.
- Real estate salespeople should be particularly sensitive to significant renovations made to any property.

5.2 The hairline crack can be caused by the upward bowing of the bottom chord on trusses (i.e., truss uplift). This bowing is believed to be caused by fluctuating heat and humidity levels that affect various portions of the truss dependent on whether a particular segment of the truss is located within the insulation of the attic or exposed.

APPENDIX

▣ Exercise 6   An Exterior Viewpoint

6.1   See chapter materials regarding rafters with particular reference to over spanning, rafter spread and condensation. See also Collar Tie, Knee Wall and Roof (subtopic Trusses).

6.2   Three possible sources of a sagging roof:

- Condensation: Plywood roof sheathing can begin to delaminate, causing loss of strength.
- Termites: Infestation can develop largely unnoticed.
- Rot: As wood rot progresses in the roof sheathing or trusses, the wood cell walls collapse leading to a loss of strength and the formation of cracks which will ultimately lead to sagging.

APPENDIX

CHAPTER 7
FINISHES AND FEATURES

Chapter Mini-Review

1. The most common type of asphalt shingle used today weighs 210 pounds per square.

✔ **True**   ◯ False

This is a true statement, but higher quality shingles are available with longer life expectancies.

2. Most asphalt shingles are self-sealing and classified by weight.

✔ **True**   ◯ False

Self-sealing is possible because a tar strip is put on the surface by the manufacturer. Asphalt shingles are classified by weight. Generally, the heavier the weight, the longer the life expectancy.

3. The life expectancy of wood shingles can extend to 40 years, depending on the shingle quality.

✔ **True**   ◯ False

This is a true statement, but practitioners are reminded that life expectancy varies based on such things as exposure to weather and shingle grade.

4. The pitch of a roof has little or no impact on how long asphalt shingles will last before having to be replaced.

◯ True   ✔ **False**

Pitch does have an effect on shingle life expectancy. Generally, the steeper the roof pitch, the longer the shingles are likely to last.

5. Roof leaks can be difficult to trace because the water does not always appear on the interior immediately below the source of the leak.

✔ **True**   ◯ False

Leaks can prove difficult as water may run along framing members or vapour barriers from higher locations within the structure.

6. A window sash is basically the frame that holds the pane of glass.

✔ **True**   ◯ False

The sash is also commonly movable as the window is opened.

7. Glazing is the process of tempering glass to increase its strength.

◯ True   ✔ **False**

Glazing refers to the act of furnishing and/or fitting panels of glass in relation to doors and windows.

8. Brick masonry walls are commonly used when constructing new residential structures in Ontario.

◯ True   ✔ **False**

Solid brick walls in residential structures were commonplace historically, but now have been replaced with framing and exterior brick veneer.

APPENDIX

CH7 MINI

9. Drywall in residential structures is usually installed over a base coat of plaster.

   ○ True   **False**

   Drywall is installed directly to wall framing studs and does not require a base coat. Plaster is an alternative wall finish that is no longer widely used in residential construction.

10. Low-e glass produces greater energy efficiency in windows due to its ability to reflect long-wave radiation.

     True   ○ False

    Low-e glass effectively reduces long wave radiation, which reduces the amount of heat entering a structure.

11. An ER of −80 represents an excellent efficiency rating for a window.

    ○ True   **False**

    A high negative rating indicates poor energy efficiency.

12. Volatile organic compounds can be toxic.

     True   ○ False

    Volatile organic compounds can be toxic and lead to health-related problems including various illnesses associated with sick building syndrome.

13. A lintel might be found above a door or a window in a typical residential structure.

     True   ○ False

    A lintel supports the load over an opening; e.g., a window or door.

14. A double hung window is constructed with two moving parts.

    ✓ **True**   ○ False

    The two moving parts include an outer part on the top half and an inner part on the bottom half.

Active Learning Exercises

CH7 EX1

▣ Exercise 1   Fill-in-the-Blanks

1.1 In a solid masonry brick wall, a wythe is a [*layer*] of brick.

1.2 [*Copper*] eavestroughs are considered the best, with a life expectancy of between 50 and 100 years.

1.3 A built-up roof is commonly called a [*tar*] and [*gravel*] roof.

1.4 Roll roofing normally has a life expectancy of [*five*] to [*ten*] years.

APPENDIX

1.5 A slider window typically travels in a wood or [*vinyl*] track.

1.6 Early glass sliding doors made with [*metal*] were very poor insulators.

1.7 On most houses, the eavestrough is attached to the [*fascia*] board.

1.8 A downspout should have a minimum discharge distance of [*six*] feet.

▣ Exercise 2   Multiple Choice

CH7 EX2

2.1 Which of the following is the most appropriate description of a casement window?

  a. Hinged at the top to swing out.

     Incorrect. A casement window is not typically hinged at the top.

  b. Windows which move up and down in their guides.

     Incorrect. This generally describes a double hung window.

  c. **Hinged at the side and opens inward or outward.**

     ✔ *CORRECT.* Casement windows are typically hinged at the side to open inward or outward.

  d. Two panes of glass sliding on a wooden track.

     Incorrect. This generally describes a slider window, not a casement window.

2.2 Which of the following is NOT correct?
This question requires that the *incorrect* option be identified.

  a. Most skylights have leaked or will leak at some point.

     This option is correct. Leakage is a long term issue with most skylights.

  b. Triple glazing is becoming more common as energy costs increase.

     This option is correct. Triple glazing has become more popular as residential owners seek increased energy efficiency.

  c. Most doors are a source of heat loss.

     This option is correct. Exterior doors are a source of heat loss and typically do not provide as high an insulation factor as adjacent insulated exterior walls.

  d. **Most manufacturers recommend the use of storm doors with insulated core metal doors.**

     ✔ *THIS IS THE INCORRECT OPTION.* Problems can arise given potential overheated air between the storm door and the insulated core metal door.

2.3 Most roof flashings are galvanized steel and are designed to keep water out. In which of the following circumstances are flashings usually necessary?

a. At changes of direction.

Incorrect. Roof flashings are typically necessary at changes of direction, but a more appropriate answer option is available.

b. At joints in material.

Incorrect. Roof flashings are typically necessary at joints in material, but a more appropriate answer option is available.

c. Where dissimilar materials meet.

Incorrect. Roof flashings are typically necessary where dissimilar materials meet, but a more appropriate answer option is available.

d. All of the above.

✔ *CORRECT.* All of the above answer options are correct.

2.4 Which of the following statements is NOT true with respect to eavestroughs and downspouts? **This question requires that the *incorrect* option be identified.**

a. Downspouts should discharge water into proper drains or onto the ground a good distance away from foundation walls.

This option is correct. Proper downspouts significantly contribute to overall drainage around a structure.

b. An important function of eavestroughs and downspouts is to collect leaves from the roof areas and discharge them away from the foundation.

✔ *THIS IS THE INCORRECT OPTION.* Eavestroughs and downspouts can become clogged by leaves and not operate properly to drain water away from the structure.

c. The proper function of eavestroughs and downspouts should contribute toward a dry basement.

This option is correct. Properly installed eavestroughs and downspouts assist by collecting and directing water away from basement walls.

d. Eavestroughs and downspouts will help protect the walls of buildings from water ordinarily running off the roof.

This option is correct. Eavestroughs and downspouts assist by collecting water and diverting the water away from walls.

2.5 Volatile organic compounds:

a. Are essential in the glazing process in window production.

Incorrect. Glazing relates to windows not volatile organic compounds.

b. May be found in building materials which off-gas emissions into the interior of a structure.

✔ *CORRECT.* Various building materials have been found to off-gas emissions. Low and no VOC materials are becoming increasingly popular in the marketplace.

c. Are only identified as a problem involving off-gasing within commercial and not residential structures.

Incorrect. Volatile organic compounds can be a potential problem in both residential and commercial structures.

d. Are no longer a health-related issue.

Incorrect. Volatile organic compounds remain a potential problem depending on materials being used in construction.

APPENDIX

2.6 A green roof has many benefits. Which is NOT one of them? **This question requires that the** *incorrect* **option be identified.**

a. **Improves the reflective quality of the roof.**	✔ *THIS IS THE INCORRECT OPTION.* A green roof is not reflective.
b. Improves stormwater runoff in and around the building.	*This option is correct.* Green roofs improve stormwater runoff in and around the building.
c. Improves the shade factor thereby reducing heat gain/loss.	*This option is correct.* Green roofs improve the shade factor thereby reducing heat gain/loss.
d. Improves air quality.	*This option is correct.* Green roofs improve air quality.

2.7 Which of the following statements is NOT true with respect to windows? **This question requires that the** *incorrect* **option be identified.**

a. Windows provide light and ventilation for homes, at the expense of some heat loss.	*This option is correct.* A trade off exists between the benefits of windows and heat loss resulting from those windows.
b. As energy costs have increased, double and triple glazed windows have become more popular.	*This option is correct.* Double and triple glazing assists in improving energy efficiency and lowering associated energy costs.
c. **The rain screen principle refers to water drainage techniques specifically involving window installations.**	✔ *THIS IS THE INCORRECT OPTION.* The rain screen principle refers to water drainage techniques involving brick veneer walls.
d. Windows may include low emissivity technology to improve energy efficiency.	*This option is correct.* Low-e (emissivity) allows for greater reflective qualities that enhance energy efficiency.

2.8 Which of the following statements is correct with respect to roofing?

a. Most roofing materials are excellent insulators.	*Incorrect.* Insulation quality varies significantly by roofing material, most with poor overall insulating quality.
b. Asphalt shingles have a life expectancy of at least 50 years.	*Incorrect.* Asphalt shingles, depending on the grade selected, have various life expectancies but none currently exceed 35 to 40 years.
c. While wind may cause shingle roof deterioration, sunlight does not affect the wear factor.	*Incorrect.* Sun, as well as wind, causes deterioration of asphalt roofs.
d. **Corrugated plastic tile is typically used for roofs over patios and light structures.**	✔ *CORRECT.* Corrugated plastic tile might be used, for example, over an exterior deck on a cottage.

APPENDIX

2.9   Which of the following statements is correct?

a.   **The steeper the roof pitch, the longer the shingled roof will typically last.**

☑ *CORRECT.* Pitch does have an impact on shingle life expectancy.

b.   Built-up roofs are designed primarily for residential structures.

Incorrect. Built-up roofs are designed primarily for commercial structures.

c.   Inert gas fills are now used in all residential and commercial windows.

Incorrect. Inert gas fills are relatively new in the marketplace, but are gaining widespread popularity.

d.   A solid masonry wall requires an interior wooden framework for support.

Incorrect. A solid masonry wall is a load-bearing component of the structure and does not require an interior wooden framework for support.

2.10   Building components that assist in keeping basement areas dry by directing water away from the foundation are the:

a.   Fibreboard.

Incorrect. Fibreboard is used internally and does not directly assist in keeping basement areas dry.

b.   Lintels.

Incorrect. Lintels are found above windows and doors.

c.   **Eavestrough/Downspouts.**

☑ *CORRECT.* The key components used for directing water away from the foundation are the eaves-trough and downspouts.

d.   Exterior Insulation and Finishing System.

Incorrect. While the exterior finishing system may assist, the primary components are included in another answer option.

  🔳 **Exercise 3   Water Stains**

3.1   The leakage source could be nearby but not necessarily directly above the damaged area. While the window may be the culprit (e.g., no casing on outside or leaky casing) the stain is at the top of the frame. Your answer should note potential problems with flashings, water backing up under the shingles, faulty installation of the skylight and the general age of the entire roof (i.e., life expectancy of asphalt shingles).

Alternatively, the leakage could be coming from the roof area, dripping down from ceiling joists into the wall cavity and running out near the window. The patching indicates either a continuing problem, a temporary fix or long term solution to the problem highlighting the need to investigate further.

3.2   A wind driven rain can pass though the brick wall. A one inch air space is left between the brick and the inside framing materials. Accordingly, rain can run down the inside of the brick face or the outer surface of the sheathing and exit through the holes.

APPENDIX

3.3   Carpet dampness in the basement level will require further investigation to pinpoint the problem. Water could be entering the basement area due to improper drainage, the lack of eavestrough or the absence of downspouts. Alternatively, the problem might be coming from an entirely different area of the house. For example, it could be in some way connected to the water staining in the master bedroom. Water may be following wall cavities to the lower level.

APPENDIX

CHAPTER 8
MECHANICAL SYSTEMS AND INSULATION

Chapter Mini-Review

1. Ground fault circuit interrupters are used for certain bathroom outlets and installations near water; e.g., swimming pools.

 True   False

The ground fault circuit interrupter is a device designed to shut off power to a circuit when there is a flaw in the system; i.e., electrical leakage.

2. Hot water tanks are typically insulated to prevent water leakage during operation.

 True   **False**

Hot water tanks are typically insulated to increase energy efficiency.

3. Plumbing repairs or improvements are typically costly owing to the fact that most plumbing components are enclosed within structures.

 True   False

Water distribution and waste drainage systems are typically enclosed within interior walls.

4. A traditional open wood fireplace can take more heat away from a structure than it generates.

 True   False

The warm air from the structure that goes up the chimney typically can represent more heat loss than the radiant heat gained from the flames.

5. RSI-Value is the metric equivalent of R-Value.

 True   False

R-value (or its metric equivalent RSI-Value) is a numerical representation of thermal resistance.

6. Knob-and-tube wiring in a residential structure does not typically pose problems when attempting to obtain home insurance.

 True   **False**

Problems can arise with knob-and-tube wiring particularly due to overloading and other modernization within older houses.

7. Water testing is mandatory for all residential water wells in Ontario within six months of purchasing the property.

 True   **False**

Bacteriological testing of existing water wells is not mandatory, but is essential in detecting the presence of bacteria.

8. Class 5 sewage systems can only be used for residential cottage purposes.

 True   **False**

Class 5 sewage systems (holding tanks) can apply to any property and typically are used where a Class 4 system is inappropriate; e.g., small lot size or restricted clearances.

APPENDIX

9. A leaching (absorption) bed is most commonly associated with a Class 4 system.

    ✔ **True**   ◯ False

   The leaching bed and septic tank make up a complete Class 4 system.

10. A raised absorption bed is typically used where topography/soils does not permit sufficient filtering and/or drainage.

    ✔ **True**   ◯ False

    Approved sand and soil filtering materials are brought to the site.

11. Standards concerning R-2000 houses are developed and enforced by the Ministry of Housing in Ontario.

    ◯ True   ✔ **False**

    The federal government oversees R-2000 standards through Natural Resources Canada.

12. Convection refers to the conveyance or transferral of a substance thorough a solid material.

    ◯ True   ✔ **False**

    Convection refers to the movement of a gas or liquid given changes in density.

Active Learning Exercises

■ **Exercise 1   Technical Terms (Fill-in-the-Blanks)**

1.1 The size of the service entrance cable determines how much

     electricity   is available to the house.

1.2 An R-value is a numerical representation of   *thermal*

     resistance .

1.3 Of wood shavings insulation, mineral wool or cellulose fibre,   *cellulose*

     fibre   has the highest R-value.

1.4 Two 100-amp fuses in the main disconnect would normally indicate

     100   amp service. *(the 100 amp fuses are not added together)*

1.5 An octopus furnace is normally referred to as a   *gravity*   furnace.

APPENDIX

1.6 High efficiency furnaces have an efficiency in the mid to high | **90%** | range.

1.7 There must be adequate venting in a plumbing system to permit

| *waste water to drain freely* | .

1.8 Modern boilers are normally | *closed* | systems.

1.9 Grounded outlets have one major difference from ungrounded outlets, that being the

| *third (ground) wire* | .

1.10 In a hot water tank, the more water that can be drawn off without depleting the hot water supply is referred to as the | *recovery* | | *rate* | .

CH8 EX2 ■ **Exercise 2 Multiple Choice**

2.1 Which of the following statements is true with respect to the electrical service supplied to a house?

  a. The resistance of any material to the flow of electricity is measured in amps.

      Incorrect. Resistance is measured in ohms. The electrical current is measured in amps.

  b. Distribution panels are used in large commercial structures, but are not used in residential homes.

      Incorrect. Distribution panels are found in both commercial and residential structures.

  c. Electrical power entering the typical house goes into a main disconnect, which has two fuses or two circuit breakers.

      ✔ *CORRECT.* Sometimes, the two fuses are connected together to look like one big circuit breaker.

  d. Both a. and c. are correct.

      Incorrect. One of these options is an incorrect answer, therefore, d. is incorrect.

APPENDIX

2.2 Which of the following statements is NOT correct with respect to knob-and-tube wiring systems? This question requires that the *incorrect* option be identified.

CH8 EX2

a.	Knob-and-tube systems must be replaced in existing residential property.	✔ *THIS IS THE INCORRECT OPTION.* While replacement is recommended and, in fact, may be required by certain insurers, no mandatory requirement exists.
b.	The system gets its name from the ceramic knobs by which the wire is secured and the tubes that are used where wires pass through wood framing members.	*This option is correct.* The system was named based on its component parts.
c.	Breakdown of the insulation on knob-and-tube wiring is most often the reason it has to be replaced.	*This option is correct.* Insulation breakdown is a serious concern in regard to knob-and-tube wiring.
d.	Knob-and-tube wiring was used residentially until approximately 1950.	*This option is correct.* Knob-and-tube wiring was extensively used in the pre-1950 era.

2.3 Which of the following statements is NOT correct with respect to the seasonal efficiency of heating systems? This question requires that the *incorrect* option be identified.

a.	A conventional system is about 55–60% seasonally efficient.	*This option is correct.* A conventional system is typically 55–60% seasonally efficient.
b.	A mid efficiency system operates optimally at approximately 80% efficiency.	*This option is correct.* Mid efficiency furnaces vary somewhat but generally are around 80% efficient.
c.	A high efficiency system operates above the 90% range.	*This option is correct.* High efficiency furnaces vary somewhat but generally are around 90% efficient.
d.	A gravity furnace operates at the same level as a high efficiency system.	✔ *THIS IS THE INCORRECT OPTION.* A gravity furnace has a very low efficiency rate and are generally viewed as obsolete.

2.4 Which of the following statements is correct with respect to a septic tank system?

a.	The septic tank is a water tight container usually made of fiberglass, concrete or steel.	*Incorrect.* Another option is the correct answer for this question.
b.	The septic tank serves as a holding tank which allows heavy solids to settle to the bottom.	*Incorrect.* Another option is the correct answer for this question.
c.	Liquids are ultimately discharged from the tank into a tile bed.	*Incorrect.* Another option is the correct answer for this question.
d.	All of the above.	✔ *CORRECT.* All of the answer options provided are correct.

APPENDIX

2.5 Which of the following statements is NOT correct? **This question requires that the *incorrect* option be identified.**

a. Galvanized steel piping was used in plumbing systems up to approximately 1950.

This option is correct. Galvanized steel piping was widely used in Canada until the 1950's.

b. Plastic supply piping has gained considerable popularity in recent years.

This option is correct. Plastic supply piping is now commonly used in new house construction.

c. **Adequate venting is required to minimize noise factor when water is passing through piping.**

✅ *THIS IS THE INCORRECT OPTION.* Venting does not impact noise, but rather allows for water to freely drain through the house waste system.

d. A pressure tank provides relatively even water pressure to the house.

This option is correct. Water pressure will vary somewhat, but generally a pressure tank provides relatively even pressure for the water distribution system.

2.6 Convection:

a. **Involves the movement of a gas or liquid given changes in the density of that medium.**

✅ *CORRECT.* Convection involves the movement of a gas or liquid given changes in the density of that medium.

b. Is dramatically accelerated when heat travels through highly conductive materials such as window frames.

Incorrect. This statement relates to conduction, not convection.

c. Is the transmission of energy through space via a straight line.

Incorrect. This statement relates to radiation, not convection.

d. Is a process used when conducting a bacteriological analysis of well water.

Incorrect. Convection is not related to bacteriological analysis.

2.7 Which of the following is NOT typically analyzed in an energy audit? **This question requires that the *incorrect* option be identified.**

a. Sources of air leakage and general condition of insulation.

This option is correct. An energy audit would typically include sources of air leakage and general condition of insulation.

b. Furnace and duct distribution system.

This option is correct. An energy audit would typically include an inspection of the furnace and duct distribution system from an energy efficiency perspective.

c. **Electrical distribution panel.**

✅ *THIS IS THE INCORRECT OPTION.* The electrical distribution panel would not normally form part of an energy audit.

d. Water heater.

This option is correct. An energy audit would typically include an inspection of the water heater from an energy efficiency perspective.

APPENDIX

■ **Exercise 3   Commentary**

CH8 EX3

3.1   The ground fault circuit interrupter could be a possible cause. Bathroom receptacles utilize ground fault circuit interrupters which shut off power automatically if power leakage amounting to as little as .005 amps occurs. See additional chapter discussion regarding ground fault circuit interrupters.

3.2   The minimum system size is dictated by bedrooms in the residence. A waste disposal system utilizing a septic bed is not a Class 3 (cesspool) but rather a Class 4. See chapter topics relating to onsite sewage systems.

3.3   The R-value is lower in the basement area than on exterior walls in the upper portions, due in part to the insulating quality of earth around the foundation.

3.4   The house location is not the key factor, but rather whether or not the house has separate sewers (sanitary and storm). With combination sewers, a large volume of storm water can back up into basements.

CHAPTER 9
THE APPRAISAL PROCESS

Chapter Mini-Review

1. Two purposes of an appraisal involve the transfer of ownership and the extension of credit.

    True   ◯ False

   Ownership transfer and extension of credit are two of five major purposes for an appraisal.

2. Form reports in Ontario can only be completed by fee appraisers.

   ◯ True   **False**

   Fee appraisers can complete form reports, but so also can other individuals with appropriate credentials and/or experience.

3. Narrative reports tend to be lengthy.

    True   ◯ False

   Narrative reports provide a logical and systematic presentation of all pertinent facts, theoretical premises and explanations leading to a final opinion of value.

4. A letter of opinion is best described as a brief, unsubstantiated estimate of value.

    True   ◯ False

   The practice of drafting letters of opinion is now discouraged given liability issues.

5. The effective date of an appraisal can differ from the inspection date of that appraisal.

    True   ◯ False

   As an example, an appraiser may inspect a property as of the current date, but provide an estimate of value based on an historical date. For example, the historical date may be required to establish value for taxation issues.

6. Step 1 in the appraisal process involves establishing an appraisal plan.

   ◯ True   **False**

   Establishing an appraisal plan is part of Step 2: Preliminary Inspection and Planning the Work.

7. The age cycle of a neighbourhood consists of four phases.

   ◯ True   **False**

   The age cycle consists of three phases: growth, stability and decline.

8. The factors taken into consideration when analyzing a neighbourhood in relation to a single family home appraisal will typically differ from those for a retail or a farm operation.

    True   ◯ False

   Factors would differ. For example, neighbourhood analysis for a retail operation could take into account such things as retail competition and trading area. A farm analysis might include distance to market and crops grown in the area.

APPENDIX

9. Site analysis normally involves assessing various factors including locational and physical considerations.

 True   False

Other factors that are also taken into consideration are legal/governmental and economic.

10. Analysis of site improvements only includes improvements on the site.

 True   **False**

Analysis of site improvements can include both improvements on the site and improvements to the site.

11. Reconciliation typically involves taking estimates derived from two or more approaches to value and averaging these amounts to arrive at a final estimate of value.

 True   **False**

Reconciliation is based on careful analysis and judgement, not simply on a mathematical calculation.

12. An appraiser's certification can involve various statements such as: *the appraiser has no present or contemplated interest in the property* and *that a personal inspection of the property has been made.*

 True   False

The examples provided are typical of what might be included in an appraiser's certification, but significant variations are found in the marketplace.

13. A comparative market analysis is a form of appraisal.

 True   **False**

A comparative market analysis is not an appraisal, but merely a form designed to assist the seller in establishing a listing price.

14. The *Residential Market Comparison Guide* (OREA Form 260) provides space for recommendations concerning both maximum list price and probable selling price.

 True   False

The form also provides space for an estimate of selling costs. Important: Inclusion of such information is optional.

15. Assessors use the traditional three approaches to value in much the same fashion as appraisers when estimating value.

 True   False

Assessors do use the traditional approaches to estimate value, but are subject to certain legislation restrictions in that regard which go beyond the scope of this course.

16. The assessment notice includes a property's assessment and the taxes payable arising from that assessment.

 True   **False**

The assessment notice does not include a statement of taxes owed or any demand concerning payment of those taxes.

APPENDIX

Active Learning Exercises

■ Exercise 1   Multiple Choice

1.1 The estimation of value for an insurance claim or expropriation is best described as:

a. **The purpose of the appraisal.**

✔ *CORRECT.* An insurance claim or expropriation represents one of five major purposes for an appraisal.

b. A limiting condition in an appraisal.

Incorrect. A limiting condition in an appraisal is a qualifying statement typically included at the end of the report.

c. Step Four in the appraisal process.

Incorrect. Step 4 involves applying one of three approaches to value within the appraisal.

d. The certification signed by the appraiser.

Incorrect. The certification involves statements made by the appraiser (e.g., that he or she has made a personal inspection) and does not directly relate to reasons for the appraisal as stated in this question.

1.2 The appraisal report (OREA Form 700) illustrated in this chapter:

a. Does not require the personal inspection of the subject property by the appraiser.

Incorrect. One of the pre-printed items included with the certification states that the appraiser has personally inspected the subject property.

b. **Includes a limiting condition that refers to environmental defects.**

✔ *CORRECT.* One of the limiting conditions at the end of the appraisal form refers to environmental defects.

c. Is designed specifically for use with residential condominiums.

Incorrect. This form is designed for single family residential properties. Another OREA form (Form 701) is used with residential condominiums.

d. Includes provisions for using the income approach to value.

Incorrect. The form includes the cost and direct comparison approaches, but not the income approach. The income approach would not typically apply to single-family residential properties.

1.3 A loss of value that arises from the perception of a problem:

a. Does not apply for residential appraisals, only commercial valuations.

Incorrect. Perception can affect both residential and commercial valuations.

b. Is most commonly referred to as a detrimental condition.

Incorrect. Detrimental conditions refer to physical conditions, not perceptions of a problem.

c. **Is most commonly referred to as a stigma.**

✔ *CORRECT.* Stigmas involve perception.

d. Is only considered in narrative reports and not form reports.

Incorrect. Stigmas can be considered in any appraisal.

APPENDIX

1.4 The date to which an appraisal applies is referred to as the: `CH9` `EX1`

   a. Inspection date.

                                               Incorrect. The inspection date is often the date on which the appraisal applies, but need not be.

   b. **Effective date.**   ✔ *CORRECT.* The effective date is the date on which the appraisal applies.

   c. Market value date.   *Incorrect.* No such term is used in relation to appraisals.

   d. Data collection date.   *Incorrect.* The date or dates on which data is collected may be the date on which an appraisal applies, but need not be.

1.5 The term typically used to describe when a neighbourhood becomes built up and prices stabilize is:

   a. Growth.   *Incorrect.* Growth refers to a situation in which a neighbourhood is under development.

   b. Decline.   *Incorrect.* Decline is typically associated with buildings that pass their prime economic life and general neighbourhood conditions are worsening.

   c. Prosperity.   *Incorrect.* No such term is used in relation to the age (life) cycle of a neighbourhood.

   d. **Stability.**   ✔ *CORRECT.* Stability refers to a time period in the age (life) cycle of neighbourhood when the area is built up and prices stabilize.

1.6 A step in the appraisal process that necessitates obtaining information about general area trends as well as site and improvement specifics is described as:

   a. Step 1.   *Incorrect.* Step 1 concerns defining the problem.

   b. Step 2.   *Incorrect.* Step 2 involves the preliminary inspection and planning the work.

   c. **Step 3.**   ✔ *CORRECT.* Step 3 is the data collection and analysis stage in which the neighbourhood, site and improvements are analyzed.

   d. Step 4.   *Incorrect.* Steps 4, 5 and 6 involve applying the approaches to value.

1.7 A statistical method to establish value through computer searching of extensive property files in a database is commonly referred to as a (an):

   a. Automated market review.   *Incorrect.* No such term is used in relation to computer generated valuations.

   b. **Automated valuation model.**   ✔ *CORRECT.* Automated valuation models are now being used by lenders and assessors.

   c. Computer-enabled browser.   *Incorrect.* A computer-enabled browser may be involved in the process, but the actual valuation process involving a database has a specific title. See other answer options.

   d. Comparative market analysis.   *Incorrect.* A comparative market analysis refers to a form used by practitioners to assist the seller in establishing the listing price.

APPENDIX

1.8 The process by which an appraiser evaluates and selects from two or more alternative conclusions or indications to arrive at a single-value estimate is normally referred to as:

a. Approach to estimate value.

Incorrect. Three approaches to estimate value are used (direct comparison, cost and income) but none of these specifically refer to the question as posed.

b. Limiting condition.

Incorrect. A limiting condition qualifies the appraisal in some way, but is not directly related to arriving at a single-value estimate.

c. Final estimate of value.

Incorrect. The final estimate of value is a result of the process, not the process itself.

d. **Reconciliation.**

✓ *CORRECT.* Reconciliation correctly describes the process of evaluating and selecting from two or more alternate conclusions to arrive at a single-value estimate.

1.9 Assessors use three traditional approaches to valuation. Which is NOT one of them? **This question requires that the *incorrect* option be identified.**

a. **Direct Assessment Approach.**

✓ *THIS IS THE INCORRECT OPTION.* No such term is used when discussing approaches to valuation.

b. Cost Approach.

This option is correct. The cost approach is one of three traditional approaches to valuation.

c. Direct Comparison Approach.

This option is correct. The direct comparison approach is one of three traditional approaches to valuation.

d. Income Approach.

This option is correct. The income approach is one of three traditional approaches to valuation.

1.10 When conducting a site analysis, patterns of land use and access to transportation are commonly referred to as:

a. Legal/governmental factors.

Incorrect. Legal/governmental factors generally refer to lawful and restrictive uses relating to a property.

b. Economic factors.

Incorrect. Economic factors relate to such issues as prices of comparable sites, tax burden, utility costs and service costs.

c. Physical factors.

Incorrect. Physical factors involve considerations such as typography, climatic conditions and services/utilities.

d. **Locational factors.**

✓ *CORRECT.* Locational factors involve considerations such as land use pattern, corner influences and accessibility to the site.

APPENDIX

▣ Exercise 2　Appraisal Form

2.1　An appraiser might be asked to inspect property and establish a value for a prior date; e.g., capital gains tax or a fire loss that occurred one or more months ago. A relocation company might be interested in establishing value as of a specific date to align with corporate relocation records; e.g., a few days or weeks prior to the actual date of inspection. For most appraisals, the inspection date and the effective date would be the same.

> **NOTE**　Caution is strongly advised in all matters concerning effective dates that significantly pre-date the inspection date; e.g., a situation involving capital gains tax. Under such circumstances, an appraiser might be asked to establish a value for several years previous to the inspection. The appraiser should have experience in such appraisals, have supporting documentation relating to that period and confidently establish the condition, size and other attributes of both the property and comparables used. Appraisers undertaking such appraisals should also ensure that extensive documentation is retained in support of the valuation.

2.2　Creativity is encouraged, as an extensive answer range is possible. Selected negative factors located on or near the site are provided by way of suggestion only:

- A residential property fronting onto a busy arterial road with extensive traffic noise.
- An existing easement on the property (i.e., sewer main through the rear yard that prevents the possibility of an inground pool).
- Various houses adjacent to the property that are of a much lower value (Principle of Regression).
- An inconsistent use on an abutting property; e.g., a convenience store open 24 hours a day immediately adjacent to a residential home.
- A lot that is low and prone to flooding and/or poor water drainage.
- A well-maintained house that is situated within a neighbourhood of poorly maintained properties.
- A property having a mutual side drive when all adjacent homes, while comparable in size, appearance and general condition, have private drives.

2.3　Creativity is encouraged, as an extensive answer range is possible. Selected negative factors located are provided by way of suggestion only:

- Outdated features/facilities, particularly in the kitchen and bathroom. (A detailed discussion of loss in value due to obsolescence is covered later in this Section.)
- The overall configuration of the house may be poor; e.g., room placement is unusual, bathroom is directly off the living room, a small, steep stairway, etc.
- Mechanical equipment may be old and/or not in working order; e.g., furnace, water heater, dishwasher, etc.
- Interior condition may be poorly maintained and in need of decorating.
- Electrical service may be out-of-date (e.g., knob-and-tube wiring) and/or inadequate (e.g., 60-amp service).
- Selected rooms may be very small; e.g., a third bedroom that will not accommodate any type of furniture other than a small single bed.
- A damp basement and/or musty smell within the house indicating the presence of moisture within the structure.

APPENDIX

Exercise 3   Assessment (True/False)

1. MPAC has responsibility for assessment delivery services throughout Ontario.

    True   ◯ False

   Services include preparation of the assessment rolls for municipalities.

2. The assessment system establishes four standard property classes, but also provides for various optional classes.

   ◯ True   False

   The assessment system has seven standard classes, along with various optional classes. These may be further refined to more clearly articulate uses and address properties requiring special treatment.

3. The valuation date is the day on which all Ontario properties are valued for assessment purposes.

    True   ◯ False

   For example, this valuation date for all Ontario properties for the 2007 taxation year was January 1, 2006.

4. Assessment rolls do not list the current value established by assessors for specific properties, as such information is confidential.

   ◯ True   False

   Current value is published in the assessment roll.

5. The Notice of Property Assessment does not include procedures for assessment appeal.

   ◯ True   False

   Assessment appeal procedures are referred to on the notice.

6. Assessors routinely monitor building permits to determine where renovations and new construction are taking place.

    True   ◯ False

   Many, but not all improvements to a property, can be assessed for taxation purposes.

APPENDIX

CHAPTER 10
DIRECT COMPARISON APPROACH

Chapter Mini-Review

1. Certain information can be obtained from a land titles office regarding comparable sales in the marketplace.

    True   ◯ False

   Land registry records typically include selected sale particulars.

2. A key to the successful use of the direct comparison approach is the selection of highly comparable property sales for comparison purposes.

    True   ◯ False

   Probably, the most significant factor in using this approach is the ability to find highly comparable property sales. Lack of these is a significant limitation when using this approach.

3. If the feature in the comparable is poorer than the subject property, a minus adjustment is made.

   ◯ True   **False**

   A plus adjustment is made if the feature in the comparable is poorer than the subject property.

4. If the subject property has a fireplace (valued at $9,000 but costs $11,500) and the comparable does not have a fireplace, a plus adjustment of $11,500 is made to the comparable.

   ◯ True   **False**

   The plus adjustment would be based on value, not cost. A plus adjustment of $9,000 is needed.

5. Beneficial financing associated with a comparable property may have to be adjusted, if the subject property does not have similar financing.

    True   False

   Financing terms can positively or negatively impact value.

6. If both the subject property and a comparable back onto the same golf course, but are located on different areas of the course, an adjustment to location may be required.

    True   False

   An adjustment may be required given a significant difference. For example, the comparable may have a protective screen (to stop golf balls) partially blocking the already limited view, while the subject property has an elevated panoramic view of the course and two small lakes.

7. The time resale method used in time adjustments relies on finding comparable properties that have sold and then resold within a short period of time.

   ● **True**   ◯ False

   The time resale method can be effective, assuming that such property sales can be found in the marketplace.

APPENDIX

8. If construction quality in the subject property is significantly better than that found in a comparable, a minus adjustment to the comparable would normally be required.

    ○ True   ✔ False

A plus adjustment would be made, not a minus adjustment.

9. If a local market was experiencing rising prices and a recently constructed home (typical of homes which are increasing in price) was selected as a comparable, any adjustment to that comparable for time would be a minus amount.

    ○ True   ✔ False

A plus adjustment would be required to allow for the rise in prices since the comparable was constructed.

10. Lot size adjustments are always calculated on a per front foot/metre basis.

    ○ True   ✔ False

Lot size adjustments are typically made based on the per front foot/metre basis, but other methods can be used; e.g., per square foot basis for industrial buildings.

11. Estimating value for a unique property can be difficult using the direct comparison approach, as few comparables may be available.

    ✔ True   ○ False

Lack of recent, comparable sales can significantly impact the reliability of a value estimate.

12. The fact that some information is sometimes difficult to obtain regarding a comparable property (e.g., the motivation of the seller) can be a weakness when applying the direct comparison approach.

    ✔ True   ○ False

Motivation of the seller is a good example, as a comparable may have sold at market value given that the seller was reasonably motivated, while another comparable may have sold for a much lower price given dire financial circumstances surrounding that particular seller.

APPENDIX

Active Learning Exercises

Exercise 1   Direct Comparison Approach: 13 Maple Street

Sales Analysis

Item	Subject	Comparable 1		Comparable 2		Comparable 3	
Address	13 Maple Street	42 Main Street		36 Reid Street		239 Apple Crescent	
Distance To Subject		2 Blocks		3 Blocks		4 Blocks	
Date Sold		6 Months Ago		Last Week		2 Weeks Ago	
Sale Price		208,500		222,000		223,800	
Days On Market							
Time Adjustment		+10,425					
Time Adjusted Price		218,925		222,000		223,800	
Location						Ravine Lot	−7,000
Lot Size	55 x 120	50 x 120	+9,875	60 x 115	−9,875	55 x 125	
House Style	Bungalow			Bungalow		Bungalow	
Age of House	4 Years						
Total Sq. Footage	1,205 sq. ft.	1,140 sq. ft.	+6,029	1,260 sq. ft.	−5,101	1,205 sq. ft.	
Family Room							
Bedrooms							
Bathrooms	1 – 4 pc.	1–4 pc. 1–2 pc.	−1,500	1 – 4 pc.		1–4 pc. 1–2 pc.	−1,500
Basement/% Finished							
Rec Room	Yes	No	+5,000	No	+5,000	No	+5,000
Garage/Parking	No	1-Car	−4,000	No		No	
Interior Condition							
Exterior Condition							
Fireplace	Yes – L.R.	Yes – L.R.		No	+2,000	Yes – L.R.	
Central Air	No	No		Yes	−2,000	No	
Walkout	No	No		No		Yes	−1,500
Total Adjustments		+15,404		−9,976		−5,000	
Totally Adj. Sale Price		$234,329		$212,024		$218,800	

Comments, Reconciliation And Estimate Of Value By The Direct Comparison Approach

Comparable 3 required the least number and amount of adjustments followed closely by Comparable 2. Both are recent sales.

Comparable 1 required more adjustments, including a substantial time adjustment, but indicated a value close to the range indicated by the

2 best comparables.

Based on the above information and analysis, a value by the Direct Comparison Approach is estimated to be: ($ .... 218,000 ....)

APPENDIX

■ **Exercise 2   New Comparables**

Sales Analysis

Item	Subject	Comparable 1		Comparable 2		Comparable 3	
Address	13 Maple Street	193 Westway		38 Weller St.		202 Glendon Ave.	
Distance To Subject		3 Blocks		5 Blocks		1 Block	
Date Sold		6 Months Ago		1 Year Ago		1 Year Ago	
Sale Price		226,500		209,000		221,000	
Days On Market							
Time Adjustment			+11,325		+20,900		+22,100
Time Adjusted Price		237,825		229,900		243,100	
Location				Corner	+4,000		
Lot Size	55 x 120	60 x 120	−9,875	65 x 110	−19,750	57.5 x 120	−4,938
House Style	Bungalow	Bungalow		Bungalow		Bungalow	
Age of House	4 Years	4 Years		4 Years		4 Years	
Total Sq. Footage	1,205 sq. ft.	1,290 sq. ft.	−7,884	1,205 sq. ft.		1,325 sq. ft.	−11,130
Family Room							
Bedrooms							
Bathrooms	1 – 4 pc.	1–4 pc. 1–2 pc.	−1,500	1–4 pc.		1–4 pc. 1–2 pc.	−1,500
Basement/% Finished							
Rec Room	Yes	No	+5,000	Yes		Yes	
Garage/Parking	No	1 1/2 Car	−6,000	1 Car	−4,000	1 Car	−4,000
Interior Condition							
Exterior Condition							
Fireplace(s)	Yes – L.R.	Yes – L.R.		No	+2,000	No	+2,000
Central Air	No	No		No		No	
Deck	No	Yes	−2,500	No		No	
Total Adjustments		−22,759		−17,750		−19,568	
Totally Adj. Sale Price		$215,066		$212,150		$223,532	

Comments, Reconciliation And Estimate Of Value By The Direct Comparison Approach

All 3 comparables required substantial adjustments, including a large time adjustment. I would give the greatest weight to Comparable 1, the most recent sale. It is also within the range indicated by the other 2 comparables. ....

....

....

....

....

....

Based on the above information and analysis, a value by the Direct Comparison Approach is estimated to be: ($...................215,000...................)

2.2   The comparables in **Exercise 1** provide a better indication of market value. The comparables are more recent sales and are most similar to the subject property.

APPENDIX

Exercise 3   The Older Three Bedroom Sidesplit

CH10 EX3

Sales Analysis

Item	Subject	Comparable 1		Comparable 2		Comparable 3	
Address	29 Brock Street	38 Elgin Avenue		128 Maple Lane		218 Maxwell Avenue	
Distance To Subject		4 Blocks		2 Blocks		2 Blocks	
Date Sold		5 Months Ago		Last Week		3 Weeks Ago	
Sale Price		152,300		156,500		162,900	
Days On Market							
Time Adjustment							
Time Adjusted Price		152,300		156,500		162,900	
Location	Good	Fair	+6,000			Excellent	−6,000
Lot Size	60 x 115	55 x 110	+4,500	60 x 120		64 x 110	−3,600
House Style	Sidesplit	Backsplit		Sidesplit		Backsplit	
Age of House							
Total Sq. Footage	123 sq. m.	120 sq. m.	+2,100	112 sq. m.	+7,700	123 sq. m.	
Family Room							
Bedrooms							
Bathrooms							
Basement/% Finished							
Rec Room							
Garage/Parking	1–Car	2–Car	−10,000	2–Car	−10,000	No	+10,000
Interior Condition							
Exterior Condition							
Fireplace(s)	No	Yes	−2,000	No		No	
Total Adjustments		+600		−2,300		+400	
Totally Adj. Sale Price		$152,900		$154,200		$163,300	

Comments, Reconciliation And Estimate Of Value By The Direct Comparison Approach

Comparable 2 is the most similar to the subject, being a sidesplit, and also requiring the fewest adjustments. It was also the most recent sale. The value indicated by Comparable 2 was also supported by the other two comparables.

Based on the above information and analysis, a value by the Direct Comparison Approach is estimated to be: ($........................154,000....................)

APPENDIX

CHAPTER 11
THE COST APPROACH

Chapter Mini-Review

1. The cost approach is most suitable to situations in which various highly comparable property sales are available to compare with the subject property being appraised.

   ○ True   ✔ **False**

   The reverse is true. The cost approach can be most suitable when no comparable property sales are available.

2. The estimated age in years as indicated by the condition and utility of a structure is referred to as its effective age for purposes of calculating depreciation.

   ✔ **True**   ○ False

   Effective age is indicated by the overall condition and utility of a structure, as distinct from its actual age. The effective age is often less than the actual age if improvements have been made to the structure.

3. Replacement cost is generally preferred to reproduction cost when appraising older structures.

   ✔ **True**   ○ False

   Practical difficulties arise if reproduction cost is used in older structures given inherent complex calculations.

4. Physical deterioration can be broadly grouped under *functional* and *external* for purposes of calculating depreciation.

   ○ True   ✔ **False**

   Obsolescence, not physical deterioration, can be grouped under functional and external.

5. A weak real estate market can potentially be viewed as economic obsolescence for purposes of calculating depreciation.

   ✔ **True**   ○ False

   Economic obsolescence involves broad economic issues such as a weak real estate market.

6. If the replacement cost of a building is $187,500, its effective age is 15 years, its actual age is 10 years and its economic life is 60 years, the depreciation using the age-life method would be $44,550.

   ○ True   ✔ **False**

   The correct answer is $46,875 (15/60 x $187,500).

7. Incurable items under physical deterioration may be physically or technically possible to remedy, but normally not economically sound to do so.

   ✔ **True**   ○ False

   Incurable items are not economically sound to cure.

8. A 100-amp service that may be easily converted to a 200-amp service might be viewed as a curable item under functional obsolescence.

   ✔ **True**   ○ False

   The conversion would be judged as curable as the cost would not typically exceed the added utility gained by this change.

APPENDIX

CH11 MINI

9. The term superadequacy refers to an overimprovement that does not realize any economic benefit, such as excess structural reinforcement in walls and ceilings that accrues no benefit to the property or its value.

 True   ◯ False

Superadequacy is a factor that offers no real benefit to the value of the structure and, consequently, to the overall value of the property.

10. The cost approach is highly reliable, regardless of the age of the structure.

◯ True   **False**

The cost approach is less reliable with older structures, given certain judgements and assumptions that must be made, complexities involved with depreciation calculations and the potential for differing estimates depending on the specific methods used.

11. Depreciation, in one form or another, can result in loss of value even if a house is not occupied.

 True   ◯ False

Many forms of depreciation occur regardless of whether a house is occupied or not.

12. A furnace has an effective age of 15 years, an economic life of 25 years and a replacement cost of $2,290. Based on this information, the depreciation would be $1,174.

◯ True   **False**

The correct answer is $1,374 (15/25 × $2,290).

13. Locational obsolescence involves the loss in value attributed to forces beyond the property's boundaries.

 True   ◯ False

Locational obsolescence could involve a residential home negatively impacted by an adjacent retail operation.

14. The observed condition (breakdown) method is the simplest method of estimating accrued depreciation.

◯ True   **False**

This method is the most complex method. Flat depreciation or economic age-life depreciation methods are easier to apply.

15. If the replacement cost is $377,500, the site value is $244,000 and the accrued depreciation is $63,400, the estimated value of this property would be $621,500.

◯ True   **False**

The estimated value would be $558,100 (244,000 + (377,500 − 63,400)).

APPENDIX

CH11 **EX1** ## Active Learning Exercises

■ ### Exercise 1 Multiple Choice

1.1 If site values have been increasing by 1% per month, what time adjustments should be made for two lots, one selling 3 months ago for $155,000 and the other for $150,000 6 months ago?

a. **$4,650 and $9,000** ✔ *CORRECT.* A plus adjustment of $4,650 ((.01 × 155,000) × 3) and $9,000 ((.01 × 150,000) × 6).

b. $6,169 and $9,000 *Incorrect.* Check math.

c. $4,437 and 8,358 *Incorrect.* Check math.

d. −$4,437 and −$8,358 *Incorrect.* Check math and also note that a plus adjustment is required, not a minus adjustment.

1.2 If site values have been decreasing by 1% per month and a comparable sale for $140,000 four months ago is judged 3% superior to the subject property, what associated adjustments should be applied to that comparable in arriving at an adjusted price?

a. −$5,400 and −$4,000 *Incorrect.* Check math.

b. $1,400 and $4,200 *Incorrect.* Check math. Also, minus adjustments are required for both.

c. **−$5,600 and −$4,200** ✔ *CORRECT.* A minus adjustment of $5,600 ((.01 × $140,000) × 4) and minus adjustment of $4,200 (.03 × $140,000).

d. −$5,600 and $4,000 *Incorrect.* Check math. Also, minus adjustments are required for both.

1.3 A lot sold 8 months ago for $240,000 and resold 4 months ago for $284,000. What monthly percentage increase in value applies to that sale?

a. 2.33% per month. *Incorrect.* Check math.

b. **4.58% per month.** ✔ *CORRECT.* Increase for four-month period is 18.33% ($44,000 ÷ 240,000); one month is 4.58%

c. 5.46% per month. *Incorrect.* Check math.

d. 6.05% per month. *Incorrect.* Check math.

1.4 A lot sold 6 months ago for $326,000 and resold last month for $385,690. What monthly percentage increase in value applies to that sale?

a. 3.45% *Incorrect.* Check math.

b. 2.95% *Incorrect.* Check math.

c. **3.66%** ✔ *CORRECT.* Increase for five month period is $59,690 or 18.3%. Increase per month is 3.66%.

d. 5.02% *Incorrect.* Check math.

APPENDIX

1.5 In the economic age-life method, the effective age and the remaining economic life, when combined, comprise the:

CH11 EX1

a. Accrued depreciation.

Incorrect. Accrued depreciation is not comprised of effective age combined with remaining economic life. However, accrued depreciation can be calculated using effective age and remaining economic life.

b. **Economic life.**

✔ *CORRECT.* The effective age and remaining economic life, together, comprise the economic life of a structure.

c. Actual age.

Incorrect. Actual age is the chronological age.

d. Replacement cost.

Incorrect. Replacement cost does not directly relate to this question. Select another answer option.

1.6 Small, curable items are those items that:

a. **A typical buyer would probably repair or replace when taking possession of a property.**

✔ *CORRECT.* Curable items are those that are economically sound to repair or replace.

b. Would not be replaced during the economic life of the building.

Incorrect. Most small, curable items are readily repaired or replaced and would not be avoided during the economic life of the building.

c. Would not be economically sound to cure.

Incorrect. Curable items are economically sound to cure.

d. Relate solely to economic obsolescence.

Incorrect. Economic obsolescence is focused on obsolescence due to overall economic trends and does not relate directly to small, curable items.

1.7 Costing manuals:

a. Typically provide residential costs only.

Incorrect. Costing manuals are available for both residential and commercial structures and related components.

b. **Typically include unit costs for a range of building structures.**

✔ *CORRECT.* Costing manuals typically include unit costs for a range of building structures.

c. Include only figures for reproduction cost.

Incorrect. Costing manuals typically focus on replacement costs.

d. None of the above.

Incorrect. One of the answer options is correct.

APPENDIX

1.8 Locational obsolescence:

a.	**Is one of two sub-categories under external obsolescence.**	✓ *CORRECT.* The other sub-category under external obsolescence is economic obsolescence.
b.	Relates primarily to economic conditions in the general vicinity of the subject property.	*Incorrect.* This description relates to economic obsolescence, not locational obsolescence.
c.	Does not apply in the case of new houses.	*Incorrect.* Locational obsolescence can apply to new as well as resale houses.
d.	Is always calculated using the economic age-life depreciation method.	*Incorrect.* Other methods are available to estimate depreciation arising from locational obsolescence; e.g., the observed condition (breakdown) method.

1.9 An appraiser details various metric measurements concerning improvements located on a property at 154 Main Street. What is the total replacement cost if the main structure measures 16.32 x 12.50 metres and replacement cost is $978.32 per square metre?

a.	$193,429	*Incorrect.* The correct answer is calculated by multiplying 204 square metres by $978.32.
b.	**$199,577**	✓ *CORRECT.* The correct answer is calculated by multiplying 204 square metres by $978.32.
c.	$207,682	*Incorrect.* The correct answer is calculated by multiplying 204 square metres by $978.32.
d.	$197,622	*Incorrect.* The correct answer is calculated by multiplying 204 square metres by $978.32.

1.10 Based on the following information, what is the accrued depreciation using the economic age-life depreciation method?

- *Residential Structure*: actual age: 15 years; effective age: 10 years; remaining economic life: 30 years; and replacement cost $183,482.
- *Single-Car Garage*: actual age: 10 years; effective age: 10 years; remaining economic life: 15 years; and replacement cost of $24,580.
- *Swimming Pool*: actual age: 5 years; effective age: 5 years; remaining economic life: 10 years; replacement cost $29,585.

a.	$51,582	*Incorrect.* Check math. Reminder: The economic life equals effective age + remaining economic life.
b.	$88,682	*Incorrect.* Check math. Reminder: The economic life equals effective age + remaining economic life.
c.	$58,392	*Incorrect.* Check math. Reminder: The economic life equals effective age + remaining economic life.
d.	**$65,564**	✓ *CORRECT.* The correct answer is obtained by totalling the calculated depreciation for each item.

APPENDIX

Exercise 2   Matching

i.	Objective Value	Cost to Create
c.	Site Value	Abstraction Method
e.	Incurable	Not Economically Sound to Cure
g.	Replacement Cost	Comparative Square Metre/Foot Method
d.	Superadequacy	No Contribution to Value
a.	Physical Deterioration	Breakdown—Structures/Components
f.	Reproduction Cost	Exact Replica

No Match: b. Economic Life; h. Long-Lived.

Exercise 3   Site Valuation (Time Adjustment)

SALE	SALE DATE	SALE PRICE	TIME ADJUSTMENT	ADJUSTED SALE PRICE
1	8 months ago	$211,000	8,440	219,440
2	6 months ago	$212,800	6,384	219,184
3	4 months ago	$217,000	4,340	221,340
4	2 months ago	$218,600	2,186	220,786

Estimate of Value:

Final estimate of value will vary based on your evaluation of the adjusted prices. Remember that Sale #4 was judged most comparable, however, the other sales must be taken into consideration. An appraiser would have other factors to consider, but based solely on the information provided, a reasonable estimate of value might be $221,000 as Sales #3 and #4 were most recent, Sales #3 and #4 required the least amount of time adjustment, and Sale #4 was most comparable.

Exercise 4   Replacement Cost

STRUCTURE	MEASUREMENT	TOTAL SQ. FT.	REPLACEMENT COST	TOTAL COST
Main Building	26 x 42 ft.	1,092	$180.00/sq.ft.	$196,560
Addition	14 x 26 ft.	364	$120.00/sq.ft.	43,680
Garage	16 x 21 ft.	336	$47.00/sq.ft.	15,792
Other Improvements:				
Storage Shed			$9,000	9,000
Total Replacement Cost				**$265,032**

APPENDIX

■ Exercise 5   Accrued Depreciation

A recreational cottage has an actual age of 10 years, an estimated effective age of 5 years and a remaining economic life of 30 years. The replacement cost new is $97,700. A frame boat house was added to the property 5 years ago and has an effective age of 3 years with a remaining economic life of 17 years. The replacement cost new is $27,500. The accrued depreciation for both main and accessory structures is:

STRUCTURE	EFFECTIVE AGE ÷ ECONOMIC LIFE	REPLACEMENT COST	DEPRECIATION
House	5/35	$97,700	$13,957
Boat House	3/20	27,500	4,125
Total Accrued Depreciation			**$18,082**

APPENDIX

CHAPTER 12
THE INCOME APPROACH

Chapter Mini-Review

1. The appraisal procedure for the income approach consists of five steps.

     ○ True   ✔ **False**

    The appraisal procedure consists of six steps.

2. Direct capitalization involves the determination of operating cash flows for a specified holding period plus the reversionary value at point of sale.

     ○ True   ✔ **False**

    This statement describes yield capitalization, not direct capitalization.

3. An appraiser, when reviewing the owner's operating statements, must stabilize expenses on an annual basis for purposes of a reconstructed operating statement.

     ✔ **True**   ○ False

    Stabilizing expenses is required, as certain costs may be incurred every four or five years, and should be annualized to reflect proper pro-rating.

4. Business tax should be included as an operating expense within a reconstructed operating statement.

     ○ True   ✔ **False**

    Business tax is excluded when developing a reconstructed operating statement.

5. If a free suite is provided to a superintendent or a janitor, market rent for that unit must be included in potential gross (rental) income.

     ✔ **True**   ○ False

    The market rent must be included in potential gross income and then deducted as an operating expense.

6. A deduction for vacancy and credit losses must apply both to potential gross (rental) income and to other income.

     ○ True   ✔ **False**

    Depending on the circumstances, the deduction for vacancy and bad debt can be applied to just the potential gross (rental) income or to other income as well.

7. If the effective gross income is $489,092, the gross operating expenses are $397,000 and the capitalization rate is 9.27%, the estimate of value calculation is $993,441.

     ✔ **True**   ○ False

    The net operating income is $92,092, which is divided by the cap rate of 9.27% (.0927) = $993,441.

8. When estimating the potential gross (rental) income of a commercial property, the appraiser should use actual rent, not market rent.

     ○ True   ✔ **False**

    The reverse is true. The appraiser should use market rent, not actual rent.

APPENDIX

9. A relatively small upward or downward movement (e.g., 1%) in the cap rate can have a significant impact on the estimate of value.

 ✔ **True**   ◯ False

This is a correct statement. For example, if a property has a net operating income of $237,000, the estimate of value based on an 8% cap rate is $2,962,500 while the same NOI capitalized at 9% is $2,633,333. Note also that a larger cap rate produces a lower estimated value.

10. A disadvantage of the income approach is the difficulty of selecting an appropriate capitalization rate.

 ✔ **True**   ◯ False

Often, this difficulty arises from lack of adequate comparable sales upon which to determine an applicable capitalization rate.

11. The income approach is best suited to income-producing properties that are owner occupied.

 ◯ True   ✔ **False**

The income approach is not well suited to owner-occupied properties given additional adjustments and assumptions that must be made.

12. Gross operating expense is subtracted from effective gross income to arrive at net operating income.

 ✔ **True**   ◯ False

Net operating income is then used to arrive at an estimate of value using an appropriate capitalization rate.

Active Learning Exercises

■ **Exercise 1   Cap Rate: Thirty-Unit Apartment Building**

1.1   Calculate the capitalization rate for all six properties.

SALE	SALE PRICE	NET OPERATING INCOME (NOI)	CAPITALIZATION RATE
1	2,100,000	196,300	.0935 or 9.35%
2	1,980,000	193,450	.0977 or 9.77%
3	1,700,000	164,050	.0965 or 9.65%
4	1,863,000	172,550	.0926 or 9.26%
5	1,986,000	184,490	.0929 or 9.29%
6	2,150,000	183,600	.0854 or 8.54%

1.2   Given that Sales #1 and #4 were most comparable, the most weight would be placed on the respective cap rates: 9.35% and 9.26%. Based on that assumption, a reasonable conclusion would be 9.30. In the real world, the cap rate selected would also be impacted by other factors not directly addressed in this question.

1.3   The value is:

$187,000 ÷ .0930 = **$2,010,752.69** (rounded to $2,011,000)

■ Exercise 2   Cap Rate Calculations

2.1   **$873,171**

$393,000–303,500 = $ 89,500
$89,500 ÷ .1025 = $873,171

2.2   **8.09%**

$72,600 ÷ 897,000 = .0809 or 8.09%

2.3   **$41.11**

$293,000–244,900 = $48,100
$48,100 ÷ .0975 = $493,333
$493,333 ÷ 12,000 = $41.11 per square foot

2.4

ADDRESS	SALE PRICE	NOI	DEGREE OF COMPARABILITY	CAP RATE
136 West St.	193,500	18,965	High	.0980 or 9.80%
210 Westcott St.	186,000	21,050	Low	.1131 or 11.31%
13821 Main	189,500	14,861	Low	.0784 or 7.84%
336 Perimeter Rd.	202,500	17,500	Medium	.0864 or 8.64%
98 Walkers Lane	201,600	19,300	High	.0957 or 9.57%
971 River Road	186,000	19,943	Medium	.1072 or 10.72%
2 Express Pkwy.	200,600	19,694	High	.0982 or 9.82%

Greatest emphasis is placed on properties with highest comparability. Analysis indicates a capitalization rate of .0975. (Answers will vary slightly based on individual judgement.)

2.5

ADDRESS	SALE PRICE	NOI	DEGREE OF COMPARABILITY	CAP RATE
298 East Ave.	193,500	24,328	Low	.1257 or 12.57%
89 Foundry Road	189,330	21,050	Low	.1112 or 11.12%
336 Gateway Park	210,300	20,300	Low	.0965 or 9.65%

The Foundry Road property is judged slightly more comparable than the other two and greatest weight is placed upon this capitalization rate. A reasonable range of values appears to be as follows:

Range of Capitalization Values   **.0965 to .1257**

Upper Range of Value $22,565 ÷ .0965
= $233,834 (rounded to $234,000)
$234,000 ÷ 12,500 = **$18.72 per square foot**

Lower Range of Value $22,565 ÷ .1257
= $179,515 (rounded to $180,000)
$180,000 ÷ 12,500 = **$14.40 per square foot**

NOTE: Lower and upper estimates will vary based on the range of cap rates selected. Extreme caution is always advised when insufficient good comparables are available and/or a unique type of property is being valued. In this instance, the property should also be analyzed in terms of the cost approach and direct comparison approach to provide a full perspective prior to any final indication of value.

APPENDIX

■ Exercise 3   The Retail Store

Various critical comments can be levelled against the use of this information. The following represents most, but not all, possibilities.

1. *Regarding the government-sourced information:*
- What was the source of information used by the regional representatives in obtaining cap rates?
- If a valid source, were the gross incomes, effective incomes and net operating incomes calculated using methods consistent with accepted procedures for reconstructing operating statements?
- Is the information dated and how large a sample was secured?
- How comparable are the properties used in deriving a cap rate for this unique, older retail store?

The bottom line: Don't rely on secondary information unless it can be fully investigated.

2. *Regarding Jamieson's adjustments:*
- The adjustment may be valid based on Jamieson's experience, but always stick to the facts. The building is somewhat unique and setting a cap rate may prove difficult.
- The plaza is really run down. Is this adequately reflected in the cap rate chosen?
- Adjustments should be made on empirical facts.

3. *Regarding the owner's representations:*
- How was the $20,000 NOI arrived at? An income and expense analysis is required using accepted procedures for reconstructed worksheets.

4. *Regarding the use of a cap rate:*
- A small upward or downward cap rate adjustment will have a dramatic impact on indicated value.
- The cap rate will not take into consideration important factors such as debt service and tax liabilities.
- Given the uniqueness of the property, a reliable cap rate may be difficult given the lack of comparables for this particular type of property.

■ Exercise 4   1287 Western Avenue

OPERATING EXPENSES

Payment Type	Annual Payment
Property Taxes	$9,300
Water	3,800
Fire Insurance	9,300
Minor Repairs and Maintenance	12,570
Electricity for Common Areas	6,590
Landscaping Contract	5,300
Janitor's Salary	39,800
Hall Repainting—Annualized	2,450
Exterior Trim—Annualized	950
Painting of Suites—Annualized	3,850
Main Lobby Decorating—Annualized	870
Management Fee (2.5%)	6,078
Total Operating Expenses	**$100,858**

APPENDIX

CAPITALIZATION RATE

CH12 EX4

SALE	SALE PRICE	NOI	CAP RATE
1	1,496,660	149,870	.1001 or 10.01%
2	1,522,600	157,500	.1034 or 10.34%
3	1,621,400	164,840	.1017 or 10.17%

From an appraiser's perspective, a selected capitalization rate might be: .1025 or 10.25%. Answers will vary slightly based on individual judgement.

Potential Gross (Rental) Income	$240,480
Less: Vacancy and Credit Losses	−9,619
Add: Other Income	+ 12,240
Effective Gross Income	**243,101**
Less: Operating Expenses	−100,858
Net Operating Income	**= 142,243**

Indicated Value by the Income Approach $142,243 ÷ .1025
= **$1,387,737** (rounded to $1,388,000)

APPENDIX

CHAPTER 13
MORTGAGE FUNDAMENTALS

Chapter Mini-Review

1. The mortgagor gives or lends the money and registers the mortgage against the property in the land registry office.

    True   **False**

   The mortgagee gives or lends the money; the mortgagor receives the funds and must perform all covenants under the mortgage.

2. A chattel mortgage is given on movable objects or personal property.

    True   False

   Chattel mortgages are registered based on procedures set out in the *Personal Property Security Act*.

3. Subsequent mortgagees, over and above the first mortgagee, have the right to be notified regarding default action being taken by the first mortgagee, but cannot make payments on behalf of the mortgagor to stave off such action.

    True   **False**

   A subsequent encumbrancer can make payments to protect his/her position in relation to the first mortgagee and stave off action by that first mortgagee.

4. A lease that is entered into prior to the registration of a mortgage generally has priority over that mortgage.

   True (checked)   False

   Alternatively, a lease entered into after registration would not take priority over the mortgage, unless some arrangement was made to the contrary.

5. The requirement that a mortgagor will provide insurance on the buildings is one of the implied covenants under the *Land Registration Reform Act*.

    True   False

   This implied covenant is one of several detailed under the 'three implied covenants' set out in the *Land Registration Reform Act*.

6. The mortgagee can only assign a mortgage with the express written consent of the mortgagor.

    True   **False**

   A mortgage can be sold, transferred or assigned by a mortgagee without the consent of the mortgagor. However, the mortgagor must be notified of the assignment.

7. A mortgagee can only pursue legal remedies for mortgage default once he or she has exhausted all non-legal remedies.

    True   **False**

   While non-legal remedies may be pursued, the mortgagee is under no legal obligation to use such means and may pursue legal remedies immediately upon default.

CH13 MINI

8. A legal remedy in which the mortgagor forfeits his or her equity of redemption along with any equity that he or she may have in the property is referred to as a judicial sale.

   ○ True   **False**

   A legal remedy in which the mortgagor forfeits the equity of redemption is referred to as a foreclosure.

9. Under a power of sale, the mortgagee can force the sale of the mortgaged property when default occurs.

    True   ○ False

   Power of sale is the most frequently used remedy for default.

10. Money markets are typically associated with short term borrowing with capital markets focused on longer term borrowing.

     True   ○ False

    The mortgage market is one of many components making up the Canadian capital market.

11. The secondary market is focused on sub-prime lending involving higher risk levels with borrowers having B and C level credit.

    ○ True   **False**

    The sub-prime market is part of the primary market, not the secondary market.

12. Mortgage brokers in Ontario are regulated by the Financial Services Commission of Ontario.

     True   ○ False

    The Financial Services Commission of Ontario enforces provisions relating to mortgage brokers as set out in the *Mortgage Brokerages, Lenders and Administrators Act, 2006.*

13. High ratio mortgages can only be insured by Canada Mortgage and Housing Corporation.

    ○ True   **False**

    Currently, other insurers include Genworth Financial Canada and AIG United Guaranty.

14. Creditor life insurance is another name for mortgage default insurance.

    ○ True   **False**

    Creditor life insurance provides insurance protection for the borrower (e.g., disability coverage) while mortgage default insurance provides protection for the lender should the borrower fail to meet obligations set out in the mortgage.

APPENDIX

Active Learning Exercises

■ Exercise 1   Multiple Choice

1.1   A chattel mortgage:

a.   **May be registered pursuant to procedures set out in the *Personal Property Security Act*.**   ✔ *CORRECT.* Chattels are registered under the *Personal Property Security Act*.

b.   May be registered pursuant to procedures set out in the *Mortgages Act*.   *Incorrect.* The *Mortgages Act* does not deal with chattel mortgages.

c.   May be registered pursuant to procedures set out in the *Mortgage Brokerages, Lenders and Administrators Act, 2006*.   *Incorrect.* The *Mortgage Brokerages, Lenders and Administrators Act, 2006* focuses on regulatory controls impacting mortgage brokers.

d.   Is not normally registered in the Province of Ontario.   *Incorrect.* While a chattel mortgage need not be registered, prudent lenders avail themselves of registration provisions set out in provincial legislation.

1.2   Under a judicial sale:

a.   The mortgagor must release all interests that he or she may have in the land at the point of electing to involve the Court in the sale.   *Incorrect.* The mortgagor is not required to release all interests in the land at point of involving the Court in the sale of the property.

b.   **Any surplus, after obligations to encumbrancers are satisfied, would be paid to the mortgagor (subject to court and related costs).**   ✔ *CORRECT.* Any surplus would be awarded to the mortgagor.

c.   The Court evicts the mortgagor and takes possession of the property.   *Incorrect.* No eviction takes place. The property is offered for sale by the Court.

d.   The mortgagor does not receive any surplus after obligations to encumbrancers and court costs are paid.   *Incorrect.* The mortgagor does receive any surplus.

1.3   Mortgagor Jones has an existing first mortgage with Lender Inc. that is coming due and she wants to renew. However, Jones also has an existing second mortgage and wants that second mortgage to remain as such, while replacing the existing first. Which of the following privileges is needed relating to the second mortgage to accommodate this?

a.   Prepayment.   *Incorrect.* Prepayment does not apply to situations in which the second mortgagee is agreeing to maintain a specific priority in relation to the first mortgagee.

b.   Transfer.   *Incorrect.* A transfer does not apply to this situation.

c.   Renewal.   *Incorrect.* While the question addresses the topic of mortgage renewal, a specific privilege is required to handle this situation.

d.   Postponement.   ✔ *CORRECT.* A postponement clause provides that the mortgagee agrees to postpone his/her priority in favour of a prior mortgage that is being replaced.

APPENDIX

1.4 Mortgagor Smith has encountered significant financial problems and wants to be released from all interests in a mortgaged property. The mortgagee agrees to take over the property with no further action against Smith for monies owed. This arrangement is best described as a:

CH13 EX1

a. Foreclosure.

Incorrect. Foreclosure is a legal action to cause forfeiture of the mortgagor's equity of redemption.

b. Quit Claim Deed.

✅ *CORRECT.* The quit claim deed can be an expedient means to remedy a default situation.

c. Power of Sale.

Incorrect. A power of sale involves default followed by putting the property up for sale.

d. Judicial Sale.

Incorrect. A judicial sale involves default followed by a Court putting the property up for sale.

1.5 When a mortgagee takes possession of a property due to the mortgagor's default, he or she:

a. Must respect the legal rights of a tenant, if any, now occupying the property.

✅ *CORRECT.* The legal rights to be respected will vary based on the terms of the tenancy arrangement and the timing of this tenancy in relation to the mortgage.

b. Is not permitted to take any other legal action against the mortgagor.

Incorrect. The legal right to take possession may be accompanied by other legal actions; e.g., foreclosure.

c. Must not hire agents for upkeep or repair of the property.

Incorrect. The mortgagor may hire agents for upkeep and repair.

d. Is not governed by provisions of the *Mortgages Act*.

Incorrect. Certain provisions in the *Mortgages Act* apply to possession by a mortgagee.

1.6 A mortgage broker:

a. Is regulated under the *Real Estate and Business Brokers Act*.

Incorrect. Mortgage brokers are regulated under the *Mortgage Brokerages, Lenders and Administrators Act, 2006*.

b. Can represent either the lender or the borrower.

✅ *CORRECT.* A mortgage broker can represent either party subject to regulatory requirements.

c. Can only represent the lender.

Incorrect. A mortgage broker can represent the lender or the borrower.

d. Cannot receive any payment from borrowers for services performed in securing financing.

Incorrect. A mortgage broker can receive payment from either a lender or borrower, provided that regulatory requirements are met.

APPENDIX

1.7 Which of the following is a correct statement regarding provisions set out in the *Mortgages Act?*

a. A mortgagee is free to use insurance money received relating to damage to the mortgaged property in whatever way he or she sees fit.

Incorrect. Funds received relating to insurance must, at the mortgagee's discretion, be applied in making good the loss to the mortgaged property.

b. A mortgagee can pursue both the original mortgagor and a new buyer of a home who assumes the mortgage for any default of that mortgage.

Incorrect. The mortgagee must pursue one or the other.

c. When funds are received under a power of sale, payment of rent deposits to tenants must be made prior to paying costs relating to the power of sale action.

Incorrect. Costs relating to the power of sale action are paid before rent deposits of tenants are addressed.

d. **A copy of the mortgage must be received by the mortgagor (or his/her agent) within 30 days of signing.**

✔ *CORRECT.* A true copy must be received within 30 days of signing.

1.8 The secondary mortgage market:

a. Focuses on higher risk borrowers with B and C level credit.

Incorrect. The market segment dealing with higher risk borrowers is referred to as sub-prime lending (part of the primary mortgage market).

b. **Involves the trading of existing mortgages.**

✔ *CORRECT.* Typically, sales involve mortgage portfolios of primary lenders that are sold to investment companies and pension funds.

c. Is not involved with securitization of mortgages.

Incorrect. The secondary market is directly involved in mortgage securitization.

d. Focuses on new loans for property financing and rehabilitation of existing structures.

Incorrect. The primary market focuses on new loans for property financing and rehabilitation of existing structures.

APPENDIX

Exercise 2   Matching

d.	Subsequent Encumbrancers	Right to Prevent Default and Right to be Notified
e.	Equity of Redemption	Right to Redeem the Property
a.	Common Expenses	Type of Lien Registered by a Condominium Corporation
c.	Holdback	Construction Lien Act
f.	Quit Claim Deed	Release any Rights in a Parcel of Land
b.	Prepayment	Privilege Granted by a Mortgagee to a Mortgagor

No Match: g. Legal Occupancy of the Mortgaged Property by the Mortgagee

Exercise 3   Power of Sale

Discharge of all principal money due relating to the mortgage.	3
Payment to the tenants of rent deposits made pursuant to the *Residential Tenancies Act* where the rent deposit was not applied in payment for the last rent period and the residue shall be paid to the mortgagor.	5
Discharge of all interest and costs relating to the mortgage.	2
Payment of all expenses incurred in any sale or attempted sale.	1
Payment of amounts to subsequent encumbrances based on their priority.	4

APPENDIX

CHAPTER 14
MORTGAGE LENDING PRACTICES

Chapter Mini-Review

1. Credit reports typically provide a credit score that can range from 600 to 1000.

   ○ True   **False**

   The range is between 300 and 900.

2. Lenders may require a Notice of Assessment issued by the Canada Revenue Agency to verify income of prospective borrowers.

    True   ○ False

   Other acceptable documents could include T4s or T4As, income tax return and/or employer letter/pay stubs.

3. A mortgage commitment typically sets out terms and conditions for acceptance by the borrower that is valid for a specified time period.

    True   ○ False

   Terms and conditions will vary based on circumstances relating to the borrower and the property.

4. If a high ratio mortgage is obtained for $227,500 and the mortgage default premium is 2.75% of the mortgage, the amount due for this insurance would be $625.63.

   ○ True   **False**

   Decimal point placed incorrectly. The insurance premium would be $6,256.25.

5. With a variable rate mortgage, the payment may be adjusted on a periodic basis to reflect changes in interest rates.

    True   ○ False

   Variable rate mortgages typically have payment adjustments reflecting interest rate changes, while fixed rate mortgages have a 'fixed' payment over the specified term.

6. Opening of several credit accounts within a short period of time can adversely impact a credit score.

    True   ○ False

   Interestingly, not only can opening several credit accounts affect the score, so also can a number of credit report requests by creditors.

7. A guarantor on a mortgage agrees to perform and carry out covenants outlined in the mortgage document.

    True   ○ False

   He or she also agrees to make payments on dates set out in the mortgage document.

8. The Canada Small Business Financing Program is a provincial program designed to assist entrepreneurs by way of loans.

   ○ True   **False**

   The Canada Small Business Financing Program is a federal program, not a provincial program.

9. A seller take back can be an effective alternate source of mortgage funds when a property has limited appeal and the number of competing properties is increasing.

 ✔ True   ◯ False

The seller take back can also be effective given that the seller is motivated to sell and buyers for the mortgage are available, should the seller wish to subsequently sell the STB.

10. An increase in the capitalization rate by a lender has the net effect of increasing a property's value for lending purposes.

◯ True   ✔ False

An increasing capitalization rate effectively lowers the value being established for lending purposes.

11. A bridge loan is an interim form of financing used for commercial properties, but not for residential properties.

◯ True   ✔ False

Bridge financing can be effective for either commercial or residential properties.

12. A gap loan could involve a lender providing funds to assist a developer who is facing construction delays and, consequently, is unable to receive construction advances to address immediate costs.

 ✔ True   ◯ False

A gap loan is so named as it normally 'fills in the gap' while awaiting construction advances and/or permanent financing.

13. A line of credit is normally granted by a lender based on past performance of the borrower client and that borrower's strength of covenant (personal or corporate).

 ✔ True   ◯ False

A line of credit can be effective in providing interim financing as needed.

APPENDIX

CH14 EX1

Active Learning Exercises

■ Exercise 1   Mortgage Default Insurance Calculations

PURCHASE PRICE	DOWN PAYMENT	MORTGAGE AMOUNT	LTV (%)	PREMIUM (%)	PREMIUM ($)
$343,250	$53,250	$290,000	84%	1.75	$5,075.00
243,700	21,000	222,700	91	3.25	7,237.75
210,000	47,000	163,000	78	1.00	1,630.00
167,000	9,000	158,000	95	3.25	5,135.00

CH14 EX2

■ Exercise 2   Mortgage Balance and Recalculation

2.1   The monthly payment would be $1,263.92.

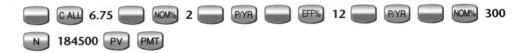

2.2   The outstanding balance after 5 years would be $167,440.70.

1 [INPUT] 60 ⬭ [AMORT] [=] [=] [=]

2.3   The monthly payment would need to be increased by $37.67 to $1,301.59 in order to arrange a mortgage for $190,000.

190000 [PV] [PMT]

CH14 EX3

■ Exercise 3   Interest Paid

Alternative A: Monthly Payment: $1,666.13 Total Interest Paid = $174,869.37

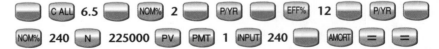

Alternative B: Monthly Payment: $1,406.30 Total Interest Paid = $196,889.91

Alternative C: Monthly Payment: $1,424.05 Total Interest Paid = $197,213.55

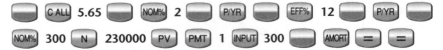

APPENDIX

■ Exercise 4   Principal and Interest

4.1   Bi-Weekly Payment: $633.83

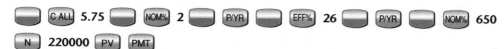

4.2   Interest Paid in First Payment: $480.20   Principal Paid in First Payment: $153.63

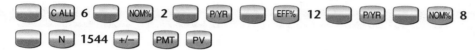

■ Exercise 5   Unknown Principal Amount

The outstanding principal today is $117,812.26

■ Exercise 6   The Reconstructed Operating Statement

6.1

Potential Gross (Rental) Income	$443,800
Less: Vacancy and Credit Losses	−17,752
Effective Rental Income	**426,048**
Add: Other Income	+ 22,190
Gross Operating Income	**448,238**
Less: Operating Expenses	−379,500
Net Operating Income	**= 68,738**

Estimate of Value ($68,738 ÷ .0925)   **= $743,114** *(rounded)*

Amount of Mortgage ($743,114 x .75)   **= $557,336** *(rounded)*

6.2

Potential Gross (Rental) Income	$443,800
Less: Vacancy and Credit Losses	−22,190
Effective Rental Income	**421,610**
Add: Other Income	+ 22,190
Gross Operating Income	**443,800**
Less: Operating Expenses	−379,500
Net Operating Income	**= 64,300**

Estimate of Value ($64,300 ÷ .0950)   **= $676,842** *(rounded)*

Amount of Mortgage ($676,842 x .70)   **= $473,789** *(rounded)*

APPENDIX

CH14 EX7

■ Exercise 7   Debt Coverage Ratio

7.1   Estimated Value Based on 9.5 Cap Rate: $37,393 ÷ .095 = $393,611 (rounded)

Maximum Loan: $393,611 x .75 = $295,208 (rounded)

7.2   Monthly Mortgage Payment: $2,489.80 (using HP 10BII)

Annual Debt Service: 2,489.80 x 12 = $29,878 (rounded)

Debt Coverage Ratio: 37,393 ÷ 29,878 = 1.25

The mortgage falls within the DCR guidelines established by National Lending Inc.

CH14 EX8

■ Exercise 8   Risk and Cap Rates

	LENDER A	LENDER B	LENDER C
CAP RATE	10.25 *Established by risk analysis*	9.55 *Market cap rate*	9.75 *Established by risk analysis*
LOAN-TO-VALUE RATIO	60%	75%	70%
VALUE ESTIMATE	$37,500 ÷ .1025 = $365,854 (rounded)	$37,500 ÷ .0955 = 392,670 (rounded)	$37,500 ÷ .0975 = $384,615 (rounded)
MORTGAGE	$365,854 x .60 = $219,512 (rounded)	$392,670 x .75 = $294,503 (rounded)	$384,615 x .70 = $269,231 (rounded)

Lender B will advance the largest mortgage.

CH14 EX9

■ Exercise 9   Specialized Financing Products

9.1   Gap Loan vs. Bridge Financing

Gap loans and bridge financing are forms of interim financing. A gap loan is sometimes used when the developer has received construction advances (based on the cost of the development) and is awaiting permanent financing based on the projected income stream. In some instances, the developer is unable to immediately meet required leasing objectives and the permanent lender will not advance all funds under the permanent mortgage (based on income stream). The gap loan provides interim financing until the lease requirements are met. Just as the gap loan fills the void between construction and permanent financing, the bridge loan assists developers between advances on construction by either an interim or permanent lender; i.e., the loan bridges the distance between advances.

APPENDIX

9.2 Standby Loan vs. Letter of Guarantee

CH14 EX9

A standby loan is arranged usually with the specific intent of not utilizing the loan but rather providing a backup to the developer to secure other interim financing. In a sense, the standby loan performs the same function as a letter of guarantee. Given that such a loan can be arranged, the developer can then seek more attractive terms for other interim or permanent financing. The letter of guarantee is commonly associated with development projects involving municipalities; e.g., a plan of subdivision, and concerns regarding the developer's ability to complete all servicing requirements as set out in the subdivision agreement. The letter of guarantee from a lender assures the existence of funds and the lender's commitment to fulfill financial obligations of the developer, if necessary.

APPENDIX

CHAPTER 15
TRADING AND AGENCY RELATIONSHIPS

Chapter Mini-Review

1. A seller representation agreement is often referred to in the marketplace as a listing agreement.

   ✔ **True**   ◯ False

   REBBA 2002 uses the term 'representation agreement' when referring to agreements between agents and seller principals.

2. Agency describes a relationship in which one party (the agent) accepts responsibility for representing another (a third party).

   ◯ True   ✔ **False**

   The agent accepts responsibility for representing a principal, not a third party.

3. The term agent refers to a salesperson registered pursuant to REBBA 2002.

   ◯ True   ✔ **False**

   The term 'agent' refers to a brokerage registered pursuant to REBBA 2002.

4. An agency relationship created by agreement can either be express or implied.

   ✔ **True**   ◯ False

   Agency relationships can be implied, but all practitioners are strongly advised to create express (written) agreements and avoid potential problems.

5. An agent's authority can be granted retroactively.

   ✔ **True**   ◯ False

   Ratification is one of four methods by which agency can be created.

6. While agency relationships are commonplace, situations can arise in which a buyer or seller is provided only selected services as a customer.

   ✔ **True**   ◯ False

   REBBA 2002 provides that agents may be involved with service agreements with customers, as distinct from representation agreements with clients.

7. The terms agency and representation are generally analogous for purposes of discussing agency relationships as they impact real estate brokerage.

   ✔ **True**   ◯ False

   REBBA 2002 does not refer to agency, but does use the term representation. The general intent is that these two terms are analogous.

8. A real estate brokerage's actual agency authorities are typically set out in writing in a representation agreement.

   ✔ **True**   ◯ False

   Actual authorities (set out in writing) should be clearly differentiated from implied authorities, which are assumed.

9. A real estate brokerage's agency authority is subject to only three limitations.

 True   **False**

Four limitations are identified including contract, delegation, purchase price and expense.

10. Real estate agency relationships are generally assumed to give rise to fiduciary obligations.

 True   ◯ False

This assumption is based on the Supreme Court's decision that agency relationships are deemed to give rise to fiduciary obligations.

11. A fiduciary relationship, which is enforceable by the courts, can only be created by written agreement.

◯ True   **False**

An agency relationship is determined by the facts and need not be in writing. However, practitioners are strongly encouraged to have all agency relationships established by express (written) agreement.

12. A major element in determining if a fiduciary relationship has been established is whether or not the client has agreed to pay remuneration.

◯ True   **False**

A fiduciary relationship can be established when agents are working gratuitously for clients.

13. Real estate brokerages are not permitted to accept commissions from anyone other than the principal in a transaction, unless full disclosure is made to that client.

 True   ◯ False

This requirement of disclosure flows from one of the five fiduciary obligations; namely, the obligation to not make a secret profit.

14. A salesperson who claims to have special expertise will be judged in court according to that higher standard.

 True   ◯ False

Individuals who profess to have a higher standard will be judged according to that standard.

15. A salesperson employed by a brokerage owes a customer both honesty and confidentiality when fulfilling his/her duty of care.

◯ True   **False**

A salesperson owes honesty and reasonable care/skill to customers. Confidentiality is an obligation owed to clients.

16. An agency relationship can only be terminated by operation of law.

◯ True   **False**

An agency relationship can be terminated by an act of the parties or by operation of law.

APPENDIX

CH15 EX1

Active Learning Exercises

▣ Exercise 1: Agency (Matching)

b.	*Fiduciary Relationship*	*Client*
f.	*Adopts Agent's Actions*	*Ratification*
d.	*Representation Agreement*	*Express Agreement*
a.	*Third Party*	*Customer*
c.	*Common Law*	*Excludes Quebec*

No Match: e. Estoppel

CH15 EX2

▣ Exercise 2: Authorities and Obligations (Fill-in-the-Blanks)

2.1   Actual authorities are typically set out by way of a (an)

        express   agreement.

2.2   A brokerage selecting various advertising and promotion methods relating to a seller representation agreement is usually operating under a (an)

        implied   authority.

2.3   Certain   *regulatory*   obligations are established under REBBA 2002, as distinct from common law.

2.4   Two elements essential in a fiduciary relationship are *trust* and

        confidence   .

2.5   A general obligation that requires a brokerage to possess the necessary abilities to perform agency duties is best described by the phrase

        care and skill (competence)   .

2.6   A brokerage that avoids conflicts of interest is adhering to agent obligations commonly grouped under the category of

        fiduciary obligations   .

APPENDIX

▣ Exercise 3: Duty of Care/Standard of Care

CH15 **EX3**

Identify which of the following circumstances are examples of duty of care in the marketplace:

☑ The salesperson informs the buyer customer that many buyers seek out the services of a home inspector.

☑ The salesperson takes accurate room measurements and includes these on the seller representation agreement.

☑ The customer asks about arranging a new mortgage and the salesperson provides the buyer with a list of lenders that typically lend on that type of property.

☐ The seller client asks the salesperson not to divulge that a marital dispute is the primary reason for listing the home.

☑ The salesperson, when asked by the buyer about legal matters involving the house purchase, advises the client to seek appropriate expert advice.

▣ Exercise 4: Multiple Choice

CH15 **EX4**

4.1 Which of the following terms best describes duties performed by a real estate brokerage in seller representation?

a. Middleman Role.   *Incorrect.* A middleman role assumes a non-agency relationship.

b. General Agency.   *Incorrect.* General agency refers to an agent that has the general authority to stand in for another.

c. Special Agency.   ✓ *CORRECT.* The term *special agency* is used given unique agency limitations (special authority) typically placed on a real estate brokerage.

d. Third Party Agency.   *Incorrect.* No such agency relationship exists.

4.2 Which of the following best describes the key difference between clients and customers?

a. The duty of care owed to customers exceeds that owed to clients.   *Incorrect.* Duty of care owed to clients is more expansive than those owed to customers.

b. The term *client* relates to an agency relationship, while *customer* refers to a non-agency relationship.   ✓ *CORRECT.* This differentiation is widely accepted in Canadian common law jurisdictions.

c. Clients are owed greater fiduciary obligations than those owed to customers.   *Incorrect.* Customers are not owed fiduciary obligations.

d. No significant differences exist between fiduciary duties owed to clients and customers.   *Incorrect.* Fiduciary obligations is a key distinguishing factor. These are owed to clients, but not to customers.

APPENDIX

CH15 EX4

4.3 A seller permits a salesperson employed by a brokerage to show his property, agrees that the brokerage will represent his interests and discusses remuneration to be paid. However, the seller does not sign the seller representation agreement provided to him. The property is subsequently sold to a buyer by that brokerage. This situation is best described as:

a. Creating agency by oral agreement.	✔ **CORRECT.** An oral agreement is acceptable for purposes of agency law, but discouraged from a practical perspective.
b. Establishing an agency relationship by operation of law.	*Incorrect.* Creating agency by operation of law typically involves a situation where a duty is imposed on one party to act on behalf of another.
c. A good example of a salesperson performing his/her general obligation of confidentiality.	*Incorrect.* The fiduciary duty of confidentiality has no relevance to this particular situation.
d. A good example of duty of care, as it applies in the marketplace.	*Incorrect.* Duty of care is not relevant to this particular situation.

4.4 A salesperson, when listing a property, elects to focus most of her advertising efforts on the Internet rather than print media, given the particular features of the home. The seller is not aware of this specific advertising decision. This action is best described as:

a. An actual authority.	*Incorrect.* An actual authority is expressly stated, typically in a seller representation agreement.
b. An express agreement.	*Incorrect.* An express agreement refers to a written or oral agreement between principal and agent setting out actual authorities.
c. An implied authority.	✔ **CORRECT.** Implied authorities are not specifically set out, but are necessary to get the job done.
d. A legislated authority.	*Incorrect.* While certain authorities are legislated, this particular situation does not directly apply. See *Regulatory Obligations* for additional discussion.

4.5 A buyer's representative is unaware of potential water problems within a particular neighbourhood, but accidentally overhears the seller customer discussing his problems with water quality and adequate supply. The listing brokerage has made no mention of this matter. The prospective buyer client is keenly interested in the property. After leaving the property, the salesperson informs the buyer regarding what was overheard. This scenario is best described by which of the following general obligations?

a. Obedience.	*Incorrect.* Obedience involves obeying the lawful instructions of the client.
b. Negotiate Favourable Terms.	*Incorrect.* Negotiating favourable terms is a general obligation, but is not directly relevant to this particular situation.
c. Confidentiality.	*Incorrect.* Confidentiality is a general obligation, but is not directly relevant to this particular situation.
d. Disclosure.	✔ **CORRECT.** The salesperson has an obligation to disclose pertinent information about the property to his/her client.

APPENDIX

4.6 A salesperson is instructed by the seller client not to divulge mould problems associated with the listed property. The salesperson agrees once the seller assures him that the problem has gone away. Further, evidence of any problem is not readily visible from a cursory inspection. The buyer, as a customer, discovers the problem subsequent to completion of the sale and takes legal action. Regardless of the outcome, which of the following general or fiduciary obligations will be most closely scrutinized by the Courts?

a.	**Obedience.**	✔ *CORRECT.* Obedience is the obligation under close scrutiny and, more specifically, the requirement that an agent and its representatives have to follow the client's lawful instructions.
b.	Loyalty.	*Incorrect.* Loyalty focuses on placing the client's interests above all else, except the law, and is not directly relevant to this particular situation.
c.	Conflict.	*Incorrect.* Personal conflict relates to conflicts involving the brokerage/client relationship and is not directly relevant to this particular situation.
d.	Confidentiality.	*Incorrect.* This obligation involves not divulging information given by the client in confidence and is not directly relevant to this particular situation.

4.7 A buyer client is pursuing legal recourse, because the salesperson failed to inform her that the basement apartment in the purchased home was not legal. The salesperson, in his defense, argues that he only recently obtained his salesperson's registration and can't be expected to know about such matters. Which of the following statements best describes the merits of the salesperson's argument?

a.	The argument has legal merit, as recently registered salespersons are not expected to have such knowledge.	*Incorrect.* A duty of care is owed and that duty must comply with an objective standard and is not altered by arguing lack of knowledge.
b.	**The argument has little legal merit, as a duty of care is owed regardless of experience level.**	✔ *CORRECT.* Level of experience is not a consideration. Duty of care is determined based on what a reasonably well-informed registrant would do under the circumstances.
c.	The argument has legal merit, as the standard of care is subjectively interpreted by the Courts.	*Incorrect.* Duty of care is established by an objective standard.
d.	The argument has little legal merit, as a salesperson cannot be held liable for inaccurate statements.	*Incorrect.* A salesperson can be held liable for inaccurate statements as a representative of the brokerage.

APPENDIX

CHAPTER 16
REPRESENTATION

Chapter Mini-Review

1. Agency relationships can be grouped under two main categories: single representation and multiple representation.

     ✔ **True**   ◯ False

    REBBA 2002 sets out compliance requirements for representation agreements (agreements involving single representation) and multiple representation.

2. In single representation, the brokerage and its representatives owe the client both general and fiduciary obligations.

    ✔ **True**   ◯ False

    While the term 'representation' is not defined in REBBA 2002, it is generally viewed as analogous to agency and, therefore, duties would include both general and fiduciary obligations (as well as regulatory obligations set out in the Act and Regulations).

3. Typically, the brokerage representing the seller assumes that the co-operating brokerage is NOT representing the buyer, but instead is treating that buyer as a customer.

    ◯ True   ✔ **False**

    The brokerage representing the seller typically assumes that the co-operating brokerage is representing the buyer.

4. According to REBBA 2002, a brokerage and its representatives must be fair and honest to the buyer as a customer, but duties do not extend to offering conscientious service.

    ◯ True   ✔ **False**

    Section 5 of the Code of Ethics requires that the brokerage and its representatives provide conscientious and competent service to both clients and customers.

5. In single buyer representation, one of the common law obligations to the client is to disclose, in a timely manner, all relevant facts known to the brokerage and its representatives about the property or transaction.

     ✔ **True**   ◯ False

    This is one of several obligations under common law that are owed in single buyer representation.

6. When offering single representation, a brokerage and its representatives must represent the interests of the client, but do not owe a duty of care to that client.

    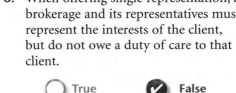 ◯ True   ✔ **False**

    Duty of care is owed to both clients and customers. The duty applies to everything done for a client, but is more limited in the case of customers.

APPENDIX

7. One of the challenges for brokerages involved with multiple representation is to handle conflicting instructions from two principals.

 True   ◯ False

Multiple representation places the brokerage in a difficult situation given competing interests of buyer and seller.

8. A salesperson representing a client, who suggests in confidence to the customer that he or she could work in his or her best interests at the same time, faces the legal perils of implied representation.

 True   ◯ False

Implied multiple representation can have serious legal consequences.

9. If two salespeople within a brokerage are representing competing buyers, they must follow disclosure procedures as set out for all multiple representation situations.

 True   ◯ False

Statutory disclosure requirements regarding multiple representation apply to competing buyers, but not to competing sellers.

10. If ABC Realty Inc. represents the seller and XYZ Real Estate Ltd. is appointed as a sub-agent, then XYZ Real Estate Ltd. owes the same general, fiduciary and regulatory obligations to the seller as does ABC Realty Inc.

 True   ◯ False

The sub-agent owes the same duties to the client as the agent.

Active Learning Exercises

 Exercise 1   Multiple Choice

CH16 EX1

1.1 Provisions in REBBA 2002 (General Regulation and the Code of Ethics) regarding multiple representation:

a. Require that only single representation can be offered by brokerages in Ontario.

Incorrect. Brokerages can offer single representation or multiple representation.

b. Do not require a written agreement between the brokerage and the client.

Incorrect. A written agreement must be provided, but the buyer or seller is not required to sign it.

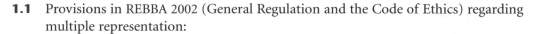

c. **Require that clients provide consent in writing to multiple representation.**

✔ *CORRECT.* Consent is required pursuant to General Regulation, Sec. 22.

d. Require that customers provide consent in writing to multiple representation.

Incorrect. Customers are not directly involved in the consent process.

APPENDIX

CH16 EX1

1.2 Which of the following is most correct in the case of single representation?

a. General and fiduciary duties are owed to a seller client, but not a duty of care.

Incorrect. A duty of care is also owed to the seller.

b. **Regulatory obligations can apply to both customers and clients.**

✔ *CORRECT.* These obligations are set out in REBBA 2002.

c. Fiduciary duties are owed to both buyer and seller.

Incorrect. This statement describes multiple representation, not single representation.

d. The brokerage representing a seller client must have a signed seller representation agreement.

Incorrect. A seller representation agreement under REBBA 2002 can be signed or unsigned by the seller, but must be prepared in writing by the registrant.

1.3 Salesperson Lee, on behalf of ABC Realty Inc., lists the seller's property and then locates a suitable new home for his client. The new home is listed by another salesperson in the same brokerage. If Lee represents the seller (now a buyer) in purchasing this listed property, he is facing a situation legally referred to as:

a. **Sequential Representation.**

✔ *CORRECT.* Sequential representation is aptly named, as it refers to successive representation relationships involving the same person.

b. Concurrent Representation.

Incorrect. Concurrent representation involves representing both buyer and seller at the same time.

c. Limited Representation.

Incorrect. No such term is currently in use.

d. Customer Representation.

Incorrect. No such term is used, as customers are not represented.

1.4 Which of the following is NOT a true statement regarding multiple representation? **This question requires that the *incorrect* option be identified.**

a. The brokerage and its representatives must act impartially to protect the interests of both clients.

This option is correct. Impartiality is required in multiple representation.

b. Implied multiple representation may be recognized by the Court based on the facts, and not simply based on what documents have been signed by the buyer or seller.

This option is correct. Implied multiple representation can be recognized by the Court based on facts, not necessarily what is in writing.

c. One of the limitations regarding disclosure is that the seller's brokerage and its representatives will not disclose the seller's motivation or any personal information, unless so instructed by the seller.

This option is correct. Such information can only be disclosed when the brokerage is so instructed by the seller.

d. **Imputed knowledge, from a legal perspective, refers to the fact that all registrants within a brokerage share each other's confidences.**

✔ *THIS IS THE INCORRECT OPTION.* Imputed knowledge, such as confidential knowledge, is deemed to be shared with all registrants within a brokerage.

APPENDIX

1.5 A salesperson, on behalf of the brokerage, agrees to represent the seller when listing his home and then also agrees to represent a buyer in the purchase of that home. The most appropriate term describing this circumstance is:

a. Multiple Representation.	✔ *CORRECT.* A brokerage representing both buyer and seller in the same trade is referred to as multiple representation.
b. Duty of Care.	*Incorrect.* Duty of care involves duties owed to client and customer.
c. Sequential Representation.	*Incorrect.* Sequential representation involves representing the same person in successive transactions.
d. Single Representation.	*Incorrect.* Single representation does not apply, as two clients are being represented.

1.6 The salesperson, as a representative of a brokerage, has been working first with the seller as a client and then with a buyer client under a multiple representation relationship for more than a week attempting to put a deal together. The problem revolves around the offered price and the closing date. To move things along, the salesperson casually mentions to the buyer that the seller is getting anxious and will probably accept a lower price, if the seller's closing date is met. The seller has not given the salesperson authority to make that statement. Which of the following best describes this situation?

a. Even a minor advantage given to one client over the other can dramatically tip the negotiating scale.	✔ *CORRECT.* The registrant involved with multiple representation can influence negotiations by not being completely impartial.
b. Conflicting instructions from buyer and seller clients involved in the same trade rarely result in a conflict for the salesperson and the brokerage.	*Incorrect.* Such instructions can often result in a conflict for the salesperson and the brokerage.
c. The first client can have a disadvantage in a multiple representation, as more confidential information is normally provided by that client than by the second client.	*Incorrect.* This is a true statement, but does not apply to the scenario as presented.
d. The salesperson does not need the client's authority to divulge this information.	*Incorrect.* The salesperson must obtain permission, as such information is confidential and detrimental to the principal when disclosed.

APPENDIX

1.7 Which of the following statements is correct?

a. A seller brokerage involved in multiple representation with seller and buyer clients owes its ultimate allegiance and loyalty to the seller, as the seller will typically be paying the commission.

Incorrect. Allegiance and loyalty are owed to both.

b. **A service agreement can be effective in avoiding multiple representation when a salesperson in a brokerage is working with a seller client and is approached by a buyer to purchase the seller's property.**

✓ *CORRECT.* Customer service agreements (e.g., OREA Forms 201 and 310) generally describe services provided to the customer.

c. Representing competing buyers is described as a form of sequential representation.

Incorrect. Representing competing buyers is a form of concurrent representation and is viewed as multiple representation for purposes of REBBA 2002.

d. Offers, but not counter-offers, are to be communicated promptly to the buyer or seller under single representation.

Incorrect. Both offers and counter-offers are to be communicated promptly to the buyer or seller.

 ■ **Exercise 2   Multiple Representation**

Identify which of the following circumstances are examples of multiple representation.

☑ Two salespersons in the same brokerage representing different clients in the same transaction.

☐ Two salespersons from different brokerages representing buyer and seller clients in the same transaction.

☑ Two salespersons from different branches of the same brokerage representing different clients in the same transaction.

☐ Two salespersons from the same brokerage; one representing the seller as a client and the other providing services to a customer in the same transaction.

☑ A salesperson from a brokerage representing a seller client and an appraiser from the same brokerage providing an evaluation of the seller client's home to a buyer who wishes to purchase the seller's home.

APPENDIX

■ Exercise 3   Obligations to Seller and Buyer (Fill-in-the-Blanks)

CH16 EX3

ABC Realty Inc. has listed a unique, six-outlet bistro operation called Bistro Best. Salesperson Lee of ABC Realty Inc. obtains the seller's consent to involve another brokerage as a sub-agent to market the enterprise. Salesperson Martin, employed by XYZ Real Estate Ltd. (the sub-agent) interests ACME Holdings Inc. as a customer in looking at the property and has an appropriate agreement signed with ACME. Based on this scenario, check off which obligations (general, fiduciary and regulatory), as well as duty of care, apply to the respective brokerages.

ANALYSIS	Seller Bistro Best		Buyer ACME Holdings Inc.	
	Obligations*	Duty of Care**	Obligations*	Duty of Care**
ABC Realty Inc.	■	■		■
Salesperson Lee	■	■		■
Other Salespeople at ABC Realty Inc.	■	■		■
XYZ Real Estate Ltd.	■	■		■
Salesperson Martin	■	■		■
Other Salespeople at XYZ Real Estate Ltd.	■	■		■

* Includes general, fiduciary and regulatory obligations.

** *Reminder:* Duty of care to the client applies to everything that is done and that ought to be done for the client. Duty of care to the customer is limited to providing information and performing functions (if any), along with limited disclosure and privacy obligations.

APPENDIX